# QUICKBOOKS® ONLINE PLUS:
# A COMPLETE COURSE
# 2016

# QUICKBOOKS® ONLINE PLUS: A COMPLETE COURSE 2016

Janet Horne, M.S.
Los Angeles Pierce College

PEARSON

Boston  Columbus  Indianapolis  New York  San Francisco  Hoboken

Amsterdam  Cape Town  Dubai  London  Madrid  Milan  Munich  Paris  Montreal  Toronto

Delhi  Mexico City  Sao Paulo  Sydney  Hong Kong  Seoul  Singapore  Taipei  Tokyo

Vice President, Business Publishing: Donna Battista
Editor-in-Chief: Ashley Dodge
Senior Sponsoring Editor: Neeraj Bhalla
Vice President, Product Marketing: Maggie Moylan
Director of Marketing, Digital Services and Products: Jeanette Koskinas
Field Marketing Manager: Natalie Wagner
Product Marketing Assistant: Jessica Quazza
Team Lead, Program Management: Ashley Santora
Team Lead, Project Management: Jeff Holcomb
Associate Team Lead, Project Management: Alison Kalil
Creative Director: Blair Brown
Art Director: Jonathan Boylan
Vice President, Director of Digital Strategy and Assessment: Paul Gentile

Manager of Learning Applications: Paul DeLuca
Digital Editor: Sarah Peterson
Director, Digital Studio: Sacha Laustsen
Digital Studio Manager: Diane Lombardo
Digital Studio Project Manager: Andra Skaalrud
Digital Studio Project Manager: Alana Coles
Digital Studio Project Manager: Robin Lazrus
Digital Content Team Lead: Noel Lotz
Digital Content Project Lead: Elizabeth Geary
Full-Service Project Management and Composition: Integra
Cover Designer: Integra
Cover Art: Keo/Shutterstock.com
Printer/Binder: RR Donnelley/Menasha
Cover Printer: Phoenix Color/Hagerstown

Microsoft and/or its respective suppliers make no representations about the suitability of the information contained in the documents and related graphics published as part of the services for any purpose. All such documents and related graphics are provided "as is" without warranty of any kind. Microsoft and/or its respective suppliers hereby disclaim all warranties and conditions with regard to this information, including all warranties and conditions of merchantability, whether express, implied or statutory, fitness for a particular purpose, title and non-infringement. In no event shall Microsoft and/or its respective suppliers be liable for any special, indirect or consequential damages or any damages whatsoever resulting from loss of use, data or profits, whether in an action of contract, negligence or other tortious action, arising out of or in connection with the use or performance of information available from the services.

The documents and related graphics contained herein could include technical inaccuracies or typographical errors. Changes are periodically added to the information herein. Microsoft and/or its respective suppliers may make improvements and/or changes in the product(s) and/or the program(s) described herein at any time. Partial screen shots may be viewed in full within the software version specified.

Microsoft® and Windows® are registered trademarks of the Microsoft Corporation in the U.S.A. and other countries. This book is not sponsored or endorsed by or affiliated with the Microsoft Corporation.

Reprinted with permission ©Intuit Inc. All rights reserved.

**Library of Congress Cataloging-in-Publication Data**

Names: Horne, Janet, author.
Title: QuickBooks Online Plus : a complete course 2016 / Janet Horne.
Description: Boston, MA : Pearson Education, [2017] |
    Includes index.
Identifiers: LCCN 2016017145 | ISBN 9780134229263 | ISBN 0134229266
Subjects: LCSH: QuickBooks. | Small business–Accounting–Computer programs. |
    Small business–Finance–Computer programs.
Classification: LCC HF5679 .H66389 2017 | DDC 657/.9042028553–dc23
LC record available at https://lccn.loc.gov/2016017145

1  16

**PEARSON**

ISBN 10:    0-13-422926-6
ISBN 13: 978-0-13-422926-3

To my family

# BRIEF TABLE OF CONTENTS

# TABLE OF CONTENTS

## Chapter 3—Sales and Receivables: Service Items

# Contents

## Chapter 4—Payables and Purchases

## Chapter 5—General Accounting and End-of-Period Procedures

# Contents

## Chapter 6—Sales and Receivables: Product and Service Items

# Contents xiii

## Chapter 7—Payables, Purchases, and Inventory

## Chapter 8—General Accounting, End-of-Period Procedures, and Budgets

## Chapter 9—Payroll

## Appendix A: Create a Company Using QuickBooks Desktop

## Appendix B: Go Mobile

## Appendix C: Additional Features

## Index

# PREFACE

***QuickBooks Online Plus: A Complete Course 2016*** is a comprehensive instructional learning resource. The text provides training using *QuickBooks Online Plus* accounting program (for simplicity, the program is referred to as *QuickBooks Online* in the text).

## DISTINGUISHING FEATURES

Throughout the text, emphasis is placed on the use of QuickBooks Online Plus's innovative approach to recording accounting transactions based on a business form rather than using the traditional journal format. This approach, however, is correlated to traditional accounting through adjusting entries, end-of-period procedures, and use of the "behind the scenes" journal. QuickBooks Online is Cloud-based and allows students to access QuickBooks Online from any computer with a Web browser. The text uses a tutorial-style training method to guide the students in the use of QuickBooks Online in a step-by-step manner and is designed to help students transition from training to using *QuickBooks Online Plus* in an actual business.

When using the text, students practice entries and explore QuickBooks Online using the Intuit Test Drive Company. After completing a drill, students use a company that they create in Chapter 2, Your Name's Beach Barkers, to enter transactions, prepare reports, and analyze data. At the end of each chapter, there are additional transactions that students complete without step-by-step instructions.

The text provides:
- ❖ Comprehensive exploration of QuickBooks Online Plus
- ❖ Reinforcement of accounting concepts
- ❖ Opportunity to work in a Cloud-based environment
- ❖ Exploration of error correction and resulting ramifications
- ❖ Introduction to and a thorough exploration and use of many of QuickBooks Online's features
- ❖ Experience in recording transactions for service and inventory businesses
- ❖ Transactions ranging from simple to complex that simulate real-world occurrences
- ❖ Use of Online Payroll Subscription
- ❖ Creation of a company for use in QuickBooks Online
- ❖ Printing of business forms and reports
- ❖ Opportunity to learn how to customize QuickBooks Online:
  - ▪ Forms
  - ▪ Settings
  - ▪ Reports

- ❖ Screen shots used liberally to show:
    - ▪ QuickBooks Online screens
    - ▪ Completed transactions
    - ▪ Reports
- ❖ Extensive assignment material including:
    - ▪ Drill using Intuit's Test Drive Company
    - ▪ Do using the company created in Chapter 2
    - ▪ Additional Transactions near the end of each chapter for reinforcement
    - ▪ End-of-chapter questions (true/false, multiple-choice, fill-in, computer assignment)

## ORGANIZATIONAL FEATURES

**QuickBooks Online Plus: A Complete Course 2016** is designed to present accounting concepts and their relationship to *QuickBooks Online Plus.* While completing each chapter, students:

- ❖ Learn underlying accounting concepts
- ❖ Receive hands-on training using a Cloud-based program, QuickBooks Online Plus
- ❖ Create and use a company
- ❖ Analyze and record transactions for service and inventory businesses
- ❖ Complete transactions and accounting for two full monthly business cycles
- ❖ Prepare Payroll using QuickBooks Online Payroll
- ❖ As the students gain experience in using QuickBooks Online in the early chapters, the transactions, QuickBooks Online features used, and material presented become more complex and sophisticated in the later chapters

### Text Organization
- ❖ Chapter 1: An Introduction to QuickBooks Online
- ❖ Chapter 2: Create a Company in QuickBooks Online
- ❖ Chapter 3: Focus on Receivables when providing Services
- ❖ Chapter 4: Focus on Payables when providing Services
- ❖ Chapter 5: End-of-Period Procedures including adjusting entries, owner withdrawals and investments, and closing entries
- ❖ Chapter 6: Focus on Receivables when selling Inventory Items, use Locations and Classes, accept Credit Cards for Customer Payments, collect Sales Tax, give Customer Sales Discounts, and record NSF Checks
- ❖ Chapter 7: Focus on Payables when purchasing and paying for Inventory items, prepare Purchase Orders, use a Company Credit Card, record Purchase and Merchandise Discounts, make Sales Tax Payments
- ❖ Chapter 8: End-of-Period Procedures, make Inventory Adjustments, prepare Budgets
- ❖ Chapter 9: Payroll
- ❖ Three Appendices:
    - ▪ Create a Company Using QuickBooks Desktop
    - ▪ Go Mobile
    - ▪ Additional Features

<u>**Chapter Organization**</u>
- ❖ The Intuit Test Drive Company is used to drill, practice, and explore transaction analysis and entry within each chapter
- ❖ In Chapter 2 students create a company that will be used in each chapter in conjunction with the Test Drive Company
- ❖ Using the company created, Your Name's Beach Barkers, students continue to analyze and record transactions that graduate from simple to complex and that are more in-depth than those in the drills
- ❖ Near the end of every chapter, additional transactions are entered without step-by-step instructions being provided
- ❖ At the end of every chapter, the concepts and applications learned are reinforced by completing:
  - True/False questions
  - Multiple-Choice questions
  - Fill-in questions
  - Computer Assignment questions

## COURSES

***QuickBooks Online Plus: A Complete Course 2016*** is designed for a one-term course in microcomputer accounting. This text covers using QuickBooks Online Plus for two monthly accounting cycles. In the first chapters, accounting for selling service items is featured. In the later chapters, both service items and inventory items are sold. Preparing payroll and creating a new company are also included. When using the text, students should be familiar with the accounting cycle and how it is related to a business. No prior knowledge of or experience with computers, Windows, or QuickBooks Online is required; however, an understanding of accounting is essential to successful completion of the coursework.

If training using QuickBooks Premier Accountant Desktop is desired, the text ***QuickBooks 2015: A Complete Course*** is available. It, too, is designed for a one-term course in microcomputer accounting.

## SUPPLEMENTS FOR THE INSTRUCTOR

Pearson Education maintains a Web site where student and instructor materials may be downloaded for classroom use at **www.pearsonhighered.com/horne**. The ***Instructor's Resource Center*** contains the following:

Student and Instructor Access:
- ❖ Data Files for Students and Instructors that include:
  - Excel Files used to Import Company Data to Create a Company (Chapter 2)
  - QuickBooks Desktop File that may be used to Create a Company (Appendix A)
  - Logos for Your Name's Beach Barkers (Added to Company in Chapter 6) and Shape Up (Used for Computer Exams for each chapter)

Instructor Only Access:
- ❖ Instructor's Resource Manual (IM) materials include:
  - ▪ Answers to the End-of-Chapter Questions
  - ▪ A Checklist with totals for all documents printed in the text
  - ▪ Excel files containing all the reports prepared in the text
  - ▪ Instructor's Manual Materials, which include:
    - • Assignment Sheets for full- and short-term courses
    - • IM Preface for instructors
    - • IM Table of Contents listing all the materials available
    - • Teaching suggestions
  - ▪ Textbook errata, which is posted as errors are discovered
- ❖ PowerPoint Presentations containing lectures for each chapter in the text
- ❖ Instructor's Solutions Manual containing Adobe .pdf files for all the printouts prepared in the text (In the chapters of the text, some reports are shown in a partial display due to space limitations. The full copies of the printed reports are included in this folder. While instructors may customize the printing required by students, everything that students are asked to print within the text is included in this folder.)
- ❖ Test Bank containing folders for:
  - ▪ Written Exams containing exams and keys for each area of study
  - ▪ Computer Exams for each Chapter
  - ▪ Bonus Practice Set covering the entire text that may be used for additional practice or as a comprehensive QuickBooks Online exam

> If you need assistance with QuickBooks, go to **https://help.QuickBooks.intuit.Com/** and click on one of the Topics, Tutorials, or Blog.

## PROGRAM UPDATES

At the time of writing all materials were current and consistent with QuickBooks Online Plus. However, Intuit continually updates and changes the program. Every month, the updates for the month are posted by Intuit. The changes are listed as Release Notes on the login screen for QuickBooks Online. To obtain more in depth information about the changes, click on the Release Notes and you will be taken to a document that describes them in more detail.

## ERRATA AND INSTRUCTOR COMMENTS

While I strive to write an error-free textbook, it is inevitable that some errors will occur. As I become aware of any errors, they will be added to an errata sheet that is posted in the Instructor's Resource Center on the Pearson Web site at **www.pearsonhighered.com/horne**. Once an errata is posted, instructors should feel free to share that information with their students and to check back periodically to see if any new items have been added. If you or your students discover an error, or have suggestions and/or concerns, I would appreciate it if the instructors would contact me and let me know what they are. My email address for instructors is also shown in the Instructor's Resource Center.

## ACKNOWLEDGMENTS

I wish to thank my colleagues for testing and reviewing the manuscript, the professors who use the text and share their thoughts and suggestions with me, and my students for providing me with a special insight into problems encountered in training. All of your comments and suggestions are greatly appreciated. A special thank you goes to Cheryl Bartlett for her proofreading and comments. In addition, I would like to thank Donna Battista, Ellen Geary, Neeraj Bhalla, Karen Carter, Alison Kalil and the production team at Pearson Education for their editorial support and assistance.

# INTRODUCTION TO QUICKBOOKS ONLINE PLUS

**1**

## LEARNING OBJECTIVES

At the completion of this chapter, you will be able to:

1. Open QuickBooks Online Plus and access the Test Drive Company
2. Understand the definition of Cloud-Based Computing
3. Have knowledge of the QuickBooks versions available for use
4. Explain the differences between manual and computerized accounting
5. Identify areas of the QuickBooks Online Home Page
6. Know how to use the Top- and Left-Navigation Bars
7. Open and close a business document
8. Understand system requirements for QuickBooks Online Plus
9. Recognize the Drill Button as an instruction to complete a task in the Test Drive Company
10. Use Help, Search, and Create
11. Access Settings via the Gear icon
12. Prepare a report
13. Know what an App is
14. Find and use Keyboard Shortcuts

## MANUAL AND COMPUTERIZED ACCOUNTING

The work performed to keep the books for a business is the same whether you use manual or computerized accounting. Transactions need to be analyzed, recorded in a journal, and posted to a ledger. Business documents such as invoices, checks, bank deposits, and credit/debit memos need to be prepared and distributed. Reports to management and owners for information and decision-making purposes need to be prepared. Records for one business period need to be closed before recording transactions for the next business period.

In a manual system, each transaction that is analyzed must be entered by hand into the appropriate journal (the book of original entry where all transactions are recorded) and posted to the appropriate ledger (the book of final entry that contains records for all of the accounts used in the business). A separate business document such as an invoice or a check must be prepared and distributed. In order to prepare a report, the accountant or bookkeeper must go through the journal or ledger and look for the appropriate amounts to include in the report. Closing the books must be done item by item via closing entries that are recorded in the journal and posted to the appropriate ledger accounts. After the closing entries are recorded, the ledger accounts must be ruled and balance sheet accounts must be reopened with Brought Forward Balances being entered.

When using a computerized system and a program such as QuickBooks Online Plus, the transactions must still be analyzed and recorded. QuickBooks Online Plus operates from a business document point of view. As a transaction occurs, the necessary business document (an invoice or a check, for example) is prepared. Based on the information in the business document, QuickBooks Online Plus records the necessary debits and credits behind the scenes in the Journal. If an error is made when entering a transaction, QuickBooks Online Plus allows the user to access the business document, register, or journal to return to the business document and make the correction. Reports are prepared with the click of the mouse.

## VERSIONS OF QUICKBOOKS

This text uses QuickBooks Online Plus. For training purposes, the program name will be shown as QuickBooks Online or QBO. Other versions of QuickBooks Online and QuickBooks Desktop software are available. It is important to know about them so you may make an informed decision regarding your software purchase/subscription when you are finished with the class and your educational trial version expires. QuickBooks accounting software is divided into three categories: Online, Desktop, and Self-Employed. The following information describes the features available for each of the software programs and provides the pricing at the time of this writing. All prices are subject to change and may not match the amounts shown in the text.

### QuickBooks Online

Four versions of the software are offered for a monthly subscription rate. Each of the QuickBooks Online programs includes different levels of features. All of the programs use an online account, provide automatic data backup, and provide bank-level security and encryption.

**Simple Start** allows full-user access to one person. Up to two accountants may be added as users for no additional charge. You may track income and expenses, process unlimited invoices and estimates, charge sales tax, print checks, record transactions, download bank and credit card transactions, import data from QuickBooks Desktop, import and export lists to/from Excel, access your data from a smartphone or tablet. More than 20 reports may be prepared. At the time of this writing, subscription rates are $12.95 per month.

**Essentials** includes everything from Simple Start but adds the capability to have access for three users with permission controls (can setup users and limit access to certain areas of the company or you may allow full access to everything). Includes payables—vendors, bills, payments, and scheduled payments. Setup invoices to automatically bill on a recurring schedule, compare sales profitability with industry trends, enables delayed charges and credits. More than 40 reports may be prepared. At the time of this writing, subscription rates are $26.95 per month.

**Plus** includes everything from Simple Start and Essentials but adds the capability to have access for five users with permission controls (may have up to 25 users total for additional fees). Maintain and track inventory using FIFO (first in first out), create and send purchase orders, create budgets, use class tracking to categorize income and expenses, track sales and profitability for each location. Employees and subcontractors may have limited access to enter time worked (time-tracking). More than 65 reports may be prepared. (This is the program you will use for the course.) At the time of this writing, subscription rates are $39.95 per month.

**Accountant** is essentially a portal for accountants to use for central access to clients' QuickBooks Online companies. Accountants may work with clients using any of the QuickBooks Online programs. It has features for managing the accountant's practice and books, as well as special accountant-only tools that may be used inside clients' QuickBooks Online companies. There is a special navigation bar that provides access to Your Practice (clients, team, and ProAdvisor) and Your Books (the accounting firm's company file). When an accountant has been added as a user to a client's company, the accountant can access the company, make corrections, reclassify transactions, write off invoices, and prepare reports. You may offer your clients QuickBooks Online subscriptions and get a wholesale price for the subscription that you pay each month. If you wish, you may bill the client a different rate for the subscription. If the client pays Intuit directly, then there will not be a 50% discount given. At the time of this writing, a 180-day subscription is valid for accounting professionals only and is free as long as you have either an active ProAdvisor membership or at least one current QuickBooks Online client.

## Additional Subscriptions For QuickBooks Online

QuickBooks Online has a large variety of extras available that may be added to the program. Some of the most important and widely-used subscriptions are for payroll and online payment processing. In addition, QuickBooks Online works with a wide variety of Apps (discussed later in the chapter).

**Payroll** is a subscription to pay W-2 employees and file payroll taxes. It may be added to any of the QuickBooks Online versions. At the time of this writing, Enhanced Payroll or Full Service Payroll may be bundled with either QuickBooks Online Essentials or QuickBooks Online Plus for an additional fee per month.

**Online Payments** can be used with all versions of QuickBooks Online to accept online payments. This includes Visa, MasterCard, American Express, Discover, and ACH (bank payments). At the time of this writing, you may select a Pay as You Go plan and pay fees for each transaction—Card Swiped: 2.40% + 25¢; Card Keyed: 3.40% + 25¢; ACH/bank transfers & check 50¢ each. You may select a Monthly Rate plan and pay $19.95 per month and fees of Card Swiped: 1.6% + 25¢; Card Keyed: 3.2% + 25¢; and 50¢ per ACH (bank payments) transaction.

## QuickBooks Desktop

There are three desktop versions available. Essentially all of the programs include many of the same capabilities and are complete accounting programs that enable a company to create invoices, track sales and expenses, manage accounts payable, prepare sales and tax reports, automatically download bank transactions, calculate and rebill job costs, calculate discounts by customer, prepare purchase orders, manage and track inventory using the average cost method, track bounced checks, and many other capabilities. In addition, you may use Income Tracker and Bill Tracker to monitor the income and outflow of your money, Insights on the Homepage to get the full picture of your business performance, and Company Snapshots to get a real-time view of your business. Accountant Collaboration Tools are available for use when working with your accountant.

**Pro** includes more than 100 reports. At the time of this writing, you may purchase the program for a special price of $219.95 for a one-time payment or select an annual subscription for of $199.95 per year and get support, data backup, and updates included.

**Premier** includes more than 150 industry specific reports and contains everything that is in Pro as well as industry-specific features. From Premier you may toggle to another edition of QuickBooks including Accountant, Contractor, Manufacturing & Wholesale, Nonprofit, Professional Services, Retail, and Pro. At the time of this writing, you may purchase the program for a one-time payment of $379.95 or select an annual subscription for a special price of $299.95 per year and get support, data backup, and updates included.

**Enterprise Solutions** contains all of the features included in Premier, but is designed for a larger business. You can track more than 100,000 customers, vendors, inventory items, and employees, use online backup and data protection, cloud hosting is available for a fee, use Advanced Reporting to access all of your QuickBooks data to create any report needed, consolidate reports from multiple company files, and create custom reports with ODBC-compliant applications using a direct connection to the QuickBooks database. At the time of this writing, there are three subscription levels available Silver, Gold, and Platinum. Pricing is based on the number of users (up to 30). The prices for one user are: Silver $75.60 per month or $900 per year, Gold $98.10 per month or $1,170 per year (also includes a more powerful functionality to pay and file taxes, pay employees, and streamline payroll with QuickBooks Enhanced Payroll), and Platinum $120.60 per month or $1,440 per year (includes everything in Gold along with valuable tools for manufacturers, wholesalers, contractors, retailers, advanced inventory, and advanced pricing).

**Accountant** (the full name of the program is ProAdvisor Deluxe) QuickBooks Accountant Desktop PLUS software is included. ProAdvisor Deluxe contains everything in that is in the Premier version of QuickBooks Desktop and has an Accountant menu that provides access to the Accountant Center; Chart of Accounts; Fixed Asset Item List; Batch Enter, Delete, and Void transactions; Client Data Review (allows the accountant to reclassify transactions, write-off multiple invoices, fix incorrect sales tax payments, troubleshoot inventory issues, identify list item changes, view changes to account balances, match unapplied vendor and customer payments/credits and clear up the Undeposited Funds account); Make and send General Journal Entries; Reconcile, prepare a Working Trial Balance; Set a Closing Date; Condense Data; Ask Client about Transaction; View Conversation List; Manage Fixed Assets; QuickBooks File Manager and Statement Writer; ProAdvisor Program information; and Online Accountant Resources. At the time of this writing, the program is available for $349 per year and includes QuickBooks Accountant Desktop program, support, training and certification, and discounts on QuickBooks products. In addition, there is a ProAdvisor Premium Program available that contains everything in the Deluxe program and includes QuickBooks Enterprise Accountant, QuickBooks for Mac, and QuickBooks Point of Sale Multi-Store software for $549 per year.

## Additional Subscriptions For QuickBooks Desktop

QuickBooks Desktop has a large variety of extras available that may be added to the program. Some of the most important and widely-used subscriptions are for payroll and payment processing. In addition, QuickBooks works with a wide variety of Apps.

**Enhanced Payroll** integrates with QuickBooks, just enter hours to process pay checks, pay by check or direct deposit, electronically file W-2's, includes payroll tax forms.  At the time of this writing, subscription rates are $25.97 per month (regular rate of $51.95) plus $1.50 per employee per month.

**Full-Service Payroll** includes all the features of Enhanced Payroll and also allows previous payroll data to be added to QuickBooks, payroll taxes are completed and filed for you, and offers a guarantee of no tax penalties. At the time of this writing, subscription rates are $55.97 per month (regular rate of $111.95) plus $2.00 per employee per month.

**Payment Processing** email invoices with a Pay Now link directly from QuickBooks, accept ACH bank transfers and all major credit cards, which include Visa, MasterCard, American Express, and Discover. As soon as an invoice is paid, QuickBooks auto-deposits the payment and updates your books automatically. At the time of this writing, you may pay per transaction for $0.00 per month and transaction fees of Card Swipe 2.4% + 25¢, Card Keyed 3.4% + 25¢, and ACH (bank payments) and checks 50¢ each. You may subscribe and pay monthly rates of $19.95 and transaction rates of Card Swiped 1.6% + 25¢, Card Keyed 3.2% + 25¢, and ACH (bank payments) and checks 50¢ each.

## QuickBooks Self-Employed

Program access is for one user with no access available for accountants—think Quicken for business. The program is used to track income and expenses, has the ability to separate business from personal spending, calculates estimated quarterly taxes, tracks mileage, classifies expenses by Schedule C categories, and downloads transactions from your bank and credit card accounts. Limited reporting is available. At the time of this writing subscription rates are $9.99 per month. You may also bundle the program with TurboTax that includes one federal and one state tax return filing for $16.99 per month.

## WHAT IS QUICKBOOKS ONLINE PLUS?

The difference between a cloud-based accounting program and a desktop program is essentially where you access and use the program and where you store and access your data. Desktop accounting has the program and data stored on your computer's hard drive. Cloud-based accounting provides program access, use, and storage over the Internet.

Since QuickBooks Online Plus uses the Cloud (Internet) to provide access to and use of the program and to record, save, and store your data, no software is downloaded and USB drives or storage media are not necessary. Cloud storage has data encryption that is extremely secure—think banks, financial institutions, brokerage firms, and Turbo Tax level security. Because QuickBooks Online Plus is web-based, it may be used in the office or on the go.

Essentially, QuickBooks Online Plus is a database of tables and fields that organize financial activity so users can utilize the data to communicate with vendors, customers, and others. When transactions have been recorded in QuickBooks Online Plus, you may create reports that show the results of operations, make financial and management decisions based on recorded information, and use information to complete additional forms and documents.

Remember, in the text QuickBooks Online Plus will be referred to as QuickBooks Online or QBO.

## QUICKBOOKS ONLINE PLUS SYSTEM REQUIREMENTS

To use QuickBooks Online Plus, an Internet connection is required (high-speed connection recommended). Supported browsers include: Chrome, Internet Explorer 10, Firefox, and Safari 6.1. QuickBooks Online is also accessible via Chrome on Android and Safari on iOS 7. The QuickBooks Online mobile app works with the iPhone, iPad, and Android phones and tablets (not all features are available on mobile devices).

## TRAINING IN QUICKBOOKS ONLINE PLUS

The Educational Trial Version of QuickBooks Online allows you to work with one company only. In addition to the trial version, there is a Test Drive Company that may be used for practice. Therefore, when working through the text, you will have two companies accessible for use during your training: QuickBooks Online Test Drive, Craig's Design & Landscaping Services, and an original company, Your Name's Beach Barkers, that you will create and use beginning in Chapter 2. The QuickBooks Online Test Drive Company will be used to explore the program and to enter transactions for practice. Anything entered into the Test Drive Company is not saved once you exit Test Drive. Beginning in Chapter 2, once you have practiced the transaction and or types of entries in the Test Drive Company, you will access Your Name's Beach Barkers and record and save similar transactions.

**DRILL BUTTON:** When practicing using the Test Drive Company, transactions to be entered will be marked with the DRILL BUTTON.

**DO BUTTON:** When entering transactions in the company you create, the transactions will be marked with the DO BUTTON

In Chapter 1, you will explore QuickBooks Online using the Test Drive Company. Once a company is created in Chapter 2, you will DRILL to enter transactions for practice using Test Drive; and then DO to enter transactions that are saved to your company. Beginning in Chapter 2 you will see side headings specifying DRILL and DO. The side headings will always be followed by the appropriate button.

## DATES

The dates used in training will be specified when you begin to record transactions. When using the Test Drive Company, you may find dates displayed that are different from those you see in the text. The Test Drive Company is programmed to automatically change the transaction dates. During the course of training, it is extremely important to use the date range indicated in the book. If you use the current date, you may not get the same information in your reports as shown in the text.

## IMPORTANT NOTE

QuickBooks Online is constantly evolving and new features, apps, and procedures change frequently. Everything in the text is correct at the time of this writing; however, by the time of publication some changes to the program may occur. QuickBooks Online has Labs available where you may experiment with proposed additions, changes, and enhancements to the program. These experiments may or may not become part of QuickBooks at any given time. Since the Labs are for testing, the features in the Labs will not be included in the text unless they become adopted before publication. Whenever possible, changes will be incorporated into the text but some of the updates will not be able to be included until the next edition of the text.

## WINDOWS AND BROWSERS

All computers use an operating system in conjunction with the software applications. Windows 7 is the operating system used in the text. Various screen shots will show procedures using Windows 7. Throughout the text, Chrome is used as the Browser. The exception to this will be using Internet Explorer when importing a company file from QuickBooks Desktop.

## ACCESS QUICKBOOKS ONLINE TEST DRIVE—DRILL

Since QuickBooks Online is a cloud-based program, you will need to open your Internet browser in order to access the program, the Test Drive Company—Craig's Design & Landscaping Services—and the company that you create in Chapter 2. As mentioned earlier, QuickBooks Online supports a variety of browsers including Chrome, Internet Explorer, Firefox, and Safari. Any supported browser may be used.

 Open QuickBooks Online Test Drive Company

> Open your Internet browser
> Enter **https://qbo.intuit.com/redir/testdrive** in the URL and press **Enter**

> Enter the numbers/words shown on the Security Verification screen, click **Continue**
> • If you make a mistake or cannot read the information, you will be given another set of numbers/words and may try again.
> • Each time you access Test Drive the Security Verification screen will show a different set of numbers/words. Occasionally, you may have to enter more than one Security Verification code in order to access the Test Drive Company.

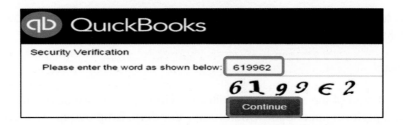

You will see the Home page for Craig's Design and Landscaping Services

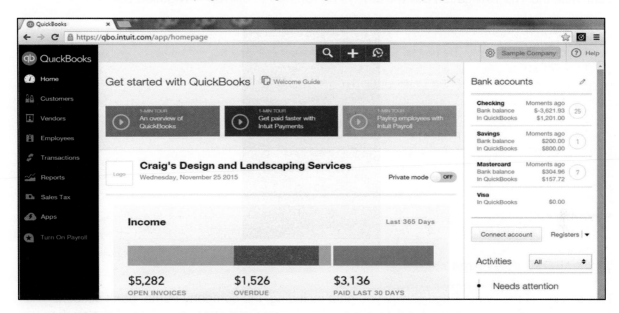

## INTRODUCTION TO THE HOME PAGE

QuickBooks Online Home Page is the key to working with company information, data, and lists; recording transactions; and preparing reports. The Home Page is divided into three primary sections—Top-Navigation Bar, Information/Display Area, and Left-Navigation Bar. These are discussed briefly below and then explored more fully within the chapter.

### Top-Navigation Bar

This bar contains several icons that are listed and described below. In the text, this will be referred to as the Top-Navigation Bar.

The three icons at the top-center of the Home Page are used to perform functions:

Is used to **Search** Transactions

Is used to **Create** Transactions

Is used to show **Recent** Transactions

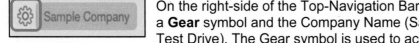 On the right-side of the Top-Navigation Bar on the Home Page you will see a **Gear** symbol and the Company Name (Sample Company is shown in the Test Drive). The Gear symbol is used to access Settings, Lists, Tools, and Your Company information.

**Help** is next to Gear and is used to ask for information about or to learn how to perform a task in QuickBooks Online

### Left-Navigation Bar

This bar is on the left-side of the screen. In addition to Home, there are seven tabs that are used to access Centers and perform actions for: Customers, Vendors, Employees, Transactions, Reports, Sales Tax, and Apps. Except for Chapter 1, the Left-Navigation Bar will be called the Navigation Bar, while the Top-Navigation Bar will always be referred to as Top-Navigation Bar.

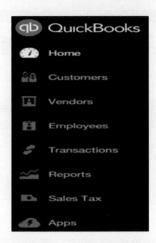

### Information/Display Area

This section of the Home Page shows you data including: the company name, bank account information, activities, and graphical data regarding income and expenses. A brief explanation follows:

**Company Name** is shown below the Top-Navigation Bar

### Craig's Design and Landscaping Services

**Company information graphs** include information regarding the company. Each graph allows you to get more information including detailed reports or transaction information.

➢ **Income** is referred to as a Money Bar and provides information regarding open, overdue, and paid invoices.

➢ **Expenses** gives a breakdown of types of expenses.

➤ **Profit and Loss** shows a graph showing income, expenses, and net income for a period of time. (Remember the dates you see may be different from the dates below.)

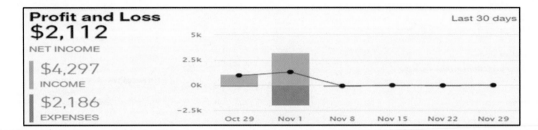

➤ **Bank Accounts** (displays bank account names and balances) and **Activities** (shows tasks that need to be or have been completed) are shown on the far-right side of the screen under the Gear and Help symbols.

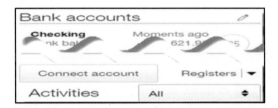

## EXPLORE THE TOP-NAVIGATION BAR—DRILL

To gain an understanding of the Top-Navigation Bar, it is important to test the features and tasks available.

 Explore each of the following capabilities on the Top-Navigation Bar:

Search

 Use Search to find an invoice

Click the **Search** icon 🔍 at the top of the Home Page
- You may search by Transaction Number, Date, or Amount.
Enter Invoice Number **1037**

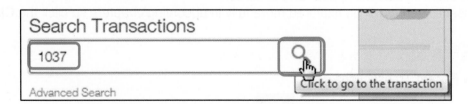

Click the search icon next to the invoice number. The invoice will be displayed.

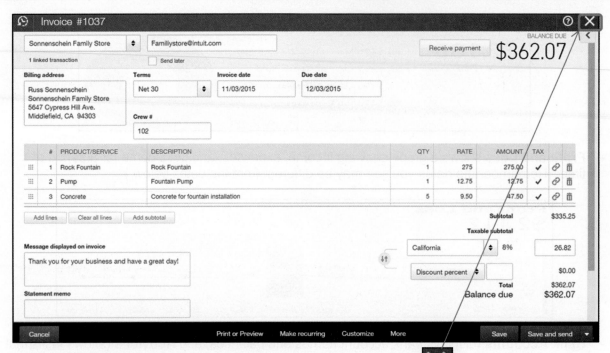

Look at the information provided in the Invoice and then click  (the **Close** button) on the invoice to close it

## Create

   Explore the Create screen

Click the Create icon ➕ to enter transactions.
- Note: When you click the Create icon, it changes to an ✖.
Transactions are divided into areas for Customers, Vendors, Employees, and Other.
Click **Invoice** in the Customers section of the Create screen

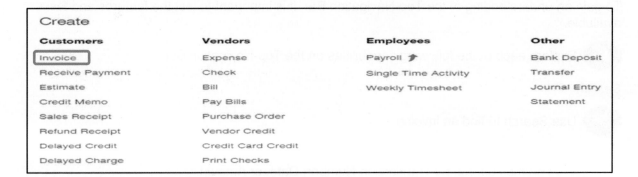

- A blank invoice will appear on the screen.
Transaction entry will be explored more fully in upcoming chapters so click the **Close** button

## Recent Transactions

View Recent Transactions

Click the **Recent Transactions** 🔄 icon to view and/or access recent transactions
Click the Credit Card Expense transaction for $34.00

- Dates will be different from the ones shown in the text.

| Recent Transactions | | | |
|---|---|---|---|
| Credit Card Expense | 11/28/2015 | $34.00 | |
| Credit Card Expense | 11/09/2015 | $42.40 | Hicks Hardware |
| Credit Card Expense | 11/15/2015 | $19.99 | Squeaky Kleen Car Wash |
| Credit Card Expense | 11/08/2015 | $19.99 | Squeaky Kleen Car Wash |
| Credit Card Expense | 11/08/2015 | $18.97 | Bob's Burger Joint |
| Credit Card Credit | 11/17/2015 | $900.00 | |
| Check No.Debit | 11/01/2015 | $19.99 | Squeaky Kleen Car Wash |
| Cash Expense | 10/30/2015 | $3.86 | Bob's Burger Joint |
| Cash Expense | 10/25/2015 | $19.99 | Squeaky Kleen Car Wash |
| Cash Expense | 10/25/2015 | $5.66 | Bob's Burger Joint |
| | | | More... |

Review the information shown on the Expense form, and then click the **Close** button

## Gear

 Access information for Your Company, Lists, Tools, and Profile

Click the **Gear**  icon
- This is used to access, edit, and enter information for your settings, lists, tools, and company.

Click **Account and Settings**

**Craig's Design and Landscaping Services**

| Your Company | Lists | Tools | Profile |
|---|---|---|---|
| Account and Settings | All Lists | Import Data | User Profile |
| Manage Users | Products and Services | Import Desktop Data | Feedback |
| Custom Form Styles | Recurring Transactions | Export Data | Privacy |
| Chart of Accounts | Attachments | Reconcile | |
| QuickBooks Labs | | Budgeting | 🔒 Sign Out |
| | | Audit Log | |
| | | Order Checks ↗ | |

View the information shown for Company Settings
- To make changes to the settings, you would click the pencil ✏ icon to Edit.

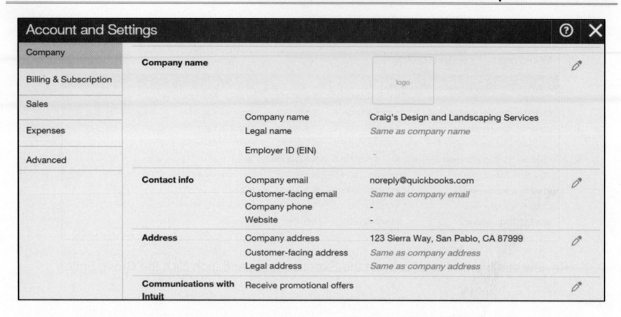

- Note the other Account and Settings tabs for Billing & Subscription, Sales, Expenses, and Advanced. These areas will be explored fully as you work through the text.

Click the **Close** button on the Account and Settings page

 Explore Help

Click the **Help** icon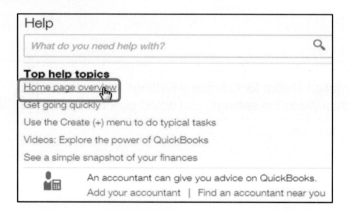

- On Help, you may type in words or phrases and click the Search icon or you may click one of the topics displayed.

Click **Home page overview**

Scroll through the information presented
- Anything displayed in blue may be clicked to access other Help items.

Click the **Close** button for Help to exit

## LEFT-NAVIGATION BAR—DRILL

The Left-Navigation Bar allows you to navigate through QuickBooks Online, access lists, and perform actions. Each area of the Navigation Bar is explored in this section.

 Click each of the areas on the Left-Navigation Bar to explore them

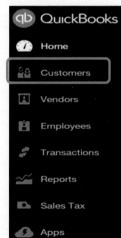

**Customers**

 View the Customers Center

> Click **Customers** on the Left-Navigation Bar to display the Customers Center
> View the Customers Center
> - Information about all of your customers is shown. This includes names, phone numbers, open balance amounts, and actions that may be performed.
> - Customers may be added, edited, or made inactive.
> - Note the dashboard. It includes a money bar that displays the amounts and number of transactions for estimates, unbilled activities, open invoices, overdue invoices, and payments received.
> - Icons are available to print, export to Excel, and change Settings.
> - Settings is used to customize the information shown.

Click the drop-down list arrow for Action for Amy's Bird Sanctuary
View the list of actions that may be performed when the suggested action is Receive payment

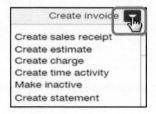

Scroll through the Customers Center until you find Cool Cars with the suggested action of Create invoice
Click the drop-down list arrow and view the action list

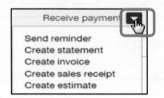

To exit the Customers Center, click a different tab on the Top- or Left-Navigation Bars

## Vendors

 View the Vendors Center

Click **Vendors** on the Left-Navigation Bar to display the Vendors Center.
View the Vendors Center
- Information is shown for all of your vendors. This includes names, phone numbers, email addresses, open balance amounts, and actions that may be performed.
- Vendors may be added, edited, or made inactive.
- The dashboard includes a money bar that displays the amounts and number of transactions for purchase orders, open bills, overdue bills, and payments made.
- Icons are available to print, export to Excel, and change Settings.
- Settings is used to customize the information shown.

Click the drop-down list arrow for **Action** for Bob's Burger Joint
View the list of actions that may be performed when the suggested action is "Create bill"

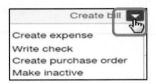

Scroll through the Vendors Center until you find Brosnahan Insurance Agency with the
suggested action of Make payment
Click the drop-down list arrow and view the action list

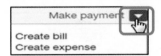

To exit the Vendors Center, click a different tab on the Top- or Left-Navigation Bars

## Employees

 View the Employees Center

Click **Employees** on the Left-Navigation Bar to display the Employees Center
View the Employees Center
- Information is shown for all of your employees. This includes names, phone numbers, email addresses, and actions that may be performed.
- Employees may be added, edited, or made inactive.
- The dashboard includes a money bar that displays payroll amounts for employee, employer, and net pay.
- Icons are available to print and to change Settings.
- Settings is used to customize the information shown.

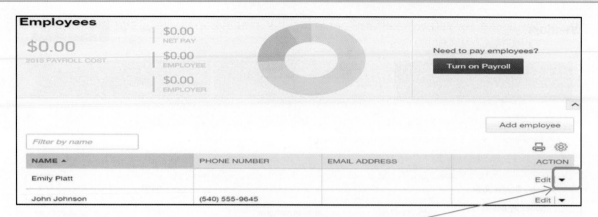

Click the drop-down list arrow for **Action** for Emily Platt
View the list of actions that may be performed when Payroll has not been activated

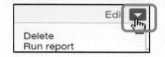

Click **Turn on payroll**
View the Employees Center

- When payroll is turned on in the Test Drive Company, payroll may be run and an Action column will not be shown.
- Information shown for all employees includes names, pay rate, pay method, and status.
- After you turn on payroll in the Test Drive Company, different employees are shown.

To exit the Employees Center, click a different tab on the Top- or Left-Navigation Bars

## Transactions

 View the categories in Transactions

Click **Transactions** on the Left-Navigation Bar to display the subcategories for Transactions
- Transactions subcategories are Banking, Sales, Expenses, and Chart of Accounts.
- Each of the areas allows transaction entry, editing, and actions.
Click **Banking** in the Transactions section of the Navigation Bar to access the Banking Center and view your bank feeds
- The money bar/dashboard includes information for your banking accounts including the bank balances and your QuickBooks balances.

- In this center you can perform batch actions, match transactions, add transactions, and add new bank accounts.
- Icons are available to print and to change Settings.
- Settings is used to customize the information shown.

To exit Banking Transactions, click a different tab on the Top- or Left-Navigation Bars
Click **Sales** in the Transactions section of the Left-Navigation Bar to access the Sales Center and view sales transactions

- The money bar/dashboard lists estimates, unbilled activities, open invoices, overdue invoices, and payments received.
- Individual transaction information includes the Date, Type, Number, Customer, Due Date, Balance, Total, Status, and Action.
- In this center you can perform batch actions, add transactions, import transactions and click individual transactions to drill down and see the details.
- Icons are available to print, export to Excel, and change Settings.
- Settings is used to customize the information shown.

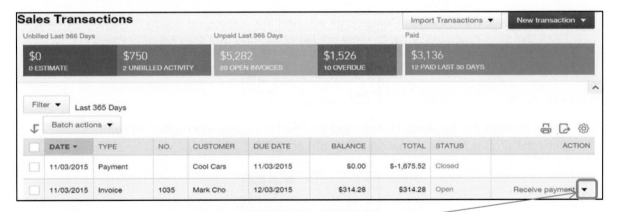

Click the drop-down list arrow for **Action** for Mark Cho
View the list of actions that may be performed when the suggested action is Receive payment

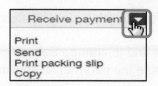

Scroll through the Sales Center until you find Pye's Cakes with the suggested action of Print
Click the drop-down list arrow and view the action list

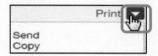

To exit the Sales Center, click a different tab on the Top- or Left-Navigation Bars
Click **Expenses** in the Transactions section of the Navigation Bar to view a list of recent
  expense transactions
- Individual transaction information includes the Date, Type, Number, Payee, Category,
  Total, and Action.
- In this center you can perform batch actions, add transactions, import transactions and
  click individual transactions to drill down and see the details.
- You may create a new transaction, make a payment, export to Excel, or drill down to see
  the details of an individual transaction.
- Icons are available to print, export to Excel, and change Settings.
- Settings is used to customize the information shown.

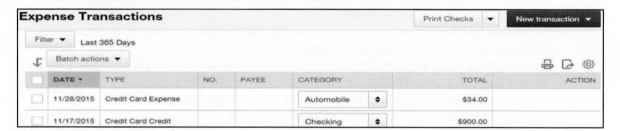

Scroll through the Expense Center until you find the suggested action of Make Payment
Click the drop-down list arrow to view the list of actions that may be performed

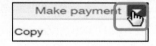

Scroll through the Expense Center until you find the suggested action of Print
Click the drop-down list arrow and view the action list

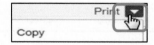

To exit the Expense Center, click a different tab on the Top- or Left-Navigation Bars
Click **Chart of Accounts** in the Transactions section of the Navigation Bar to access the
  Chart of Accounts
- You will see the Account Name, Type, Detail Type, QuickBooks Balance, Bank Balance
  (if appropriate), and the Action column.
- You may Run Reports, add New Accounts, View the Account Register (individual
  account information), Edit and Delete Accounts.

- Icons are available to edit, print, and change Settings (customize information shown).

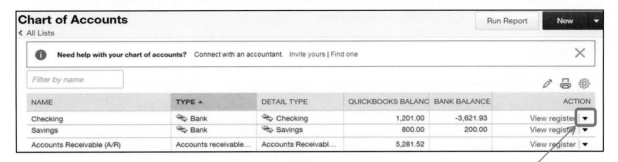

| NAME | TYPE ▲ | DETAIL TYPE | QUICKBOOKS BALANC | BANK BALANCE | ACTION |
|------|--------|-------------|-------------------|--------------|--------|
| Checking | Bank | Checking | 1,201.00 | -3,621.93 | View register ▼ |
| Savings | Bank | Savings | 800.00 | 200.00 | View register ▼ |
| Accounts Receivable (A/R) | Accounts receivable... | Accounts Receivabl... | 5,281.52 | | View register ▼ |

Click the Checking account drop-down list arrow for Action next to View register
Click the drop-down list arrow and view the action list

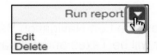

Scroll through the Chart of Accounts until you find Retained Earnings with the suggested
action of Run Report
Click the drop-down list arrow and view the action list

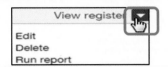

To exit the Chart of Accounts, click a different tab on the Top- or Left-Navigation Bars

## Reports

 View the Reports Center

Click **Reports** to access the Reports Center.
- All of the reports available in QuickBooks Online may be prepared from this center.
- The dashboard at the top of the screen provides information for the Net Income, Income, and Expenses.
- There are five tabs that you may click to access different reports: Recommended, Frequently Run, My Custom Reports, Management Reports, and All Reports.

Click the tab for **All Reports**
- You will see the respective report categories and descriptions.

- If you use different program features, payroll for example, your listing may be different from those shown in the text. If Payroll is on, the last category is Manage Payroll. If Payroll is off, it is Manage Employees.

---

### All Reports

**Business Overview**

These reports show different perspectives of how your business is doing.

**Manage Accounts Receivable**

These reports let you see who owes you money and how much they owe you so you can get paid.

**Manage Accounts Payable**

These reports show what you owe and when payments are due so you can take advantage of the time you have to pay bills but still make payments on time.

**Accountant Reports**

These are reports accountants typically use to drill down into your business details and prepare your tax returns.

**Manage Products and Inventory**

These reports will help you understand how much inventory you have and how much you are paying and making for each of your inventory items.

**Review Sales**

These reports group and total sales in different ways to help analyze your sales to see how you're doing and where you make your money.

**Review Expenses and Purchases**

These reports total your expenses and purchases and group them in different ways to help you understand what you spend.

**Manage Sales Tax**

These reports help you manage the sales taxes you collect and then pay the tax agencies.

**Manage Payroll**

These reports help you manage employee activities and payroll.

---

Click on the various categories to see the reports listed for each one
To exit Reports, click a different tab on the Top- or Left-Navigation Bars

## Taxes

If you do not have Payroll turned on, the Left-Navigation Bar will be Sales Tax. If you have Payroll turned on, the Left-Navigation Bar will be Taxes and will have two sub-categories: Sales Tax and Payroll Tax

 Explore the Sales Tax Center

Click **Taxes** and **Sales Tax** or click **Sales Tax** on the Navigation Bar to open the Sales Tax Center
- The Sales Tax Center is used to track and pay sales tax.
- It is divided into two sections: Sales Tax Owed and Recent Sales Tax Payments.
- Important reminder: always use the Sales Tax Center to record your Sales Tax payments. If you pay sales taxes as a bill or write a check, the payments will not appear in the Recent Payments list.
- Information is displayed with the most recent date shown first.

To exit the Sales Tax Center, click a different tab on the Top- or Left-Navigation Bars

## Payroll Tax

 Explore the Payroll Tax Center

Click **Taxes** and **Payroll Tax** on the Left-Navigation Bar to open the Payroll Tax Center
- If you do not have Payroll turned On, click **Employees** on the Navigation Bar, then click the **Turn on Payroll** button.

The Payroll Tax Center is divided into two sections: Taxes and Forms
- The Taxes side allows you to Pay Taxes and view the Tax Type, Due Date, and E-Payment Cutoff Date and Time. There are other tasks that may be performed as well.
- The Due Date and E-Payment Cutoff dates are changed frequently and will not match the text.
- The Forms side allows you to access a variety of both blank and archived Forms.

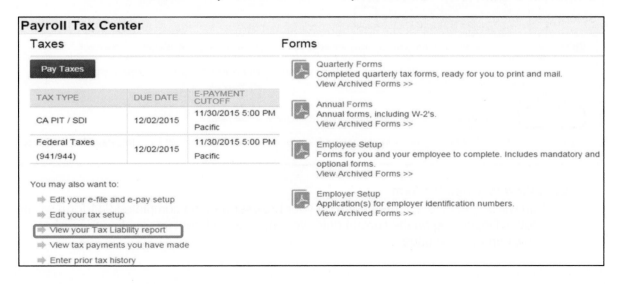

Click **View your Tax Liability report** to prepare the report
- Note the information displayed regarding the Taxes, Tax Amounts, Tax Paid, and Tax Owed.

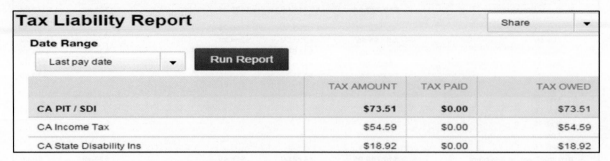

| Tax Liability Report | | Share ▼ | |
|---|---|---|---|
| **Date Range** | | | |
| Last pay date ▼   Run Report | | | |
| | TAX AMOUNT | TAX PAID | TAX OWED |
| **CA PIT / SDI** | **$73.51** | **$0.00** | **$73.51** |
| CA Income Tax | $54.59 | $0.00 | $54.59 |
| CA State Disability Ins | $18.92 | $0.00 | $18.92 |

Click **Payroll Tax** on the Left-Navigation Bar or the Back ⬅ button on your browser to return to the Payroll Tax Center
Click **Quarterly Forms** in the Forms section of the Center
- You will see an explanation regarding the Quarterly forms available and a portal to the form in blue.
Click **941**

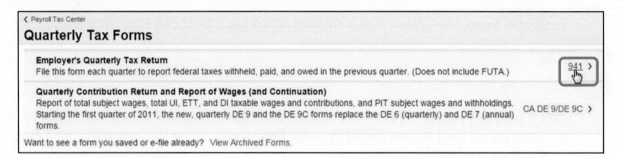

The Employer's Quarterly Tax Return screen will be shown
- You may click the drop-down list arrow for "Select the period" to display a different date range.

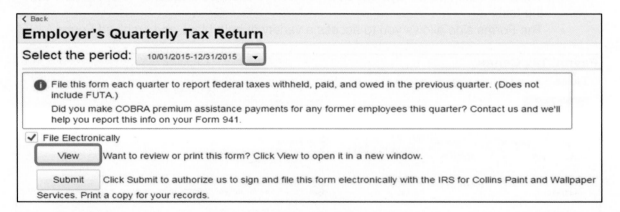

Click **View** to review the form
- You will be taken to a separate tab on your browser and the completed 941 form will be shown. Depending on the current date, you may see different information than what shows on the next page.

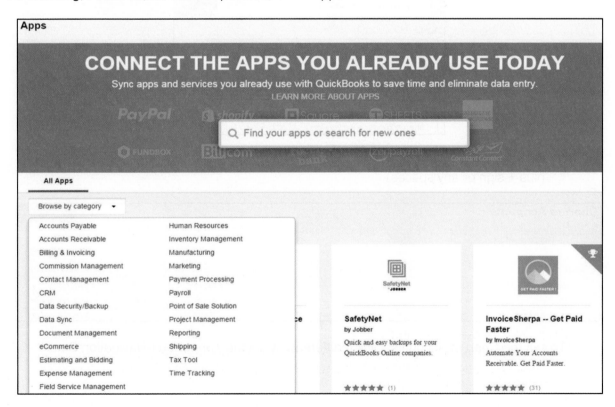

Partial Form

To exit Form 941 Employer's Quarterly Federal Tax Return, click **Close** on the browser tab

To exit the Payroll Tax Center, click a different tab on the Top- or Left-Navigation Bars

## Apps

Not available in the Test Drive Company

Once you create a company, you may click **Apps** to go to the App Center. There are hundreds of apps available that integrate and work with QuickBooks Online. Some apps are free while others charge a fee.

Apps may be selected by category (shown on the screen shot) or by apps grouped together based on Trending, Featured, Newest, Top Rated, or All Apps.

## USE HELP TO FIND KEYBOARD SHORTCUTS—DRILL

To save time, you may use the keyboard rather than the mouse or track pad to Go To, Work with Forms, Move Between Fields, Enter Dates in Fields, Change Dates in a Calendar, Calculate Amounts and Rates, Choose Items in Drop-Down Lists, Respond to Messages, Enter Transactions in a Register, Adjust Print Alignment, and Move Around in Journal Entries.

 Use Help to find out about Keyboard Shortcuts

Click **Help** on the Top-Navigation Bar
Enter the phrase **Keyboard shortcuts**, click the **Search** icon

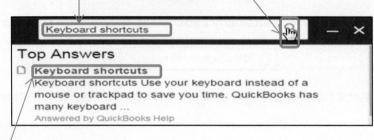

Click **Keyboard shortcuts** listed in the Top Answers
- A keyboard shortcut is a group of key strokes that will enable you to go to something quickly.
- Read and scroll through the information provided.

Click **Go To** in the information displayed to view a keyboard shortcut chart
After scrolling through the Keyboard Shortcuts, click the **Close** button to exit Help

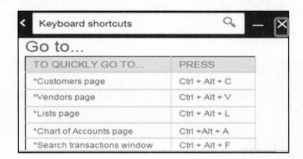

Use the keyboard shortcut **Ctrl + Alt + A** to access the Chart of Accounts (do not type the plus + sign or any spaces)

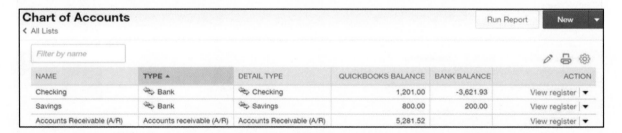

To exit the Chart of Accounts, click a different tab on the Top- or Left-Navigation Bars

## EXIT QUICKBOOKS ONLINE AND THE TEST DRIVE COMPANY—DRILL

Click the **Close** button on your Web browser to exit both QuickBooks Online and the Test Drive Company, Craig's Design and Landscaping Services

## SUMMARY

Chapter 1 provides general information regarding QuickBooks Online Plus. In this chapter, various QuickBooks Online features were examined. The Test Drive Company provided by Intuit was used to explore the different elements, operations, and characteristics of QuickBooks Online Plus in preparation for beginning work in Chapter 2.

# END-OF-CHAPTER QUESTIONS

## TRUE/FALSE

ANSWER THE FOLLOWING QUESTIONS IN THE SPACE PROVIDED BEFORE THE QUESTION NUMBER.

_____ 1. The Top-Icon Bar is at the top of the Home Page.

_____ 2. Cloud-Based Computing uses the Internet to provide program access.

_____ 3. You must have a password to login to the Test Drive Company.

_____ 4. You may use Search to find a transaction.

_____ 5. Select Reports on the Left-Navigation Bar to access the reports available for QuickBooks Online.

_____ 6. You must pay a monthly fee to access the Test Drive Company.

_____ 7. A mouse is used to click on a keyboard shortcut.

_____ 8. Payroll taxes are always active.

_____ 9. QuickBooks is available in Online and Desktop versions.

_____ 10. On the Create screen, click Invoice under Customer to access a blank invoice.

## MULTIPLE CHOICE

WRITE THE LETTER OF THE CORRECT ANSWER IN THE SPACE PROVIDED BEFORE THE QUESTION NUMBER.

_____ 1. Company Settings are accessed by clicking the ___.
A. Search icon
B. Gear icon
C. Plus icon
D. Home on the Left-Navigation Bar

_____ 2. Supported browsers for QuickBooks Online include ___.
A. Chrome
B. Internet Explorer
C. Firefox
D. All of the above

_____ 3. Clicking Create opens a list of tasks that may be completed for ___.
A. Company Settings
B. Accounts Payable
C. Vendors
D. Accountants

_____ 4. The Company Name is displayed ___.
   A. Under the Income Bar
   B. In the Information and Display Area
   C. On the Left-Navigation Bar
   D. On the browser tab

_____ 5. You may Search by ___.
   A. Amount
   B. Date
   C. Transaction
   D. All of the above

_____ 6. Bank Accounts and Activities are shown on the ___.
   A. Home Page
   B. Left-Navigation Bar
   C. Top-Navigation Bar
   D. None of the above

_____ 7. The Money Bar for ___ includes information for Purchase Orders
   A. Customers
   B. Vendors
   C. Home Page
   D. All of the above

_____ 8. To save transactions in QuickBooks Online, you use ___.
   A. A USB drive
   B. The hard disk in the computer
   C. The Cloud
   D. All of the above

_____ 9. To give commands without using the mouse, you use a(n) ___.
   A. Keyboard Shortcut
   B. Navigation Bar
   C. Menu
   D. Icon

_____ 10. There are hundreds of external ___ available that integrate and work with QuickBooks Online.
   A. Commands
   B. Tasks
   C. Apps
   D. All of the above

## FILL-IN

IN THE SPACE PROVIDED, WRITE THE ANSWER THAT MOST APPROPRIATELY COMPLETES THE SENTENCE.

1. Click _____ on the Left-Navigation Bar and _____ to access the Sales Center.

2. To keep the books for a business, accounting transactions need to be _____, _____, and _____.

3. QuickBooks Online uses the _____ or the _____ to provide program access and data storage.

4. In the Customer Center there are icons to print, export to Excel, or change _____.

5. Click Customers on the _____ to access the Customers Center.

## COMPUTER ASSIGNMENT

USE THE QUICKBOOKS ONLINE TEST DRIVE COMPANY TO LOOK UP INFORMATION, THEN WRITE THE ANSWERS TO THE FOLLOWING EXERCISES IN THE SPACE PROVIDED

1. What is the Keyboard Shortcut to Open the Chart of Accounts?       _____

2. Which icon do you click in order to Print Checks?       _____

3. Which icon do you click in order to Manage Users?       _____

4. You may Search by Date, Amount, or ___.       _____

5. You click ___ on the ___-Navigation Bar to Access All Reports.       _____

6. View Reports to determine which report shows you the company Assets, Liabilities, and Equity?       _____

7. The other name for the Profit and Loss report is ___. (View Reports if you need to look up this information.)       _____

8. What are the four categories for Transactions on the Left-Navigation Bar?       _____
_____
_____
_____

9. You can find the list of Keyboard Shortcuts by using ___.       _____

10. What three areas of information are graphically displayed on the Home Page?_____
_____
_____

# CREATE A COMPANY

## LEARNING OBJECTIVES

At the completion of this chapter, you will be able to:

1. Activate the Educational Trial Version of QuickBooks Online Plus
2. Create a company in QuickBooks Online Plus
3. Import Lists from Excel files
4. Change Settings for a new company
5. Edit the imported Customers and Vendors Lists
6. Add Fixed Assets
7. Edit accounts in the imported Chart of Accounts
8. Edit the Products and Services List
9. Understand that you can import a company from QuickBooks Desktop
10. Print, export to Excel, and use email to submit lists and reports.

## TRAINING TUTORIAL

The following tutorial is a step-by-step guide to setting up the fictitious company Your Name's Beach Barkers. Company information, accounts, items, customers, and vendors, and other details must be provided before transactions may be recorded in QuickBooks.

Please note that QuickBooks Online is updated on a regular basis. If your screens are not always an exact match to the text, check with your instructor to see if you should select something that is similar to the text.

## TRAINING PROCEDURES

To maximize the training benefits, you should:

1. Read the entire chapter *before* beginning the tutorial within the chapter.
2. Answer the end-of-chapter questions.
3. Be aware that transactions to be entered are given within a **MEMO**.
4. If you have practice drills to perform, they will be marked by ▶ .
5. To complete a practice drill, you will open the Test Drive Company, Craig's Design & Landscaping Services.
6. The entries to be completed in the chapter for Your Name's Beach Barkers will be indicated by ▶ .
7. When you have completed a section, put a check mark next to the final step.
8. If you do not complete a section, put the date in the margin next to the last step completed. This will make it easier to know where to begin when training is resumed.
9. You may not finish the entire chapter in one computer session.
10. **Remember no work is saved in the Test Drive Company. If you do not finish the chapter or a section within one work session, you will need to re-enter information into the Test Drive Company.**
11. As you complete your work, proofread carefully and check for accuracy. Double-check amounts of money and the accounts, items, and dates used.

12.  Check with your instructor to find out how completed work will be submitted. You may be asked to print or email documents and/or reports to your instructor or your instructor may wish to access your QuickBooks Online account and view your work within the program. Instructions for printing, exporting, and/or emailing are presented within the chapter.

13.  There is a checklist at the end of the chapter that lists everything that is printed and/or exported to Excel when working through the chapter. There is a blank line next to each document listed so you can mark it when it has been printed and/or completed.

## DATES

Throughout the text, the year used for the screen shots is 2016. Check with your instructor to see what year to use for the transactions. Sometimes, the difference in the computer and text dates will cause a slight variation in the way QuickBooks' screens are displayed and they may not match the text exactly. If you cannot change a date that is provided by QuickBooks, accept it and continue with your training. Instructions are given where this occurs. The main criterion is to be consistent with the year you use throughout the text. QuickBooks Online inserts the current date into a transaction, be aware of this and be sure to use the date indicated in the text. When you use the Test Drive Company, know that it is programmed for automatic date changes and that the dates shown in the text will not match the ones you see on your computer screen.

## IMPORTANT NOTE

QuickBooks Online is constantly evolving and new features, apps, and procedures change frequently. Everything in the text is correct at the time of this writing; however, by the time of publication some changes to the program may occur. QuickBooks Online has Labs available where you may experiment with proposed additions, changes, and enhancements to the program. These experiments may or may not become part of QuickBooks at any given time. Since the Labs are for testing, the features in the Labs will not be included in the text unless they become adopted before publication. Whenever possible, changes will be incorporated into the text but do note that some of the updates will not be able to be included until the next edition of the text.

## WINDOWS AND BROWSERS

All computers use an operating system in conjunction with the software applications. Windows 7 is the operating system used in the text. Various screen shots will show procedures using Windows 7. Throughout the text, Chrome is used as the Browser. The exception to this will be using Internet Explorer when a company file is imported from and exported to QuickBooks Desktop.

## TRIAL VERSION, TEST DRIVE, DRILL AND DO BUTTONS

The Educational Trial Version of QuickBooks Online allows you to work with one company only. As a result of this, when you work through the chapters, you will be directed to use the Test Drive Company, Craig's Design and Landscaping Services, to practice a task before you enter it into Your Name's Beach Barkers. When you work in the Test Drive Company, you cannot save your work so use of the company is strictly for practice and learning. Sometimes, you will have to make entries into the Test Drive Company before you can practice a task. Instructions will be given when this occurs. There will be instances in which you will not be able to practice a task before completing it in Your Name's Beach Barkers. Instructions will be given when this happens.

As you work through the chapter, remember the differences between the Drill and Do buttons. In this chapter, you will get reminders regarding which button to use when you switch from drilling to doing.

**DRILL BUTTON:** When practicing using the Test Drive Company, transactions to be entered will be marked with the DRILL BUTTON.

**DO BUTTON:** When entering transactions in the company you create, Your Name's Beach Barkers, the transactions will be marked with the DO BUTTON.

## CREATE YOUR QUICKBOOKS ONLINE EMAIL ACCOUNT—DO

Before you can create a company and use QuickBooks Online, you need to have an email account established that you will use to login to QuickBooks. The email will be your Intuit ID. If you use a different Web browser, go Incognito, use a different computer, or try to work with the mobile app, you will be required to authenticate your access by answering an email sent to your Intuit ID address. You may use your personal email or you may create an email account specifically for this text. Whichever email account you use, you should give it and your QuickBooks Online Password to your instructor. This will be a backup in case you forget your password. It may also be used by your instructor to open your company and check your work.

For illustration purposes, an email account using Gmail will be created specifically for the QBO Educational Trial Version.

_DO_

Create a Gmail Account for QuickBooks Online

Open your Internet browser
- The screenshots and instructions are given for Google Chrome. Internet Explorer will be similar.
There are three ways to access your Web browser:
    Click the **Start** button, click **All Programs**, click the **Google Chrome** folder, and click
        **Google Chrome**
    Click the **Chrome** icon on the Taskbar
    Click the **Chrome** shortcut on the Desktop
If Google does not show when Chrome is launched, enter **www.google.com** as the URL, press **Enter**

- The https:// is inserted automatically.
Click the **Sign in** button
- If you see **Add Account**, click it.   
Click **Create Account**

Enter the information required:

Type your actual First Name in the First text box

Type your actual Last Name in the Last text box

In Choose your username, enter your new email address:

**YourNameTestQBO**

- Use your real first and last name. For example, Joe Smith's username would be: JoeSmithTestQBO.
- When using the Educational Trial Version of QuickBooks Online, Intuit would appreciate it if the word "Test" is part of the email address. That will help delineate the Educational Trial Version.
- @gmail.com is automatically entered.

Enter the same password you will use to login to Intuit in the Create a password text box

- The password should contain at least eight mixed-case letters, a number, and a symbol to be a strong password. In fact, an eight-character password with numbers, symbols, and mixed-case letters is harder to guess because it has 30,000 times as many possible combinations as an eight-character password using all lower case letters.

Re-enter your password in the Confirm your password text box

To enter your Birthday, click the drop-down list arrow ⬍ for Month

Click on the Month of your birthday

Enter the Day and Year of your birth

Click the drop-down list arrow ⬍ for Gender

Click **Male**, **Female**, or **Other**

Enter your Mobile phone number

Enter your current email address

To "Prove you're not a robot," enter the numbers shown in the picture in Type the text:

Click the drop-down list arrow for Location, click **United States**

Click the **I agree to the Google Terms of Service and Privacy Policy** check box

- To read the Terms and Policy, click **Terms of Service** and **Privacy Policy**.

Click the **Next step** button [Next step]

You will get a Welcome screen

Click **Continue**

- Your Gmail account is now active and ready to use. The first time you access your email, you will get a few information screens. You may read them, click Next to view more, or click the Close button to close the information screens.
- Unless instructed otherwise, give your email address and QuickBooks password to your instructor.
- Since your instructor will have full access to this Gmail account, it is recommended that you use it only for QuickBooks Online.
- <u>Before</u> you activate the program and create the company, read the following information for Company Profile and Begin Working in QuickBooks Online.

## COMPANY PROFILE: YOUR NAME'S BEACH BARKERS—READ

Your Name's Beach Barkers is a fictitious company that provides boarding in the Dog House, playtime at Dog Day Camp, grooming in the Dog Salon, and training at Dog School. Your Name's Beach Barkers is located in Venice, California, and is a sole proprietorship owned by you. You are involved in all aspects of the business. Your Name's Beach Barkers has four employees—Ray Butler, Heather Giacchi, and Gail Henry, and Evan Jones—who may be referred to during transaction descriptions. (Employee names and details will be added in the Payroll chapter.)

The company operates using the accrual-basis of accounting. Accrual-basis accounting matches the income and the expenses of a period in order to arrive at an accurate figure for net income or net loss. Revenue is earned at the time the service is performed or the sale is made no matter when the actual cash is received. An expense is recorded at the time the bill is received or the purchase is made regardless of the actual payment date. The other accounting method available is Cash-basis accounting, which records income or revenue at the time cash is received no matter when the sale was made or the service performed. In cash-basis accounting, an expense is not recorded until it is paid.

## BEGIN WORKING IN QUICKBOOKS ONLINE—READ

In the tutorial all transactions are listed in memos. Always enter the date of the transaction as specified in the memo. If the transaction does not have a date given, use the memo date for the transaction. By default, QuickBooks Online automatically enters the current date of the computer or the last transaction date used. In many instances, this will not be the same date as the transaction in the text. When necessary, customer, vendor, account, and products and services names will be given in the transaction. If a memo contains more than one transaction, there will be a visual separation between them.

> **MEMO**
> **DATE:** The transaction date is listed here
>
> Transaction details are given in the body of the memo. Names, the type of transaction, amounts of money, and any other details needed are listed here.

Even when you are given instructions on how to enter a transaction step by step, you should always refer to the memo for transaction details. Once a specific type of transaction has been entered in a step-by-step manner, additional transactions will be made without having instructions provided. Of course, you may always refer to instructions given for previous transactions for ideas or for the steps used to enter those transactions. Always double-check the date and the year used for the transaction. Using an incorrect date will cause reports to have different totals and contain different transactions than those shown in the text.

You should complete the next two sections at the same time. Do not begin Activate QuickBooks Online Plus Educational Trial Version unless you also have enough time to complete Create Your Name's Beach Barkers.

## ACTIVATE QUICKBOOKS ONLINE PLUS EDUCATIONAL TRIAL VERSION—DO

Once you have created your email account that you will use as your Intuit ID, you will need to set up your QuickBooks account and activate your QuickBooks Online Plus Educational Trial Version. Once the program is activated you will have use of the software for five months. You may import company data for the first 60 days. When the trial period is over, you will be able to see your data for a period of time; but you will not be able to access it unless you subscribe to QuickBooks Online Plus. The company created in QuickBooks Online Plus may not be used in other versions of QuickBooks Online.

### DO

Activate QuickBooks Online Plus Educational Trial Version

      Enter **quickbooks.intuit.com/start/retail_sui** in the URL of your Web browser
      Press **Enter**
      Using the Access Code card information provided in your book, enter your License number
         and Product number
      Click **I agree to the Terms of Service**
      Click **Set Up Account**

Complete the Sign Up for QuickBooks form:

    Email Address: Enter the Email Address you just created

    First name: Enter your real first name

    Last name: Enter your real last name

    Mobile number: Enter your cell or home phone number including the area code.

    Password: Enter the same password that you created for your email address

    Confirm Password: Enter the same password again.

Click **Create Account**

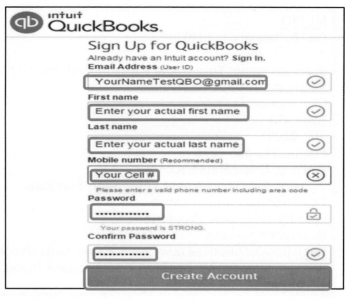

The Creating your QuickBooks account is shown:

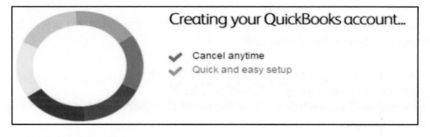

Next you will be taken to a screen to Set Up Beach Barkers

Continue with the next section immediately

## CREATE YOUR NAME'S BEACH BARKERS—DO

Once you have created your Intuit ID and activated the QuickBooks Online Educational Trial Version, you will begin to create your company. Please note that the information provided here is strictly focused on the Educational Trial Version of QuickBooks Online Plus. If you do not setup your company immediately after registering, or install the 30-day Trial Version or a subscription version of the program, the screens shown will be different from the ones displayed in the text. However, most of the information required will be similar to the text.

**MEMO**
**DATE:** January 1, 2016

Business name: **Your Name's Beach Barkers** (Use your real name)
Address: **1302 Pacific Avenue**
City: **Venice**
State: **CA**
ZIP: **92091**
Phone: **310-555-2275**
Website: **BeachBarkers.com**
Industry: **Pet Care (except Veterinary) Services**
Sell: **Products and services**
Industry Type: **Sole Proprietor**
Business Age: **Less than 1 Year**
Keep track of business now?, click **Excel, QuickBooks Desktop, Pen and paper**
"What matters to your business?" screen, click **Invoicing, Expense tracking, and Mobile
    office**

<u>DO</u>

*prepaid subsumption
ends 9-1-18*

On the screens shown in QuickBooks Online, perform the following steps to enter the
information provided in the Memo box

Click at the end of your Email address in Business name
**Backspace** until you remove your Email address
- If your email address is followed by the word Company, also delete the word Company.
Key in the company name **Your Name's Beach Barkers**
- Remember to use your real name. For example, the author's business name would be:
    Janet Horne's Beach Barkers.
- The Logo for Beach Barkers will be added later in the text.
Press **Tab**, enter the Address **1302 Pacific Avenue**
Press **Tab**, enter the City **Venice**
Press **Tab**, enter the State **CA**
Press **Tab**, enter the ZIP **92091**
Press **Tab**, enter the Business phone **310-555-2275**
Press **Tab**, enter the Website **BeachBarkers.com**
Verify that you entered all of the information correctly

*Couldn't
enter
this email
"please enter
valid entry"*

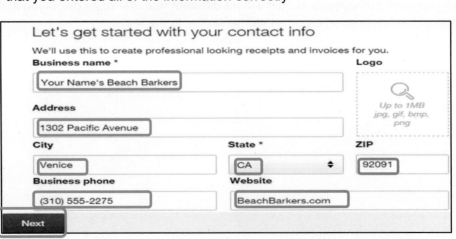

- If you get different screens from the ones shown in the chapter, provide the information that you have available and continue the setup.

Click **Next**

Click in the text box for "Industry"

Type the word **Pet**

- QuickBooks Online has a lot of different industries that may be selected. Selecting the correct industry enables QuickBooks Online to create a Chart of Accounts that is specific to the industry.

Click **Pet Care (except Veterinary) Services** to select the Industry    *couldnt find*

Click the drop-down arrow for "What do you sell?"

Click **Products and services**

- In a later chapter we will be working with inventory items so it is appropriate to select Products and services for what we sell.

Click the drop-down list arrow for "Business type"

Click **Sole proprietor**

If your screen asks different questions including:

> Do you have an accountant, bookkeeper, or tax pro?, click **No**
>
> Do you want to import data from QuickBooks for Windows or Mac?, click **No**
>
> Do you have-W-2 employees?, click **Yes**
>
> How do you like to get paid?, click **Cash, Check, Credit Card**

Click the drop-down list arrow for "Business age"

Click **Less than 1 year**

Verify that you entered all of the information correctly

**Tell us a bit more about your business**

We'll use what we know about businesses like yours to jumpstart your setup.

**Industry ***

Pet Care (except Veterinary) Services

**What do you sell? ***      **Business type**

Products and services      Sole proprietor

**Business age**

Less than 1 year

Previous    Next

Click **Next**

On the "How do you keep track of your business now?" screen, click **Excel, QuickBooks Desktop, and Pen and paper**

**How do you keep track of your business now?**

Choose all that apply. We'll show you how to get everything into your books.

| ✓ Excel | ✓ QuickBooks Desktop |
| Google | Online banking |
| ✓ Pen and paper | Other software |

Previous    Next

Click **Next**

On the "What matters to your business?" screen, click **Invoicing**, **Expense tracking**, and **Mobile office**

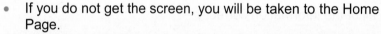

Click **Next**

- You will see a series of screens while QuickBooks is creating your company.

If you see the screen "Your QuickBooks is ready," click **Let's dive in**

- If you do not get the screen, you will be taken to the Home Page.

If you continue with the next section at this time, be sure to use Your Name's Beach Barkers

## VIEW INFORMATION PROVIDED BY QUICKBOOKS ONLINE—DO

When QuickBooks Online creates your company, it creates a Chart of Accounts, a list of Products and Services, and Company Settings based on the type of Industry you selected when creating Your Name's Beach Barkers.

_DO_

 View the Chart of Accounts and the Products and Services List in **Your Name's Beach Barkers**

Click the **Gear** icon on the Top-Navigation Bar

In the column for Settings, click **Chart of Accounts**

Scroll through the Chart of Accounts and view all of the accounts created by QuickBooks Online

Click the **Gear** icon again

In the column for Lists, click **Products and services**

Scroll through the list of Products and services to see what QuickBooks Online created

## PURGE COMPANY INFORMATION—DO

Within the first 60 days of activating your QuickBooks Online account, you may purge data, import data using Excel, and import data using QuickBooks Desktop as many times as you wish. If you want to redo any of the setup and/or data import, you will need to repeat the purge process.

If we accept all of the information provided by QBO, there will be a lot of time-consuming editing to perform. Since we are within the first 60 days of our subscription, we can purge the company and then set it up using the Chart of Accounts and the Products and Services Lists that we prefer.

*DO*

*doesn't appear in URL*

 Purge **Your Name's Beach Barkers** by performing the following steps

Make sure your QuickBooks Online Plus company, Your Name's Beach Barkers, is open
On the URL of your Web browser enter **https://qbo.intuit.com/app/purgecompany**
Press **Enter**
- If your number of accounts or the number of days left are different from what is shown below, do not be concerned.

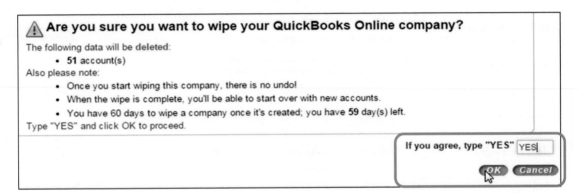

⚠ **Are you sure you want to wipe your QuickBooks Online company?**

The following data will be deleted:
- **51 account(s)**

Also please note:
- Once you start wiping this company, there is no undo!
- When the wipe is complete, you'll be able to start over with new accounts.
- You have 60 days to wipe a company once it's created; you have **59 day(s) left**.

Type "YES" and click OK to proceed.

If you agree, type "YES"  [YES]

OK   Cancel

Enter the word **YES**; and then, click **OK**
For "What type of business is this?" click the drop-down list arrow and scroll through the list of businesses until you get to Miscellaneous Services, click **Pet Care Services**

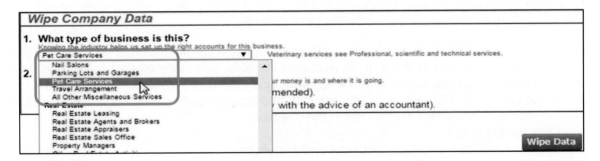

*Wipe Company Data*

1. **What type of business is this?**
   Knowing the industry helps us set up the right accounts for this business.
   [Pet Care Services ▼]        Veterinary services see Professional, scientific and technical services.

2. [dropdown list:]
   Nail Salons
   Parking Lots and Garages
   **Pet Care Services**
   Travel Arrangement
   All Other Miscellaneous Services
   Real Estate
   Real Estate Leasing
   Real Estate Agents and Brokers
   Real Estate Appraisers
   Real Estate Sales Office
   Property Managers

   ur money is and where it is going.
   mended).
   y with the advice of an accountant).

   **Wipe Data**

For "Create accounts based on my industry?" make sure that **Create accounts based on my industry (recommended)** is selected
Click **Wipe Data**

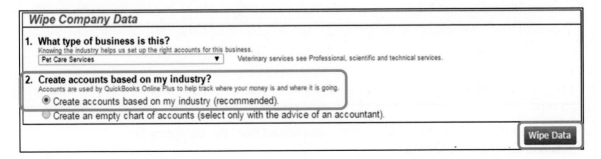

*Wipe Company Data*

1. **What type of business is this?**
   Knowing the industry helps us set up the right accounts for this business.
   [Pet Care Services ▼]        Veterinary services see Professional, scientific and technical services.

2. **Create accounts based on my industry?**
   Accounts are used by QuickBooks Online Plus to help track where your money is and where it is going.
   ● Create accounts based on my industry (recommended).
   ○ Create an empty chart of accounts (select only with the advice of an accountant).

   **Wipe Data**

## VIEW CHART OF ACCOUNTS AND PRODUCT SERVICE LIST—DO

Once the purge has been completed, it is important to see which accounts and products and services have been automatically created by QuickBooks Online.

*DO*

View the Chart of Accounts and the Products and Services List in **Your Name's Beach Barkers**

Click the **Gear** icon
In the column for Settings, click **Chart of Accounts**
Scroll through the Chart of Accounts and view all of the accounts created by QBO

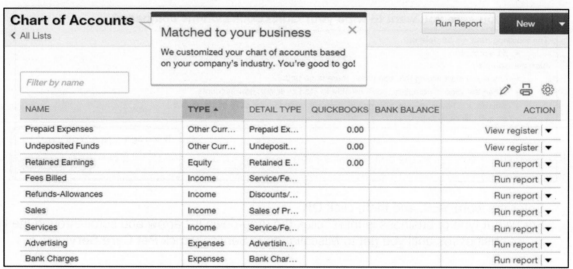

| NAME | TYPE ▲ | DETAIL TYPE | QUICKBOOKS | BANK BALANCE | ACTION |
|---|---|---|---|---|---|
| Prepaid Expenses | Other Curr... | Prepaid Ex... | 0.00 | | View register \| ▼ |
| Undeposited Funds | Other Curr... | Undeposit... | 0.00 | | View register \| ▼ |
| Retained Earnings | Equity | Retained E... | 0.00 | | Run report \| ▼ |
| Fees Billed | Income | Service/Fe... | | | Run report \| ▼ |
| Refunds-Allowances | Income | Discounts/... | | | Run report \| ▼ |
| Sales | Income | Sales of Pr... | | | Run report \| ▼ |
| Services | Income | Service/Fe... | | | Run report \| ▼ |
| Advertising | Expenses | Advertisin... | | | Run report \| ▼ |
| Bank Charges | Expenses | Bank Char... | | | Run report \| ▼ |

**Partial Chart of Accounts**

- You will notice that a lot of accounts that you will use are not included. Accounts such as Checking, Accounts Receivable, Accounts Payable, and many others are missing. Some missing accounts will be added when importing your Chart of Accounts, Customers List, Vendors List, Products and Services List, and adding opening balances. Other accounts will be added and/or edited later in the chapter.

Click the **Gear** icon
In the column for Lists, click **Products and Services**
View the two items on the list

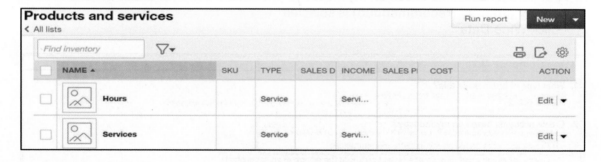

| | NAME ▲ | SKU | TYPE | SALES D | INCOME | SALES P | COST | ACTION |
|---|---|---|---|---|---|---|---|---|
| ☐ | Hours | | Service | | Servi... | | | Edit \| ▼ |
| ☐ | Services | | Service | | Servi... | | | Edit \| ▼ |

- This proves that the previous data was wiped from the company file.

Close QuickBooks Online:

Click the **Gear** icon
In the "Your Company" column, click **Sign Out**

## COMPANY SETTINGS—DRILL

Now that you have purged Your Name's Beach Barkers, it is appropriate to edit some of the settings selected by QuickBooks. This is required because not all of the settings will be what you want.

There are four areas in Account and Settings that need to be edited. These are: Company, Sales, Expenses, and Advanced. (You may find setting tabs for Billing & Subscription and/or Payments shown. If either tab is shown on your screen, simply disregard it.)

Beginning in this section, you will start to use the Test Drive Company to practice a task prior to entering material in Your Name's Beach Barkers.

*DRILL*

 Open the **Test Drive Company** and practice customizing settings

Enter **https://qbo.intuit.com/redir/testdrive** in the URL of your Web browser
Enter the word/numbers shown for Security Verification
- Remember, the word/numbers will be different each time you access the Test Drive Company. If you make a mistake, you will be given a different Security Verification word/number.

Click **Continue**
Click the **Gear** icon at the top of the screen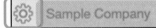
In the Settings column, click **Account and Settings**

Craig's Design and Landscaping Services

| Your Company | Lists | Tools | Profile |
|---|---|---|---|
| Account and Settings | All Lists | Import Data | User Profile |
| Manage Users | Products and Services | Import Desktop Data | Feedback |
| Custom Form Styles | Recurring Transactions | Export Data | Privacy |
| Chart of Accounts | Attachments | Reconcile | |
| QuickBooks Labs | | Budgeting | 🔒 Sign Out |
| | | Audit Log | |
| | | Order Checks ⬈ | |

- The Company Settings will be displayed. Sections shown are Company name, Contact info, Address, and Communications with Intuit.
- Notice the Pen icon. 🖉 Anytime you want to edit a setting, you click the Pen icon. Click the **Pen** icon for Company name

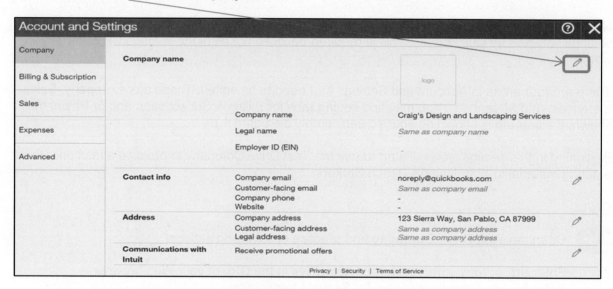

Click in the text box for **Company name**
Backspace until Craig's Design and Landscaping Services is erased
Enter **Your Name's Beach Barkers**

- Use your real name.
- Verify that the Legal name check box contains a check mark. This indicates that the Company name and the Legal name are the same.

Tab to or click in the text box for **Employer ID (EIN)**
Enter **11-2222222**

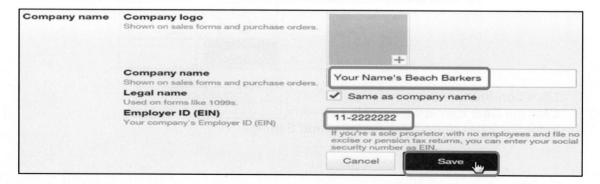

Click the **Save** button

- Your Name's Beach Barkers is shown as the Company name. The Employer ID (EIN) shows 11-2222222.

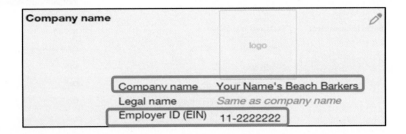

- There are no additional changes that need to be made to the Company settings.

Click the **Billing & Subscription** tab

- This shows you information about your account and has sections for Accounting, Payroll, Payments, and Checks.

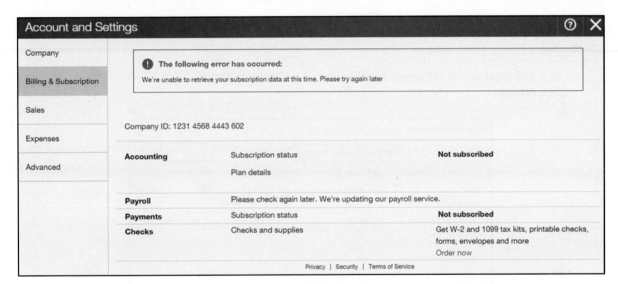

- At this time, there are no changes that need to be made to Billing & Subscription settings.

Click the **Sales** tab

- This screen enables you to select settings for sales transactions. Sections include Customize, Sales form content, Products and services, Messages, Online delivery, and Statements.

Click the **Pen** icon for Sales form content

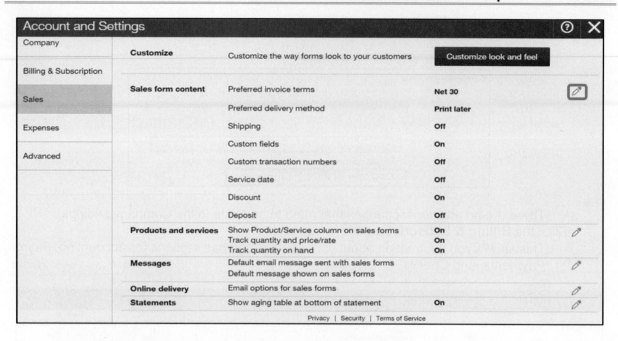

Click the drop-down list arrow for "Preferred delivery method"
Click **None**

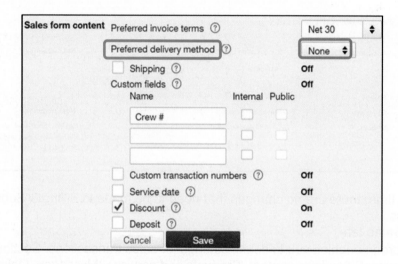

No other changes are required for this section, click **Save**
Click the **Pen** icon for **Statements**
Click the check box for "Show aging table at bottom of statement" to remove the check mark
Click the **Question mark** symbol for "Show aging table at bottom of statement" to see the
     explanation for this setting

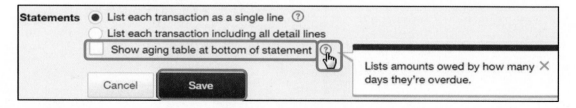

Click the **Save** button
Click the **Expenses** tab

- This screen enables you to select settings for expense transactions. Sections include Bills and expenses and Purchase orders.

Click the **Pen** icon for Bills and expenses

Click the drop-down list arrow for "Default bill payment terms"

Click **Net 30**

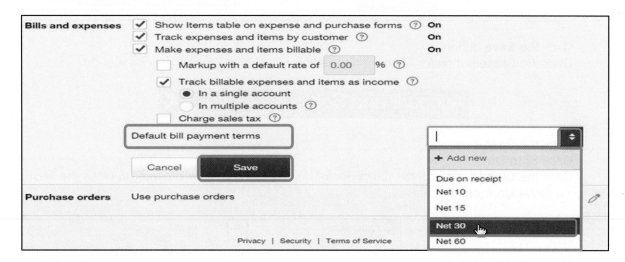

Click the **Save** button

Click the **Advanced** tab

- This screen enables you to select advanced settings. Sections include Accounting, Company type, Chart of accounts, Categories, Automation, Time tracking, Currency, and Other preferences.

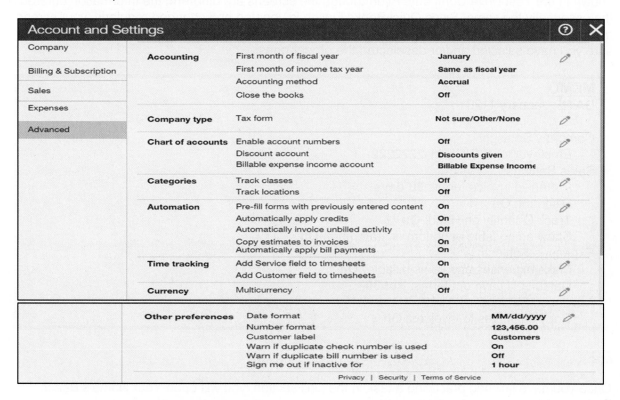

Click the **Pen** icon for Company type

Click the drop-down list arrow for Tax form

Click **Sole proprietor (Form 1040)**

Click the **Save** button
Click the **Close** button for Account and Settings

Click the **Gear** icon
Click **Sign Out**
Click the **Close** button on the QuickBooks tab at the top of your browser to close the Test
    Drive Company

## COMPANY SETTINGS—DO

Now that the Drill using the Test Drive Company is complete, you will open QuickBooks Online and make the changes shown in the Memo box. As you work through this section, you will notice that the screens shown for QuickBooks Online Educational Trial Version are not the same as the ones shown in the Test Drive Company. Even though the screens are different, the information entered is the essentially the same. Since QuickBooks Online is updated and changed regularly, your screens may differ from the ones shown here. It is important that you verify each of the settings to make sure you have selected and/or deselected the proper ones.

> **MEMO**
> **DATE:** January 1, 2016
>
> Company Settings:
>     Employer's ID (EIN): **11-2222222**
> Sales Settings:
>     Preferred invoice terms: **30 days**
>     Discount: **On**
>     Track Quantity on Hand: **On**
>     Show aging table at bottom of statement: **Off**
> Expenses Settings:
>     Make expenses and items billable: **On**
>     Default bill payment terms: **Net 30**
> Advanced Settings:
>     Copy estimates to invoices: **Off**

*DO*

Once you have finished practicing a task in the Drill section, you will open Your Name's Beach Barkers and enter the information in the company.

Open <u>**Your Name's Beach Barkers**</u> and change the Company Settings

Open QuickBooks Online
Type **qbo.intuit.com** in the URL, press **Enter**
Enter your Intuit ID (Email account name) and your Password, click **Sign In**

Click the **Gear** icon at the top of the screen
In the Settings column, click **Company Settings**

- As you will notice, at the time of this writing the Educational Trial Version of QuickBooks Online Plus has different screens than the Test Drive.
- For Test Drive, your column heading was "Your Company." The first item in the column was "Account and Settings." In the Educational Trial Version, the column heading is "Settings." The first item in the column is "Company Settings."
- Even though the names and some of the following screens are different from the Test Drive Company, the information to be entered for Your Name's Beach Barkers is the same.

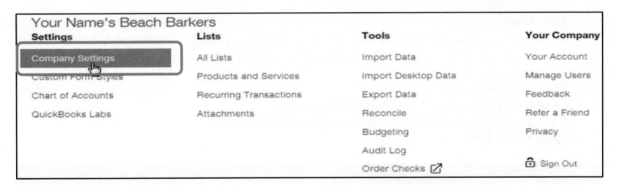

- The five tabs shown at the time of this writing are Company, Sales, Expenses, Payments, and Advanced. The Test Drive had a tab for Billing & Subscription rather than Payments.

Click the **Company** tab on the left of the screen
Verify the information provided

- Notice that the Employer's ID (EIN) is missing.

Click the **Pen** icon 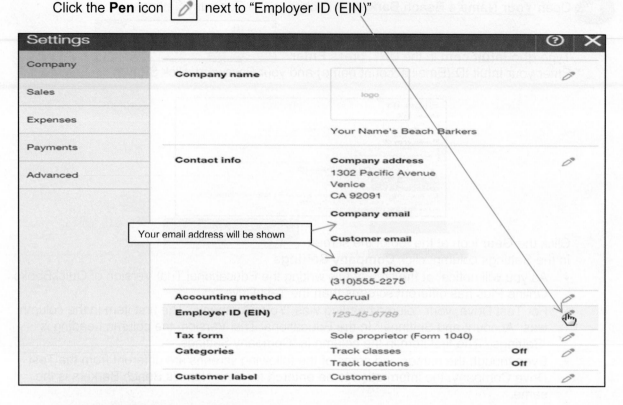 next to "Employer ID (EIN)"

Enter **11-2222222** for the Employer ID
Click **Save**
- The Employer ID (EIN) was the only change for the Company Settings. Verify that it was changed and that all of your settings match the ones shown in the Memo. Make any necessary changes.

Click the **Sales** tab
Click the **Pen** icon 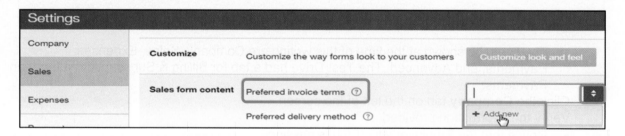 for "Sales Form Content"
Click the drop-down list arrow for "Preferred invoice terms"
Click **+ Add New**

For Name, enter **Net 30**
Tab to or click in the text box for "days," enter **30**

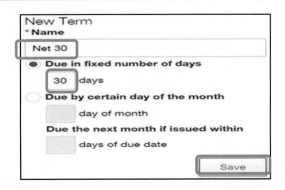

Click **Save**

Click the check box for **Discount** to insert a check mark

There are no other changes required for Sales Form Content, click **Save** for that section

- Even though we will not be selling products until later in the text, we will be importing products with a quantity on hand.

Click the **Pen** icon for "Products and services"

Click the check box for "Track quantity on hand" to insert a check mark

Click **Save**

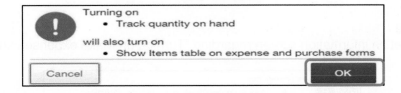

After you click Save, you will get the following screen:

Turning on
- Track quantity on hand

will also turn on
- Show Items table on expense and purchase forms

Cancel      OK

Click **OK**

To change "Show aging table at bottom of statement" to **Off**, click the **Pen** icon for "Statements"

Click the check box for "Show aging table at bottom of statement" to remove the check mark

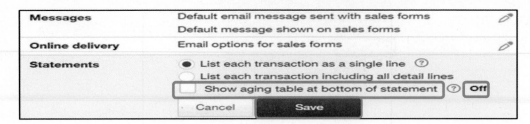

Click **Save**

Verify all of your Sales Settings

- If the information does not match the following screen, make any necessary changes.

**Sales Settings**:

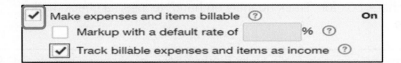

Click the **Expenses** tab

Click the **Pen** icon for "Bills and expenses"

Click the check box for "Make expenses and items billable" to insert a check mark

- Make sure "Track billable expenses and items as income" has a check mark.

Click the drop-down list arrow for "Default bill payment terms"

Click **Net 30**

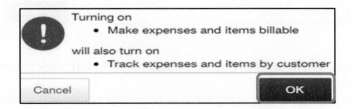

Click **Save**

You will get an information screen regarding "Turning on Make expenses and items billable"

Click **OK**

Verify all of your Expenses Settings

- If the information does not match the following screen, make any necessary changes.

**Expenses Settings**:

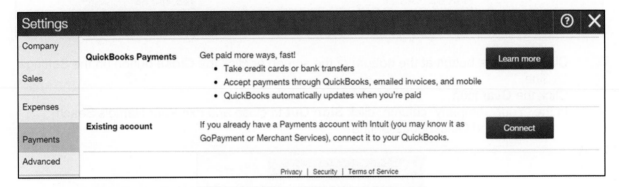

| Bills and expenses | Show Items table on expense and purchase forms | On |
| | Track expenses and items by customer | On |
| | Make expenses and items billable | On |
| | Default bill payment terms | Net 30 |
| Purchase orders | Use purchase orders | Off |

Click the **Payments** tab

- There are no changes to be made.

| Settings | | | | ⊘ ✕ |
|---|---|---|---|---|
| Company | **QuickBooks Payments** | Get paid more ways, fast! | | Learn more |
| Sales | | • Take credit cards or bank transfers | | |
| | | • Accept payments through QuickBooks, emailed invoices, and mobile | | |
| Expenses | | • QuickBooks automatically updates when you're paid | | |
| | **Existing account** | If you already have a Payments account with Intuit (you may know it as | | Connect |
| Payments | | GoPayment or Merchant Services), connect it to your QuickBooks. | | |
| Advanced | | Privacy \| Security \| Terms of Service | | |

Click the **Advanced** tab

Click the **Pen** icon for "Automation"

Since Your Name's Beach Barkers does not use estimates, click the check box for "Copy estimates to invoices" to remove the check mark

Click **Save**

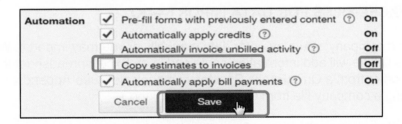

| Automation | ✔ | Pre-fill forms with previously entered content ⊘ | On |
| | ✔ | Automatically apply credits ⊘ | On |
| | ☐ | Automatically invoice unbilled activity ⊘ | Off |
| | ☐ | Copy estimates to invoices | Off |
| | ✔ | Automatically apply bill payments ⊘ | On |
| | Cancel | Save | |

Verify all of your Advanced Settings

- If the information does not match the following screen, make any necessary changes.

**Advanced Settings**:

| Accounting | First month of fiscal year | January | ✏ |
| | First month of income tax year | Same as fiscal year | |
| | Close the books | Off | |
| Chart of accounts | Enable account numbers | Off | ✏ |
| | Discount account | Discounts given | |
| | Billable expense income account | Billable Expense Income | |
| Automation | Pre-fill forms with previously entered content | On | ✏ |
| | Automatically apply credits | On | |
| | Automatically invoice unbilled activity | Off | |
| | Copy estimates to invoices | Off | |
| | Automatically apply bill payments | On | |
| Time tracking | Add Service field to timesheets | Off | ✏ |
| | Add Customer field to timesheets | On | |
| Currency | Multicurrency | Off | ✏ |
| Other preferences | Date format | MM/dd/yyyy | ✏ |
| | Number format | 123,456.00 | |
| | Warn if duplicate check number is used | On | |
| | Warn if duplicate bill number is used | Off | |
| | Sign me out if inactive for | 1 hour | |

Click the **Done** button at the bottom of the screen or click the **Close** button on the Settings line

Click the **Gear** icon

In the "Your Company" column, click **Sign Out** to close and exit Your Name's Beach Barkers and QuickBooks Online

# DOWNLOAD EXCEL FILES FOR DATA IMPORT—DO

When you create a company, you may enter data manually or you may import it. When importing data, QuickBooks Online will add information contained in an Excel spreadsheet that is properly formatted for import or from a QuickBooks Desktop company file. (See Appendix A for information regarding importing a company file from QuickBooks Desktop.)

The Excel files that you will use to import Customers, Vendors, Chart of Accounts, and Products and Services when creating Your Name's Beach Barkers are available on the Pearson Web site **http://www.pearsonhighered.com/horne/**. A QuickBooks Desktop company file is also posted for download in case your instructor specifies using this method. There is also a folder for importing company logos that will be used in Chapter 6. Depending on your Internet browser, your version of Windows, your storage location, and a variety of other variables, your screens may not always match those shown in the text. If you find differences and are not sure if you are proceeding correctly, check with your instructor.

## _DO_

 Download Excel Import files and QuickBooks Desktop company file

Insert your USB drive into your computer or ask you professor for specific directions to be used at your school

Open your Web browser

Enter the address http://www.pearsonhighered.com/horne/

- Sometimes it is difficult to read "horne." Remember the name is HORNE.
- Note: At the time of this writing, a temporary cover image was posted. The actual cover will change when the site is finalized.
- When completing the following steps, be sure to use the section for the QuickBooks Online Plus text.
- Check with your instructor to determine if you will use a different procedure.
- **IMPORTANT**: Depending on your version of Windows and the Web browser you use, your screens may be different from the examples shown. If so, complete the download using the prompts from your program. Ask your instructor for assistance if necessary. Since QuickBooks Online Plus prefers Google Chrome for the browser, Chrome is used for the file download.

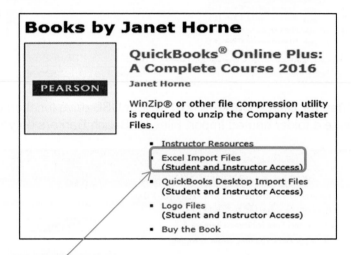

Click **Excel Import Files**

- You will see a tab with excel_imports (10).zip at the bottom-left side of the browser page.
- The number shown on your file may not be (10). Accept whatever number is shown.

Click the drop-down list arrow next to **excel_imports (10).zip**

Click **Open**

Click **Extract all files**

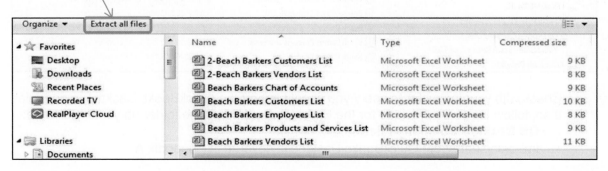

Click the **Browse** button
- Make sure your USB drive is inserted into your computer.

Scroll through the list of storage locations shown, click the letter shown for your USB drive, click **OK**
- If your USB drive location is not shown, click **Computer** to expand the list of storage locations.
- The text uses **F:** as the USB drive location. Your location may be different.

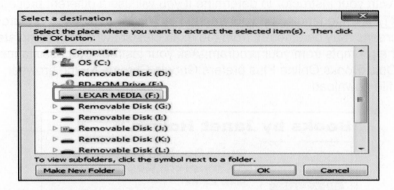

Enter **Import Files for Beach Barkers** next to your USB drive location (F:\ in the example)
- This will create a folder named Import Files for Beach Barkers on your USB drive.

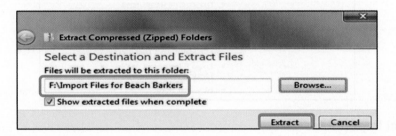

Click **Extract**

If you do not see the files, double-click the folder **Import Files for Beach Barkers**
- You will see the Excel files that you will use for importing data into QuickBooks Online Plus.

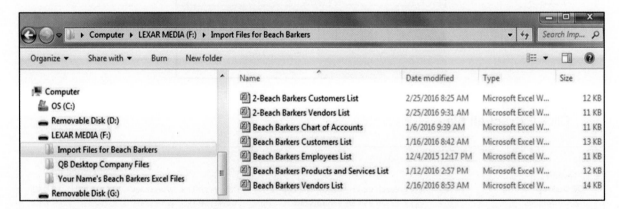

Check with your instructor to see if you should import the QuickBooks Desktop Import Files
If so, follow the steps provided for the Excel files and name the folder on your USB Drive:
>       **QB Desktop Company Files**
- Importing data from QuickBooks Desktop is covered in Appendix A.

## IMPORT COMPANY DATA—READ

In addition to the accounts and lists QuickBooks Online creates for you automatically, there are two ways to set up the important lists and data for your QuickBooks Online company. You may import a copy of your company file directly from QuickBooks Desktop or you may import data from lists in Excel. Since not everyone will have access to QuickBooks Desktop, those steps will be given in Appendix A. This chapter will focus on importing Excel spreadsheets that contain data for Your Name's Beach Barkers.

Unlike drills in later chapters, the drills in this chapter will use the Excel spreadsheets for Your Name's Beach Barkers for practice in importing data. Beginning in Chapter 3, practice assignments will not include any information from Your Name's Beach Barkers.

## IMPORT AND EDIT THE CUSTOMERS LIST—DRILL

When you import customer data, you will be able to add your customers and some of their account information. Not everything you want in your customers' accounts can be imported. Once you import your Customers List from Excel, you will need to edit your customer accounts and add any missing information.

### DRILL

 Open the **Test Drive Company** following the steps presented earlier and practice importing lists from Excel

#### Import Customers List

The first list to import is the Customers List.

 Use the **Test Drive Company** and import the Customers List you downloaded

> Now that the Test Drive Company is open, click the **Gear** icon, click **Import Data** in the Tools column
> - You will see a list of the data that may be imported: Customers, Vendors, Accounts, and Products and Services. The lists will be imported in the order that they are shown on this screen.
>
> Click **Customers**

> - There are three steps to import a file: Upload, Map Data, and Import. These steps are illustrated as you complete the Customers Import.
> Click the **Browse** button for "Select a CSV or Excel file to upload"

Click the location of your USB drive
- In this example, the location is (F:).

Double-click the folder **Import Files for Beach Barkers**

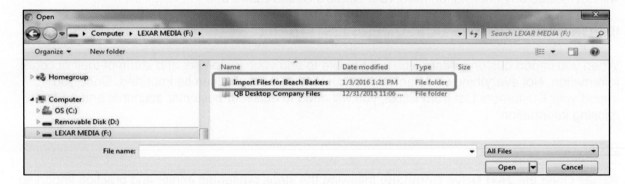

Click the file **Beach Barkers Customers List**
Click the **Open** button

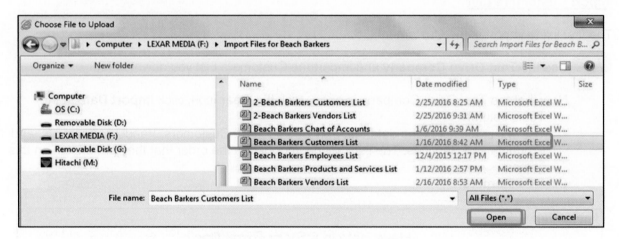

The file name will be inserted into the text box

- If you need to select a different file, simply click the Browse button; then click the correct file.

Once you have entered the name of the correct file, click the **Next** button

This screen shows the MAP DATA information

- Map Data is used to match the data in the Excel file to the appropriate fields of information for QuickBooks Online.
- A field contains information for a specific category. For example, the field "Name" will contain the names of your customers.

Scroll through the list of fields and view the QuickBooks Online Field and Your Field names

- If there is no Excel field available in QuickBooks Online, you will see No Match.
- For example, to import a customer's Mobile number, click the drop-down list arrow for No Match next to the QuickBooks Online Field name "Mobile," scroll through the list; and then, if available, click the field name for the customer's mobile phone number in the Excel file.
- There are no fields available in your import file for the customer's mobile phone number, so leave as No Match.

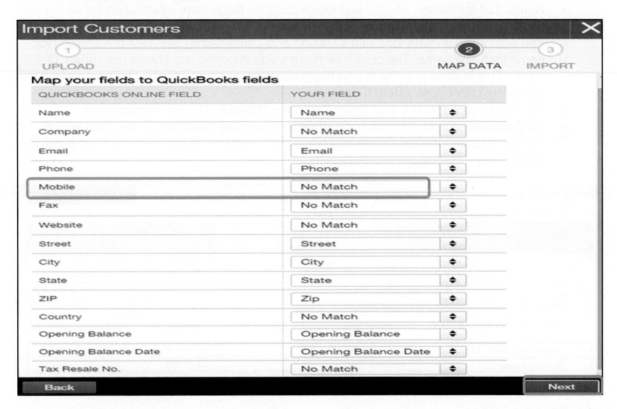

- If there are errors and you cannot link the data, your information will be shown in red.

Click the **Next** button

The records of each customer in the Customers List are shown

- A record contains all of the information for one customer.

If there are errors, your information will be shown in red and must be changed it in order to import

- For example, if the Opening Balance Date for Dori Anderson had been entered as 12/31/2015, it would be shown in red. QuickBooks Online requires that the date be entered as Year, Month, Day.

| ✓ | NAME | EMAIL | PHONE | STREET | CITY | STATE | ZIP | OPENING BALANCE | OPENING BALANCE DATE |
|---|------|-------|-------|--------|------|-------|-----|-----------------|----------------------|
| ✓ | Anderson, Do | DoriAnd@754 | 213-555-7091 | 395 Brooks C | Venice | CA | 90202 | 2500 | 12/31/2015 |

Since all records are correct, click the **Import** button
- You will get a message telling you how many customers were imported.

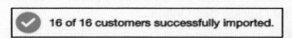

Click **Customers** on the Left-Navigation Bar

- In Chapter 1 this was referred to as the Left-Navigation Bar. From this point forward, it will be referred to as the Navigation Bar.

Scroll through the Customers List
- Did you notice the customers you imported? Dori Anderson and Larry Bailey were two of the customers imported and are shown below Amy's Bird Sanctuary, an original customer.
- Notice that the Name, Phone, and Open Balance fields have information for all the customers, including the new ones.
- The original customers for Craig's Design and Landscaping Services are shown first name then last name. The customer names you imported are shown last name, first name. This is done in order to sort the customers alphabetically by last name when you are using Your Name's Beach Barkers.
- You may notice that the Test Drive Company shows the Phone number with parentheses around the area code while the imported customers are shown with a hyphen between the area code and telephone number. Do not be concerned about the differences.

Partial List

### Edit Customers List

Because there is information for customers that is not imported, all of your customers will need to be edited. The information entered will be used when you record transactions for the customers.

 Continue to use the **Test Drive Company** and edit the Customers List that you imported

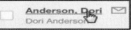

Point to **Anderson, Dori**
When you see the name underlined, click the left-mouse button
- Dori's account information will be shown.
- Not all information that you want to include for a customer is able to be imported. So, imported customers need to be edited.
- These selections will be used when you record transactions for the customers.

Click the **Edit** button

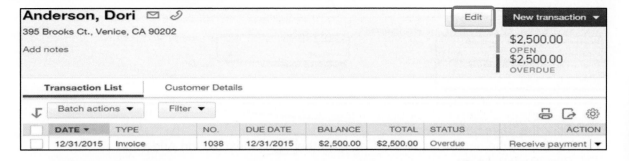

For "Print on check as" click the check box to remove the check mark for "Use display name"

- QuickBooks Online will use the information for "First Name" and "Last Name" when using the customer, Dori Anderson.

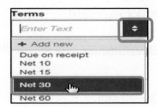

Click the **Payment and billing** tab

Click the drop-down list arrow for "Preferred payment method," then click **Check**

Click the drop-down list arrow for "Terms," click **Net 30**

Click the drop-down list arrow for "Preferred delivery method," click **None**

- The Opening balance was entered when you imported the Customers List so nothing needs to be entered for this.

View the changes

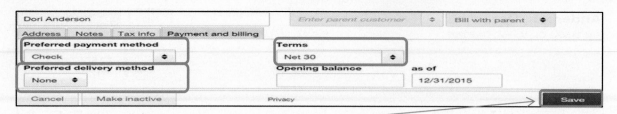

Click the **Save** button

To display the entire Customers List, click the  next to Dori Anderson

Click **Bailey, Larry**

Use the steps presented for Dori Anderson and change Larry's account to include:

Remove check mark from "Print on check as"

Preferred payment method: **Check**

Terms: **Net 30**

"Preferred delivery method: **None**

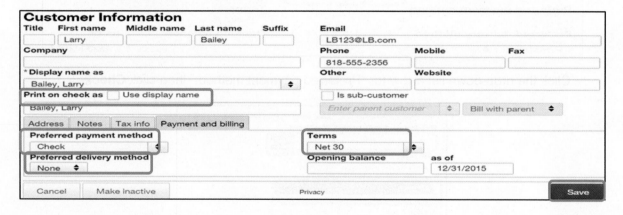

Click **Save**

## Print and/or Export Customers List

The Customers List may be printed and/or exported to Excel.

 Continue to use the **Test Drive Company** and complete the steps listed below to print or export the Customers List

Click **Customers** on the Navigation Bar

To print a copy of the Customers List, click the **Printer** icon

- You will see a copy of your Customers List.

Partial List

Verify the information for printing
- Your printer and other details may not match the screen shot shown above. If necessary, check with your instructor about appropriate print settings.

Since printing is not required for the drill, click **Cancel**
- If you see the Customer List displayed on a separate tab, click the Close arrow on the Customer List tab.

To export the list to Excel, click the **Export to Excel** icon
At the bottom of your browser window, you will see customer (number).xls
Click the drop-down list arrow for customer
- Customer (16).xls may not be an exact match for your file name.

Click **Open**

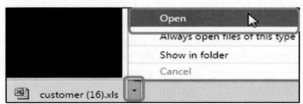

You will see the Customers List in Excel
- The spreadsheet may or may not open in Protected View.

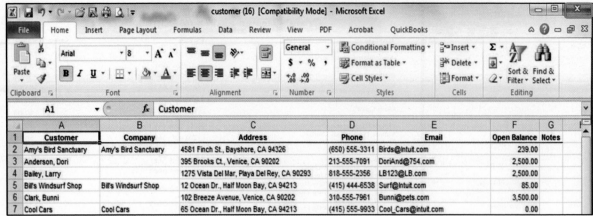

Partial List

Click the top **Close** button to close Excel without saving the spreadsheet
If you get a message regarding saving, click **Don't Save**

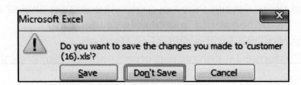

Return to the Test Drive Company, close, and exit the program:
  Click the **Gear** icon
  Click **Sign Out**
- Once you close the Test Drive Company, all of the customers you imported will be
  erased from Craig's Design and Landscaping Services.

## IMPORT AND EDIT THE CUSTOMERS LIST—DO

Now that you have practiced importing and editing your Customers List, you will import it into Your
Name's Beach Barkers. Once you have successfully imported your list, you will edit all of your
customers to include missing information. Finally, you will review printing, exporting, and emailing
your Customers List. The Customers List remains as part of the company file and does not
disappear when you close and exit Your Name's Beach Barkers.

---

**MEMO**
**DATE:** January 1, 2016

Import the Customers List
Edit all customers to include:
  Print on Check: remove check for "Use display name"
  Click **Payment and Billing** tab:
    Preferred payment method: **Check**
    Terms: **Net 30**
    Preferred delivery method: **None**

---

_DO_

Open **Your Name's Beach Barkers** following the steps presented earlier and import lists
from Excel

## Import Customers List

The first list to import is the Customers List.

 Use **Your Name's Beach Barkers** and import the Customers List using the Excel spreadsheet you downloaded

With Your Name's Beach Barkers open, click the **Gear** icon
Click **Import Data** in the Tools column
- You will see a list of the data that may be imported: Customers, Vendors, Accounts, and Products and Services.

Click **Customers**

- As you learned in practice, there are three steps to import a file: Upload, Map Data, and Import. These steps are illustrated as you complete the Customers Import into Your Name's Beach Barkers.

Click the **Browse** button for "Select a CSV or Excel file to upload"

Click the location of your USB drive
- In this example, the location is (F:).

Double-click the folder **Import Files for Beach Barkers**

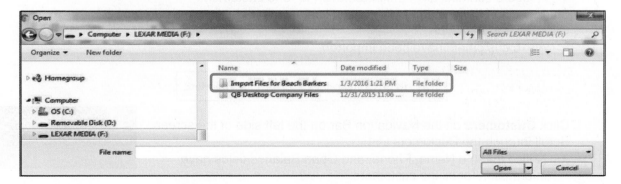

Click the file **Beach Barkers Customers List**
Click the **Open** button

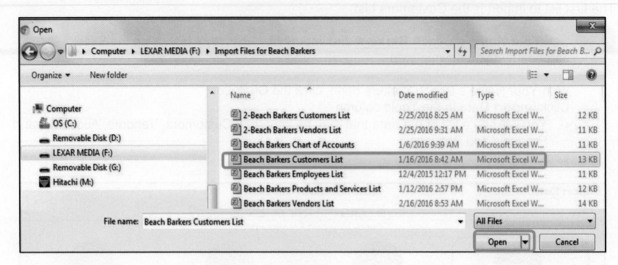

The file name will be inserted into the text box

- If you need to select a different file, click the Browse button; then click the correct file.
Click the **Next** button once you have entered the name of the correct file
- As you saw in the Drill, this screen shows the MAP DATA information and is used to match the data in an Excel file with the appropriate fields of information for QuickBooks Online.
- Remember, a field contains information for a specific category. For example, the field "Name" will contain the names of your customers.

Scroll the list of fields and view the QuickBooks Online Field and Your Field names
Click the **Next** button
The records of each customer in the Customers List are shown
- A record contains all of the information for one customer.

Since none of the customer information is shown in red, all records are correct
Click the **Import** button
- All 16 customers have been imported.

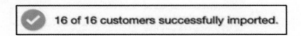

16 of 16 customers successfully imported.

Click **Customers** on the Navigation Bar on the left side of the screen
Scroll through the Customers List
- Notice that the Name, Phone, and Open Balance fields have information for all the customers.

Partial List

## Edit Customers List

Because there is information for customers that are not imported, all of your customers will need to be edited. This information will be used when you record transactions for the customers.

 Edit the Customers List

> Point to **Anderson, Dori**
> When you see the name underlined, click the left-mouse button
> - Dori's account information will be shown.
> Click the **Edit** button

> Click the check box on "Print on check as" to remove the check mark for "Use display name"
> - Any checks written to Dori Anderson will have her first name then her last name on the Payee line.
> - Since most customers are individuals and not businesses, business forms should include the first and last name. Notice that Company is blank. If the customer were a business, you would not want a First Name and Last Name; you would use a Company name.

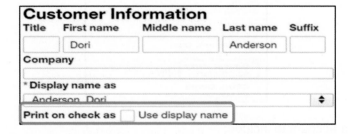

> Click the **Payment and billing** tab

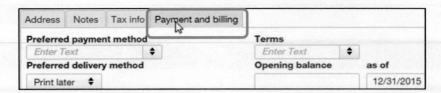

Click the drop-down list arrow for "Preferred payment method," click **Check**

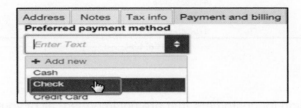

Click the drop-down list arrow for "Terms," click **Net 30**

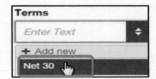

- The Opening balance was entered when you imported the Customers List so nothing needs to be entered. The "as of" date will show the current date.

View the changes

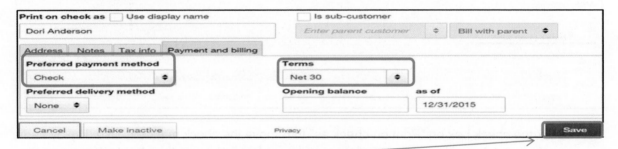

Click the **Save** button

To display the entire Customers List, click the [image] next to Dori Anderson

- Notice that the Account Balance is shown below each customer's name.

Click **Bailey, Larry**

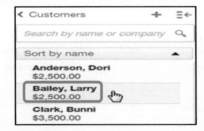

Change Larry's account to include:

    Print on check: **Larry Bailey**

    Preferred payment method: **Check**

    Terms: **Net 30**

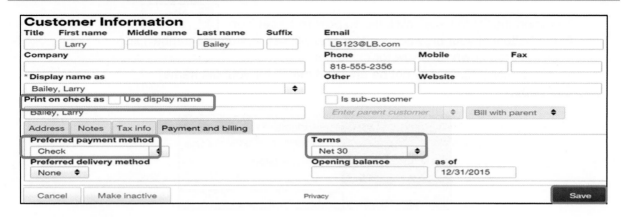

Click **Save**

Repeat for <u>all</u> remaining customers

When finished editing all of the customers, click **Customers** on the Navigation Bar

- Each professor will have individual requirements for submitting work. Check with your instructor to determine which documents will be submitted and how they should be submitted. Instructions for printing and exporting to Excel are shown. If your instructor uses a different method, obtain instructions from your professor.

## Print and/or Export Customers List

Once the Customers List has been edited, it is important to print and/or export the List to Excel.

 Continue to use **Your Name's Beach Barkers** and complete the steps listed below to print or export the Customers List

To print a copy of the Customers List, click the **Printer** icon
Make the appropriate selections on the Print menu:

    Destination: should be the printer you will be using

    Pages: All

    Copies: 1

    Layout: Portrait

    Color: Black and white

    Options: Two-sided if available for your printer

Click **Print**

To export the list to Excel, click the **Export to Excel** icon
At the bottom of your browser window, you will see customer (number).xls
Click the drop-down list arrow for customer
- Customer (15).xls may not be an exact match for your file name.

Click **Open**

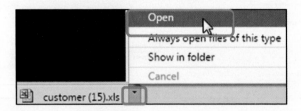

You will see the Customers List in Excel
- The file may open in Protected View. If your file is shown in Protected View, it cannot be saved, click **Enable Editing**.

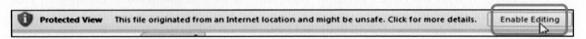

Scroll through the Excel file to view the customer information

| | A | B | C | D | E | F | G |
|---|---|---|---|---|---|---|---|
| | **Customer** | **Company** | **Address** | **Phone** | **Email** | **Open Balance** | **Notes** |
| | Anderson, Dori | | 395 Brooks Ct., Venice, CA 90202 | 213-555-7091 | DoriAnd@754.com | 2,500.00 | |
| | Bailey, Larry | | 1275 Vista Del Mar, Playa Del Rey, CA 90293 | 818-555-2356 | LB123@LB.com | 2,500.00 | |
| | Clark, Bunni | | 102 Breeze Avenue, Venice, CA 90202 | 310-555-7961 | Bunni@pets.com | 3,500.00 | |
| | Evans, Keith | | 90123 | 310-555-6314 | KEvans@evans.com | 0.00 | |
| | Gilbert, Oscar | | 1839 A Street, Santa Monica, CA 90123 | 310-555-8763 | OG@abc.com | 500.00 | |
| | Gucci, Gloria | | 795 Ocean Avenue, Venice, CA 90202 | 310-555-9875 | GloriaG@123.com | 0.00 | |
| | Montez, Annabelle | | 719 4th Avenue, Santa Monica, CA 90123 | 310-555-8015 | Amontez@xyz.com | 800.00 | |
| | Norbert, Viv | | 125 23rd Avenue, Venice, CA 90202 | 310-555-8651 | VivN@gva.com | 2,900.00 | |
| | Phillips, Eric | | 2190 State Street, Brentwood, CA 90049 | 310-555-1275 | EricPhil@098.com | 1,500.00 | |
| | Quint, Brad | | 6 Northstar Street, Marina Del Rey, CA 90295 | 310-555-9642 | BradQ@385.com | 1,800.00 | |
| | Rodriquez, Ricardo | | 851 4th Court, Santa Monica, CA 90202 | 213-555-5421 | RR@bde.com | 900.00 | |
| | Stark, Colleen | | 5519 Via Donte, Marina Del Rey, CA 90296 | 310-555-6482 | CoStark@beach.com | 3,200.00 | |
| | Summer, Matthew | | 2210 Pacific Avenue, Marina Del Rey, CA 90295 | 213-555-2594 | MattS@qwe.com | 150.00 | |
| | Vines, Pamela | | 119 Via Marina, Marina Del Rey, CA 90295 | 310-555-1354 | PamV@mail.com | 750.00 | |
| | Williams, Taylor | | 3211 Ocean Front Walk, Venice, CA 90202 | 310-555-8042 | Taylor@wil.com | 3,650.00 | |
| | Wilson, Katie | | 4157 Via Marina, #3, Venice, CA 90202 | 213-555-7908 | Kw@587.com | 2,850.00 | |

Click **File** at the top of the Excel screen, and then click **Save As**

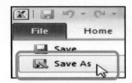

Click the location of your USB drive
- F: is the location in this illustration.

Right click in the open pane below QB Desktop Company Files
Point to **New,** then click **Folder**

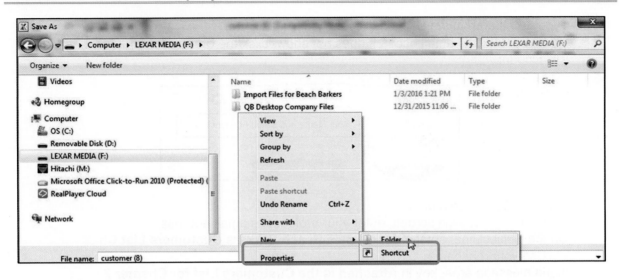

Type **Your Name's Beach Barkers Excel Files** as the name of the folder, press **Enter**
- Your actual First and Last Name's should be used rather than "Your Name's."

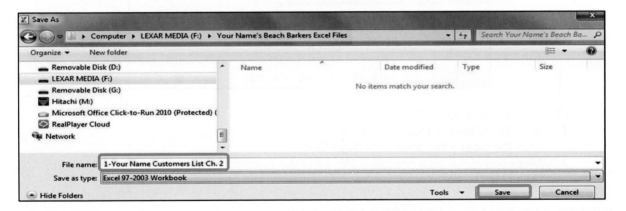

Double-click the folder to open it
Click in the text box for **File name**
Enter **1-Your Name Customers List Ch. 2** as the file name
- Your actual First and Last Name should be used.
Click the **Save** button

## Email Customers List

Each instructor will have his or her method for the submission of assignments. One way to submit your work is by email. Check with your instructor to see if you should email the Customers List. If so, use your Intuit ID email account for the email.

 To email **Your Name's Beach Barkers** Customers List, open a new Tab on your browser to email this report

At the top of your browser click the small, empty tab to open a new Tab

Type **gmail.com** in the URL on the new tab, press **Enter**
- If your Intuit ID email account does not show, click the graphic for your Intuit email account.

Click the **Compose** button
On the New Message screen, enter your professor's email address
On the Subject line, enter **Your Name's Beach Barkers Customers List Ch. 2**
- Use your real name.

In the message area, key in **Attached is the Customers List for Chapter 2**
Click the **Paperclip** icon
Click **1-Your Name's Customers List Ch. 2** from the list of files in the Your Name's Beach Barkers Excel Files folder on your USB drive
Click **Open**
When the file has been attached, click the **Send** button
- If your instructor wants you to submit your work in batches, add all of the file names in your message. Click the paperclip icon and select each file to be attached. When all the files have been attached, click **Send**.

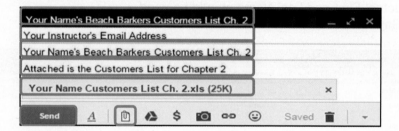

Close your email account
To close Your Name's Beach Barkers:
    Click the **Gear** icon, then click **Sign Out**
- When you close your company file, all of the customers will remain as part of your company.

## IMPORT AND EDIT THE VENDORS LIST—DRILL

When you import vendor data, you will be able to add your vendors and some of their account information. As with customers, not everything you want in your vendors' accounts can be imported. Once you import your Vendors List from Excel, you will need to edit your vendor accounts and add any missing information.

In this section, you will practice importing, editing, and printing, the Vendors List. As was stated previously, you will be using the Excel files for Your Name's Beach Barkers to practice importing. In Chapter 3, you will not use any material from Your Name's Beach Barkers in the Test Drive Company.

## DRILL

 Open the **Test Drive Company** following the steps presented earlier; then, practice importing the Vendors List from Excel

### Import the Vendors List

The second list to import is the Vendors List.

Use the **Test Drive Company** and import the Vendors List you downloaded

Now that the Test Drive Company is open, click the **Gear** icon
Click **Import Data** in the Tools column
Click **Vendors**

Click the **Browse** button for "Select a CSV or Excel file to upload"

Click the location of your USB drive
- In this example, the location is (F:).
Double-click the folder **Import Files for Beach Barkers**

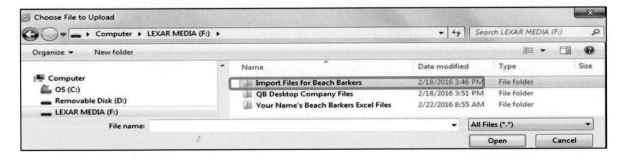

Click the file **Beach Barkers Vendors List**
Click the **Open** button

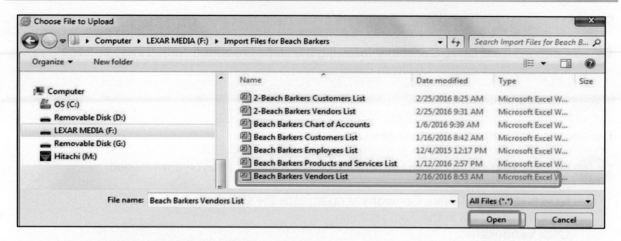

The file name will be inserted into the text box

- If you need to select a different file, click the Browse button; then click the correct file.

Click the **Next** button

This screen shows the MAP DATA information and is used to match the data in the Excel file to the appropriate fields of information for QuickBooks Online

- Remember, a field contains information for a specific category. For example, the field "Name" will contain the names of your vendors.

Scroll the list of fields and view the QuickBooks Online Field and Your Field names

- Just as with customers, if there is no Excel field available in QuickBooks Online, you will see No Match.

Click the **Next** button

The records of each vendor in the Vendors List are shown

- A record contains all of the information for one vendor.
- As with customers, if there are errors, the information will be shown in red. You must change it in order to import your vendors.

Since all records are correct, click the **Import** button

- You will see a message "10 of 11 vendors successfully imported." Because we are using the Test Drive Company, the Vendors List already contains United States Treasury as a vendor. When you import the Vendors List, you will get an error message stating that United States Treasury is a duplicate.

Click the **Close** button to end the Vendors List import

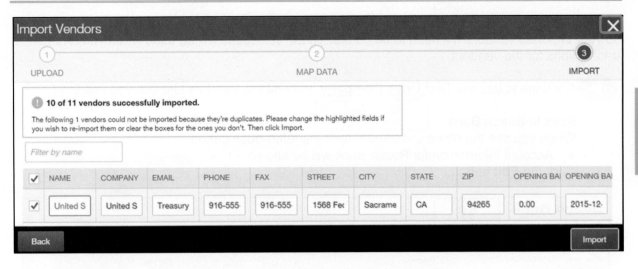

Click **Vendors** on the Navigation Bar on the left side of the screen

Scroll through the Vendors List

- Did you notice the vendors you imported? Beach Bank and Bow-Wow Supplies were imported and are shown along with Bob's Burger Joint and other original vendors.
- Notice that the Name, Phone, Email, and Open Balance fields have information for all the vendors, including the new ones.
- Just as with customers, you will notice that the phone numbers are displayed differently.

**Partial List**

## Edit Vendors List

If a Vendor is a business, Company should show a company name. If the vendor were an individual, you would not use a Company name just the "First name" and "Last name." If the vendor is a company that uses a person's name on checks, as in Books by Bessie, you would want both the "Company" and the "First name" and "Last name" fields to have information.

When you import Vendors from Excel into QuickBooks Online, you are required to use a name field, which enters information into the "First name" and "Last name" fields. To include information for "Company" your import file should include that field as well. Since our imported vendors are all companies, the First name and Last name should be removed from each vendor's record.

In addition to editing the vendors' names, there are selections for vendors that may not be imported, so your imported vendors will need to be edited. These selections will be used when you record transactions for the vendors.

 Continue to use the **Test Drive Company** and edit the Vendors List that you imported

> Point to **Beach Bank**

When you see the name underlined, click the left-mouse button
- Account information for Beach Bank will be shown.

Click the **Edit** button

Click in the "First name" field to highlight **Beach**, press **Delete** key or backspace to remove the name

Repeat to remove Bank from the "Last name" field
- The only additional information that we want to include is Terms of 30 days.

Click the drop-down list arrow for "Terms"

Click **Net 30**

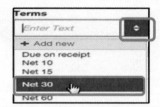

View the changes and note the other fields available:

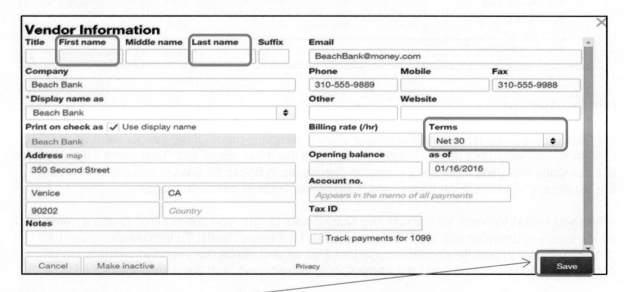

Click the **Save** button

Click **Vendors** on the Navigation Bar
Point to Bow-Wow Supplies when you see the name underlined, click **Bow-Wow Supplies**
Click the **Edit** button
Click in the "First name" text box and delete the First name
Repeat to delete the "Last name"
Click the drop-down list arrow for "Terms," click **Net 30**

2

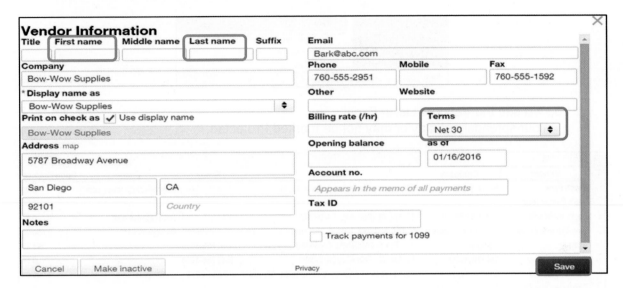

Click **Save**

## Print and/or Export Vendors List

The Vendors List may be printed and/or exported to Excel.

 Continue to use the **Test Drive Company** and complete the steps listed below to print or export the Vendors List

Click **Vendors** on the Navigation Bar
To print a copy of the Vendors List, click the **Printer** icon
- You will see a copy of your Vendors List.

**Craig's Design and Landscaping Services**

| Vendor | Phone | Email | Open Balance |
|---|---|---|---|
| Beach Bank<br>Beach Bank | 310-555-9889 | BeachBank@money.com | $0.00 |
| Bob's Burger Joint | | | $0.00 |
| Books by Bessie<br>Books by Bessie | (650) 555-7745 | Books@Intuit.com | $0.00 |
| Bow-Wow Supplies<br>Bow-Wow Supplies | 760-555-2951 | Bark@abc.com | $2,000.00 |
| Brosnahan Insurance Agency<br>Brosnahan Insurance Agency | (650) 555-9912 | | $241.23 |
| Cal Telephone<br>Cal Telephone | (650) 555-1616 | | $0.00 |
| Canine Supplies<br>Canine Supplies | 310-555-6971 | Canine@ssi.com | $3,000.00 |
| Chin's Gas and Oil<br>Chin's Gas and Oil | | | $0.00 |
| Cigna Health Care<br>Cigna Health Care | (520) 555-9874 | | $0.00 |
| Computers by Jenni<br>Computers by Jenni | (650) 555-8721 | Msfixit@Intuit.com | $0.00 |
| Diego's Road Warrior Bodyshop<br>Diego's Road Warrior Bodyshop | | | $755.00 |
| Dog Toy Town<br>Dog Toy Town | 310-555-6464 | Toys@xyz.com | $0.00 |
| EDD<br>EDD | | | $0.00 |

**Partial Report**

Since printing is not required for the drill, click **Cancel**
To export the list to Excel, click the **Export to Excel** icon
At the bottom of your browser window, you will see vendor (number).xls
- The screen shot shows vendor (1).xls. The number you see may not be 1.
Click the drop-down list arrow for vendor
Click **Open**

You will see the Vendors List in Excel
- Your spreadsheet may or may not be marked Protected.

| | A | B | C | D | E | F |
|---|---|---|---|---|---|---|
| 1 | **Vendor** | **Company** | **Address** | **Phone** | **Email** | **Open Balance** |
| 2 | Beach Bank | Beach Bank | 350 Second Street, Venice, CA 90202 | 310-555-9889 | BeachBank@money.com | 0.00 |
| 3 | Bob's Burger Joint | | | | | 0.00 |
| 4 | Books by Bessie | Books by Bessie | 15 Main St., Palo Alto, CA 94303 | (650) 555-7745 | Books@Intuit.com | 0.00 |
| 5 | Bow-Wow Supplies | Bow-Wow Supplies | 5787 Broadway Avenue, San Diego, CA 92101 | 760-555-2951 | Bark@abc.com | 2,000.00 |
| 6 | Agency | Agency | P.O. Box 5, Middlefield, CA 94482 | (650) 555-9912 | | 241.23 |
| 7 | Cal Telephone | Cal Telephone | 10 Main St., Palo Alto, CA 94303 | (650) 555-1616 | | 0.00 |
| 8 | Canine Supplies | Canine Supplies | 10855 Western Avenue, Los Angeles, CA 90012 | 310-555-6971 | Canine@ssi.com | 3,000.00 |
| 9 | Chin's Gas and Oil | Chin's Gas and Oil | | | | 0.00 |
| 10 | Cigna Health Care | Cigna Health Care | | (520) 555-9874 | | 0.00 |
| 11 | Computers by Jenni | Computers by Jenni | 1515 Main St., Middlefield, CA 94482 | (650) 555-8721 | Msfixit@Intuit.com | 0.00 |
| 12 | Bodyshop | Bodyshop | | | | 755.00 |
| 13 | Dog Toy Town | Dog Toy Town | 1970 College Boulevard, Hollywood, CA 90028 | 310-555-6464 | Toys@xyz.com | 0.00 |
| 14 | EDD | EDD | | | | 0.00 |

Partial List

Click the top **Close** button [X] in the upper right corner of the title bar to close Excel
without saving
To close the Test Drive company:
Click the **Gear** icon
Click **Sign Out**
- Once you close the Test Drive Company, all of the vendors you imported will be erased
from Craig's Design and Landscaping Services.

## IMPORT, EDIT, AND PRINT/EXPORT THE VENDORS LIST—DO

Now that you have practiced importing and editing vendors, you will import your Vendors List into
Your Name's Beach Barkers. Once the list is imported successfully, you will edit the vendors.
Finally, you will review printing, exporting to Excel, and emailing your Vendors List.

| MEMO |
|---|
| **DATE:** January 1, 2016 |
| |
| Import the Vendors List |
| Edit all vendors to include: Terms: **Net 30** |

_DO_

 Open **Your Name's Beach Barkers** following the steps presented earlier; then, import the Vendors List from Excel

Import Vendors List

The second list to import is the Vendors List.

 Use **Your Name's Beach Barkers** and import the Vendors List you downloaded

Click the **Gear** icon
Click **Import Data** in the Tools column
Click **Vendors**

Click the **Browse** button for "Select a CSV or Excel file to upload"

Click the location of your USB drive
• In this example, the location is (F:).
Double-click the folder **Import Files for Beach Barkers**

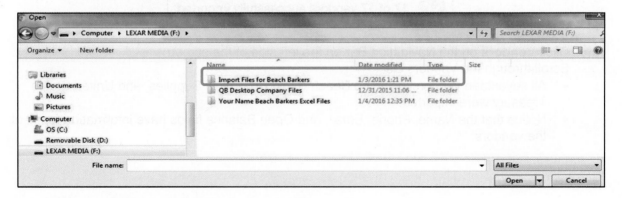

Click the file **Beach Barkers Vendors List**
Click the **Open** button

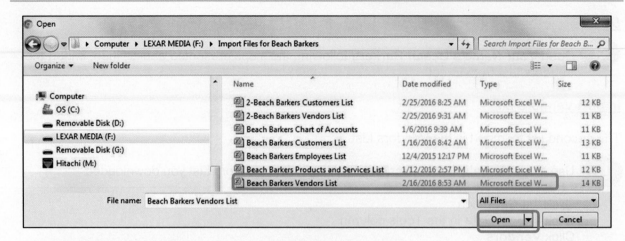

The file name will be inserted into the text box

- If you need to select a different file, simply click the Browse button; then click the correct file.

Once you have entered the name of the correct file, click the **Next** button

This screen shows the MAP DATA information and is used to match the data in the Excel file to the appropriate fields of information for QuickBooks Online

- If there are errors and you cannot link the data, your information will be shown in red.

Click the **Next** button

The records of each vendor in the Vendors List are shown

- As with customers, if there are errors, the information will be shown in red. You must change it in order to import your vendors.

Since all records are correct, click the **Import** button

- You will a message regarding the number of vendors imported.

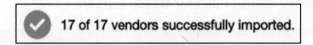

17 of 17 vendors successfully imported.

Click **Vendors** on the Navigation Bar on the left side of the screen

Scroll through the Vendors List

- All seventeen vendors including Beach Bank, Bow-Wow Supplies, and United States Treasury were imported.
- Notice that the Name, Phone, Email, and Open Balance fields have information for all of the vendors.

| VENDOR ▲  /  COMPANY | PHONE | EMAIL | OPEN BALANCE | ACTION |
|---|---|---|---|---|
| **Beach Bank** ✉<br>Beach Bank | 310-555-9889 | BeachBank@money.com | $0.00 | Create bill ⏐ ▼ |
| **Bow-Wow Supplies** ✉<br>Bow-Wow Supplies | 760-555-2951 | Bark@abc.com | $2,000.00 | Make payment ⏐ ▼ |
| **Canine Supplies** ✉<br>Canine Supplies | 310-555-6971 | Canine@ssi.com | $3,000.00 | Make payment ⏐ ▼ |
| **Dog Toy Town** ✉<br>Dog Toy Town | 310-555-6464 | Toys@xyz.com | $0.00 | Create bill ⏐ ▼ |
| **Employment Development [**<br>Employment Development Depa | 310-555-8877 | EDD@ca.gov | $0.00 | Create bill ⏐ ▼ |
| **Garcia's Advertising** ✉<br>Garcia's Advertising | 310-555-1879 | AdsbyG@promo.com | $0.00 | Create bill ⏐ ▼ |
| **Health Insurance, Inc.** ✉<br>Health Insurance, Inc. | 310-555-7412 | Health@ins.com | $0.00 | Create bill ⏐ ▼ |
| **Kennel Equipment, Inc.** ✉<br>Kennel Equipment, Inc. | 310-555-1156 | Kennel@pet.com | $0.00 | Create bill ⏐ ▼ |
| **Marina Water District** ✉<br>Marina Water District | 310-555-5462 | Water@utilities.com | $0.00 | Create bill ⏐ ▼ |
| **Morales Auto Repair** ✉<br>Morales Auto Repair | 310-555-1873 | Autos@beach.com | $0.00 | Create bill ⏐ ▼ |
| **Puppy Treats** ✉<br>Puppy Treats | 213-555-4365 | puptreat@123.com | $0.00 | Create bill ⏐ ▼ |
| **Quality Insurance** ✉<br>Quality Insurance | 213-555-8175 | Ins@ins.com | $0.00 | Create bill ⏐ ▼ |
| **Southern California Gas Co**<br>Southern California Gas Compa | 800-555-6282 | SCGC@utilities.com | $0.00 | Create bill ⏐ ▼ |
| **State Board of Equalization**<br>State Board of Equalization | 916-555-0000 | Equalization@ca.gov | $0.00 | Create bill ⏐ ▼ |
| **Training Supplies & Equipm**<br>Training Supplies & Equipment | 310-555-2915 | Training@456.com | $300.00 | Make payment ⏐ ▼ |
| **United States Treasury** ✉<br>United States Treasury | 916-555-1234 | Treasury@us.gov | $0.00 | Create bill ⏐ ▼ |
| **Venice Rentals** ✉<br>Venice Rentals | 310-555-9354 | Rentals@Venice.com | $0.00 | Create bill ⏐ ▼ |

## Edit Vendors List

As you learned in the Drill, if a Vendor is a business, Company should show a company name. If the vendor were an individual, you would not use a Company name just the "First name" and "Last name." If the vendor is a company that uses a person's name on checks, for example, Roger Wilson for the First and Last names and Wilson Co. for the Company name, you would want both the "Company" and the "First name" and "Last name" fields to have information.

When you import Vendors from Excel into QuickBooks Online, you are required to use a name field, which enters information into the "First name," "Middle name," and "Last name" fields. To include information for "Company" your import file should include that field as well. Since our imported vendors are all companies, the First name, Middle name, and Last name should be removed from each vendor's record.

In addition to editing the vendors' names, there are selections for vendors that may not be imported, so your imported vendors will need to be edited. These selections will be used when you record transactions for the vendors.

Continue to use **Your Name's Beach Barkers** and change the terms for each vendor to Net 30.

Point to **Beach Bank**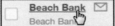
When you see the name underlined, click the left-mouse button
- Account information for Beach Bank will be shown.

Click the **Edit** button

Click in the "First name" field to highlight **Beach**, press **Delete** key or backspace to remove the name
Repeat to remove Bank from the "Last name" field
- The only additional information that we want to include is Terms of 30 days.

Click the drop-down list arrow for "Terms"
Click **Net 30**

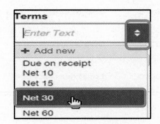

View the changes and note the other fields available:

Click the **Save** button
Click **Vendors** on the Navigation Bar
Click **Bow-Wow Supplies**

Delete the First name and Last name
Click the drop-down list arrow for "Terms," click **Net 30**

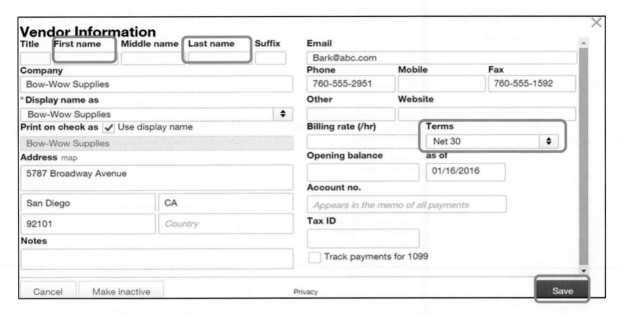

Click **Save**
Repeat for <u>all</u> of the vendors in the list
- Note: When you edit Dog Toy Town, Employment Development Department, and any other vendors with three words or more words in the name, you will need to delete the First, Middle, and Last names.

## Print, Export, and Email Vendors List

Once the Vendors List has been edited, it is important to print and/or export the List to Excel.

 Continue to use **Your Name's Beach Barkers** and complete the steps listed below to print or export the Vendors List

Click **Vendors** on the Navigation Bar
- You will see a copy of your Vendors List.
- As was mentioned for the Customers List, each professor will have individual requirements for submitting work. Check with your instructor to determine which documents will be submitted and how they should be submitted. Instructions for printing and exporting to Excel are shown. If your instructor uses a different method, obtain instructions from your professor.

Follow the steps listed below to print or export the Vendors List
To print a copy of the Vendors List, click the **Printer** icon
Make the appropriate selections on the Print menu:
  Destination: should be the printer you will be using
  Pages: All
  Copies: 1
  Layout: Portrait
  Color: Black and white
  Options: Two-sided if available for your printer
- Your printer and other details may not match the screen shot shown. If necessary, check with your instructor about appropriate print settings.

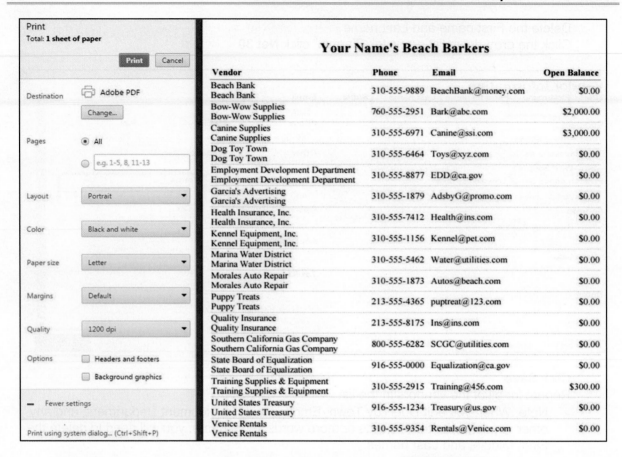

Click **Print**
To export the list to Excel, click the **Export to Excel** icon
At the bottom of your browser window, you will see vendor (number).xls
- Vendor (7).xls may not be an exact match for your file name.

Click the drop-down list arrow for vendor
Click **Open**

| Open |
| Always open files of this type |
| Show in folder |
| Cancel |

vendor (7).xls

You will see the Vendors List in Excel
- The file may open in Protected View.

- If the file is in Protected View it cannot be saved; click **Enable Editing**.

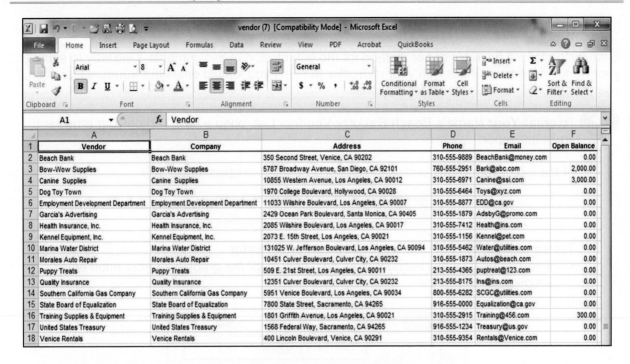

Click **File** at the top of the Excel screen, and then click **Save As**

Click the location of your USB drive
- F: is the location used in this illustration.

If it is necessary to open the folder, double-click **Your Name's Beach Barkers Excel Files**

Click in the text box for **File name**

Enter **2-Your Name Vendors List Ch. 2** as the file name
- Use your real first and last name.

Click the **Save** button

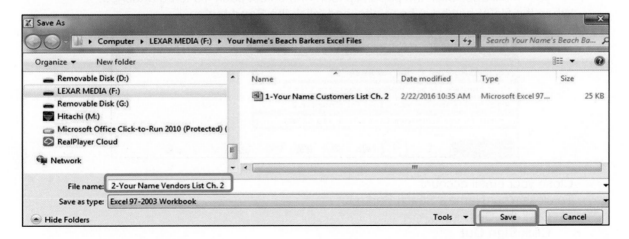

**Email Vendors List**

Each instructor will have his or her method for the submission of assignments. One way to submit your work is by email. Check with your instructor to see if you should email the Vendors List. If so, use your Intuit ID email account for the email.

 To email **Your Name's Beach Barkers** Vendors List, open a new Tab on your browser to email this report

At the top of your browser click the small, empty tab to open a new Tab

Type **gmail.com** in the URL on the new tab, press **Enter**
- If your Intuit ID email account does not show, click the graphic for your Intuit email account.

Click the **Compose** button
On the New Message screen, enter your professor's email address
On the Subject line, enter **Your Name's Beach Barkers Vendors List Ch. 2**
- Use your real name.
In the message area, key in **Attached is the Vendors List for Chapter 2**
Click the **Paperclip** icon
Click **2-Your Name Vendors List Ch. 2** from the list of files in the Your Name's Beach Barkers Excel Files folder on your USB drive
Click **Open**
- If your instructor wants you to submit your work in batches, add all of the file names in your message. Click the paperclip icon and select each file to be attached.
When the file(s) has/have been attached, click the **Send** button

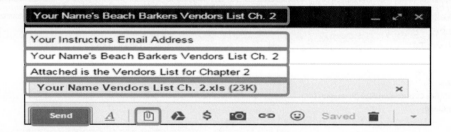

Close your email account
To close Your Name's Beach Barkers:
    Click the **Gear** icon
    Click **Sign Out**
- All the information you entered into your company file is saved as part of the file.

## IMPORT AND EDIT THE CHART OF ACCOUNTS—DRILL

The third list to be imported is the Chart of Accounts. Even though you are using the Test Drive Company, you will practice importing the accounts for Your Name's Beach Barkers that you downloaded.

### _DRILL_

 Open the **Test Drive Company** following the steps presented earlier; then, practice editing and importing the Chart of Accounts from Excel

### Edit Account

When importing a Chart of Accounts, it is important that the accounts QuickBooks Online generates do not conflict with the accounts you are importing. For example, if you have an expense account named Supplies and you are trying to import an asset account also named Supplies, the two accounts will be in conflict because they have the same name.

 As you use the **Test Drive Company**, you will need to edit an account before you import the Chart of Accounts

The imported Chart of Accounts uses Supplies as an asset account
To avoid, conflict with account names, change the name of the existing expense account
Supplies to **Supplies Expense**
Click **Transactions** on the Navigation Bar, click **Chart of Accounts**
Scroll through the Chart of Accounts until you see the expense Supplies
Click the drop-down list arrow for "Supplies"
Click **Edit**

Add **Expense** to the Name:
Click at the end of Supplies
Click a second time to remove the highlighting
Press **Space**, key in the word **Expense**, press **Tab**

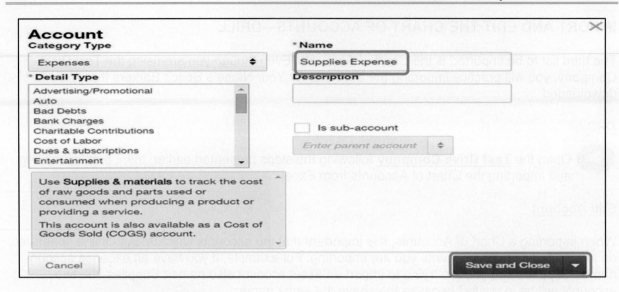

Click **Save and Close**
- If your screen shows Save and New, click the drop-down list arrow next to the button; then click Save and Close.

## Import Chart of Accounts

Now that conflicting account names have been changed, it is appropriate to import the Chart of Accounts.

 Continue to use the **Test Drive Company** and practice importing the Chart of Accounts

Click the **Gear** icon, click **Import Data** in the Tools column, and click **Accounts**

Click the **Browse** button for "Select a CSV or Excel file to upload"

Click the location of your USB drive

- In this example, the location is (F:).
Double-click the folder **Import Files for Beach Barkers**

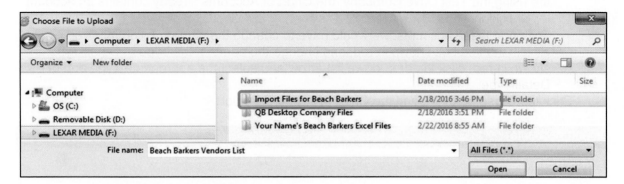

Click the file **Beach Barkers Chart of Accounts**
Click the **Open** button

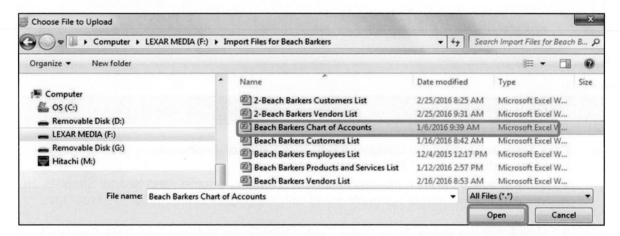

The file name will be inserted into the text box

- If you need to select a different file, simply click the Browse button; then click the correct file.
Once you have entered the name of the correct file, click the **Next** button
This screen shows the MAP DATA information used to match the data in the Excel file to the fields for QuickBooks Online
Click the **Next** button
The records for each account are shown

- As with customers and vendors, if there are errors, the information will be shown in red. You must change it in order to import your accounts.
Click the **Import** button

- You will see a message "22 of 23 accounts successfully imported." The error message states that "1 accounts could not be imported because they're duplicates." Because we are using the Test Drive Company, the Chart of Accounts already contains an account for Checking.
- To import these accounts, we would have to change the names. To do this, you would click in the text box shown in red, and change the name. If the Type or Detail Type is shown in red, click the drop-down list arrow and select the appropriate Type and/or Detail Type.

Click the **Close** button to end the Chart of Accounts import

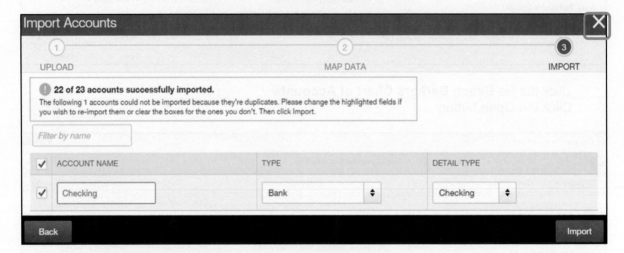

Click **Transactions** on the Navigation Bar, click **Chart of Accounts**
Scroll through the Chart of Accounts

- Did you notice the accounts you imported? Cleaning Supplies and Kennel Supplies are included in the Chart of Accounts along with the original accounts for the Test Drive Company.
- Notice that the Name, Type, Detail Type, QuickBooks Balance, and Bank Balance fields have information for all the original accounts.

## Edit Chart of Accounts

Even though you have had QuickBooks setup some accounts and have imported additional accounts, many of the accounts will need to be edited. Some of the required editing includes adding Opening Balances for asset and liability accounts, changing the account Detail Type, making accounts subaccounts, adding accounts, and deleting accounts.

Continue using the **Test Drive Company** and practice adding opening balances and creating subaccounts

For this practice, you will add opening balances to Cleaning Supplies and Kennel Supplies and make them subaccounts of Supplies
Make sure the Chart of Accounts is open

- If it is not open, click **Transactions** on the Navigation Bar, and click **Chart of Accounts**.

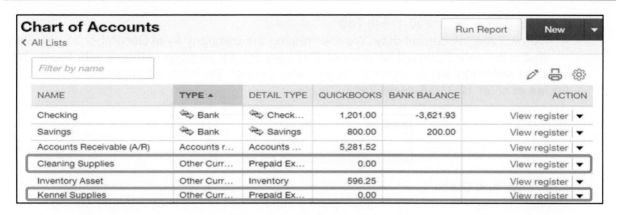

Click the drop-down list arrow for Cleaning Supplies
Click **Edit**

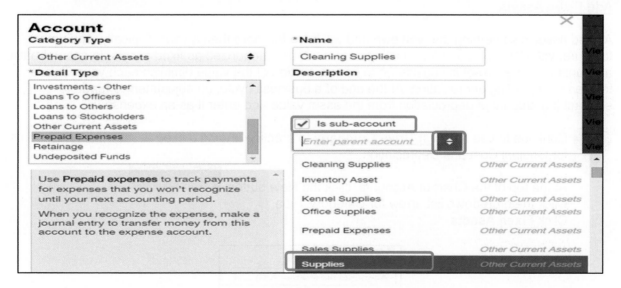

Look at the Account information for Cleaning Supplies
- Note that the Category Type is Other Current Assets—something that will be used or converted to cash within one year.
- The Detail Type is Prepaid Expenses—something that will become an expense once it is used. While you have it on hand, it is something you own so it is categorized as an asset.

Click the check box to mark **Is sub-account**
Click the drop-down list arrow, scroll through the list of accounts, click **Supplies**
- Occasionally, the Test Drive doesn't show the accounts you imported in the list of accounts. If this is the case, simply read through the steps or select a different account for practice.

Tab to **Balance**, enter **750**, press **Tab**
- You will see the current date. We are creating the company as of December 31, 2015 so that is the date that <u>must</u> be entered. Pay <u>very careful attention</u> to this or your Profit and Loss statement will be incorrect as you work through the following chapters.

For **as of** enter **12/31/15**, press **Tab**

Click **Save and Close**

Repeat the steps to make Kennel Supplies a subaccount of Supplies with an opening balance of 1895 as of 12/31/15

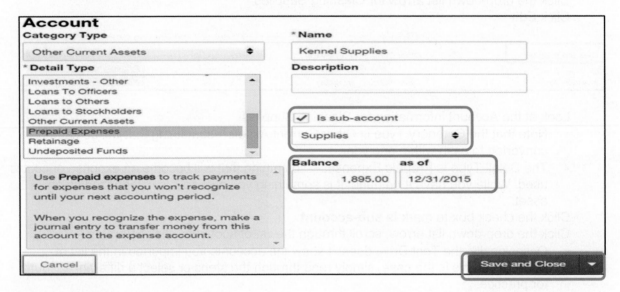

## Add Fixed Assets

A fixed asset is something that you own and will have for more than a year. Typically, equipment, furniture, vehicles, and other long-lasting assets will be categorized as fixed assets. In accrual-basis accounting, a fixed asset is considered to have a portion of the value diminish each year. This is tracked by recording depreciation. At the end of a business cycle, an adjustment is made to subtract the amount of depreciation from the asset value and enter it as an expense.

 Continue to use the **Test Drive Company** to practice adding a fixed asset with subaccounts for Original Cost and Depreciation

At the top of the Chart of Accounts, click the **New** button
Click the drop-down list arrow for Category Type
Click **Fixed Assets**

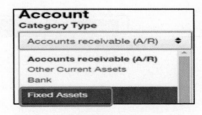

For Detail Type, scroll through the list, then click **Machinery & Equipment**
- QBO inserts Machinery & Equipment as the Name.

Tab to **Name**, delete **Machinery & Equipment**, and enter **Kennel Equipment**

Click the check box for "Track depreciation of this asset"

Enter the Original Cost **20300**
- QBO inserts the comma, decimal point, and two zeros.

Tab to **as of**, enter **123115**
- QBO inserts the /.

Press **Tab**

Enter the Depreciation as **2030** (do <u>not</u> put a – in front of the amount)

Tab to **as of**, enter **123115**

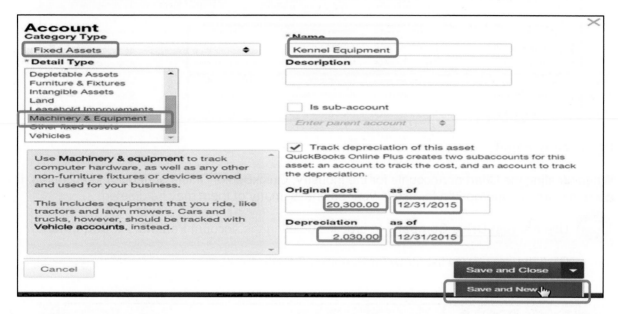

Click **Save and New**
- If your screen shows Save and Close, click the drop-down list arrow next to the button; then click Save and New.

Repeat the steps to add **Equipment**, Original Cost **8000**, as of **12/31/15**, Depreciation **800**, as of **12/31/15**

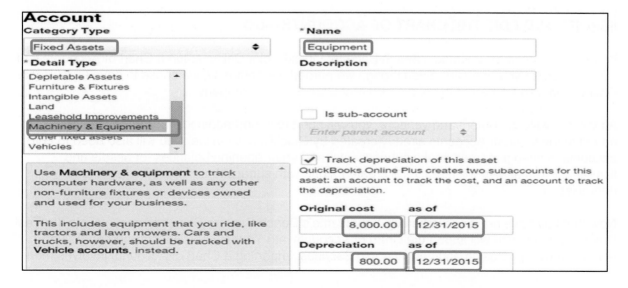

Click **Save and Close**

- If necessary, click the drop-down list arrow for Save and New.

View the changes to the Chart of Accounts

- Note that the Book Value is shown as the balance for Equipment and Kennel Equipment with the amount of depreciation and the original cost shown beneath. (Book Value is calculated: Cost - Depreciation = Book Value)

| Supplies | Other Curr... | Prepaid Ex... | 0.00 | View register | ▼ |
|---|---|---|---|---|---|
| Cleaning Supplies | Other Curr... | Prepaid Ex... | 750.00 | View register | ▼ |
| Kennel Supplies | Other Curr... | Prepaid Ex... | 1,895.00 | View register | ▼ |
| Uncategorized Asset | Other Curr... | Other Curr... | 0.00 | View register | ▼ |
| Undeposited Funds | Other Curr... | Undeposit... | 2,062.52 | View register | ▼ |
| Equipment | Fixed Assets | Machinery ... | 7,200.00 | View register | ▼ |
| Depreciation | Fixed Assets | Accumulat... | -800.00 | View register | ▼ |
| Original cost | Fixed Assets | Machinery ... | 8,000.00 | View register | ▼ |
| Kennel Equipment | Fixed Assets | Machinery ... | 18,270.00 | View register | ▼ |
| Depreciation | Fixed Assets | Accumulat... | -2,030.00 | View register | ▼ |
| Original cost | Fixed Assets | Machinery ... | 20,300.00 | View register | ▼ |

## Delete an Account

When creating the Chart of Accounts for the industry, QuickBooks Online added some accounts. If accounts are not appropriate for use in your business, many of them may be deleted.

 Use the **Test Drive Company** to practice deleting the account **Penalties & Settlements**

Click the drop-down list arrow for Penalties & Settlements
Click **Delete**

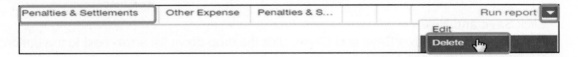

| Penalties & Settlements | Other Expense | Penalties & S... | | | Run report | ▼ |
|---|---|---|---|---|---|---|
| | | | | | Edit | |
| | | | | | Delete | |

Click **Yes** on the warning screen
Close the Test Drive Company

## IMPORT AND EDIT THE CHART OF ACCOUNTS—DO

When you created Your Name's Beach Barkers, QuickBooks Online setup a Chart of Accounts that was created for your industry. Even though we purged the company, we chose to have QuickBooks Online establish a Chart of Accounts for a Pet Care Service company.

As you did with customers and vendors, you will need to import additional accounts that will be added to the Chart of Accounts already created by QuickBooks Online. You will also need to edit accounts to change names, make subaccounts, and enter opening balances for assets and liabilities. Fixed assets will need to be created along with subaccounts for original cost and depreciation.

Now that you have practiced importing Your Name's Beach Barkers Chart of Accounts into the Test Drive Company, you will import the Chart of Accounts into Your Names Beach Barkers. As you learned in Craig's Design and Landscaping Services, importing a Chart of Accounts involves more than the actual import. Accounts will need to be edited and added. In addition opening balances will need to be entered for Assets and Liabilities.

> **MEMO**
> **DATE:** January 1, 2016
>
> Edit:
>     Change the name of the Expense account **Supplies** to **Supplies Expense**
> Import the chart of Accounts
> Add:
>     Fixed Assets (Chart provided in that section)
>     Opening Balances for Assets and Liabilities (Chart provided in that section)

<u>*DO*</u>

 Open **Your Name's Beach Barkers** as previously instructed and change account names, import the Chart of Accounts, add accounts, and edit accounts.

## Edit Account Name

When importing a Chart of Accounts, it is important that the accounts QuickBooks Online generates do not conflict with the accounts you are importing. For example, if you have an expense account named Supplies and you are trying to import an asset account also named Supplies, the two accounts will be in conflict because they have the same name.

 Use **Your Name's Beach Barkers** and change account names

Click **Transactions** on the Navigation Bar, click **Chart of Accounts**
Scroll through the accounts until you get to the Expense account Supplies
- Since our imported Chart of Accounts uses Supplies as an asset account, change the name of the expense account Supplies to **Supplies Expense** prior to importing the Chart of Accounts from Excel.
Click the drop-down list arrow for Supplies
Click **Edit**

| Supplies | Expenses | Supplies &... | | | Run report |
|---|---|---|---|---|---|
| Supplies - Cleaning | Expenses | Supplies &... | | Edit | |
| | | | | Delete | |

Add **Expense** to the Name:
    Click at the end of Supplies
    Click a second time to remove the highlighting
    Press **Space**, key in the word **Expense**, press **Tab**

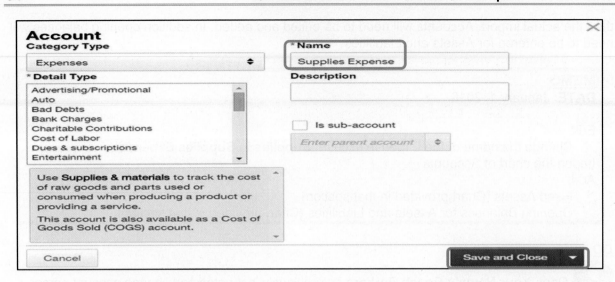

Click **Save and Close**
- If your screen shows Save and New, click the drop-down list arrow next to the button; then click Save and Close.

| Supplies Expense | Expenses | Supplies &... | | Run report ▼ |

Repeat the steps above to rename the asset **Prepaid Expenses** to **Prepaid Insurance**
- The Detail Type is Prepaid Expenses— A Prepaid Expense something that is paid for and will be used within one year. While you have it on hand, it is something you own so it is categorized as an asset. As it is used up, the amount used will become an expense.

To enter the Balance for Prepaid Insurance, click in the Balance text box, enter **1200**
Tab to "as of" and enter **123115**, press **Tab**

Click **Save and Close**
- Click the drop-down list arrow if it does not show.

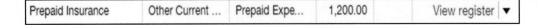

| Prepaid Insurance | Other Current ... | Prepaid Expe... | 1,200.00 | View register ▼ |

Import Chart of Accounts

Now that conflicting account names have been changed, it is appropriate to import the Chart of Accounts.

 Use **Your Name's Beach Barkers** and import the Chart of Accounts

Click the **Gear** icon, click **Import Data** in the Tools column, and then click **Accounts**

Click the **Browse** button for "Select a CSV or Excel file to upload"

Click the location of your USB drive
- In this example, the location is (F:).

If necessary, double-click the folder **Import Files for Beach Barkers**

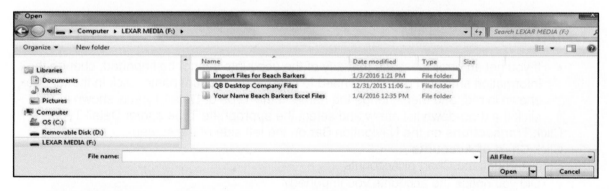

Click the file **Beach Barkers Chart of Accounts**
Click the **Open** button

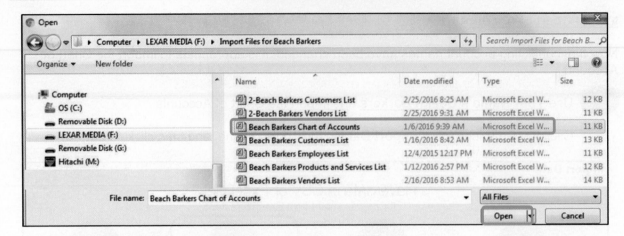

The file name will be inserted into the text box

- If you need to select a different file, click the Browse button; then click the correct file.

Once you have entered the name of the correct file, click the **Next** button

The MAP DATA information is shown, click the **Next** button

The records for each account are shown

- As with customers and vendors, if there are errors, the information will be shown in red. Anything shown in red must be changed in order to import your accounts.

You will get a message that 23 records are ready to be imported

Click the **Import** button

You will see a message "23 of 23 accounts successfully imported."

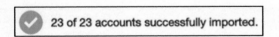

- If you get an error message that any of the accounts cannot be imported, change the information shown in red. If you need to change an account name, click in the text box shown in red; and then change the name. If the Type or Detail Type is shown in red, click the drop-down list arrow and select the appropriate Type and/or Detail Type.

Click **Transactions** on the Navigation Bar on the left side of the screen

Click **Chart of Accounts**

Scroll through the Chart of Accounts

- Did you notice the accounts you imported?
- Notice that the Name, Type, Detail Type, QuickBooks Balance, and Bank Balance fields have information for all the accounts, including the new ones.

## Edit Chart of Accounts

Even though you have had QuickBooks setup some accounts and have imported additional ones, many of the accounts will need to be edited. Some of the required editing includes adding Opening

Balances for asset and liability accounts, changing the account Detail Type, and making accounts subaccounts. In addition, there will still be accounts that need to be added and other accounts will need to be deleted.

 Use **Your Name's Beach Barkers** and edit the Chart of Accounts

With the Chart of Accounts still showing on the screen, edit the asset and liability accounts shown in the following chart, make subaccounts as indicated, add opening balances, and add As of dates
- Only the asset and liability accounts will be edited at this point. Other accounts will need to be edited after the Products and Services are imported.

| Account | Type | Detail Type | Subaccount of: | Opening Balance | As of Date |
|---|---|---|---|---|---|
| Checking | Bank | Checking | | 45,385.00 | 12/31/15 |
| Cleaning Supplies | Other Current Asset | Prepaid Expenses | Supplies | 750.00 | 12/31/15 |
| Kennel Supplies | Other Current Asset | Prepaid Expenses | Supplies | 1,895.00 | 12/31/15 |
| Office Supplies | Other Current Asset | Prepaid Expenses | Supplies | 350.00 | 12/31/15 |
| Sales Supplies | Other Current Asset | Prepaid Expenses | Supplies | 500.00 | 12/31/15 |
| Equipment Loan | Long Term Liability | Notes Payable | Loans Payable | 2,000.00 | 12/31/15 |
| Furniture & Fixtures Loan | Long Term Liability | Notes Payable | Loans Payable | 2,500.00 | 12/31/15 |

In the Chart of Accounts, click the drop-down list arrow for Checking, click **Edit**
Click in the text box for **Balance**, enter **45385** for the Balance
- QBO inserts the comma, decimal point, and two zeros.
Tab to **as of**, enter **123115**, press **Tab**
- QBO inserts the /.

Click **Save and Close**
- If Save and New is shown, click the drop-down list arrow; then click Save and Close.

Make Cleaning Supplies a subaccount of Supplies, add the Balance, and as of date:

Click the drop-down list arrow for **Cleaning Supplies**, click **Edit**

Click the check box for "Is sub-account"

Click the drop-down list arrow, click the asset account **Supplies**

Tab to **Balance**, enter **750**, tab to **as of**, enter **123115**, press **Tab**

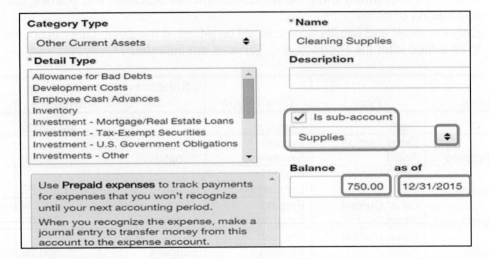

Click **Save and Close**

Repeat for the remaining assets and liabilities shown in the chart

When all changes to assets and liabilities have been made, the Chart of Accounts will show:
- For better display of the Chart of Accounts, the print version of the assets and liabilities is shown in the following screen shot.
- Note that Supplies shows a balance of 0.00. When you prepare reports later in the chapter, Supplies will show a balance that represents the total of all the subaccounts.

## Your Name's Beach Barkers

**Chart of Accounts**

| Name | Type | Detail Type | Balance |
|---|---|---|---|
| Checking | Bank | Checking | 45,385.00 |
| Accounts Receivable (A/R) | Accounts receivable (A/R) | Accounts Receivable (A/R) | 27,500.00 |
| Prepaid Insurance | Other Current Assets | Prepaid Expenses | 1,200.00 |
| Supplies | Other Current Assets | Prepaid Expenses | 0.00 |
|    Cleaning Supplies | Other Current Assets | Prepaid Expenses | 750.00 |
|    Kennel Supplies | Other Current Assets | Prepaid Expenses | 1,895.00 |
|    Office Supplies | Other Current Assets | Prepaid Expenses | 350.00 |
|    Sales Supplies | Other Current Assets | Prepaid Expenses | 500.00 |
| Uncategorized Asset | Other Current Assets | Other Current Assets | 0.00 |
| Undeposited Funds | Other Current Assets | Undeposited Funds | 0.00 |
| Accounts Payable (A/P) | Accounts payable (A/P) | Accounts Payable (A/P) | 5,300.00 |
| Payroll Liabilities | Other Current Liabilities | Payroll Tax Payable | 0.00 |
| Loans Payable | Long Term Liabilities | Notes Payable | 0.00 |
|    Equipment Loan | Long Term Liabilities | Notes Payable | 2,000.00 |
|    Furniture & Fixtures Loan | Long Term Liabilities | Notes Payable | 2,500.00 |

## Add Fixed Assets

As mentioned in the drill, a fixed asset is something that you own and will have for more than a year. Typically, equipment, furniture, vehicles, and other long-lasting assets will be categorized as fixed assets. In accrual-basis accounting, a fixed asset is considered to have a portion of the value diminish each year. This is tracked by recording depreciation. At the end of a business cycle, an adjustment is made to subtract the amount of depreciation from the asset value and enter it as an expense.

 Continue to use **Your Name's Beach Barkers** and add Fixed Assets

Use the following chart to add fixed assets with subaccounts for Original Cost and Depreciation

| Account | Type | Detail Type | Original Cost | As of | Depreciation | As of |
|---|---|---|---|---|---|---|
| ~~Office~~ Equipment | Fixed Assets | Machinery & Equipment | 8,000 | 12/31/15 | 800 | 12/31/15 |
| Furniture & Fixtures | Fixed Assets | Furniture & Fixtures | 15,000 | 12/31/15 | 1,500 | 12/31/15 |
| Kennel Equipment | Fixed Assets | Machinery & Equipment | 20,300 | 12/31/15 | 2,030 | 12/31/15 |
| Vehicles | Fixed Assets | Vehicles | 32,000 | 12/31/15 | 3,200 | 12/31/15 |

At the top of the Chart of Accounts, click the **New** button
Click the drop-down list arrow for Category Type
Click **Fixed Assets**

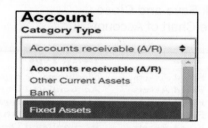

For Detail Type, click **Machinery & Equipment**
- QBO inserts Machinery & Equipment as the Name.
Change the Name to **Equipment**
Click the check box to mark "Track depreciation of this asset"
Click in the text box for Original Cost, enter **8000**
- QBO inserts the comma, decimal point, and two zeros.
Tab to **as of**, enter **123115**
- QBO inserts the /.
Press **Tab**
Enter the Depreciation as **800** (do <u>not</u> put a – in front of the amount)
Tab to **as of**, enter **123115**

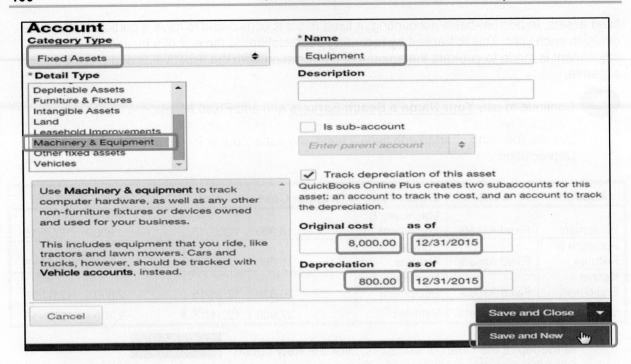

Click **Save and New**
Repeat the steps to add **Furniture & Fixtures**, **Kennel Equipment**, and **Vehicles**
After adding Vehicles, click **Save and Close**
View the fixed assets in the Chart of Accounts:

| Name | Type | Detail Type | Balance |
|---|---|---|---|
| Equipment | Fixed Assets | Machinery & Equipment | 7,200.00 |
| Depreciation | Fixed Assets | Accumulated Depreciation | -800.00 |
| Original cost | Fixed Assets | Machinery & Equipment | 8,000.00 |
| Furniture & Fixtures | Fixed Assets | Furniture & Fixtures | 13,500.00 |
| Depreciation | Fixed Assets | Accumulated Depreciation | -1,500.00 |
| Original cost | Fixed Assets | Furniture & Fixtures | 15,000.00 |
| Kennel Equipment | Fixed Assets | Machinery & Equipment | 18,270.00 |
| Depreciation | Fixed Assets | Accumulated Depreciation | -2,030.00 |
| Original cost | Fixed Assets | Machinery & Equipment | 20,300.00 |
| Vehicles | Fixed Assets | Vehicles | 28,800.00 |
| Depreciation | Fixed Assets | Accumulated Depreciation | -3,200.00 |
| Original cost | Fixed Assets | Vehicles | 32,000.00 |

- There are more changes that need to be made to the Chart of Accounts. These will be completed after your Products and Services List has been imported.
  Close Your Name's Beach Barkers as previously instructed

## IMPORT PRODUCTS AND SERVICES LIST—DRILL

The last list to be imported is the one that contains the products and services you sell. QuickBooks Online uses the Products and Services List to match the items sold with appropriate income accounts.

When working in the Test Drive Company, there will be many products and services shown. As you did with the other imported lists, you will practice importing using the **Test Drive Company**, Craig's Design and Landscaping Services, before importing the list into Your Name's Beach Barkers.

_DRILL_

 Open the **Test Drive Company** following the steps presented earlier; then, import the Products and Services List from Excel

Click the **Gear** icon, click **Import Data** in the Tools column, and click **Products and Services**

Click the **Browse** button for "Select a CSV or Excel file to upload"
Click the location of your USB drive
- (F:) in this example.

If necessary, double-click the folder **Import Files for Beach Barkers**
Click the file **Beach Barkers Products and Services List**
Click the **Open** button

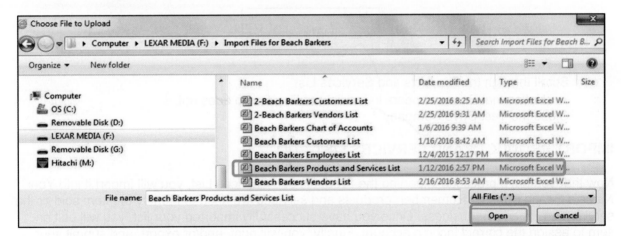

The file name will be inserted into the text box

Click the **Next** button
Since nothing is highlighted in red, click **Next** for MAP DATA

Scroll through Items shown on the IMPORT screen
- Notice that Day Camp shows red for Income Account and Bones does not show anything marked in red.
- Since we did not re-import the Chart of Accounts, some of the Income Accounts in our Products and Services List are missing and are marked in red.
- Since this is practice, we will disregard the errors.

Click the **Import** button to import the 15 records that are ready to be imported

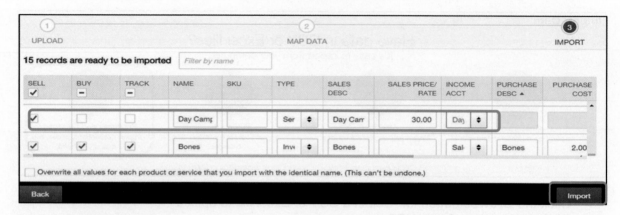

Click the **Close** button on the screen stating that "9 of 15 products and services successfully imported."
Click the **Gear** icon
Click **Products and Services** in the Lists column

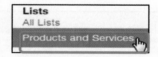

Scroll through the Products and Services List
- Notice that Bones appears in the list but Day Camp does not.

Close the Test Drive Company

## IMPORT PRODUCTS AND SERVICES LIST—DO

Now that you have practiced importing the Products and Services List, you will import it into Your Name's Beach Barkers. Remember, products and services are used to identify the item sold or the service performed in a business. Once you have successfully imported your list, you will edit an item to assign the correct income account. Finally, you will print, and/or export, and submit your Products and Services List.

> **MEMO**
> **DATE:** January 1, 2016
>
> Edit a Service item: **Hours** and change the Income account to **Hours**
> Import the Products and Services List

**DO**

Open **Your Name's Beach Barkers** following the steps presented earlier and import the Products and Services List from Excel

<u>Edit an Item</u>

Before importing the Products and Services List into <u>**Your Name's Beach Barkers**</u>, edit the item "Hours" and link it to the appropriate income account

Once Your Name's Beach Barkers is open, click the **Gear** icon
- Before importing the Products and Services List, it is important to view and, if necessary, edit the existing list.

Click **Products and Services** in the List column

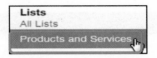

- Note that there are two items shown: Hours and Services.

To link the item Hours to the appropriate income account, click **Edit** next to Hours
Click the drop-down list arrow for "Income account"
Scroll through the accounts shown, click the income account **Hours**

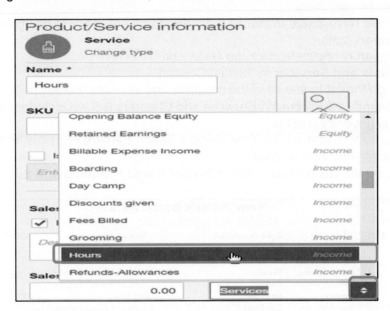

Click **Save & Close**

<u>Import the Products and Services List</u>

Products and Services are used to indicate what item is sold or service performed. The imported list has the services you provide and the products you have in inventory.

Import the Products and Services List into <u>**Your Name's Beach Barkers**</u>

Click the **Gear** icon, click **Import Data** in the Tools column, and click **Products and Services**
Click the **Browse** button for "Select a CSV or Excel file to upload"
- You should return to the list of Import Files shown on your USB drive. If not, follow the steps presented earlier for accessing these files.

Click the file **Beach Barkers Products and Services List**

Click the **Open** button
The file name will be inserted into the text box

Click the **Next** button
Since nothing is highlighted in red, click **Next** for MAP DATA
Scroll through the Items shown on the IMPORT screen
None of the fields have anything shown in red
- Because you have imported your Chart of Accounts, all of the necessary accounts are available for matching.
- You should have a screen stating that 15 records are ready to be imported.
Click the **Import** button
Once the import is complete, click the **Gear** icon
Click **Products and Services** in the List Column
Scroll through the list to see all of the products and services you will be selling
- Note: Chapters 3-5 focus on Services and Chapters 6-8 will include both Services and Products (inventory) items.
Print, and/or export, and submit Your Name's Beach Barkers Products and Services List Ch. 2 as previously instructed
- If you save the file in Excel, name it **3-Your Name Products and Services List Ch. 2**.

### Your Name's Beach Barkers

Products and services

| Name | SKU | Type | Sales description | Income account | Sales Price | Cost | Quantity |
|---|---|---|---|---|---|---|---|
| Boarding | | Service | Boarding | Boarding | 55 | | |
| Bones | | Inventory item | Bones | Sales of Product Income | | 2 | 350 |
| Brushes | | Inventory item | Brushes | Sales of Product Income | | 5 | 35 |
| Collars | | Inventory item | Collars | Sales of Product Income | | 10 | 650 |
| Day Camp | | Service | Day Camp | Day Camp | 30 | | |
| Dog Food-Canned | | Inventory item | Dog Food-Canned | Sales of Product Income | | 2.50 | 485 |
| Dog Food-Dry | | Inventory item | Dog Food-Dry | Sales of Product Income | | 7 | 400 |
| Grooming | | Service | Grooming | Grooming | | | |
| Hours | | Service | | Hours | | | |
| Leashes | | Inventory item | Leashes | Sales of Product Income | | 10 | 450 |
| Services | | Service | | Services | | | |
| Sweaters | | Inventory item | Sweaters | Sales of Product Income | | 15 | 325 |
| Toys & Treats | | Inventory item | Toys & Treats | Sales of Product Income | | 2 | 3450 |
| Training 1 | | Service | One-Hour Session | Training | 75 | | |
| Training 2 | | Service | Five One-Hour Sessions | Training | 350 | | |
| Training 3 | | Service | Ten One-Hour Sessions | Training | 650 | | |
| Vitamins | | Inventory item | Vitamins | Sales of Product Income | | 3 | 450 |

Do not close QuickBooks Online or Your Name's Beach Barkers

## FINALIZE THE CHART OF ACCOUNTS—DO

Once the Product and Services List has been imported, the Chart of Accounts should be finalized. The Opening Balance Equity account needs to be renamed and some of the income and expense accounts need to be reorganized as subaccounts.

The last part of the company creation is to finalize the Chart of Accounts. As stated, you will need to rename and add subaccounts. Finally, you will print and/or export, and submit your Chart of Accounts. When this is completed, you will be ready to go to Chapter 3 and begin to enter transactions for Your Name's Beach Barkers.

Since all data entered previously disappears when you close the Test Drive Company and you have already practiced renaming files and making subaccounts, you will not complete a drill.

---

**MEMO**
**DATE:** January 1, 2016

Change Account Names:
**Opening Balance Equity** to **Your Name, Capital**
**Discounts given** to **Sales Discounts** (make it a subaccount of Services)
**Shipping and delivery expense** to **Shipping & Delivery**
**Supplies-Cleaning** to **Cleaning Supplies Expense** (make it a subaccount of Supplies Expense)
Create Subaccounts of **Services**:
**Boarding**, **Day Camp**, **Fees Billed**, **Grooming**, **Hours**, **Refunds-Allowances**, and **Training**
Add Account:
Type: **Cost of Goods Sold**; Detail Type: **Supplies & Materials**; Name: **Purchases Discounts**; Subaccount of **Cost of Goods Sold**
Create Subaccounts of **Insurance Expense**:
**Insurance-Disability** and **Insurance-Liability**
Create Subaccount of **Supplies Expense**:
**Kennel Supplies Expense**, **Office Supplies Expense**, and **Sales Supplies Expense**
Delete Accounts:
**Meals and Entertainment**, **Travel**, **Travel Meals**, **Other Portfolio Income**, and **Penalties & Settlements**

---

<u>DO</u>

Finalize the Chart of Accounts for **Your Name's Beach Barkers**

Open the Chart of Accounts as previously instructed
Scroll through the accounts to view opening balances and subaccounts

- When you see Opening Balance Equity, note the 142,362.50 for the QuickBooks balance. As you enter opening balances for the asset and liability accounts, the amounts are also entered into this equity account. Remember, you must have a debit and a credit for each transaction. If you debit the asset for the amount of the opening balance, the Opening Balance Equity account is credited. For a liability, Opening Balance Equity is debited and the liability is credited.
- Remember: Assets = Liabilities + Owner's Equity.

Click **View register** for Opening Balance Equity
Point to **–Split–** on the first entry for $3,200.00

- The two accounts used and the amounts are shown. Vehicles:Depreciation $-3,200.00 and Opening Balance Equity $3,200.
- QuickBooks Online does not show columns for Debits and Credits. Instead, columns are named Increase and Decrease and the transactions are shown based on the entry's effect on the account. In this transaction, the amount of the depreciation reduced the amount of equity.

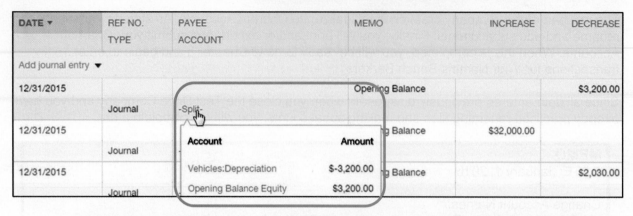

- Note the second transaction. If you were to point to –Split-, you would see that the Original Cost of Vehicles is entered for $32,000.00. It is shown in the Increase column, because the value of the asset (something you own) increases the value of equity. While the amount of depreciation decreases the overall value of Vehicles and the Opening Balance.

Click **Back to Chart of Accounts**

Rename **Opening Balance Equity** to **Your Name, Capital**
Click the drop-down list arrow for Opening Balance Equity, click **Edit**
Delete **Opening Balance Equity** from the Name
Enter **Your Name, Capital**, click **Save and Close**
- Use your actual first and last name.

| Your Name, Capital | Equity | Opening B... | 142,362.50 |

Rename "Discounts given" to **Sales Discounts** using the same procedures as Opening Balance Equity
- The Category and Detail Type remain the same.
Make Sales Discounts a subaccount of Services

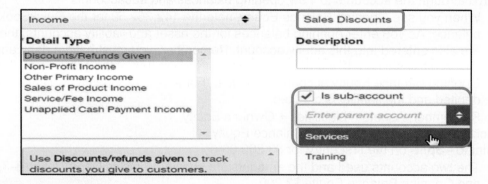

Click **Save and Close**
Follow the instructions provided previously to:
Rename "Shipping and delivery expense" to **Shipping & Delivery**

Rename "Supplies – Cleaning" to **Cleaning Supplies Expense** and make it a subaccount of
   Supplies Expense

Make the following income accounts subaccounts of Services: **Boarding**, **Day Camp**, **Fees
   Billed**, **Grooming**, **Hours**, **Refunds-Allowances**, and **Training**

| Services | Income | Service/Fee I... |
|---|---|---|
| Boarding | Income | Service/Fee I... |
| Day Camp | Income | Service/Fee I... |
| Fees Billed | Income | Service/Fee I... |
| Grooming | Income | Service/Fee I... |
| Hours | Income | Service/Fee I... |
| Refunds-Allowances | Income | Discounts/R... |
| Sales Discounts | Income | Discounts/R... |
| Training | Income | Service/Fee I... |

Add a new account **Purchases Discounts**; Type: **Cost of Goods Sold**; Detail Type:
   **Supplies & Materials**; subaccount of: **Cost of Goods Sold**

## Account

**Category Type**

Cost of Goods Sold

**Name**

Purchases Discounts

**Detail Type**

Cost of labor - COS
Equipment Rental - COS
Other Costs of Services - COS
Shipping, Freight & Delivery - COS
Supplies & Materials - COGS

**Description**

✔ Is sub-account

Cost of Goods Sold

Use **Supplies & materials - COGS** to track
the cost of raw goods and parts used or
consumed when producing a product or
providing a service.

Make **Insurance-Disability** and **Insurance-Liability** subaccounts of the expense account
   "Insurance "

| Insurance | Expenses | Insurance |
|---|---|---|
| Insurance - Disability | Expenses | Insurance |
| Insurance - Liability | Expenses | Insurance |

Make **Kennel Supplies Expense**, **Office Supplies Expense**, and **Sales Supplies
   Expense** subaccounts of "Supplies Expense"

| Supplies Expense | Expenses | Supplies & M.. |
|---|---|---|
| Cleaning Supplies Expense | Expenses | Supplies & M.. |
| Kennel Supplies Expense | Expenses | Supplies & M.. |
| Office Supplies Expense | Expenses | Supplies & M.. |
| Sales Supplies Expense | Expenses | Supplies & M.. |

Delete the account **Meals and Entertainment**

Click the drop-down list arrow for Meals and Entertainment, click **Delete**

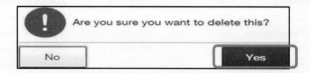

Click **Yes** on the warning screen

> ! Are you sure you want to delete this?
>
> No　　　　　　　　　Yes

Repeat the steps to delete **Travel**, **Travel Meals**, **Other Portfolio Income**, and **Penalties & Settlements**
- You will no longer see the accounts that were deleted. However, they still remain in your Chart of Accounts as inactive (deleted) accounts.

View the Deleted/Inactive accounts

Click the Settings [⚙] icon in the Chart of Accounts

Click **Include inactive** in the Other section ☑ Include inactive

Scroll through the Chart of Accounts, notice the accounts marked (deleted) with an Action of Make Active

| Meals and Entertainment (deleted) | Expenses | Entertainment M... | | | Make active ▼ |
| Travel (deleted) | Expenses | Travel | | | Make active ▼ |
| Travel Meals (deleted) | Expenses | Travel Meals | | | Make active ▼ |

Do not print or export the Chart of Accounts
Close Your Name's Beach Barkers then continue to the next section

## PRINT, EXPORT, AND EMAIL REPORTS—DRILL

In addition to printing from lists, you may print a list from Reports. This will be done to print the Chart of Accounts. In addition, once a QuickBooks Online company has been created, it is important to prepare reports to make sure all information came through correctly. These reports include: Account List, Trial Balance, Journal, Profit and Loss, and Balance Sheet.

### *DRILL*

Practice the steps for printing and exporting a report.

 Open the **Test Drive Company** and print, export, and email an Account Listing

The Test Drive Company has a problem when preparing reports
To eliminate the problem, your will turn off the QuickBooks Lab for Redesigned Reports
- When testing potential features and/or apps to include in QuickBooks Online, Intuit places them in QuickBooks Labs. If you want to experiment with one of these, you turn it on in QuickBooks Labs. The feature may or may not become a permanent part of QuickBooks Online, but you may practice with it.
- The test drive has Redesigned Reports turned ON. With this feature on, you cannot prepare reports in Craig's Design and Landscaping Services so it must be turned off.

Click the **Gear** icon

Click **QuickBooks Labs** in the Your Company column

Scroll through the list of experimental plug-ins until you find Redesigned Reports
Click the **On/Off** toggle to turn off this feature

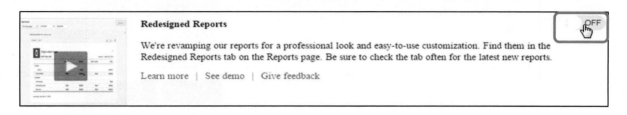

Click **No** on the message screen for "You turned off Redesigned Reports"
Click **Done** at the bottom-right side of the screen
Click **Reports** on the Left-Navigation Bar
- All of the reports available in QuickBooks Online may be prepared from this center.
- The dashboard at the top of the screen provides information for the Net Income, Income, and Expenses.
- There are five tabs that you may click to access different reports: Recommended, Frequently Run, My Custom Reports, Management Reports, and All Reports.

Click **All Reports**
- You will see the respective report categories available and their descriptions.
- Reports are organized according to business functions and grouped within the appropriate categories.

Read the description for Accountant Reports, and then click **Accountant Reports**

| Recommended | Frequently Run | My Custom Reports | Management Reports | All Reports |
|---|---|---|---|---|

## All Reports

**Business Overview**

These reports show different perspectives of how your business is doing.

**Manage Accounts Receivable**

These reports let you see who owes you money and how much they owe you so you can get paid.

**Manage Accounts Payable**

These reports show what you owe and when payments are due so you can take advantage of the time you have to pay bills but still make payments on time.

**Manage Employees**

These reports help you manage employee activities and payroll.

**Review Sales**

These reports group and total sales in different ways to help analyze your sales to see how you're doing and where you make your money.

**Review Expenses and Purchases**

These reports total your expenses and purchases and group them in different ways to help you understand what you spend.

**Accountant Reports**

These are reports accountants typically use to drill down into your business details and prepare your tax returns.

**Manage Products and Inventory**

These reports will help you understand how much inventory you have and how much you are paying and making for each of your inventory items.

Scroll through the reports to view the ones available
Read the description for Account List
Point to the small report to the left of Account List to see a popup that displays a sample of the report
Click **Account List**
View the Chart of Accounts
Read the following without completing the steps:
> To Print the list, click the **Print** button and print as previously instructed
> To Export the list to Excel, click the **Export** button, select the type **XLSX** or **XLS** for the type of Excel report, and export as previously instructed
> To Email the list to your instructor without saving, click the **Email** button, Your Name <quickbooks-email@intuit.com> is inserted by QuickBooks, enter your instructor's email address, if you wish to add a note, do so in Note:, then click **Send**

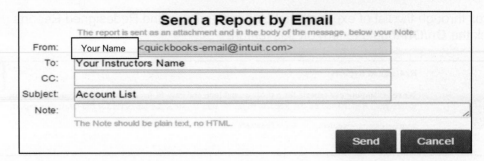

Close the Test Drive Company

## PRINT, EXPORT, AND EMAIL REPORTS—DO

Now that you have practiced printing an Account List using Reports, you will print the Account List, Trial Balance, Journal, Profit and Loss, and Balance Sheet for Your Name's Beach Barkers. These reports may be required to be submitted to your instructor.

---

**MEMO**
**DATE:** January 1, 2016

Print, export, and/or submit the following reports:
    **Account List**
    **Trial Balance**
    **Journal**
    **Profit and Loss**
    **Balance Sheet**

---

_DO_

 Return to **Your Name's Beach Barkers** and prepare, print, export, and/or email the reports listed in the Memo box

## Account List

_DO_

 Use **Your Name's Beach Barkers** to prepare the **Account List** for **12/31/15**

Open Your Name's Beach Barkers as previously instructed
Click **Reports** on the Navigation Bar
- All of the reports available in QuickBooks Online may be prepared from this center.
- The dashboard at the top of the screen provides information for the Net Income, Income, and Expenses.
- As you saw in the Test Drive Company, there are five tabs that you may click to access different reports: Recommended, Frequently Run, My Custom Reports, Management Reports, and All Reports.
Click **All Reports**
- You will see the respective report categories available and their descriptions.
- Reports are shown within each category and are organized by business functions.
Read the description for Accountant Reports
Click **Accountant Reports**

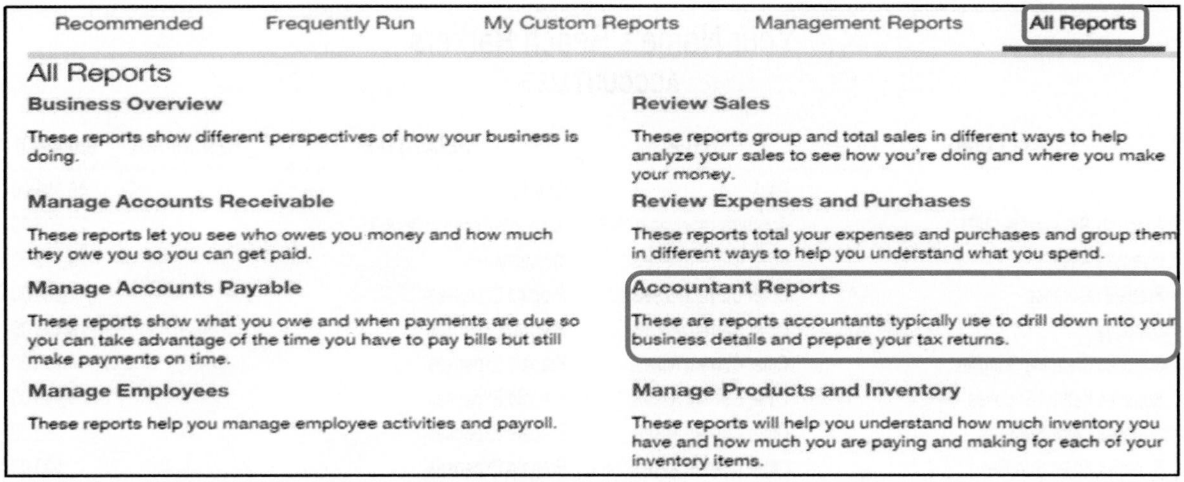

| Recommended | Frequently Run | My Custom Reports | Management Reports | **All Reports** |
|---|---|---|---|---|

**All Reports**

**Business Overview**

These reports show different perspectives of how your business is doing.

**Manage Accounts Receivable**

These reports let you see who owes you money and how much they owe you so you can get paid.

**Manage Accounts Payable**

These reports show what you owe and when payments are due so you can take advantage of the time you have to pay bills but still make payments on time.

**Manage Employees**

These reports help you manage employee activities and payroll.

**Review Sales**

These reports group and total sales in different ways to help analyze your sales to see how you're doing and where you make your money.

**Review Expenses and Purchases**

These reports total your expenses and purchases and group them in different ways to help you understand what you spend.

**Accountant Reports**

These are reports accountants typically use to drill down into your business details and prepare your tax returns.

**Manage Products and Inventory**

These reports will help you understand how much inventory you have and how much you are paying and making for each of your inventory items.

2

Scroll through the Accountant Reports to view the ones available
- Notice the description for Account List.

Click **Account List**

On the "Cash or accrual for summary reports?" make sure **Accrual basis** is selected, then click **Finish**

Compare your Chart of Accounts with the following:
- Assets, Liabilities, and Equity accounts will have balances. Income and Expense accounts will not.
- Sometimes the parent account (Supplies for example) will show the total value—shown in the following screen shot. Other times, the parent account will show 0.00. Either way, the subaccounts should show their values.
- If there are differences between your Account List and the one shown on the following page, make the appropriate corrections.
- If you need to correct an Account Name, Type, Detail Type, or Description, click the account shown in the report. You will open the Account screen that you used when editing accounts previously.
- If you need to correct an Opening Balance, Make the changes as follows: Click **Transactions** on the Navigation Bar, click **Chart of Accounts**, click the account with the incorrect balance, click **View Register**. In the Register click the transaction for **Opening Balance**, click the **Edit** button, change the amount, click **Save**.

# Your Name's Beach Barkers
## ACCOUNT LIST

| ACCOUNT | TYPE | DETAIL TYPE | DESCRIPTION | BALANCE |
|---|---|---|---|---|
| Checking | Bank | Checking | | 45,385.00 |
| Accounts Receivable (A/R) | Accounts receivable (A/R) | Accounts Receivable (A/R) | | 27,500.00 |
| Inventory Asset | Other Current Assets | Inventory | | 29,012.50 |
| Prepaid Insurance | Other Current Assets | Prepaid Expenses | | 1,200.00 |
| Supplies | Other Current Assets | Prepaid Expenses | | 3,495.00 |
| Supplies:Cleaning Supplies | Other Current Assets | Prepaid Expenses | | 750.00 |
| Supplies:Kennel Supplies | Other Current Assets | Prepaid Expenses | | 1,895.00 |
| Supplies:Office Supplies | Other Current Assets | Prepaid Expenses | | 350.00 |
| Supplies:Sales Supplies | Other Current Assets | Prepaid Expenses | | 500.00 |
| Uncategorized Asset | Other Current Assets | Other Current Assets | | 0.00 |
| Undeposited Funds | Other Current Assets | Undeposited Funds | | 0.00 |
| Equipment | Fixed Assets | Machinery & Equipment | | 7,200.00 |
| Equipment:Depreciation | Fixed Assets | Accumulated Depreciation | | -800.00 |
| Equipment:Original cost | Fixed Assets | Machinery & Equipment | | 8,000.00 |
| Furniture & Fixtures | Fixed Assets | Furniture & Fixtures | | 13,500.00 |
| Furniture & Fixtures:Depreciation | Fixed Assets | Accumulated Depreciation | | -1,500.00 |
| Furniture & Fixtures:Original cost | Fixed Assets | Furniture & Fixtures | | 15,000.00 |
| Kennel Equipment | Fixed Assets | Machinery & Equipment | | 18,270.00 |
| Kennel Equipment:Depreciation | Fixed Assets | Accumulated Depreciation | | -2,030.00 |
| Kennel Equipment:Original cost | Fixed Assets | Machinery & Equipment | | 20,300.00 |
| Vehicles | Fixed Assets | Vehicles | | 28,800.00 |
| Vehicles:Depreciation | Fixed Assets | Accumulated Depreciation | | -3,200.00 |
| Vehicles:Original cost | Fixed Assets | Vehicles | | 32,000.00 |
| Accounts Payable (A/P) | Accounts payable (A/P) | Accounts Payable (A/P) | | -5,300.00 |
| Payroll Liabilities | Other Current Liabilities | Payroll Tax Payable | | 0.00 |
| Loans Payable | Long Term Liabilities | Notes Payable | | -4,500.00 |
| Loans Payable:Equipment Loan | Long Term Liabilities | Notes Payable | | -2,000.00 |
| Loans Payable:Furniture & Fixtures Loan | Long Term Liabilities | Notes Payable | | -2,500.00 |
| Retained Earnings | Equity | Retained Earnings | | 0.00 |
| Your Name, Capital | Equity | Opening Balance Equity | | -142,362.50 |
| Billable Expense Income | Income | Service/Fee Income | | |
| Sales | Income | Sales of Product Income | | |
| Sales of Product Income | Income | Sales of Product Income | | |
| Services | Income | Service/Fee Income | | |
| Services:Boarding | Income | Service/Fee Income | | |
| Services:Day Camp | Income | Service/Fee Income | | |
| Services:Fees Billed | Income | Service/Fee Income | | |
| Services:Grooming | Income | Service/Fee Income | | |
| Services:Hours | Income | Service/Fee Income | | |
| Services:Refunds-Allowances | Income | Discounts/Refunds Given | | |
| Services:Sales Discounts | Income | Discounts/Refunds Given | | |
| Services:Training | Income | Service/Fee Income | | |
| Uncategorized Income | Income | Service/Fee Income | | |
| Cost of Goods Sold | Cost of Goods Sold | Supplies & Materials - COGS | | |

| | | |
|---|---|---|
| Cost of Goods Sold:Purchases Discounts | Cost of Goods Sold | Supplies & Materials - COGS |
| Advertising | Expenses | Advertising/Promotional |
| Automobile Expense | Expenses | Auto |
| Bank Charges | Expenses | Bank Charges |
| Commissions & fees | Expenses | Other Miscellaneous Service Cost |
| Dues & Subscriptions | Expenses | Dues & subscriptions |
| Equipment Rental | Expenses | Equipment Rental |
| Freight & Delivery | Expenses | Shipping, Freight & Delivery |
| Insurance | Expenses | Insurance |
| Insurance:Insurance - Disability | Expenses | Insurance |
| Insurance:Insurance - Liability | Expenses | Insurance |
| Interest Expense | Expenses | Interest Paid |
| Laundry | Expenses | Other Miscellaneous Service Cost |
| Legal & Professional Fees | Expenses | Legal & Professional Fees |
| License Expense | Expenses | Taxes Paid |
| Office Expenses | Expenses | Office/General Administrative Expenses |
| Other General and Admin Expenses | Expenses | Office/General Administrative Expenses |
| Promotional | Expenses | Advertising/Promotional |
| Purchases | Expenses | Supplies & Materials |
| Rent or Lease | Expenses | Rent or Lease of Buildings |
| Repair & Maintenance | Expenses | Repair & Maintenance |
| Shipping & Delivery | Expenses | Shipping, Freight & Delivery |
| Stationery & Printing | Expenses | Office/General Administrative Expenses |
| Supplies Expense | Expenses | Supplies & Materials |
| Supplies Expense:Cleaning Supplies Expense | Expenses | Supplies & Materials |
| Supplies Expense:Kennel Supplies Expense | Expenses | Supplies & Materials |
| Supplies Expense:Office Supplies Expense | Expenses | Supplies & Materials |
| Supplies Expense:Sales Supplies Expense | Expenses | Supplies & Materials |
| Taxes & Licenses | Expenses | Taxes Paid |
| Telephone Expense | Expenses | Utilities |
| Uncategorized Expense | Expenses | Other Miscellaneous Service Cost |
| Utilities | Expenses | Utilities |
| Interest Earned | Other Income | Interest Earned |
| Other Miscellaneous Income | Other Income | Other Miscellaneous Income |
| Other Ordinary Income | Other Income | Other Miscellaneous Income |
| Depreciation Expense | Other Expense | Depreciation |
| Miscellaneous | Other Expense | Other Miscellaneous Expense |

When the Chart of Accounts is correct perform one of the following

**Print**: click the **Print** button follow instructions given earlier for printing

**Export** to Excel: click the drop-down list arrow on the **Excel** button, click **Excel (XLSX or XLS)**. If you save the report, name it **4-Your Name Chart of Accounts Ch. 2**.

**Submit**: as previously instructed or email the report directly to your instructor without saving, click the **Email** button, Your Name <quickbooks-email@intuit.com> is inserted by QuickBooks, enter your instructor's email address, if you wish to add a note, do so in Note:, then click **Send**.

When finished, click **Reports** on the Navigation Bar; continue with the Trial Balance section

Trial Balance

*DO*

Continue to use **Your Name's Beach Barkers** to prepare the **Trial Balance** for **12/31/15**

    Click **Trial Balance**
- The Trial Balance proves that Debits equal Credits.
- You will see the report for the current month. Since the company was created on December 31, 2015, you will need to enter those dates for the report.

    Click in the **From:** text box, delete the beginning date, enter **123115**
- QuickBooks inserts the **/** and enters 2015 for the year.

    Click in the **To:** text box, delete the current date, enter **123115**
    Click **Run Report**

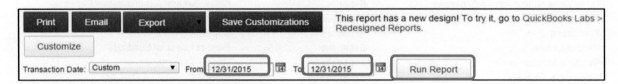

The Trial Balance appears as follows:

### Your Name's Beach Barkers
**TRIAL BALANCE**
As of December 31, 2015

| | DEBIT | CREDIT |
|---|---:|---:|
| Checking | 45,385.00 | |
| Accounts Receivable (A/R) | 27,500.00 | |
| Inventory Asset | 29,012.50 | |
| Prepaid Insurance | 1,200.00 | |
| Supplies:Cleaning Supplies | 750.00 | |
| Supplies:Kennel Supplies | 1,895.00 | |
| Supplies:Office Supplies | 350.00 | |
| Supplies:Sales Supplies | 500.00 | |
| Equipment:Depreciation | | 800.00 |
| Equipment:Original cost | 8,000.00 | |
| Furniture & Fixtures:Depreciation | | 1,500.00 |
| Furniture & Fixtures:Original cost | 15,000.00 | |
| Kennel Equipment:Depreciation | | 2,030.00 |
| Kennel Equipment:Original cost | 20,300.00 | |
| Vehicles:Depreciation | | 3,200.00 |
| Vehicles:Original cost | 32,000.00 | |
| Accounts Payable (A/P) | | 5,300.00 |
| Loans Payable:Equipment Loan | | 2,000.00 |
| Loans Payable:Furniture & Fixtures Loan | | 2,500.00 |
| Your Name, Capital | | 142,362.50 |
| Services | | 27,500.00 |
| Miscellaneous | 5,300.00 | |
| **TOTAL** | **$187,192.50** | **$187,192.50** |

    Check your balances, correct as necessary; then print, export, and submit the report as previously instructed
- If you save and name the report it should be **5-Your Name Trial Balance Ch. 2**.

Journal

*DO*

Continue to use **Your Name's Beach Barkers** to prepare the **Journal** for **12/31/15**

Click **Reports** on the Navigation Bar, repeat the steps to prepare the **Journal** From: **12/31/15** To: **12/31/15**
- Starting with the most current entry, the Journal shows all of your entries in Debit and Credit format.

Scroll through the report, is your total $199,222.50

| TOTAL | $199,222.50 | $199,222.50 |
|---|---|---|

- At this point, your only transactions are opening balances. Notice that you will have opening balances for the assets and liabilities that you entered, as well as, for each customer, vendor, and product imported. If your total does not match, make corrections in the account as instructed earlier. If the entries are in a different order, do not be concerned as long as the amounts, accounts, and totals match.

Print, export, and/or submit as previously instructed
- Name the file **6-Your Name Journal Ch. 2**.

## Profit and Loss

_DO_

Continue to use **Your Name's Beach Barkers** to prepare the **Profit and Loss** for **12/31/15**

Repeat the steps provided earlier to prepare the **Profit and Loss** report for **12/31/15**
- When you first access the report, it shows the current month. Notice that there are no balances or amounts shown. This is because the amounts used to determine income and expenses were entered for 2015, a previous year.
- Remember, the Profit and Loss (also known as Income Statement) uses income minus expenses to determine the Net Income or Net Loss for the period.
- Technically, QuickBooks Online should have put the opening balances for customers into Uncategorized Income rather than Services. The opening balances for vendors should have been entered into Uncategorized Expenses rather than Other Expenses Miscellaneous. Since these are opening balances and will not reflect on the Profit and Loss in the following year, it is alright to leave these as is rather than record adjusting entries.

### Your Name's Beach Barkers
#### PROFIT AND LOSS
##### December 31, 2015

|  | TOTAL |
|---|---|
| **Income** | |
| Services | 27,500.00 |
| **Total Income** | **$27,500.00** |
| **Gross Profit** | **$27,500.00** |
| **Expenses** | |
| **Total Expenses** | |
| **Net Operating Income** | **$27,500.00** |
| **Other Expenses** | |
| Miscellaneous | 5,300.00 |
| **Total Other Expenses** | **$5,300.00** |
| **Net Other Income** | **$ -5,300.00** |
| **Net Income** | **$22,200.00** |

Print, export, and/or submit as previously instructed
- Name the file **7-Your Name Profit and Loss Ch. 2**.

Balance Sheet

<u>*DO*</u>

 Continue to use **Your Name's Beach Barkers** to prepare the **Balance Sheet** for **12/31/15**

- Note that Total Assets equal $174,362.50 and that Total Liabilities and Equity equal $174,362.50. This proves the fundamental accounting equation that Assets = Liabilities and Equity.

## Your Name's Beach Barkers
### BALANCE SHEET
As of December 31, 2015

| | TOTAL |
|---|---|
| **ASSETS** | |
| Current Assets | |
| Bank Accounts | |
| Checking | 45,385.00 |
| **Total Bank Accounts** | **$45,385.00** |
| Accounts Receivable | |
| Accounts Receivable (A/R) | 27,500.00 |
| **Total Accounts Receivable** | **$27,500.00** |
| Other current assets | |
| Inventory Asset | 29,012.50 |
| Prepaid Insurance | 1,200.00 |
| Supplies | |
| Cleaning Supplies | 750.00 |
| Kennel Supplies | 1,895.00 |
| Office Supplies | 350.00 |
| Sales Supplies | 500.00 |
| **Total Supplies** | **3,495.00** |
| **Total Other current assets** | **$33,707.50** |
| **Total Current Assets** | **$106,592.50** |
| Fixed Assets | |
| Equipment | |
| Depreciation | -800.00 |
| Original cost | 8,000.00 |
| **Total Equipment** | **7,200.00** |
| Furniture & Fixtures | |
| Depreciation | -1,500.00 |
| Original cost | 15,000.00 |
| **Total Furniture & Fixtures** | **13,500.00** |
| Kennel Equipment | |
| Depreciation | -2,030.00 |
| Original cost | 20,300.00 |
| **Total Kennel Equipment** | **18,270.00** |
| Vehicles | |
| Depreciation | -3,200.00 |
| Original cost | 32,000.00 |
| **Total Vehicles** | **28,800.00** |
| **Total Fixed Assets** | **$67,770.00** |
| **TOTAL ASSETS** | **$174,362.50** |

| LIABILITIES AND EQUITY | TOTAL |
|---|---|
| Liabilities | |
| Current Liabilities | |
| Accounts Payable | |
| Accounts Payable (A/P) | 5,300.00 |
| **Total Accounts Payable** | **$5,300.00** |
| **Total Current Liabilities** | **$5,300.00** |
| Long-Term Liabilities | |
| Loans Payable | |
| Equipment Loan | 2,000.00 |
| Furniture & Fixtures Loan | 2,500.00 |
| **Total Loans Payable** | **4,500.00** |
| **Total Long-Term Liabilities** | **$4,500.00** |
| **Total Liabilities** | **$9,800.00** |
| Equity | |
| Retained Earnings | 22,200.00 |
| Your Name, Capital | 142,362.50 |
| Net Income | |
| **Total Equity** | **$164,562.50** |
| **TOTAL LIABILITIES AND EQUITY** | **$174,362.50** |

Print, export, and/or submit as previously instructed
- Name the file **8-Your Name Balance Sheet Ch. 2**.

Do <u>not</u> close Your Name's Beach Barkers

## ADDITIONAL TRANSACTIONS—DO

Near the end of each chapter, there will be a section containing additional transactions that will be similar to the ones you completed during the chapter. These transactions will be listed in a Memo. You must enter them without any specific instructions being provided. If you have questions about how to enter transactions, you may refer back to material presented earlier in the chapter.

In preparation for opening a second location of Your Name's Beach Barkers in Malibu, California, you will import additional Customers and Vendors.

_DO_

Continue to use **Your Name's Beach Barkers** and enter the following transactions and print, export, and submit as instructed in the Memo box

- Hint: To determine the names of the newly imported customers and vendors, you can open the Excel files that you import.

---

**MEMO**
**DATE:** December 31, 2015

Import the Excel file: 2-Beach Barkers Customers List. Edit the all of the newly imported customers: Remove check mark for Print on Check as, Payment Method: Check, Terms: Net 30. Print, export, and submit the list. Name it **9-Your Name Customers List 2 Ch. 2**

Import the Excel file: 2-Beach Barkers Vendors List. Edit all of the newly imported vendors: Remove First, Middle, and Last Names, Terms: Net 30. Print, export, and submit the list. Name it **10-Your Name Vendors List 2 Ch. 2**

---

## SUMMARY

In this chapter, an Intuit ID and email account were established; the Educational Trial Version of QuickBooks Online Plus was activated and registered; and the company, Your Name's Beach Barkers, was created. QuickBooks Online set up a Chart of Accounts for a Pet Service Business and it was modified by importing accounts. In addition to importing, accounts were also and added, edited, and deleted. Additional lists for Customers, Vendors, and Products/Services were also imported and edited. Opening Balances for accounts, customers, and vendors were entered and reports were prepared, printed, exported, and emailed.

# END-OF-CHAPTER QUESTIONS

## TRUE/FALSE

ANSWER THE FOLLOWING QUESTIONS IN THE SPACE PROVIDED BEFORE THE QUESTION NUMBER.

_____ 1. You must have an email account before you can activate the QuickBooks Online Educational Trial Version.

_____ 2. QuickBooks Online Labs are permanent additions to the program.

_____ 3. Before you can activate your Educational Trial Version of QuickBooks Online, you must identify the industry type—sole proprietorship, partnership, corporation, etc.

_____ 4. You may import data from Excel.

_____ 5. Reports are accessed by clicking the Gear button and are grouped into categories according to business functions.

_____ 6. .Each product or service must be linked to an appropriate income account.

_____ 7. Imported data never needs to be edited.

_____ 8. When you create a company and identify the type of business, QuickBooks Online creates a Chart of Accounts based on your selected type of business.

_____ 9. Company Settings must be imported from Excel.

_____10. You may import a company file from QuickBooks Desktop.

## MULTIPLE CHOICE

WRITE THE LETTER OF THE CORRECT ANSWER IN THE SPACE PROVIDED BEFORE THE QUESTION NUMBER.

_____ 1. Reports may be ___.
   A. Printed
   B. Exported to Excel
   C. Emailed
   D. All of the above

_____ 2. To edit a Company Setting, click the ___ icon.
   A. Plus
   B. Menu
   C. Pen
   D. Diamond

_____ 3. To assign a subaccount to an expense, edit ___.
   A. The Vendors List
   B. Accounts Payable
   C. The Account that will be a subaccount
   D. The Profit and Loss report

_____ 4. To access the Customers List, click Customers on the ___.
   A. Company Settings List
   B. Navigation Bar
   C. Import Data Screen
   D. On the Browser Tab

_____ 5. After you import the Chart of Accounts, edit the ___ and ___ accounts to add Opening Balances and as of dates.
   A. Asset and Liability
   B. Asset and Income
   C. Liability and Expense
   D. Income and Expense

_____ 6. Each vendor imported from Excel needs to be edited to add ___ to the Vendor.
   A. Terms
   B. Preferred Payment Method
   C. Preferred Delivery Method
   D. All of the above

_____ 7. Something that is paid for and will be used within one year is a(n) ___
   A. Expense
   B. Prepaid Expense
   C. Bill
   D. All of the above

_____ 8. A Fixed Asset is something that you will own for ___.
   A. Less than a year
   B. The life of the business
   C. More than a year
   D. All of the above

_____ 9. The ___ report proves the fundamental accounting equation: Assets = Liabilities and Equity.
   A. Balance Sheet
   B. Trial Balance
   C. Journal
   D. Chart of Accounts

_____ 10. To indicate the Preferred Invoice Terms, edit the ___ Settings.
   A. Company
   B. Sales
   C. Expenses
   D. Advanced

## FILL-IN

IN THE SPACE PROVIDED, WRITE THE ANSWER THAT MOST APPROPRIATELY COMPLETES THE SENTENCE.

1. The four data lists you may import are _____, _____, _____, and _____.

2. Once the Import file has been selected, you will get a MAP Data screen that is used to match the _____ names and _____ names.

3. To access Import Data click the _____ icon.

4. When you create a Fixed Asset account and track depreciation, you give the as of date and the amounts for _____ and _____.

5. Click_____ and _____ on the Navigation Bar to access the Chart of Accounts.

## COMPUTER ASSIGNMENT

REFER TO PRINTOUTS OR USE QUICKBOOKS ONLINE AND YOUR NAME'S BEACH BARKERS TO LOOK UP OR ENTER INFORMATION, AND THEN WRITE THE ANSWERS TO THE FOLLOWING EXERCISES IN THE SPACE PROVIDED

1. What are the three steps listed for Importing Data? _____
   _____
   _____

2. Which icon do you click in order to access Company Settings? _____

3. When editing Sales Settings, which icon do you click in order to enter "Preferred invoice terms?" _____

4. What is the balance of the Checking account? _____

5. To make Cleaning Supplies a subaccount of Supplies, you edit ___. _____

6. Which report proves that Debits equal Credits? _____

7. What does the Chart of Accounts show for the value of Kennel Equipment? _____

8. What is the Chart of Accounts balance for Your Name, Capital? _____

9. What is the Open Balance for the vendor, Canine Supplies? _____

10. What is the Income Account linked to the Service item Boarding? _____

## YOUR NAME'S BEACH BARKERS
## CHAPTER 2 CHECKLIST

The checklist below shows all of the business forms printed during training. Check each one that you printed, exported, and/or submitted.

| | | | |
|---|---|---|---|
| _____ | 1-Customers List | _____ | 6-Journal |
| _____ | 2-Vendors List | _____ | 7-Profit and Loss |
| _____ | 3-Products and Services List | _____ | 8-Balance Sheet |
| _____ | 4-Accounts List | _____ | 9-Customers List 2 |
| _____ | 5-Trial Balance | _____ | 10-Vendors List 2 |

2

# SALES AND RECEIVABLES: SERVICE ITEMS

**3**

## LEARNING OBJECTIVES

At the completion of this chapter, you will be able to:

1. Create invoices to record transactions for sales on account.
2. Create sales receipts to record cash sales.
3. Edit, void, and delete invoices and sales receipts.
4. Create credit memos.
5. Add new customers and modify customer records.
6. Record cash receipts.
7. Enter partial cash payments.
8. Display and print invoices, sales receipts, and credit memos.
9. Display, print, export, and send Customer and Sales Reports including Customer Balance Summary reports, Customer Balance Detail reports, Transaction List by Customer, and Sales by Product/Service Summary.
10. Display, print, export, and send additional reports including, Deposit Summary, Journal, and Trial Balance.

## ACCOUNTING FOR SALES AND RECEIVABLES

Rather than use a traditional Sales Journal to record sales on account using debits and credits and special columns, QuickBooks Online records sales by preparing invoices and sales receipts.

If your customer doesn't pay at the time you provide your service or sell your product, an invoice is prepared. QuickBooks Online uses an invoice to record sales transactions for accounts receivable in the Accounts Receivable Register. When a sale is "on account" this means that the customer owes you money and Accounts Receivable is used as the account.

Because cash sales do not involve accounts receivable and would be recorded in the Cash Receipts Journal in traditional accounting, the transactions are recorded on a Sales Receipt. Rather than using the Accounts Receivable account for the debit part of the transaction, Undeposited Funds is used because you received payment at the time the sale was made or the service was performed.

Depending on how your company was created, QuickBooks Online puts the money received from a cash sale and from a payment receipt—a customer's payment on account for an existing invoice – into the Undeposited Funds account. When a bank deposit is made the Undeposited Funds are placed in the Checking or Cash account.

A new customer can be added on the fly as transactions are entered. Unlike many computerized accounting programs, in QuickBooks Online, error correction is easy. A sales form may be edited, voided, or deleted in the same window where it was created. Customer information may be changed by editing the Customer in the Customer Center.

A multitude of reports are available when using QuickBooks Online. Reports for Accounts Receivable include Customer Balance Summary, Customer Balance Detail, Invoice List, and others. Sales reports provide information regarding the amount of sales and include Sales by Customer Summary, Sales by Customer Detail, Sales by Product/Service Summary and Sales by Product/Service Detail, among others. As you learned in Chapter 2, traditional accounting reports such as Trial Balance, Profit and Loss, and Balance Sheet are also available.

## TRAINING TUTORIAL

Now that the fictional company—Your Name's Beach Barkers—has been created, it is time to record transactions. This chapter focuses on recording sales—both cash and on account—customer payments, bank deposits, and other transactions for receivables and sales. In addition to recording transactions, you will also prepare several reports. Use of Your Name's Beach Barkers will continue throughout the text as you explore the different facets and capabilities of QuickBooks Online. Because you can only create and use one company in the Educational Trial Version of QuickBooks Online, new concepts and procedures will be practiced in the Test Drive Company, and then entered into Your Name's Beach Barkers.

## TRAINING PROCEDURES

Follow the same training procedures that were presented in Chapter 2. For familiarity with the procedures presented in the chapter, it is helpful to read the chapter before entering transactions. As you work through the chapter, remember that the Test Drive Company will not save your work so try to complete related sections before ending your work session. Mark your place in the textbook so you know where you left off in your training. Make sure you check your work and proofread carefully. Double-check the amounts of money, account, product/services items, and dates used.

Print, export, and submit work as directed in the chapter and by your instructor. When you prepare a business document; such as, an invoice or a sales receipt, you may print or save the document. If you prepare a report, you may print the document, export it to Excel, and/or send or submit it.

Since this is the first chapter where you will record transactions in QuickBooks Online, there are more transactions than in later chapters. This is done to provide you with a familiarity with QuickBooks Online. As you learned in Chapter 2, additional transactions will be completed near the end of the chapter. These transactions are similar to the ones you entered in the Test Drive Company and in Your Name's Beach Barkers so no step-by-step instructions will be given. If you need to refer back to the chapter materials to make the entries, you should feel free to do so. If you can enter them without looking back, you have learned how to do something on your own in QuickBooks Online.

## DATES

Remember that the year used for the screen shots is 2016. Check with your instructor to see what year to use for the transactions. Sometimes, the difference in the computer and text dates will cause a slight variation in the way QuickBooks Online screens are displayed and they may not match the text exactly. If you cannot change a date that is provided by QuickBooks Online, accept it and continue with your training. Instructions are given where this occurs. The main criterion is to be consistent with the year you use throughout the text. QuickBooks Online inserts the current date into a transaction, be aware of this and be sure to use the date indicated in the text.

In the Test Drive Company, transaction dates are programmed to change automatically so the dates shown in the text will be different from the dates shown in the Test Drive Company.

## IMPORTANT NOTE

QuickBooks Online is constantly evolving and new features, apps, and procedures change frequently. Everything in the text is correct at the time of this writing; however, by the time of publication some changes to the program may occur. QuickBooks Online has Labs available where you may experiment with proposed additions, changes, and enhancements to the program. These experiments may or may not become part of QuickBooks Online at any given time. Since the Labs are for testing, the features in the Labs will not be included in the text unless they become adopted before publication. Whenever possible, changes will be incorporated into the text but do note that some of the updates will not be able to be included until the next edition of the book.

## BEGIN TRAINING

In this chapter you will be entering transactions for accounts receivable and cash sales, receipts for payments on account, and bank deposits. As you learned in Chapter 2, much of the organization of QuickBooks Online is dependent upon lists. The two primary types of lists you will use for sales and receivables are the Customers List and the Products and Services List.

In addition to being a list, the Customers List functions as the Accounts Receivable Subsidiary Ledger. Even though QuickBooks Online does not use this term, the use of the Customers List for the Accounts Receivable Subsidiary Ledger conforms to GAAP (Generally Accepted Accounting Principles). A transaction entry for an individual customer is posted to the customer's account in the Customers List just as it would be posted to the customer's individual account in an Accounts Receivable Subsidiary Ledger.

The total of the Customers List will be equal to the balance of the Accounts Receivable account in the Chart of Accounts. The Chart of Accounts also functions as the General Ledger when using GAAP standards.

Sales are often made up of various types of income. When you created Your Name's Beach Barkers in Chapter 2, you imported a Chart of Accounts that included several accounts for income. Some of the income accounts were made subaccounts of Service Income. When recording a sale, whether for cash or on account, you sell something from your Products and Services List. The item on the list is matched with the appropriate income account. For example, if you give a dog a bath, you will use the product/services item Grooming. The income from that bath will be entered into the Services Income: Grooming account and into either Accounts Receivable or Undeposited Funds.

### ENTER, EDIT, AND VIEW A SALE ON ACCOUNT—DRILL

Because QuickBooks operates on a business form premise, a sale on account is entered via an invoice. You prepare an invoice, and QuickBooks Online records the transaction in the Journal and automatically posts it in the customer's account in the Customers List. Technically, the transaction debits Accounts Receivable (and the customer's account in the Accounts Receivable Subsidiary Ledger) and credits the appropriate Income Account.

Even though the drill is for practice the transaction will be shown in a Memo. Complete the following transaction to record sales on account.

---

**MEMO**
**DATE:** January 1, 2016

Record Dukes Basketball Camp's Weekly Gardening Service for $150.

---

*DRILL*

 Open the **Test Drive Company** as previously instructed and practice entering sales transactions on account

- If you get a message regarding allowing cookies, simply re-enter the Security Verification and click Continue.
- If the Security Verification that you enter is not recognized, you may have to enter a second or even third code number.

## Enter a Sale on Account

 Practice preparing an Invoice in the **Test Drive Company**

Click the **Plus** icon

On the Create screen, click **Invoice** in the Customers Column
- An invoice is used to record a sale on account.
- A sale on account is basically a customer's charge account with the company. This is sometimes referred to as a credit sale even though a credit card is not used at the time of purchase. A transaction recorded on an invoice means that the customer will pay for the purchase at a later time.

| Create | | | |
|---|---|---|---|
| **Customers** | **Vendors** | **Employees** | **Other** |
| Invoice | Expense | Payroll 🏃 | Bank Deposit |
| Receive Payment | Check | Single Time Activity | Transfer |
| Estimate | Bill | Weekly Timesheet | Journal Entry |
| Credit Memo | Pay Bills | | Statement |
| Sales Receipt | Purchase Order | | |
| Refund Receipt | Vendor Credit | | |
| Delayed Credit | Credit Card Credit | | |
| Delayed Charge | Print Checks | | |

After clicking Invoice, a blank invoice will appear on the screen
- Notice the different fields for information. Much of this will be completed once you choose a customer. For example, in the text box for the PRODUCT/SERVICE field, you will select a products/services item from a drop-down list and then enter other required information such as Quantity and Rate.

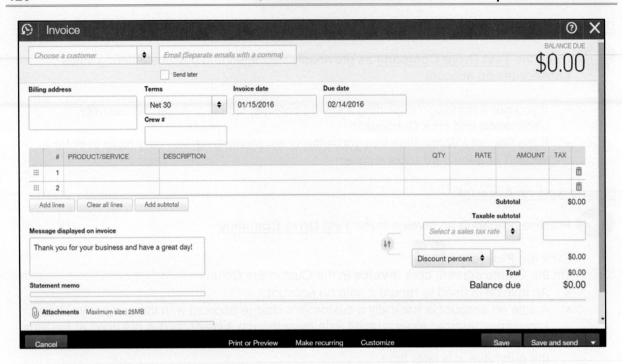

Click the drop-down list arrow for "Choose a customer," then click **Dukes Basketball Camp**

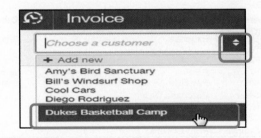

- Note that the customer's name, email address, billing address, and terms were inserted. Tab to or click in "Invoice date," delete the current date, enter **01/01/16**, press **Tab**
- The Due date now shows 01/31/2016.
- Note: Throughout the text, dates may be given with or without the / between sections; for example, 01/01/16 or 010116. The year may be shown and entered as 16 or 2016. Either method works because QuickBooks Online automatically inserts / between the date segments and includes 2016 for the year.

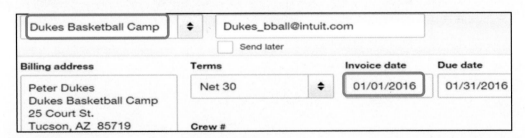

Click in the PRODUCT/SERVICE Column, you will see "Enter Text" and a drop-down list arrow

Click the drop-down list arrow, click **Gardening**

- The Item name, Description, and Quantity are entered by QuickBooks Online. The quantity entered, is always 1.

Tab to the Rate column, enter the weekly rate for Dukes Basketball Camp of **150**, press **Tab**

- The Amount column now shows 150. The Subtotal, Total, and Balance Due are $150.00.

- There is a text box for "Message displayed on invoice." It contains the company's standard message.
- Since this is a service, there is no Sales Tax. No Discount on the sale has been given. The amounts for those two fields is 0.00.

Click the **Save** button at the bottom of the invoice

- You will see a message: Invoice 1038 saved.

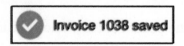

Click the **Print or Preview** button at the bottom of the screen and view your choices for printing

Click **Print or Preview** to view the invoice

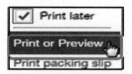

- The completed invoice will be shown exactly how it will be printed.

3

---

**Craig's Design and Landscaping Services**

123 Sierra Way
San Pablo, CA 87999
noreply@quickbooks.com

# INVOICE

| **BILL TO** | | **INVOICE #** 1038 |
| Peter Dukes | | **DATE** 01/01/2016 |
| Dukes Basketball Camp | | **DUE DATE** 01/31/2016 |
| 25 Court St. | | **TERMS** Net 30 |
| Tucson, AZ 85719 | | |

| ACTIVITY | QTY | RATE | AMOUNT |
|---|---|---|---|
| **Landscaping:Gardening**<br>Weekly Gardening Service | 1 | 150.00 | 150.00 |

| Thank you for your business and have a great day! | **BALANCE DUE** | **$150.00** |

---

Click the **Close and remove from print queue** button at the bottom of the invoice
- Since the entries for the Test Drive are practice, there is no need to print them unless instructed to do so by your professor.

Do <u>not</u> close the Test Drive Company

## Edit and Correct Errors

If an error is discovered while entering invoice information, it may be corrected. While there are several ways to correct errors a simple way is to point to the error, highlight it by dragging the mouse through the error, then type the correction or press the Delete key to remove completely.

 Use the **Test Drive Company** to practice editing and making corrections to Invoice # 1038

With Invoice 1038 on the screen, click the drop-down list arrow for the Customer
Click **John Melton**
Click in the "Invoice date" column, the date will be highlighted, type the new date **01/10/16**, and then press **Tab**
- Note that the invoice now shows the Name, Email, Address, and Terms for John Melton. The Invoice date shows 01/10/2016 with a Due date of 02/09/2016.

Click in the "QTY" column and enter a quantity of **4**, press **Tab**
- Note that the Rate remains at 150 and that the Amount is recalculated by QuickBooks Online.

Click the **Cancel** button at the bottom of the invoice to cancel the changes you made to Invoice 1038
Click **Yes** for "Do you want to leave without saving?"
- This cancels the changes you entered and Invoice 1038 will still be for Duke's Basketball Camp.

Do <u>not</u> close the Test Drive Company

## View the Invoice

 View the completed invoice for Dukes Basketball Camp in the **Test Drive Company**

Click **Customers** on the Navigation Bar
Click on the Customer Name: **Dukes Basketball Camp**
- View the Transaction List and note Invoice 1038.

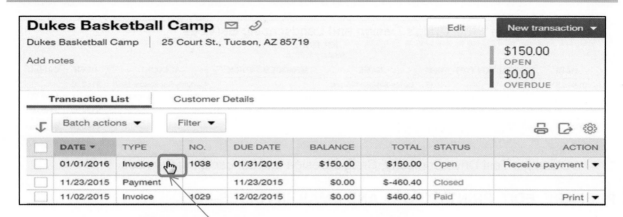

To open the invoice, click anywhere in the information for the invoice
Click the **Close** button at the top of the invoice
Do not close the Test Drive Company

## VIEW THE INVOICE IN A JOURNAL—DRILL

Because QuickBooks operates on a business form premise, a sale on account is entered via an invoice. You prepare an invoice and when you save the it, QuickBooks Online records the transaction in the Journal and automatically debits Accounts Receivable and the individual customer's account in the Customers List and then credits the appropriate Income Account.

### DRILL

Continue to use the **Test Drive Company** and view the invoice you prepared in the Journal

Click the **Gear** icon, click **QuickBooks Labs** in the Your Company column
Scroll down to Redesigned Reports, click the **ON** button to toggle to **OFF**
Click **No** on the message "You turned off Redesigned Reports," click **Done**
Click **Reports** on the Navigation Bar
Click **All Reports**, click **Accountant Reports**, click **Journal**
- The transactions were entered for January 1, 2016.
For the report date, click in From: delete the date shown, enter **01/01/16**
Repeat the steps to enter **01/01/16** in To:
Click **Run Report**
- As you view the report, note the date of 01/01/2016. If your invoice does not show in this report, it means you entered the incorrect date when recording the transaction. Click **Customers** on the Navigation bar, click Duke's Basketball Camp, and click the invoice in the Transaction List for the Customer. Change the date to **01/01/16**, click **Save and Close**. Prepare the Journal again with 01/01/16 for the dates, and you should see your invoice.
- If you find errors in an invoice shown in the report, click the word **Invoice**. You will return to the invoice. Make any necessary corrections, click **Save and Close**. You will return to the Journal and will see the corrections made.
- Depending on the programmed date changes in the Test Drive Company, the number of transactions and the Total may be different from the screen shot shown on the next page.

Close the Test Drive Company, Craig's Design and Landscaping Services

## PREPARE, EDIT, PRINT/EXPORT AND EMAIL INVOICES—DO

Now that you have practiced creating an invoice, you will record several sales on account for Your Name's Beach Barkers. Once you complete an invoice, check it carefully and correct any errors following the steps illustrated in the drill. When your invoices have been entered, you will print, and/or save as a pdf file, and submit them.

---

**MEMO**

**DATE:** January 1, 2016

Gloria Gucci made a reservation for her dog, Mishka, for one day of Day Camp. Create Invoice 1015.

Pamela Vines brought in her dog, Wolf, for Ten One-Hour Sessions of Training, Invoice 1016.

Eric Phillips brought in his dog, Frank, for three days of Boarding, Invoice 1017.

---

<u>**DO**</u>

 Open **Your Name's Beach Barkers** and prepare invoices to record sales on account

Open Your Name's Beach Barkers as previously instructed
Click the **Plus** icon in the Top-Navigation Bar
On the Create screen, click **Invoice** in the Customers Column
- Remember, an invoice is used to record a sale on account.
- As was previously stated, a sale on account is basically a customer's charge account with the company. This is sometimes referred to as a credit sale even though a credit card is not used at the time of purchase. A transaction recorded on an invoice means that the customer will pay for the purchase at a later time.

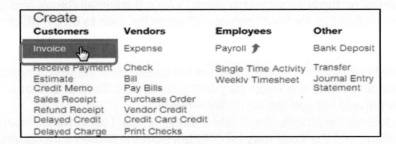

After clicking Invoice, a blank invoice will appear on the screen
Click the drop-down list arrow for "Choose a customer," then click **Gucci, Gloria**
- In the text, customers are usually referred to by first name then last name even though they are organized by the last name in the Customers List.

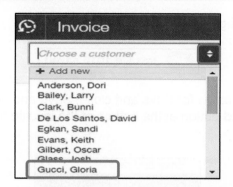

- Note that the customer's name, email address, billing address, and terms were inserted.
Tab to or click in "Invoice date," delete the current date, enter **01/01/16**, press **Tab**
- The Due date now shows 01/31/2016.

Click in the PRODUCT/SERVICE Column, you will see "Enter Text" and a drop-down list
 arrow
Click the drop-down list arrow, click **Day Camp**

- The Item name, Description, Quantity 1, and Rate are entered by QuickBooks.
- The Amount column shows 30.00. The Subtotal, Total, and Balance Due are $30.00.

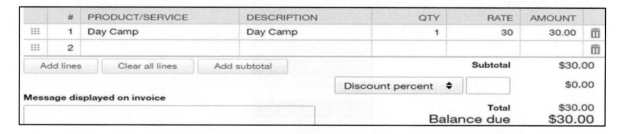

- Since this is a service, there is no Sales Tax. We have not set up sales tax so it does not
 appear on the invoice.
- No Discount on the sale has been given. The amount for the field is 0.00.
The text box for "Message displayed on invoice" is empty
- When creating the company, you did not set up a standard message.
Click in the text box for "Message displayed on invoice" and enter **Thank you for your
 business!**
Click the **Save** button at the bottom of the invoice to save the invoice in QuickBooks Online

- You will see a message: Invoice 1015 saved.

Click the drop-down list arrow for Save and close, Save and new, or Save and send
Click the **Save and Send** button at the bottom of the invoice to send a copy of your invoice
without previewing

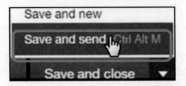

You will see the email message and a small copy of the invoice
- Note that the email address is the customer's email. This is what you want for a real
business; however, in our fictitious business we do not want to send this email.
Click the **Cancel** button

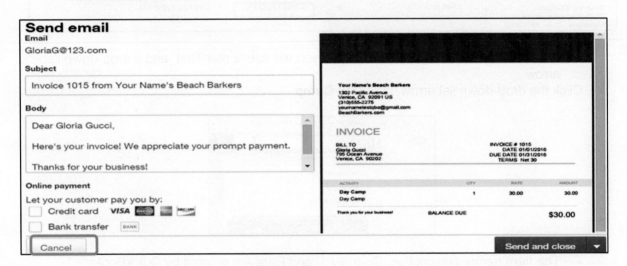

Click the **Print or Preview** button at the bottom of the screen and view your choices for
printing
Click **Print or Preview** to view the invoice

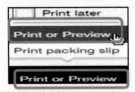

- The preview of the invoice is shown.
- At the bottom of the invoice, you will see the message that you entered.

**Your Name's Beach Barkers**

1302 Pacific Avenue
Venice, CA 92091 US
(310)555-2275    → Your email address

BeachBarkers.com

# INVOICE

| BILL TO | | |
|---|---|---|
| Gloria Gucci | INVOICE # | 1015 |
| 795 Ocean Avenue | DATE | 01/01/2016 |
| Venice, CA 90202 | DUE DATE | 01/31/2016 |
| | TERMS | Net 30 |

| ACTIVITY | QTY | RATE | AMOUNT |
|---|---|---|---|
| **Day Camp** | 1 | 30.00 | 30.00 |
| Day Camp | | | |

| Thank you for your business! | BALANCE DUE | **$30.00** |
|---|---|---|

Click the **Printer** icon at the top of the invoice to print the invoice

To save a pdf copy of the invoice that may be emailed, click the **Save** icon,

   Create a new folder on your USB drive named   Your Name's Beach Barkers Documents

   Create a folder inside Your Name's Beach Barkers Documents and name it **Your Name Chapter 3**

Name the document **1-Your Name Invoice 1015 Gloria Gucci**

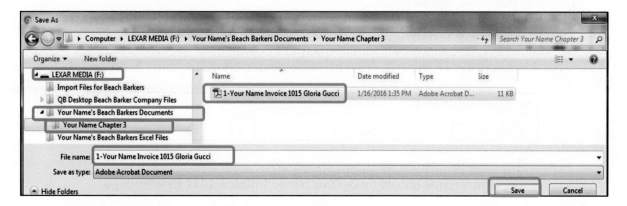

Click the **Save** button on the Save As screen
- If Adobe Reader opens and shows the document, close it.

Click the **Close** button at the bottom of the preview invoice on your screen

Click **Save and new** at the bottom of the invoice to save it in QuickBooks Online and go to a new invoice

Refer to the Memo for the information needed to record the invoice for Pamela Vines

To prepare the invoice for Pamela Vines, repeat the steps as shown for Gloria Gucci to record, print, and/or save the memo

- Remember, Pamela's invoice is for Ten One-Hour Training Sessions. Use the item Training 3 and a quantity of 1, <u>not</u> Training 1 with a quantity of ten.

- Did you remember to key in **Thank you for your business!** in the "Message displayed on invoice" text box?

- The invoice below is shown as it appears after recording. It looks different than the invoice preview that was displayed for Gloria Gucci, but it contains the same information.

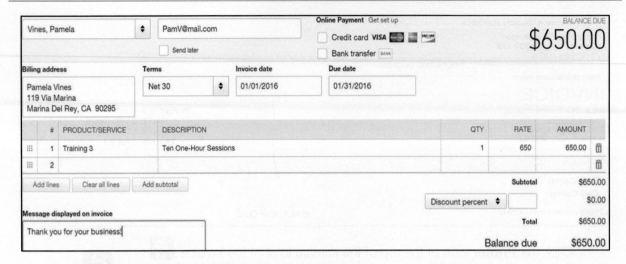

- Did you print and/or save the invoice as a pdf file?
- The document name should be **2-Your Name Invoice 1016 Pamela Vines**.

Click **Save and new**

- If you do not see Save and new, click the drop-down list arrow next to the save command displayed. Remember the save commands are: Save and close, Save and new, and Save and send.

Refer to the Memo for the information needed to record the invoice for Eric Phillips

Repeat the steps shown previously to record, print, and/or save the memo

- Remember, Eric's invoice is for three days of Boarding.

After you select the PRODUCT/SERVICE Boarding, tab to QTY, enter **3**, press **Tab**

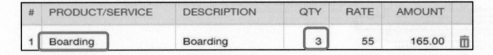

Print and/or save the invoice as shown previously

- The document name should be **3-Your Name Invoice 1017 Eric Phillips**.

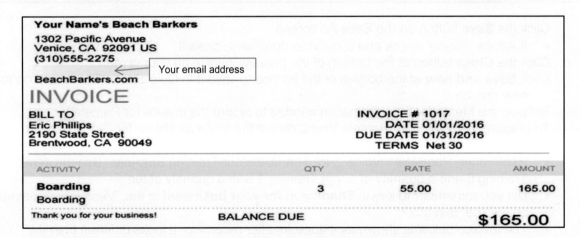

Click **Save and close** to save in QuickBooks Online and to close Invoices

- If you do not see Save and close, click the drop-down list arrow next to the save command displayed. Remember the save commands are: Save and close, Save and new, and Save and send.

Do <u>not</u> close Your Name's Beach Barkers

## VIEW THE INVOICES IN A JOURNAL—DO

Now that you have prepared several invoices, you should review them in the Journal.

*DO*

 View the three invoices you prepared in the Journal of **Your Name's Beach Barkers**

> Click **Reports** on the Navigation Bar
> Click **All Reports**, click **Accountant Reports**, click **Journal**
> - The transactions were entered for January 1, 2016.
> If necessary, change the date by clicking in From: deleting the date shown, entering **01/01/2016**
> Change the Date for To: **01/01/2016**
> Click **Run Report**
> - As you view the report, note the date of 01/01/2016. If an invoice does not show in this report, it means you entered the incorrect date when recording the transaction. Click **Customers** on the Navigation bar, click the customer whose invoice you did not see, and click the invoice in the Transaction List for the Customer. Change the date to **01/01/16**, preview, print and/or save your invoice, then click **Save and close** on the invoice to save it in QuickBooks Online. Prepare the Journal again with the correct dates, and you should see your invoice.
> - If you find errors in an invoice shown in the report, click the word **Invoice**. You will return to the invoice. Make any necessary corrections, preview and save/print the invoice, then click **Save and close** to save in QuickBooks Online. You will return to the Journal and will see the corrections made.

### Your Name's Beach Barkers
#### JOURNAL
##### January 1, 2016

| DATE | TRANSACTION TYPE | NUM | NAME | MEMO/DESCRIPTION | ACCOUNT | DEBIT | CREDIT |
|------|------------------|-----|------|------------------|---------|-------|--------|
| 01/01/2016 | Invoice | 1015 | Gucci, Gloria | | Accounts Receivable (A/R) | $30.00 | |
| | | | | Day Camp | Services:Day Camp | | $30.00 |
| | | | | | | $30.00 | $30.00 |
| 01/01/2016 | Invoice | 1016 | Vines, Pamela | | Accounts Receivable (A/R) | $650.00 | |
| | | | | Ten One-Hour Sessions | Services:Training | | $650.00 |
| | | | | | | $650.00 | $650.00 |
| 01/01/2016 | Invoice | 1017 | Phillips, Eric | | Accounts Receivable (A/R) | $165.00 | |
| | | | | Boarding | Services:Boarding | | $165.00 |
| | | | | | | $165.00 | $165.00 |
| **TOTAL** | | | | | | **$845.00** | **$845.00** |

> Close Your Name's Beach Barkers without printing, exporting, or emailing the Journal—unless instructed otherwise by your professor

## ENTER AND ADD ITEMS FOR A SALE ON ACCOUNT—DRILL

Frequently, an invoice prepared for a customer will contain more than one item. The procedures for preparing this type of invoice are the same. You simply select additional lines in the invoice to add more Products/Service items.

> **MEMO**
> **DATE:** January 1, 2016
>
> Amy's Bird Sanctuary is designing a new enclosure that will include a fountain where the birds can get a drink of water. The fountain was donated by a local charity. Craig's Design and Landscaping Services is doing the work. Prepare an invoice for 5 hours of Custom Design to design the new enclosure, 5 hours to pour the concrete, and 5 hours to install the fountain.

*DRILL*

 Open the **Test Drive Company**, prepare an invoice, and add a new sales item

Click the **Plus** icon

On the Create screen, click **Invoice** in the Customers Column

Click the drop-down list arrow for Choose a customer, then click **Amy's Bird Sanctuary**

Tab to or click in "Invoice date," enter **01/01/16**, press **Tab**

- The Due date now shows 01/31/2016.
- Note the information regarding Billable time on the right side of the invoice. This means that time has been spent for Custom Design work.

Click **Open** on the Billable Time screen to see the details

You will get a screen that asks if you want to leave the Invoice without saving, click **Yes**

Review the Time Activity information that is shown

- The employee, John Johnson, spent five hours working on the Custom Design for Amy's Bird Sanctuary at the rate of $75.00 per hour. This activity is called Time Tracking and will be used later in the text.
- The Date of 12/19/2015 that is shown may be different on your screen. The Test Drive Company, automatically changes some of the dates in the company. If your date is different, there is nothing wrong.

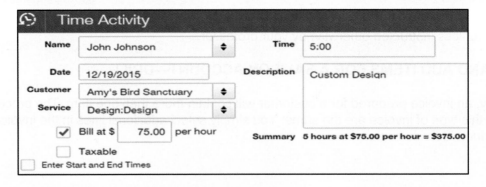

Click the **Cancel** button to return to a blank invoice

Create the invoice for Amy's Bird Sanctuary
Select **Amy's Bird Sanctuary** as the Customer and enter the Invoice date of **01/01/16**
Click [ ↻ **Add** ] or the [ Add all ] button to add the Billable Time item to the invoice

| | # | PRODUCT/SERVICE | DESCRIPTION | QTY | RATE | AMOUNT | TAX | | |
|---|---|---|---|---|---|---|---|---|---|
| ⠿ | 1 | Design:Design | Custom Design | 5 | 75 | 375.00 | | 🔗 | 🗑 |
| ⠿ | 2 | | | | | | | | 🗑 |
| Add lines | | Clear all lines | Add subtotal | | | **Subtotal** | | **$375.00** | |

- The five hours of Custom Design has been added to the invoice.

In the second line, click in PRODUCT/SERVICE; you will see Enter Text and a drop-down
list arrow

Click the drop-down list arrow, click **Concrete**, tab to QTY, enter **5**, press **Tab**, enter the
RATE of **75**, press **Tab**

- Since this is for the labor of installing concrete, if you see a check mark in the **Tax**
column, click the check mark to remove it.
- Notice that another line appears in the invoice. If a line did not appear, you would click
the **Add Lines** button.

Click in PRODUCTS/SERVICES for Line 3, click the drop-down list arrow, and scroll through
the Product/Service List to find the correct item for the installation of the fountain

- The only item for Installation is for landscaping.

Since there is not an appropriate item, click **+ Add new** to add one

- When you create a new item while preparing an invoice, it is referred to as adding "on
the fly."

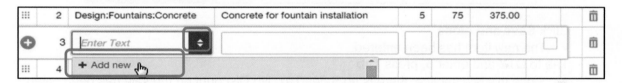

- You can add three types of Products/Services items: Inventory, Non-inventory, and
Service.

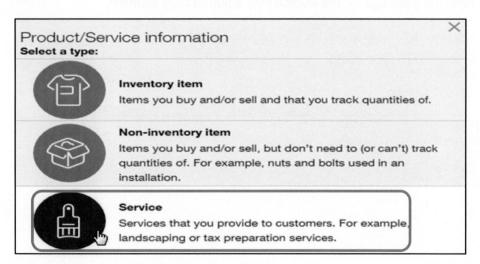

Click **Service**
Enter the Name **Fountain Installation**

Tab to or click in the text box for "Description on sales forms" under Sales Information and key in **Fountain Installation**

Tab to Sales price/rate, enter **75**

Click the drop-down list arrow for Income account

Scroll through the list of accounts, click **Services**

- If "Is taxable" has a check mark, click to deselect.

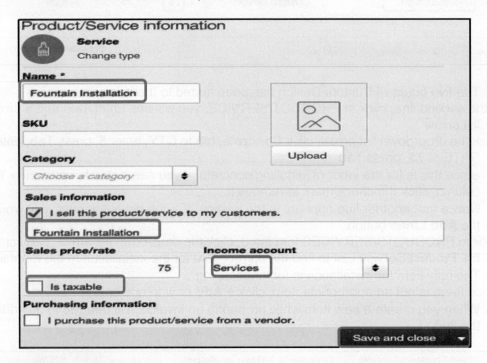

Click **Save and close**

- The new item has been entered.

Tab to QTY and enter **5**, press **Tab**

- Since this is a service, there is no Sales Tax. No Discount on the sale has been given. The amounts for those two fields are 0.00.

Review the invoice

- Note the message for the invoice was automatically inserted.

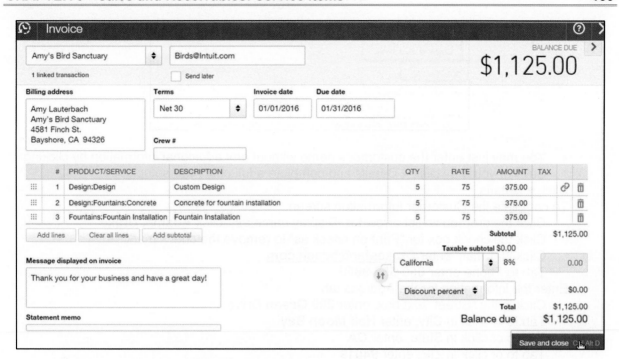

Click the drop-down list arrow for Save and close, Save and new, or Save and send
Click **Save and new** at the bottom of the invoice
- You will see a message that Invoice 1038 saved.
Do <u>not</u> close the Test Drive Company

## CREATE AN INVOICE AND ADD A NEW CUSTOMER—DRILL

QuickBooks Online allows you to add new customers at any time. In fact, you may add a customer "on the fly" while you are creating an invoice.

## <u>DRILL</u>

 Continue to use the **Test Drive Company** to practice creating an invoice and adding a new customer

A blank invoice should be on the screen
- If not, open an invoice as previously instructed.
Click the drop-down list arrow for "Choose a customer"
Click **+ Add new**

A New Customer screen will appear and the cursor will be positioned in the "Name" text box
Enter the customer's name **Drake Adams**

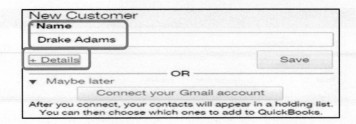

- You may just enter the customer's name without any additional information by clicking Save or you may click + Details and complete a full customer setup.

Click **+ Details**

To complete the Customer Information screen:

Click the drop-down list arrow for "Display name as," click **Adams, Drake**

Click the check box for "Print on check as" to remove the check mark

Click in "Email" enter **Drakester@beach.com**

Tab to Phone enter **650-555-9856**

Enter the information for the Address tab:

Click in the "Street" text box, enter **209 Ocean Drive**

Tab to or click in City, enter **Half Moon Bay**

Tab to or click in State, enter **CA**

Tab to or click in ZIP, enter **94019**

Make sure there is a check mark for "Same as billing address"

Click the "Payment and billing" tab

Complete the Payment and billing information:

Click the drop-down list arrow for "Preferred payment method," click **Check**

Click the drop-down list arrow for "Terms," click **Net 30**

Click the drop-down list arrow for "Preferred delivery method," click **None**

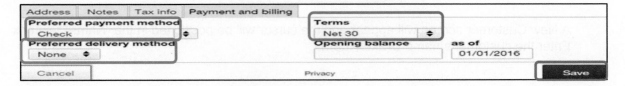

Click **Save** to add the new customer

- Note that the invoice information for Drake Adams is entered into the invoice.

Click the **Cancel** button to in the lower-left side of the invoice to close without saving
Click **Yes** on the "Do you want to leave without saving?" screen
Verify that Drake Adams has been added to your Customers List
Click **Customers** on the Navigation Bar, view the list

Do <u>not</u> close the Test Drive Company, Craig's Design and Landscaping Services

## CUSTOMER BALANCE SUMMARY REPORT—DRILL

In addition to the Journal that was prepared earlier, QuickBooks Online has a variety of reports available for Accounts Receivable and Sales. When you open Reports on the Navigation Bar and select All Reports, you will see several categories. You will notice that there are categories for Manage Accounts Receivable and Review Sales.

### *DRILL*

Use the **<u>Test Drive Company</u>** and prepare a Customer Balance Summary Report

- If you did not close the Test Drive Company, you should not have to turn off Redesigned Reports in the QuickBooks Labs. If you did close the company, go to QuickBooks Labs and turn off Redesigned Reports.

Click **Reports** on the Navigation Bar, click **All Reports**
With the report categories showing, click the **Manage Accounts Receivable** category
Within the list of reports contained in the Manage Accounts Receivable category, click
    **Customer Balance Summary**

> Manage Accounts Receivable
> **Customer Balance Summary**
> Shows each customer's total open balances.
> Run | Customize

The report will be for All Dates
- This report shows the balances for all of the customers who owe you money. Notice that customers without balances are not shown.
- Your report may differ from the one below. If you closed the Test Drive Company, you would have erased all of the entries you made.

## Craig's Design and Landscaping Services
### CUSTOMER BALANCE SUMMARY
#### All Dates

| | TOTAL |
|---|---|
| Amy's Bird Sanctuary | 1,364.00 |
| Bill's Windsurf Shop | 85.00 |
| Freeman Sporting Goods | |
| 0969 Ocean View Road | 477.50 |
| 55 Twin Lane | 85.00 |
| Total Freeman Sporting Goods | 562.50 |
| Geeta Kalapatapu | 629.10 |
| Jeff's Jalopies | 81.00 |
| John Melton | 450.00 |
| Kookies by Kathy | 75.00 |
| Mark Cho | 314.28 |
| Paulsen Medical Supplies | 954.75 |
| Red Rock Diner | 226.00 |
| Rondonuwu Fruit and Vegi | 78.60 |
| Shara Barnett | |
| Barnett Design | 274.50 |
| Total Shara Barnett | 274.50 |
| Sonnenschein Family Store | 362.07 |
| Sushi by Katsuyuki | 160.00 |
| Travis Waldron | 414.72 |
| Weiskopf Consulting | 375.00 |
| TOTAL | $6,406.52 |

Point to the amount in the TOTAL column for Amy's Bird Sanctuary

| | TOTAL |
|---|---|
| Amy's Bird Sanctuary | 1,364.00 |

When the amount shows in blue, click the amount
This will take you to the Customer Balance Detail for Amy's Bird Sanctuary
- Note that Invoice 1038 that you recorded as a drill is shown in the report. If you closed the Test Drive Company after you recorded Invoice 1038, it will not be shown.
- This process is often called "drill-down" because you are getting more specific about information. In fact, you could drill-down one more time by clicking Invoice 1038 in the Customer Balance Detail for Amy's Bird Sanctuary and go to the invoice.

## Craig's Design and Landscaping Services
### CUSTOMER BALANCE DETAIL
#### All Dates

| DATE | TRANSACTION TYPE | NUM | DUE DATE | AMOUNT | OPEN BALANCE | BALANCE |
|---|---|---|---|---|---|---|
| Amy's Bird Sanctuary | | | | | | |
| 12/01/2015 | Invoice | 1021 | 12/31/2015 | 459.00 | 239.00 | 239.00 |
| 01/01/2016 | Invoice | 1038 | 01/31/2016 | 1,125.00 | 1,125.00 | 1,364.00 |
| Total for Amy's Bird Sanctuary | | | | $1,584.00 | $1,364.00 | |
| TOTAL | | | | $1,584.00 | $1,364.00 | |

Close the Test Drive Company

## ADD INVOICE MESSAGE TO SETTINGS—DO

When you entered invoices for Your Name's Beach Barkers, you had to type a message for each invoice. When you prepared invoices in the Test Drive Company, the message was automatically inserted. The message for the invoice can be added to your settings and will automatically be inserted in your invoices.

<u>DO</u>

Open **Your Name's Beach Barkers** as previously instructed and create an Invoice message

Click the **Gear** icon, click **Company Settings**, and then click the **Sales** tab
Click the **Pen** icon for Messages
Complete the information for "Default message shown" on sales forms:
    Click the drop-down list arrow next to "Estimate"
    Click **Invoices and other sales forms**
    Click in the text box for "Default message to customers on sales forms…"
    Key in **Thank you for your business!**

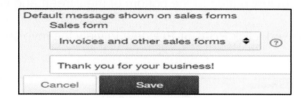

Click **Save**, click **Done**
- All of your invoices will now include this message automatically.
Continue to the next section
Do <u>not</u> close Your Name's Beach Barkers

## CREATE MULTIPLE ITEM INVOICES, NEW CUSTOMER, NEW SALES ITEMS—DO

QuickBooks Online allows you to add new customers and sales items at any time. In fact, you may add a customer and/or sales item "on the fly" while you are creating an invoice.

Many invoices include more than one sales item. As you learned in the drills, it is easy to enter transactions that include several products and/or services.

> **MEMO**
> **DATE:** January 1, 2016
>
> Bunni Clark brought her dog, Foxy, for 5 days of Boarding. While staying at Your Name's Beach Barkers, Foxy will have Five One-Hour Sessions of Training.
>
> Bunni's friend decided to bring her dog, Peaches, for 5 days of Day Camp and a One-Hour Training Session. Add the new customer, Ashley Rhodes (Email: AshR@beach.com, Phone: 310-555-1234, Address: 439 Carroll Canal, Venice, CA 90291, Preferred Payment Method: Check, Terms: Net 30).
>
> Matthew Summer wants someone to come to his home and walk his dog, Pepper, for 1 hour per day for five days. Plus, Matthew wants someone to pick up after his dog—1 hour of Poop Scoop.

<u>DO</u>

Use **Your Name's Beach Barkers** and prepare Invoices as previously instructed

Create Multiple Item Invoice

Continue to use **Your Name's Beach Barkers** and create an invoice for Bunni Clark

Click the **Plus** icon

On the Create screen, click **Invoice** in the Customers Column

Click the drop-down list arrow for Choose a customer, then click **Clark, Bunni**

- Note that the customer's name, email address, billing address, and terms were inserted.

Tab to or click in Invoice date, enter **01/01/16**, press **Tab**

- The Due date now shows 01/31/2016.

Line 1: Click in the field for PRODUCT/SERVICE, click the drop-down list arrow, click **Boarding**

Tab to QTY, enter **5**, press **Tab**

Line 2: Click in PRODUCT/SERVICE for the second line, click **Training 2** to enter the Five One-Hour Sessions, press **Tab**

- Review the invoice and note the Message: Thank you for your business!

Click the **Print or Preview** button at the bottom of the screen and view your choices for printing

In the choices displayed, click **Print or Preview** to view the invoice

View the INVOICE

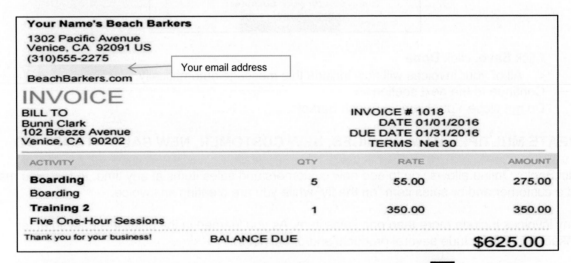

Click the **Printer** icon at the top of the invoice to print the invoice

To save a pdf copy of the invoice that may be emailed, click the **Save** icon,

- Save in Your Name's Beach Barkers Documents, Chapter 3, and name the document **4-Your Name Invoice 1018 Bunni Clark**.

Click **Save and new** at the bottom of the invoice to save in QuickBooks Online and go to a new invoice

- If you do not see Save and new, click the drop-down list arrow next to the save command displayed. Remember the save commands are: Save and close, Save and new, and Save and send.

## Add a New Customer

As you learned in the Drill, it is possible to add a new customer "on the fly" while preparing an invoice.

▶ Continue to use **Your Name's Beach Barkers**; add a new customer—Ashley Rhodes—and complete Invoice 1019

Click the drop-down list arrow for "Choose a customer"

Click **+ Add new**

A New Customer screen will appear and the cursor will be positioned in the Name text box

Enter the customer's name **Ashley Rhodes**
- You may just enter the customer's name without any additional information by clicking Save or you may click + Details and complete a full customer setup.

Click **+ Details**

To complete the Customer Information screen:

Click the drop-down list arrow for "Display name as," click **Rhodes, Ashley**

Click the check box for "Print on check as" to remove the check mark

Click in "Email" enter **AshR@beach.com**

Tab to Phone enter **310-555-1234**

Enter the information for the Address tab:

Click in the "Street" text box, enter **439 Carroll Canal**

Tab to or click in City, enter **Venice**

Tab to or click in State, enter **CA**

Tab to or click in ZIP, enter **90291**

Make sure there is a check mark for "Same as billing address"

Click the "Payment and billing" tab

Complete the Payment and billing information:

Click the drop-down list arrow for "Preferred payment method," click **Check**

Click the drop-down list arrow for "Terms," click **Net 30**

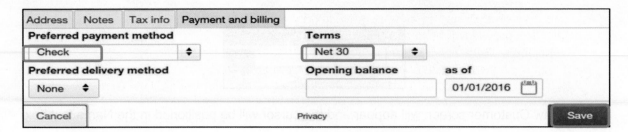

Click **Save** to add Ashley as a customer and return to the invoice
- Note that Ashley's information has been completed automatically.

Invoice Date: **01/01/16**

Complete the invoice for 5 days of Day Camp and 1 One-Hour Session of Training

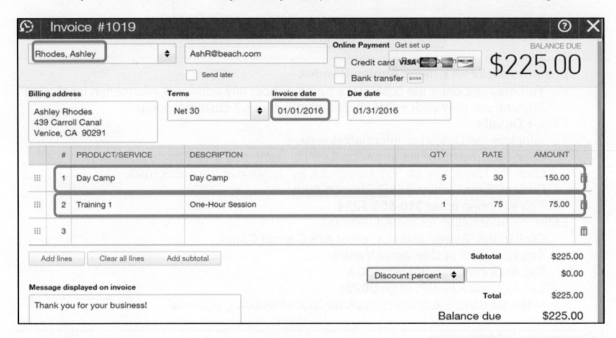

Print and/or save, and submit as previously instructed
- Name the file **5-Your Name Invoice 1019 Ashley Rhodes**.

When finished with the invoice, click **Save and new**

Do <u>not</u> close Your Name's Beach Barkers

## Add New Products/Service Items

As you learned in the Drill, it is possible to add a new sales item "on the fly" while preparing an invoice.

Continue to use **Your Name's Beach Barkers**, complete Invoice 1020 for Matthew Summer, and create two new service items

Create an invoice as previously instructed

Customer: **Matthew Summer**

Invoice date: **01/01/16**

Line 1: Click in PRODUCT/SERVICE field, click the drop-down list arrow

Click **+ Add new**, click **Service**

Enter the Name: **Dog Walking**

Click in "Description on sales forms," enter **Dog Walking**

Tab to or click in the "Sales price/rate" text box, enter the hourly rate of **15**

Click the drop-down list arrow for "Income account"

Scroll through the list of accounts to find an appropriate service account

- Since none of the accounts are actually what you want, you have two choices: select an account that is in the list and edit the account name later or exit the Product/Service information screen and the invoice, then enter a new account in the Chart of Accounts.

The account Services subaccount Fees Billed has not been associated with any of the Products/Services, click **Fees Billed** to select it for the account

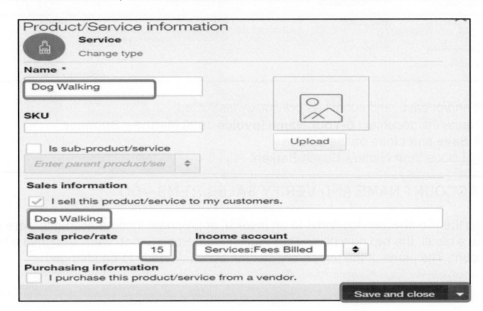

Click **Save and close** on the Product/Service information screen

Tab to QTY and enter **5**, press **Tab**

Line 2: Click in PRODUCT/SERVICE, click **+ Add new**

Repeat the steps to add another **Service** item

    Name: **Poop Scoop**

    Description: **Poop Scoop**

    Sales price/rate: **15**

    Income account: **Services:Fees Billed**

Complete the invoice

- What quantity did you use for Poop Scoop?

Print and/or save, and submit as previously instructed
- Name the document **6-Your Name Invoice 1020 Matthew Summer**.

Click **Save and close** on the invoice
Do <u>not</u> close Your Name's Beach Barkers

## CHANGE ACCOUNT NAME AND VERIFY SALES ITEMS—DO

When adding the two new service items to an invoice, appropriate income accounts were not available. As a result, the two new items Dog Walking and Poop Scoop were assigned a temporary income account. The name of the temporary income account needs to be changed.

<u>DO</u>

In the company **Your Name's Beach Barkers**, rename the Services subaccount Fees Billed to House Calls

Open the Chart of Accounts as previously instructed
Scroll through the accounts until you see Services
Click the drop-down list arrow for "Fees Billed"
Click **Edit**
Click in "Name," delete Fees Billed, and key in **House Calls**

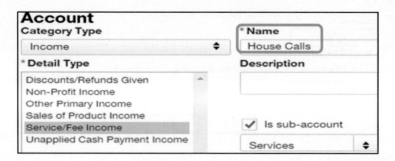

Click **Save and Close**
- Note the account House Calls in the Chart of Accounts. It has replaced Fees Billed.

Click the **Gear** icon and open Products/Services List
Click **Edit** for Dog Walking
Notice that the Income account shows Services:House Calls
Close Dog Walking
Edit Poop Scoop to verify the Income account of Services:House Calls
Exit the Products and Services List
Do <u>not</u> close Your Name's Beach Barkers

## ENTER TRANSACTIONS—DO

Now that transactions have been entered following step-by-step instructions, additional transactions should be entered without guidance. If you do not remember how to enter something, refer to steps presented earlier in the chapter.

---

<u>MEMO</u>
**DATE:** January 1, 2016

Larry Bailey brought in his dog, Wally, for a Bath and Nail trim. Add the two new items (Name: Bath, Description: Bath, Rate: 35, Income account: Services:Grooming. Name: Nails, Description: Nails, Rate: 20, Income account: Services:Grooming), Invoice 1021.

Oscar Gilbert signed up his dog, Brut, for Ten One-Hour Sessions of Training, Invoice 1022.

Annabelle Montez needs someone to come to her home and walk her dog, Salty, 1 hour a day for five days. Plus, Annabelle wants you to pick up after Salty on the fifth day of walking— 1 hour of Poop Scoop. While at home, Salty should be brushed every time he is walked. (There is a product/service item named Brushes, which is for product, a brush.) Add the new service item (Name: Brushing, Rate: 15, Description: Brushing, Income account: Services:Grooming), Invoice 1023.

A new customer brought in her dog, Lily for 1 day of Day Camp, 1 Bath, and 1 Nails. Add the new customer, Carol Russell (Email: CRuss@beach.com, Phone: 310-555-4656, Address: 3403 Strongs Drive, Marina del Rey, CA 90291, Preferred Payment Method: Check, Terms: Net 30), Invoice 1024.

---

<u>DO</u>

Continue to use **Your Name's Beach Barkers** and enter the Invoices detailed in the Memo, add any new customers, add any new service items

Refer to earlier sections in the chapter if you need step-by-step instructions to create the memos, add a new customer, and create new sales items
- Always check to make sure the Invoice date is January 1, 2016.
- Remember, when billing for Training there are three items available: Training 1 a single One-Hour Session, Training 2 a group of Five One-Hour Sessions, and Training 3 a group of Ten One-Hour Sessions. If a customer signs up for five hours of training, you would use Training 2.

- If you forget to enter a quantity, QuickBooks Online calculates the amount based on a quantity of 1.
- Always use the Products/Services List to determine the appropriate service items for the invoice. If you do not have an appropriate service item, create one.
- If you make an error, correct it.
- If instructed to do so by your professor, print, save, and submit each invoice immediately after you enter the information for it. Name the invoices just as you have been doing:

> **7-Your Name Invoice 1021 Larry Bailey**
> **8-Your Name Invoice 1022 Oscar Gilbert**
> **9-Your Name Invoice 1023 Annabelle Montez**
> **10-Your Name Invoice 1024 Carol Russell**

- To save in QuickBooks Online and go from one invoice to the next, click the **Save & new** button.
- Click **Save & close** after Invoice 1024 has been entered and printed.

- Did you create two new Service items and enter a QTY of 5 for both Dog Walking and Brushing?

| Carol Russell<br>3403 Strongs Drive<br>Marina del Rey, CA 90292 | | Net 30 ⬍ | 01/01/2016 | 01/31/2016 | | | |
|---|---|---|---|---|---|---|---|
| # | PRODUCT/SERVICE | DESCRIPTION | | | QTY | RATE | AMOUNT |
| 1 | Day Camp | Day Camp | | | 1 | 30 | 30.00 |
| 2 | Bath | Bath | | | 1 | 35 | 35.00 |
| 3 | Nails | Nails | | | 1 | 20 | 20.00 |

| Add lines | Clear all lines | Add subtotal | Subtotal | $85.00 |
|---|---|---|---|---|
| | | | Discount percent ⬍ | $0.00 |
| **Message displayed on invoice** | | | Total | $85.00 |
| Thank you for your business! | | | Balance due | $85.00 |

Do <u>not</u> close Your Name's Beach Barkers

## ANALYZE TRANSACTIONS IN THE JOURNAL—DO

Now that you have entered additional transactions, it is a good time to view the Journal. Remember, the Journal displays every transaction entered and includes information for the Transaction Type, Transaction Number, Name, Memo, Account, Debit, and Credit.

## *DO*

Prepare a Journal to view all of your entries in **Your Name's Beach Barkers**

Click **Reports** on the Navigation Bar, click **All Reports**, click **Accountant Reports**, click **Journal**
Change the Dates for the report From: **01/01/2016** and To: **01/01/2016**
Click **Run Report**
Scroll through the report to view all of the Invoices entered to date
- If you do not see one of your invoices, you probably did not use the date of 01/01/2016. To find your invoice, enter the Current Date as the date for To:, click **Run Report**, and look for the missing invoice(s). If you find them, click the word **Invoice**, and you will be returned to the actual invoice. Change the Invoice date, then click **Save and close**.
- After correcting the invoice, you will return to the Journal. Re-enter To: **01/01/16**, click **Run Report**, and verify the correction(s).
- Check the items listed in the MEMO/DESCRIPTION column and the accounts listed in the ACCOUNTS column very carefully. Using an incorrect item and/or account can be a reason for errors.

### Your Name's Beach Barkers
#### JOURNAL
January 1, 2016

| DATE | TRANSACTION TYPE | NUM | NAME | MEMO/DESCRIPTION | ACCOUNT | DEBIT | CREDIT |
|------|------------------|-----|------|------------------|---------|-------|--------|
| 01/01/2016 | Invoice | 1015 | Gucci, Gloria | | Accounts Receivable (A/R) | $30.00 | |
| | | | | Day Camp | Services:Day Camp | | $30.00 |
| | | | | | | **$30.00** | **$30.00** |
| 01/01/2016 | Invoice | 1016 | Vines, Pamela | | Accounts Receivable (A/R) | $650.00 | |
| | | | | Ten One-Hour Sessions | Services:Training | | $650.00 |
| | | | | | | **$650.00** | **$650.00** |
| 01/01/2016 | Invoice | 1017 | Phillips, Eric | | Accounts Receivable (A/R) | $165.00 | |
| | | | | Boarding | Services:Boarding | | $165.00 |
| | | | | | | **$165.00** | **$165.00** |
| 01/01/2016 | Invoice | 1018 | Clark, Bunni | | Accounts Receivable (A/R) | $625.00 | |
| | | | | Boarding | Services:Boarding | | $275.00 |
| | | | | Five One-Hour Sessions | Services:Training | | $350.00 |
| | | | | | | **$625.00** | **$625.00** |
| 01/01/2016 | Invoice | 1019 | Rhodes, Ashley | | Accounts Receivable (A/R) | $225.00 | |
| | | | | Day Camp | Services:Day Camp | | $150.00 |
| | | | | One-Hour Session | Services:Training | | $75.00 |
| | | | | | | **$225.00** | **$225.00** |
| 01/01/2016 | Invoice | 1020 | Summer, Matthew | | Accounts Receivable (A/R) | $90.00 | |
| | | | | Dog Walking | Services:House Calls | | $75.00 |
| | | | | Poop Scoop | Services:House Calls | | $15.00 |
| | | | | | | **$90.00** | **$90.00** |
| 01/01/2016 | Invoice | 1021 | Bailey, Larry | | Accounts Receivable (A/R) | $55.00 | |
| | | | | Bath | Services:Grooming | | $35.00 |
| | | | | Nails | Services:Grooming | | $20.00 |
| | | | | | | **$55.00** | **$55.00** |
| 01/01/2016 | Invoice | 1022 | Gilbert, Oscar | | Accounts Receivable (A/R) | $650.00 | |
| | | | | Ten One-Hour Sessions | Services:Training | | $650.00 |
| | | | | | | **$650.00** | **$650.00** |
| 01/01/2016 | Invoice | 1023 | Montez, Annabelle | | Accounts Receivable (A/R) | $165.00 | |
| | | | | Dog Walking | Services:House Calls | | $75.00 |
| | | | | Poop Scoop | Services:House Calls | | $15.00 |
| | | | | Brushing | Services:Grooming | | $75.00 |
| | | | | | | **$165.00** | **$165.00** |
| 01/01/2016 | Invoice | 1024 | Russell, Carol | | Accounts Receivable (A/R) | $85.00 | |
| | | | | Day Camp | Services:Day Camp | | $30.00 |
| | | | | Bath | Services:Grooming | | $35.00 |
| | | | | Nails | Services:Grooming | | $20.00 |
| | | | | | | **$85.00** | **$85.00** |
| **TOTAL** | | | | | | **$2,740.00** | **$2,740.00** |

- Is your total $2,740.00?
  To close the report without printing, click **Reports** on the Navigation Bar
  Do <u>not</u> close Your Name's Beach Barkers

## CUSTOMER BALANCE SUMMARY REPORT—DO

As you learned in the drill, the Customer Balance Summary shows the balances for all of the customers who owe you money. Customers without balances are not shown.

<u>DO</u>

Prepare, print, and/or save the Customer Balance Summary report for **Your Name's Beach Barkers**

Click **Reports** on the Navigation Bar
- The category Accountant Reports should show.
Click **<All Reports** just above the category title Accountant Reports
Click the category **Manage Accounts Receivable**
Click **Customer Balance Summary** in the Manage Accounts Receivable category report list

Manage Accounts Receivable
Customer Balance Summary
Shows each customer's total open balances.
Run | Customize

You will the report present for All Dates

### Your Name's Beach Barkers
#### CUSTOMER BALANCE SUMMARY
##### All Dates

|  | TOTAL |
| --- | --- |
| Anderson, Dori | 2,500.00 |
| Bailey, Larry | 2,555.00 |
| Clark, Bunni | 4,125.00 |
| Gilbert, Oscar | 1,150.00 |
| Gucci, Gloria | 30.00 |
| Montez, Annabelle | 965.00 |
| Norbert, Viv | 2,900.00 |
| Phillips, Eric | 1,665.00 |
| Quint, Brad | 1,800.00 |
| Rhodes, Ashley | 225.00 |
| Rodriguez, Ricardo | 900.00 |
| Russell, Carol | 85.00 |
| Stark, Colleen | 3,200.00 |
| Summer, Matthew | 240.00 |
| Vines, Pamela | 1,400.00 |
| Williams, Taylor | 3,650.00 |
| Wilson, Katie | 2,850.00 |
| **TOTAL** | **$30,240.00** |

To drill-down for Customer Balance Details for Annabelle Montez, point to the amount in the TOTAL column

|  | TOTAL |
| --- | --- |
| Montez, Annabelle | 965.00 |

When the amount shows in blue, click the amount
This will take you to the Customer Balance Detail for Annabelle Montez

### Your Name's Beach Barkers
#### CUSTOMER BALANCE DETAIL
##### All Dates

| DATE | TRANSACTION TYPE | NUM | DUE DATE | AMOUNT | OPEN BALANCE | BALANCE |
| --- | --- | --- | --- | --- | --- | --- |
| Montez, Annabelle |  |  |  |  |  |  |
| 12/31/2015 | Invoice | 1005 | 12/31/2015 | 800.00 | 800.00 | 800.00 |
| 01/01/2016 | Invoice | 1023 | 01/31/2016 | 165.00 | 165.00 | 965.00 |
| Total for Montez, Annabelle |  |  |  | $965.00 | $965.00 |  |
| TOTAL |  |  |  | $965.00 | $965.00 |  |

- Note that Invoice 1005 was prepared 12/31/12015 to enter the opening balance and Invoice 1023 was prepared for 01/01/2016.

Continue to drill-down to the invoice, point to Invoice 1023, when the invoice information turns blue, click the invoice

| Montez, Annabelle |  |  |  |  |  |  |
| --- | --- | --- | --- | --- | --- | --- |
| 12/31/2015 | Invoice | 1005 | 12/31/2015 | 800.00 | 800.00 | 800.00 |
| 01/01/2016 | Invoice | 1023 | 01/31/2016 | 165.00 | 165.00 | 965.00 |
| Total for Montez, Annabelle |  |  |  | $965.00 | $965.00 |  |

- You will be taken to Invoice 1023.
Click the **Cancel** button at the bottom of the invoice
Click**< Back to Summary Report** on Annabelle's Customer Balance Detail Report
- Verify with your instructor whether or not you should print, export, and/or submit the report.
If you are required to do so, perform one of the following:
    **Print**: click the **Print** button
    Make the appropriate selections on the Print menu:
        Destination: should be the printer you will be using
        Pages: All
        Copies: 1
        Layout: Portrait
        Color: Black and white
        Options: Two-sided if available for your printer
- Your printer and other details may not match the screen shot shown. If necessary, check with your instructor about appropriate print settings.
    **Export** to Excel: click the drop-down list arrow on the **Excel** button, click **Excel (XLSX or XLS)**. If you save the report, name it **11-Your Name Customer Balance Summary Ch. 3**.
- Remember, only reports may be exported to Excel.
    **Submit**: as previously instructed or email the report directly to your instructor without saving to a pdf file, click the **Email** button, Your Name <quickbooks-email@intuit.com> is inserted by QuickBooks Online, enter your instructor's email address, if you wish to add a note, do so in Note:, then click **Send**
    Close Your Name's Beach Barkers

## CORRECT AN INVOICE—DRILL

Errors may be corrected very easily with QuickBooks Online. Because an invoice is prepared for sales on account, corrections are made directly on the invoice. You can access the invoice via the Customers List or in the Accounts Receivable account register. The account register contains detailed information regarding each transaction that used the account. Therefore, anytime an invoice is recorded, it is posted to the Accounts Receivable register.

> **MEMO**
> **DATE:** January 7, 2016
>
> You realized that the Invoice Date for John Melton should have been January 5, 2016. In addition, he should have been billed for 15 hours of Custom Design. Correct Invoice 1007.

### *DRILL*

 Open the **Test Drive Company** and make corrections to invoices

Open the Test Drive Company as previously indicated
Click **Customers** on the Navigation Bar
Scroll through the list, point to the name **John Melton**, when the name is underlined, click it
- The Transaction List for John Melton should appear on the screen.

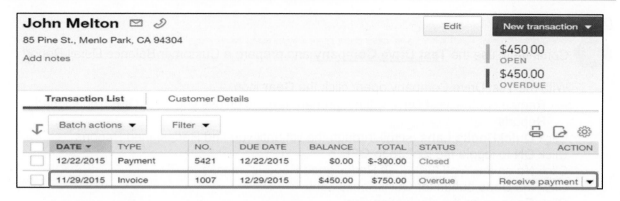

Click anywhere in the line for **Invoice 1007**
- The invoice date at the time of this writing was 11/29/2015. The Test Drive Company automatically changes dates. Therefore, the dates shown in the text will not match the date you see in the Test Drive Company.
- Invoice 1007 is opened.

Click in the "Invoice date" column, remove the date, enter **010516**, press **Tab**

Click in QTY, remove 10, enter **15**, press **Tab**

- View the changes and note that the Balance Due shows $825.00.

Click **Save and close**

Click **Yes** on the message regarding the transaction being linked to others
- Notice the Invoice 1007 shown in the register for John Melton.

Do <u>not</u> close the Test Drive Company

## CUSTOMER BALANCE DETAIL REPORT—DRILL

The Customer Balance Detail report shows all the transactions for each credit customer. The report lists unpaid invoices for each customer and includes information for the invoice date and number, due date, total, and open balance.

*DRILL*

Continue to use the **Test Drive Company** and prepare a Customer Balance Detail Report

With the Test Drive Company open, click the **Gear** icon
- Remember the Test Drive will not prepare reports unless you Turn **OFF** Redesigned Reports.

Click **QuickBooks Labs**, scroll through the list until you find Redesigned Reports

Click **ON** to toggle the feature to **OFF**

Click **No** on the "You turned off Redesigned Reports" message

Click the **Done** button for QuickBooks Labs

Click **Reports** on the Navigation Bar

Click **All Reports**, click **Manage Accounts Receivable**

Click **Customer Balance Detail**

All Dates shows for the date range of the report
- Scroll through the Customer Balance Detail Report and view the information presented.
- Notice that the invoice you edited for John Melton is included in the report.

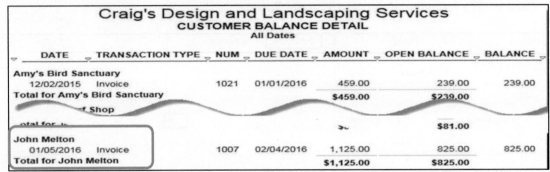

Partial Report

Continue to the next section
- You should complete the next section as part of this work session!

Do not close the Test Drive Company

## VOID AND DELETE INVOICES—DRILL

Deleting an invoice permanently removes it from QuickBooks without a trace. If you would like to correct your financial records for an invoice that you no longer want, it is more appropriate to void the invoice. When an invoice is voided, it remains in the QuickBooks system with a zero balance.

---

**MEMO**
**DATE:** January 7, 2016

John Melton decided to sell his home so he is canceling his plans for the custom design work. Void Invoice 1007.

John asked that you remove Invoice 1007 from your records. Delete the invoice.

---

*DRILL*

Continue to use the **Test Drive Company** and void an invoice and delete invoices

Void Invoice

Since you want to keep Invoice 1007 for John Melton in your records, you will void the invoice

 Use the **Test Drive Company**, refer to the Memo and the following steps to Void an invoice

With the Customer Balance Detail Report showing on the screen, click **Invoice 1007** for John Melton to drill-down directly to the invoice
- If you do not have the report on the screen, click **Customers** on the Navigation Bar, click **John Melton**, and click **Invoice 1007**.

With Invoice 1007 showing on the screen, click the **More** button at the bottom of the invoice

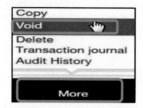

Click **Void**
Click **Yes** on the message

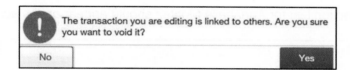

Click **OK** on the "Transaction successfully voided" screen
To view the effect of voiding the invoice, click **Customers** on the Navigation Bar
Point to John Melton, when his name is underlined, click **John Melton**
- You will see Invoice 1007 with a Balance of 0.00 and a Status of Voided.

| | | | | | | | |
|---|---|---|---|---|---|---|---|
| ☐ | 12/23/2015 | Payment | 5421 | 12/23/2015 | $-300.00 | $-300.00 | Unapplied |
| ☐ | 11/30/2015 | Invoice | 1007 | 12/30/2015 | $0.00 | $0.00 | Voided | Print ▼ |

Delete Invoice

Since John requested you delete the invoice from your records, you will delete Invoice 1007.

 Continue to use the **Test Drive Company** and delete Invoice 1007

Click **Invoice 1007** in the Register for John Melton
Repeat the steps listed for voiding an invoice, except click **Delete** when you click the **More** button
Click **Yes** on the "Are you sure you want to delete this?" screen
- You will be returned to the register. Invoice 1007 is no longer shown.

| ☐ | DATE ▼ | TYPE | NO. | DUE DATE | BALANCE | TOTAL | STATUS | ACTION |
|---|---|---|---|---|---|---|---|---|
| | | | There are no transactions matching the criteria. | | | | | |

Close the Test Drive Company

## CORRECT AN INVOICE—DO

Now that you have practiced making corrections on invoices, you will make corrections for two of Your Name's Beach Barkers invoices.

> **MEMO**
> **DATE:** January 7, 2016
>
> Invoice 1023 for Annabelle Montez should have January 5, 2016 for the date. In addition, she should have been billed for 2 hours of Poop Scoop. Correct the invoice.
>
> Invoice 1024 for Carol Russell should also be dated January 5, 2016. She should have been billed for 3 days of Day Camp and 3 Brushing. Correct the invoice.

<u>*DO*</u>

Continue to use **Your Name's Beach Barkers**

Open **Your Name's Beach Barkers** as previously indicated
Click **Customers** on the Navigation Bar
Scroll through the list, point to the name **Annabelle Montez**, when the name is underlined, click it
- The Transaction List for Annabelle Montez should appear on the screen.

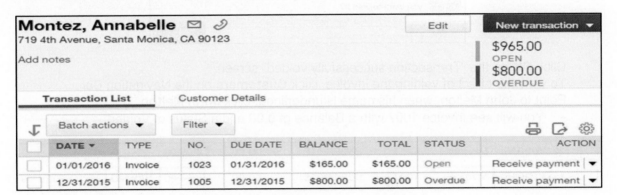

Click anywhere in the line for **Invoice 1023**, dated 01/01/2016
- Invoice 1023 is opened.

Click in the "Invoice date" column, remove the date of 01/01/2016, enter **010516**, press **Tab**
Click in QTY for Poop Scoop, remove 1, enter **2**, press **Tab**

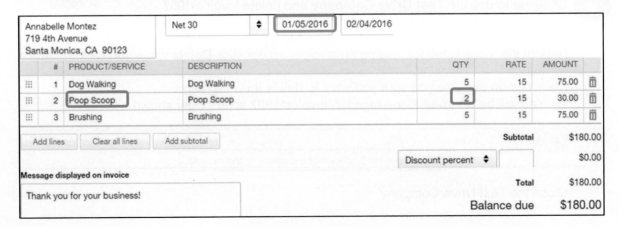

- View the changes and note that the Balance Due shows $180.00.
Print and/or save the Invoice as previously instructed
- Name the document **12-Invoice 1023 Annabelle Montez Corrected**.
Click **Save and close**
- Notice the Invoice 1023 shown in the register for Annabelle Montez.

| | | | | | | | | |
|---|---|---|---|---|---|---|---|---|
| | 01/05/2016 | Invoice | 1023 | 02/04/2016 | $180.00 | $180.00 | Open | Receive payment ▼ |
| | 12/31/2015 | Invoice | 1005 | 12/31/2015 | $800.00 | $800.00 | Overdue | Receive payment ▼ |

Click **Customers** on the Navigation Bar, refer to the Memo, and make the corrections for Carol Russell

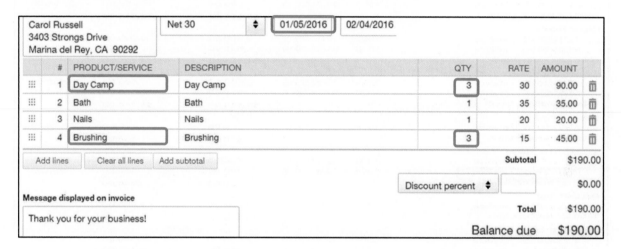

Print and/or save the corrected invoice
- Name the document **13-Invoice 1024 Carol Russell Corrected**.
Click **Save and close**
- Notice that Invoice 1024 shows in the register for Carol Russell.

| | | | | | | | | |
|---|---|---|---|---|---|---|---|---|
| | 01/05/2016 | Invoice | 1024 | 02/04/2016 | $190.00 | $190.00 | Open | Receive payment ▼ |

Do <u>not</u> close Your Name's Beach Barkers

## CUSTOMER BALANCE DETAIL REPORT—DO

As you did for practice, preparing the Customer Balance Detail Report allows you to verify the transactions for each credit customer. The report lists unpaid invoices for each customer and includes information for the invoice date and number, due date, total, and open balance.

## *DO*

 Continue to use the **<u>Your Name's Beach Barkers</u>** and prepare a Customer Balance Detail Report

With the Your Name's Beach Barkers open, click **Reports** on the Navigation Bar
- If the category Manage Accounts Receivable is not on the screen, click **All Reports**, click **Manage Accounts Receivable**.
Click **Customer Balance Detail**
All Dates shows for the date range of the report

- Scroll through the Customer Balance Detail Report and view the information presented.
- Notice that the invoices you edited for Annabelle Montez and Carol Russell are included in the report.

## Your Name's Beach Barkers
### CUSTOMER BALANCE DETAIL
#### All Dates

| DATE | TRANSACTION TYPE | NUM | DUE DATE | AMOUNT | OPEN BALANCE | BALANCE |
|------|------------------|-----|----------|--------|--------------|---------|
| **Anderson, Dori** | | | | | | |
| 12/31/2015 | Invoice | 1001 | 12/31/2015 | 2,500.00 | 2,500.00 | 2,500.00 |
| Total for Anderson, Dori | | | | **$2,500.00** | **$2,500.00** | |
| **Bailey, Larry** | | | | | | |
| 12/31/2015 | Invoice | 1002 | 12/31/2015 | 2,500.00 | 2,500.00 | 2,500.00 |
| 01/01/2016 | Invoice | 1021 | 01/31/2016 | 55.00 | 55.00 | 2,555.00 |
| Total for Bailey, Larry | | | | **$2,555.00** | **$2,555.00** | |
| **Clark, Bunni** | | | | | | |
| 12/31/2015 | Invoice | 1003 | 12/31/2015 | 3,500.00 | 3,500.00 | 3,500.00 |
| 01/01/2016 | Invoice | 1018 | 01/31/2016 | 625.00 | 625.00 | 4,125.00 |
| Total for Clark, Bunni | | | | **$4,125.00** | **$4,125.00** | |
| **Gilbert, Oscar** | | | | | | |
| 12/31/2015 | Invoice | 1004 | 12/31/2015 | 500.00 | 500.00 | 500.00 |
| 01/01/2016 | Invoice | 1022 | 01/31/2016 | 650.00 | 650.00 | 1,150.00 |
| Total for Gilbert, Oscar | | | | **$1,150.00** | **$1,150.00** | |
| **Gucci, Gloria** | | | | | | |
| 01/01/2016 | Invoice | 1015 | 01/31/2016 | 30.00 | 30.00 | 30.00 |
| Total for Gucci, Gloria | | | | **$30.00** | **$30.00** | |
| **Montez, Annabelle** | | | | | | |
| 12/31/2015 | Invoice | 1005 | 12/31/2015 | 800.00 | 800.00 | 800.00 |
| 01/05/2016 | Invoice | 1023 | 02/04/2016 | 180.00 | 180.00 | 980.00 |
| Total for Montez, Annabelle | | | | **$980.00** | **$980.00** | |
| **Norbert, Viv** | | | | | | |
| 12/31/2015 | Invoice | 1006 | 12/31/2015 | 2,900.00 | 2,900.00 | 2,900.00 |
| Total for Norbert, Viv | | | | **$2,900.00** | **$2,900.00** | |
| **Phillips, Eric** | | | | | | |
| 12/31/2015 | Invoice | 1007 | 12/31/2015 | 1,500.00 | 1,500.00 | 1,500.00 |
| 01/01/2016 | Invoice | 1017 | 01/31/2016 | 165.00 | 165.00 | 1,665.00 |
| Total for Phillips, Eric | | | | **$1,665.00** | **$1,665.00** | |
| **Quint, Brad** | | | | | | |
| 12/31/2015 | Invoice | 1008 | 12/31/2015 | 1,800.00 | 1,800.00 | 1,800.00 |
| Total for Quint, Brad | | | | **$1,800.00** | **$1,800.00** | |
| **Rhodes, Ashley** | | | | | | |
| 01/01/2016 | Invoice | 1019 | 01/31/2016 | 225.00 | 225.00 | 225.00 |
| Total for Rhodes, Ashley | | | | **$225.00** | **$225.00** | |
| **Rodriguez, Ricardo** | | | | | | |
| 12/31/2015 | Invoice | 1009 | 12/31/2015 | 900.00 | 900.00 | 900.00 |
| Total for Rodriguez, Ricardo | | | | **$900.00** | **$900.00** | |
| **Russell, Carol** | | | | | | |
| 01/05/2016 | Invoice | 1024 | 02/04/2016 | 190.00 | 190.00 | 190.00 |
| Total for Russell, Carol | | | | **$190.00** | **$190.00** | |
| **Stark, Colleen** | | | | | | |
| 12/31/2015 | Invoice | 1010 | 12/31/2015 | 3,200.00 | 3,200.00 | 3,200.00 |
| Total for Stark, Colleen | | | | **$3,200.00** | **$3,200.00** | |
| **Summer, Matthew** | | | | | | |
| 12/31/2015 | Invoice | 1011 | 12/31/2015 | 150.00 | 150.00 | 150.00 |
| 01/01/2016 | Invoice | 1020 | 01/31/2016 | 90.00 | 90.00 | 240.00 |
| Total for Summer, Matthew | | | | **$240.00** | **$240.00** | |
| **Vines, Pamela** | | | | | | |
| 12/31/2015 | Invoice | 1012 | 12/31/2015 | 750.00 | 750.00 | 750.00 |
| 01/01/2016 | Invoice | 1016 | 01/31/2016 | 650.00 | 650.00 | 1,400.00 |
| Total for Vines, Pamela | | | | **$1,400.00** | **$1,400.00** | |
| **Williams, Taylor** | | | | | | |
| 12/31/2015 | Invoice | 1013 | 12/31/2015 | 3,650.00 | 3,650.00 | 3,650.00 |
| Total for Williams, Taylor | | | | **$3,650.00** | **$3,650.00** | |
| **Wilson, Katie** | | | | | | |
| 12/31/2015 | Invoice | 1014 | 12/31/2015 | 2,850.00 | 2,850.00 | 2,850.00 |
| Total for Wilson, Katie | | | | **$2,850.00** | **$2,850.00** | |
| **TOTAL** | | | | **$30,360.00** | **$30,360.00** | |

Print and or Save the report
- Name it **14-Your Name Customer Balance Detail Ch. 3**.

Continue to the next section

## VOID AND DELETE INVOICES—DO

As you learned in the practice, deleting an invoice permanently removes it from QuickBooks. When an invoice is voided, it remains in the QuickBooks system with a zero balance.

> **MEMO**
> **DATE:** January 7, 2016
>
> Eric Phillips had a change in travel plans and will not be boarding his dog, Frank, at this time. Void Invoice 1017.
>
> Gloria Gucci's dog, Mishka, got sick and had to go to the vet rather than come to Day Camp. Delete Invoice 1015.

### DO

 Continue to use **Your Name's Beach Barkers** and void and delete invoices

### Void Invoice

Since you want to keep Invoice 1017 for Eric Phillips in your records, you will void the invoice.

 Use **Your Name's Beach Barkers**, refer to the Memo and the following steps to Void an invoice

With the Customer Balance Detail Report showing on the screen, click **Invoice 1017** for Eric Phillips to drill-down directly to the invoice
- If you do not have the report on the screen, click **Customers** on the Navigation Bar, click **Eric Phillips**, click **Invoice 1017** in his Transaction List.

With Invoice 1017 showing on the screen, click the **More** button at the bottom of the invoice

Click **Void**
Click **Yes** on the message

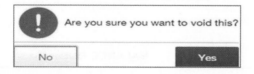

Click **OK** on the "Transaction successfully voided" screen
- You will be returned to the report. Because the report does not show voided invoices, Invoice 1017 is no longer shown.

### Delete Invoice

Since you do not want Invoice 1015 for Gloria Gucci in your records, you will delete the invoice.

Continue to use **Your Name's Beach Barkers**, refer to the Memo and the following steps to delete an invoice

>    Click **Invoice 1015** for Gloria Gucci In the Customer Balance Detail Report or access her
>        account in the Customers List, and click **Invoice 1015**
>    Repeat the steps shown for voiding, except click **Delete** after you click the **More** button
>    Click **Yes** on the "Are you sure you want to delete this?" screen
>    • You will be returned to the report. Gloria Gucci and Invoice 1015 are no longer shown.
>    Do not close Your Name's Beach Barkers

## View Individual Accounts and Print Voided Invoice

Once you delete and/or void invoices, it is helpful to look at the individual customer's account.

 Continue to use **Your Name's Beach Barkers**, return to the Customers List and view the accounts for Eric Phillips and Gloria Gucci

>    Click **Customers** on the Navigation Bar
>    Point to Phillips, Eric when his name is underlined, click **Phillips, Eric**
>    • You will see Invoice 1017 with a Balance of 0.00 and a Status of Voided.

| | 01/01/2016 | Invoice | 1017 | 01/31/2016 | $0.00 | $0.00 | Voided | | Print | ▼ |
|---|---|---|---|---|---|---|---|---|---|---|
| | 12/31/2015 | Invoice | 1007 | 12/31/2015 | $1,500.00 | $1,500.00 | Overdue | | Receive payment | ▼ |

>    • If you are required to save pdf copy and/or print the invoice, click **Print** in the register
>        and follow steps previously provided. Name the document **15-Your Name Invoice 1017
>        Eric Phillips**. Notice that it is stamped "VOID."

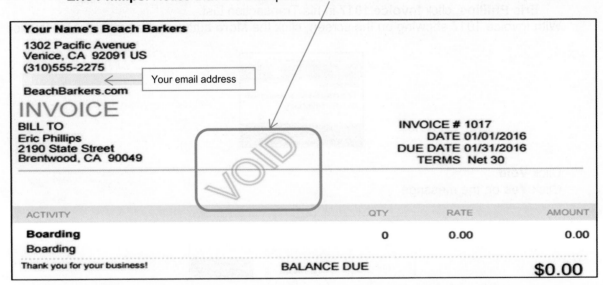

When printing from the register, QuickBooks Online opened a separate tab in your browser, click **Close** on the browser tab

Repeat the steps to access Gloria Gucci's account
• Nothing is shown for Gloria's account because the invoice was deleted and there were no other transactions in her account.

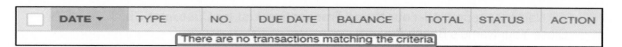

Do <u>not</u> close Your Name's Beach Barkers

## TRANSACTION LIST BY CUSTOMER—DO

As you learned in the drill, the Transaction List by Customer shows you the transactions for each customer within a certain time period and is located in the Review Sales section of All Reports.

<u>*DO*</u>

Continue to use **Your Name's Beach Barkers** and prepare a Transaction List by Customer Report

Click **Reports** on the Navigation Bar
Click **<All Reports** just above the category name, Manage Accounts Receivable
Click **Review Sales**
Click **Transaction List by Customer**
Enter the report dates From: **01/01/16** and To: **01/05/16**, click **Run Report**

### Your Name's Beach Barkers
#### TRANSACTION LIST BY CUSTOMER
##### January 1-5, 2016

| DATE | TRANSACTION TYPE | NUM | POSTING | MEMO/DESCRIPTION | ACCOUNT | AMOUNT |
|------|------------------|-----|---------|------------------|---------|--------|
| **Bailey, Larry** | | | | | | |
| 01/01/2016 | Invoice | 1021 | Yes | | Accounts Receivable (A/R) | 55.00 |
| **Total for Bailey, Larry** | | | | | | **$55.00** |
| **Clark, Bunni** | | | | | | |
| 01/01/2016 | Invoice | 1018 | Yes | | Accounts Receivable (A/R) | 625.00 |
| **Total for Clark, Bunni** | | | | | | **$625.00** |
| **Gilbert, Oscar** | | | | | | |
| 01/01/2016 | Invoice | 1022 | Yes | | Accounts Receivable (A/R) | 650.00 |
| **Total for Gilbert, Oscar** | | | | | | **$650.00** |
| **Montez, Annabelle** | | | | | | |
| 01/05/2016 | Invoice | 1023 | Yes | | Accounts Receivable (A/R) | 180.00 |
| **Total for Montez, Annabelle** | | | | | | **$180.00** |
| **Phillips, Eric** | | | | | | |
| 01/01/2016 | Invoice | 1017 | Yes | Voided | Accounts Receivable (A/R) | 0.00 |
| **Total for Phillips, Eric** | | | | | | **$0.00** |
| **Rhodes, Ashley** | | | | | | |
| 01/01/2016 | Invoice | 1019 | Yes | | Accounts Receivable (A/R) | 225.00 |
| **Total for Rhodes, Ashley** | | | | | | **$225.00** |
| **Russell, Carol** | | | | | | |
| 01/05/2016 | Invoice | 1024 | Yes | | Accounts Receivable (A/R) | 190.00 |
| **Total for Russell, Carol** | | | | | | **$190.00** |
| **Summer, Matthew** | | | | | | |
| 01/01/2016 | Invoice | 1020 | Yes | | Accounts Receivable (A/R) | 90.00 |
| **Total for Summer, Matthew** | | | | | | **$90.00** |
| **Vines, Pamela** | | | | | | |
| 01/01/2016 | Invoice | 1016 | Yes | | Accounts Receivable (A/R) | 650.00 |
| **Total for Vines, Pamela** | | | | | | **$650.00** |

You will see the voided invoice for Eric Phillips
- Because the invoice for Gloria Gucci was deleted, it does not appear in the Transaction List by Customer Report.

Print and/or save the list as previously instructed

- Name the report: **16-Your Name Transaction List by Customer Ch. 3**.
Close Your Name's Beach Barkers

## RECORD CASH SALES—DRILL

Not all sales in a business are on account. In many instances, payment is made at the time the service is performed and is entered as a cash sale. When entering a cash sale, you prepare a sales receipt rather than an invoice. QuickBooks Online records the transaction in the Journal and places the amount of cash received in an account called Undeposited Funds. The funds received remain in Undeposited Funds until you record a deposit to your bank account. Once deposited, the funds will appear in your checking or cash account.

<u>MEMO</u>
**DATE:** January 10, 2016

Cool Cars needed to have a Pest Control Service Performed. Paid with Check 4985.
A new customer—Cash Customer—needed 5 hours of Maintenance & Repair at $50 per hour. Paid with cash.

_DRILL_

Open the **Test Drive Company** and prepare sales receipts to record cash (and check) transactions

With the Test Drive Company open, practice completing sales receipts
Click the **Plus** button in the Top-Navigation Bar
Click **Sales Receipt** in the Customers menu on the Create screen

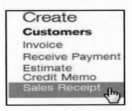

Click the drop-down list arrow for" Choose a customer," click **Cool Cars**
Tab to or click in the "Date" text box, enter the date **011016**
Click the drop-down list arrow for "Payment method," click **Check**
Tab to Reference no. and enter the check number **4985**
- Deposit to should show Undeposited Funds, if it does not, click the drop-down list arrow, then click Undeposited Funds.
As you did for invoices, select the PRODUCT/SERVICE of **Pest Control**, press **Tab**, and view the Sales Receipt

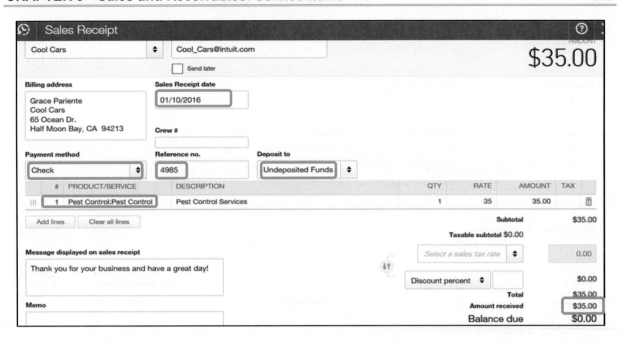

- The visual appearance of a Sales Receipt is very similar to an invoice. Sales Receipts are numbered sequentially with invoices. Some of the differences are entering the Payment method, Reference number (Check), and selecting the account for Deposit to. At the bottom of the Sales Receipt, you will see the transaction total in Amount received, and $0.00 for Balance due.

Click **Save and new** to go to a new Sales Receipt (If necessary, click the drop-down list arrow for Save and close or Save and send, then click Save and new.)

Click the drop-down list arrow for "Choose a customer" and scroll through the list of customers

Since you do not see any list for Cash Customer, click **+ Add new**

Enter **Cash Customer** for the Name

- Since a cash customer will not be used to record sales on account, there is no need to enter any details.

Click the **Save** button.

- Notice that the Billing address only includes the name Cash Customer.

Make sure the Date is **011016**, and complete the Sales Receipt as previously instructed

Be sure to enter **Cash** as the Payment method, and use a QTY of **5**, and a RATE of **50**.

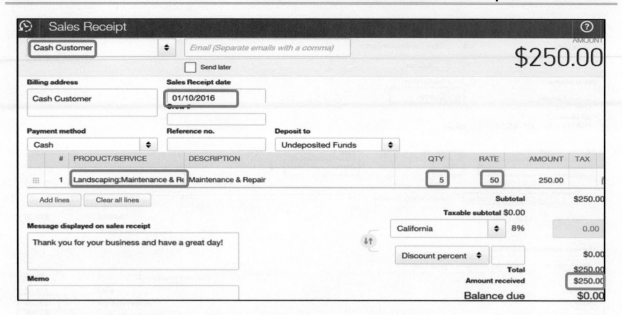

Click **Save and close**

- If you do not see Save and close, click the drop-down list arrow next to the save command displayed. Remember the save commands are: Save and close, Save and new, and Save and send.
- You should complete the next section as part of this work session!

Do <u>not</u> close the Test Drive Company you must use your work to complete the next section

## SALES BY CUSTOMER DETAIL REPORT—DRILL

To obtain information regarding sales, you prepare reports in the Review Sales category of Reports. Sales reports provide information regarding cash and credit sales. The Sales by Customer Detail report shows the sales transactions for each customer. The report lists all sales transactions—invoices and/or sales receipts—for each customer and includes information for the date, transaction type, number, products/service, memo/description, quantity, rate, account, and balance.

## *DRILL*

Continue to use the **Test Drive Company** and prepare a Sales by Customer Detail Report

With the Test Drive Company open, remember to Turn **OFF** Redesigned Reports as you did previously

Access **Reports** on the Navigation Bar, click **All Reports**, and click **Review Sales**

Click **Sales by Customer Detail** in the list of reports shown for the Review Sales category

Use the Dates From: **01/01/16** and To: **01/10/16**

- Scroll through the report and view the information presented. Only Cash Customer and Cool Cars is shown in the following report. The Test Drive Company is programmed with automatic date changes so you may have more than the two customers shown.

### Craig's Design and Landscaping Services
#### SALES BY CUSTOMER DETAIL
##### January 1-10, 2016

| DATE | TRANSACTION TYPE | NUM | PRODUCT/SERVICE | MEMO/DESCRIPTION | QTY | RATE | AMOUNT | BALANCE |
|---|---|---|---|---|---|---|---|---|
| **Cash Customer** | | | | | | | | |
| 01/10/2016 | Sales Receipt | 1039 | Landscaping:Maintenance & Repair | Maintenance & Repair | 5.00 | 50.00 | 250.00 | 250.00 |
| **Total for Cash Customer** | | | | | | | $250.00 | |
| **Cool Cars** | | | | | | | | |
| 01/10/2016 | Sales Receipt | 1038 | Pest Control:Pest Control | Pest Control Services | 1.00 | 35.00 | 35.00 | 35.00 |
| **Total for Cool Cars** | | | | | | | $35.00 | |
| **TOTAL** | | | | | | | $285.00 | |

6

Do not close the report, continue to the next section
- You should complete the next section as part of this work session!

Do not close the Test Drive Company

## CORRECT SALES RECEIPT—DRILL

As with invoices, errors in sales receipts may be corrected very easily with QuickBooks Online. Because a sales receipt is prepared for cash sales, corrections are made on the sales receipt. Since Sales Receipts are shown in the Sales by Customer Detail Report, you will access them in the report by clicking on the sales receipt. If you do not have the report on the screen, you may access the Sales Receipt by going to the customer's account in the Customers List.

> **MEMO**
> **DATE:** January 10, 2016
>
> As you review the Sales Receipts shown in the Sales by Customer Detail Report, you realize that you did not record 5 hours of Trimming for the Cash Customer on Sales Receipt 1039.

_DRILL_

 Continue to use the **Test Drive Company** and correct a sales receipt

With the Sales by Customer Detail Report showing on the screen, point to and click **Sales Receipt 1039** for Cash Customer
- Sales Receipt 1039 for Cash Customer will be shown.

Enter the second line of the sales receipt for 5 hours of Trimming as previously instructed

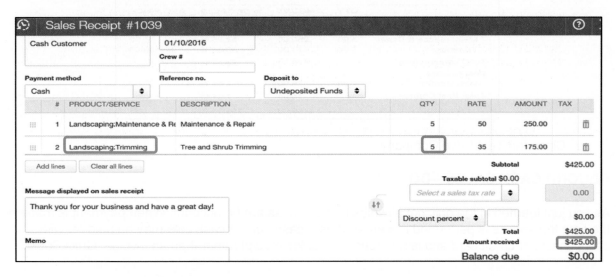

View the changes and note that the Amount Received shows $425.00.
Click **Save and close** (If necessary, click the drop-down list for Save and new or Save and send to find this.)
- If the Sales by Customer Detail Report is on the screen, you will see the additional information for Sales Receipt 1039.

| Cash Customer | | | | | | | | | |
|---|---|---|---|---|---|---|---|---|---|
| 01/10/2016 | Sales Receipt | 1039 | Landscaping:Trimming | Tree and Shrub Trimming | 5.00 | 35.00 | 175.00 | 175.00 |
| 01/10/2016 | Sales Receipt | 1039 | Landscaping:Maintenance & Repair | Maintenance & Repair | 5.00 | 50.00 | 250.00 | 425.00 |
| **Total for Cash Customer** | | | | | | | $425.00 | |

Do <u>not</u> close the Test Drive Company

## SALES BY PRODUCT/SERVICE SUMMARY—DRILL

When information regarding the sales according to the product or service, a Sales by Product/Service Summary is the appropriate report to print or view. This report enables you to see how much revenue is being generated by each product and/or service item. This provides important information for decision making and managing the business.

### *DRILL*

 Continue to use the **Test Drive Company** and prepare the Sales by Product/Service Summary Report

Open the Review Sales category in Reports and prepare the Sales by Product/Service Summary Report for January 1-10, 2016
- If you need detailed instructions on report preparation, refer to instructions provided earlier in the chapter.
- This report provides information regarding the quantity, dollar amount, percent of sales, and average price for each sales item used.
- If your report does not match the following, it may be due to the Test Drive's automatic date change. Do not worry if the information you have does not match the report shown.

### Craig's Design and Landscaping Services
#### SALES BY PRODUCT/SERVICE SUMMARY
##### January 1-10, 2016

| | QTY | AMOUNT | % OF SALES | AVG PRICE |
|---|---|---|---|---|
| **Landscaping** | | | | |
| Maintenance & Repair | 5.00 | 250.00 | 54.35 % | 50.00 |
| Trimming | 5.00 | 175.00 | 38.04 % | 35.00 |
| **Total Landscaping** | | 425.00 | 92.39 % | |
| **Pest Control** | | | | |
| Pest Control | 1.00 | 35.00 | 7.61 % | 35.00 |
| **Total Pest Control** | | 35.00 | 7.61 % | |
| **TOTAL** | | **$460.00** | **100.00 %** | |

Close the Test Drive Company

## RECORD CASH SALES—DO

As you just learned in the drill, not all sales in a business are on account. When payment is made at the time the service is performed it is entered as a cash sale. A cash sale may be paid for with cash, check, or credit card and is recorded on a sales receipt rather than an invoice. QuickBooks

Online records the transaction in the Journal and places the amount received in an account called Undeposited Funds. The funds received remain in Undeposited Funds until you record a deposit to your bank account.

| MEMO |
|---|
| DATE: January 10, 2016 |
| Keith Evans enrolled his dog, Boomer, in Ten One-Hour Sessions of Training, Check 2643. |
| A new customer, Cash Customer, brought in Fluffy for a quick brushing. Paid with Cash. |
| Dori Anderson brought in her dogs, GiGi and Precious, for 1 day of Day Camp and a Brushing. (Since there are two dogs, double the quantity.), Check 9534. |
| Another Cash Customer brought in his dog, Curly, for a Bath and Nail trimming, Check 4570. |
| Gloria Gucci brought in Mishka for a Bath. Paid with Cash. |

<u>DO</u>

Use **Your Name's Beach Barkers** to prepare sales receipts for cash (and check) sales transactions

With the Your Name's Beach Barkers open, complete the sales receipts listed in the Memo
Click the **Plus** button in the Top-Navigation Bar
Click **Sales Receipt** in the Customers menu on the Create screen
Click the drop-down list arrow for "Choose a customer," click **Evans, Keith**
Tab to or click in the text box for Sales Receipt date, enter **011016**
If Check does not show automatically, click the drop-down list arrow for Payment method, then click **Check**
Tab to Reference no., enter the check number **2643**
Deposit to should be Undeposited Funds; if it is not the account shown, click the drop-down list arrow and click **Undeposited Funds**
As you did for invoices, select the PRODUCT/SERVICE of **Training 3** for the Ten One-Hour Sessions of Training, press **Tab**, and view the Sales Receipt

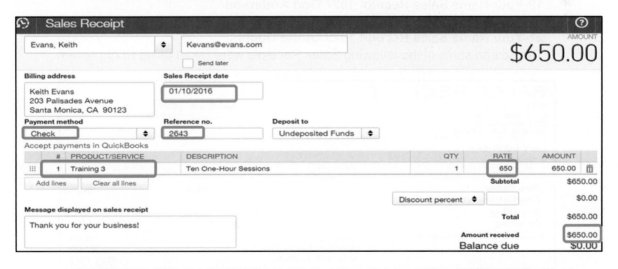

- As you learned in your drill, the visual appearance of a Sales Receipt is very similar to an invoice. Some of the differences are entering the Payment method, Reference number (Check), and selecting the account for Deposit to. At the bottom of the Sales Receipt, you will see the transaction total in Amount received, and $0.00 for Balance due.

Print and/or save as a pdf file as previously instructed
- Name the Sales Receipt: **17-Your Name Sales Receipt 1025 Keith Evans**.

Click **Save and new** (if necessary, click the drop-down list for Save and close or Save and send to find this.) to save in QuickBooks Online and go to a new Sales Receipt
Add the new Cash Customer as instructed in the drill
- Notice that the Billing address only includes the name Cash Customer.

Make sure the date is **01/10/16**, and use the information in the Memo to complete the Sales Receipt as previously instructed
Be sure to enter **Cash** as the Payment method, and use a QTY of 1 for Brushing

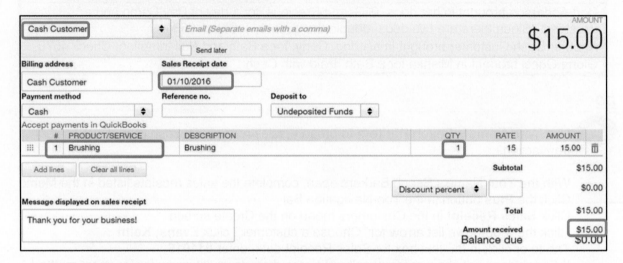

Print and/or save the sales receipt as previously instructed
- Name the Sales Receipt: **18-Your Name Sales Receipt 1026 Cash Customer**.

Click **Save and new** (If necessary, click the drop-down list for Save and close or Save and send to find this.)
Continue to enter, print, and/or save the Sales Receipts listed in the Memo
- Name the next three Sales Receipts:
  **19-Your Name Sales Receipt 1027 Dori Anderson**
  **20-Your Name Sales Receipt 1028 Cash Customer**
  **21-Your Name Sales Receipt 1029 Gloria Gucci**
- The screen shots of the following Sales Receipts were taken using Print preview.

## SALES RECEIPT

**BILL TO**
Dori Anderson
395 Brooks Ct.
Venice, CA 90202

**SALES # 1027**
**DATE 01/10/2016**

**PMT METHOD**
Check

| ACTIVITY | QTY | RATE | AMOUNT |
|---|---|---|---|
| **Day Camp** Day Camp | 2 | 30.00 | 60.00 |
| **Brushing** Brushing | 2 | 15.00 | 30.00 |

Thank you for your business!

| | |
|---|---|
| TOTAL | 90.00 |
| AMOUNT RECEIVED | 90.00 |
| BALANCE DUE | **$0.00** |

```
SALES RECEIPT
BILL TO                                    SALES #  1028
Cash Customer                              DATE  01/10/2016

PMT METHOD
Check
  ACTIVITY                    QTY      RATE          AMOUNT
  Bath                          1      35.00           35.00
  Bath
  Nails                         1      20.00           20.00
  Nails
Thank you for your business!   TOTAL                   55.00
                               AMOUNT RECEIVED         55.00
                               BALANCE DUE           $0.00
```

```
SALES RECEIPT
BILL TO                                    SALES #  1029
Gloria Gucci                               DATE  01/10/2016
795 Ocean Avenue
Venice, CA  90202

PMT METHOD
Cash
  ACTIVITY                    QTY      RATE          AMOUNT
  Bath                          1      35.00           35.00
  Bath
Thank you for your business!   TOTAL                   35.00
                               AMOUNT RECEIVED         35.00
                               BALANCE DUE           $0.00
```

Click **Save and close** as previously instructed
Continue to the next section without closing Your Name's Beach Barkers

## SALES BY CUSTOMER DETAIL REPORT—DO

To obtain information regarding sales, you prepare reports in the Review Sales category of Reports. The Sales by Customer Detail report shows the sales transactions for each customer and includes information for the date, transaction type, number, products/service, memo/description, quantity, rate, account, and balance.

## DO

Continue to use **Your Name's Beach Barkers** and prepare a Sales by Customer Detail Report

Access **Reports** on the Navigation Bar, select **Review Sales**, and **Sales by Customer Detail**
Use the Dates From: **01/01/16** and To: **01/10/16**
- Scroll through the report and view the information presented.

### Your Name's Beach Barkers
**SALES BY CUSTOMER DETAIL**
January 1-10, 2016

| DATE | TRANSACTION TYPE | NUM | PRODUCT/SERVICE | MEMO/DESCRIPTION | QTY | RATE | AMOUNT | BALANCE |
|---|---|---|---|---|---|---|---|---|
| **Anderson, Dori** | | | | | | | | |
| 01/10/2016 | Sales Receipt | 1027 | Day Camp | Day Camp | 2.00 | 30.00 | 60.00 | 60.00 |
| 01/10/2016 | Sales Receipt | 1027 | Brushing | Brushing | 2.00 | 15.00 | 30.00 | 90.00 |
| **Total for Anderson, Dori** | | | | | | | $90.00 | |
| **Bailey, Larry** | | | | | | | | |
| 01/01/2016 | Invoice | 1021 | Nails | Nails | 1.00 | 20.00 | 20.00 | 20.00 |
| 01/01/2016 | Invoice | 1021 | Bath | Bath | 1.00 | 35.00 | 35.00 | 55.00 |
| **Total for Bailey, Larry** | | | | | | | $55.00 | |
| **Cash Customer** | | | | | | | | |
| 01/10/2016 | Sales Receipt | 1028 | Nails | Nails | 1.00 | 20.00 | 20.00 | 20.00 |
| 01/10/2016 | Sales Receipt | 1026 | Brushing | Brushing | 1.00 | 15.00 | 15.00 | 35.00 |
| 01/10/2016 | Sales Receipt | 1028 | Bath | Bath | 1.00 | 35.00 | 35.00 | 70.00 |
| **Total for Cash Customer** | | | | | | | $70.00 | |
| **Clark, Bunni** | | | | | | | | |
| 01/01/2016 | Invoice | 1018 | Training 2 | Five One-Hour Sessions | 1.00 | 350.00 | 350.00 | 350.00 |
| 01/01/2016 | Invoice | 1018 | Boarding | Boarding | 5.00 | 55.00 | 275.00 | 625.00 |
| **Total for Clark, Bunni** | | | | | | | $625.00 | |
| **Evans, Keith** | | | | | | | | |
| 01/10/2016 | Sales Receipt | 1025 | Training 3 | Ten One-Hour Sessions | 1.00 | 650.00 | 650.00 | 650.00 |
| **Total for Evans, Keith** | | | | | | | $650.00 | |

**Partial Report**

- Scroll through the report and view your entries. Is your total $3,510?

Since this is a report, follow instructions given earlier to print, export, and/or email it

- Name the report **22-Your Name Sales by Customer Detail Ch. 3**.

Do not close the report, continue to the next section

Do <u>not</u> close Your Name's Beach Barkers

## CORRECT SALES RECEIPT—DO

As you learned in the drill, errors in sales receipts may be corrected very easily with QuickBooks Online. Since Sales Receipts are shown in the Sales by Customer Detail Report, access them by clicking on the sales receipt shown in the report. If you do not have the report on the screen, you may access the Sales Receipt by going to the customer's account in the Customers List.

---

**MEMO**
**DATE:** January 10, 2016

In reviewing the Sales Receipts shown in the Sales by Customer Detail Report, you realize that you did not record 1 Nail trimming for Gloria Gucci's dog. Correct Sales Receipt 1029.

---

<u>DO</u>

Continue to use **Your Name's Beach Barkers** and correct a sales receipt

With the Sales by Customer Detail Report showing on the screen, point to and click **Sales Receipt 1029** for Gloria Gucci

- Sales Receipt 1029 for Gloria Gucci will be shown.

Enter the second line of the sales receipt for 1 Nail trimming as previously instructed

```
SALES RECEIPT
BILL TO                                    SALES # 1029
Gloria Gucci                               DATE  01/10/2016
795 Ocean Avenue
Venice, CA 90202
PMT METHOD
Cash
  ACTIVITY                      QTY        RATE         AMOUNT
  Bath                           1        35.00          35.00
  Bath
  Nails                          1        20.00          20.00
  Nails
Thank you for your business!    TOTAL                    55.00
                                AMOUNT RECEIVED          55.00
                                BALANCE DUE             $0.00
```

View the changes and note that the Amount Received shows $55.00.
Save as a pdf and/or print the sales receipt
- Name it **23-Your Name Sales Receipt 1029 Gloria Gucci Corrected**.
Click **Save and close**
- If you have the Sales by Customer Detail Report on the screen, you will see the additional information for Sales Receipt 1029.

| Gucci, Gloria | | | | | | | | |
|---|---|---|---|---|---|---|---|---|
| 01/10/2016 | Sales Receipt | 1029 | Nails | Nails | 1.00 | 20.00 | 20.00 | 20.00 |
| 01/10/2016 | Sales Receipt | 1029 | Bath | Bath | 1.00 | 35.00 | 35.00 | 55.00 |
| Total for Gucci, Gloria | | | | | | | $55.00 | |

Do not close Your Name's Beach Barkers

## SALES BY PRODUCT/SERVICE SUMMARY—DO

A Sales by Product/Service Summary report enables you to see how much revenue is being generated by each product/service item.

## DO

Continue to use **Your Name's Beach Barkers** and prepare the Sales by Product/Service Summary Report

Open the Review Sales category in Reports and prepare the Sales by Product/Service Summary Report for January 1-10, 2016
- If you need detailed instructions on report preparation, refer to instructions provided earlier in the chapter.

### Your Name's Beach Barkers
### SALES BY PRODUCT/SERVICE SUMMARY
#### January 1-10, 2016

| | | TOTAL | | |
|---|---|---|---|---|
| | QTY | AMOUNT | % OF SALES | AVG PRICE |
| Bath | 4.00 | 140.00 | 3.97 % | 35.00 |
| Boarding | 5.00 | 275.00 | 7.79 % | 55.00 |
| Brushing | 11.00 | 165.00 | 4.67 % | 15.00 |
| Day Camp | 10.00 | 300.00 | 8.50 % | 30.00 |
| Dog Walking | 10.00 | 150.00 | 4.25 % | 15.00 |
| Nails | 4.00 | 80.00 | 2.27 % | 20.00 |
| Poop Scoop | 3.00 | 45.00 | 1.27 % | 15.00 |
| Training 1 | 1.00 | 75.00 | 2.12 % | 75.00 |
| Training 2 | 1.00 | 350.00 | 9.92 % | 350.00 |
| Training 3 | 3.00 | 1,950.00 | 55.24 % | 650.00 |
| TOTAL | | $3,530.00 | 100.00 % | |

- Analyze which products sell the most and which ones bring in the most revenue.

To drill-down and see the details for your most popular sales item, point to either the quantity or amount for **Brushing** and click when underlined

### Your Name's Beach Barkers
#### TRANSACTION REPORT
##### January 1-10, 2016

| DATE | TRANSACTION TYPE | NUM | CLIENT | MEMO/DESCRIPTION | QTY | RATE | AMOUNT | BALANCE |
|------|------------------|-----|--------|------------------|-----|------|--------|---------|
| 01/05/2016 | Invoice | 1024 | Russell, Carol | Brushing | 3.00 | 15.00 | 45.00 | 45.00 |
| 01/05/2016 | Invoice | 1023 | Montez, Annabelle | Brushing | 5.00 | 15.00 | 75.00 | 120.00 |
| 01/10/2016 | Sales Receipt | 1026 | Cash Customer | Brushing | 1.00 | 15.00 | 15.00 | 135.00 |
| 01/10/2016 | Sales Receipt | 1027 | Anderson, Dori | Brushing | 2.00 | 15.00 | 30.00 | 165.00 |
| **Total for Brushing** | | | | | | | **$165.00** | |
| **TOTAL** | | | | | | | **$165.00** | |

To return to the Sales by Product/Service Summary, click | **< Back to Summary Report** |
Since this is a report, follow instructions given earlier to print, export, and/or email it

- Name the report **24-Your Name Sales by Product-Service Summary Ch. 3**. Since you cannot use a / in a file name, use a hyphen – between Product and Service.

Close Your Name's Beach Barkers

## CREDIT MEMO AND REFUND RECEIPT—DRILL

Credit memos are prepared to show a reduction to a transaction recorded on an invoice. If the invoice has already been sent to the customer, it is more appropriate and less confusing to make a change to a transaction by issuing a credit memo rather than voiding or deleting the invoice and issuing a new one. A credit memo notifies a customer that a change has been made to a transaction and subtracts the amount from the amount due.

If, however, you have already received payment for the invoice or the transaction was a cash sale recorded on a sales receipt, you will prepare a refund receipt and issue a refund of the money to the customer.

---

**MEMO**
**DATE:** January 12, 2016

Red Rock Diner only used 1 Pest Control treatment rather than the two billed on Invoice 1023. Prepare a Credit Memo.

Diego Rodriguez used 3 hours of Gardening service not the 4 listed on Sales Receipt 1014. Rate is $35 per hour. Prepare a Refund Receipt with Check as the Payment Method.

---

### _DRILL_

 Use the **Test Drive Company** to prepare a credit memo and a refund receipt

### Credit Memo

The transaction for Pest Control treatment for Red Rock Diner was recorded on an invoice. To record the reduction to the amount owed, you will prepare a Credit Memo.

 Use the **Test Drive Company**, refer to the Memo and the following steps to prepare a Credit Memo for Red Rock Diner

Click the **Plus** icon in the Top-Navigation Bar, click **Credit Memo** in the Customers column
Click the drop-down list arrow for "Choose a customer," click **Red Rock Diner**

Enter the Credit Memo Date **011216**
Use **Pest Control** for the Product/Service
- The QTY automatically uses 1.

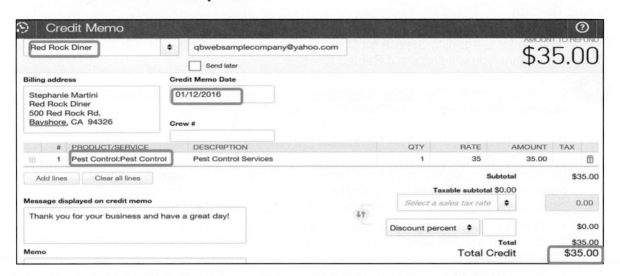

Review the Credit Memo, click **Save and close** as previously instructed
Go to the Customers List, and click **Red Rock Diner** to see the Credit Memo in the transactions list
- Notice that the Date for the Credit Memo says 01/12/16, which is the date of the Credit Memo. There is also a Payment for 0.00 shown that is dated the Current Date.
- The Payment is generated automatically by QuickBooks Online in order to match the Credit Memo to the Invoice. Changing the date for the Payment to match the date of the Credit Memo will help you identify that the Payment and Credit Memo are linked.

Click the Payment for the current date
Change the Payment date to **011216**, press **Tab**
- You will see that the Credit Memo has a check mark and that Invoice 1024 also has a check mark. When you look at the Payment column for Invoice 1024, you will see a Payment of 35.00. The payment is the amount of the credit memo. This means the Credit Memo was applied to the invoice and the amount owed will be reduced.

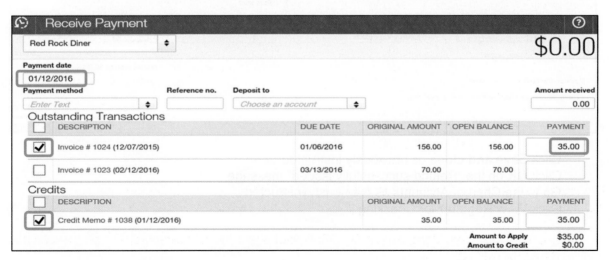

Click **Save and close**
On the message screen about modifying the transaction because it is linked, click **Yes**

You will return to Red Rock Diner's Transaction List
- Notice that the Credit Memo and Payment are shown next to each other.

## Refund Receipt

The transaction for Gardening Service for Diego Rodriguez was recorded on a sales receipt. To refund the amount, you will prepare a Refund Receipt.

 Continue to use the **Test Drive Company**, refer to the Memo and the following steps to prepare a Refund Receipt for Diego Rodriguez

Click the **Plus** icon in the Top-Navigation Bar
Click **Refund Receipt** in the Customers column
Click the drop-down list arrow for "Choose a customer," click **Diego Rodriguez**
Enter the Refund Receipt Date **011216**
Click the drop-down list arrow for "Payment method," click **Check**
- Check is used because you are writing a check for the refund.
To select the account used for the refund, click the drop-down list arrow for "Refund From"
Click **Checking**
- You will see 71 in Check no. This is the next available check in the company's checking account.
Use **Gardening** for the Product/Service
- The QTY automatically uses 1.
Tab to RATE, enter **35**, press **Tab**

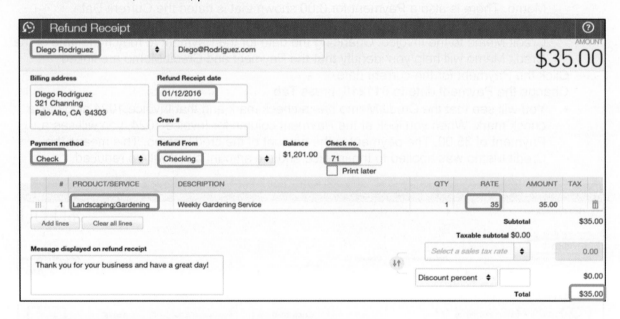

Click **Save and close** as previously instructed
Click **OK** on the "Refund successfully issued" message
Go to the Chart of Accounts as previously instructed
Click **View Register** for Checking

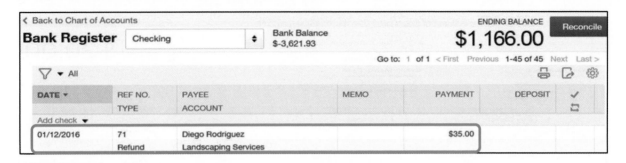

Close the Test Drive Company

## CREDIT MEMO AND REFUND RECEIPT—DO

As you just learned, credit memos are prepared to show a reduction to a transaction recorded on an invoice. A refund receipt is prepared when you have already received payment for an invoice or the transaction was a cash sale recorded on a sales receipt, you will prepare a refund receipt and issue a refund of the money to the customer.

---

**MEMO**

**DATE:** January 12, 2016

Ashley Rhodes dog, Peaches, had to go to the vet and miss a day of Day Camp recorded on Invoice 1019. Prepare a Credit Memo for one day of Day Camp.

Sales Receipt 1029 for Gloria Gucci had been corrected to include an amount for Nails to be trimmed. When bathing the dog, the nails were really fine and did not need trimming. Prepare a Refund Receipt for the Nails. Payment Method: Check.

---

## DO

 Use **Your Name's Beach Barkers** to prepare a credit memo and a refund receipt

### Credit Memo

The transaction for Ashley Rhodes was recorded on an invoice. To record the reduction to the amount owed, you will prepare a Credit Memo.

 Use **Your Name's Beach Barkers**, refer to the Memo and the instructions in the drill to prepare a Credit Memo for Ashley Rhodes

Open a **Credit Memo**
Customer: **Rhodes, Ashley**
Credit Memo Date: **011216**
Product/Service: **Day Camp**
Quantity: **1**

Review the Credit Memo

Save as a pdf or print as previously instructed

Name the file **25-Your Name Credit Memo 1030 Ashley Rhodes**

- Have you noticed that invoices, sales receipts, and credit memos are numbered sequentially?

Click **Save and close** as previously instructed

Go to Ashley's account in the Customers List, to see the Credit Memo in the transactions list

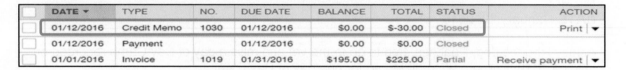

| DATE ▼ | TYPE | NO. | DUE DATE | BALANCE | TOTAL | STATUS | ACTION |
|---|---|---|---|---|---|---|---|
| 01/12/2016 | Credit Memo | 1030 | 01/12/2016 | $0.00 | $-30.00 | Closed | Print  ▼ |
| 01/12/2016 | Payment | | 01/12/2016 | $0.00 | $0.00 | Closed | |
| 01/01/2016 | Invoice | 1019 | 01/31/2016 | $195.00 | $225.00 | Partial | Receive payment  ▼ |

- Note the Credit Memo, Date, and Total shown in the Transaction List for Ashley Rhodes.
- In addition to the Credit memo, you will see a Payment. The screen shot shows the same date as the Credit Memo. On your screen, the Payment will be shown above the Credit Memo and show the current date. Changing the date for the Payment to match the date of the Credit Memo will help you identify that the Payment and Credit Memo are linked.

Click the transaction for **Payment**

Change the Payment date to **011216**

- You will see a screen for Receive Payment. QuickBooks Online created this payment so the amount of the credit could be linked and applied to the original Invoice 1019.

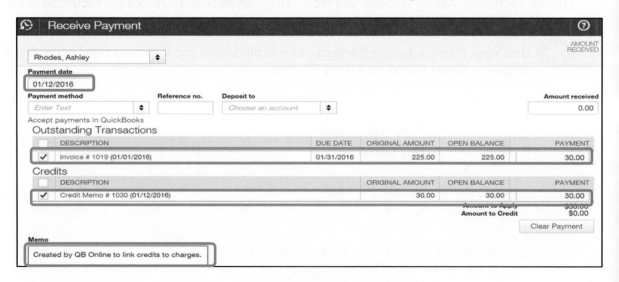

Click the **Save and close** button on the Receive Payment screen

Click **Invoice 1019** in Ashley's Transaction List
- Look in the Totals area on the invoice. Notice that it shows $30.00 for Amount received. This means that the $30.00 credit has been applied to the invoice.

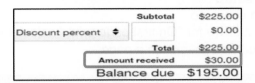

| | Subtotal | $225.00 |
|---|---|---|
| Discount percent ⬦ | | $0.00 |
| | Total | $225.00 |
| | Amount received | $30.00 |
| | Balance due | $195.00 |

Click **Save and close** as previously instructed
Continue to use Your Name's Beach Barkers to record a Refund Receipt

## Refund Receipt

The transaction for Nails for Gloria Gucci's dog was recorded on a sales receipt. To refund the amount, you will prepare a Refund Receipt.

 Continue to use **Your Name's Beach Barkers**, refer to the Memo and the instructions in the drill to prepare a Refund Receipt for Gloria Gucci

Open a **Refund Receipt**
Customer: **Gloria Gucci**
Refund Receipt Date: **011216**
Refund Method: **Check**
To select the Account used for the refund, click the drop-down list arrow for "Refund From"
Click **Checking**
- You will see 1 in Check no. This is the next available check in the company's checking account. Because this is the first check written by Your Name's Beach Barkers, the number should be 1.
Product/Service: **Nails**
- The QTY automatically uses **1**.

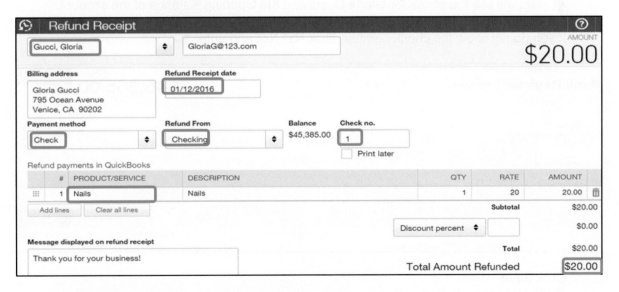

Click **Print Check** at the bottom of the Refund Receipt
Click **OK** on the "Refund successfully issued" screen

- You will be taken to a "Print checks setup" screen. This allows you to setup and align preprinted checks that are purchased from Intuit.

Since you are not using real checks, click **Standard** for the type of check, then click **Yes, I'm finished with setup**

Enter **1** as the Starting check no.

Click the drop-down list arrow for "On first page print," select **1 check**

- You can print up to three checks on a page.

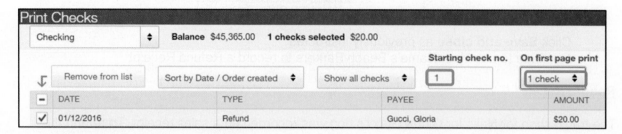

Click the **Preview and print** at the bottom of the screen and print as previously instructed

- Save the document as **26-Your Name Check 1 Gloria Gucci**.

On the "Did your checks print OK?" screen, make sure "Yes, they all printed correctly" is selected, click **Done**

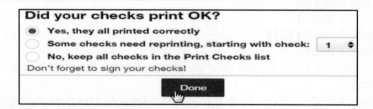

Click the **Close** button on the Print checks screen

Go to the Chart of Accounts as previously instructed

Click **View Register** for Checking

- You will see the check for Gloria Gucci and the Opening Balance of the account.
- REF NO. should have 1 for the Reference Number and Type should have Refund.

If you do not show the check number, click **Ref No.** and enter **1**

Click **Save**

Close Your Name's Beach Barkers

## RECEIVE PAYMENTS—DRILL

Since a sale on account is originally recorded on an invoice, Receive Payments is used when a customer pays you what is owed for the invoice. Frequently, new users of QuickBooks will try to record a payment receipt using a Sales Receipt, which is used only for cash sales not for payments on account.

When you record a Receive Payment from a customer who owes you money for an invoice, you see a complete list of outstanding invoices. QuickBooks Online automatically selects the invoice that has the same amount as the payment. If there isn't an invoice with the same amount, QuickBooks Online marks the oldest invoice and enters the payment amount. When customers make a full or partial payment of the amount they owe, QuickBooks Online places the money received in the Undeposited Funds account. The money stays in this account until a bank deposit is made.

3

---

**MEMO**
**DATE:** January 15, 2016

Kookies by Kathy paid Invoice 1016 in full. Check 7645 for $75.

Bill's Windsurf Shop paid a partial payment of $50 for Invoice 1027, Check 1379.

---

*DRILL*

 Open the **Test Drive Company**, refer to the Memo, and complete the following steps to prepare Payment Receipts

> Click the **Plus** icon on the Top-Navigation Bar
> Click **Receive Payment** in the Customers Column and complete the following information:
>> Customer: **Kookies by Kathy**
>> Payment date: **01/15/16**
>> Payment method: **Check**
>> Reference no.: **7645**
>> Deposit to: **Undeposited Funds**
>> • Payments received by customers are put in the Undeposited Funds account until the Bank Deposit is made. By doing this, you do not accidentally write checks or make payments using money that has not been deposited into the bank account. When the bank deposit is made, the amount will be removed from Undeposited Funds and entered into Checking.
>> Tab to Amount received, enter **75**, press **Tab**
>> • QuickBooks matched the amount of the payment to the amount of the invoice and marked the invoice with a check mark.

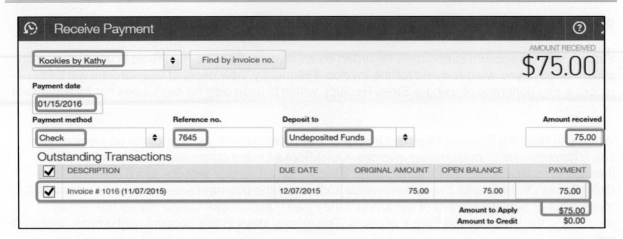

Click **Save and new** as previously instructed

Rather than enter a Customer name, click **Find by invoice no.** and enter **1027**, click **Find**

Using the information in the memo, enter the partial payment received from Bill's Windsurf Shop

- QuickBooks Online applied the $50.00 payment to Invoice 1027.

Click in the "Memo" text box and enter **Partial Payment**

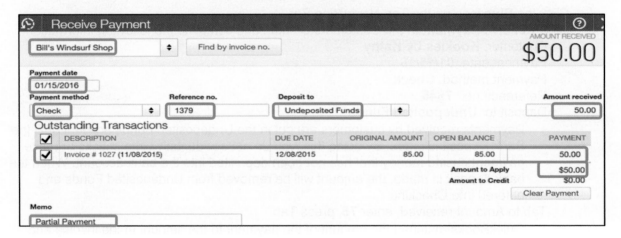

Click **Save and close** as previously instructed

## TRANSACTION DETAIL BY ACCOUNT—DRILL

This report shows all of the entries made into each account in the Chart of Accounts, which is also known as the General Ledger, during the dates specified for the report.

### *DRILL*

Continue to use the **Test Drive Company** prepare a Transactions Detail by Account Report for January 1-15, 2016

Go to QuickBooks Labs and Turn **OFF** Redesigned Reports as previously instructed
Go to Reports, click **Accountant Reports** in All Reports
Click the report **Transaction Detail by Account**
Enter the Dates From: **01/01/16** To: **01/15/16**, press **Tab**
- Look at the information shown for Accounts Receivable and Undeposited Funds shown below. Note that the payment amounts for Bill's Windsurf Shop and Kookies by Kathy were deducted from Accounts Receivable and entered into Undeposited Funds.
- If you see more than the two transactions, do not be concerned. Remember, the Test Drive Company automatically changes transaction dates.

### Craig's Design and Landscaping Services
#### TRANSACTION DETAIL BY ACCOUNT
##### January 1-15, 2016

| DATE | TRANSACTION TYPE | NUM | NAME | MEMO/DESCRIPTION | SPLIT | AMOUNT | BALANCE |
|------|-----------------|-----|------|------------------|-------|--------|---------|
| **Accounts Receivable (A/R)** | | | | | | | |
| 01/15/2016 | Payment | 1379 | Bill's Windsurf Shop | | Undeposited Funds | -50.00 | -50.00 |
| 01/15/2016 | Payment | 7645 | Kookies by Kathy | | Undeposited Funds | -75.00 | -125.00 |
| **Total for Accounts Receivable (A/R)** | | | | | | $ -125.00 | |
| **Undeposited Funds** | | | | | | | |
| 01/15/2016 | Payment | 1379 | Bill's Windsurf Shop | Partial Payment | Accounts Receivable (A/R) | 50.00 | 50.00 |
| 01/15/2016 | Payment | 7645 | Kookies by Kathy | | Accounts Receivable (A/R) | 75.00 | 125.00 |
| **Total for Undeposited Funds** | | | | | | $125.00 | |

Close the Test Drive Company

## RECEIVE PAYMENTS—DO

As you practiced in the drill, Receive Payments is used when a customer pays you what is owed for an invoice. Remember, QuickBooks Online selects the invoice that has the same amount as the payment. If there isn't an invoice with the same amount, QuickBooks marks the oldest invoice and enters the payment amount. Money received from customer payments is recorded in the Undeposited Funds account until a bank deposit is made.

> **MEMO**
> **DATE:** January 15, 2016
>
> Note: Use **Undeposited Funds** for the "Deposit to" account.
>
> Received payment in full from Larry Bailey for Invoice 1021, Check 6489 for $55.
> Bunni Clark paid her account in full, Check 4465 for $4,125.
> Received a partial payment from Oscar Gilbert for Invoice 1022, Check 1972 for $300.
> Ashley Rhodes paid Invoice 1019 in full. Check 7531 for $195.
> Received Check 6431 from Annabelle Montez for $100 as partial payment for Invoice 1023.

_DO_

Open **Your Name's Beach Barkers**, refer to the Memo, and complete the following Payment Receipts

Click the **Plus** icon on the Top-Navigation Bar
Click **Receive Payment** in the Customers Column and complete the following information:
    Customer: **Larry Bailey**
    Payment date: **01/15/16**
    Payment method: **Check**
    Reference no.: **6489**

Deposit to: **Undeposited Funds**
- Remember, payments received by customers are put in the Undeposited Funds account until the Bank Deposit is made. When the bank deposit is made, the amount will be removed from Undeposited Funds and entered into Checking.

Amount received: **55**, press **Tab**
- After pressing the Tab key, QuickBooks Online matched the amount of the payment to the amount of the invoice and marked Invoice 1021 with a check mark.

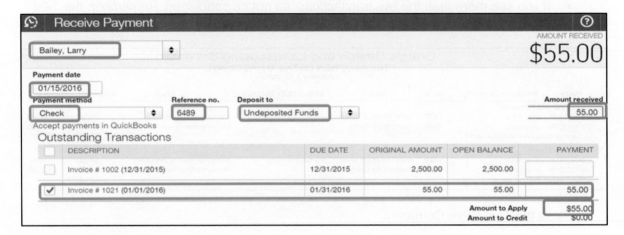

QuickBooks Online does not print Receive Payments, click **Save and new** as previously instructed

Use the information in the memo to record the payment from Bunni Clark

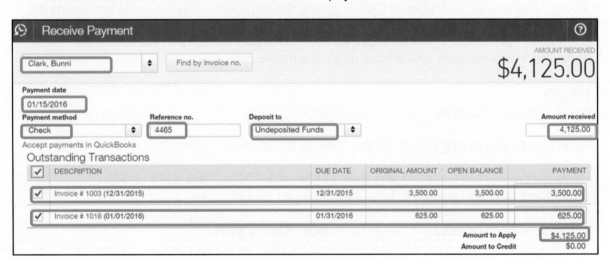

- Notice that QuickBooks Online marked both invoices.

Click **Save and new** as previously instructed
- If you get a message from QuickBooks Online for Get paid online, click **No thanks**.

Enter the Payment Receipt from Oscar Gilbert for $300
- The Payment Receipt for Oscar Gilbert does not match the total of either invoice, so QuickBooks Online marks the oldest invoice—his opening balance.

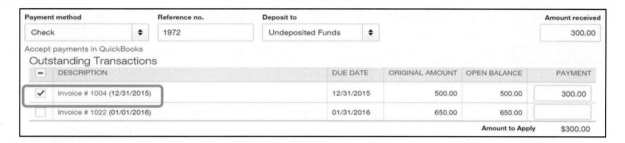

Click the check box for Invoice 1004 to remove the check
Click the check box for Invoice 1022 to mark it
- QuickBooks Online should put the payment of 300.00 in the Payment field.
Enter the memo **Partial Payment**
View the finished form

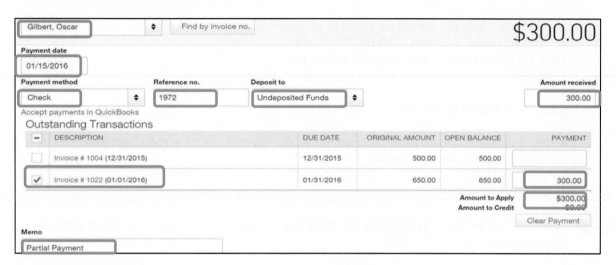

Click **Save and new**
Enter the Receive Payment for Ashley Rhodes using the information in the Memo

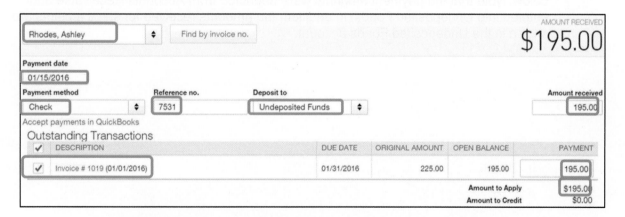

- Notice that QuickBooks Online shows the Original Amount of 225.00 and an Open Balance of 195.00. The difference between the two amounts is the amount of the $30.00 credit recorded earlier.
Record the Receive Payment for Annabelle Montez using the information in the Memo
- Be sure to include a memo Partial Payment if an invoice is not paid in full.

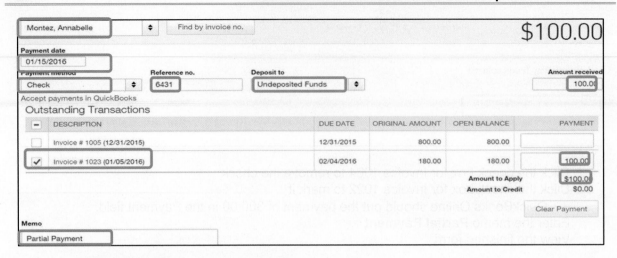

- Did you apply the partial payment to Invoice 1023?
- Did you enter a Memo of Partial Payment?

Click **Save and close** as previously instructed

Continue to use Your Name's Beach Barkers in the next section

## TRANSACTION DETAIL BY ACCOUNT—DO

As in the drill, this report shows all the entries made into each account in the Chart of Accounts during the dates specified for the report.

_DO_

Continue to use **Your Name's Beach Barkers** prepare a Transaction Detail by Account Report for January 1-15, 2016

Follow the steps presented earlier and prepare the Transaction Detail by Account Report
- Look at the information shown for Accounts Receivable and Undeposited Funds shown below. Note that the payment amounts were deducted from Accounts Receivable and entered into Undeposited Funds. In addition, the amounts received for sales receipts are shown in the Undeposited Funds account.

Your Name's Beach Barkers
TRANSACTION DETAIL BY ACCOUNT
January 1-15, 2016

| DATE | TRANSACTION TYPE | NUM | NAME | MEMO/DESCRIPTION | SPLIT | AMOUNT | BALANCE |
|---|---|---|---|---|---|---|---|
| **Checking** | | | | | | | |
| 01/12/2016 | Refund | 1031 | Gucci, Gloria | | Services:Grooming | -20.00 | -20.00 |
| **Total for Checking** | | | | | | $ -20.00 | |
| **Accounts Receivable (A/R)** | | | | | | | |
| 01/01/2016 | Invoice | 1018 | Clark, Bunni | | -Split- | 625.00 | 625.00 |
| 01/01/2016 | Invoice | 1022 | Gilbert, Oscar | | Services:Training | 650.00 | 1,275.00 |
| 01/01/2016 | Invoice | 1017 | Phillips, Eric | Voided | Services:Boarding | 0.00 | 1,275.00 |
| 01/01/2016 | Invoice | 1021 | Bailey, Larry | | -Split- | 55.00 | 1,330.00 |
| 01/01/2016 | Invoice | 1016 | Vines, Pamela | | Services:Training | 650.00 | 1,980.00 |
| 01/01/2016 | Invoice | 1020 | Summer, Matthew | | -Split- | 90.00 | 2,070.00 |
| 01/01/2016 | Invoice | 1019 | Rhodes, Ashley | | -Split- | 225.00 | 2,295.00 |
| 01/05/2016 | Invoice | 1024 | Russell, Carol | | -Split- | 190.00 | 2,485.00 |
| 01/05/2016 | Invoice | 1023 | Montez, Annabelle | | -Split- | 180.00 | 2,665.00 |
| 01/12/2016 | Credit Memo | 1030 | Rhodes, Ashley | | Services:Day Camp | -30.00 | 2,635.00 |
| 01/12/2016 | Payment | | Rhodes, Ashley | | -Split- | 0.00 | 2,635.00 |
| 01/15/2016 | Payment | 4465 | Clark, Bunni | | Undeposited Funds | -4,125.00 | -1,490.00 |
| 01/15/2016 | Payment | 6489 | Bailey, Larry | | Undeposited Funds | -55.00 | -1,545.00 |
| 01/15/2016 | Payment | 1972 | Gilbert, Oscar | | Undeposited Funds | -300.00 | -1,845.00 |
| 01/15/2016 | Payment | 6431 | Montez, Annabelle | | Undeposited Funds | -100.00 | -1,945.00 |
| 01/15/2016 | Payment | 7531 | Rhodes, Ashley | | Undeposited Funds | -195.00 | -2,140.00 |
| **Total for Accounts Receivable (A/R)** | | | | | | $ -2,140.00 | |
| **Undeposited Funds** | | | | | | | |
| 01/10/2016 | Sales Receipt | 1025 | Evans, Keith | | Services:Training | 650.00 | 650.00 |
| 01/10/2016 | Sales Receipt | 1027 | Anderson, Dori | | -Split- | 90.00 | 740.00 |
| 01/10/2016 | Sales Receipt | 1029 | Gucci, Gloria | | -Split- | 55.00 | 795.00 |
| 01/10/2016 | Sales Receipt | 1026 | Cash Customer | | Services:Grooming | 15.00 | 810.00 |
| 01/10/2016 | Sales Receipt | 1028 | Cash Customer | | -Split- | 55.00 | 865.00 |
| 01/15/2016 | Payment | 6489 | Bailey, Larry | | Accounts Receivable (A/R) | 55.00 | 920.00 |
| 01/15/2016 | Payment | 7531 | Rhodes, Ashley | | Accounts Receivable (A/R) | 195.00 | 1,115.00 |
| 01/15/2016 | Payment | 1972 | Gilbert, Oscar | Partial Payment | Accounts Receivable (A/R) | 300.00 | 1,415.00 |
| 01/15/2016 | Payment | 4465 | Clark, Bunni | | Accounts Receivable (A/R) | 4,125.00 | 5,540.00 |
| 01/15/2016 | Payment | 6431 | Montez, Annabelle | Partial Payment | Accounts Receivable (A/R) | 100.00 | 5,640.00 |
| **Total for Undeposited Funds** | | | | | | $5,640.00 | |

**Partial Report**

Print, export, and/or Email your report
To print in Landscape (11 wide by 8 ½ long), on the print menu click **Layout**, and then click
   **Landscape**
- Name the report **27-Your Name Transaction Detail by Account Ch. 3**.
Close Your Name's Beach Barkers

## BANK DEPOSIT—DRILL

When you record cash sales and the receipt of payments on account, QuickBooks Online places the money received in the Undeposited Funds account. Once the deposit has been made at the bank, it should be recorded. When the deposit is recorded, the funds are transferred from Undeposited Funds to the account selected when preparing the deposit (usually Checking). This is important because, until the money is deposited, it does not show as being available for use.

### _DRILL_

 Open and use the **Test Drive Company** and record a Bank Deposit

   With the Test Drive Company open, click the **Plus** icon
   In the Other column, click **Bank Deposit**

- The account should be Checking. If not, select it from the drop-down list.

Enter the Date: **011516**, press **Tab**

For Select Existing Payments, click the check box next to RECEIVED FROM

- This will insert check marks and select all of the transactions shown.

Click the drop-down list for PAYMENT METHOD for each payment, and click **Check**

- Normally, QuickBooks Online completes the PAYMENT METHOD automatically.
- Note that there are sections to Add New Deposits and to get Cash back.

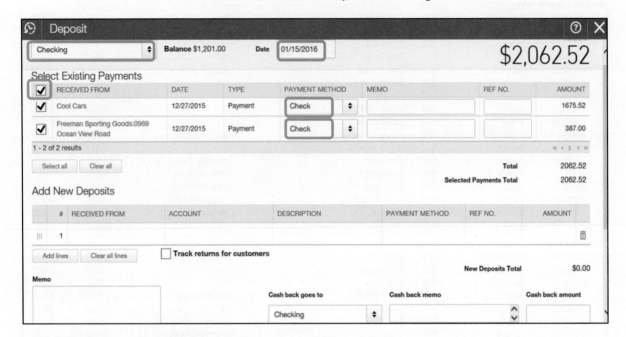

Click **Save and close** as previously instructed

Close the Test Drive Company

## BANK DEPOSIT—DO

As you practiced in the drill, when a bank deposit is recorded, the funds are transferred from Undeposited Funds to the account selected when preparing the deposit (usually Checking). This is important because, until the money is deposited, it does not show as being available for use. The bank deposit should be recorded at the time the actual deposit is made at the bank.

## _DO_

Open and use **Your Name's Beach Barkers** and record a Bank Deposit

With the Your Name's Beach Barkers open, click the **Plus** icon

In the Other column, click **Bank Deposit**

- The account should be Checking if not, select it from the drop-down list.

Enter the Date: **011516**, press **Tab**

For Select Existing Payments, click the check box next to RECEIVED FROM

- This will insert check marks and select all of the transactions shown.

Click **Print** at the bottom of the Deposit screen

Click **Print deposit summary only**

- The Deposit Summary may be saved as a pdf file and/or printed. It cannot be exported.
- Note the dates displayed on the preview. On the left side of the report, you will see "Summary of Deposits to Checking on 01/15/2016." On the right side of the report, you

will see the current date. This is an instance where QuickBooks Online inserts the
current date and you cannot remove it.

- If you save the Deposit Summary, name it **28-Your Name Bank Deposit Ch. 3**.

28

## Deposit Summary

Summary of Deposits to Checking on 01/15/2016      | Current Date |

| CHECK NO. | PMT METHOD | RECEIVED FROM | MEMO | AMOUNT |
|---|---|---|---|---|
| 2643 | Check | Evans, Keith | | 650.00 |
| | Cash | Cash Customer | | 15.00 |
| 9534 | Check | Anderson, Dori | | 90.00 |
| 4570 | Check | Cash Customer | | 55.00 |
| | Cash | Gucci, Gloria | | 55.00 |
| 6489 | Check | Bailey, Larry | | 55.00 |
| 4465 | Check | Clark, Bunni | | 4125.00 |
| 1972 | Check | Gilbert, Oscar | Partial Payment | 300.00 |
| 7531 | Check | Rhodes, Ashley | | 195.00 |
| 6431 | Check | Montez, Annabelle | Partial Payment | 100.00 |
| | | | DEPOSIT SUBTOTAL | 5640.00 |
| | | | LESS CASH BACK | |
| | | | DEPOSIT TOTAL | 5640.00 |

Click **Save and close** as previously instructed
Continue to use Your Name's Beach Barkers in the next section

## ADDITIONAL TRANSACTIONS—DO

Close to the end of each chapter, there will be a section of additional transactions that will be similar
to the ones you completed during the chapter. These transactions will be listed in a Memo. You
must enter them without any specific instructions. If you have questions about how to enter
transactions, you may refer back to material presented earlier in the chapter.

## *DO*

Continue to use **Your Name's Beach Barkers** and enter the following transactions in the
Memo boxes

Print, save, and submit as you have been requested by your instructor.
- Use the same naming structure as previously instructed: Document number, your name,
  business form and number, customer name. For example, 29-Your Name Invoice 11111
  John Doe
- If you correct and print a business document, add Corrected at the end of the document
  name.
Any cash or checks received should be placed into Undeposited Funds until the bank
  deposit is made

**MEMO**
**DATE:** January 15, 2016

Note: Use **Undeposited Funds** for the "Deposit to" account.

| |
|---|
| A new customer, Ray Childers, (Email: RC@Venice.com, Phone: 310-555-8864, Address: 35 Market Street, Venice, CA 90291, Payment method: Check, Terms: Net 30) purchased and paid for 1 Ten One-Hour Sessions of Training, 3 days of Boarding, 1 Bath, and 1 Nails for his dog, Rico, Check 3247. |
| Matthew Summer paid his account in full using Check 2756 for $240. |
| Rename the products/service item Grooming to Dental Care; Description: Dental Care, Sales price/Rate: $50, Income account: Services:Grooming. |
| Brad Quint brought his dog, Clementine, in for 5 days of Boarding, 1 Bath, 1 Nails, 4 Brushing, and 1 Dental Care. |
| Received a partial payment from Viv Norbert for Invoice 1006, Check 7383 for $1,500. |
| Create a new Account: Type: Income, Detail type: Service/Fee Income, Name: Transportation, Subaccount of: Services. |
| Received payments on account from Taylor Williams, Check 1679; Colleen Stark, Check 2811; and Katie Wilson, Check 3145. All were paid in full. |
| Keith Evans needs to have his dog, Boomer, walked for an hour, brushed, poop scoop, and taken to the vet for shots. Use the appropriate products/services. All quantities are 1 except 3 Transportation to the vet. |

Continue recording, saving, and printing transactions.

**MEMO**
**DATE:** January 17, 2016

| |
|---|
| Viv Norbert brought in her dog, Barney, to have 1 Dental Care, 1 Bath, 1 Nails, and paid Cash. |
| Rename Brushing to Coat Brushing. |
| Gloria Gucci signed up Mishka for 5 days of Day Camp and 5 Coat Brushing. Since she was having car problems, she had you pick up and return Mishka each day. Bill for 10 hours of Transportation. |
| Keith Evans did not need 1 hour of transportation used on January 15, 2016. Prepare the appropriate business form. |
| Cash Customer brought in her dog for 1 day Boarding, 1 Dental Care, 1 Bath, and 1 Nails, Check 2050. |
| Make the Bank Deposit. |
| Gloria Gucci was charged for 5 days of Boarding, change to 5 days of Day Camp. |

Continue to use Your Name's Beach Barkers

## VIEW SALES—DO

In addition to a variety of reports for sales, QuickBooks Online allows you to view all of your sales transactions. You may view all of the transactions or you may specify a specific date range. Information is shown for the Transaction Date, Type, No., Customer, Due Date, Balance, Total, Status, and Actions available to be performed.

*DO*

 Continue to use **Your Name's Beach Barkers** to view all sales transactions

Click **Transactions** on the Navigation Bar
- You will notice that there are selections for Banking, Sales, Expenses, and Chart of Accounts.

Click **Sales**
- All sales transactions are shown for the Last 365 days from the most recent date to the oldest date.

To specify the date range, click the **Filter** button
Enter the From date **12/31/15** and To date **01/17/16**
Click **Apply**

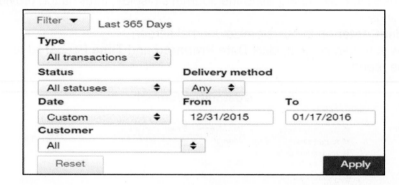

Click the Printer icon to print, the Export icon to export to Excel, or the Settings icon to customize the fields displayed

*38*   Print in Landscape orientation, export to Excel, and/or submit as previously instructed
- If you save the report, name it **38-Your Name Sales Transaction List Ch. 3**.

Continue to use Your Name's Beach Barkers to complete reports

## JOURNAL—DO

Even though QuickBooks Online displays registers and reports in a manner that focuses on the transaction—for example, entering a sale on account via an invoice—it still keeps a Journal. The Journal records each transaction and lists the accounts and the amounts for debit and credit entries. In many instances, going through the Journal entries will help you find errors in your transactions. Always check the transaction dates, the account names, and the items listed in the Memo column. If a transaction does not appear in the Journal, it may be due to using an incorrect date or forgetting to enter it. Remember, only the transactions entered within the report dates will be displayed.

In your concepts course, you may have learned that the General Journal was where all entries were recorded in debit/credit format. In QuickBooks Online, you do record some non-recurring debit/credit transactions as a Journal Entry and then display all debit/credit entries no matter where the transactions were recorded in the Journal Report.

Continue to use **Your Name's Beach Barkers** and prepare a Journal Report

Open **Reports** as previously instructed
Use the category **Accountant Reports**
Click **Journal**
The dates are from **01/01/16** to **Current Date**

- Previously prepared reports, have the Date and Time Prepared shown as a footer. Your instructor may wish to have this information to determine when you completed your work. If your instructor does not want this in your report, you may customize the footer and remove it.

Click the **Customize** button at the top of the report

- This is used to make changes to the Journal's display, information provided, among other things.

Click **Header/Footer** on the Customize Journal screen
In the Show in footer: section, click **Date Prepared** and **Time Prepared** to remove them from the report

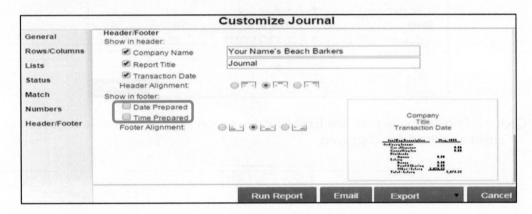

Click the **Run Report** button

- Make sure the dates are still From: 01/01/16 and To: Current Date.
- Just in case the date was not changed for the Payment transactions generated by QuickBooks Online for Credit Memos, the current date is used.
- Also, if there are any transactions missing due to date errors, they should show when the current date is the end date of the report.

Scroll through the report to view the transactions

- Many of the columns do not display in full or may make the report print on two-pages wide. Columns may need to be resized in order to adjust the column width.

Resize the width of the MEMO/DESCRIPTION column so there is not as much width to that column
Position the cursor on the sizing arrow ⬇ between MEMO/DESCRIPTION and ACCOUNT

- The cursor turns into a plus with arrows pointing left and right.

Hold down the primary (left) mouse button

Drag the cursor from the sizing arrow between MEMO/DESCRIPTION and ACCOUNT to the <u>left</u> until you have reduced the amount of space in MEMO/DESCRIPTION
- You will see a dotted vertical line while you are dragging the mouse and holding down the primary mouse button.
- You may make columns larger by pointing to the sizing arrow and dragging to the <u>right</u>.
- QuickBooks Online will not let you make the columns too small. If you try to make the column too small, QuickBooks Online will not let you resize it.

Scroll through the Journal and view all of the transactions shown in Debit/Credit format
Verify your total

| TOTAL | $40,205.00 | $40,205.00 |
|---|---|---|

If the totals do not match, make corrections. Double-check dates, amounts, accounts, and items used in the transactions
When the totals are correct, print, export, and/or submit as previously instructed
- If you print, use Landscape for the Layout.
- Name the report **39-Your Name Journal Ch. 3**.

Do <u>not</u> close Your Name's Beach Barkers

## TRIAL BALANCE—DO

When all sales transactions have been entered, it is important to prepare and print the Trial Balance and verify that the total debits equal the total credits.

<u>*DO*</u>

Continue to use **Your Name's Beach Barkers** and prepare a Trial Balance

Return to Reports
Click **Trial Balance** in the Accountant Reports Category
Dates From: **010116** To: **011716**
Click the **Customize Report** button and change **Header/Footer** so **Date Prepared**, **Time Prepared**, and **Report Basis** do not print
Print, export, and/or submit as previously instructed
- If you print, use Portrait for the Layout.
- Name the report **40-Your Name Trial Balance Ch. 3**.

## Your Name's Beach Barkers
### TRIAL BALANCE
#### As of January 17, 2016

| | DEBIT | CREDIT |
|---|---|---|
| Checking | 63,580.00 | |
| Accounts Receivable (A/R) | 14,930.00 | |
| Inventory Asset | 29,012.50 | |
| Prepaid Insurance | 1,200.00 | |
| Supplies:Cleaning Supplies | 750.00 | |
| Supplies:Kennel Supplies | 1,895.00 | |
| Supplies:Office Supplies | 350.00 | |
| Supplies:Sales Supplies | 500.00 | |
| Undeposited Funds | 0.00 | |
| Equipment:Depreciation | | 800.00 |
| Equipment:Original cost | 8,000.00 | |
| Furniture & Fixtures:Depreciation | | 1,500.00 |
| Furniture & Fixtures:Original cost | 15,000.00 | |
| Kennel Equipment:Depreciation | | 2,030.00 |
| Kennel Equipment:Original cost | 20,300.00 | |
| Vehicles:Depreciation | | 3,200.00 |
| Vehicles:Original cost | 32,000.00 | |
| Accounts Payable (A/P) | | 5,300.00 |
| Loans Payable:Equipment Loan | | 2,000.00 |
| Loans Payable:Furniture & Fixtures Loan | | 2,500.00 |
| Retained Earnings | | 22,200.00 |
| Your Name, Capital | | 142,362.50 |
| Services:Boarding | | 770.00 |
| Services:Day Camp | | 420.00 |
| Services:Grooming | | 885.00 |
| Services:House Calls | | 225.00 |
| Services:Training | | 3,025.00 |
| Services:Transportation | | 300.00 |
| TOTAL | $187,517.50 | $187,517.50 |

Close Your Name's Beach Barkers and QuickBooks Online

## SUMMARY

In this chapter, recording cash and credit sales was practiced using the Test Drive Company and then entered in Your Name's Beach Barkers using sales receipts and invoices. Credit memos and refund receipts were issued. Customer accounts were added and revised. Invoices and sales receipts were edited, deleted, and voided. Cash payments were received and bank deposits were made. All the transactions entered reinforced the QuickBooks Online concept of using the business form to record transactions rather than enter information in journals. However, QuickBooks does not disregard traditional accounting methods. Instead, it performs this function in the background. The Journal was accessed and printed. The fact that the Customers List functions as the Accounts Receivable Ledger and that the Chart of Accounts is the General Ledger in QuickBooks Online was pointed out. The importance of reports for information and decision-making was illustrated. Exploration of the various sales and accounts receivable reports allowed information to be viewed from a sales standpoint and from an accounts receivable perspective. Sales reports emphasized both cash and credit sales according to the product/service generating the revenue. Accounts Receivable reports focused on amounts owed by credit customers. The traditional trial balance emphasizing the equality of debits and credits was prepared.

# END-OF-CHAPTER QUESTIONS

## TRUE/FALSE

ANSWER THE FOLLOWING QUESTIONS IN THE SPACE PROVIDED BEFORE THE QUESTION NUMBER.

_____ 1. An invoice is prepared to record a sale on account.

_____ 2. Using an incorrect date will not affect the results of reports.

_____ 3. The Customers List functions as the General Ledger in QuickBooks Online.

_____ 4. An invoice may be exported to Excel.

_____ 5. A new product/service item cannot be added when creating a sales receipt.

_____ 6. A Customer Balance Summary Report shows you the balances for all customers who owe you money.

_____ 7. You may record the sale of more than one item on both invoices and sales receipts.

_____ 8. You can add a new customer on the fly.

_____ 9. An invoice may not be deleted.

_____ 10. Payment receipts are not printed in QuickBooks Online.

## MULTIPLE CHOICE

WRITE THE LETTER OF THE CORRECT ANSWER IN THE SPACE PROVIDED BEFORE THE QUESTION NUMBER.

_____ 1. Reports may be ___.
A. Printed
B. Exported to Excel
C. Emailed
D. All of the above

_____ 2. Receive Payments is used to record a(n) ___.
A. Payment for an Invoice
B. Cash Sale
C. Refund
D. Bank Deposit

_____ 3. The Sales by Customer Detail Report shows information about ___ for each customer.
A. Credit Sales
B. Cash Sales
C. Sales on Account
D. All of the above

_____ 4. A Credit Memo is prepared to record a reduction to a transaction recorded on a(n) ___.
    A. Sales Receipt
    B. Invoice
    C. Deposit Slip
    D. Payment Receipt

_____ 5. When payment is made at the time of purchase, the transaction is recorded on a(n) ___.
    A. Invoice
    B. Payment Receipt
    C. Sales Receipt
    D. Refund Receipt

_____ 6. When a payment is made for a sale on account, it may be a ___ payment.
    A. Full
    B. Partial
    C. Both A and B
    D. Pay in advance

_____ 7. QuickBooks Online does not print ___.
    A. Invoices
    B. Sales Receipts
    C. Credit Memo and/or Refund Receipts
    D. Receive Payments

_____ 8. To view all entries recorded in Debit/Credit format, you prepare a ___.
    A. Journal
    B. Trial Balance
    C. Customer Balance Summary
    D. Transaction List Report

_____ 9. The Customers List functions as the ___.
    A. General Ledger
    B. Accounts Receivable Ledger
    C. Income Account
    D. Primary Account

_____ 10. When receiving a partial payment for an invoice, QuickBooks selects the ___ invoice.
    A. Most recent
    B. Largest balance
    C. Oldest
    D. None of the above

## FILL-IN

IN THE SPACE PROVIDED, WRITE THE ANSWER THAT MOST APPROPRIATELY COMPLETES THE SENTENCE.

1. To refund money to a customer, you prepare a _____. To decrease an amount owed for an invoice, you prepare a _____.

2. The_____ Report prints the current date that cannot be changed at the top of the report.

3. The report that shows all of the entries made into each account in the Chart of Accounts is _____ .

4. Cash and checks received from customers are entered into the _____ account until the bank deposit is made.

5. The **Plus** icon is located on the _____ Bar.

## COMPUTER ASSIGNMENT

REFER TO PRINTOUTS OR USE QUICKBOOKS ONLINE AND YOUR NAME'S BEACH BARKERS TO LOOK UP OR ENTER INFORMATION, AND THEN WRITE THE ANSWERS TO THE FOLLOWING EXERCISES IN THE SPACE PROVIDED

1. How much was the bank deposit on January 17, 2016? _____

2. What business document did you complete to record Keith Evans' purchase of 1 hour Dog Walking, 1 Brushing, 1 Poop Scoop, and 3 hours Transportation on January 15, 2016? _____

3. Prepare a Sales by Product/Service Summary report for January 1-17, 2016. Which sales item had the largest quantity and which item generated the largest amount of Revenue? _____ _____

4. How much does Keith Evans owe as of January 17, 2016? _____

5. What business form did you use to record the reduction of one day of Day Camp for Ashley Rhodes? _____

6. What account was used for Receive Payments from Larry Bailey? _____

7. Prepare a Customer Balance Summary report as of January 17, 2016. Which customer(s) has/have the largest balance? _____ _____

8. How much is the largest customer balance? _____

9. How much does Gloria Gucci owe on her account on January 18, 2016? _____

10. Go to Reports, Review Sales, and prepare a Sales by Customer Summary report for January 1-17, 2016. What is the total? _____

# CHAPTER 3 CHECKLIST

The checklist below shows all of the business forms printed during training. Check each one that you printed, exported, and/or submitted.

| | |
|---|---|
| _____ 1-Invoice 1015 Gloria Gucci | _____ 21-Sales Receipt 1029 Gloria Gucci |
| _____ 2-Invoice 2016 Pamela Vines | _____ 22-Sales by Customer Detail Ch. 3 |
| _____ 3-Invoice 1017 Eric Phillips | _____ 23-Sales Receipt 1029 Gloria Gucci Corrected |
| _____ 4-Invoice 1018 Bunni Clark | _____ 24-Sales by Product/Service Summary Ch. 3 |
| _____ 5-Invoice 1019 Ashley Rhodes | _____ 25-Credit Memo 1030 Ashley Rhodes |
| _____ 6-Invoice 1020 Matthew Summer | _____ 26-Check 1 Gloria Gucci |
| _____ 7-Invoice 1021 Larry Bailey | _____ 27-Transaction Detail by Account Ch. 3 |
| _____ 8-Invoice 1022 Oscar Gilbert | _____ 28-Bank Deposit |
| _____ 9-Invoice 1023 Annabelle Montez | _____ 29-Sales Receipt 1032 Ray Childers |
| _____ 10-Invoice 1024 Carol Russell | _____ 30-Invoice 1033 Brad Quint |
| _____ 11-Customer Balance Summary Ch. 3 | _____ 31-Invoice 1034 Keith Evans |
| _____ 12-Invoice 1023 Annabelle Montez Corrected | _____ 32-Sales Receipt 1035 Viv Norbert |
| _____ 13-Invoice 1024 Carol Russell Corrected | _____ 33-Invoice 1036 Gloria Gucci |
| _____ 14-Customer Balance Detail Ch. 3 | _____ 34-Credit Memo 1037 Keith Evans |
| _____ 15-Invoice 1017 Eric Phillips | _____ 35-Sales Receipt 1038 Cash Customer |
| _____ 16-Transaction List by Customer Ch. 3 | _____ 36-Bank Deposit |
| _____ 17-Sales Receipt 1025 Keith Evans | _____ 37-Invoice 1036 Gloria Gucci Corrected |
| _____ 18-Sales Receipt 1026 Cash Customer | _____ 38-Sales Transaction List Ch. 3 |
| _____ 19-Sales Receipt 1027 Dori Anderson | _____ 39-Journal Ch. 3 |
| _____ 20-Sales Receipt 1028 Cash Customer | _____ 40-Trial Balance Ch. 3 |

# PAYABLES AND PURCHASES

## LEARNING OBJECTIVES

At the completion of this chapter you will be able to:

1. Understand the concepts for computerized accounting for payables.
2. Enter, edit, correct, delete, and pay bills.
3. Add new vendors and new accounts.
4. View and access transactions in the Vendor's Register.
5. Understand when to record and pay bills, write checks, and enter expense transactions.
6. Understand the concept of Prepaid Expenses.
7. Print checks individually or as a batch.
8. Enter vendor credits.
9. Void and delete checks.
10. View Transaction Audit History.
11. Pay for expenses using petty cash.
12. Purchase an asset with a company check.
13. View all Expense Transactions.
14. Display, print, export, and/or submit reports, including Transaction List by Vendor, Purchases by Vendor Detail, Check Detail, Unpaid Bills, and Vendor Balance Summary.
15. Use a date range to control the data displayed in a report.

## ACCOUNTING FOR PAYABLES AND PURCHASES

At this point in your training, most of the accounting for purchases and payables is simply entering and paying bills or writing checks for expenses incurred in the operation of the business. Purchases are for things used in the operation of the business. Some transactions will be in the form of cash purchases, and others will be purchases on account. Essentially, in QuickBooks Online if you purchase something and pay for it later, you record a Bill and pay for it through Pay Bills—a purchase/payment on account. If you receive a bill in the mail, a water bill for example, and pay for it without recording a bill, you write a check. If you purchase something and pay for it at the time of purchase using cash, credit card, or handwritten check, you record an Expense and your method of payment.

Bills can be paid when they are received or when they are due. Rather than use cumbersome journals, QuickBooks Online continues to focus on recording transactions based on the business document; therefore, you use the Bill and Pay Bills features of the program to record the receipt and payment of bills. QuickBooks Online keeps track of bill due dates and shows the number of Overdue bills on the Vendors Dashboard. Payments can be made by recording payments in the Pay Bills window. If you have a bill, such as rent, that is paid for by a check and not entered as a bill, you use Write Checks. A small cash purchase can be recorded by recording an expense and using Petty Cash for the payment. Even though QuickBooks Online focuses on recording transactions on the business forms used, all transactions are recorded behind the scenes in the Journal.

QuickBooks Online uses a Vendor List for all vendors with which the company has an account. QuickBooks Online does not refer to the Vendor List as the Accounts Payable Ledger; yet, that is exactly what it is. The total of the Vendor List/Accounts Payable Ledger will match the total of the Accounts Payable account in the Chart of Accounts/General Ledger.

As in Chapter 3, corrections can be made directly on the business form, in the Vendor's Register, or within the account. New accounts and vendors may be added on the fly as transactions are entered. Reports illustrating vendor balances, unpaid bills, purchases and vendor details, transaction history, check detail, and accounts payable registers may be viewed, printed, and exported.

## TRAINING TUTORIAL

Now that the fictional company—Your Name's Beach Barkers—has been used to record sales transactions, this chapter focuses on recording purchases and payments, writing checks, and using Petty Cash. In addition to recording transactions, you will also prepare several reports. Use of Your Name's Beach Barkers will continue throughout the text as you explore the different facets and capabilities of QuickBooks Online. Because you can only create and use one company in the Educational Trial Version of QuickBooks Online, new concepts and procedures will be practiced in the Test Drive Company, and then entered into Your Name's Beach Barkers just as you did in Chapters 2 and 3.

## TRAINING PROCEDURES

Follow the same training procedures that were presented in Chapters 2 and 3. Remember that the Test Drive Company will not save your work so try to complete related sections before ending your work session. Mark your place in the textbook so you know where you left off in your training. Make sure you check your work and proofread carefully. Double-check the amounts of money, accounts, product/services items, and dates used.

Print, export, and submit work as directed in the chapter and by your instructor. When you prepare a business document such as a check, you may print or save the document. You may not print bills or expense entries. If you prepare a report, you may print the document, export it to Excel, and/or submit it.

Just as you did in Chapter 3, you will enter additional transactions near the end of the chapter. These transactions are similar to the ones you entered in the Test Drive Company and in Your Name's Beach Barkers so no step-by-step instructions will be given. If you need to refer back to the chapter materials to make the entries, you should feel free to do so. If you can enter them without looking back, you have learned how to do something on your own in QuickBooks Online.

## DATES

Remember that the year used for the screen shots is 2016. Continue to use the same year that you used in Chapters 2 and 3. When QuickBooks Online inserts the current date into a transaction, be aware of this and be sure to use the date indicated in the text. When using the Test Drive Company, remember that it is programmed to change dates automatically so the dates of the screen shots in the text will not match the ones on your screen.

## IMPORTANT NOTE

QuickBooks Online is constantly evolving and new features, apps, and procedures change frequently. Everything in the text is correct at the time of this writing; however, by the time of publication some changes to the program may occur. Whenever possible, changes will be incorporated into the text but do note that some of the updates will not be able to be included until the next edition of the book.

## BILLS, CHECKS, EXPENSES

QuickBooks Online has three ways to record purchases and expenses: Bills, Checks, and Expenses. During this chapter, all three ways will be explored.

### Bills and Bill Payments

If you receive a Bill for an expense or an asset that is a prepaid expense--think office supplies—and plan to pay it at a later time, you record the transaction as a Bill. When you pay for the Bill, you use Pay Bills. Using Pay Bills matches the Bill and the Bill Payment and QuickBooks Online automatically writes the Check. You may also use a credit card to pay a bill. (This will be discussed in a later chapter.)

### Checks

If you buy something or pay for an expense without recording it as a bill, you prepare a Check in QuickBooks Online.

### Expenses

If you buy something or pay for an expense without recording a bill or writing a check in QuickBooks Online, you record an Expense. When you record Expenses, payment would be made using Petty Cash or a credit card. If you wrote the check by hand and not in QuickBooks Online, you would also record the payment in Expenses.

## BEGIN TRAINING

In this chapter, you will be entering bills incurred by the company in the operation of the business. You will also be recording the payment of bills, purchases using checks, and expenses using petty cash.

The Vendors List keeps information regarding the vendors with whom you do business; and, in addition to being a list, the Vendors List functions as the Accounts Payable Subsidiary Ledger. Even though QuickBooks does not use this term, the use of the Vendors List for the Accounts Payable Subsidiary Ledger conforms to GAAP (Generally Accepted Accounting Principles). A transaction entry for an individual vendor is posted to the vendor's account in the Vendors List just as it would be posted to the vendor's individual account in an Accounts Payable Subsidiary Ledger.

The balance of the Vendors List will be equal to the balance of the Accounts Payable account in the Chart of Accounts. The Chart of Accounts also functions as the General Ledger when using GAAP standards.

As in the previous chapters, all transactions are listed in memos. The transaction date will be the same as the memo date unless specified otherwise within the transaction. Vendor names, when necessary, will be given in the transaction. Unless other terms are provided, the terms are Net 30.

Purchases and payables are usually for items that are used in the operation of the business. The Vendors List includes the vendor names and other related information. The expense accounts in the Chart of Accounts are most frequently the ones selected. In the course of the chapter, the creation and use of Petty Cash will be included as will the purchase of an asset by writing a check.

## ENTER, EDIT, AND VIEW BILLS—DRILL

QuickBooks provides accounts payable tracking. Entering bills as soon as they are received is an efficient way to record your liabilities. On the Bill screen, you will enter the vendor, vendor's address, terms, bill date, due date, bill number, account details, and/or item details. The Account details section is used when recording a bill for an expense; while, the Item details section is used when purchasing Inventory Items. When you record a bill, it is a purchase on account. When you enter the bill, QuickBooks Online will enter a Debit to the Expense Account and a Credit to Accounts Payable in the Journal.

> **MEMO**
> **DATE:** January 18, 2016
>
> Record the bill from Lee Advertising for $150.00. Memo: Monthly Advertising. Terms Net 30.

### *DRILL*

 Open the **Test Drive Company** as previously instructed and practice entering bills

### Enter Bill

 Practice recording Bills in the **Test Drive Company**

On the Top-Navigation Bar, click the **Plus** icon
On the Create screen, click **Bill** in the Vendors Column

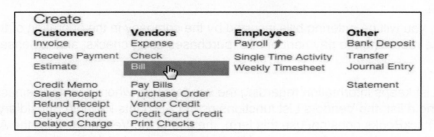

- A bill is used to record a purchase on account and is basically the company's charge account with a vendor's company. A transaction recorded on a bill means that you will pay for the purchase at a later time.

Click the drop-down list arrow for Choose a Vendor
Click **Lee Advertising**

- If the text box for Terms is blank, click the drop-down list arrow, click **Net 30**.

Tab to Bill date, enter **011816**, press **Tab**

- If there are no lines for entry under "Account details" and you see ▶ Account details click it to Expand the section.

Click in Line 1 in the ACCOUNT text box, click the drop-down list arrow, click **Advertising**
Tab to AMOUNT, enter **150**, press **Tab**
Click in "Memo" text box, enter **Monthly Advertising** to identify the reason for the transaction

- As you gain more experience with the layout of the forms used in QuickBooks Online, you will not see as many details highlighted in quotation marks.
- When you print the Journal, Monthly Advertising will show in the MEMO/DESCRIPTION column.

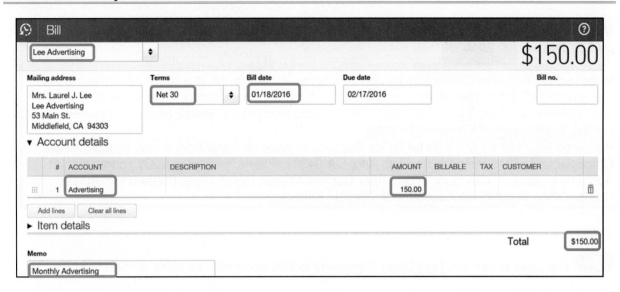

> Click **Save and close**
> * Remember, if you see Save and new or Save and send, click the drop-down list arrow and then click Save and close.
>
> Continue using the Test Drive Company

## Edit and Correct Errors

If an error is discovered for a bill, you may return to the bill and correct it.

 Practice correcting a Bill in the **Test Drive Company**

> Forgot to record 452 for the Bill no.
> Click **Vendors** on the Navigation Bar
> Click **Lee Advertising**
> Click **Bill** in the Transaction List for Lee Advertising
> Enter the Bill no. **452**

> Click **Save and new**
> Do <u>not</u> close the Test Drive Company

## ENTER BILLS, ADD ACCOUNT, AND ADD NEW VENDOR—DRILL

As with invoices, bills with multiple items may be prepared, vendors may be added on the fly, and new accounts may be added while entering a bill.

MEMO
**DATE:** January 18, 2016

Received Bill 890 from Computers by Jenni for a one-month rental of a computer while ours is being repaired, $150. The bill also includes $250 for Computer Repairs. Terms Net 30. Add a new expense account: Type: Expenses, Detail Type: Equipment Rental, Name: Computer Rental, Subaccount of Equipment Rental.

Received Bill 7182 for $349.00 for Office Supplies to have on hand from a new vendor, Jones Office Supplies (275 Main Street, Palo Alto, CA 94303, Phone: 650-555-1232, Terms: Net 30. Add a new account: Category Type: Other Current Assets, Detail Type: Prepaid Expenses, Name: Office Supplies, Subaccount of: Prepaid Expenses.

*DRILL*

 Continue to use the **Test Drive Company** to add accounts, vendors, and record bills

Create Multiple Item Bill and Add New Account

When there is more than one charge on a bill, you simply continue using the next line in Accounts.

 Use the **Test Drive Company** to record the bills in the Memo

> With a new **Bill** showing on the screen, click the drop-down list arrow for Vendor
> Click **Computers by Jenni**
> Terms: **Net 30**
> Bill date: **01/18/16**
> Bill no.: **890**
> For Line 1: click in the ACCOUNT text box, click the drop-down list arrow
> Click **+Add new**
> Create a new Account:
> Category Type: **Expenses**
> Detail Type: **Equipment Rental**
> Name: **Computer Rental**
> Subaccount of: **Equipment Rental**
> Click **Save and Close**

Tab to AMOUNT and enter **150**
For Line 2: click in the ACCOUNT text box, click the drop-down list arrow
Click the Expense account **Maintenance and Repair: Computer Repairs**
- Do not click the Maintenance and Repair that is a subaccount of Job Expenses and Cost of Labor.

Tab to AMOUNT and enter **250**
Enter the Memo: **One-Month Computer Rental and Computer Repairs**

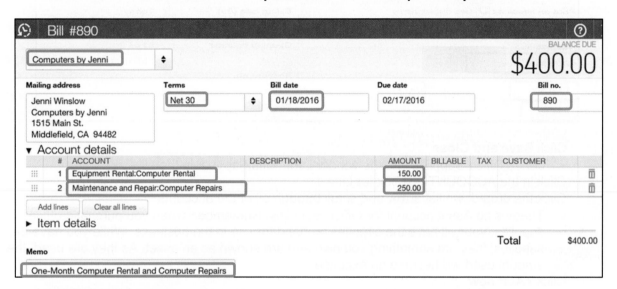

Click **Save and new**
- Remember, if Save and new isn't shown, click the drop-down list arrow next to Save and close or Save and send.

Do <u>not</u> close the Test Drive Company

## Purchase Prepaid Expenses, Add New Vendor and New Account

The accrual method of accounting matches the expenses of a period against the revenue of the period. Frequently, when in training, there may be difficulty in determining whether something is recorded as an expense or as an asset (a prepaid expense). When you buy or pay for something to have on hand and it will eventually be used up, it is recorded as an asset. After it is used, an adjusting entry is made to transfer the amount to an expense account. For example, when you purchase office supplies to have on hand, it is called a prepaid expense and is recorded in the asset account Office Supplies. At the end of the period, an adjusting entry is made to transfer the amount of office supplies used to the expense account Supplies: Office Supplies Expense.

 Continue using the **Test Drive Company** to record the bill from a new vendor, Jones Office Supplies

Click in the Choose a Vendor text box, click the drop-down list arrow, and click **+Add new**
Enter the name **Jones Office Supplies**
Click **+Details**
Delete **Jones** from "First name," delete **Office** from "Middle name," and delete **Supplies** from "Last name"
Enter **Jones Office Supplies** in "Company"
Complete the Vendor information using the information in the Memo

Click **Save and Close**

- Jones Office Supplies and the vendor information appear in the bill.

Click in the ACCOUNT text box for Line 1

Click the drop-down list arrow and scroll through all of the accounts

- There is no Asset account for Office Supplies. Remember, when you purchase office supplies, you will have the supplies on hand for use in the business. While you have the supplies, they are something you own and are shown as an asset. As they are used, the amount used will become an expense.

Click **+Add new**

Use the information in the Memo to create the new account

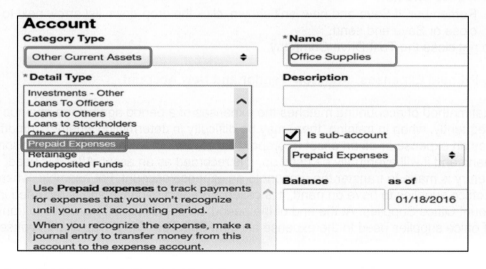

Refer to the Memo and complete the bill

- The transaction is self-explanatory so there is no need to enter a transaction memo.

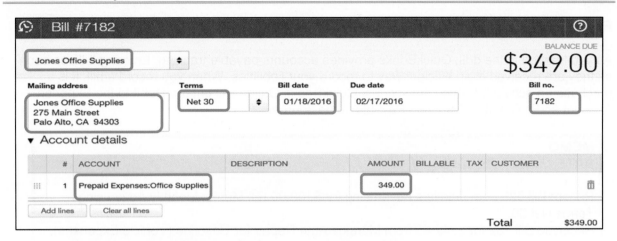

Click **Save and close** or the drop-down list arrow and then the command
Do <u>not</u> close the Test Drive Company, continue to the next section

## TRANSACTIONS LIST BY VENDOR REPORT—DRILL

To obtain information regarding transactions by vendor, you prepare a Transaction List by Vendor Report. This allows you to view the vendors with recorded transactions. The type of transaction is identified; for example, the word *Bill* appears when you have entered the transaction as a bill. The transaction date, any invoice numbers or memos entered when recording the transaction, the accounts used, and the transaction amounts appear in the report.

## *DRILL*

 Continue to use the **Test Drive Company** to prepare the Transaction List by Vendor

As you have done for previous reports, turn **OFF** Redesigned Reports in QuickBooks Labs
Click the **Gear** icon, click **QuickBooks Labs**
Scroll to Redesigned Reports, click **ON** to toggle to **OFF**, click **Done**
Click **Reports** on the Navigation Bar
Select **All Reports**, and then select **Review Expenses and Purchases**
Scroll through the list of reports available in this category, click **Transaction List by Vendor**
Enter the dates From: **01/01/2016** and To: **01/18/16**, click **Run Report**
Scroll through the report to see all of the Vendor Transactions for January 1-18
   • The partial report shown below only shows the bills you entered.

### Craig's Design and Landscaping Services
**TRANSACTION LIST BY VENDOR**
January 1-28, 2016

| DATE | TRANSACTION TYPE | NUM | POSTING | MEMO/DESCRIPTION | ACCOUNT | AMOUNT |
|------|------------------|-----|---------|------------------|---------|--------|
| **Computers by Jenni** | | | | | | |
| 01/18/2016 | Bill | 890 | Yes | One-Month Computer Rental and Computer Repairs | Accounts Payable (A/P) | 400.00 |
| **Jones Office Supplies** | | | | | | |
| 01/18/2016 | Bill | 7281 | Yes | | Accounts Payable (A/P) | 349.00 |
| **Lee Advertising** | | | | | | |
| 01/18/2016 | Bill | 452 | Yes | Monthly Advertising | Accounts Payable (A/P) | 150.00 |

Close the Test Drive Company

## ENTER, EDIT, AND VIEW BILLS—DO

As you learned in the drill, QuickBooks provides accounts payable tracking. Entering bills as soon as they are received is an efficient way to record your liabilities. When you record a bill, it is a purchase on account. Behind the scenes, QuickBooks Online will enter a Debit to the Expense Account and a Credit to Accounts Payable in the Journal.

> ### MEMO
> **DATE:** January 18, 2016
>
> Record Bill 525 from Garcia's Advertising for $100.00 Bill Memo: Monthly Advertising. Terms Net 30.
>
> Received Bill 762 for $342.45 from Morales Auto Repair for Gasoline (Vehicle Expenses), $79.95. The bill also includes Belts and Timing Repair for $262.50. (Add a new Expense Account: Vehicle Repair, Detail Type: Repair & Maintenance, Subaccount of Repair & Maintenance). Bill Memo: Gasoline and Repair.
>
> Received Bill 890 for $275 from a new vendor, Computer Town (2239 Abbott-Kinney Drive, Venice, CA 90291, Email: ComputerTown@data.com, Phone: 310-555-8816, Fax: 310-555-6188, Terms: Net 30) for a one-month rental of a computer (Equipment Rental) while ours is being repaired, $75. The bill also includes $200 for Computer Repairs. Bill Memo: One-Month Computer Rental and Computer Repair. Add a new expense account: Type: Expenses, Detail Type: Repair & Maintenance, Name: Computer Repair, Subaccount of Repair & Maintenance.
>
> Record Bill 4953 from Quality Insurance for an additional $600 of Insurance. Terms Net 30. Bill Memo: Additional Insurance.
>
> Received Bill 286 for $425.23 for Office Supplies to have on hand—a prepaid expense—from a new vendor, Super Office (2175 Main Street, Santa Monica, CA 90405, Email: SuperOffice@beach.com, Phone: 310-555-3275, Fax: 310-555-5723, Web site: www.SuperOffice.com, Terms: Net 30, no Bill Memo necessary.

*DO*

Open **Your Name's Beach Barkers** as previously instructed and enter the bills in the Memo

*Enter Bill*

When entering the following transactions, the Terms will be Net 30. Because the terms were included for each vendor's record, Net 30 should appear automatically in your bills.

Enter a Bill in **Your Name's Beach Barkers**

Click the **Plus** icon

On the Create screen, click **Bill** in the Vendors Column

- A bill is used to record a purchase on account and is basically the company's charge account with a vendor's company. A transaction recorded on a bill means that you will pay for the purchase at a later time.

Click the drop-down list arrow for Vendor

Click **Garcia's Advertising**

Tab to Bill date, enter **011816**, press **Tab**

Enter the Bill no. **525**

Click in Line 1 in the ACCOUNT text box, click the drop-down list arrow, click **Advertising**

Tab to AMOUNT, ENTER **100**, press **Tab**

Tab to or click in the Memo text box and enter **Monthly Advertising**

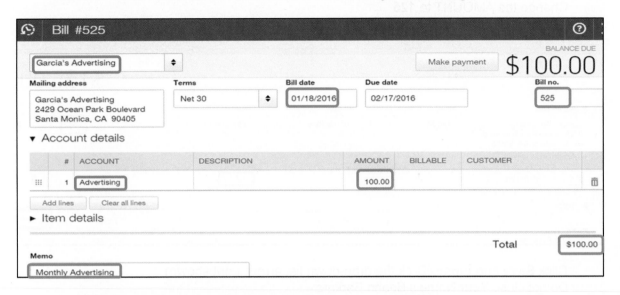

- QuickBooks Online does not print the Bills that you record.
  Click **Save and close** (Click the drop-down list arrow if it is not shown)
  Do <u>not</u> close Your Name's Beach Barkers

## Edit and Correct Errors

If an error is discovered for a bill, you may return to the bill and correct it.

 Correct the bill for Garcia's Advertising

Click the **Recent Transactions** icon on the Top-Navigation Bar

- Using the Recent Transactions List displays a list of the most recent transactions and is a fast way to access them. The order of the transactions displayed may be different from the one shown below.

Click **Bill No. 525** for **Garcia's Advertising** on the list of Recent Transactions

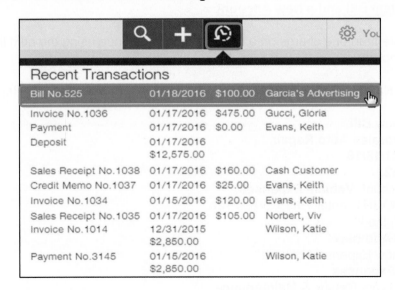

- You are returned to Bill No. 525.

Change "Bill no." to **2525**
Change the AMOUNT to **125**

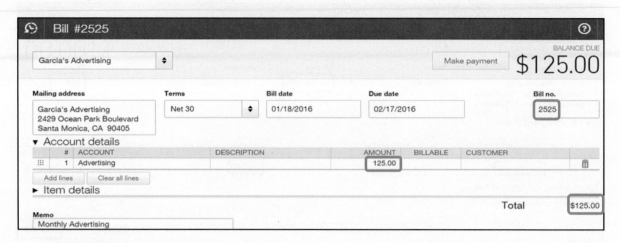

Click **Save and close** (Click the drop-down list arrow if not shown)
Do not close Your Name's Beach Barkers

## Change Account Name

In the Chart of Accounts, there is an expense account named Automobile Expense. It should be renamed to Vehicle Expenses.

Continue to use **Your Name's Beach Barkers**

Open the Chart of Accounts as previously instructed
Scroll through the Account List until you get to Automobile Expense
Click the drop-down list arrow for Automobile Expense, click **Edit**
Change the "Name" to **Vehicle Expenses**
Click **Save and Close** (Click the drop-down list arrow if not shown)
Do not close Your Name's Beach Barkers

## Create Multiple Item Bill and a New Account

When there is more than one charge on a bill, you simply continue using the next line in the Account details section.

Use **Your Name's Beach Barkers** to record the bill from Morales Auto Repair

Create a new **Bill**
Vendor: **Morales Auto Repair**
Bill date: **01/18/16**
Bill no.: **762**
Line 1: Account: **Vehicle Expenses**
Tab to AMOUNT, enter **79.95**, press **Tab**
Complete Line 2:
Account: **+Add new**
Create a new Expense Account:
      Type: **Expenses**
      Detail Type: **Repair & Maintenance**
      Name: **Vehicle Repair**

Subaccount of: **Repair & Maintenance**
Return to the bill and enter the amount for Line 2: **262.50**
Memo: **Gasoline and Repair**

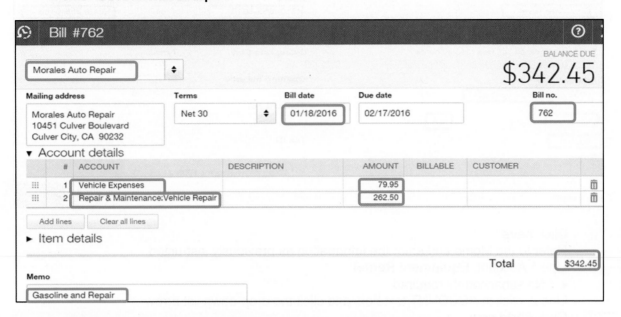

Click **Save and new**, do <u>not</u> close Your Name's Beach Barkers

## Enter Bill, Add New Vendor and New Account

When recording a bill, you may enter an account on the fly.

 Continue using **Your Name's Beach Barkers** to record the bill from Computer Town

Add a New Vendor, Computer Town
Click the drop-down list arrow for "Choose a vendor"
Click **+Add new**
Enter the Name **Computer Town**
Click **+Details**
Delete **Computer** from the First name and **Town** from the Last name
Enter **Computer Town** for Company
Refer to the Memo and enter the other details as previously instructed

**Vendor Information**

| Title | First name | Middle name | Last name | Suffix |
|---|---|---|---|---|

Company
Computer Town

*Display name as*
Computer Town

Print on check as ✓ Use display name
Computer Town

Address *map*
2239 Abbott-Kinney Drive

Venice                    CA

90291                    Country

Notes

Email
ComputerTown@data.com

Phone                Mobile                    Fax
(310) 555-8816                        (310) 555-6188

Other                Website

Billing rate (/hr)        Terms
Net 30

Opening balance        as of
01/18/2016

Account no.
Appears in the memo of all payments

Tax ID

☐ Track payments for 1099

Cancel                    Privacy                    Save

Click **Save**
Refer to the Memo and enter the information as previously instructed
Line 1 Account: **Equipment Rental**
- No subaccounts required.
Line 2, click in ACCOUNT text box, and click the drop-down list arrow
Click **+Add new**
Use the Memo information and previous instructions to create a new Expense Account
    **Computer Repair**
Complete the Bill as instructed
For the Memo, enter **One-Month Computer Rental and Computer Repair**

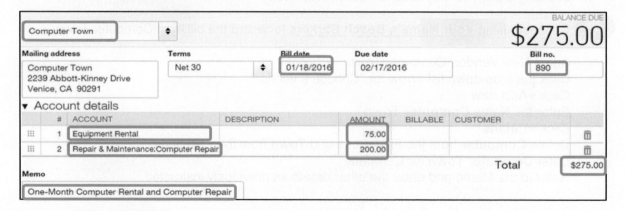

Click **Save and new**
Do <u>not</u> close Your Name's Beach Barkers

## Purchase Prepaid Expenses

As presented in the Drill, the accrual method of accounting matches the expenses of a period against the revenue of the period. When you buy or pay for something to have on hand and it will eventually be used up, it is recorded in an asset account that is a prepaid expense. At the end of the period, an adjusting entry is made to transfer the amount used from the asset account to the expense account.

 Continue using **Your Name's Beach Barkers** to record the bill from Quality Insurance

Enter Bill **4953** from **Quality Insurance** as previously instructed
For Line 1, use the Asset Account: **Prepaid Insurance**
- Prepaid Insurance is a prepaid expense and is an asset until it is used up.

Amount: **600**
Memo: **Additional Insurance**

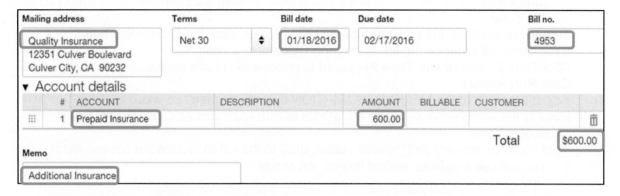

Click **Save and new**
Refer to the Memo and follow the steps previously presented to add a new vendor, Super
Office and prepare a bill for Office Supplies to have on hand
- Did you use the Asset Account Supplies: Office Supplies?
- If you were to look at the account setup, you would find the Detail Category listed as
Prepaid Expenses. That is because while we have the supplies on hand, they are
something we own.

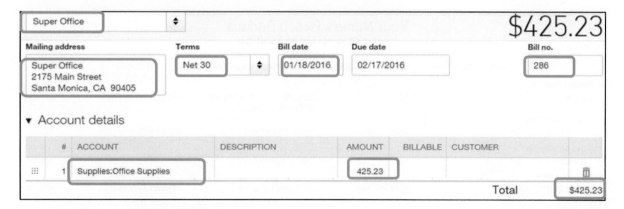

Click **Save and close**
Do <u>not</u> close Your Name's Beach Barkers

## TRANSACTIONS LIST BY VENDOR REPORT—DO

A Transaction List by Vendor Report is prepared to view the vendors and transaction details that
have been recorded.

<u>DO</u>

Continue to use **Your Name's Beach Barkers** to prepare the Transaction List by Vendor

Click **Reports** on the Navigation Bar
Select **All Reports**

- If you are within a report category, you will click **<All Reports**.

Click **Review Expenses and Purchases**

Scroll through the list of reports available in this category, click **Transaction List by Vendor**

Enter the dates From: **01/01/16** and To: **01/18/16**, click **Run Report**

Scroll through the report to see all of the Vendor Transactions for January 1-18, 2016

- Check with your professor to see if you should remove the Date and Time Prepared from the footer.

To remove the date and time prepared from the footer, click the **Customize** button

Click **Header/Footer** on the left side of the Customize screen

Click **Date Prepared** and **Time Prepared** to remove the check marks

Click **Run Report**

Adjust the width of the MEMO/DESCRIPTION column so it isn't so wide

Point to the sizing arrow between MEMO/DESCRIPTION and ACCOUNT until you get a double arrow

Hold down the primary (left) mouse button, drag to the left to reduce the column width

- You will see a dashed vertical line as you resize.

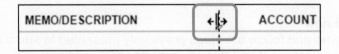

View the Report

- Notice that the Bill Memos you entered on the bills appear in the Memo/Description column. You did not enter a Bill Memo for the transaction with Super Office so nothing appears in the Memo/Description column for that bill.

## Your Name's Beach Barkers
### TRANSACTION LIST BY VENDOR
#### January 1-18, 2016

| DATE | TRANSACTION TYPE | NUM | POSTING | MEMO/DESCRIPTION | ACCOUNT | AMOUNT |
|---|---|---|---|---|---|---|
| **Computer Town** | | | | | | |
| 01/18/2016 | Bill | 890 | Yes | One-Month Computer Rental and Computer Repair | Accounts Payable (A/P) | 275.00 |
| **Garcia's Advertising** | | | | | | |
| 01/18/2016 | Bill | 2525 | Yes | Monthly Advertising | Accounts Payable (A/P) | 125.00 |
| **Morales Auto Repair** | | | | | | |
| 01/18/2016 | Bill | 762 | Yes | Gasoline and Repair | Accounts Payable (A/P) | 342.45 |
| **Quality Insurance** | | | | | | |
| 01/18/2016 | Bill | 4953 | Yes | Additional Insurance | Accounts Payable (A/P) | 600.00 |
| **Super Office** | | | | | | |
| 01/18/2016 | Bill | 286 | Yes | | Accounts Payable (A/P) | 425.23 |

As you did with reports in Chapter 3, print, email, and or export the report

- Verify with your instructor whether or not you should print, export, and/or submit the report. You may submit a report by clicking the Email button or by printing to a PDF file and attaching it to an email.

If you are required to do so, perform one of the following:

**Print**: click the **Print** button and make the appropriate selections on the Print menu

**Export** to Excel: click the drop-down list arrow on the **Excel** button, click **Excel (XLSX or XLS)**. If you save the report, name it **1-Your Name Transaction List by Vendor Ch. 4**.

- Remember, only reports may be exported to Excel.

**Email**: Sends the report directly to your instructor without saving to a pdf file, click the **Email** button, Your Name <quickbooks-email@intuit.com> is inserted by

QuickBooks, enter your instructor's email address, if you wish to add a note, do so in
Note:, then click **Send**

Close Your Name's Beach Barkers

## ENTER VENDOR CREDIT—DRILL

A Vendor Credit is prepared to record a reduction to a transaction between your company and a
vendor. If you make a return or were billed for more than you used, you will receive a credit memo
from a vendor acknowledging a change to the amount owed. In QuickBooks Online, you complete a
Vendor Credit to record the receipt of the Vendor's Credit Memo. The amount of the vendor credit is
deducted from the amount owed.

---

**MEMO**
**DATE:** January 20, 2016

Received Credit Memo 201 from Robertson & Associates for one-half hour less time than
originally billed for Legal & Professional Fees:Accounting. Reduce the amount from $315 to
$275

---

### *DRILL*

 Open the **Test Drive Company** and record the Vendor Credit from Robertson & Associates

Open the Vendors List, click **Robertson & Associates**
In the Register for Robertson & Associates, click the **Bill** for **315**
View the Bill and then close it
Click the **Plus** icon on the Top-Navigation Bar
In the Vendors column, click **Vendor Credit**
- Even though the Vendor Credit is for a different purpose, many of the procedures used
  in recording the form are the same as when you record bills. Step-by-step instructions
  will be given when there are differences in methods and/or procedures.
Complete the Vendor Credit:
Vendor: **Robertson & Associates**
Payment Date: **01/20/16**
Ref no.: **201**
- When the vendor changes an amount owed from a customer (Test Drive Company), the
  vendor (Robertson & Associates) issues a credit memo to you. This is entered as the
  Reference number for the Vendor Credit.
In Line 1, click in the column for ACCOUNT
Scroll through the account list, select **Legal & Professional Fees: Accounting**
- The original bill had an amount of $315. The credit memo adjusted for that amount.
  Since the amount of the adjustment was not given in the memo, it needs to be
  calculated: 315-275 = 40.
Enter the amount of the adjustment: **40**
Enter the Memo: **Reduce time billed**

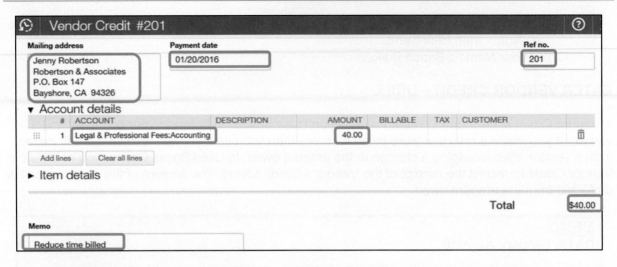

Click **Save and close** (click the drop-down if necessary)
Do not close the Test Drive Company

## VIEW VENDOR REGISTER—DRILL

A Vendor Credit will be shown in the individual vendor's register. Open the Register for Robertson & Associates and view the Vendor Credit.

### *DRILL*

Continue to use the **Test Drive Company** and view the Vendor Credit in the Register

The register for **Robertson & Associates** should still be on the screen
- If it is not on the screen, open the Vendors List and the Vendor Register as previously instructed.
You will see the Vendor Credit for 01/20/2016

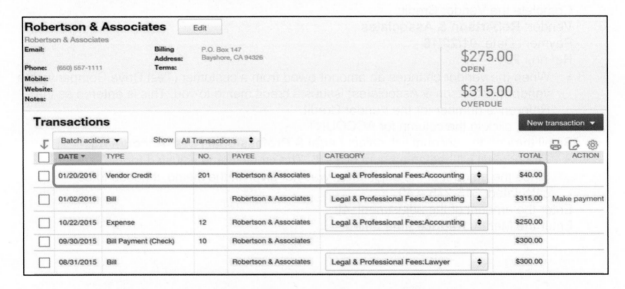

- You will see the Vendor Credit along with other transactions for Robertson & Associates. Some of the transactions shown are areas that you have not yet studied or used. Do not

worry if you don't understand everything displayed at this time. As you advance through the text, these areas will be presented.
- If the dates shown on the transactions are different from the ones shown above, do not be concerned. The Test Drive Company is programmed to automatically change the transaction dates.

Do **not** close the Test Drive Company, continue and complete the next section

## UNPAID BILLS REPORT—DRILL

It is possible to get information regarding unpaid bills by simply preparing a report. QuickBooks Online prepares an Unpaid Bills Report listing information for each unpaid bill. This includes the Transaction Date, Transaction Type, Number, Due Date, number of days Past Due, Amount of the original bill, and the Open Balance. Evaluating the Unpaid Bills Report enables you to determine which bills should be paid and to know which bills are overdue.

### *DRILL*

 Continue to use the **Test Drive Company** and view the Unpaid Bills Report

4

> To prepare reports in the Test Drive Company, follow the procedures presented earlier to turn **OFF** Redesigned Reports
>
> Access **Reports**, click **All Reports**
> - If you see **<All Reports** above a report category, you click it. Otherwise, click **All Reports**.
>
> Click the category **Manage Accounts Payable**
> Click **Unpaid Bills**
> - The report is displayed for All Dates.
> - Look at the information shown for Robertson & Associates. Notice that the Bill for $315.00 subtracts the Vendor Credit of $40.00 resulting in a total of $275.00.

| | | | | | | |
|---|---|---|---|---|---|---|
| **Craig's Design and Landscaping Services** | | | | | | |
| **UNPAID BILLS** | | | | | | |
| All Dates | | | | | | |
| DATE | TRANSACTION TYPE | NUM | DUE DATE | PAST DUE | AMOUNT | OPEN BALANCE |
| **Brosnahan Insurance Agency** | | | | | | |
| **(650) 555-9912** | | | | | | |
| 12/26/2015 | Bill | | 01/05/2016 | 23 | 241.23 | 241.23 |
| Total for Brosnahan Insurance Agency | | | | | **$241.23** | **$241.23** |
| **Diego's Road Warrior Bodyshop** | | | | | | |
| 12/31/2015 | Bill | | 01/30/2016 | -2 | 755.00 | 755.00 |
| Total for Diego's Road Warrior Bodyshop | | | | | **$755.00** | **$755.00** |
| **Norton Lumber and Building Materials** | | | | | | |
| **(650) 363-6578** | | | | | | |
| 01/02/2016 | Bill | | 01/02/2016 | 26 | 205.00 | 205.00 |
| Total for Norton Lumber and Building Materials | | | | | **$205.00** | **$205.00** |
| **PG&E** | | | | | | |
| **(888) 555-9465** | | | | | | |
| 11/18/2015 | Bill | | 12/18/2015 | 41 | 86.44 | 86.44 |
| Total for PG&E | | | | | $86.44 | $86.44 |
| **Robertson & Associates** | | | | | | |
| **(650) 557-1111** | | | | | | |
| 01/02/2016 | Bill | | 01/02/2016 | 26 | 315.00 | 315.00 |
| 01/20/2016 | Vendor Credit | 201 | | 0 | -40.00 | -40.00 |
| Total for Robertson & Associates | | | | | **$275.00** | **$275.00** |
| **TOTAL** | | | | | **$1,562.67** | **$1,562.67** |

> Do **not** close the Unpaid Bills Report
> Do **not** close the Test Drive Company, continue and complete the next section

## VOID AND DELETE BILLS—DRILL

As with invoices, bills may be deleted. Once a bill is deleted, it does not show as a transaction. If you want to keep the bill in your records, it must be voided manually by entering an amount of 0.00 and Void for the Memo.

> <u>MEMO</u>
> **DATE:** January 21, 2016
>
> In reviewing the Unpaid Bills Report, you realize that the bill for Diego's Road Warrior Bodyshop should have been voided because we decided not to do the repairs on the truck. Void the bill.
>
> The transaction with Norton Lumber and Building materials for $205 was cancelled. Delete the bill.

### *DRILL*

 Continue to use the **Test Drive Company** and Void and Delete bills

### <u>Void Bill</u>

 Use the **Test Drive Company** and the Unpaid Bills Report to access and then void a bill

> Using the Unpaid Bills Report, click the Bill for Diego's Road Warrior Bodyshop
> - At the time of this writing, a bill does not have a Void command. As a result, you will void the bill manually.
> With the bill open on the screen, enter **0.00** for the AMOUNT
> Enter **Void** in the Memo text box
> - Note: Because the Test Drive Company is programmed to automatically change dates, the Bill date will be different from the screen shot.

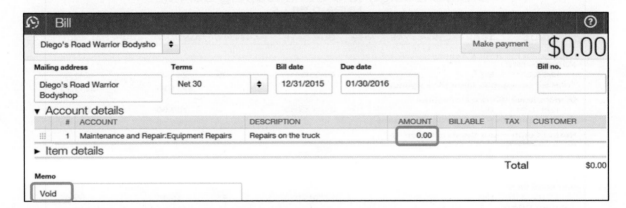

> Click **Save and close** (Click the drop-down list arrow if necessary)
> You are returned to the Unpaid Bills Report.
> - Notice that the bill for Diego's Road Warrior Bodyshop no longer shows in the Unpaid Bills Report.

### <u>Delete Bill</u>

 Use the **Test Drive Company** and the Unpaid Bills Report to access and then delete a bill

With the Unpaid Bills Report on the screen, click the bill for Norton Lumber and Building Materials

Click the **More** button at the bottom of the bill for Norton Lumber and Building Materials

Click **Delete**

Click **Yes** on the message "The transaction you are editing is linked to others. Are you sure you want to delete it?"

You are returned to the Unpaid Bills Report

* The bill for Norton Lumber and Building Materials no longer shows.

Open **Vendors**

Click **Diego's Road Warrior Bodyshop**

| | 12/31/2015 | Bill | Diego's Road Warrior Bodyshop | Maintenance and Repair:Equipmer ⬍ | $0.00 |

* The transaction still shows in the Register and has a total of 0.00.

Open the Register for **Norton Lumber and Building Materials**

* The deleted transaction for a bill for $205.00 does not show.

Do <u>not</u> close the Test Drive Company, continue with the next section

## PAY BILLS—DRILL

When using QuickBooks Online, a transaction that is recorded on a Bill must be paid using the Pay Bills feature of the program. QuickBooks Online will write the check and match it to the bill. If you simply write a check, the bill payment and bill are not matched, the expense account used for the check is increased, and the bill still shows in the Unpaid Bills Report.

Using Pay Bills enables you to determine which bills to pay, the method of payment—check or credit card—and the payment account. When determining which bills to pay, QuickBooks Online displays the bills, with the oldest first, shows the Open Balance, allows you to apply a Credit, shows the Payment Amount, and the Total Amount. The total amount for bills paid is shown along with the current payment account balance.

> <u>MEMO</u>
> **DATE:** January 21, 2016
>
> In reviewing the Unpaid Bills Report, you marked the bills from PG&E and Robertson & Associates for payment. Pay the bills.

<u>*DRILL*</u>

 Continue to use the **<u>Test Drive Company</u>** and Pay Bills

Click the **Plus** icon on the Top-Navigation Bar

Click **Pay Bills** in the Vendor column

On the Pay Bills screen, click the drop-down list arrow for Payment account

Click **Checking**

Enter the Payment Date: **01/21/16**

* Because of the programmed date change, the transaction dates and the number of overdue bills may be different than shown.

Click the bill for **PG&E**

* Notice that the PAYMENT amount of 86.44 has been entered and shows as the total for the Open Balance, Payment, and Total Amount columns.

- The CREDIT APPLIED column shows *Not available*, which means that there is no vendor credit for this bill.

Click the check box for **Robertson & Associates**
- As soon as the transaction is marked, the $40.00 Credit is applied and the Payment of $275 is automatically calculated and entered by QuickBooks Online.
- Note the totals for the Open Balance, Credit Applied, Payment, and Total Amount columns.
- At the bottom of the Bill Payment screen, the "Current account balance" for Checking is shown, the amount of "Total payment" is subtracted, and the "New account balance" is calculated and entered by QuickBooks Online.

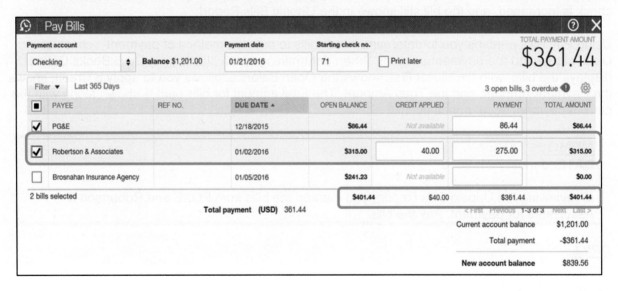

Click **Save and close** (or drop-down list arrow if necessary)
Close the Test Drive Company

## ENTER VENDOR CREDIT—DO

A Vendor Credit is prepared to record a reduction to a transaction between your company and a vendor. With QuickBooks Online, you complete a Vendor Credit to record a credit memo received from a vendor acknowledging a change to an amount owed. The amount of the vendor credit is deducted from the amount owed.

> **MEMO**
> **DATE:** January 20, 2016
>
> When we received the office supplies from Super Office, five reams of paper had water damage. We returned the paper and received Credit Memo 725 from Super Office for $21.55.

*DO*

Open **Your Name's Beach Barkers** and record the Vendor Credit from Super Office

Open Your Name's Beach Barkers as previously instructed
Click the **Plus** icon on the Top-Navigation Bar
In the Vendors column, click **Vendor Credit**
Complete the Vendor Credit to **Super Office**
Payment Date: **01/20/16**
Ref no.: **725**

- When the vendor changes an amount owed from a customer (Your Name's Beach Barkers), the vendor (Super Office) issues a credit memo to you. The number of the Super Office Credit Memo is entered as the Reference number for the Vendor Credit.

In Line 1, click in the column for ACCOUNT
Scroll through the account list, select the Asset account **Supplies:Office Supplies**

- Because the office supplies were purchased to have on hand, they were originally entered into the asset account. The return of the paper reduces the amount of office supplies on hand so the asset account is used for the Vendor Credit.

Enter the amount of the adjustment: **21.55**
Click in the "Memo" text box and enter **Returned defective paper**

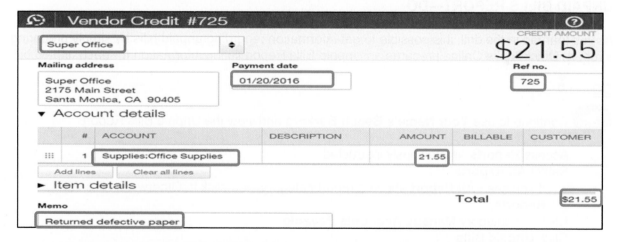

Click **Save and close** (click drop-down list arrow if necessary)
Do <u>not</u> close Your Name's Beach Barkers

## VIEW VENDOR REGISTER—DO

A Vendor Credit will be shown in the individual vendor's register. Open the Register for Super Office and view the Vendor Credit.

> Continue to use **Your Name's Beach Barkers** and view the Vendor Credit in the Vendor's Register
>
> Open the Vendors List and the register for Super Office as previously instructed
> You will see the Vendor Credit for 01/20/2016

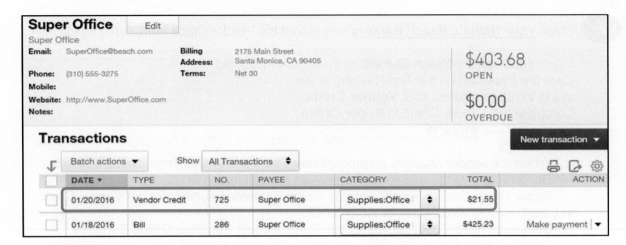

- You will see the Vendor Credit along with the bill you entered earlier in the chapter.
- In the column for CATEGORY you will see the account used in the transaction.

Do not close Your Name's Beach Barkers

## UNPAID BILLS REPORT—DO

As you learned in the drill, it is possible to get information regarding unpaid bills by simply preparing a report. QuickBooks Online prepares an Unpaid Bills Report listing information for each unpaid bill.

_DO_

> Continue to use **Your Name's Beach Barkers** and view the Unpaid Bills Report
>
> Access **Reports** as previously instructed
> Select **All Reports**
> - If you see **<All Report** above a report category, you click it. Otherwise, click **All Reports**.
> Click the category **Manage Accounts Payable**
> Click **Unpaid Bills**
> - The report is displayed for All Dates.
> - The number of days Past Due is calculated on the date of the computer so the numbers in your report will be different from the screen shot.
> - As you look at the Past Due column in the screen shot, you will see some bills with a – in front of the number. That is the number of days until the bill is due. The number of days shown without a – indicate the number of days overdue. The Past Due number of days is based on the current date so the days shown will not match the text.
> - Look at the information shown for Super Office. Notice that the Bill for $425.23 subtracts the Vendor Credit of $21.55 resulting in a total of $403.68.

### Your Name's Beach Barkers
#### UNPAID BILLS
##### All Dates

| DATE | TRANSACTION TYPE | NUM | DUE DATE | PAST DUE | AMOUNT | OPEN BALANCE |
|---|---|---|---|---|---|---|
| **Bow-Wow Supplies** 760-555-2951 | | | | | | |
| 12/31/2015 | Bill | | 12/31/2015 | 29 | 2,000.00 | 2,000.00 |
| Total for Bow-Wow Supplies | | | | | **$2,000.00** | **$2,000.00** |
| **Canine Supplies** 310-555-6971 | | | | | | |
| 12/31/2015 | Bill | | 12/31/2015 | 29 | 3,000.00 | 3,000.00 |
| Total for Canine Supplies | | | | | **$3,000.00** | **$3,000.00** |
| **Computer Town** (310) 555-8816 | | | | | | |
| 01/18/2016 | Bill | 890 | 02/17/2016 | -19 | 275.00 | 275.00 |
| Total for Computer Town | | | | | **$275.00** | **$275.00** |
| **Garcia's Advertising** 310-555-1879 | | | | | | |
| 01/18/2016 | Bill | 2525 | 02/17/2016 | -19 | 125.00 | 125.00 |
| Total for Garcia's Advertising | | | | | **$125.00** | **$125.00** |
| **Morales Auto Repair** 310-555-1873 | | | | | | |
| 01/18/2016 | Bill | 762 | 02/17/2016 | -19 | 342.45 | 342.45 |
| Total for Morales Auto Repair | | | | | **$342.45** | **$342.45** |
| **Quality Insurance** 213-555-8175 | | | | | | |
| 01/18/2016 | Bill | 4953 | 02/17/2016 | -19 | 600.00 | 600.00 |
| Total for Quality Insurance | | | | | **$600.00** | **$600.00** |
| **Super Office** (310) 555-3275 | | | | | | |
| 01/18/2016 | Bill | 286 | 02/17/2016 | -19 | 425.23 | 425.23 |
| 01/20/2016 | Vendor Credit | 725 | | 0 | -21.55 | -21.55 |
| Total for Super Office | | | | | **$403.68** | **$403.68** |
| **Training Supplies & Equipment** 310-555-2915 | | | | | | |
| 12/31/2015 | Bill | | 12/31/2015 | 29 | 300.00 | 300.00 |
| Total for Training Supplies & Equipment | | | | | **$300.00** | **$300.00** |
| TOTAL | | | | | **$7,046.13** | **$7,046.13** |

Remove the Date and Time Prepared from the report footer

Print, export, and/or email or submit the report as required by your professor

- Name the report **2-Your Name Unpaid Bills Ch. 4**.

Do <u>not</u> close the Unpaid Bills Report or Your Name's Beach Barkers

## VOID AND DELETE BILLS—DO

As with invoices, bills may be deleted. Once a bill is deleted, it does not show as a transaction. If you want to keep a bill in your records, you must manually void it by entering an amount of 0.00. It is important to include a Memo that says Void.

> <u>MEMO</u>
> **DATE:** January 21, 2016
>
> In reviewing the Unpaid Bills Report, you realize that the bill from Quality Insurance was sent in error. Void the bill.
>
> After voiding the bill, you spoke with Quality Insurance and decided it would be better if the bill did not appear in the company records. Delete the bill.

### <u>DO</u>

Continue to use **Your Name's Beach Barkers** and Void and Delete bills

<u>Void Bill</u>

 Use <u>**Your Name's Beach Barkers**</u> and the Unpaid Bills Report to access and void a bill

Using the Unpaid Bills Report, click the bill for Quality Insurance
With the bill open on the screen, enter **0.00** for the AMOUNT
Delete the Memo of Additional Insurance and enter **Void**

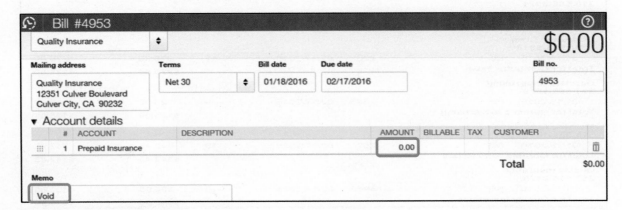

Click **Save and close**
- Notice that the bill for Quality Insurance no longer shows in the Unpaid Bills Report.

<u>Delete Bill</u>

 Use <u>**Your Name's Beach Barkers**</u> and the Vendor Register to access and then delete a bill

Open the Vendor Register for Quality Insurance as previously instructed
- View the Bill in the Register. It shows a Total of $0.00.
Click the bill to open it
Click the **More** button at the bottom of the bill for Quality Insurance
Click **Delete**
Click **Yes** on the message "Are you sure you want to delete this?"
You are returned to the Quality Insurance Account Register
- No transactions are shown.
Do <u>not</u> close Your Name's Beach Barkers

## PAY BILLS—DO

As you explored in the drill, when using QuickBooks Online, a transaction that is recorded on a Bill must be paid using the Pay Bills feature of the program. If you simply write a check, the bill payment and bill are not matched, the expense account used for the check is increased, and the bill still shows in the Unpaid Bills Report. In addition, using Pay Bills enables you to determine which bills to pay, the method of payment—check or credit card—and the payment account.

> <u>**MEMO**</u>
> **DATE:** January 21, 2016
>
> When reviewing the Unpaid Bills Report, you marked the bills from Super Office and Training Supplies & Equipment for payment in full. Pay a partial payment of $500 each to Bow-Wow Supplies and Canine Supplies. Pay the bills.

_DO_

Continue to use **Your Name's Beach Barkers** and Pay Bills

Click the **Plus** icon on the Top-Navigation Bar
Click **Pay Bills** in the Vendor column
On the Pay Bills screen, click the drop-down list arrow for "Payment account"
Click **Checking**
Enter the Payment Date of **01/21/16**

- Notice the red flags on the bills due 12/31/2015. Those were opening balances that were entered when the company was created in Chapter 2.

Click the bill for **Training Supplies & Equipment**

- Notice that the PAYMENT amount of 300.00 has been entered and shows as the total for the Open Balance, Payment, and Total Amount columns.
- The Credit Applied column shows _Not available_, which means that there is no vendor credit for this bill.
- Look at the Current account balance of $63,580.00 at the bottom of the Pay Bills screen. Beneath that the amount of the Total payment of $300.00 is subtracted to reach a New account balance of $63,280.00.

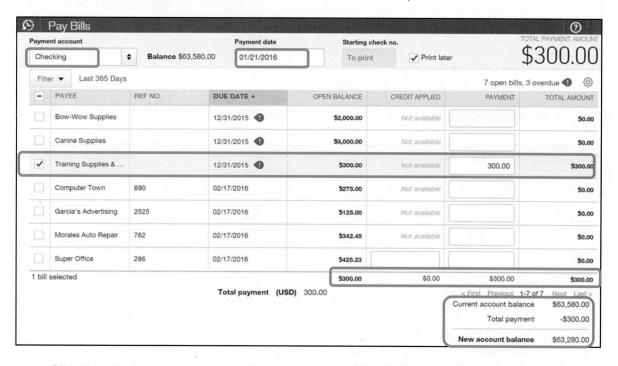

Click the check box for **Super Office**

- As soon as the transaction is marked, the $21.55 Credit is applied and the Payment of $403.68 is automatically calculated and entered by QuickBooks Online.

Click **Bow-Wow Supplies** to mark, click in the PAYMENT text box
Delete the Payment Amount of $2,000.00 and enter **500**, press **Tab**
Repeat the steps for the partial payment of $500 to Canine Supplies

- Note the totals for the Open Balance, Credit Applied, Payment, and Total Amount columns.
- Look at the Current account balance of $63,580.00 at the bottom of the Pay Bills screen. Beneath that the amount of the Total payment of $1,703.68 is subtracted to reach a New account balance of $61,876.32.

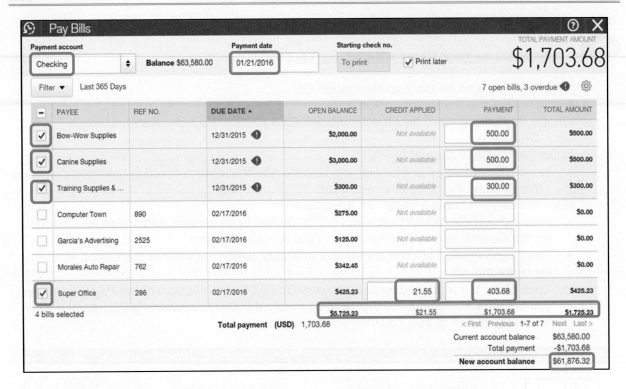

Click **Save and print**
- You will see the list of the 4 checks selected.
- Notice that the Starting check no. is 2. Remember, you wrote the refund check Gloria Gucci in Chapter 2.

Click **Print setup** at the bottom of the screen
Click **Standard** as the type of check
Click **Yes, I'm finished with setup**
Click **Preview and print**
- The four checks will appear in the preview. Note that three checks will print on one page and the fourth check will print on the next page.

---

01/21/2016

Training Supplies & Equipment                                    **300.00

Three hundred and 00/100••••••••••••••••••••••••••••••••••••••••••••••••••••••••••••••

   Training Supplies & Equipment
   1801 Griffith Avenue
   Los Angeles, CA  90021


01/21/2016

Super Office                                                     **403.68

Four hundred three and 68/100•••••••••••••••••••••••••••••••••••••••••••••••••••••••••

   Super Office
   2175 Main Street
   Santa Monica, CA  90405


01/21/2016

Bow-Wow Supplies                                                 **500.00

Five hundred and 00/100•••••••••••••••••••••••••••••••••••••••••••••••••••••••••••••••

   Bow-Wow Supplies
   5787 Broadway Avenue
   San Diego, CA  92101

---

01/21/2016

Canine  Supplies                                                 **500.00

Five hundred and 00/100•••••••••••••••••••••••••••••••••••••••••••••••••••••••••••••••

   Canine  Supplies
   10855 Western Avenue
   Los Angeles, CA  90012

---

If the checks printed correctly, make sure **Yes, they all printed correctly** is selected
- On the screen for "Did your checks print OK?" there are selections for: "Yes, they all printed correctly," "Some checks need reprinting, starting with check: 2" (2 is shown but the number may be changed), or "No, keep all checks in the Print Checks list."

If your checks printed correctly, click **Done**
- If not, make the appropriate selection and reprint.
- If you print to a PDF file so you can email the checks to your instructor, use the name **3-Your Name Checks 2-5**.

Click the **Close** button at the top of Print Checks
Do <u>not</u> close Your Name's Beach Barkers

## EDIT BILLS USING VENDOR REGISTER—DO

Once you have paid a bill, the bill payment shows in the Vendor's Register. In the Register, the TYPE will be Bill Payment (Check).

## <u>DO</u>

Continue to use **<u>Your Name's Beach Barkers</u>** to view bill payments in the Vendor Register

Open the Vendor Register for **Bow-Wow Supplies** as previously instructed

- You will see two transactions in the Register for Bow-Wow Supplies. A Bill for $2,000.00, which was entered as the Opening Balance when the company was created in Chapter 2. The second transaction is for Bill Payment (Check) for $500.00, which is the amount of payment made.

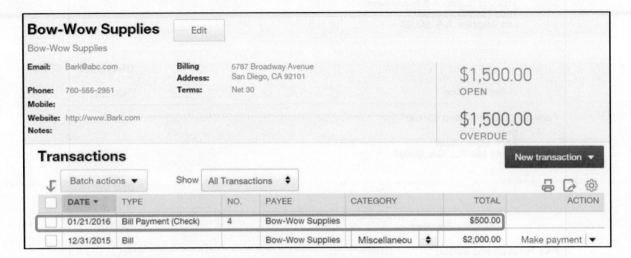

Click the **Bill Payment (Check)** to open the transaction
- You will see Check #4 for the bill payment.
- Note the Vendor Name, Bow-Wow Supplies, the account used, Checking, and the Balance for Checking. In the Outstanding Transactions, the bill for which partial payment was made is shown.
- Since this is a partial payment, it is good to note that in the Memo

Click in the Memo text box, enter **Partial Payment**

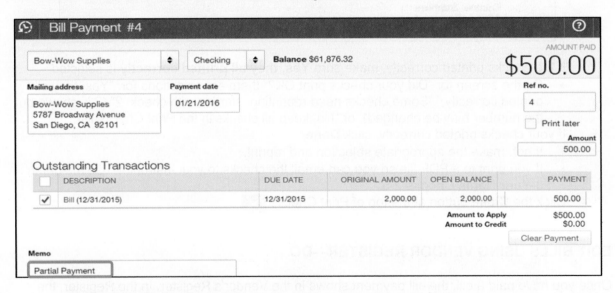

Click **Save and close** (or click the drop-down list arrow if necessary)

Click **Yes** on "The transaction you are editing is linked to others. Are you sure you want to modify it?"

Repeat the steps to insert a Memo of **Partial Payment** for Canine Supplies

Review the Bill Payments for Training Supplies & Equipment
- Note that the Total for both the Bill and the Bill Payment match.

Close the Register

Open the Register for Super Office
- You will see three transactions: Bill, Vendor Credit, and Bill Payment. The Total of the Bill Payment and the Vendor Credit equal the amount of the original Bill.

### Super Office   Edit

**Transactions**

| | DATE | TYPE ▾ | NO. | PAYEE | CATEGORY | | TOTAL |
|---|---|---|---|---|---|---|---|
| ☐ | 01/21/2016 | Bill Payment (Check) | 3 | Super Office | | | $403.68 |
| ☐ | 01/20/2016 | Vendor Credit | 725 | Super Office | Supplies:Office Supplies | ◆ | $21.55 |
| ☐ | 01/18/2016 | Bill | 286 | Super Office | Supplies:Office Supplies | ◆ | $425.23 |

Do not close Your Name's Beach Barkers

## BILL PAYMENT LIST—DO

When a bill is paid, it will be included in the Bill Payment List in the Manage Accounts Payable Reports Category. This report shows all of the bills paid during a specified date range and indicates the account used for payment, the date of the payment, the check number, the vendor, the amount of each check, and the total amount of all checks written to pay bills.

### DO

Continue to use **Your Name's Beach Barkers** to prepare the Bill Payment List Report

Open **Reports** as previously instructed
In the Manage Accounts Payable category, click **Bill Payment List**
The report dates are From: **01/01/16** To: **01/21/16**, click **Run Report**

### Your Name's Beach Barkers
#### BILL PAYMENT LIST
##### January 1-21, 2016

| DATE | NUM | VENDOR | AMOUNT |
|---|---|---|---|
| **Checking** | | | |
| 01/21/2016 | 2 | Training Supplies & Equipment | -300.00 |
| 01/21/2016 | 3 | Super Office | -403.68 |
| 01/21/2016 | 4 | Bow-Wow Supplies | -500.00 |
| 01/21/2016 | 5 | Canine Supplies | -500.00 |
| **Total for Checking** | | | **$ -1,703.68** |

Remove the Date and Time Prepared from the report footer
Print, export, and/or email or submit the report as required by your professor
- Name the report **4-Your Name Bill Payment List Ch. 4**.
Close the Bill Payment List and Your Name's Beach Barkers

## WRITE CHECKS TO PAY BILLS—DRILL

Although it is more efficient to record and pay bills using Bills and Pay Bills, QuickBooks Online also allows a check to be written to pay for routine payments such as utilities. (Remember, if you record a bill in Bills, you must use Pay Bills to write the bill payment check.) When you write a check, it is not entered as a bill and the expense for which the check is being written is included in the ACCOUNT text box.

> **MEMO**
> **DATE:** January 22, 2016
>
> Write Check 71 to pay the $108.95 telephone bill to Cal Telephone.
> Write Check 72 to pay the gas and electric bill to PG&E for $79.50.

*DRILL*

  Open the **Test Drive Company** and write the checks indicated in the Memo

Once the Test Drive Company is open, click the **Plus** icon
Click **Check** in the Vendors column
Click the drop-down list arrow for "Choose a payee," click **Cal Telephone**
Use **Checking** as the account
Enter the Payment date **01/22/16**
Click in the ACCOUNT column for Line 1, click the drop-down list arrow
Scroll through the list of accounts
Click **Telephone**, a subaccount of Utilities
Tab to AMOUNT and enter **108.95**, press **Tab**

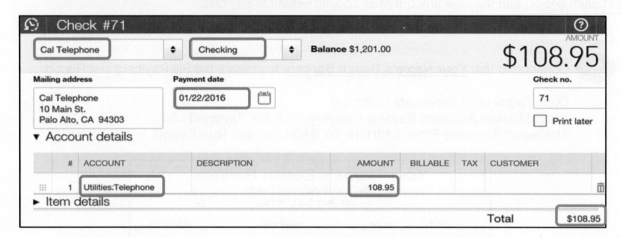

Click **Save and new**
Prepare Check 72 to PG&E using the information provided in the Memo
- You will get information regarding a Bill for $86.44 to be added to the check. Do <u>not</u> add this to the check. To close the pane, click the ▶ icon.

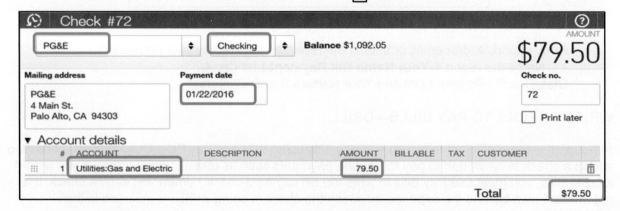

Click **Save and close** (click the drop-down list arrow if necessary)

Open the Vendor Register for PG&E

- You will see Check 72 shown for $79.50. The TYPE shows Check and there are no bills that correspond to that amount. Also notice that there is a Bill shown for $114.09 and a Bill Payment (Check) for the same amount.

**PG&E**  Edit

**Transactions**  New transaction ▼

| | DATE ▾ | TYPE | NO. | PAYEE | CATEGORY | | TOTAL | ACTION |
|---|---|---|---|---|---|---|---|---|
| ☐ | 01/22/2016 | Check | 72 | PG&E | Utilit | ⬍ | $79.50 | |
| ☐ | 01/02/2016 | Bill Payment (Check) | 6 | PG&E | | | $114.09 | |
| ☐ | 12/18/2015 | Bill | | PG&E | Utilit | ⬍ | $114.09 | |
| ☐ | 11/19/2015 | Bill | | PG&E | Utilit | ⬍ | $86.44 | Make payment ▼ |

Do <u>not</u> close the Test Drive Company

## EDIT CHECKS—DRILL

Mistakes can occur in business—even on a check. QuickBooks allows for checks to be edited at any time.

> **MEMO**
> **DATE:** January 22, 2016
>
> When reviewing Check 72 to PG&E, you realize the amount should have been $97.50. Edit the check.

### DRILL

Continue to use the **Test Drive Company** and edit the check to PG&E

Click **Check 72** in the Vendor Register for PG&E to open it
Click in the AMOUNT text box, delete the **79.50**, and enter **97.50**
Click **Save and close** (click the drop-down list arrow if necessary)
View the corrected check in the Register

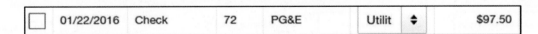

| | | | | | | | |
|---|---|---|---|---|---|---|---|
| ☐ | 01/22/2016 | Check | 72 | PG&E | Utilit | ⬍ | $97.50 |

Close the Test Drive Company

## WRITE CHECKS TO PAY BILLS—DO

As you just practiced, it is more efficient to record and pay bills using Bills and Pay Bills. However, QuickBooks Online also allows a check to be written to pay for routine payments such as utilities.

<u>MEMO</u>
**DATE:** January 22, 2016

| Write a check to pay the $175.95 monthly water bill to Marina Water District. Check Memo: Monthly Water. |
| Write a check to Southern California Gas Company to pay the monthly gas bill of $145.50. Check Memo: Monthly Gas-Heating |
| Write a check to Cal Electric (2945 Venice Boulevard, Venice, CA 90291, Email: CalElectric@power.com, Phone: 800-555-7223, Website: http://www.CalElectric.com, Terms: Net 30) for $89.75 for the monthly electric bill. Check Memo: Monthly Electricity |
| Record the bill to Cal Electric a second time. Everything should be identical. |

<u>DO</u>

Open **Your Name's Beach Barkers** and write the checks indicated in the Memo

Once Your Name's Beach Barkers is open, click the **Plus** icon
Click **Check** in the Vendors column
Payee: **Marina Water District**
Use **Checking** as the account
Enter the Payment date **01/22/16**
- We will print the checks as a batch (group) later.
Print later should have a check mark; if it does not, click it to mark
Click in the ACCOUNT column for Line 1, click the drop-down list arrow
Scroll through the list of accounts
There is not an account for Water, so click **+Add new**
    Category Type: **Expenses**
    Detail Type: **Utilities**
    Name: **Water**
    Subaccount of: **Utilities**
    Click **Save and Close** (click the drop-down list arrow if necessary)
Tab to AMOUNT and enter **175.95**, press **Tab**
Even though the transaction is self-explanatory enter the Memo: **Monthly Water**

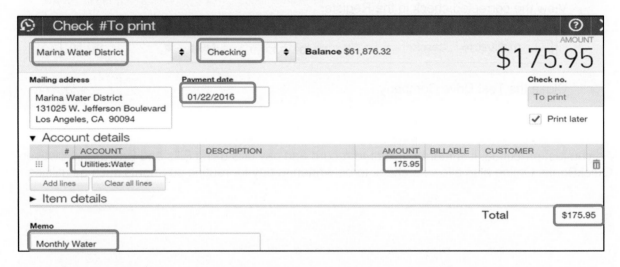

Click **Save and new**
Prepare Check 7 to Southern California Gas Company using the information provided in the Memo

Create a new account: **Gas-Heating** a subaccount of Utilities as you enter the bill

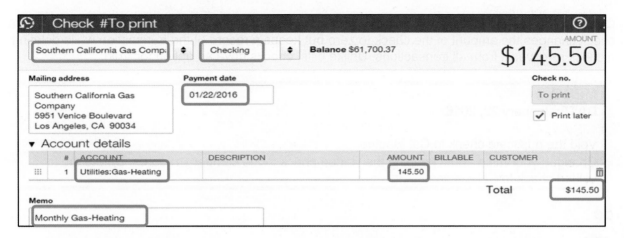

Click **Save and new**
Write a check to the new vendor, Cal Electric, following the steps presented earlier
- Did you add a new vendor and a new account?

Click **Save and new**
Enter the Check to **Cal Electric** a second time
- When a vendor has a bill that has been recorded, frequently, the information on the previous bill will be inserted when preparing a new bill for the vendor. If that is the information you want, you do not have to make any changes to the bill.
- Notice that the check is an exact duplicate of the previous one.

**Duplicate Check**

Click **Save and close** and continue to the next section
Do <u>not</u> close Your Name's Beach Barkers

## VOID AND DELETE CHECKS—DO

QuickBooks Online allows checks to be voided and deleted. As with other business forms, voiding a check changes the amount of the check to zero but keeps a record of the transaction while deleting a check removes it from all transactions. Unlike bills, checks have an option for Void.

> <u>MEMO</u>
> **DATE:** January 22, 2016
>
> Void the duplicate check to Cal Electric.
> Changed your mind about keeping the voided check in the company records. Delete the voided check to Cal Electric.

<u>*DO*</u>

 Continue to use **Your Name's Beach Barkers** to void and delete checks

<u>Void Check</u>

 Void the duplicate check to Cal Electric

Access the duplicate check in the Cal Electric Vendor Register
Click on the top **Check** to open it
With the check to Cal Electric showing on the screen, click the **More** button at the bottom of the check
Click **Void**
Click **Yes** on the "Are you sure you want to void this?" screen
Click **OK** on the "Transaction successfully voided" screen
* The check appears in the Vendor Register and has 0.00 for the total.

|  | 01/22/2016 | Check |  | Cal Electric | Utilities:Electric | ◆ | $0.00 |
|---|---|---|---|---|---|---|---|
|  | 01/22/2016 | Check |  | Cal Electric | Utilities:Electric | ◆ | $89.75 |

<u>Delete Check</u>

 Delete the voided check to Cal Electric

After thinking about keeping the voided check to Cal Electric, you decided to delete it
Click the Check for 0.00 in the Vendor Register for Cal Electric to open it
Click the **More** button at the bottom of the check
Click **Delete**
Click **Yes** on the "Are you sure you want to delete this?" screen
* The voided check does not appear in the Vendor Register. The only check shown is for $89.75.
Do <u>not</u> close Your Name's Beach Barkers

## EDIT CHECKS—DO

Mistakes can occur in business—even on a check. QuickBooks allows for checks to be edited at any time.

> **MEMO**
> **DATE:** January 22, 2016
>
> When reviewing the check to Southern California Gas Company to pay the monthly gas bill, you realized that the amount of the check should be $189.50.

<u>**DO**</u>

Continue to use Your Name's Beach Barkers and edit the check to Southern California Gas Company

Click the **Recent Transactions** icon on the Top-Navigation Bar
Click anywhere in the line for **Check** for **Southern California Gas Company** to open the check

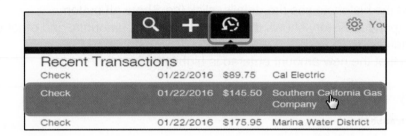

Change the AMOUNT to **189.50** following steps previously presented
Click **Save and close**
Go to the Vendor Register for Southern California Gas Company
Verify the Total for the Check

| | 01/22/2016 | Check | | Southern California Gas Company | Utilities:Gas-Heating | ⬍ | $189.50 |
|---|---|---|---|---|---|---|---|

Do <u>not</u> close Your Name's Beach Barkers

## VIEW AUDIT HISTORY—DO

Because QuickBooks is so flexible, a company must institute a system for cash control. For example, if the check for $145.50 to Southern California Gas Company had been printed, QuickBooks Online would allow a second check for $189.50 to be printed. In order to avoid any impropriety, more than one person should be designated to review checks. As a matter of practice, in a small business the owner or a person other than the one writing checks should sign them. Pre-numbered checks should be used, and any checks printed but not mailed should be submitted along with those for signature.

As a further safeguard, QuickBooks automatically tracks all the additions, deletions, and modifications made to transactions in in the Audit History for the transaction.

<u>**DO**</u>

Continue to use **<u>Your Name's Beach Barkers</u>** and view the Audit History for the check to Southern California Gas Company

Click the Check for **Southern California Gas Company** in the Vendor Register for Southern California Gas Company

Click the **More** button

Click **Audit History**

- You will see the collapsed transaction information that includes current date, time, and person editing the transaction. For example, the author's transaction history shows as follows:

To expand the history to see the details, click the **Show all** button

- The expanded history shows the transaction dates, amounts, and other check information.
- Notice that the new amount entered is highlighted.

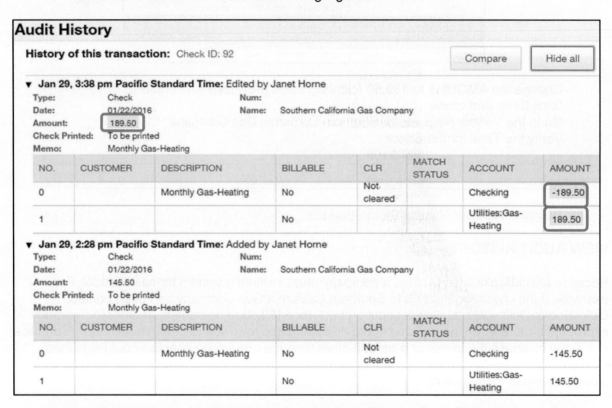

Click the **Compare** button to have each part of the transaction compared

After you look at the comparison of each line, click **Show changes only**

- The only the changes made are shown and the change is highlighted.

| FIELD | JAN 29, 2:28 PM PACIFIC STANDARD TI... | JAN 29, 3:38 PM PACIFIC STANDARD TI... |
|---|---|---|
| AMOUNT: | 145.50 | 189.50 |
| Line NO. 0 | | |
| AMOUNT | -145.50 | -189.50 |
| Line NO. 1 | | |
| AMOUNT | 145.50 | 189.50 |

Do not close Your Name's Beach Barkers

## PRINT CHECKS—DO

QuickBooks Online allows you to print checks as they are entered or they may be printed at a later time. To write a batch (group) of checks and then print them all at the same time, the check box for Print Later is selected. The appropriate check number is indicated during printing. When you use a standard check, three checks print on a page.

### DO

Continue to use **Your Name's Beach Barkers** and print checks

Click the **Plus** icon, click **Print Checks** in the Vendors column
- Information shown on Print Checks includes: The payment method/account: Checking, Balance: $61,421.12, 3 checks selected: $455.20, Starting check no.: 6. In addition, the three checks you entered for Marina Water District, Southern California Gas Company, and Cal Electric, are shown along with the Date, Type, and Amount.

Click the **Preview and print** button at the bottom of the screen
- If you print and save to a PDF file, name the document **5-Your Name Checks 6-8**. View the printed checks

```
                                                              01/22/2016


            Marina Water District                            **175.95
One hundred seventy-five and 95/100••••••••••••••••••••••••••••••••••••••••••


        Marina Water District
        131025 W. Jefferson Boulevard
        Los Angeles, CA  90094

      Monthly Water


                                                              01/22/2016



            Southern California Gas Company                  **189.50
One hundred eighty-nine and 50/100••••••••••••••••••••••••••••••••••••••••••


        Southern California Gas Company
        5951 Venice Boulevard
        Los Angeles, CA  90034

      Monthly Gas-Heating


                                                              01/22/2016


            Cal Electric                                     **89.75

Eighty-nine and 75/100•••••••••••••••••••••••••••••••••••••••••••••••••


        Cal Electric
        2945 Venice Boulevard
        Venice, CA  90291

      Monthly Electricity
```

Click the **Close** button on the Print preview
- You will get a screen for "Did your checks print OK?" with selections for: "Yes, they all printed correctly," "Some checks need reprinting, starting with check: 6" (6 is shown but the number may be changed), or "No, keep all checks in the Print Checks list."
If your checks printed correctly, make sure "Yes, they all printed correctly" is selected, then click **Done**
- If not, make the appropriate selection and reprint.
Click the **Close** button at the top of Print Checks ✕
Do <u>not</u> close Your Name's Beach Barkers

## EDIT VENDOR AND REPRINT CHECK--DO

Even if a check has been printed, it may be edited and reprinted.

> **MEMO**
> **DATE:** January 22, 2016
>
> As you review the checks just printed, you notice that the address for Marina Water District is incorrect. Change the address to 13125 W. Jefferson Boulevard and reprint Check 6.

<u>*DO*</u>

Continue to use <u>**Your Name's Beach Barkers**</u> and edit the vendor Marina Water District and reprint check 6

Open the Vendor List, click the vendor **Marina Water District**, click the **Edit** button
Change the address number to **13125**, click **Save**
In the register, click **Check 6** to reopen it

Click **Print check**
Change the Starting check no. to **6**
Click **Print and preview** and print the check as previously instructed
- If you print and save to a PDF file, name the document:
  **6-Your Name Check 6-Corrected**.
Close the Print preview, click **Done** on the "Did your checks print OK?" screen
Click the **Close** button at the top of Print Checks

## CHECK DETAIL REPORT—DO

Once checks have been printed, it is important to review information about them. The Check Detail Report provides detailed information regarding Checks prepared to pay for bills and expenses. The information shown includes the Date, Transaction Type, Number, Name, Memo/Description, CLR (means the check has been cleared), and Amount.

_DO_

Continue to use **Your Name's Beach Barkers** to prepare the Check Detail Report

Open **Reports** and the category for **Review Expenses and Purchases**
Click **Check Detail**
Customize the report to remove the date and time prepared
Enter the report dates From: **01/01/16** To: **01/22/16**
View the Check Detail Report
- Note that the checks prepared in Pay Bills have the Transaction Type of Bill Payment (Check) while the checks that you wrote without recording a bill have the Transaction Type of Check.
- As you look at the Amount column, you will see two amounts for each check. Some of the amounts have a – in front of the number while others do not.
- Remember the fundamental accounting equation: Assets = Liabilities + Equity.
- Also remember that Debit = Left and Credit = Right.
- Since Assets are on the left of the = sign, an increase to an asset is entered as a Debit and a decrease is entered as a Credit. Conversely, Accounts Payable is a Liability and is on the right of the = sign. An increase to Accounts Payable would be a Credit and a decrease would be a Debit.
- Think about the Bill Payment transactions. Evaluate Check 3 to Super Office. The original bill was:

**BILL:**

| DEBIT | | CREDIT | |
|---|---|---|---|
| Office Supplies, | $300 | Accounts Payable, | $300 |

- The bill payment is:

**BILL PAYMENT**

| DEBIT | | CREDIT | |
|---|---|---|---|
| Accounts Payable, | $300 | Checking, | $300 |

- Ultimately, the bill and bill payment finalize the transaction as an increase to the asset Office Supplies and a decrease to the asset Checking.

- Think about the Check transactions. Evaluate Check 6 to Marina Water District:

**CHECK**

| DEBIT | | CREDIT | |
|---|---|---|---|
| Utilities: Water, | $175.95 | Checking, | $175.95 |

- For an Expense, such as water, an increase in an expense—the cost of doing business—would ultimately decrease Net Income (Income – Expenses = Net Income). Since Net Income increases Equity, an Expense would decrease Equity so an increase in an expense would be a Debit.

### Your Name's Beach Barkers
### CHECK DETAIL
January 1-22, 2016

| DATE | TRANSACTION TYPE | NUM | NAME | MEMO/DESCRIPTION | CLR | AMOUNT |
|---|---|---|---|---|---|---|
| **Checking** | | | | | | |
| 01/21/2016 | Bill Payment (Check) | 2 | Training Supplies & Equipment | | | -300.00 |
| | | | | | | -300.00 |
| 01/21/2016 | Bill Payment (Check) | 3 | Super Office | | | -403.68 |
| | | | | | | -403.68 |
| 01/21/2016 | Bill Payment (Check) | 4 | Bow-Wow Supplies | Partial Payment | | -500.00 |
| | | | | | | -500.00 |
| 01/21/2016 | Bill Payment (Check) | 5 | Canine Supplies | Partial Payment | | -500.00 |
| | | | | | | -500.00 |
| 01/22/2016 | Check | 6 | Marina Water District | Monthly Water | | -175.95 |
| | | | | | | 175.95 |
| 01/22/2016 | Check | 7 | Southern California Gas Company | Monthly Gas-Heating | | -189.50 |
| | | | | | | 189.50 |
| 01/22/2016 | Check | 8 | Cal Electric | Monthly Electricity | | -89.75 |
| | | | | | | 89.75 |

Print, export, and or email the report as instructed by your professor
- If you save the report, name it **7-Your Name Check Detail Ch. 4**.
Close Your Name's Beach Barkers

## PETTY CASH—READ

Frequently, a business will need to pay for small expenses with cash. These might include expenses such as postage, office supplies, and miscellaneous expenses. For example, rather than write a check for postage due of 75 cents, you would use money from petty cash. QuickBooks Online allows you to establish and use a petty cash account to track these small expenditures. Normally, a Petty Cash Voucher or Petty Cash Ticket is prepared; and, if available, the receipt(s) for the transaction is (are) stapled to it. In QuickBooks Online when you record an Expense you can scan a receipt and attach it electronically to the transaction.

It is important in a business to keep accurate records of the petty cash expenditures. Procedures for control of the Petty Cash fund need to be established to prohibit access to and unauthorized use of the cash. Periodically, the petty cash expenditures are recorded so that the records of the company accurately reflect all expenses incurred in the operation of the business.

## PETTY CASH—DRILL

There are times when you need a small amount of cash to pay for something. To account for this money, you establish the Petty Cash account to record transactions whenever the cash is spent. Petty Cash must have money in order to pay for small expenses. After withdrawing cash from the bank, you record the funding of Petty Cash by transferring money from your Checking account into Petty Cash. Alternatively, you can write a check for the amount and then go to the bank and cash it.

---

**MEMO**
**DATE:** January 23, 2016

Withdrew $100 in cash from Checking to have Petty Cash on hand. Create a new account: Category Type: Banking, Detail Type: Cash on Hand, Name: Petty Cash. Record the transfer of $100 from Checking into Petty Cash.

Use Petty Cash to pay for Squeaky Kleen Car Wash, $19.95.

---

### DRILL

Open the **Test Drive Company** and practice creating and using Petty Cash

### Create and Fund Petty Cash Account

When you create the Petty Cash Account to have cash on hand, you have to get money for use in the account. This may be done by cashing a check or making a cash withdrawal at the bank. To account for this money, you create a Petty Cash account to record transactions whenever the cash is spent. You record the funding of Petty Cash by transferring money from your Checking account into Petty Cash.

Use the **Test Drive Company** and add and fund the account Petty Cash

> Open the Chart of Accounts as previously instructed
> Click **New**
> Add Petty Cash:
> > Category Type: **Bank**
> > Detail Type: **Cash on hand**
> > Name: **Petty Cash**
> > - Do not enter a Balance.

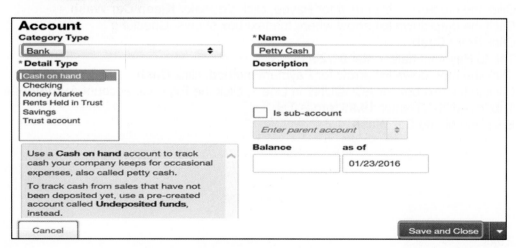

Click **Save and Close** (click the drop-down list arrow if necessary)
Click the **Plus** icon
Click **Transfer** in the Other column
Click the drop-down list arrow for Transfer Funds From, click **Checking**
- Notice that the Balance of the Checking account shows $1,201.00.
Click the drop-down list arrow for Transfer Funds To, click **Petty Cash**
- Notice that the Balance of the Petty Cash account shows $0.00.
Click in the text box for Transfer Amount, enter **100**, press **Tab**
Change the date to **01/23/16**, press **Tab**
Enter the Memo **Establish Petty Cash**

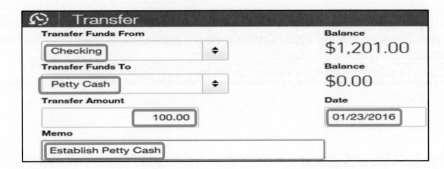

Click **Save and close** (click the drop-down list arrow if necessary)
- When you return to the Chart of Accounts, you will see the balance of Checking is now $1,101.00 and the balance of Petty Cash is $100.00.

| Checking | 🐟 Bank | 🐟 Checking | 1,101.00 |
| Petty Cash | Bank | Cash on hand | 100.00 |

Do <u>not</u> close the Test Drive Company, continue and complete the next section

## Petty Cash Transaction

When you have the cash on hand for Petty Cash and you pay for small purchases or expenses, you will record the transaction as an Expense.

 Continue to use the **Test Drive Company** and record a Petty Cash transaction

Click the **Plus** icon, click **Expense** in the Vendors column
Click the drop-down list arrow for Payee, click **Squeaky Kleen Car Wash**
Click the drop-down list arrow where the text box shows "Checking"
Click **Petty Cash**
Tab to Payment date, enter **01/23/16**
Click the drop-down list arrow for Payment method, click **Cash**
Click in the text box for ACCOUNT in Line 1, click the Expense account **Automobile**
Tab to AMOUNT enter **19.95**, press Tab
Enter the Memo **Car Wash**

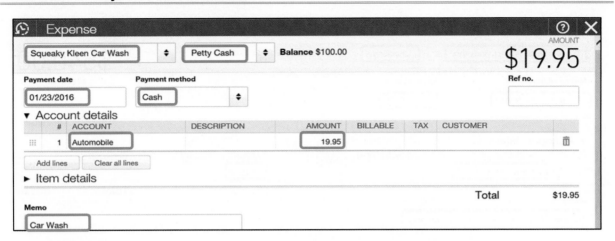

Click **Save and close** (click the drop-down list arrow if necessary)
Return to the Chart of Accounts
- Note the balance of Petty Cash of $80.05.

| Checking | 🔁 Bank | 🔁 Checking | 1,101.00 |
|---|---|---|---|
| Petty Cash | Bank | Cash on hand | 80.05 |

Do **not** close the Test Drive Company

## PURCHASE ASSET WITH COMPANY CHECK—DRILL

Not all purchases will be transactions on account and not all checks will be written to pay for bills and expenses. If something is purchased and paid for with a check, a check is written and the purchase is recorded.

---

**MEMO**
**DATE:** January 23, 2016

Purchased a custom truck liner with a 10-year warranty for the back of the truck. Paid for it by writing a check for $540.00.

---

*DRILL*

 Open the **Test Drive Company** and record the purchase of the truck liner

Click the **Plus** icon, click **Check** in the Vendors Column
Payee: **Diego's Road Warrior Bodyshop**
Account: **Checking**
Date: **012316**
- If you see a message regarding Add to Check, close it by clicking  **>** .
For ACCOUNT, click the Fixed Asset, **Truck: Original Cost**
- This account is used since the truck liner has a 10-year warranty.
Enter the AMOUNT of **540**
Enter **Custom Truck Liner with 10-Year Warranty** as the Memo

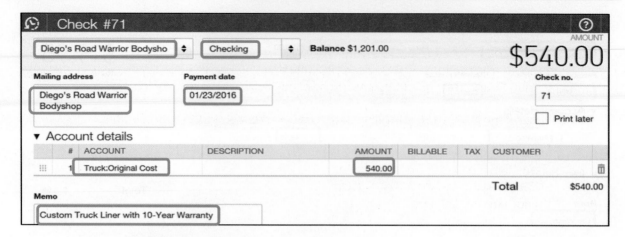

Click **Save and close** (or the drop-down list arrow)
Open the Chart of Accounts as previously instructed
View the Account Register for Truck:Original Cost
- Note the two transactions, Check 71 for $540.00 and a Journal entry for the Opening Balance of $13,495.00.

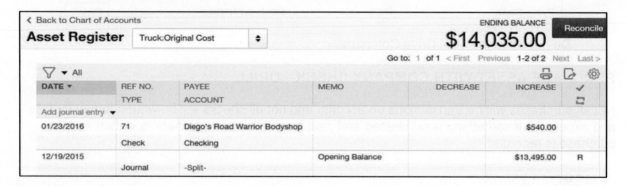

Close the Test Drive Company

## PETTY CASH—DO

As you learned in the drill, there are times when you need a small amount of cash to pay for something. To account for this money, you establish and fund the Petty Cash account to record transactions whenever the cash is spent.

---

**MEMO**

**DATE:** January 23, 2016

Withdrew $100 in cash from Checking to have Petty Cash on hand. Create a new account: Category Type: Bank, Detail Type: Cash on Hand, Name: Petty Cash. Record the transfer of $100 from Checking into Petty Cash.

Used $6.47 from Petty Cash to pay for 1 ream of paper that you purchased from Super Office to use immediately for flyers that you will print and give to your customers.

---

_DO_

 Open **Your Name's Beach Barkers** then create and use Petty Cash

## Create and Fund Petty Cash Account

To account for money to have on hand to pay for small expenses, you establish the Petty Cash account and record transactions whenever the cash is spent. Once the account has been created, you record the funding of Petty Cash by cashing a check or withdrawing cash at the bank.

 Use **Your Name's Beach Barkers** to add and fund the Petty Cash account

Open the Chart of Accounts as previously instructed, click **New**
Add Petty Cash as previously instructed
- Refer to the Memo for account details.
- Do <u>not</u> enter a Balance.

Click **Save and Close**
Click the **Plus** icon
Click **Transfer** in the Other column
Transfer Funds From: **Checking**
- Notice that the Balance of the Checking account shows $61,421.12.
Transfer Funds To: **Petty Cash**
- Notice that the Balance of the Petty Cash account shows $0.00.
Transfer Amount: **100**
Date **01/23/16**
Memo: **Establish Petty Cash**

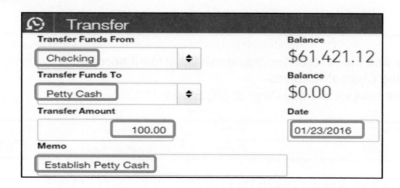

Click **Save and close** (click the drop-down list arrow if necessary)

- When you return to the Chart of Accounts, you will see the balance of Checking is $61,321.12 and the balance of Petty Cash is $100.00.

| Checking | Bank | Checking | 61,321.12 |
| Petty Cash | Bank | Cash on hand | 100.00 |

Do <u>not</u> close Your Name's Beach Barkers

## Petty Cash Transaction

When you have cash on hand for Petty Cash and you pay for small purchases or expenses, you will record the transaction as an Expense.

 Continue to use **Your Name's Beach Barkers** to record a Petty Cash transaction

Click the **Plus** icon, click **Expense** in the Vendors column
Payee: **Super Office**
Click the drop-down list arrow where the text box shows "Checking," click **Petty Cash**
Payment date: **01/23/16**
Click the drop-down list arrow for Payment method, click **Cash**
Click in the text box for ACCOUNT in Line 1, click the Supplies Expense subaccount **Office Supplies Expense**
- Since the paper is for immediate use, it is an expense. Earlier in the chapter, you recorded a transaction for office supplies to have on hand. Because you were going to have the supplies available for future use, they were recorded in the Asset account Office Supplies.
Amount: **6.47**
Enter the Memo **Paper for Flyers**

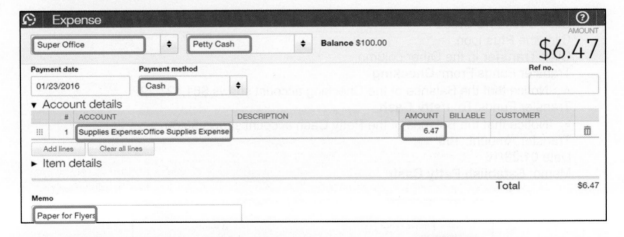

Click **Save and close** (click the drop-down list arrow if necessary)
Return to the Chart of Accounts
- Note the balance of Petty Cash of $93.53.

| Checking | Bank | Checking | 61,321.12 |
| Petty Cash | Bank | Cash on hand | 93.53 |

Do <u>not</u> close Your Name's Beach Barkers

## PURCHASE ASSET WITH COMPANY CHECK—DO

As you learned in the drill, if something is purchased and paid for with a check, a check is written and the purchase is recorded.

> **MEMO**
> **DATE:** January 23, 2016
>
> Wrote Check 9 for $862.92 to purchase a printer for the office from Computer Town.

*DO*

 Open **Your Name's Beach Barkers** and record the printer purchase

Refer to the Memo and prepare the Check as previously instructed
- If you see a message regarding Add to Check, close it by clicking [ **>** ].

Click **Print Later** to remove the check mark

Enter **9** for Check no.

Account: Fixed Asset **Equipment: Original Cost**
- Since you will have the printer for over a year, it is a fixed asset.

Memo: **Purchase Printer**

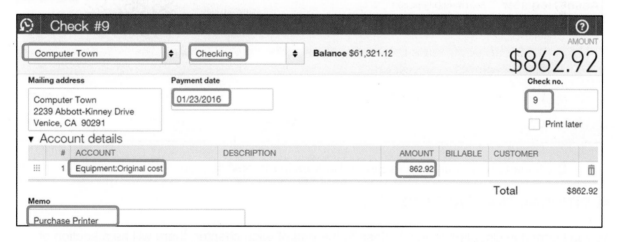

Click **Print Check** at the bottom of the screen
- You get a message that the check was saved.
- If you are not sure that QuickBooks Online remembered to use Standard Checks, click **Print setup**, make sure that Standard is selected, then click **Yes, I'm finished with setup**.

Click **Preview and print** at the bottom of the screen
- You will see a preview of the check.

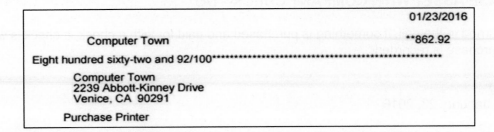

Print as previously instructed
- If you save the check as a PDF document to email to your instructor, name it
  **8-Your Name Check 9 Computer Town**.

Click **Close** on the screen
On the "Did your checks print OK?" screen, click **Done**
Click the **Close** button at the top of the Print Checks screen
Open the Chart of Accounts as previously instructed
View the Account Register for Equipment:Original Cost
- Note the two transactions, Check 9 for $862.92 and a Journal entry for the Opening
  Balance of $8,000.00.

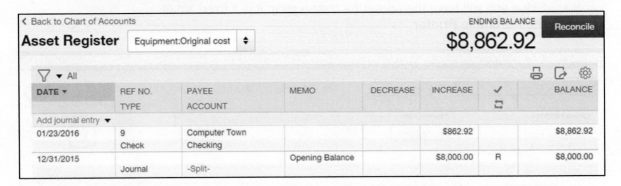

Continue to use Your Name's Beach Barkers in the next section

## ADDITIONAL TRANSACTIONS—DO

As you learned in Chapters 2 and 3, close to the end of each chapter, there will be a section of additional transactions that will be similar to ones you completed during the chapter. These transactions will be listed in Memos. You will enter them without any specific instructions. If you have questions about how to enter transactions, you may refer back to material presented earlier in the chapter.

### _DO_

Continue to use **Your Name's Beach Barkers** and enter the following transactions in the Memo boxes

Add Memos to transactions where appropriate
Print, save, and submit as you have been requested to do by your instructor
- When you enter a batch of checks or write several checks in Pay Bills, print the batch. When you enter single checks, print them when they are entered. Assign the next available check number. The last check written before this section was Check Number 9.

- Use the same naming structure as previously instructed: Document number, your name, business form and number, vendor name. For example, 29-Your Name Check 1234 John Doe.

---

**MEMO**

**DATE:** January 24, 2016

Received Bill 276 from Canine Supplies for the purchase of Kennel Supplies to have on hand, $189.00.

Received Bill 425 for $75 from Garcia's Advertising for a newspaper ad.

Paid <u>cash</u> for an oil change from Morales Auto Repair, $29.95. (Vehicle Expenses)

Received Bill 564 for $175.00 for the purchase of Cleaning Supplies to <u>have on hand</u> from a new vendor, Supplies Unlimited (7291 E. Los Angeles Street, Los Angeles, CA 90012, Email: Supplies@orders.com, Phone: 310-555-8529, Fax: 310-555-9258, Website: www.SuppliesUnlimited.com, Terms: Net 30).

Change the name of the Fixed Asset Account Equipment to Office Equipment.

Wrote Check 10 to Super Office for the purchase of a new Fax machine—Office Equipment, $322.92.

Paid the rent of $1,500 to Venice Rentals.

The January 18, 2016 vehicle repair by Morales Auto Repair was $50 less than originally billed. Received Credit Memo 725 from them.

---

Continue recording, saving, and printing transactions

---

**MEMO**

**DATE:** January 27, 2016

Note: Use this date for the remaining transactions

Paid the monthly telephone bill of $129.95 to Beach Telephone Company (425 Rose Avenue, Venice, CA 90291, Phone: 800-555-6554, Website: www.BeachTelephone.com, Terms: Net 30).

Had to take a load of towels to the laundromat to wash and dry. Paid $6.50 in cash to a new vendor, Lulu's Laundry (2151 Lincoln Boulevard, Venice, CA 90291, Phone: 310-555-8789, Terms: Net 30).

Transfer an additional $50 to Petty Cash.

Make partial payments of $200 to Bow-Wow Supplies and $300 to Canine Supplies toward their opening balances. Pay the full amount owed to Morales Auto Repair. Pay Garcia's Advertising for Bill 2525.

---

Continue to use Your Name's Beach Barkers to complete reports

## VIEW EXPENSES—DO

In addition to a variety of reports relating to expenses, QuickBooks Online allows you to view all of your expense transactions. You may view all of the transactions, specify a date range and/or type of transactions. Information is shown for the Transaction Date, Type, No., Payee, Category, Total, and Actions available to be performed.

*DO*

Continue to use **Your Name's Beach Barkers** to view all expense transactions

Click **Transactions** on the Navigation Bar
- Notice that there are selections for Banking, Sales, Expenses, and Chart of Accounts.

Click **Expenses**
- All sales transactions are shown for the Last 365 days from the most recent date to the oldest date.

To specify the date range, click the **Filter** button

Enter the From date **12/31/15** and To date **01/27/16**

Click **Apply**

Click the **Settings** icon 🔧 next to the print and export icons, click **Show More**
- Columns displayed have a check mark. You may deselect any of these columns. You may select other Columns to display by clicking on them.

Click the Columns for **Balance** and **Status** to add them to the List

Print in Landscape orientation, export to Excel, and/or submit as previously instructed
- If you save the report, name it **13-Your Name Expense Transaction List Ch. 4**.

Continue to use Your Name's Beach Barkers to complete reports

## VENDOR BALANCE SUMMARY—DO

QuickBooks Online has two Vendor Balance Reports available in the Manage Accounts Payable Category in Reports. There is a Summary Report that shows unpaid balances for vendors and a Detail Report that lists each transaction for a vendor. In order to see how much is owed to each vendor, prepare a Vendor Balance Summary report.

*DO*

Continue to use **Your Name's Beach Barkers** and prepare a Vendor Balance Summary Report

Open the **Manage Accounts Payable** report category in All Reports as previously instructed

Click **Vendor Balance Summary**
- By default, the report is prepared for All Dates. You may select an As of Date if you wish.

### Your Name's Beach Barkers
#### VENDOR BALANCE SUMMARY
##### All Dates

|                      | TOTAL      |
| -------------------- | ---------- |
| Bow-Wow Supplies     | 1,300.00   |
| Canine Supplies      | 2,389.00   |
| Computer Town        | 275.00     |
| Garcia's Advertising | 75.00      |
| Supplies Unlimited   | 175.00     |
| **TOTAL**            | **$4,214.00** |

- Do your Vendor Balances match the ones shown in the above report? If not, go back through your entries in the Expense Transactions List and verify your entries with the information given in the text.

Remove the Date Prepared and Time Prepared, if instructed to do so by your professor

Print, export, and/or submit as previously instructed
- If you print, use Portrait for the Layout.
- Name the report **14-Your Name Vendor Balance Summary Ch. 4**.

Continue to use Your Name's Beach Barkers to complete reports

## UNPAID BILLS—DO

As you learned earlier in the chapter, it is possible to get information regarding unpaid bills by preparing the Unpaid Bills Report. Evaluating the Unpaid Bills Report enables you to determine which bills should be paid and to know which bills are overdue.

### *DO*

Continue to use **Your Name's Beach Barkers** and prepare the Unpaid Bills Report

Click **Unpaid Bills** in the Manage Accounts Payable section in All Reports
- By default the report is prepared for All Dates.
- Scroll through the report and note which bills are past due. If there is a minus (-) in front of the number, it means the number of days until the bill is due. Remember, the number of days shown in Past Due is calculated based on the current date. The number of days you see will not match the following report.
- If you have made a partial payment for a bill, you will see a difference between the Amount of the bill and the Open Balance. The Open Balance tells you the remaining amount that needs to be paid for the bill.

### Your Name's Beach Barkers
#### UNPAID BILLS
All Dates

| DATE | TRANSACTION TYPE | NUM | DUE DATE | PAST DUE | AMOUNT | OPEN BALANCE |
|---|---|---|---|---|---|---|
| **Bow-Wow Supplies** 760-555-2951 | | | | | | |
| 12/31/2015 | Bill | | 12/31/2015 | 31 | 2,000.00 | 1,300.00 |
| **Total for Bow-Wow Supplies** | | | | | **$2,000.00** | **$1,300.00** |
| **Canine Supplies** 310-555-6971 | | | | | | |
| 12/31/2015 | Bill | | 12/31/2015 | 31 | 3,000.00 | 2,200.00 |
| 01/24/2016 | Bill | 276 | 02/23/2016 | -23 | 189.00 | 189.00 |
| **Total for Canine Supplies** | | | | | **$3,189.00** | **$2,389.00** |
| **Computer Town** (310) 555-8816 | | | | | | |
| 01/18/2016 | Bill | 890 | 02/17/2016 | -17 | 275.00 | 275.00 |
| **Total for Computer Town** | | | | | **$275.00** | **$275.00** |
| **Garcia's Advertising** 310-555-1879 | | | | | | |
| 01/24/2016 | Bill | 425 | 02/23/2016 | -23 | 75.00 | 75.00 |
| **Total for Garcia's Advertising** | | | | | **$75.00** | **$75.00** |
| **Supplies Unlimited** (310) 555-8529 | | | | | | |
| 01/24/2016 | Bill | 564 | 02/23/2016 | -23 | 175.00 | 175.00 |
| **Total for Supplies Unlimited** | | | | | **$175.00** | **$175.00** |
| **TOTAL** | | | | | **$5,714.00** | **$4,214.00** |

Remove the Date Prepared and Time Prepared, if instructed to do so by your professor
Print, export, and/or submit as previously instructed
- If you print, use Portrait for the Layout.
- Name the report **15-Your Name Unpaid Bills Ch. 4**.

Continue to use Your Name's Beach Barkers to complete reports

## BILL PAYMENT LIST—DO

As you learned earlier in the chapter, when a bill has been paid, it is shown in the Bill Payment List in the Manage Accounts Payable Reports Category.

### DO

 Continue to use **Your Name's Beach Barkers** to prepare the Bill Payment List Report

> In the Manage Accounts Payable category, click **Bill Payment List**
> The report dates are From: **01/01/16** To: **01/27/16**
> Remove the Date and Time Prepared from the report footer
> Print, export, and/or email or submit the report as required by your professor
> * If you print, use Portrait for the Layout.
> * Name the report **16-Your Name Bill Payment List Ch. 4**.
> Continue to use Your Name's Beach Barkers to complete reports

## TRANSACTIONS LIST BY VENDOR—DO

Now that you have entered the transactions for Chapter 4, it is important to view information for vendor transactions. To do this, you prepare a Transaction List by Vendor Report. The report displays the vendors that have recorded transactions.

### DO

 Continue to use **Your Name's Beach Barkers** to prepare the Transaction List by Vendor

> Access the **Review Expenses and Purchases** report category
> Click **Transaction List by Vendor**
> Use the Dates From: **010116** To: **012716**
> * Scroll through the report and view the transactions listed for each vendor. If a vendor does not appear in the report, you may have used transaction dates outside the date range or the vendor may not have any transactions recorded.
> Remove the Date Prepared and Time Prepared, if instructed to do so by your professor
> Print, export, and/or submit as previously instructed
> * If you print, use Landscape for the Layout.
> * Name the report **17-Your Name Transaction List by Vendor Ch. 4**.
> Continue to use Your Name's Beach Barkers to complete reports

## CHECK DETAIL—DO

As you learned earlier in the chapter, once checks have been printed, it is important to review information about them. The Check Detail Report provides detailed information regarding Checks prepared and Petty Cash expenditures made to pay for bills and expenses.

### DO

 Continue to use **Your Name's Beach Barkers** and prepare the Check Detail Report

> In the report category **Review Expenses and Purchases**, click **Check Detail**
> Enter the Dates From: **010116** and To: **012716**, and then click **Run Report**

- Your report should show Checks 2-16 and three Petty Cash expenditures. This report does not show Check 1 because it was not used to pay a bill or an expense. It was written to give a refund in Chapter 3.

Remove the Date Prepared and Time Prepared, if instructed to do so by your professor
Print, export, and/or submit as previously instructed

- If you print, use Portrait for the Layout.
- Name the report **18-Your Name Check Detail Ch. 4**.

Continue to use Your Name's Beach Barkers to complete reports

## JOURNAL—DO

As you learned in Chapter 3, QuickBooks Online records every entry behind the scenes in debit and credit format. Preparing the Journal report will display this information. In many instances, going through the Journal entries and checking transaction dates, account names, and products/services listed in the Memo column will help you find errors in your transactions. If a transaction does not appear in the Journal, it may be due to using an incorrect date or forgetting to enter it.

In your concepts course, you may have learned that the General Journal was where all entries were recorded in debit/credit format. In QuickBooks Online, you do record some debit/credit transactions as Journal Entries and then display all debit/credit entries no matter where the transactions were recorded in the Journal Report.

## _DO_

 Continue to use **Your Name's Beach Barkers** and prepare a Journal Report

Return to **All Reports**, select **Accountant Reports**, and click **Journal**
Enter the Dates From: **010116** To: **Current Date**

- Scroll through the report and note the transaction dates. If any transactions are dated later than January 27, 2016, they should appear. If necessary change any incorrect transaction dates.
- Look at the debits and credits carefully, the debit entry is not always shown first.

Verify your Total:

| TOTAL | $47,968.27 | $47,968.27 |
|---|---|---|

To see the entries for sales and customer payments entered in Chapter 3, enter the Dates:
From: **010116** To: **011716**

Verify your Total:

| TOTAL | $40,205.00 | $40,205.00 |
|---|---|---|

To see the entries for bills and expenses entered in Chapter 4, enter the Dates:
From: **011816** To: **012716**
Verify your Total:

| TOTAL | $7,763.27 | $7,763.27 |
|---|---|---|

- By looking at the totals for the three different time periods, it may help you isolate where an error occurred and enable you to make corrections. Double-check dates, amounts, accounts, and products/services used in the transactions.

Remove the Date Prepared and Time Prepared, if instructed to do so by your professor

When the totals are correct, print, export, and/or submit the Journal for <u>January 18-27, 2016</u> (Chapter 4 entries) as previously instructed

- If you print, use Landscape for the Layout.
- Name the report **19-Your Name Journal Ch. 4**.

Continue to use Your Name's Beach Barkers to complete reports

## TRIAL BALANCE—DO

When all sales transactions have been entered, it is important to prepare the Trial Balance to verify that the total debits equal the total credits.

## <u>DO</u>

Continue to use **Your Name's Beach Barkers** and prepare a Trial Balance

Click **Trial Balance** in the Accountant Reports Category
Enter the Dates From: **010116** To: **012716**
Click **Run Report**
Compare your Trial Balance with the one shown on the next page
Remove the Date Prepared, Time Prepared, and Report Basis if instructed to do so by your professor
When the totals are correct, print, export, and/or submit the Trial Balance as of
January 27, 2016 (Chapter 4 entries) as previously instructed

- If you print, use Portrait for the Layout.
- Name the report **20-Your Name Trial Balance Ch. 4**.

## Your Name's Beach Barkers
### TRIAL BALANCE
As of January 27, 2016

| | DEBIT | CREDIT |
|---|---|---|
| Checking | 57,537.88 | |
| Petty Cash | 107.08 | |
| Accounts Receivable (A/R) | 14,930.00 | |
| Inventory Asset | 29,012.50 | |
| Prepaid Insurance | 1,200.00 | |
| Supplies:Cleaning Supplies | 925.00 | |
| Supplies:Kennel Supplies | 2,084.00 | |
| Supplies:Office Supplies | 753.68 | |
| Supplies:Sales Supplies | 500.00 | |
| Undeposited Funds | 0.00 | |
| Furniture & Fixtures:Depreciation | | 1,500.00 |
| Furniture & Fixtures:Original cost | 15,000.00 | |
| Kennel Equipment:Depreciation | | 2,030.00 |
| Kennel Equipment:Original cost | 20,300.00 | |
| Office Equipment:Depreciation | | 800.00 |
| Office Equipment:Original cost | 9,185.84 | |
| Vehicles:Depreciation | | 3,200.00 |
| Vehicles:Original cost | 32,000.00 | |
| Accounts Payable (A/P) | | 4,214.00 |
| Loans Payable:Equipment Loan | | 2,000.00 |
| Loans Payable:Furniture & Fixtures Loan | | 2,500.00 |
| Retained Earnings | | 22,200.00 |
| Your Name, Capital | | 142,362.50 |
| Services:Boarding | | 770.00 |
| Services:Day Camp | | 420.00 |
| Services:Grooming | | 885.00 |
| Services:House Calls | | 225.00 |
| Services:Training | | 3,025.00 |
| Services:Transportation | | 300.00 |
| Advertising | 200.00 | |
| Equipment Rental | 75.00 | |
| Laundry | 6.50 | |
| Rent or Lease | 1,500.00 | |
| Repair & Maintenance:Computer Repair | 200.00 | |
| Repair & Maintenance:Vehicle Repair | 212.50 | |
| Supplies Expense:Office Supplies Expense | 6.47 | |
| Telephone Expense | 129.95 | |
| Utilities:Electric | 89.75 | |
| Utilities:Gas-Heating | 189.50 | |
| Utilities:Water | 175.95 | |
| Vehicle Expenses | 109.90 | |
| TOTAL | $186,431.50 | $186,431.50 |

Close Your Name's Beach Barkers

## SUMMARY

In this chapter, accounting for purchases and expenses was performed. By the end of the chapter, bills were recorded and paid, checks were written, small expense transactions were entered, and reports were prepared. The petty cash fund was established and used for payments of small expense items. Checks were voided and deleted. Accounts were added and modified. New vendors were added. The Vendors List and individual Vendor Registers were used to access transactions. Transaction Audit History was viewed and discussed. An asset was purchased with a company check. All expense transactions were viewed. Reports were prepared for Transaction List by Vendor and Check Details. Unpaid Bills and Vendor Balance Summary Reports provided information regarding bills that had not been paid.

# END-OF-CHAPTER QUESTIONS

## TRUE/FALSE

ANSWER THE FOLLOWING QUESTIONS IN THE SPACE PROVIDED BEFORE THE QUESTION NUMBER.

_____ 1. When a bill has been recorded, you may pay it using Pay Bills or by writing a check manually.

_____ 2. You may access a Bill by clicking the Recent Transactions icon.

_____ 3. You can add a new account while recording a bill.

_____ 4. The Pay Bills window does not tell you which bills are overdue.

_____ 5. On the Pay Bills Screen, QuickBooks Online inserts the amount for Credit Applied when the bill is selected for payment.

_____ 6. A prepaid expense is an asset.

_____ 7. A bill must be voided manually.

_____ 8. The Bill Payment List report tells you which bills have not been paid.

_____ 9. A Vendor Credit increases the amount you owe a vendor.

_____10. When you use Compare to view an Audit History for a transaction, the original transaction amount is highlighted.

## MULTIPLE CHOICE

WRITE THE LETTER OF THE CORRECT ANSWER IN THE SPACE PROVIDED BEFORE THE QUESTION NUMBER.

_____ 1. When you record a bill, it <u>must</u> be paid ___.
   A. With Petty Cash
   B. By writing a Check
   C. Using Pay Bills
   D. All of the above

_____ 2. Which of the following would not be a prepaid expense?
   A. Equipment Rental
   B. Insurance
   C. Office Supplies
   D. None of the above

_____ 3. To pay for a bill that has not been recorded, you use ___.
A. Pay Bills
B. Bills
C. Check
D. Accounts Payable

_____ 4. If a bill payment amount does not match any of the bill amounts, QuickBooks Online applies it to ___.
A. The newest bill
B. The oldest bill
C. Splits the amount among all bills owed to the vendor
D. Vendor Credits

_____ 5. You may view the Audit History of a transaction in the following ways:
A. Show All
B. Compare
C. Collapsed
D. All of the above

_____ 6. To pay for small expenses using cash, you use the ___ account.
A. Cash
B. Transfer
C. Petty Cash
D. Undeposited Funds

_____ 7. The report that you prepare to determine which bills to pay is the ___ report.
A. Expenses List
B. Vendor Balance Detail
C. Bill Payment List
D. Unpaid Bills

_____ 8. If you purchase something and pay for it later, you record a ___.
A. Bill
B. Petty Cash Future Expense form
C. Check with a later date
D. Future Payment form

_____ 9. Which report shows every transaction recorded in Debit/Credit format?
A. Trial Balance
B. Journal
C. Transaction List by Vendor
D. Expenses List

_____ 10. To see the unpaid balances for vendors, you prepare a ___ report.
A. Unpaid Bills
B. Vendor Balance Summary
C. Vendor Balance Detail
D. Any of the above

## FILL-IN

IN THE SPACE PROVIDED, WRITE THE ANSWER THAT MOST APPROPRIATELY COMPLETES THE SENTENCE.

1.  When referring to GAAP standards, the Vendors List functions as the _____ Ledger in QuickBooks Online.

2.   The report that provides detailed information regarding Checks prepared and Petty Cash expenditures is the _____ report.

3.  If you fund Petty Cash by making a cash withdrawal at the bank, you enter it in the Petty Cash account by a completing a(n) _____ in QuickBooks Online.

4.  When you record the Telephone Bill, in the Journal QuickBooks Online enters a _____ to an Expense Account and a _____ to Accounts Payable.

5.  You remove the date prepared and time prepared from a report footer by clicking the _____ button.

## COMPUTER ASSIGNMENT

REFER TO PRINTOUTS OR USE QUICKBOOKS ONLINE AND YOUR NAME'S BEACH BARKERS TO LOOK UP OR ENTER INFORMATION, AND THEN WRITE THE ANSWERS TO THE FOLLOWING EXERCISES IN THE SPACE PROVIDED

1. What is the balance of Petty Cash on January 24, 2016?                _____

2. What business form did you complete to record the purchase of the Fax machine from Super Office?                _____

3. What is the total of the Bill Payment List on January 27, 2016?                _____

4. How much was the check for Morales Auto Repair on January 27, 2016?                _____

5. What business form did you complete to record the reduction of the amount owed to Morales Auto Repair on January 24, 2016?                _____

6. Which Vendor had the most transactions recorded for January, 2016?                _____

7. What was the Bill number and amount of the Bill Payment check prepared for Garcia's Advertising on January 27, 2016?                _____

                _____

8. For the purchase of the Fax machine from Super Office, what account is used in the Journal for the debit:                _____
and the credit:                _____

9. What is the balance of the Checking account after recording Check 11?                _____

10. For the transaction with Lulu's Laundry, the account debited in the Journal is:                _____
and the account credited is:                _____

# CHAPTER 4 CHECKLIST

The checklist below shows all of the business forms printed during training. Check each one that you printed, exported, and/or submitted.

| | |
|---|---|
| _____ 1-Transaction List by Vendor Ch. 4 | _____ 11-Check 12 Beach Telephone Company |
| _____ 2-Unpaid Bills Ch. 4 | _____ 12-Checks 13-16 |
| _____ 3-Checks 2-5 | _____ 13-Expense Transactions List Ch. 4 |
| _____ 4-Bill Payment List Ch. 4 | _____ 14-Vendor Balance Summary Ch. 4 |
| _____ 5-Checks 6-8 | _____ 15-Unpaid Bills Ch. 4 |
| _____ 6-Check 6 Corrected | _____ 16-Bill Payment List Ch. 4 |
| _____ 7-Check Detail Ch. 4 | _____ 17-Transaction List by Vendor Ch. 4 |
| _____ 8-Check 9 Computer Town | _____ 18-Check Detail Ch. 4 |
| _____ 9-Check 10 Super Office | _____ 19-Journal Ch. 4 |
| _____ 10-Check 11 Venice Rentals | _____ 20-Trial Balance Ch. 4 |

4

# GENERAL ACCOUNTING AND END-OF-PERIOD PROCEDURES

**5**

## LEARNING OBJECTIVES

At the completion of this chapter, you will be able to:

1. Complete the end-of-period procedures.
2. Record Journal Entries for depreciation and the adjusting entries required for accrual-basis accounting.
3. Record owner's equity transactions for a sole proprietor including capital investment, owner withdrawals, and transfer of net income into the capital account.
4. Reconcile the bank statement, record bank service charges, automatic payments, and mark cleared transactions.
5. Print reports including Statement of Cash Flows, Journal, Trial Balance, Profit & Loss, and Balance Sheet.
6. Close the end of a period.

## GENERAL ACCOUNTING AND END-OF-PERIOD PROCEDURES

As previously stated, QuickBooks Online operates from the standpoint of a business document rather than an accounting form, journal, or ledger. While QuickBooks Online does incorporate all of these items into the program, in many instances they operate behind the scenes. QuickBooks Online does not require special closing procedures at the end of a period. At the end of the fiscal year, QuickBooks Online transfers the Net Income into Retained Earnings and allows you to protect the data for the year by assigning a closing date to the period. Once a period is closed, all of the transaction detail is maintained and viewable, but it will not be changed unless Yes is clicked on a warning screen.

Even though a formal closing does not have to be performed within QuickBooks Online, when you use accrual-basis accounting, several transactions must be recorded to reflect all expenses and income for the period. For example, bank statements must be reconciled and any charges or bank collections need to be recorded. During the business period, the accountant for the company will review things such as adjusting entries, depreciation schedules, owner's equity adjustments, and so on. The changes and adjustments may be entered directly into the company or they may be made by the accountant using QuickBooks Online Accountant. Once necessary adjustments have been made, reports reflecting the end-of-period results of operations should be prepared.

## TRAINING TUTORIAL AND PROCEDURES

Continue to use the Test Drive Company for practice and the fictional company, Your Name's Beach Barkers, to record end-of-period transactions, adjustments, and reconciliations; to assign a closing date; and to prepare reports. In certain sections of the chapter, transactions will need to be entered into the Test Drive Company before you can complete a drill. When working with Equity accounts, the material entered into Your Name's Beach Barkers is more complex than the entries for the Test Drive Company. Instructions are given to guide you through the process.

Just as you did in Chapters 2, 3,and 4, you will enter additional transactions near the end of the chapter. These transactions are similar to the ones you entered in the Test Drive Company and in

Your Name's Beach Barkers so no step-by-step instructions will be given. If you need to refer back to the chapter materials to make the entries, you should feel free to do so. If you can enter them without looking back, you have learned how to do something on your own in QuickBooks Online.

## DATES

Remember that the year used for the screen shots is 2016. Continue to use the same year that you used in Chapters 2, 3, and 4. When QuickBooks Online inserts the current date into a transaction, be aware of this and be sure to use the date indicated in the text. There are instances, the Reconciliation report for example, where QuickBooks Online uses the current date no matter what date you insert. The rule is, if you cannot change a date, accept the date given. Don't forget that the Test Drive Company is programmed to automatically change dates and that the dates shown in the text will not match the ones shown on your computer. When using the Test Drive Company, you may have to use the current date in some of the practices in order to access the desired data. Instructions will be given when this occurs.

## IMPORTANT NOTE

QuickBooks Online is constantly evolving and new features, apps, and procedures change frequently. Everything in the text is correct at the time of this writing; however, by the time of publication some changes to the program may occur. Whenever possible, changes in QuickBooks Online will be incorporated into the text but do note that some of the updates will not be able to be included until the next edition of the book.

## ADJUSTMENTS FOR ACCRUAL-BASIS ACCOUNTING

As previously stated, the accrual-basis of accounting matches the income and the expenses of a period in order to arrive at an accurate figure for net income or net loss. Thus, the revenue is earned at the time the service is performed or the sale is made no matter when the actual cash is received. The cash-basis of accounting records income or revenue at the time cash is received no matter when the sale was made or the service performed. The same holds true when a business buys things or pays bills. In accrual-basis accounting, the expense is recorded at the time the bill is received or the purchase is made regardless of the actual payment date. In cash-basis accounting, the expense is not recorded until it is paid. In QuickBooks Online, the Accounting Method selected by default in Settings is Accrual. It may be changed to Cash.

To illustrate the effect on the Profit and Loss between Accrual-Basis and Cash-Basis accounting, use the following example. Record $1,000 of sales on account and one year of insurance for $600 in November: Using accrual-basis accounting, you would record $1,000 as income or revenue and $600 as a prepaid expense in an asset account—Prepaid Insurance. Every month, an adjusting entry for $50 would be made to record the amount of insurance used for the month. In cash-basis accounting, when the $1,000 payment on account is received in March, that is when you record income. When using the cash-basis of accounting, you would have no income and $600 worth of insurance recorded as an expense for November with nothing else recorded for insurance until the following November. The income of $1,000 would not be shown in November. A Statement of Profit & Loss prepared in November would show:

| November | Accrual | | Cash | |
|---|---|---|---|---|
| Income | | $1,000 | | $ 0 |
| Insurance Expense | ($600/12) = | -50 | | -600 |
| Net Profit (Loss) | Profit | $950 | Loss | -$600 |

When using accrual-basis accounting, there are several internal transactions that must be recorded. These entries are called adjusting entries. Some items used in a business are purchased and or paid for in advance. When this occurs, they are recorded as an asset and are called prepaid expenses. As these are used, they become expenses of the business. For example, insurance for the entire year would be used up month by month and should, therefore, be a monthly expense. Commonly, the insurance is billed and paid for six months or the entire year. Until the insurance is used, it is an asset. Each month, the portion of the insurance used becomes an expense for the month. (Refer to the preceding chart.) Another example for adjusting entries is in regard to equipment. Since it does wear out and will eventually need to be replaced, rather than wait until replacement to record the use of the equipment, an adjusting entry is made to allocate the use of equipment as an expense for a period. This is called depreciation.

## ADJUSTING ENTRIES: PREPAID EXPENSES—DRILL

A prepaid expense is an item that is paid for in advance. Examples of prepaid expenses include: Insurance—policy is usually for six months or one year; Office Supplies—buy to have on hand and use as needed. (This is different from supplies that are purchased for immediate use.) As noted earlier, a prepaid expense is an asset until it is used. As the insurance or supplies are used, the amount used becomes an expense for the period. In accrual-basis accounting, an adjusting entry is made in the General Journal at the end of the period to allocate the amount of prepaid expenses (assets) used to expenses.

The Test Drive Company does not always have accounts or recorded transactions that are needed to illustrate some of the concepts presented in the text. Prior to recording an adjusting entry for insurance, a bill for insurance must be entered.

---

**MEMO**
**DATE**: January 30, 2016

Record the bill from Brosnahan Insurance Agency for one-year's insurance premium of $900.
Record the monthly adjustment for Prepaid Insurance.

---

## *DRILL*

 Open the **Test Drive Company**

Record a Bill for Insurance as instructed in Chapter 4
Vendor: **Brosnahan Insurance Agency**
Bill date: **01/30/16**
Account: **Prepaid Expenses**
- You will erase the Account: Insurance and the Amount: 241.23 that were entered because of a previous transaction.
Amount: **900**
Click **Save and close**
- Remember, if the Save command you want to use does not show, click the drop-down list, and then, click the correct command.
- Depending on your computer and other variables, the keyboard shortcut of **Ctrl+Alt+D** may be used to **Save and close** the transaction. (Think of D for Done.)
Calculate the amount of the adjusting entry—One-year premium ÷ months = amount:
          $900 ÷ 12 = $75
Click the **Plus** icon
Click **Journal Entry** in the Other column

- A Journal Entry requires both a debit and a credit just as you did when you recorded a General Journal Entry in your concepts course.

Enter the date: **01/30/16**, press **Tab**

- The Journal Entry number **1** is shown.

Line 1: Click in the ACCOUNT text box for

Click the drop-down list arrow, scroll through the accounts, click the Expense account

   **Insurance**

Tab to DEBITS, and enter the amount of the adjusting entry **75**

Tab to DESCRIPTION, enter **Adjusting Entry, January**

Line 2: Tab to or click in ACCOUNT, scroll through the accounts, click **Prepaid Expenses**

- Credits of 75 and the Description are automatically entered by QuickBooks Online. If they do not appear automatically, simply enter them as instructed for the Debit entry.

- This adjusting entry decreases the asset Prepaid Expenses by $75 and increases the expense Insurance.

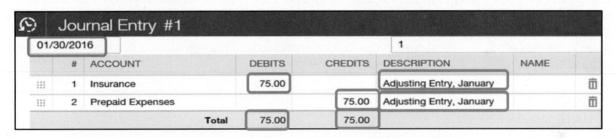

- Notice that the amounts for Debits equal the amounts for Credits.

Click **Save and close**

- If the Save command you want to use does not show, click the drop-down list, and then, click the correct command.

- Depending on your computer and other variables, the keyboard shortcut of **Ctrl+Alt+D** may be used for Save and close.

Open the Chart of Accounts as previously instructed; open the Register for Prepaid Expenses

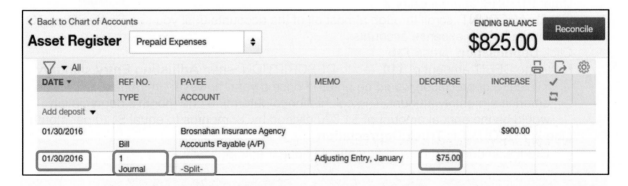

- You will see the Bill that you recorded and Journal Entry 1. For Journal Entry 1, rather than see the Account name, you see the word –Split– for the Journal entry. This means that the transaction was split between two or more accounts. In this case, Insurance and Prepaid Expenses were the accounts used.

Click **Back to Chart of Accounts** (just above the words Asset Register)

Scroll down to the expense account Insurance, click **Run report**

On the Account QuickReport, enter the date From: **01/30/16** To: **01/30/16**, click **Run Report**

## Craig's Design and Landscaping Services
### ACCOUNT QUICKREPORT
January 30, 2016

| DATE | TRANSACTION TYPE | NUM | NAME | MEMO/DESCRIPTION | ACCOUNT | CLR | AMOUNT | BALANCE |
|------|------------------|-----|------|------------------|---------|-----|--------|---------|
| **Insurance** | | | | | | | | |
| 01/30/2016 | Journal Entry | 1 | | Adjusting Entry, January | Insurance | | 75.00 | 75.00 |
| **Total for Insurance** | | | | | | | $75.00 | |
| **TOTAL** | | | | | | | $75.00 | |

Do not close the Test Drive Company, complete the next section

## ADJUSTING ENTRIES—DEPRECIATION—DRILL

Equipment and other long-term assets lose value over their lifetime. Unlike supplies—where you can actually see, for example, the paper supply diminishing—it is very difficult to see how much of a truck has been "used up" during the month. To account for the fact that machines do wear out and need to be replaced, an adjustment is made for depreciation. This adjustment correctly matches the expenses of the period against the revenue of the period.

> **MEMO**
> **DATE**: January 30, 2016
>
> Record a Journal Entry for the depreciation of the Truck, $110.

## *DRILL*

 Continue to use the **Test Drive Company**

Click the **Plus** icon; click **Journal Entry** in the Other column
Record a Journal Entry as instructed previously
Date: **01/30/16**, Journal Entry **2**
Line 1: ACCOUNT, scroll through almost all of the accounts until you see Depreciation at the end of the expense accounts
Click **Depreciation**, press **Tab**
Enter the DEBIT amount of **110**, tab to DESCRIPTION, enter **Adjusting Entry, January**
- Typically, depreciation would be entered once a year; however, in the text, we will be entering a monthly amount. The calculation to determine one month's depreciation would be the annual amount of $1,320 divided by 12 months to equal $110 per month.
Line 2: ACCOUNT is **Truck:Depreciation**
- Credits amount and Description should appear automatically.

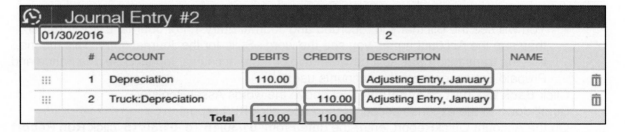

Click **Save and close** (Remember the keyboard shortcut of **Ctrl+Alt+D** may be used to Save and close the transaction)

Open the Chart of Accounts and view the effect of the adjusting entry for depreciation

| Truck | Fixed Assets | Vehicles | 13,385.00 |
|---|---|---|---|
| Depreciation | Fixed Assets | Accumulated Depreciation | -110.00 |
| Original Cost | Fixed Assets | Vehicles | 13,495.00 |

- The amount of the Original Cost does not change. Accumulated Depreciation contains the amount of the adjusting entry. The overall Book Value of the asset is now $13,385, which reflects the value of the asset. (Original cost $13,495 minus the Depreciation $110 equals the Book Value $13,385.)

Scroll down to the Depreciation expense account, click **Run Report**
Enter the dates From: **013016** To: **013016**, click **Run Report**

### Craig's Design and Landscaping Services
**ACCOUNT QUICKREPORT**
January 30, 2016

| DATE | TRANSACTION TYPE | NUM | NAME | MEMO/DESCRIPTION | ACCOUNT | CLR | AMOUNT | BALANCE |
|---|---|---|---|---|---|---|---|---|
| **Depreciation** | | | | | | | | |
| 01/30/2016 | Journal Entry | 2 | | Adjusting Entry, January | Depreciation | | 110.00 | 110.00 |
| **Total for Depreciation** | | | | | | | **$110.00** | |
| **TOTAL** | | | | | | | **$110.00** | |

Do <u>not</u> close the Test Drive Company, complete the next section

## PREPARE THE JOURNAL—DRILL

Once Journal Entries have been recorded, it is important to view them. As you learned in earlier chapters, even with the special ways in which transactions are entered in QuickBooks Online through invoices, bills, checks, etc., the Journal is still the book of original entry. All transactions recorded for the company may be viewed in the Journal even if they were entered elsewhere. The Journal may be viewed or printed at any time.

## _DRILL_

Continue to use the **Test Drive Company** and prepare the Journal

Click the **Gear** icon, click **QuickBooks Labs**, turn **OFF** Redesigned Reports, click **Done**
Click **Reports** on the Navigation Bar, click **All Reports**, click **Accountant Reports**, and
    click **Journal**
Enter the Dates From: **013016** and To: **013016**, click **Run Report**

### Craig's Design and Landscaping Services
**JOURNAL**
January 30, 2016

| DATE | TRANSACTION TYPE | NUM | NAME | MEMO/DESCRIPTION | ACCOUNT | DEBIT | CREDIT |
|---|---|---|---|---|---|---|---|
| 01/30/2016 | Bill | | Brosnahan Insurance Agency | | Accounts Payable (A/P) | | $900.00 |
| | | | | | Prepaid Expenses | $900.00 | |
| | | | | | | **$900.00** | **$900.00** |
| 01/30/2016 | Journal Entry | 1 | | Adjusting Entry, January | Insurance | $75.00 | |
| | | | | Adjusting Entry, January | Prepaid Expenses | | $75.00 |
| | | | | | | **$75.00** | **$75.00** |
| 01/30/2016 | Journal Entry | 2 | | Adjusting Entry, January | Depreciation | $110.00 | |
| | | | | Adjusting Entry, January | Truck:Depreciation | | $110.00 |
| | | | | | | **$110.00** | **$110.00** |
| **TOTAL** | | | | | | **$1,085.00** | **$1,085.00** |

- The transactions you entered for the insurance bill and the two adjusting entries should be shown. If you have additional transactions, it is because the Test Drive Company is programmed to change the transaction dates.

Close the Test Drive Company

## ADJUSTING ENTRIES: PREPAID EXPENSES—DO

As you learned in the drill, a prepaid expense is an item that is paid for in advance. Examples of prepaid expenses include: Insurance—policy is usually for six months or one year; Office Supplies—buy to have on hand and use as needed. (This is different from supplies that are purchased for immediate use.) In accrual-basis accounting, a Journal Entry is recorded at the end of the period to allocate the amount of prepaid expenses (assets) used to expenses.

| MEMO |
| --- |
| **DATE**: January 30, 2016 |
| Calculate and record the monthly adjustment for Prepaid Insurance for your vehicle. Create a new expense account: Category Type: Expenses, Detail Type: Insurance, Name: Vehicle Insurance, Subaccount of: Insurance (an Expense account). |
| Record the adjusting entry for the amount of Sales Supplies used, $100. |
| After taking inventory, you calculate that you have $825 of Cleaning Supplies on hand. Record the adjusting entry. |

_DO_

Open **Your Name's Beach Barkers** and record adjusting entries for prepaid expenses

Click the **Plus** icon
Click **Journal Entry** in the Other column
Enter the date: **01/30/16**, press **Tab**
- The Journal Entry number **1** is shown.
Click in the ACCOUNT text box for Line 1
- This adjusting entry is to record the amount of Vehicle Insurance used for the month.
Click the drop-down list arrow, scroll through the accounts, there is no account for **Vehicle Insurance**
Click **+Add new**
Create a new expense account using the information in the Memo and following the same procedures detailed in previous chapters
Using the $1,200 in the Prepaid Insurance account for the one-year premium amount, calculate the amount of the adjusting entry
- One-year premium ÷ months = amount:
  $1,200 ÷ 12 = $100
Tab to DEBITS, and enter the amount of the adjusting entry **100**
Tab to DESCRIPTION, enter **Adjusting Entry, January**
Tab to or click in ACCOUNT in Line 2, scroll through the accounts, click **Prepaid Insurance**
- The Credit of 100 and the Description are automatically entered by QuickBooks Online. If they do not appear automatically, simply enter them as instructed for the Debit entry.
- This adjusting entry decreases the asset Prepaid Insurance by $100 and increases the expense Vehicle Insurance by $100.

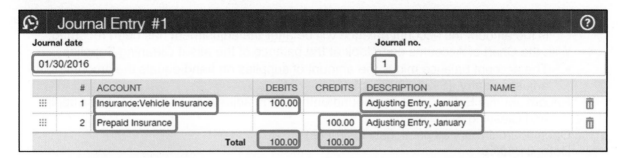

Click **Save and close**
- If the Save command you want to use does not show, click the drop-down list, and then, click the correct command or use the keyboard shortcut of **Ctrl+Alt+D**.

Open the Chart of Accounts as previously instructed, and then click **View Register** for Prepaid Insurance

- You will see the Opening Balance for Prepaid Insurance and Journal Entry 1. Rather than see the Account name, you see the word –Split- for the Journal entry. This means that the transaction was split between two or more accounts. In this case, Vehicle Insurance and Prepaid Insurance were the accounts used.
- If you see a message in the Balance column for "Only displayed when date/stat sort," click the heading for **Date** (you will see 12/31/2015 transaction first), then click it again to reverse and show the 01/30/2016 transaction first.

Click **Back to Chart of Accounts** (just above the words Asset Register)

Scroll down to the Insurance Expense subaccount Vehicle Insurance, click **Run report**

On the Account QuickReport, enter the date From: **01/30/16** To: **01/30/16**, click **Run Report**

### Your Name's Beach Barkers
#### ACCOUNT QUICKREPORT
**January 30, 2016**

| DATE | TRANSACTION TYPE | NUM | NAME | MEMO/DESCRIPTION | ACCOUNT | CLR | AMOUNT | BALANCE |
|------|------------------|-----|------|------------------|---------|-----|--------|---------|
| **Insurance** | | | | | | | | |
| **Vehicle Insurance** | | | | | | | | |
| 01/30/2016 | Journal Entry | 1 | | Adjusting Entry, January | Insurance:Vehicle Insurance | | 100.00 | 100.00 |
| Total for Vehicle Insurance | | | | | | | **$100.00** | |
| Total for Insurance | | | | | | | **$100.00** | |
| TOTAL | | | | | | | **$100.00** | |

Reopen the Chart of Accounts

Prior to preparing the Journal Entry, calculate the amount of the adjusting entries
- The transaction for Sales Supplies states that the amount of <u>supplies used</u> is $100. That is the amount of the adjustment to be recorded.

- The transaction for Cleaning Supplies states that there is $825 of <u>supplies on hand</u>. That is the amount the account balance will be <u>after</u> the adjustment has been recorded.

With the Chart of Accounts open look at the balance of the asset Cleaning Supplies

- The account balance minus the amount of supplies on hand equals the amount of the adjusting entry. ($925 - $825 = $100)

Record Journal Entry 2 as a compound entry for the adjusting entries for Office Supplies and Cleaning Supplies

Open Journal Entry as previously instructed

Date: **01/30/16**

Journal no.: **2**

Line 1: Account: **Sales Supplies Expense**, Debit: **100**, Description: **Adjusting Entry, January**

Line 2: Account: **Sales Supplies**, Credit: **100**, Description: **Adjusting Entry, January**

Line 3: Account: **Cleaning Supplies Expense**, Debit: **100**, Description: **Adjusting Entry, January**

Line 4: Account: **Cleaning Supplies**, Credit: **100**, Description: **Adjusting Entry, January**

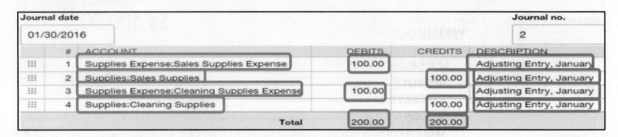

| Journal date | | | | | Journal no. |
|---|---|---|---|---|---|
| 01/30/2016 | | | | | 2 |
| # | ACCOUNT | DEBITS | CREDITS | DESCRIPTION | |
| 1 | Supplies Expense:Sales Supplies Expense | 100.00 | | Adjusting Entry, January | |
| 2 | Supplies:Sales Supplies | | 100.00 | Adjusting Entry, January | |
| 3 | Supplies Expense:Cleaning Supplies Expense | 100.00 | | Adjusting Entry, January | |
| 4 | Supplies:Cleaning Supplies | | 100.00 | Adjusting Entry, January | |
| | Total | 200.00 | 200.00 | | |

Click **Save and new** (Ctrl+Alt+S)

Do <u>not</u> close Your Name's Beach Barkers, complete the next section

## ADJUSTING ENTRIES—DEPRECIATION—DO

Equipment and other long-term assets lose value over their lifetime. To account for the fact that machines wear out and need to be replaced, an adjustment is made for depreciation. This adjustment correctly matches the expenses of the period against the revenue of the period.

> **MEMO**
> **DATE**: January 30, 2016
>
> Record a Journal Entry for one-month's depreciation of the Vehicle, $275.

*(handwritten note in left margin: Could not create account)*

## DO

Continue to use **Your Name's Beach Barkers**

Record a Journal Entry as instructed previously

Date: **01/30/16**, Journal Entry **3**

Line 1: Account: **Depreciation Expense**, Debit: **275**, Description: **Adjusting Entry, January**

- Typically, depreciation would be entered once a year; however, in the text, we will be entering a monthly amount. The calculation to determine one month's depreciation would be the annual amount of $3,300 divided by 12 months to equal $275 per month.

For Line 2, Account: **Vehicles:Depreciation**, Credit: **275**, Description: **Adjusting Entry, January**

| Journal date | | | | | Journal no. | | | |
|---|---|---|---|---|---|---|---|---|
| 01/30/2016 | | | | | 3 | | | |
| | # | ACCOUNT | DEBITS | CREDITS | DESCRIPTION | | NAME | |
| ⠿ | 1 | Depreciation Expense | 275.00 | | Adjusting Entry, January | | | 🗑 |
| ⠿ | 2 | Vehicles:Depreciation | | 275.00 | Adjusting Entry, January | | | 🗑 |
| | | Total | 275.00 | 275.00 | | | | |

Click **Save and close** (Ctrl+Alt+D)
Return to the Chart of Accounts and view the effect of the adjusting entry for depreciation

| *Name* | *Type* | *Detail type* | |
|---|---|---|---|
| Vehicles | Fixed Assets | Vehicles | 28,525.00 |
| Depreciation | Fixed Assets | Accumulated Depreciation | -3,475.00 |
| Original cost | Fixed Assets | Vehicles | 32,000.00 |

- The amount of the Original Cost does not change. Accumulated Depreciation contains the amount of the adjusting entry. The overall Book Value of the asset is now $28,525, which reflects the value of the asset: Original cost $32,000 minus Depreciation $3,475 (Opening Balance $3,200 plus adjusting entry $275) equals the Book Value $28,525.

Scroll down to the Depreciation Expense account, click **Run Report**
Enter the dates From: **013016** To: **013016**, click **Run Report**

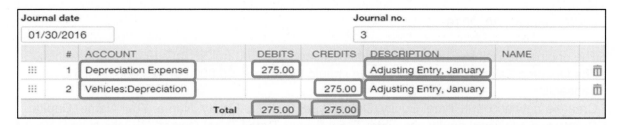

**Your Name's Beach Barkers**
**ACCOUNT QUICKREPORT**
January 30, 2016

| DATE | TRANSACTION TYPE | NUM | NAME | MEMO/DESCRIPTION | ACCOUNT | CLR | AMOUNT | BALANCE |
|---|---|---|---|---|---|---|---|---|
| **Depreciation Expense** | | | | | | | | |
| 01/30/2016 | Journal Entry | 3 | | Adjusting Entry, January | Depreciation Expense | | 275.00 | 275.00 |
| **Total for Depreciation Expense** | | | | | | | $275.00 | |
| **TOTAL** | | | | | | | $275.00 | |

Close Your Name's Beach Barkers

## EDIT, CREATE, AND TRANSFER BALANCES FOR EQUITY ACCOUNTS—DRILL

When a company is created in QuickBooks Online, all of the values of the opening balances are entered into the Opening Balance Equity account. Other than Retained Earnings, the Test Drive Company does not show any other Equity accounts. Typically, you will have owner's equity accounts for the owner's investment and drawing accounts. In QuickBooks Online, Opening Balance Equity cannot have subaccounts so the Owner's Equity section needs to have accounts created and amounts transferred.

5

> **MEMO**
> **DATE:** January 30, 2016
>
> The original deposit to Checking should have been $35,000 not $5,000. Edit the transaction.
>
> The Opening Balance for Notes Payable should have been $5,000 not $25,000. Edit the transaction.
>
> Create a new account: Type: Equity, Detail Type: Owner's Equity, Name: Your Name, Capital.
>
> Create two additional equity accounts: Type: Equity, Detail Type: Owner's Equity, Name: Your Name, Investment, Subaccount of: Your Name, Capital and Type: Equity, Detail Type: Owner's Equity, Name: Your Name, Drawing, Subaccount of: Your Name, Capital.
>
> Transfer the amount of the Opening Balance Equity account to Your Name, Capital and Your Name, Investment.

## DRILL

 Open the **Test Drive Company** to edit transactions, add accounts, and transfer the balance of the Opening Balance Equity account to Capital accounts

## Edit Transactions

Sometimes, the information shown in the Test Drive Company needs to be changed in order to facilitate the presentation of concepts and functions in QuickBooks Online.

 Edit transactions for Opening Balance Equity

    Open the Opening Balance Equity Account Register
    • Scroll through all of the transactions until you get to the very last entry, the Deposit for Checking for $5,000.
    Click the **Transaction**
    Click the **Edit** button
    Change the $5,000 shown in New Deposits to **35,000**
    Click **Save and close**
    Click **Yes** on the message regarding editing a transaction that has been reconciled
    Scroll through the Opening Balance Equity Register until you see an Opening Balance for $25,000
    Point to word **–Split–**
    • The two accounts used in the transaction will appear on a pop-up screen. They are: Notes Payable and Opening Balance Equity.
    Click the **Transaction**
    Click the **Edit** button, change the entries for Debits and Credits to **5,000**
    Click **Save and close**
    Click **Yes** on the message for editing a transaction that has been reconciled
    Click **<Back to Chart of Accounts**, located just above the words "Equity Register"
    Continue using the Test Drive Company to complete the next section

## Add Equity Accounts

When a company is created, it may not have all of the accounts you need or want. New accounts may be added at any time.

 Add Equity accounts
    Click **New** at the top of the Chart of Accounts

Add the new equity account: **Your Name, Capital**
Category Type: **Equity**
Detail Type: **Owner's Equity**
Name: **Your Name, Capital**
- Use your real name.

Click **Save and new**

Add two additional equity accounts: Your Name, Investment and Your Name, Drawing using the information provided in the Memo
- Use your actual name instead of "Your Name" in the accounts.
- Both accounts are Subaccounts of Your Name, Capital.
- There are no opening balances for the accounts.

Click **Save and close** after creating the last account
View the Equity section in the Chart of Accounts

| Opening Balance Equity | Equity | Opening Balance Equity | 40,662.50 | View register ▼ |
|---|---|---|---|---|
| Retained Earnings | Equity | Retained Earnings | 0.00 | Run report ▼ |
| Your Name, Capital | Equity | Owner's Equity | 0.00 | View register ▼ |
| Your Name, Drawing | Equity | Owner's Equity | 0.00 | View register ▼ |
| Your Name, Investment | Equity | Owner's Equity | 0.00 | View register ▼ |

Continue using the Test Drive Company to complete the next section

## Transfer Opening Balance Equity into Capital Accounts

Once you have the appropriate capital accounts, you may transfer the amount of the owner's original investment into the Your Name, Investment account. Then, transfer the remaining balance in the Opening Balance Equity into Your Name's Capital.

Create Journal Entries to transfer the owner's original investment and the Opening Balance Equity into the appropriate Capital accounts

Open Journal Entry as previously instructed
Date: **013016**
Line 1: Account: **Opening Balance Equity**, Debit: **35,000**, Description: **Transfer Owner Investment**
- Because this was used as your only equity/capital account it will have a credit balance. Transferring the owner's investment will decrease the balance of the account. That is done by debiting Opening Balance Equity.

Line 2: Account: **Your Name, Investment**, Credit: **35,000**, Description: **Transfer Owner Investment**

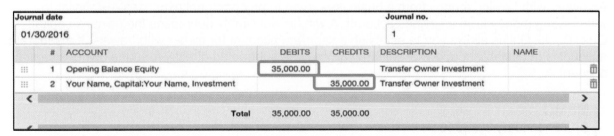

Click **Save and close**
View the results of the transaction

| Opening Balance Equity | Equity | Opening Balance Equity | 5,662.50 |
|---|---|---|---|
| Retained Earnings | Equity | Retained Earnings | 0.00 |
| Your Name, Capital | Equity | Owner's Equity | 35,000.00 |
| Your Name, Drawing | Equity | Owner's Equity | 0.00 |
| Your Name, Investment | Equity | Owner's Equity | 35,000.00 |

Follow the steps presented and record another Journal Entry to transfer the remaining amount of Opening Balance Equity, 5,662.50, to Your Name, Capital

| Journal date | | | | | Journal no. | |
|---|---|---|---|---|---|---|
| 01/30/2016 | | | | | 2 | |
| # | ACCOUNT | DEBITS | CREDITS | DESCRIPTION | | NAME |
| 1 | Opening Balance Equity | 5,662.50 | | Transfer to Capital Account | | |
| 2 | Your Name, Capital | | 5,662.50 | Transfer to Capital Account | | |
| | Total | 5,662.50 | 5,662.50 | | | |

Click **Save and close**
View the results of the transaction

| Opening Balance Equity | Equity | Opening Balance Equity | 0.00 |
|---|---|---|---|
| Retained Earnings | Equity | Retained Earnings | 0.00 |
| Your Name, Capital | Equity | Owner's Equity | 40,662.50 |
| Your Name, Drawing | Equity | Owner's Equity | 0.00 |
| Your Name, Investment | Equity | Owner's Equity | 35,000.00 |

- The balance of Opening Balance Equity is now 0.00, which indicates that all of the equity entered for opening balances when the company was created has now been transferred into the Capital account.
- The amount of the original investment shows in Your Name, Investment, a subaccount of Your Name, Capital.
- The balance of Your Name, Capital is equal to the previous balance for Opening Balance Equity.

Do not close the Test Drive Company, continue and complete the next section

## OWNER WITHDRAWALS—DRILL

In a sole proprietorship an owner cannot receive a paycheck because he or she owns the business. An owner withdrawing money from a business—even to pay personal expenses—is similar to withdrawing money from a savings account. A withdrawal simply decreases the owner's capital. QuickBooks Online allows you to establish a separate account for owner withdrawals. If a separate account is not established, owner withdrawals may be subtracted directly from the owner's capital account.

---

**MEMO**
**DATE**: January 30, 2016

Record the monthly withdrawal of $1,000.

---

_DRILL_

 Continue to use the **Test Drive Company** to record an owner withdrawal

- If you did not continue training immediately after completing the previous section, you will have to re-enter the account for Your Name, Capital and Your Name, Drawing. Your Equity section will not match the one shown below, but you will be able to practice entering an owner withdrawal.

Click the **Plus** icon, click **Check** in the Vendors column
Since the owner is not a customer, vendor, or employee, leave the Payee blank
Use **Checking** to pay the check
Payment date: **013016**
Click **Print later** to remove the check mark
Line 1: Account: **Your Name, Drawing**, Amount: **1,000**
Memo: **Monthly Withdrawal**

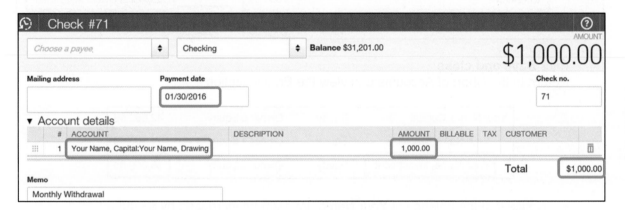

Click **Save and close**
Return to the Chart of Accounts and view the Equity section

| Opening Balance Equity | Equity | Opening Balance Equity | 0.00 |
|---|---|---|---|
| Retained Earnings | Equity | Retained Earnings | 0.00 |
| Your Name, Capital | Equity | Owner's Equity | 39,662.50 |
| Your Name, Drawing | Equity | Owner's Equity | -1,000.00 |
| Your Name, Investment | Equity | Owner's Equity | 35,000.00 |

Do <u>not</u> close the Test Drive Company, continue and complete the next section

## CASH INVESTMENT BY OWNER—DRILL

An owner may decide to invest more of his or her personal cash in the business at any time. The new investment is entered into the owner's investment account and into cash. The investment should be recorded in a Journal Entry.

---

**MEMO**
**DATE**: January 30, 2016

Record an additional cash investment of $3,000.

---

*DRILL*

Continue to use the **Test Drive Company** and record a cash investment by the owner

Prepare a Journal Entry as previously instructed using the information provided in the Memo
Transaction Accounts: **Checking** and **Your Name, Investment**
- If you did not continue training immediately after completing the previous section, you
  will have to re-enter the account for Your Name, Capital and Your Name, Investment.
  Your Equity section will not match the one shown below, but you will be able to practice
  entering an owner's additional investment.
Transaction Description: **Additional Owner Investment**

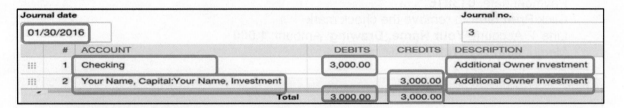

| Journal date | | | | | Journal no. |
|---|---|---|---|---|---|
| 01/30/2016 | | | | | 3 |

| | # | ACCOUNT | DEBITS | CREDITS | DESCRIPTION |
|---|---|---|---|---|---|
| ⋮⋮⋮ | 1 | Checking | 3,000.00 | | Additional Owner Investment |
| ⋮⋮⋮ | 2 | Your Name, Capital:Your Name, Investment | | 3,000.00 | Additional Owner Investment |
| | | Total | 3,000.00 | 3,000.00 | |

Click **Save and close**
Return to the Chart of Accounts and view the Equity section

| Your Name, Capital | Equity | Owner's Equity | 42,662.50 |
|---|---|---|---|
| Your Name, Drawing | Equity | Owner's Equity | -1,000.00 |
| Your Name, Investment | Equity | Owner's Equity | 38,000.00 |

- Notice that the balance of Your Name, Investment increased by $3,000.
Do <u>not</u> close the Test Drive Company, continue and complete the next section

## NON-CASH INVESTMENT BY OWNER—DRILL

In addition to a cash investment, an owner may make non-cash investments; such as, reference
books, equipment, tools, buildings, and so on. Additional investments by an owner are added to
owner's equity. In the case of a sole proprietorship, the investment is added to the Capital account
for Investments.

---

**MEMO**
**DATE**: January 30, 2016

Record an investment of $5,000 worth of office furniture.

---

*DRILL*

Continue to use the **Test Drive Company** and record a non-cash investment by the owner

Create a new fixed asset account for Furniture
Click **New** at the top of the Chart of Accounts
Category Type: **Fixed Assets**, Detail Type: **Furniture & Fixtures**, Name: **Furniture**
Click **Track depreciation of this asset** to select
Original Cost: **0.00**, as of: **013016**
Depreciation: **0.00**, as of: **013016**

Click **Save and Close** to save Furniture and the sub-accounts for Depreciation and Original Cost

Prepare a Journal Entry as previously instructed using the information provided in the Memo

Transaction Accounts: **Furniture: Original Cost** and **Your Name, Investment**

Description: **Investment by Owner**

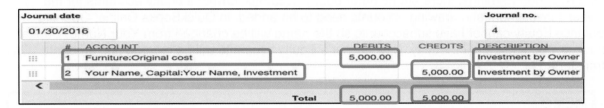

| Journal date | | | | | | Journal no. | |
|---|---|---|---|---|---|---|---|
| 01/30/2016 | | | | | | 4 | |
| | # | ACCOUNT | DEBITS | CREDITS | DESCRIPTION | | |
| ⫶ | 1 | Furniture:Original cost | 5,000.00 | | Investment by Owner | | |
| ⫶ | 2 | Your Name, Capital:Your Name, Investment | | 5,000.00 | Investment by Owner | | |
| < | | | | | | | |
| | | Total | 5,000.00 | 5,000.00 | | | |

Click **Save and close**

Do <u>not</u> close the Test Drive Company, continue and complete the next section

## PREPARE THE JOURNAL—DRILL

Once Journal Entries have been recorded, it is important to view them. All the transactions recorded for Owner's Equity for January 30, 2016 will show in the Journal.

## *DRILL*

Continue to use the **Test Drive Company** and prepare the Journal

Click the **Gear** icon, click **QuickBooks Labs**, turn **OFF** Redesigned Reports, click **Done**

Go to Reports, click **All Reports**, click the category **Accountant Reports**, click **Journal**

Enter the Dates From: **01/30/16** To: **01/30/16**, click **Run Report**

- All of the transactions entered on January 30, 2016 for Owner's Equity will be shown. If you have other transactions shown as well, it may be due to the Test Drive Company automatically changing transaction dates. Disregard transactions that you did not enter.

### Craig's Design and Landscaping Services
#### JOURNAL
#### January 30, 2016

| DATE | TRANSACTION TYPE | NUM | NAME | MEMO/DESCRIPTION | ACCOUNT | DEBIT | CREDIT |
|---|---|---|---|---|---|---|---|
| 01/30/2016 | Journal Entry | 1 | | Transfer Owner Investment | Opening Balance Equity | $35,000.00 | |
| | | | | Transfer Owner Investment | Your Name, Capital:Your Name, Investment | | $35,000.00 |
| | | | | | | $35,000.00 | $35,000.00 |
| 01/30/2016 | Journal Entry | 2 | | Transfer to Capital Account | Opening Balance Equity | $5,662.50 | |
| | | | | Transfer to Capital Account | Your Name, Capital | | $5,662.50 |
| | | | | | | $5,662.50 | $5,662.50 |
| 01/30/2016 | Check | 71 | | Monthly Withdrawal | Checking | | $1,000.00 |
| | | | | | Your Name, Capital:Your Name, Drawing | $1,000.00 | |
| | | | | | | $1,000.00 | $1,000.00 |
| 01/30/2016 | Journal Entry | 3 | | Additional Owner Investment | Checking | $3,000.00 | |
| | | | | Additional Owner Investment | Your Name, Capital:Your Name, Investment | | $3,000.00 |
| | | | | | | $3,000.00 | $3,000.00 |
| 01/30/2016 | Journal Entry | 4 | | Investment by Owner | Furniture:Original cost | $5,000.00 | |
| | | | | Investment by Owner | Your Name, Capital:Your Name, Investment | | $5,000.00 |
| | | | | | | $5,000.00 | $5,000.00 |
| **TOTAL** | | | | | | **$49,662.50** | **$49,662.50** |

Close the Test Drive Company

## CREATE AND TRANSFER BALANCES FOR EQUITY ACCOUNTS—DO

When Your Name's Beach Barkers was created in QuickBooks Online, all of the values of the opening balances were entered into the Opening Balance Equity account. In Chapter 2, Opening Balance Equity was changed to Your Name, Capital to help you identify the equity section. Other than Retained Earnings, there are no other equity accounts. Owner's equity accounts for the owner's investment and drawing accounts need to be added. In QuickBooks Online, Opening Balance Equity cannot have subaccounts so the name will be changed from Your Name, Capital back to Opening Balance Equity. New Owner's Equity accounts will be created and amounts transferred.

| MEMO |
| --- |
| **DATE:** January 30, 2016 |
| Change Your Name, Capital to Opening Balance Equity. |
| Create a new account: Type: Equity, Detail Type: Owner's Equity, Name: Your Name, Capital. |
| Create two additional equity accounts: Type: Equity, Detail Type: Owner's Equity, Name, Your Name, Investment, Subaccount of: Your Name, Capital and Type: Equity, Detail Type: Owner's Equity, Name: Your Name, Drawing, Subaccount of: Your Name, Capital. |
| Transfer the Opening Balance Equity account balance to Your Name, Capital and Your Name, Investment. |

### DO

 Open **Your Name's Beach Barkers** to edit transactions, add accounts, and transfer the balance of the Opening Balance Equity account to Capital accounts

### Change Account Name

 Change the name of Opening Balance Equity

Open the Chart of Accounts, edit Your Name, Capital
Change the name to **Opening Balance Equity**, click **Save and Close**

### Add Equity Accounts

 Add Equity accounts

Click **New** at the top of the Chart of Accounts
Add the new equity account: **Your Name, Capital**
Category Type: **Equity**
Detail Type: **Owner's Equity**
Name: **Your Name, Capital**
- Use your real name.
Click **Save and new**
Add two additional equity accounts: Your Name, Investment and Your Name, Drawing using the information provided in the Memo
- Use your actual name in the account not the words Your Name.
- Both accounts are Subaccounts of Your Name, Capital.
- There are no opening balances for the accounts.
Click **Save and close** after creating the last account
View the Equity section in the Chart of Accounts

- If your Equity accounts are shown in a different order, do not be concerned. The equity accounts are shown in alphabetical order. If your name begins with a letter before "O" your capital accounts will be shown first.

| Opening Balance Equity | Equity | Opening Balance Equity | 142,362.50 |
|---|---|---|---|
| Retained Earnings | Equity | Retained Earnings | 0.00 |
| Your Name, Capital | Equity | Owner's Equity | 0.00 |
| Your Name, Drawing | Equity | Owner's Equity | 0.00 |
| Your Name, Investment | Equity | Owner's Equity | 0.00 |

Continue using Your Name's Beach Barkers to complete the next section

## Transfer Opening Balance Equity into Capital Accounts

Once you have the appropriate capital accounts, you may transfer the amount of the owner's original investment into the Your Name, Investment account. Then, transfer the remaining balance in the Opening Balance Equity into Your Name, Capital.

 Create a compound Journal Entry 4 to transfer the owner's original investment and the Opening Balance Equity into the appropriate Capital accounts

View the Register for Opening Balance Equity
Scroll through the register until you find the Deposit transaction for Checking
The amount shown, $45,385.00, is the amount of your original investment
Open Journal Entry as previously instructed
Date: **013016**
Journal no.: **4**
Line 1: Account: **Opening Balance Equity**, Debit: **142,362.50**, Description: **Close Opening Balance Equity**
- Because this was used as your only equity/capital account it will have a credit balance. You debit Opening Balance Equity to remove the balance, which will close the account.
Line 2: Account: **Your Name, Investment**, Credit: **45,385** (you will change the amount shown for the credit to the investment amount), Description: **Transfer Owner Investment**
Line 3: Account: **Your Name, Capital**, Credit: **96,977.50**, Description: **Close Opening Balance Equity**
- QuickBooks calculates the amount in Line 3 by subtracting the investment of $45,385 from the Opening Balance Equity of $142,362.50.

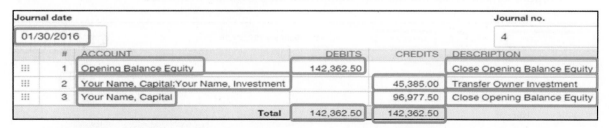

| Journal date | | | | | Journal no. | |
|---|---|---|---|---|---|---|
| 01/30/2016 | | | | | 4 | |
| # | ACCOUNT | DEBITS | CREDITS | DESCRIPTION | | |
| 1 | Opening Balance Equity | 142,362.50 | | Close Opening Balance Equity | | |
| 2 | Your Name, Capital:Your Name, Investment | | 45,385.00 | Transfer Owner Investment | | |
| 3 | Your Name, Capital | | 96,977.50 | Close Opening Balance Equity | | |
| | Total | 142,362.50 | 142,362.50 | | | |

Click **Save and close**
If you return to the account register, click **<Back to the Chart of Accounts**
View the results of the transaction
- Because QBO generally alphabetizes account names within a category, equity for example, the accounts with Your Name may be shown before Opening Balance Equity.

| Opening Balance Equity | Equity | Opening Balance Equity | 0.00 |
|---|---|---|---|
| Retained Earnings | Equity | Retained Earnings | 0.00 |
| Your Name, Capital | Equity | Owner's Equity | 142,362.50 |
| Your Name, Drawing | Equity | Owner's Equity | 0.00 |
| Your Name, Investment | Equity | Owner's Equity | 45,385.00 |

- The balance of Opening Balance Equity is now 0.00, which indicates that all of the equity entered for opening balances when the company was created has now been transferred into the Capital account.
- The amount of the original investment shows in Your Name, Investment, a subaccount of Your Name, Capital.
- The balance of Your Name, Capital is equal to the previous balance for Opening Balance Equity.

Do <u>not</u> close Your Name's Beach Barkers, continue and complete the next section

## OWNER WITHDRAWALS—DO

In a sole proprietorship an owner cannot receive a paycheck because he or she owns the business. A withdrawal decreases the owner's capital whenever the owner withdraws money from the business. QuickBooks Online allows you to establish a separate account for owner withdrawals. If a separate account is not established, owner withdrawals may be subtracted directly from the owner's capital account.

> **MEMO**
> **DATE**: January 30, 2016
>
> Record your semi-monthly withdrawal of $500.

<u>*DO*</u>

Continue to use **Your Name's Beach Barkers** and record an owner withdrawal

Click the **Plus** icon, click **Check** in the "Vendors" column
Since the owner is not a customer, vendor, or employee, leave the Payee blank
Use **Checking** to pay the check
Payment date: **013016**
Click **Print later** to remove the check mark
Prepare Check 17 for the monthly withdrawal as previously instructed

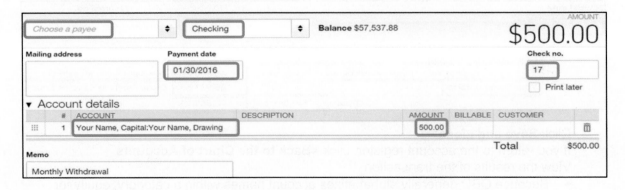

Click **Print check**
Check No. **17**, click **Preview and print**, print the check

- If you save the check as a pdf file, name it **1-Your Name Check 17**.

Click **Close** on Print Preview, click **Done** on Checks Print OK, click **Cancel** on the print check screen

Return to the Chart of Accounts and view the Equity section

| Your Name, Capital | Equity | Owner's Equity | 141,862.50 |
| Your Name, Drawing | Equity | Owner's Equity | -500.00 |
| Your Name, Investment | Equity | Owner's Equity | 45,385.00 |

Do <u>not</u> close Your Name's Beach Barkers

## CASH INVESTMENT BY OWNER—DO

An owner may make additional investments in the business at any time. A cash investment is entered into the owner's investment account and into cash. Since an additional investment is made by the owner and there are no business forms available for owner investments, a Journal Entry is recorded.

> **MEMO**
> **DATE**: January 30, 2016
>
> You had a Certificate of Deposit that matured. Rather than keep the money in your personal bank account, you invested the $3,000 into Your Name's Beach Barkers.

<u>DO</u>

Continue to use **Your Name's Beach Barkers** to record a cash investment by the owner

Prepare Journal Entry 5 as previously instructed
Transaction Description: **Additional Owner Investment**

| Journal date | | | | | Journal no. | |
|---|---|---|---|---|---|---|
| 01/30/2016 | | | | | 5 | |
| | # | ACCOUNT | DEBITS | CREDITS | DESCRIPTION | |
| | 1 | Checking | 3,000.00 | | Additional Owner Investment | |
| | 2 | Your Name, Capital:Your Name, Investment | | 3,000.00 | Additional Owner Investment | |
| | | Total | 3,000.00 | 3,000.00 | | |

Click **Save and close**
Return to the Chart of Accounts and view the Equity section

| Your Name, Capital | Equity | Owner's Equity | 144,862.50 |
| Your Name, Drawing | Equity | Owner's Equity | -500.00 |
| Your Name, Investment | Equity | Owner's Equity | 48,385.00 |

- Notice that the balance of Your Name, Investment increased by $3,000.

Do <u>not</u> close Your Name's Beach Barkers

## NON-CASH INVESTMENT BY OWNER—DO

In addition to a cash investment, an owner may make non-cash investments. Additional investments by an owner are added to owner's equity. In the case of a sole proprietorship, the investment is added to the Capital account for Investments.

> **MEMO**
> **DATE**: January 30, 2016
>
> Rather than use the new computer and printer you just purchased at home, you decided to use it and invest it in Your Name's Beach Barkers. Record an investment of $2,500 worth of Office Equipment.

**DO**

Continue to use **Your Name's Beach Barkers** and record a non-cash investment

Prepare Journal Entry 6 as previously instructed
Transaction Accounts: **Office Equipment: Original Cost** and **Your Name, Investment**
Description: **Additional Investment**

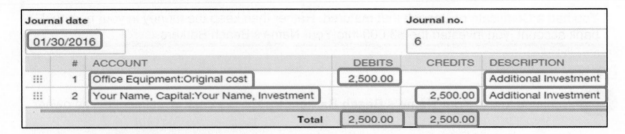

| Journal date | | | | | | |
|---|---|---|---|---|---|---|
| 01/30/2016 | | | | Journal no. | 6 | |
| | # | ACCOUNT | DEBITS | CREDITS | DESCRIPTION | |
| ⠿ | 1 | Office Equipment:Original cost | 2,500.00 | | Additional Investment | |
| ⠿ | 2 | Your Name, Capital:Your Name, Investment | | 2,500.00 | Additional Investment | |
| | | Total | 2,500.00 | 2,500.00 | | |

Click **Save and close**
Return to the Chart of Accounts and view the Equity section

| Your Name, Capital | Equity | Owner's Equity | 147,362.50 |
|---|---|---|---|
| Your Name, Drawing | Equity | Owner's Equity | -500.00 |
| Your Name, Investment | Equity | Owner's Equity | 50,885.00 |

- Notice that the balance of Your Name, Investment increased by $2,500.

Do <u>not</u> close Your Name's Beach Barkers

## PREPARE THE JOURNAL—DO

All the transactions recorded for adjusting entries and for Owner's Equity for January 30, 2016 will show in the Journal.

**DO**

Continue to use **Your Name's Beach Barkers** to prepare the Journal report

Go to Reports, use the category **Accountant Reports**, select **Journal**
Enter the Dates From: **01/30/16** To: **01/30/16**, click **Run Report**
Remove the Date Prepared and Time Prepared from the Footer

## Your Name's Beach Barkers
### JOURNAL
#### January 30, 2016

| DATE | TRANSACTION TYPE | NUM | NAME | MEMO/DESCRIPTION | ACCOUNT | DEBIT | CREDIT |
|------|------------------|-----|------|------------------|---------|-------|--------|
| 01/30/2016 | Journal Entry | 1 | | Adjusting Entry, January | Insurance:Vehicle Insurance | $100.00 | |
| | | | | Adjusting Entry, January | Prepaid Insurance | | $100.00 |
| | | | | | | **$100.00** | **$100.00** |
| 01/30/2016 | Journal Entry | 2 | | Adjusting Entry, January | Supplies Expense:Sales Supplies Expense | $100.00 | |
| | | | | Adjusting Entry, January | Supplies:Sales Supplies | | $100.00 |
| | | | | Adjusting Entry, January | Supplies Expense:Cleaning Supplies Expense | $100.00 | |
| | | | | Adjusting Entry, January | Supplies:Cleaning Supplies | | $100.00 |
| | | | | | | **$200.00** | **$200.00** |
| 01/30/2016 | Journal Entry | 3 | | Adjusting Entry, January | Depreciation Expense | $275.00 | |
| | | | | Adjusting Entry, January | Vehicles:Depreciation | | $275.00 |
| | | | | | | **$275.00** | **$275.00** |
| 01/30/2016 | Journal Entry | 4 | | Close Opening Balance Equity | Opening Balance Equity | $142,362.50 | |
| | | | | Transfer Owner Investment | Your Name, Capital:Your Name, Investment | | $45,385.00 |
| | | | | Close Opening Balance Equity | Your Name, Capital | | $96,977.50 |
| | | | | | | **$142,362.50** | **$142,362.50** |
| 01/30/2016 | Check | 17 | | Monthly Withdrawal | Checking | | $500.00 |
| | | | | | Your Name, Capital:Your Name, Drawing | $500.00 | |
| | | | | | | **$500.00** | **$500.00** |
| 01/30/2016 | Journal Entry | 5 | | Additional Owner Investment | Checking | $3,000.00 | |
| | | | | Additional Owner Investment | Your Name, Capital:Your Name, Investment | | $3,000.00 |
| | | | | | | **$3,000.00** | **$3,000.00** |
| 01/30/2016 | Journal Entry | 6 | | Additional Investment | Office Equipment:Original cost | $2,500.00 | |
| | | | | Additional Investment | Your Name, Capital:Your Name, Investment | | $2,500.00 |
| | | | | | | **$2,500.00** | **$2,500.00** |
| **TOTAL** | | | | | | **$148,937.50** | **$148,937.50** |

Print in landscape orientation, export, and/or send/submit the report as previously instructed
- If you save or export it to Excel, name it: **2-Your Name Journal Ch. 5**.

Do <u>not</u> close Your Name's Beach Barkers

## BALANCE SHEET—DO

A Balance Sheet proves the fundamental accounting equation: Assets = Liabilities + Owner's Equity. When the adjustments for the period have been recorded, a balance sheet should be prepared. The Balance Sheet shows, as of the report dates, the balance in each balance sheet account with subtotals provided for assets, liabilities, and equity.

## <u>DO</u>

Continue to use **Your Name's Beach Barkers** to prepare the Balance Sheet report

Access Accountant Reports, click **Balance Sheet**
Enter the Dates From: **010116** To: **013116**, click **Run Report**

## Your Name's Beach Barkers
### BALANCE SHEET
#### As of January 31, 2016

| | TOTAL |
|---|---|
| **ASSETS** | |
| **Current Assets** | |
| **Bank Accounts** | |
| Checking | 60,037.88 |
| Petty Cash | 107.08 |
| **Total Bank Accounts** | **$60,144.96** |
| **Accounts Receivable** | |
| Accounts Receivable (A/R) | 14,930.00 |
| **Total Accounts Receivable** | **$14,930.00** |
| **Other current assets** | |
| Inventory Asset | 29,012.50 |
| Prepaid Insurance | 1,100.00 |
| Supplies | |
| Cleaning Supplies | 825.00 |
| Kennel Supplies | 2,084.00 |
| Office Supplies | 753.68 |
| Sales Supplies | 400.00 |
| **Total Supplies** | **4,062.68** |
| Undeposited Funds | 0.00 |
| **Total Other current assets** | **$34,175.18** |
| **Total Current Assets** | **$109,250.14** |
| **Fixed Assets** | |
| **Furniture & Fixtures** | |
| Depreciation | -1,500.00 |
| Original cost | 15,000.00 |
| **Total Furniture & Fixtures** | **13,500.00** |
| **Kennel Equipment** | |
| Depreciation | -2,030.00 |
| Original cost | 20,300.00 |
| **Total Kennel Equipment** | **18,270.00** |
| **Office Equipment** | |
| Depreciation | -800.00 |
| Original cost | 11,685.84 |
| **Total Office Equipment** | **10,885.84** |
| **Vehicles** | |
| Depreciation | -3,475.00 |
| Original cost | 32,000.00 |
| **Total Vehicles** | **28,525.00** |
| **Total Fixed Assets** | **$71,180.84** |
| **TOTAL ASSETS** | **$180,430.98** |

| LIABILITIES AND EQUITY | |
|---|---|
| **Liabilities** | |
| **Current Liabilities** | |
| **Accounts Payable** | |
| Accounts Payable (A/P) | 4,214.00 |
| **Total Accounts Payable** | **$4,214.00** |
| **Total Current Liabilities** | **$4,214.00** |
| **Long-Term Liabilities** | |
| **Loans Payable** | |
| Equipment Loan | 2,000.00 |
| Furniture & Fixtures Loan | 2,500.00 |
| **Total Loans Payable** | **4,500.00** |
| **Total Long-Term Liabilities** | **$4,500.00** |
| **Total Liabilities** | **$8,714.00** |
| **Equity** | |
| Opening Balance Equity | 0.00 |
| Retained Earnings | 22,200.00 |
| Your Name, Capital | 96,977.50 |
| Your Name, Drawing | -500.00 |
| Your Name, Investment | 50,885.00 |
| **Total Your Name, Capital** | **147,362.50** |
| Net Income | 2,154.48 |
| **Total Equity** | **$171,716.98** |
| **TOTAL LIABILITIES AND EQUITY** | **$180,430.98** |

- Notice that Total Assets of $180,430.98 equal the Total Liabilities and Equity.
- As you review the Equity section, you will see that Opening Balance Equity is 0.00. Your Name, Capital shows $96,977.50, Drawing is -$500, and Investment is $50,885.00. You will also see amounts in Retained Earnings and in Net Income. These will be discussed later in the chapter.

Print in Portrait, export, and/or send/submit as previously instructed

- The file name should be **3-Your Name Balance Sheet Ch. 5**.

Close Your Name's Beach Barkers

*See "ask a question"*

## BANK RECONCILIATION—READ

Each month, the checking account should be reconciled with the bank statement to make sure that the balances agree. The bank statement will rarely have an ending balance that matches the balance of the checking account. This is due to several factors: outstanding checks (written by the business but not yet paid by the bank), deposits in transit (deposits that were made too late to be included on the bank statement), bank service charges, interest earned on checking accounts, collections made by the bank, and errors made in recording checks and/or deposits by the company or by the bank.

Many companies sign up for online banking and use the bank feeds that are matched to recorded transactions. Since Your Name's Beach Barkers is not a real company, we cannot sign up for online banking. As a result, Bank Feeds and Online Banking will not be included in the chapter.

In order to have an accurate amount listed as the balance in the checking account, it is important that the differences between the bank statement and the checking account be reconciled. If something such as a service charge or a collection made by the bank appears on the bank statement, it needs to be recorded in the checking account.

Reconciling a bank statement is an appropriate time to find any errors that may have been recorded in the checking account. The reconciliation may be out of balance because a transposition was made (recording $94 rather than $49), a transaction was recorded backwards, a transaction was recorded twice, or a transaction was not recorded at all. If a transposition was made, the error may be found by dividing the difference by 9. For example, if $94 was recorded and the actual transaction amount was $49, you would subtract 49 from 94 to get 45. The number 45 can be evenly divided by 9, so your error was a transposition.

## RECONCILE CHECKING—DRILL

To reconcile the bank statement, you Reconcile the Checking account. The Opening Balance should match either the amount of the final balance on the last reconciliation or the starting balance of the account.

> **MEMO:**
> **DATE:** January 31, 2016
>
> Begin the Reconciliation of the Checking account. Use the Current Date, an Ending Balance of $5,441.39.
> ---
> Select the first 10 checks, the 3 deposits, and the first 3 items for Deposits and Other Credits.
> ---
> Add the Vendor: **Bay Town Bank**.
> ---
> As you record an automatic loan payment of $92.12—Principal $75.45, Interest: $16.67, add an account: Category Type: Expenses, Detail Type: Interest Paid, Name: Interest Expense.
> ---
> Complete the Reconciliation.

## *DRILL*

 Use the **Test Drive Company** to reconcile the Checking account

To access the Reconciliation, click the **Gear** icon, click **Reconcile**, in the Tools column

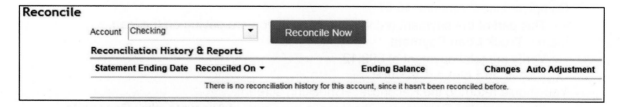

Account: **Checking**
Click the **Reconcile Now** button

Enter information for the Checking account on the Start Reconciling screen
Statement Ending Date: **Current Date**

- As you have experienced, the Test Drive Company automatically changes transaction dates. As a result, you will need to use the current date for the bank reconciliation.
- When you use the educational trial version of QuickBooks Online, the Start Reconciling screen will have an area where you can record Bank Charges and Interest Earned. That information will be presented when you reconcile the bank statement for Your Name's Beach Barkers.

Enter the Ending Balance: **5,441.39**

- This means the balance of the bank statement.

Click **OK**
Click the first 15 items listed under Checks and Payments

- The transactions should begin with Robertson & Associates for $300 and end with Chin's Gas and Oil for $52.14.

Click the first 3 items listed for Deposits and Other Credits and the last three Deposits

- If you look at the summary area in the lower-left of the reconcile screen, you will see amounts for Beginning Balance, Checks and Payments, Deposits and Other Credits, Statement Ending Balance, Cleared Balance, and Difference. The Difference is the same amount as the unrecorded automatic loan payment of $92.12.

| ▼ | Edit Information from Statement | Beginning Balance | 5,000.00 |
| | | 15  Checks and Payments | 1,447.79 |
| | Service Charge | 6  Deposits and Other Credits | |
| | Interest Earned | | 1,981.30 |
| | | Statement Ending Balance | 5,441.39 |
| | | Cleared Balance | 5,533.51 |
| | | Difference | -92.12 |

To record an automatic loan payment that does not appear in your reconciliation screen, click the **Plus** icon, click **Check** in the Vendors column
Click in the drop-down list arrow for Payee
The bank does not appear as a vendor, click **+ Add new**
Enter the vendor name, **Bay Town Bank**, click **Save**

- If you do not want to track payments to the bank, you do not have to add a vendor or enter a payee name on the check.

Checking should appear next to the vendor name with a Balance of $1,201.00
Date: **Current Date**

- For illustration, the text will use **01/31/16** for the date.

If marked, click Print Later to remove the check mark, remove the Check no.
Line 1: Account: **Loan Payable** Amount: **75.45**

- This is the amount of the loan principle you are paying to reduce the loan amount.

Line 2: Account: click the drop-down list arrow then click **+Add new**
Category Type: **Expenses**, Detail type: **Interest Paid**, Name: **Interest Expense**
Click **Save and Close** (Click the drop-down if it doesn't show)
Complete Line 2 Amount: **16.67**

- This part of the payment records the interest you are paying on the loan.

Memo: **Truck Loan Payment**

- Verify the total payment of $92.12.

Click **Save and close (**Ctrl+Alt+D)
You should return to the Reconcile – Checking screen

- If not, open the Register for Checking in the Chart of Accounts, click **Reconcile**.
- If the previously marked 15 checks and 6 deposits/credits are no longer selected, click them again to reselect.

Scroll through the list of Checks and Payments until you find the loan payment to Bay Town Bank, click to select
- Note the information in the gray summary area at the bottom of the reconcile screen. When you have a Difference of 0.00, the Reconciliation is complete

## Reconcile - Checking

For statement ending on:  01/31/2016                                                    ☑ Hide transactions after the statement's end date

### Checks and Payments

| ☐ | 🗐 | Date ▲ | Type | Num | Name | Amount |
|---|---|--------|------|-----|------|--------|
| ☑ | | 12/23/2015 | Bill Pay... | 7 | Hicks Hardware | 250.00 |
| ☑ | | 12/26/2015 | Expense | 8 | Hicks Hardware | 24.36 |
| ☑ | | 01/04/2016 | Check | ... | Tony Rondonuwu | 100.00 |
| ☑ | | 01/04/2016 | Cash Pu... | ... | Bob's Burger Joint | 5.66 |
| ☑ | | 01/04/2016 | Cash Pu... | ... | Squeaky Kleen... | 19.99 |
| ☑ | | 01/05/2016 | Cash Pu... | ... | Chin's Gas and... | 52.14 |
| ☐ | | 01/05/2016 | Check | 70 | Chin's Gas and... | 185.00 |
| ☐ | | 01/06/2016 | Bill Pay... | 11 | Hall Properties | 900.00 |
| ☐ | | 01/07/2016 | Check | 2 | Mahoney Mugs | 18.08 |
| ☐ | | 01/07/2016 | Expense | 13 | Hicks Hardware | 215.66 |
| ☐ | | 01/09/2016 | Cash Pu... | ... | Bob's Burger Joint | 3.86 |
| ☑ | | 01/31/2016 | Check | ... | Bay Town Bank | 92.12 |

### Deposits and Other Credits

| ☐ | 🗐 | Date ▲ | Type | Num | Name | Amount |
|---|---|--------|------|-----|------|--------|
| ☑ | | 10/19/2015 | Payment | 1053 | Bill's Windsurf Shop | 175.00 |
| ☑ | | 12/19/2015 | Payment | 5664 | 55 Twin Lane | 86.40 |
| ☑ | | 12/19/2015 | Sales R... | 1008 | Kate Whelan | 225.00 |
| ☐ | | 12/21/2015 | Payment | ... | Amy's Bird Sanct... | 105.00 |
| ☐ | | 01/06/2016 | Payment | 1886 | Cool Cars | 694.00 |
| ☐ | | 01/08/2016 | Sales R... | 10264 | Dylan Sollfrank | 337.50 |
| ☐ | | 01/11/2016 | Payment | ... | 55 Twin Lane | 50.00 |
| ☐ | | 01/11/2016 | Payment | 2064 | Travis Waldron | 103.55 |
| ☑ | | 01/11/2016 | Deposit | ... | | 218.75 |
| ☑ | | 01/12/2016 | Deposit | ... | | 408.00 |
| ☑ | | 01/13/2016 | Deposit | ... | | 868.15 |

| ▼ Edit Information from Statement | | |
|---|---|---|
| | Beginning Balance | 5,000.00 |
| | 16  Checks and Payments | 1,539.91 |
| Service Charge | 6  Deposits and Other Credits | |
| Interest Earned | | 1,981.30 |
| | Statement Ending Balance | 5,441.39 |
| | Cleared Balance | 5,441.39 |
| | Difference | 0.00 |

[ Finish Now ]   [ Finish Later ]   [ Cancel ]

**Partial Reconciliation**

Once the reconciliation is complete, click **Finish Now**
- You should return to the Reconciliation screen and see your reconciliation listed in the Reconciliation History & Reports.

Click the row with your reconciliation information to view the Reconciliation Report
- In the Reconciliation Report, you will see three sections: Summary, Details, and Additional Information. Summary provides information regarding the Reconciliation amounts and the Checking account balance. The Details section shows the Cleared transactions for Checks and Payments and Deposits and Other Credits. The Additional Information section shows the Uncleared transactions for Checks and Payments and Deposits and Other Credits.

Close the Test Drive Company

## RECONCILE CHECKING—DO

When you Reconcile the Checking account, you are matching the entries in your Checking account with the entries shown on your bank statement. Since this is the first time Your Name's Beach Barkers Checking account has been reconciled, the Opening Balance is the starting balance of the account. The bank reconciliation for Your Name's Beach Barkers is more complex than the reconciliation you performed for practice. As a result, the procedures to Reconcile Checking have been divided into sections marked with green side headings.

---

**MEMO:**
**DATE:** January 31, 2016

Reconciliation the Checking account. The bank statement is dated January 22, 2016.

---

## *DO*

 Use **Your Name's Beach Barkers** to reconcile the Checking account

## Bank Statement Information

Some information appearing on the bank statement is entered into the Begin Reconciliation window. This information includes the statement date, ending balance, bank service charges, and interest earned.

 Use the following bank statement for Your Name's Beach Barkers as you follow the written instructions to reconcile the checking account (Do <u>not</u> try to reconcile the bank statement without following the instructions provided.)

<table>
<tr><td colspan="5" style="text-align:center">Beach Bank<br>350 Second Street<br>Venice, CA 90202<br>310-555-9889</td></tr>
<tr><td colspan="5">Your Name's Beach Barkers<br>1302 Pacific Avenue<br>Venice, CA 92091</td></tr>
<tr><td colspan="2">Account: 123-321-4566</td><td colspan="3" style="text-align:right">January 22, 2016</td></tr>
<tr><td>Beginning Balance, 1/1/2016</td><td></td><td></td><td></td><td style="text-align:right">$45,385.00</td></tr>
<tr><td>1/12/2016 Check 1</td><td></td><td style="text-align:right">$20.00</td><td></td><td style="text-align:right">45,365.00</td></tr>
<tr><td>1/15/2016 Deposit</td><td style="text-align:right">5,640.00</td><td></td><td></td><td style="text-align:right">51,005.00</td></tr>
<tr><td>1/15/2016 Equipment Loan Pmt.: Principal<br>    $29.41. Interest $8.33:</td><td></td><td style="text-align:right">37.74</td><td></td><td style="text-align:right">50,967.26</td></tr>
<tr><td>1/15/2016 Service Charge</td><td></td><td style="text-align:right">8.00</td><td></td><td style="text-align:right">50,959.26</td></tr>
<tr><td>1/15/2016 Interest</td><td style="text-align:right">37.85</td><td></td><td></td><td style="text-align:right">50,997.11</td></tr>
<tr><td>1/21/2016 Check 2</td><td></td><td style="text-align:right">300.00</td><td></td><td style="text-align:right">50,697.11</td></tr>
<tr><td>1/21/2016 Check 3</td><td></td><td style="text-align:right">403.68</td><td></td><td style="text-align:right">50,293.43</td></tr>
<tr><td>1/21/2016 Check 4</td><td></td><td style="text-align:right">500.00</td><td></td><td style="text-align:right">49,793.43</td></tr>
<tr><td>1/21/2016 Check 5</td><td></td><td style="text-align:right">500.00</td><td></td><td style="text-align:right">49,293.43</td></tr>
<tr><td>Ending Balance, 1/22/2016</td><td></td><td></td><td></td><td style="text-align:right">$49,293.43</td></tr>
</table>

## Begin Reconciliation

As you learned in the practice, the first part of the reconciliation is to enter the bank statement information.

 Begin the Checking Account Reconciliation for **Your Name's Beach Barkers**

> Click the **Gear** icon, click **Reconcile**, in the Tools column
> Account: **Checking**

**Reconcile**

| Account | Checking ▾ | Reconcile Now |
| --- | --- | --- |

**Reconciliation History & Reports**

| Statement Ending Date | Reconciled On ▾ | Ending Balance | Changes | Auto Adjustment |
| --- | --- | --- | --- | --- |
| | There is no reconciliation history for this account, since it hasn't been reconciled before. | | | |

Click the **Reconcile Now** button

Enter the Bank Statement information for the Checking account on the Start Reconciling
   screen

Statement Ending Date: **01/22/16**

- There will be two bank statements for reconciliation in this chapter, one now and one as
  part of the Additional Transactions toward the end of the chapter.
- QuickBooks Online inserts the Beginning Balance of $45,385.00.

Enter the Ending Balance: **49,293.43**

- This is the ending balance shown on the bank statement.

Enter the Service Charge: **8.00**, Tab to Date and enter **01/22/16**, Account: **Bank Charges**

Enter the Interest Earned: **37.85**, Date: **01/22/16**, Account: **Interest Earned**

- Double-check the dates for Service Charge and Interest Earned to make sure you used
  01/22/2016.

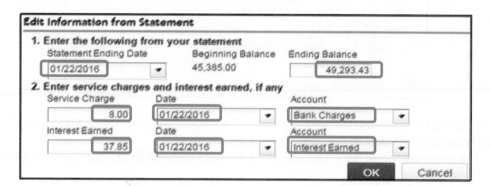

Click **OK**

- You are taken to Reconcile – Checking. Notice that the Service Charge and Interest are
  shown with a check mark and the statement information entered is shown in the gray
  summary area.
- As you look at the statement information, you will see a Cleared Balance of 45,414.85
  and a Difference of 3,878.58. If you take the Beginning Balance, subtract the service
  charge and add the interest earned, that becomes the Cleared Balance. Subtract the
  Statement Ending Balance and the Cleared Balance to determine the Difference. When
  you complete the Bank Reconciliation, the Difference <u>must</u> be 0.00.

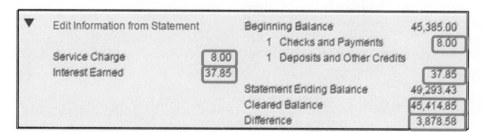

Do <u>not</u> close Your Name's Beach Barkers, continue to the next section

- If you do not have time to complete the Bank Reconciliation, click Finish Later to save
  your work up to this point. <u>DO NOT</u> click Finish Now!

## Mark Cleared Transactions

Once bank statement information for service charges and interest has been entered, compare the
checks and deposits listed on the statement with the transactions for the checking account. An item
may be marked individually by clicking the check box for the deposit or the check.

Continue with **Your Name's Beach Barkers** Checking Account Reconciliation and mark cleared checks and deposits

Compare the bank statement with the **Reconcile - Checking** window
Click the items that appear on both statements
- If you are unable to complete the reconciliation in one session, click the **Finish Later** button to leave the reconciliation and return to it later.
- Under _no_ circumstances should you click **Finish Now** until the reconciliation is complete and the Difference is 0.00.

Click in the check box for the Refund to Gloria Gucci to mark
- If you click on any other part of the transaction, you will be taken to the Refund Receipt.

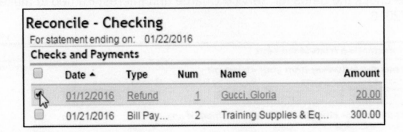

Refer to the Bank Statement and select all of the Checks, Payments, and Deposits shown in the Reconcile – Checking screen
- The automatic loan payment of $37.74 has not been recorded so it will not be shown in Reconcile – Checking.

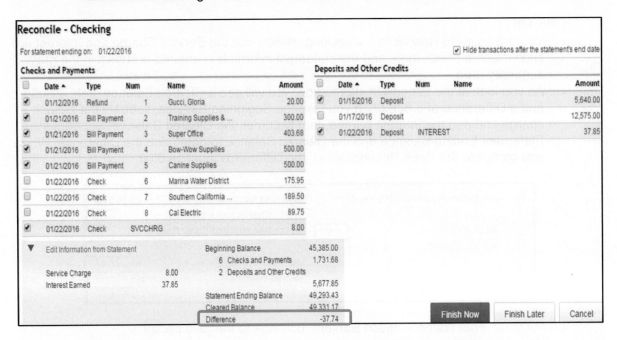

- Notice the Difference of **-37.74**.

Continue to use Your Name Beach Barkers to complete the next section

## Adjusting Entries—Bank Reconciliation

When you have an automatic loan payment setup with the bank, the payment amount will be deducted from your bank account each month. To account for this, you will need to enter the loan payment.

With **Your Name's Beach Barkers** Reconcile - Checking window still showing, enter the automatic loan payment

Click the **Plus** icon and click **Check** from the Vendors column
Record the check as previously instructed
Payee: **Beach Bank**
Payment Account: **Checking**
Payment date: **01/22/2016**
Click **Print later** to unmark
Check no.: Leave Blank
Line 1: Account: **Equipment Loan**, Amount: **29.41**
Line 2: Account: **Interest Expense**, Amount: **8.33**
Memo: **Equipment Loan Payment**

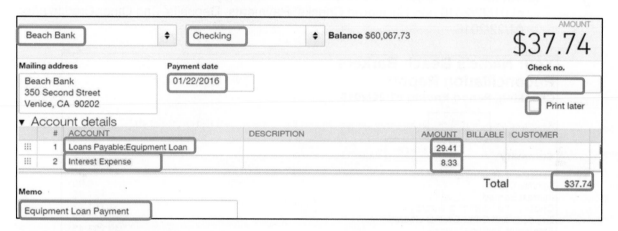

Click **Save and close**
- You should return to the Reconcile – Checking screen. If not, access the Checking Account Register in the Chart of Accounts and click **Reconcile**.
- If your 7 Checks and Payments and 2 Deposits and Other Credits are no longer selected, click them again.

Click the Check you just entered for Beach Bank
- The Difference is now 0.00. If your difference is not, find and correct your errors, make sure you marked only those checks and deposits listed in the Bank Statement.

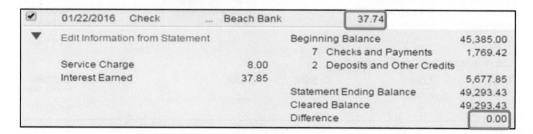

With a Difference of 0.00, click **Finish Now**
After clicking Finish Now, you will return to the original Reconcile screen
You will see the list of all the reconciliation reports you have prepared
Do **not** close Your Name's Beach Barkers continue with the next section

## Reconciliation Report

 Prepare the Reconciliation Report for **Your Name's Beach Barkers**

In the Reconciliation History & Reports listing, click **01/22/2016**
- For Reconciled On, you will see the current date. Accept the date shown.

| Reconciliation History & Reports | | | | |
|---|---|---|---|---|
| Statement Ending Date | Reconciled On ▾ | Ending Balance | Changes | Auto Adjustment |
| 01/22/2016 | 02/08/2016 | 49,293.43 | | |

The report is divided into three sections:

    **Summary**—summarizes Checking account information
    **Details**—lists the Checks and Payments cleared and Deposits and Other Credits cleared
    **Additional Information**—lists Uncleared Checks, Payments, Deposits, and Credits as of 01/22/2016 and Uncleared Checks, Payments, Deposits, and Other Credits after 01/22/2016

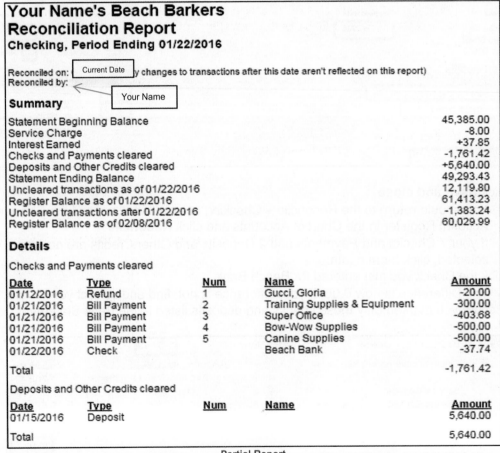

**Your Name's Beach Barkers**
**Reconciliation Report**
**Checking, Period Ending 01/22/2016**

Reconciled on: [ Current Date ] y changes to transactions after this date aren't reflected on this report)
Reconciled by: ← [ Your Name ]

**Summary**

| | |
|---|---|
| Statement Beginning Balance | 45,385.00 |
| Service Charge | -8.00 |
| Interest Earned | +37.85 |
| Checks and Payments cleared | -1,761.42 |
| Deposits and Other Credits cleared | +5,640.00 |
| Statement Ending Balance | 49,293.43 |
| Uncleared transactions as of 01/22/2016 | 12,119.80 |
| Register Balance as of 01/22/2016 | 61,413.23 |
| Uncleared transactions after 01/22/2016 | -1,383.24 |
| Register Balance as of 02/08/2016 | 60,029.99 |

**Details**

Checks and Payments cleared

| Date | Type | Num | Name | Amount |
|---|---|---|---|---|
| 01/12/2016 | Refund | 1 | Gucci, Gloria | -20.00 |
| 01/21/2016 | Bill Payment | 2 | Training Supplies & Equipment | -300.00 |
| 01/21/2016 | Bill Payment | 3 | Super Office | -403.68 |
| 01/21/2016 | Bill Payment | 4 | Bow-Wow Supplies | -500.00 |
| 01/21/2016 | Bill Payment | 5 | Canine Supplies | -500.00 |
| 01/22/2016 | Check | | Beach Bank | -37.74 |
| Total | | | | -1,761.42 |

Deposits and Other Credits cleared

| Date | Type | Num | Name | Amount |
|---|---|---|---|---|
| 01/15/2016 | Deposit | | | 5,640.00 |
| Total | | | | 5,640.00 |

Partial Report

Print as previously instructed
- If you print to a pdf file, save it as **4-Your Name Reconciliation Report Ch. 5**.
- You cannot export this report to Excel.

Click **Close** on the report
Do <u>not</u> close Your Name's Beach Barkers

## VIEW CHECKING ACCOUNT REGISTER—DO

Once the Checking account and bank statement have been reconciled, it is wise to scroll through the Checking account register to view the effect of the reconciliation on the account. You will notice a column with a check mark. As you scroll through the register, transactions that were reconciled are marked with an R.

 Continue to use **Your Name's Beach Barkers** and view the Checking account register

> Open the Chart of Accounts and click **View Register** for Checking
> Scroll through the transactions
> * Notice that the Service Charge, Interest, and Equipment Loan Payment are shown and marked with an R. All of the other transactions selected during the reconciliation are also marked with an R.
> Change the column widths to display information in full
> Adjust the width of the PAYEE column
> Point to the sizing arrow between PAYEE and MEMO and until you get a double arrow
> Hold down the primary (left) mouse button, drag to the right to enlarge the column width
> * You will see a dark vertical line as you resize.

> Repeat the steps and widen the MEMO column
> Make the columns for PAYMENT and DEPOSIT narrower by dragging to the left

| DATE ▼ | REF NO.<br>TYPE | PAYEE<br>ACCOUNT | MEMO | PAYMENT | DEPOSIT | ✓<br> | BALANCE |
|---|---|---|---|---|---|---|---|

> Scroll through the register and note that you can see Payees and Memos in full

| DATE | REF NO.<br>TYPE | PAYEE<br>ACCOUNT | MEMO | PAYMENT | DEPOSIT | | BALANCE |
|---|---|---|---|---|---|---|---|
| 01/22/2016 | Check | Beach Bank<br>-Split- | Equipment Loan Payment | $37.74 | | R | $61,413.23 |
| 01/22/2016 | SVCCHRG<br>Check | <br>Bank Charges | Service Charge | $8.00 | | R | $61,450.97 |
| 01/22/2016 | 8<br>Check | Cal Electric<br>Utilities:Electric | Monthly Electricity | $89.75 | | | $61,458.97 |
| 01/22/2016 | 7<br>Check | Southern California Gas Company<br>Utilities:Gas-Heating | Monthly Gas-Heating | $189.50 | | | $61,548.72 |
| 01/22/2016 | 6<br>Check | Marina Water District<br>Utilities:Water | Monthly Water | $175.95 | | | $61,738.22 |
| 01/22/2016 | INTEREST<br>Deposit | <br>Interest Earned | Interest Earned | | $37.85 | R | $61,914.17 |
| 01/21/2016 | 5<br>Bill Payment | Canine Supplies<br>Accounts Payable (A/P) | Partial Payment | $500.00 | | R | $61,876.32 |
| 01/21/2016 | 4<br>Bill Payment | Bow-Wow Supplies<br>Accounts Payable (A/P) | Partial Payment | $500.00 | | R | $62,376.32 |

**Partial Register**

Continue to use Your Name's Beach Barkers in the next section

5

## PREPARE AND CUSTOMIZE STATEMENT OF CASH FLOWS—DO

A report that details the amount of cash flow in a business is the Statement of Cash Flows. This report organizes information regarding cash in three areas of activities: Operating Activities, Investing Activities, and Financing Activities. The report also projects the amount of cash at the end of a period. Rather than be required to remove the Date Prepared and Time Prepared from a report every time you prepare it, QuickBooks Online allows you to customize each report as it is prepared.

Continue to use **Your Name's Beach Barkers** to prepare a Statement of Cash Flows

> Access the Accountant Reports as previously instructed
> Click **Statement of Cash Flows**
> When the report appears, click the **Customize** button
> Remove the Date Prepared and Time Prepared from the Footer as previously instructed
> Click **Run Report**
> Click **Save Customizations**
> * Customizing in this order saves the removal of the Date and Time Prepared and nothing else. If you change the dates before saving the customizations, the date range will be saved as well. Since you do not want your report to use the dates for January 1-31, 2016 every time it is prepared, it is important to use the sequence presented above for customization.
> Review the "Save Report Customizations" screen
> Keep the Name of custom report as Statement of Cash Flows
> * Each report, such as the Journal, Trial Balance, etc., must be customized individually.
> * Once customized, the report is accessed in the "My Custom Reports" section of Reports.

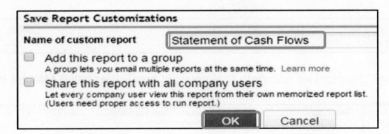

> Click **OK**
> Continue preparing the Statement of Cash Flows
> Dates From: **01/01/16** To: **01/31/16**, click **Run Report**
> * As you review the following report, you will see that the Operating Activities section details the cash generated in the operation of the business; the Investing Activities section details the cash spent on your business; and the Financing Activities section details loan financing and owner's equity. You will see the Net cash increase (or decrease) for the period, the cash at the beginning of the period, and the cash at the end of the period.
> * If your report has a line after Accounts Payable for Total Adjustments to reconcile net Income to Net Cash proceeds, that is fine.

### Your Name's Beach Barkers
### STATEMENT OF CASH FLOWS
#### January 2016

| | TOTAL |
|---|---|
| **OPERATING ACTIVITIES** | |
| Net Income | 2,176.00 |
| Adjustments to reconcile Net Income to Net Cash provided by operations: | |
| Accounts Receivable (A/R) | 12,570.00 |
| Prepaid Insurance | 100.00 |
| Supplies:Cleaning Supplies | -75.00 |
| Supplies:Kennel Supplies | -189.00 |
| Supplies:Office Supplies | -403.68 |
| Supplies:Sales Supplies | 100.00 |
| Vehicles:Depreciation | 275.00 |
| Accounts Payable (A/P) | -1,086.00 |
| **Net cash provided by operating activities** | **$13,467.32** |
| **INVESTING ACTIVITIES** | |
| Office Equipment:Original cost | -3,685.84 |
| **Net cash provided by investing activities** | **$ -3,685.84** |
| **FINANCING ACTIVITIES** | |
| Loans Payable:Equipment Loan | -29.41 |
| Opening Balance Equity | -142,362.50 |
| Your Name, Capital | 96,977.50 |
| Your Name, Capital:Your Name, Drawing | -500.00 |
| Your Name, Capital:Your Name, Investment | 50,885.00 |
| **Net cash provided by financing activities** | **$4,970.59** |
| **Net cash increase for period** | **$14,752.07** |
| Cash at beginning of period | 45,385.00 |
| **Cash at end of period** | **$60,137.07** |

Print in Portrait orientation, export, and/or send/submit as previously instructed
- If you save the report, name it: **5-Your Name Statement of Cash Flows Ch. 5**.

Do not close Your Name's Beach Barkers

## CLOSING ENTRIES—READ

In accounting, there are four closing entries made in order to close the books for a period. They include closing all income accounts, all expense accounts, and the drawing account into Income Summary. The final entry is to close the Income Summary account and transfer the net income or net loss into the owner's capital account.

In QuickBooks Online, setting a closing date will replace closing the income and expense accounts. QuickBooks Online does not close the owner's drawing account so a closing entry is recorded as a Journal Entry. Rather than use an Income Summary account, QuickBooks Online automatically transfers Net Income into Retained Earnings. Retained Earnings contains the amount of all Net Income earned and is separate from Your Name, Capital. According to GAAP, a sole proprietorship net income should be included in the owner's capital account not in retained earnings.

Due to the account requirements in the Test Drive Company, the closing entry for Drawing will be recorded in Your Name's Beach Barkers. All of the other closing entries will be practiced using the Test Drive Company. Reports will be prepared to obtain closing entry information.

## CLOSE DRAWING—DO

The closing entry for Drawing transfers the amount of owner withdrawals into Your Name, Capital. Rather than create the necessary accounts and transactions in the Test Drive Company, you will record the closing entry in Your Name's Beach Barkers. In the later part of the chapter, you will record and close an additional withdrawal.

 Continue to use **Your Name's Beach Barkers** to close Your Name, Drawing

Open the Chart of Accounts and view the balance for Your Name, Drawing

| Your Name, Capital | Equity | Owner's Equity | 147,362.50 |
| Your Name, Drawing | Equity | Owner's Equity | -500.00 |
| Your Name, Investment | Equity | Owner's Equity | 50,885.00 |

Click the **Plus** icon, click **Journal Entry** in the Other column
Enter the Date: **01/31/16**
Journal no.: **7**
- The Journal number 7 should appear automatically, if not, enter it.
Line 1: Account: **Your Name, Capital**, Debits: **500**, Description: **Close Drawing**
- Remember that a withdrawal reduces owner's equity and that a reduction to owner's equity is recorded as a debit.
Line 2: Account: **Your Name, Drawing**, Credits: **500**, Description: **Close Drawing**

| Journal date | | | | | Journal no. |
|---|---|---|---|---|---|
| 01/31/2016 | | | | | 7 |
| # | ACCOUNT | DEBITS | CREDITS | DESCRIPTION | |
| 1 | Your Name, Capital | 500.00 | | Close Drawing | |
| 2 | Your Name, Capital:Your Name, Drawing | | 500.00 | Close Drawing | |
| | Total | 500.00 | 500.00 | | |

Click **Save and close**
View the account in the Chart of Accounts
- The balance for Your Name, Drawing is 0.00.

| Your Name, Capital | Equity | Owner's Equity | 147,362.50 |
| Your Name, Drawing | Equity | Owner's Equity | 0.00 |
| Your Name, Investment | Equity | Owner's Equity | 50,885.00 |

Close Your Name's Beach Barkers

## ENTER TRANSACTION INTO THE TEST DRIVE COMPANY—DRILL

In order to manipulate the Test Drive Company and learn how to transfer Net Income, an additional transaction needs to be entered.

 Open the **Test Drive Company**

Enter an Invoice for Cool Cars, Invoice Date: **010116**
Line 1: Product/Service: **Concrete**, Description: **Concrete for fountain installation**, QTY: **1**, Rate: **1,639.95**, Tax: Click to remove check mark
Click **Save and close** and continue in the next section using the Test Drive Company

## PROFIT AND LOSS—DRILL

Since the income, expenses, and adjustments for the period have been entered, a Profit & Loss report can be prepared. This report is also known as the Income Statement and shows Income minus Expenses equals Net Income (or Net Loss). As an introduction to end-of-period reports and the transfer of Net Income and Retained Earnings into Capital, you will use the Test Drive Company for practice. As you have learned, the transaction dates in the Test Drive Company are programed to change automatically. As a result of this, your reports may not match the ones shown in the text. If this happens, simply use the amounts you see in your reports for practice.

Continue to use the **Test Drive Company** to prepare a Profit and Loss report

Turn **OFF** Redesigned Reports in QuickBooks Labs
Access **Accountant Reports** as previously instructed
Click **Profit and Loss**
Enter the Dates From: **010115** To: **Current Date**, click **Run Report**
- Due to the automatic date changes in the Test Drive Company, use the From date of January 1, 2015 and the current date for the To date. Otherwise, the amounts shown in the reports for this drill will be different from the text.
- If your amount for Net Income is not an exact match, do not be concerned, simply continue with the closing entries using the amounts shown in your report.

| Net Income | $3,282.41 |
|---|---|

- Write down the amount of the Net Income.
Do <u>not</u> close the Test Drive Company

## BALANCE SHEET—DRILL

As you learned in earlier chapters, the Balance Sheet proves the fundamental accounting equation: Assets = Liabilities + Owner's Equity. Because of the automatic date changes in the Test Drive Company, reports will not match the text unless you use a date range from January 1, 2015 until the current date.

 Continue to use **Your Name's Beach Barkers** and prepare the Balance Sheet

Return to Accountant Reports, click **Balance Sheet**
Enter the Dates From: **01/01/15** To: **Current Date**, click **Run Report**
Scroll down to the Equity section of the report
- If your amounts for Net Income and Retained Earnings are not an exact match with the following, do not be concerned, simply continue with the closing entries using the amounts shown in the Equity section on your report.

| Equity | |
|---|---|
| Opening Balance Equity | -9,337.50 |
| Retained Earnings | 384.49 |
| Net Income | 2,897.92 |
| Total Equity | $ -6,055.09 |

- When you view the Balance Sheet for January, 2015 until the Current Date, you will see Retained Earnings for $384.49 and Net Income of $2,897.92. When you add the Retained Earnings and the Net Income together, they equal the amount of net income shown in the Profit and Loss report. ($384.49 + $2,897.92 = $3,282.41)
- Again, if your numbers do not match the ones shown, do not be concerned.
Do <u>not</u> close the Test Drive Company

## TRANSFER NET INCOME—DRILL

At the end of the year, Net Income is transferred into Retained Earnings by QuickBooks Online. Because Craig's Design and Landscape is a sole proprietorship, the amount of Net Income should be included in the Open Balance Equity account not Retained Earnings. A Journal Entry needs to be recorded to transfer Net Income into Opening Balance Equity. If you had Your Name, Capital available for use, this is the account you would use for the transfer of Net Income.

Continue to use the **Test Drive Company** to transfer Net Income and Retained Earnings into Opening Balance Equity

Click the **Plus** icon, click **Journal Entry** in the Other column
Enter the Date: **Current Date**
- The screen shot uses the date of 01/31/2016.

Journal no.: **1**
Line 1: Account: **Retained Earnings**, Debits: **3,282.41**, Description: **Transfer Net Income and Retained Earnings**
- At the end of the year, QuickBooks Online automatically transfers Net Income into Retained Earnings. In order to transfer the Net Income into Opening Balance Equity, you will debit Retained Earnings to transfer both the amount of Net Income and the current amount shown in Retained Earnings. In the future, you would only need to transfer the amount of Net Income.
- The amount of the transaction is calculated by adding the amount shown in Retained Earnings to the amount of Net Income. Again, if your amounts do not match the text, either enter the amounts in your report or just continue by reading the information.

Line 2: Account: **Opening Balance Equity**, Credits: **3,282.41**, Description: **Transfer Net Income and Retained Earnings**
- Opening Balance Equity is used for the account because the Test Drive Company does not save the Owner's Equity capital accounts you created earlier in the chapter. When you transfer the Net Income and Retained Earnings for Your Name's Beach Barkers later in the chapter, Your Name, Capital will be the account used.

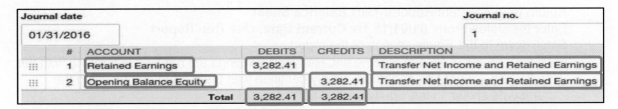

| Journal date | | | | | | Journal no. |
|---|---|---|---|---|---|---|
| 01/31/2016 | | | | | | 1 |
| | # | ACCOUNT | DEBITS | CREDITS | DESCRIPTION | |
| ⠿ | 1 | Retained Earnings | 3,282.41 | | Transfer Net Income and Retained Earnings | |
| ⠿ | 2 | Opening Balance Equity | | 3,282.41 | Transfer Net Income and Retained Earnings | |
| | | Total | 3,282.41 | 3,282.41 | | |

Click **Save and Close**, click the drop down-list arrow if necessary
- You should return to the Balance Sheet. If not, prepare the Balance Sheet again.
- If you get a Message from webpage that the report request could not be completed, click **OK**. Click **Reports** on the Navigation bar, and prepare the Balance Sheet again.

View the Equity section

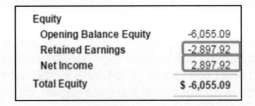

| Equity | |
|---|---|
| Opening Balance Equity | -6,055.09 |
| Retained Earnings | -2,897.92 |
| Net Income | 2,897.92 |
| Total Equity | $ -6,055.09 |

- Analyze the Equity section in the Balance Sheet. The previous amount of Retained Earnings, $384.49, was transferred into Opening Balance Equity. The current amount of Net Income, $2,897.92, shows as a negative in Retained Earnings and as a positive in Net Income.

Change the dates of the Balance Sheet to **01/01/2017** and **Current day and month 2017**
- If the current year happens to be 2017, then use 2018 as the year for this report.

Run the Report

| Equity | |
|---|---|
| Opening Balance Equity | -6,055.09 |
| Retained Earnings | 0.00 |
| Net Income | |
| Total Equity | $ -6,055.09 |

- Amounts for Retained Earnings and Net Income are no longer shown.

Do <u>not</u> close the Test Drive Company

## CLOSE THE BOOKS—DRILL

Rather than record closing entries for income and expense accounts, QuickBooks Online uses a closing date to indicate the end of a period. Once a closing date is assigned, income and expenses are effectively closed. If a transaction involving income or expenses is recorded after the closing date, it is considered part of the new period and will not be used in the calculation of net income (or loss) for the previous period. Conversely, income and expenses for a closed period will not be included in the new period.

If an error is found in a transaction for a closed period, it may be changed but only after acknowledging a warning.

 Continue to use the **Test Drive Company** and close the books for the period

Click the **Gear** icon
Click **Account and Settings** in the Your Company column
- In Your Name's Beach Barkers, you would click **Company Settings**.

Click the **Advanced** tab
Click the **Pen** icon for Accounting
Click the **Close the books** check box to select
Enter the Closing date **Current date**, press **Tab**
- The screen shot shows 01/31/16. Because transaction dates change in the Test Drive Company, you should use the current date.

Accept the selection of Allow changes after viewing a warning

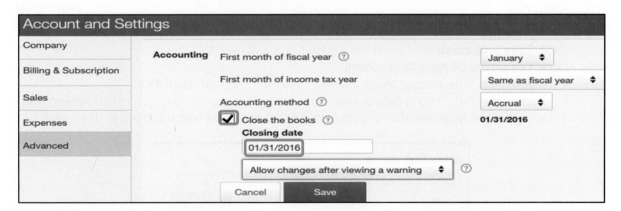

Click **Save**
Click the **Done** button in the lower-right side of the Account and Settings screen or click the **Close** button at the top-right of the screen
Do <u>not</u> close the Test Drive Company

## EDIT CLOSED PERIOD TRANSACTION—DRILL

Even though the month of January has been closed, transactions still appear in the account registers, the Journal, and so on. If it is determined that an error was made in a previous period, QuickBooks Online allows a correction to be made. In order to save an edited transaction, Yes must be clicked on a warning screen. Changes to transactions involving income or expenses will necessitate changing the amount of net income transferred into the owner's capital account.

> **MEMO**
> **DATE:** Current date
>
> Edit Invoice 1038 to Cool Cars. Rate should be $1,739.95.

 Continue to use the **Test Drive Company** to edit an invoice from a closed period and correct the amount of Net Income transferred.

> Click the **Recent Transactions** icon
> Click **Invoice No. 1038** to Cool Cars to open it
> Change the RATE to **1739.95**, press **Tab**

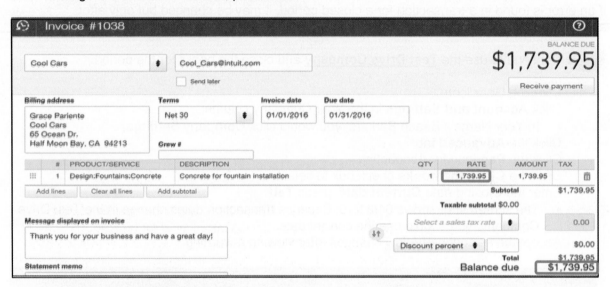

> Click **Save and close**
> Click **Yes** on the Closing date screen
> • If you get a "The transaction is linked to others…" screen, click **Yes**.
> • Sometimes the Closing date screen appears before the Transaction linked screen and sometimes it appears after it. Just click Yes no matter in which order it is displayed.

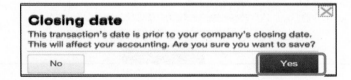

> The change in income must be included in the Journal Entry to transfer the Net Income and Retained Earnings into Opening Balance Equity, edit the transaction
> Click the **Recent Transactions** icon next to the Plus icon on the Top-Navigation Bar
> Select the Journal Entry

- • The Journal Entry No. may be different from 1. Select the entry shown.

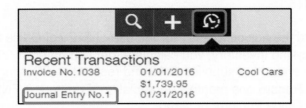

Calculate the amount of the revised Journal entry:

    Change in income: New invoice Total $1,739.95 minus $1,639.95 original invoice Total
        equals an additional $100.00 in income

    The additional income of $100.00 is added to the original transfer amount of $3,282.41
        to equal $3,382.41

Correct the adjusting entry

Line 1: Change Debits to **3382.41**

Line 2: Change Credits to **3382.41**

Click **Save and close**

Click **Yes** on the Closing date screen

To view the changes to Net Income, prepare a Balance Sheet for **01/01/15** to **Current Date**

| Equity | |
|---|---|
| Opening Balance Equity | -5,955.09 |
| Retained Earnings | -2,997.92 |
| Net Income | 2,997.92 |
| Total Equity | $ -5,955.09 |

Close the Test Drive Company

## ADDITIONAL TRANSACTIONS—DO

Record the additional transactions using Your Name's Beach Barkers. All transactions to be recorded were either completed as drills using the Test Drive Company or as transactions for Your Name's Beach Barkers. When you record closing transactions for Drawing and Net Income and Retained Earnings, be sure to use Your Name, Capital as the account rather than Opening Balance Equity.

_DO_

Open **Your Name's Beach Barkers**, enter the transactions in the Memo boxes, complete a Bank Reconciliation, and record Closing Entries for January 31, 2016

Print as instructed within the Memos

When recording Journal Entries, provide appropriate descriptions

**MEMO**
**DATE:** January 31, 2016

| |
|---|
| Journal Entry 8: Record the adjusting entry for the use of $125 of Office Supplies. |
| Journal Entry 9: After taking inventory, you calculate that you have $1,950 of Kennel Supplies on hand. Calculate the amount of supplies used and record the adjusting entry. |
| Journal Entries 10-12: Record one month's depreciation: Furniture & Fixtures, $125; Kennel Equipment, $170, and Office Equipment, $100. |
| Journal Entry 13: Record your additional cash investment of $2,000. |
| Journal Entry 14: You purchased kennel equipment to board dogs at your home. You decided not to do that and are investing the kennel equipment of $850 into Your Name's Beach Barkers. Record the investment. |
| Withdrew $600 for the second part of your monthly withdrawal. Print Check 18. (If you save as a pdf, name it **6-Your Name Check 18**. |
| Use the following Bank Statement to Reconcile the Checking account. Print the Reconciliation report. If saved as a pdf, name it **7-Your Name Reconciliation Report (2) Ch. 5**. |

This is the bank statement for January 31, 2016:

**Beach Bank**
350 Second Street
Venice, CA 90202
310-555-9889

**Your Name's Beach Barkers**
**1302 Pacific Avenue**
**Venice, CA 92091**

| Account: 123-321-4566 | | | January 30, 2016 |
|---|---|---|---|
| **Beginning Balance, 01/23/2016** | | | **$49,293.43** |
| 1/17/2016 Deposit | 12,575.00 | | 61,868.43 |
| 1/22/2016 Check 6 | | 175.95 | 61,692.48 |
| 1/22/2016 Check 7 | | 189.50 | 61,502.98 |
| 1/22/2016 Check 8 | | 89.75 | 61,413.23 |
| 1/23/2016 Transfer | | 100.00 | 61,313.23 |
| 1/23/2016 Check 9 | | 862.92 | 60,450.31 |
| 1/24/2016 Check 10 | | 322.92 | 60,127.39 |
| 1/24/2016 Check 11 | | 1,500.00 | 58,627.39 |
| 1/27/2016 Check 12 | | 129.95 | 58,497.44 |
| 1/27/2016 Transfer | | 50.00 | 58,447.44 |
| 1/27/2016 Check 13 | | 200.00 | 58,247.44 |
| 1/27/2016 Check 15 | | 292.45 | 57,954.99 |
| 1/30/2016 Furniture & Fixtures Loan Pmt: Principal: $36.76, Interest: 10.42 | | 47.18 | 57,907.81 |
| 1/30/2016 Service Charge | | 8.00 | 57,899.81 |
| 1/30/2016 Interest | 41.08 | | 57,940.89 |
| **Ending Balance, 1/30/2016** | | | **$57,940.89** |

When the reconciliation is complete, print and/or save the Reconciliation Report
• If saved as a pdf, name it **7-Your Name Reconciliation Report (2) Ch. 5**.
Continue recording, saving, and printing transactions in the following Memo

> **MEMO**
> **DATE:** January 31, 2016
>
> Journal Entry 15: Close Your Name, Drawing. (This should be for the amount of the second withdrawal.)
>
> Prepare, print, export, and/or send/submit the Profit and Loss report. Remove the Date Prepared, Time Prepared, and Report Basis. Save the Customization. Continue with the report preparation for January 1-31, 2016. Name it **8-Your Name Profit and Loss Ch. 5**.
>
> Prepare and print the Balance Sheet report. Remove the Date Prepared, Time Prepared, and Report Basis. Save the Customization. Continue with the report preparation for January 1-31, 2016. Name it **9-Your Name Balance Sheet Ch. 5**.
>
> Journal Entry 16: Transfer the Net Income and Retained Earnings into Your Name, Capital. Instructions follow

Instructions to transfer Net Income and Retained Earnings into Your Name, Capital:
Look at the **$22,200.00** balance of Retained Earnings on the Balance Sheet

- The $22,200 is the amount of Retained Earnings entered for the value of the beginning balances for Customers of $27,500.00 minus the beginning balances for Vendors of $5,300.00 as of 12/31/2015.

Look at the amount for Net Income **$1,544.66**

- Do the math: Add the Retained Earnings $22,200.00 and the Net Income $1,544.66 = $23,744.66.

Record the Journal Entry 16 for **$23,744.66**

> Close the Period 01/31/2016.
>
> Forgot to include 10 days of Day Camp on Invoice 1016 to Pamela Vines. Add it to the invoice and reprint. If you save, name it **10-Your Name Invoice 1016 Pamela Vines Corrected**.
>
> Adjust Journal Entry 16, the closing entry for transferring Net Income and Retained Earnings, to include the extra income earned for the correction to Invoice 1016. (Did you increase the amount of the Journal Entry to transfer Net Income and Retained Earnings by $300?)

Continue to use Your Name's Beach Barkers

## PROFIT AND LOSS—DO

When the transactions and adjustments for the month are complete, it is helpful to prepare the Profit and Loss report to see your amount of Net Income or Net Loss. Remember Income minus Expenses equal Net Profit or Net Loss. Even though you printed the report when recording the additional transactions, a correction to an invoice was made after printing the report.

### *DO*

Continue to use **Your Name's Beach Barkers** to prepare the Profit and Loss report for January 1-31, 2016

Access Reports as previously instructed
Click **My Custom Reports** to see all of the reports that have been customized
Click **Profit and Loss** to select the report

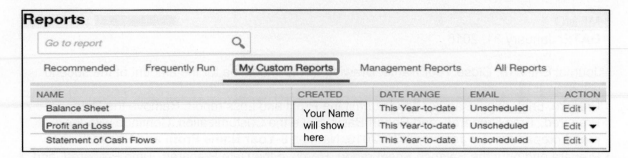

Dates are From: **010116** To: **013116**, run the report
- Scroll through the report. Review income and expenses. View the change to Net Income.

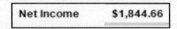

Net Income          $1,844.66

Print, export, and/or send/submit the report
- If you save the report, name it **11-Your Name Profit and Loss Ch. 5 Revised**.

Continue to use Your Name's Beach Barkers

## BALANCE SHEET—DO

After completing all of the adjustments for the month, you need to prepare a revised Balance Sheet to prove that assets are equal to liabilities and owner's equity. Because this report is for a month, the adjustment for Net Income will appear in both Retained Earnings and Net Income. If, however, this report were prepared for the year, neither account would have balances.

## DO

Continue to use **Your Name's Beach Barkers** to prepare the Profit and Loss report for January 1-31, 2016 and January 1-31, 2017

Click **Balance Sheet** in My Custom Reports
Dates From: **010116** To: **013116**, Run Report
- View and analyze the Equity section after all the adjusting entries have been made:
  After the transfer of Opening Balance Equity to Your Name, Capital, the balance of
    Opening Balance Equity is 0.00.
  The original amount of Retained Earnings, $22,200, was transferred to Your Name,
    Capital and no longer shows as part of Retained Earnings. The amount of Net
    Income transferred to Retained Earnings for the year 2016 shows as -1,844.66.
  Your Name, Capital shows $119,922.16, which is the total of the capital without including
    the Investment.
  Your Name, Drawing was closed into Your Name, Capital so it has a balance of 0.00.
  Your Name, Investment contains the balance of $53,735.00, which shows how much
    you have invested in Your Name's Beach Barkers.
  Net Income and Retained Earnings were transferred to Your Name, Capital. Since you
    are still in the same year as the adjusting transaction date, the amount of Net Income
    shows as 1,844.66 and the amount of Retained Earnings shows as -1,844.66.

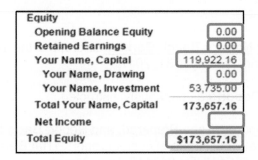

Print, export, and/or send/submit the report
- If you save the report, name it **12-Your Name Balance Sheet 2016 Ch. 5**.

To see the results of transferring Net Income/Retained Earnings into Capital, change the report dates From: **01/01/17** To: **01/31/17**, Run the Report

- Note that the amount shown for Retained Earnings, Drawing, and Opening Balance Equity is 0.00. Nothing is shown for Net Income. The amounts shown for Your Name, Capital; Your Name, Investment; and Total Your Name, Capital are all still the same as in the 2016 report.

| Equity | | |
|---|---|---|
| Opening Balance Equity | 0.00 | |
| Retained Earnings | 0.00 | |
| Your Name, Capital | 119,922.16 | |
| Your Name, Drawing | 0.00 | |
| Your Name, Investment | 53,735.00 | |
| Total Your Name, Capital | | 173,657.16 |
| Net Income | | |
| Total Equity | | $173,657.16 |

Print, export, and/or send/submit the report

- If you save the report, name it **13-Your Name Balance Sheet 2017 Ch. 5**.

Continue to use Your Name's Beach Barkers

*last report*

## JOURNAL—DO

At the end of each chapter, you will always print a Journal so you can view all of the transactions entered during the report dates. As with previous Journals, check each entry carefully, pay close attention to dates, accounts, memos, and amounts. If a transaction does not appear in the Journal, you may have used a current date that is outside the date range of the report.

## DO

▶ Continue to use **Your Name's Beach Barkers** to prepare the Journal for January 1-31, 2016

Access **Accountant Reports** as previously instructed
Click **Journal**
Remove the Date Prepared and Time Prepared from the Footer,
Click **Save Customizations**, Name of custom report: **Journal**, click **OK**
Enter the Dates From: **010116** To: **013116**, Run Report
If need be, adjust the width of the Name, Memo/Description, and Account columns so more entries display on one line

- Do your totals for Debits and Credits match the following? If not, double check your entries for correct amounts, dates, accounts, memos.

| TOTAL | $226,634.28 | $226,634.28 |
|-------|-------------|-------------|

Print in Landscape Orientation, export, and/or send/submit the report
- If you save the report, name it **14-Your Name Journal Ch. 5**.
Continue to use Your Name's Beach Barkers

## TRIAL BALANCE—DO

A Trial Balance is printed to prove that debits still equal credits. Post-closing reports are typically prepared as of the last day of the fiscal year after all closing entries for the year have been recorded. Since our closing was simply for a period, this means that income and expenses will be shown in the Trial Balance and in the Profit & Loss reports for January. When you prepare a Trial Balance for the first of the next fiscal year, income and expense accounts will not be shown.

_DO_

Continue to use **Your Name's Beach Barkers** to prepare the Trial Balance for January 1-31, 2016 and January 1-31, 2017

Access **Accountant Reports** as previously instructed
Click **Trial Balance**
Remove the Date Prepared, Time Prepared, and Report Basis from the Footer
Click **Save Customizations**, Name of custom report: **Trial Balance**, click **OK**
Enter the Dates From: **010116** To: **013116**, Run Report
- Does your Trial Balance match the following? If not, double check your entries for correct amounts, dates, accounts, memos. Remember, you can click on an account shown in the Trial Balance and access the account register.

## Your Name's Beach Barkers
### TRIAL BALANCE
As of January 31, 2016

| | DEBIT | CREDIT |
|---|---|---|
| Checking | 61,415.89 | |
| Petty Cash | 107.08 | |
| Accounts Receivable (A/R) | 15,230.00 | |
| Inventory Asset | 29,012.50 | |
| Prepaid Insurance | 1,100.00 | |
| Supplies:Cleaning Supplies | 825.00 | |
| Supplies:Kennel Supplies | 1,950.00 | |
| Supplies:Office Supplies | 628.68 | |
| Supplies:Sales Supplies | 400.00 | |
| Undeposited Funds | 0.00 | |
| Furniture & Fixtures:Depreciation | | 1,625.00 |
| Furniture & Fixtures:Original cost | 15,000.00 | |
| Kennel Equipment:Depreciation | | 2,200.00 |
| Kennel Equipment:Original cost | 21,150.00 | |
| Office Equipment:Depreciation | | 900.00 |
| Office Equipment:Original cost | 11,685.84 | |
| Vehicles:Depreciation | | 3,475.00 |
| Vehicles:Original cost | 32,000.00 | |
| Accounts Payable (A/P) | | 4,214.00 |
| Loans Payable:Equipment Loan | | 1,970.59 |
| Loans Payable:Furniture & Fixtures Loan | | 2,463.24 |
| Opening Balance Equity | | 0.00 |
| Retained Earnings | 1,844.66 | |
| Your Name, Capital | | 119,922.16 |
| Your Name, Capital:Your Name, Drawing | | 0.00 |
| Your Name, Capital:Your Name, Investment | | 53,735.00 |
| Services:Boarding | | 770.00 |
| Services:Day Camp | | 720.00 |
| Services:Grooming | | 885.00 |
| Services:House Calls | | 225.00 |
| Services:Training | | 3,025.00 |
| Services:Transportation | | 300.00 |
| Advertising | 200.00 | |
| Bank Charges | 16.00 | |
| Equipment Rental | 75.00 | |
| Insurance:Vehicle Insurance | 100.00 | |
| Interest Expense | 18.75 | |
| Laundry | 6.50 | |
| Rent or Lease | 1,500.00 | |
| Repair & Maintenance:Computer Repair | 200.00 | |
| Repair & Maintenance:Vehicle Repair | 212.50 | |
| Supplies Expense:Cleaning Supplies Expense | 100.00 | |
| Supplies Expense:Kennel Supplies Expense | 134.00 | |
| Supplies Expense:Office Supplies Expense | 131.47 | |
| Supplies Expense:Sales Supplies Expense | 100.00 | |
| Telephone Expense | 129.95 | |
| Utilities:Electric | 89.75 | |
| Utilities:Gas-Heating | 189.50 | |
| Utilities:Water | 175.95 | |
| Vehicle Expenses | 109.90 | |
| Interest Earned | | 78.93 |
| Depreciation Expense | 670.00 | |
| **TOTAL** | **$196,508.92** | **$196,508.92** |

Print in Portrait Orientation, export, and/or send/submit the report
- If you save the report, name it **15-Your Name Trial Balance Ch. 5**.

Change the report dates From: **01/01/17** To: **01/31/17**
- You will see the same information and account totals for all of the Asset, Liability, and Equity accounts. Nothing is shown for Income or Expense accounts because the report dates are for the next fiscal year.

This results in a Total of $190,504.99 for both Debit and Credit columns
- This is different from the totals shown for the 2016 Trial Balance.

Do not save or print the report

Close Your Name's Beach Barkers

5

## SUMMARY

In this chapter the focus was on performing the accounting functions for the end of a period. Journal Entries were prepared to record the adjusting entries for supplies used, insurance, and depreciation. Bank and Checking Account Reconciliations were performed and transactions for automatic payments were recorded during the reconciliation. The use of Net Income, Retained Earnings, Opening Balance Equity, and Owner's Equity accounts for Capital, Investment, and Drawing was explored, adjusted, transferred, and interpreted for a sole proprietorship. Owner withdrawals and additional investments were recorded. A period was closed and a transaction was changed after the closing. Further adjustments required because of a change after closing were made for Net Income/Retained Earnings. Reports were customized and prepared to provide data for analysis and examination of the results of business operations and end-of-period adjustments.

# END-OF-CHAPTER QUESTIONS

## TRUE/FALSE

ANSWER THE FOLLOWING QUESTIONS IN THE SPACE PROVIDED BEFORE THE QUESTION NUMBER.

_____ 1. You record the amount of supplies on hand as the amount of the adjusting entry for supplies used.

_____ 2. Once a report has been customized, it may be accessed in Accountant Reports.

_____ 3. Additional investments made by an owner may be cash or non-cash items.

_____ 4. An owner's withdrawal is recorded as a payroll expense.

_____ 5. Accrual-basis accounting matches the income from the period and the expenses for the period in order to determine the net income or net loss for the period.

_____ 6. Depreciation is recorded for the decrease in value of a fixed asset.

_____ 7. A Statement of Cash Flows organizes information regarding cash activities and projects the amount of cash at the end of a period.

_____ 8. A Balance Sheet is prepared to prove the equality of debits and credits.

_____ 9. You cannot record an automatic loan payment when you reconcile a bank statement.

_____ 10. A Reconciliation Report prints the last two bank reconciliation reports automatically.

## MULTIPLE CHOICE

WRITE THE LETTER OF THE CORRECT ANSWER IN THE SPACE PROVIDED BEFORE THE QUESTION NUMBER.

_____ 1. The report that proves Assets = Liabilities + Owner's Equity is the \_\_\_.
   A. Trial Balance
   B. Income Statement
   C. Profit & Loss Report
   D. Balance Sheet

_____ 2. If the adjusting entry to transfer Net Income and Retained Earnings into the owner's capital account is made prior to the end of the year, the Balance Sheet shows \_\_\_.
   A. Retained Earnings
   B. Net Income
   C. Both Net Income and Retained Earnings
   D. None of the above because the Net Income and Retained Earnings have been transferred into capital

5

_____ 3. A bank statement may ___.
   A. show service charges or interest not yet recorded
   B. be missing deposits in transit or outstanding checks
   C. show automatic payments
   D. all of the above

_____ 4. If you donate a desk to Your Name's Beach Barkers, it is recorded in Your Name, Investment account and in ___.
   A. Checking
   B. Furniture: Original Cost
   C. Store Supplies
   D. Owner's Donations

_____ 5. Prepaid Insurance is recorded as a(n) ___ in a(n) ___ account.
   A. Prepaid Expense, Asset
   B. Prepaid Expense, Expense
   C. Asset, Asset
   D. Expense, Expense

_____ 6. In Your Name's Beach Barkers, what account should be used to record owner investments?
   A. Your Name, Capital
   B. Your Name, Investments
   C. Opening Balance Equity
   D. Retained Earnings

_____ 7. To close income and expense accounts in QuickBooks Online, you ___.
   A. Record adjusting entries for each account
   B. Do not have to do anything
   C. Enter a closing date on the Advanced tab in Settings
   D. Transfer the total income and total expenses to Retained Earnings

_____ 8. Which report calculates the Net Income or Net Loss?
   A. Trial Balance
   B. Profit and Loss
   C. Statement of Cash Flows
   D. Balance Sheet

_____ 9. After editing an invoice in a closed period, you record the change in income by editing the adjusting entry.
   A. For the Closing Date
   B. For transferring Net Income and Retained Earnings into the Capital account
   C. You do not edit anything, you record another adjusting entry
   D. Both A and B

_____ 10. To record the decrease in value of something you own, you record ___.
   A. Depreciation
   B. Depreciation Expense
   C. A Net Loss
   D. Both A and B

## FILL-IN

IN THE SPACE PROVIDED, WRITE THE ANSWER THAT MOST APPROPRIATELY COMPLETES THE SENTENCE.

1. In a sole proprietorship, an owner's paycheck is considered a(n) _____.

2. In Your Name's Beach Barkers the entry to transfer Net Income to Capital is made by debiting _____ and crediting _____.

3. The _____ -basis of accounting records income or revenue at the time cash is received and expenses at the time they are paid.

4. A _____ is prepared to record an automatic loan payment from the bank.

5. After removing the date prepared, time prepared, and report basis from a report footer you click the _____ button to save the change for future reports.

## COMPUTER ASSIGNMENT

REFER TO PRINTOUTS OR USE QUICKBOOKS ONLINE AND YOUR NAME'S BEACH BARKERS TO LOOK UP OR ENTER INFORMATION, AND THEN WRITE THE ANSWERS TO THE FOLLOWING EXERCISES IN THE SPACE PROVIDED

5

1. What was the amount of Net Income shown on the Profit and Loss report prior to closing the period? (Printed Document 8) _____

2. What business form did you complete to record the owner's withdrawals? _____

3. What was the amount of the adjusting entry for Kennel Supplies? _____

4. What was the total amount of owner withdrawals for January? _____

5. Where did you record the automatic loan payment for Furniture & Fixtures? _____

6. What is the amount of Total Assets in the Balance Sheet for 2016 prepared after all closing entries and adjustments? (Printed Document 12) _____

7. What was the amount of the adjusting entry to transfer Net Income and Retained Earnings after correcting Invoice 1016? _____

8. What two accounts did you transfer the Opening Balance Equity into? _____
   _____

9. What account do you Debit when closing Your Name, Drawing? _____

10. What is the amount of Net Income shown on the Balance Sheet for 2017? _____

# CHAPTER 5 CHECKLIST

The checklist below shows all of the business forms printed during training. Check each one that you printed, exported, and/or submitted.

| | |
|---|---|
| _____ 1-Check 17 | _____ 9-Balance Sheet Ch. 5 |
| _____ 2-Journal Ch. 5 | _____ 10-Invoice 1016 Pamela Vines Corrected |
| _____ 3-Balance Sheet Ch. 5 | _____ 11-Profit and Loss Ch. 5 Revised |
| _____ 4-Reconciliation Report Ch. 5 | _____ 12-Balance Sheet 2016 Ch. 5 |
| _____ 5-Statement of Cash Flows Ch. 5 | _____ 13-Balance Sheet 2017 Ch. 5 |
| _____ 6-Check 18 | _____ 14-Journal Ch. 5 |
| _____ 7-Reconciliation Report (2) Ch. 5 | _____ 15-Trial Balance Ch. 5 |
| _____ 8-Profit and Loss Ch. 5 | |

# SALES AND RECEIVABLES: PRODUCT AND SERVICE ITEMS

# 6

## LEARNING OBJECTIVES

At the completion of this chapter, you will be able to:

1. Enter sales on account and cash sales of products and services.
2. Set up Sales Tax.
3. Prepare invoices and sales receipts that include sales tax.
4. Record sales discounts.
5. Create delayed charges and then convert them into invoices.
6. Add a Logo to business documents.
7. Customize business forms.
8. Record transactions for two locations.
9. Record transactions using classes.
10. Record transactions for customers using debit and credit cards.
11. Add and edit customers and accounts.
12. Add new products and services.
13. Add new terms.
14. Record NSF transactions.
15. Prepare, customize, and memorize reports.

## ACCOUNTING FOR SALES AND RECEIVABLES

In Chapter 3, information was presented, transactions were entered, and reports were created for cash and credit sales of services. When a sale was on account, an invoice was prepared. When the customer paid the amount due for the invoice, a payment receipt was recorded. If the sale was paid for at the time of purchase, a sales receipt was prepared. Whether the transaction is for a service item or a product, the same forms are still prepared.

When you sell a product, you will have an inventory of products on hand that are ready to be sold. QuickBooks Online keeps track of the quantity of products on hand, maintains the value of the inventory, and uses the FIFO (First In, First Out) method of calculating the cost of goods sold.

In addition to recording sales transactions, customer discounts for early payment, sales tax, and non-sufficient funds checks are part of running a business. Transactions for these situations are included in this chapter.

Once again, reports will be prepared to manage accounts receivable, review sales, manage products and inventory, and provide standard accountant information.

## TRAINING TUTORIAL AND PROCEDURES

Continue to use the Test Drive Company for practice and the fictional company, Your Name's Beach Barkers, to record sales on account and cash sales of products and services, receive payments, prepare credit memos and refunds, process non-sufficient funds checks, record early payment sales discounts, create and use locations, record sales tax, and customize business forms and reports. In certain sections of the chapter, transactions may need to be entered into the Test Drive Company before you can complete a drill.

Just as you did in Chapters 2-5, you will enter additional transactions near the end of the chapter. These transactions are similar to the ones you entered in the Test Drive Company and in Your Name's Beach Barkers so no step-by-step instructions will be given. If you need to refer back to the chapter materials to make the entries, you should feel free to do so. If you can enter them without looking back, you have learned how to do something on your own in QuickBooks Online.

Because recording sales information and managing inventory is the life-blood of the company, it is extremely important to have an in-depth understanding of this. As a result, there will be a few more transactions completed in this chapter than you did in some of the other chapters.

**Pay careful attention to quantities, amounts, and dates as you work through the chapter. A careless error can require a tremendous amount of effort to correct.**

## DATES

Remember that the year used for the screen shots is 2016. Continue to use the same year that you used in Chapters 2-5. Beginning in Chapter 6 through the rest of the chapters, the month used will be <u>February</u>. If QuickBooks Online inserts the current date into a transaction, be aware of this and be sure to use the date indicated in the text.

## IMPORTANT NOTE

As has been stated in earlier chapters, QuickBooks Online is constantly evolving and new features, apps, and procedures change frequently. Everything in the text is correct at the time of this writing; however, by the time of publication some changes to the program may occur.

## CUSTOMIZE QUICKBOOKS ONLINE

In the first part of the text, you used QuickBooks Online's basic formats and business forms. You learned how to customize reports and save them for future use. There are other areas of customization that may be used. From this point forward, we will use a logo for Your Name's Beach Barkers and will create and use customized business forms.

## DOWNLOAD LOGO FILES—DO

A company logo is a small picture that will appear on the Home Page in QuickBooks Online and in printed business documents. In order to include a logo for Your Name's Beach Barkers, you will need to download the .jpg logo files posted for your use on the Pearson Web site: **http://www.pearsonhighered.com/horne/**. You will follow procedures that are very similar to the Excel and QuickBooks File downloads covered in Chapter 2.

## <u>DO</u>

 Download Logo files

Insert your USB drive into your computer or ask you professor for specific directions to be used at your school
Open your Web browser
Enter the address **http://www.pearsonhighered.com/horne/**
- Sometimes it is difficult to read "horne." Remember the name is HORNE.

- Note: At the time of this writing, a temporary cover image was posted. The actual cover will change when the site is finalized.
- When completing the following steps, be sure to use the section for the QuickBooks Online Plus text.
- Check with your instructor to determine if you will use a different procedure.
- **IMPORTANT**: Depending on your version of Windows and the Web browser you use, your screens may be different from the examples shown. If so, complete the download using the prompts from your program. Ask your instructor for assistance if necessary. Since QuickBooks Online Plus prefers Google Chrome for the browser, Chrome is used for the file download.

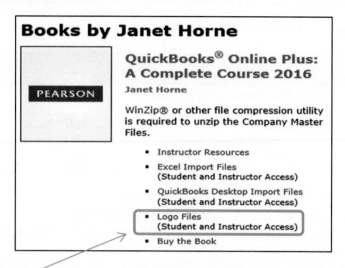

Click **Logo Files**
- You will see a tab with logo_imports.zip at the bottom-left side of the browser page. Click the drop-down list arrow next to **logo_imports.zip**

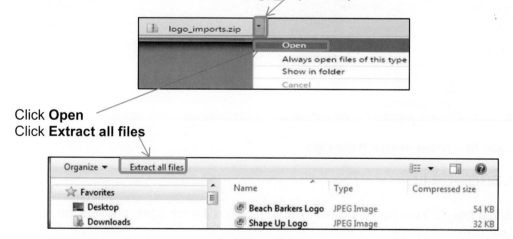

Click **Open**
Click **Extract all files**

Click the **Browse** button
- Make sure your USB drive is inserted into your computer.
Scroll through the list of storage locations shown, click the letter shown for your USB drive, click **OK**
- If your USB drive location is not shown, click **Computer** to expand the list of storage locations.
- The text uses **F:** as the USB drive location. Your location may be different.

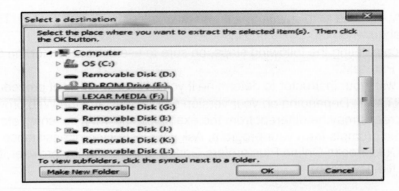

Enter **Logo Files** next to Your USB drive location (F:\ in the example)

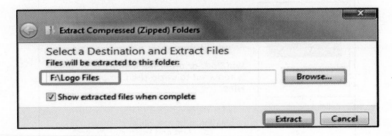

Click **Extract**
If you do not see the files, double-click the folder **Logo Files**
- You will see the Logo files that you will use for importing small pictures into Your Name's Beach Barkers and Your Name's Shape Up Center.

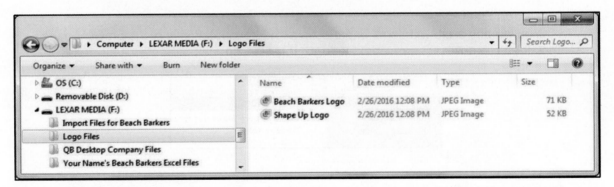

You are now ready to import the logo

## IMPORT LOGO—DRILL

Before adding a logo to Your Name's Beach Barkers, you will once again practice the procedure using the Test Drive Company.

### DRILL

Open the **Test Drive Company** as previously instructed

Click the **Gear** icon
In the column for Your Company, click **Account and Settings**, and, if necessary, click the **Company** tab
Click the **Pen** icon for Company name

Click the **+** in the lower-right corner of the empty logo

On the "Choose file to Upload" screen, scroll through the list of storage locations on the left side of the pane, click your USB drive
Double-click the **Logo Files** folder
Click **Beach Barkers Logo**, then click **Open**
- The logo will be inserted into the logo box.

Click **Save** for the Company name section
Click **Done** on the Account and Settings page
- The logo should appear on the Home Page (if it doesn't do not worry, sometimes the Test Drive Company is a little sluggish in displaying the logo). It will also appear on your printed business documents.
Do <u>not</u> close the Test Drive Company, continue with the next section

## CUSTOMIZE BUSINESS FORMS—DRILL

In the earlier chapters within the text, all business forms were prepared and printed using the standard formats provided in QuickBooks Online. In this section, you will explore and practice customizing an invoice. You may choose to create a new style so you can switch between the standard invoice and your customized invoice or you may Edit the Standard Master document.

### *DRILL*

Continue to use the **<u>Test Drive Company</u>** to customize the Standard Master form

Click the **Gear** icon, click **All Lists** in the Lists column
- You will see all of the lists used in QuickBooks Online.
Click **Custom Form Styles**
- You will see one style, Standard, listed.
Click **Edit** for the Standard Master form
On the Customize form style screen, the **Style** tab should be selected, if not, click to select
Click each of the styles to see how the invoice changes
- Airy is the style used as Standard.
Continue to use **Airy** for the style
On the right side, beneath the Logo box, click the third color in the left column to change the color of the shaded areas on the form
Click the **Appearance** tab on the left side
In the Logo crop, resize, align section, click **Medium**
In the Logo placement section, click **Right**
Click the **Header** tab

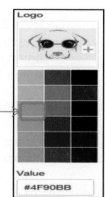

In the Company section, click **Country** and **Email** to remove the check marks
In the Custom section, click the check box to remove the selection of Crew #
Click the **Activity Table** tab
In the Columns section make the following changes
> For **Description** change the width to approximately **53**, click the **+** and then the **–** to reach the desired width
> - If your numbers are slightly different, it is not problem. You are just trying to make room for Quantity to show on one line.
> For **Quantity** change the Label Qty to **Quantity**, width should be approximately **11**

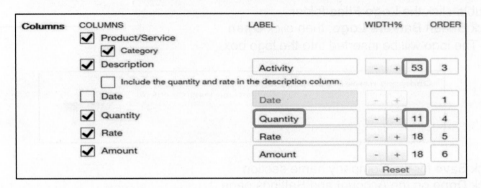

Click the **Footer** tab, change the Message to customer to: **Thank you for your business!**
Click the **Preview or print** button
- Do not be concerned if your dates do not match the preview shown.

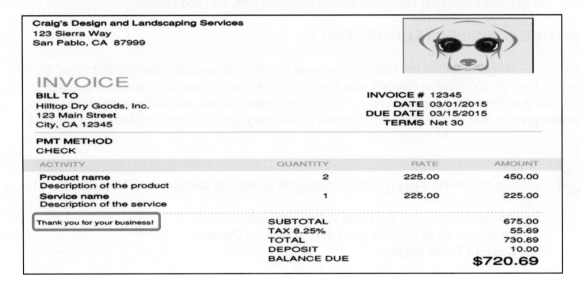

Click the **Save** button
- The revised Standard Master form will be used automatically for invoices, sales receipts, among others.
Close the Test Drive Company

## IMPORT LOGO—DO

The Logo you are adding for Your Name's Beach Barkers will appear on printed business forms. These include invoices, sales receipts, purchase orders, etc.

*DO*

Open the **Your Name's Beach Barkers** as previously instructed

Click the **Gear** icon
In the Settings column, click **Company Settings**, and, if necessary, click the **Company** tab
Click the **Pen** icon for Company name
Click the **+** in the lower-right corner of the empty logo

On the "Choose file to Upload" screen, scroll through the list of storage locations on the left
    side of the pane, click your USB drive
Double-click the **Logo Files** folder
Click **Beach Barkers Logo**, then click **Open**
- The logo will be inserted into the logo box.

Click **Done** on the Settings page
- The logo should appear on the Home Page (if it doesn't do not worry, sometimes
  QuickBooks Online is a little sluggish in displaying the logo). It will also appear on your
  printed business documents.
Do <u>not</u> close Your Name's Beach Barkers, continue with the next section

## CUSTOMIZE BUSINESS FORMS—DO

In the earlier chapters within the text, all business forms were prepared and printed using the
standard formats provided in QuickBooks Online. In this section, you will customize the Standard
form so it will be used automatically for printed business documents.

*DO*

Continue to use the **Your Name's Beach Barkers** to customize the Standard Master Form

Click the **Gear** icon; click **All Lists** in the Lists column
- You will see all of the lists used in QuickBooks Online.
Click **Custom Form Styles**
- You will see one style, Standard, listed.
Click **Edit** for the Standard Master form
On the Customize form style screen, the **Style** tab should be selected, if not, click to select
Click each of the styles to see how the invoice changes
- Airy is the style used as Standard.
Continue to use **Airy** for the style

On the right side, beneath the Logo box, click the third color in the left column to change the color of the shaded areas on the form

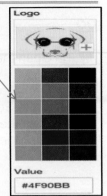

- Please note that sometimes the color change works very well and other times it does not change. The main thing to know is that you may customize your forms.
- If you change the color and still get the default blue, accept it and continue working.

Click the **Appearance** tab on the left side

In the Logo crop, resize, align section, click **Medium**

In the Logo placement section, click **Right**

Click the **Header** tab

In the Company section, click **Country** to remove the check mark

Make sure the following items have a check mark so they will be included on the form:
Company name, Address, Email, Website, and Phone

Click the **Activity Table** tab

In the Columns section make the following changes

**Description** change the width to approximately **53** by clicking the **+** and/or **−** to change the width

Quantity change the Label to **Quantity**, width should be approximately **11**

- As in the Test Drive Company, the exact number isn't important. You just want Quantity to be able to be on one line.

Click the **Footer** tab, leave the "Message to customer" as: **Thank you for your business!**

- If you do not see the Message, enter it now.

Click the **Preview or print** button to view a sample of the Invoice

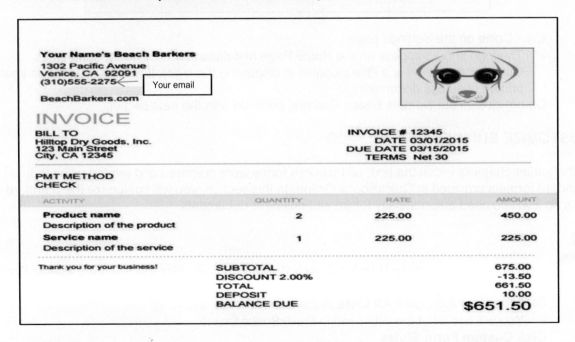

Click the **Save** button

- As a note: Future screen shots in the text will show youremail@gmail.com for the email address; however, your QuickBooks email address should be included on all of your business forms.
- As mentioned, occasionally the custom color for the business form does not change from blue. If that happens, show your instructor that you have customized the form and continue with whatever color appears.

Close Your Name's Beach Barkers

## CATEGORIZING TRANSACTIONS—READ

QuickBooks Online allows you to track income and expenses for separate parts of your business. You may track transactions by assigning a Location for different business locations, departments, regions, offices, divisions, among others. For example, if customers purchased items from different stores (locations), you would record separate invoices or sales receipts for each store. This allows you to determine the business results for each store.

The other method of categorizing transactions is into classes. With classes, you can assign the entire transaction to a class and get the same information as using a location. If this is selected, you would need to prepare different invoices or sales receipts for each class used (think of departments as an example). If you assign each line of a transaction to a class then you can enter multiple items from different classes (departments for example) all on the same invoice or sales receipt.

It is possible to use both location and class tracking within one business. For example, if you had two different stores and you wanted to track the income and expenses for each store, you would create a location. To further track income and expenses by department, you could assign a class for each department within the store locations. You would then prepare separate invoices or sales receipts for each location; while including several classes on the same business document.

## ADD NEW LOCATIONS—DRILL

If you have more than one location, you may track and categorize data for the individual areas. Location tracking will track individual and group transactions.

### *DRILL*

 Open the **Test Drive Company** as previously instructed and create Locations

Click the **Gear** icon, click **Account and Settings** in the Your Company column
Click the **Advanced** tab
Click the **Pen** icon for Categories
Click **Track locations**
Click the drop-down list arrow for Location label
- You will see choices for Business, Department, Division, Location, Property, Store, and Territory.
To select the name of the location, click **Store**, click **Save**
- Track locations shows **On**.
Click **Done**
Click the **Gear** icon again
In the Lists column, click **All Lists**
Click the category **Store** on the Lists screen
- If you see Location, that means that you didn't save the name of the location as Store.
- Nothing is shown for Stores. Each store location needs to be added to the list.
Click **New** to add your store locations
Click in the Name text box, enter **Bayshore** for the Store Information

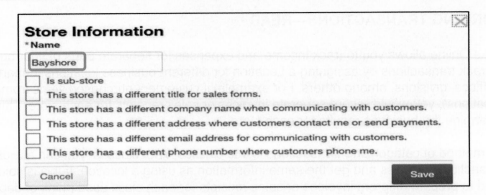

- Since this is the original company location, nothing else needs to be changed.
Click **Save**
Click **New** again
Click in the Name text box, enter **Middlefield**
Click **This store has a different address where customers contact me or send payments**
Enter the address: **789 West Avenue**, press **Tab**
Enter the city: **Middlefield**, press **Tab**
Enter the Zip code: **94482**

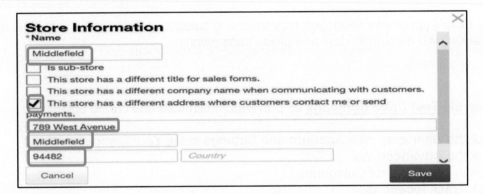

- Nothing else needs to be entered for the practice.
Click **Save**
- There are now two store locations shown for the Test Drive Company. You will select one of these stores when you enter information for invoices, sales receipts, etc.

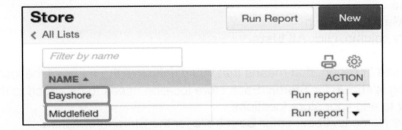

Do <u>not</u> close the Test Drive Company continue to the next section

## ADD NEW CLASSES—DRILL

Since you are using Locations to differentiate between stores, you may assign classes to differentiate between departments.

_DRILL_

Continue to use the **Test Drive Company** to create classes

Click the **Gear** icon, click **Account and Settings** in the Your Company column
Click the **Advanced** tab
Click the **Pen** icon for Categories
Click **Track classes**

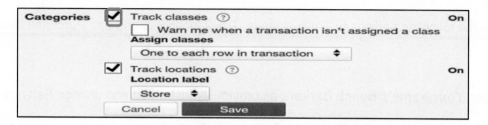

- Unlike locations, classes are not allowed to select a descriptive name; such as, departments, or enter alternate address and other contact information.
- You are allowed to determine where classes will be assigned, either to each row in a transaction or to each transaction.

Since you are using locations for each transaction, use **One to each row in transaction**
Click **Save**
Click **Done** for Account and Settings

- If you return to Store, click **<All Lists**, which is shown beneath Store. If not, click the Gear icon, click All Lists to return to the Lists for the Test Drive Company.

On the page of Lists, click **Classes**
Since no classes are shown, click **New**
In the Name text box, enter **Design**, click **Save**

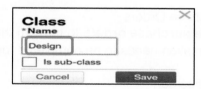

Repeat the steps to add **Fountains**, and **Landscaping** as classes

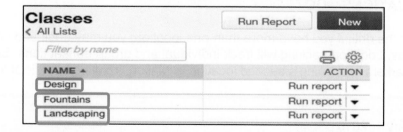

- When you close the Test Drive Company, you will erase the locations and classes. You will need to re-enter them when you return for drills and practice. Instructions will be given when you need to do this.

Close the Test Drive Company

## CHANGE SETTINGS—DO

When you have a number of settings that need to be changed, it is more efficient to change them all at the same time. Since you are adding Locations and Classes and need to activate Purchase Orders, these will all be changed at the same time.

---

**MEMO**
**DATE:** February 1, 2016

Change the following settings to Track classes, Track locations, and use Purchase Orders.

---

_DO_

 Open **Your Name's Beach Barkers** as previously instructed and change Settings

> Click the **Gear** icon, click **Company Settings** in the Settings column; if necessary, click the **Company** tab
> - You will notice that the information on the Company tab is quite different from the information displayed in the Test Drive Company.
> On the Company tab, click the **Pen** icon for Categories
> Click **Track classes** to turn **On**
> Leave the selection for Assign classes as **One to each row in transaction**
> Click **Track locations** to turn **On**
> Use **Location** as the label
> - In addition to the current Venice location, you are opening the new Malibu location this month.
> Click **Save**
> - Track classes and Track locations both say On.
> Click the **Expenses** tab
> Click the **Pen** icon for Purchase Orders
> Click the check box for **Use purchase orders** to turn **On** the feature
> - None of the other information needs to be completed for Purchase orders.
> Click **Save**
> Click **Done** on the Settings screen
> Do <u>not</u> close Your Name's Beach Barkers

## ADD NEW LOCATIONS—DO

As you learned in the drill, if you have more than one location, you may track and categorize data for individual areas. Location tracking will track individual and group transactions. Since Your Name's Beach Barkers is opening a second location in Malibu, it will be beneficial to track locations.

---

**MEMO**
**DATE:** February 1, 2016

Add Venice to the list of locations.

Add Malibu to the list of locations. Include the following information: Address: 24183 Pacific Coast Hwy, Malibu, 90265; Telephone: 424-555-3647.

---

<u>*DO*</u>

 Open <u>**Your Name's Beach Barkers**</u> as previously instructed and create a new location

Click the **Gear** icon
In the Lists column, click **All Lists**
Click **Locations** to add the Venice and Malibu locations
- Nothing is shown for Locations. Each store location needs to be added to the list.
Click **New**
Click in the Name text box, enter **Venice** for the Location Information

- Since this is the original company location, nothing else needs to be changed.
Click **Save**
Click **New** again
Click in the Name text box, enter **Malibu**
Click **This location has a different address where customers contact me or send payments**
Enter the address: **24183 Pacific Coast Hwy**, press **Tab**
Enter the city: **Malibu**, press **Tab**
Enter the Zip code: **90265**

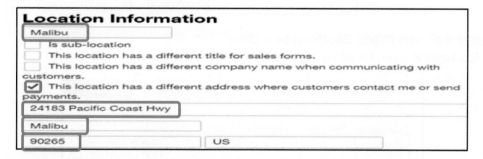

Scroll down the Location Information screen, and click **This location has a different phone number where customers phone me.** to select
Enter the phone number **424-555-3647**
Click **Save**
- There are now two locations shown for the Your Name's Beach Barkers. You will select one of these locations when you enter information for invoices, sales receipts, etc.

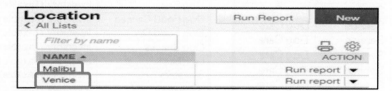

Do <u>not</u> close Your Name's Beach Barkers continue to the next section

## ADD NEW CLASSES—DO

Since you are using Locations to differentiate between Venice and Malibu, you may assign Classes to differentiate between departments or areas in the business. Assigning classes for Dog Care and

Boutique will enable you to determine the profitability of each of the two areas in the business. You could further delineate with Classes or Sub-classes for Grooming, Boarding, Dog Walking, Day Care, etc.; but, for now, you really just want to know information for the two classes.

---

**MEMO**
**DATE:** February 1, 2016

Add two Classes: Dog Care and Boutique.

---

_**DO**_

Continue to use **Your Name's Beach Barkers** and create classes

With the Location List showing on the screen, click **<All Lists**
- If you do not see the Location List, click the Gear icon, click All Lists in the List Column.

On the page of Lists, click **Classes**
Since no classes are shown, click **New**
In the Name text box, enter **Dog Care**, click **Save**
- Dog Care is used for all service items and do not have tax.

Repeat the steps to add **Boutique** as a class
- Boutique is used for all inventory items and are taxed.

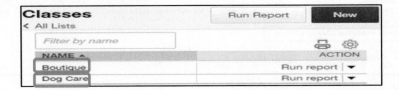

When you add a Class to a sales form, use the following charts to determine the Class:

| ITEM | TYPE | CLASS |
|------|------|-------|
| Bath | Service | Dog Care |
| Boarding | Service | Dog Care |
| Coat Brushing | Service | Dog Care |
| Day Camp | Service | Dog Care |
| Dental Care | Service | Dog Care |
| Dog Walking | Service | Dog Care |
| Hours | Service | Dog Care |
| Nails | Service | Dog Care |
| Poop Scoop | Service | Dog Care |
| Services | Service | Dog Care |
| Training 1 | Service | Dog Care |
| Training 2 | Service | Dog Care |
| Training 3 | Service | Dog Care |
| Transportation | Service | Dog Care |

| ITEM | TYPE | CLASS |
|------|------|-------|
| Bones | Inventory (Taxable) | Boutique |
| Brushes | Inventory (Taxable) | Boutique |
| Collars | Inventory (Taxable) | Boutique |
| Dog Bed | Inventory (Taxable) | Boutique |
| Dog Food-Canned | Inventory (Taxable) | Boutique |
| Dog Food-Dry | Inventory (Taxable) | Boutique |
| Dog Snacks | Inventory (Taxable) | Boutique |
| Leashes | Inventory (Taxable) | Boutique |
| Sweaters | Inventory (Taxable) | Boutique |
| Vitamins | Inventory (Taxable) | Boutique |

Do <u>not</u> close Your Name's Beach Barkers, continue to the next section

## DEBIT AND CREDIT CARDS—READ

Accepting debit and credit cards has become the normal practice in most businesses. Debit and Credit card sales are treated the same whether they are used to pay for a cash sale or a payment receipt for an invoice. When a Debit Card is accepted for payment, it is treated just like a payment by check and the amount of the sale/payment is placed into the Undeposited Funds account. When the actual bank deposit is made, the amount is deposited into the checking or bank account.

Credit cards actually increase the consumer's buying power and impulse purchasing, which may result in a higher sales amount than a purchase made by cash, check, or debit card. In addition, if a customer does not pay his/her bill, the credit card company is responsible for trying to collect the payment. When a company allows customers to have accounts, the company has to try to get payments from them if they are delinquent with their payments. If customers do not pay what is owed, the amounts owed may have to be written off as bad debts. This results in the loss of income. Many companies chose to pay the bank fees for processing credit cards rather than try to get payments from delinquent customers.

When credit card payments are recorded in QuickBooks Online, they are placed in the Undeposited Funds account until the bank deposit is recorded. In QuickBooks Online the bank fees charged for processing the credit cards are deducted directly from the bank account. When a company accepts credit cards, the payments may be processed by enrolling in a QuickBooks Payment plan. Since our company is fictitious, you will not be enrolling or participating in an actual payment plan. However, debit and credit cards will be added to the Payment Methods List so you can learn how to record those payments later in the chapter. Please note that all debit and credit card information in the book is fictitious and is not to be used for any other purposes than training within the textbook.

## ADD PAYMENT METHODS—DO

When you created Your Name's Beach Barkers in Chapter 2, you identified methods of payment as Cash, Check, and Credit Card without creating payment methods for specific types of credit cards. Nor did you select Debit Card as a payment method. You may add new payment methods to the Payment Methods List. Since the Test Drive Company already has extensive Payment Methods, you will only create Payment Methods for Your Name's Beach Barkers.

> **MEMO**
> **DATE:** February 1, 2016
>
> Add Payment Methods: Debit Card, MasterCard, and Visa. Delete the Payment Method: Credit Card.

*DO*

 Continue to use **Your Name's Beach Barkers** to add additional Payment Methods

> With the Classes list still showing on the screen, click **<All Lists**
> • If you do not see the Classes List, click the Gear icon, click All Lists in the List Column.
> On the Lists screen, click **Payment Methods**
> • You should see Cash, Check, and Credit Card as the Payment Methods.
> Click **New**
> Enter **Debit Card** as the Name for the New Payment Method, click **Save**

Repeat the steps to enter **MasterCard**
Click **This is a credit card** to identify the payment method as a credit card

Repeat to add **Visa** as a credit card
- Since you have designated specific credit cards, MasterCard and Visa, you will use those payment methods for credit cards receipts. If you accept other credit cards and do not have a specific payment method, you would either select Credit Card as the payment method or create a specific payment method for the credit card.

To delete the Credit Card payment method, click the drop-down list arrow for **Credit Card**
Click **Delete**
Click **Yes** on the message "Are you sure you want to delete this?"
View your Payment Methods

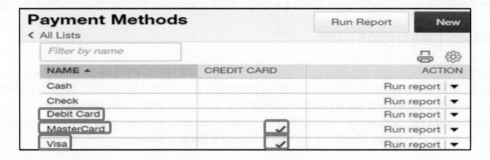

Do not close Your Name's Beach Barkers, continue with the next section

## SALES TAX—DO

A sales tax is a fee, usually a percentage of the sale, charged by government agencies on the sale of products and services. Our company is based in California, which does not charge sales tax for services provided. However, we do have a Doggie Boutique where we will sell inventory items and collect sales tax on those sales.

When collecting sales tax, the customer pays the tax as an add-on to the purchase price. The business collecting the tax forwards the tax amount to the appropriate government agencies. In order to keep track of the sales taxes collected, you use the Sales Tax Center in QuickBooks Online. In the Sales Tax Center, you set up your specific agencies, tax rates, and settings. When it is time to pay the sales tax due to the government agencies, you view and pay the sales tax you owe in the Sales Tax Center.

Since the Test Drive Company has already set up the Sales Tax Center, you will not practice this procedure.

> MEMO
> **DATE:** February 1, 2016
>
> Set up the Sales Tax Center to collect a single tax rate of 8%. Sales Tax. Name: California Sales Tax, Agency name: State Board of Equalization, Rate: 8%.

<u>DO</u>

Continue to use **Your Name's Beach Barkers** to set up the Sales Tax Center

Click **Sales Tax** on the Navigation Bar
- You will see the Sales Tax Center.

Click the **Set Up Sales Tax Rates** button
Accept the Sales Tax Settings selected
Accept Single tax rate
Enter the Tax name: **California Sales Tax**, press **Tab**
Enter the Agency name: **State Board of Equalization**, press **Tab**
Enter the Rate: **8**

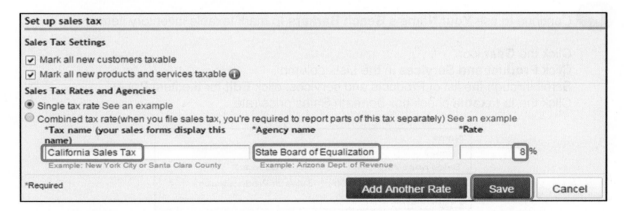

Click **Save**
- Now that the Sales Tax has been established, the Sales Tax Center has sections for Sales Tax Owed and Recent Sales Tax Payments. No tax information is shown because no transactions recorded have included sales tax.

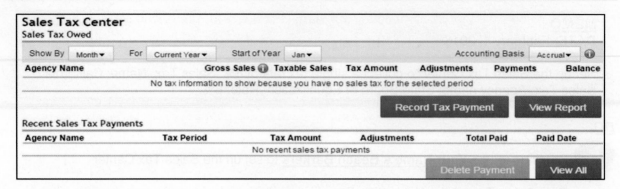

Do <u>not</u> close Your Name's Beach Barkers

## MARK INVENTORY ITEMS TAXABLE—DO

In order for sales tax to be calculated, the inventory items need to be marked Taxable. To do this you use the Products and Services List and mark each inventory item separately. When you add new inventory items, you mark them when they are created. This has already been done in the Test Drive Company; so, once again, you will not practice this procedure.

<u>MEMO</u>
**DATE:** February 1, 2016

Access the Products and Services List and individually mark taxable items: Bones, Brushes, Collars, Dog Food-Canned, Dog Food-Dry, Leashes, Sweaters, Toys & Treats, and Vitamins.

<u>DO</u>

Continue to use **Your Name's Beach Barkers** to mark taxable inventory items

Click the **Gear** icon
Click **Product and Services** in the Lists column
Scroll through the list of Products and services, click **Edit** for the item Bones
Click the **Is taxable** check box beneath Sales price/rate

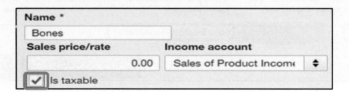

Click **Save and close**
* Bones is now marked with a ✓ in the Taxable column.

Refer to the Memo and repeat the steps to mark all of the inventory items as taxable
Print, export, and submit the Products and Services List in Landscape orientation as previously instructed

- If you save the list, name it: **1-Your Name Products and Services List Ch. 6**. Close Your Name's Beach Barkers

## INVENTORY—READ

When your company sells inventory items, QuickBooks Online will keep track of each item, the number of items on hand, and the value of the items. When you create inventory items, you tell QuickBooks Online the cost you paid for the item. This price will be used to value your inventory items at that time. As you purchase additional inventory items, you may pay more than you originally did. To account for this when recording sales of inventory items, QuickBooks Online uses the FIFO (First In, First Out) method of inventory valuation.

While you have the inventory on hand, the value of the items (calculated on the price you paid for the item) is shown in the Inventory Asset Account (something you own). When you sell the merchandise, the value of the amount sold (calculated on the price you paid for the item) is removed from Inventory Asset Account and entered into the Cost of Goods Sold account. This means when you sell merchandise, the amount used for inventory asset and cost of goods sold will be calculated based on the initial price you paid for the item. Once those items are sold, the next price you paid will be used for the calculation. For example:

### Original Widgets:
> Current Inventory: 10 Widgets
> Price Paid: $2 each
> Widget Value: $20
> Widget Value Inventory Asset: $20 (value of widgets in-stock)
> Widget Value Cost of Goods Sold: $0 (value of widgets sold)

### Purchase Additional Widgets:
> Purchase: 5 Widgets
> Price Paid: $3 each
> Widget Value: $15
> Total Widget Value Inventory Asset: $35 (Original $20 and new $15 = $35)
> Widget Value Cost of Goods Sold: $0

### Sell Widgets:
> Sell: 8 Widgets
> FIFO Selling Cost: $2
> Widget Value Inventory Asset: $19
> (remaining 2 original Widgets @ $2 = $4 and 5 new Widgets @ $3 = $15)
> Widget Value Cost of Goods Sold: $16 (8 Widgets @ $2 = $16)

### Sell Additional Widgets:
> Sell: 5 Widgets
> FIFO Selling Cost: $13 (2 original Widgets @ $2 = $4 and 3 new Widgets @ $3 = $9)
> Widget Value Inventory Asset: $6 (Leaves 2 new Widgets @ $3 = $6)
> Widget Value Cost of Goods Sold: $22

## VIEW QUANTITY ON HAND OF PRODUCTS—DRILL

Prior to recording sales transactions for products/inventory items, it is helpful to know how much quantity is on hand. One way to do this is to prepare an Inventory Valuation Summary report.

6

*DRILL*

Open the **Test Drive Company** and prepare an Inventory Valuation Summary report

As in previous chapters, go to QuickBooks Labs and turn **OFF** Redesigned Reports
Click **Reports** on the Navigation bar
Click the report category for **Manage Products and Inventory**
Click **Inventory Valuation Summary**
Because of QuickBooks automatic date changes, use the **Current Date** for the report
- The information shown includes the Quantity, the Asset Value, and the Average Cost.
- Pay special attention to the quantities on hand.

**Craig's Design and Landscaping Services**
**INVENTORY VALUATION SUMMARY**
Current Date

| | QTY | TOTAL ASSET VALUE | AVG COST |
|---|---|---|---|
| **Design** | | | |
| Fountains | | | |
| Pump | 25.00 | 250.00 | 10.00 |
| Rock Fountain | 2.00 | 250.00 | 125.00 |
| Total Fountains | | 500.00 | |
| **Total Design** | | 500.00 | |
| Landscaping | | | |
| Sprinklers | | | |
| Sprinkler Heads | 25.00 | 18.75 | 0.75 |
| Sprinkler Pipes | 31.00 | 77.50 | 2.50 |
| Total Sprinklers | | 96.25 | |
| **Total Landscaping** | | 96.25 | |
| **TOTAL** | | $596.25 | |

Close the report without printing
Do <u>not</u> close the Test Drive Company

## ENTER SALES ON ACCOUNT—DRILL

As you did for service items, when you record a sale on account, you complete an invoice when you sell products/inventory items. Since products that are sold incur sales tax, the tax is also included on the invoice. Because you closed the Test Drive Company, remember that you will not have locations, classes, or custom business forms for use in in the drill.

**MEMO**
**DATE:** February 1, 2016

Travis Waldron purchased 1 Pump, 1 Rock Fountain, and 25 Rocks @ $50 each. Record an invoice for his fountain.

Add 5 hours of Design to the invoice for Travis Waldron.

Kate Whelan had 5 sprinkler pipes, 25 sprinkler heads, and 3 hours of installation.

*DRILL*

Continue to use the **Test Drive Company** and prepare Invoices for sales on account

Click the **Plus** icon, click **Invoice** in the Customers column
Select the customer: **Travis Waldron**
Date: **Current Date**

- Once again because of the automatic date change in the Test Drive Company, you will need to use the Current Date on your invoices.

Record the transaction shown in the Memo

Once the Product/Service information has been entered, click the drop-down arrow for **Select a sales tax rate**

Click **California** to insert a tax rate of 8%

- You will see $123.20 as the amount of sales tax. (Do the math: Taxable Subtotal of $1,540 * .08 = $123.20)

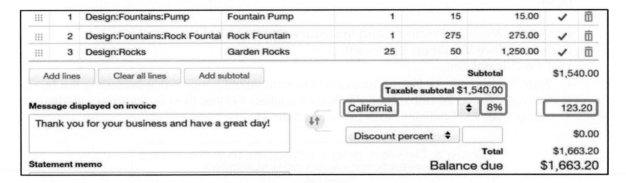

Add 5 Hours of Design service to the invoice on Line 4

- Notice that the Taxable subtotal of $1,540.00 did not change, nor did the Sales Tax amount of $123.20 change. Services are not taxable items.

Click **Save and new**

Enter the invoice to **Kate Whelan**

Use the **Current Date**

Use the information in the Memo to record the invoice for Kate Whelan

Use **California** for the Tax Rate

- Notice Sprinkler Pipes and Sprinkler Heads are marked for tax and Installation is not.

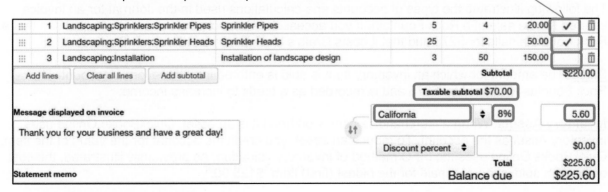

Click **Save and close**

Do <u>not</u> close the Test Drive Company

## VIEW INVENTORY VALUATION SUMMARY—DRILL

To see the effect of the sales of products on the inventory, once again prepare the Inventory Valuation Summary.

### DRILL

Continue to use the **Test Drive Company** and prepare an Inventory Valuation Summary report

Access the **Manage Products and Inventory** report category
Click **Inventory Valuation Summary**
Use the **Current Date**
- Note the quantity for the products and the amount of change since preparing the two invoices: Pump 24 rather than 25; Rock Fountain 1 rather than 2, Sprinkler Heads 0 rather than 25, Sprinkler Pipes 26 rather than 31.

| Craig's Design and Landscaping Services | | | |
|---|---|---|---|
| **INVENTORY VALUATION SUMMARY** | | | |
| Current Date | | TOTAL | |
| | QTY | ASSET VALUE | AVG COST |
| **Design** | | | |
| **Fountains** | | | |
| Pump | 24.00 | 240.00 | 10.00 |
| Rock Fountain | 1.00 | 125.00 | 125.00 |
| Total Fountains | | 365.00 | |
| **Total Design** | | 365.00 | |
| **Landscaping** | | | |
| **Sprinklers** | | | |
| Sprinkler Heads | 0.00 | 0.00 | |
| Sprinkler Pipes | 26.00 | 65.00 | 2.50 |
| Total Sprinklers | | 65.00 | |
| **Total Landscaping** | | 65.00 | |
| **TOTAL** | | $430.00 | |

Do <u>not</u> close the Test Drive Company
Read the next section then continue to use the Test Drive Company to prepare the Journal

## INVENTORY ASSETS, COST OF GOODS SOLD, SALES TAX LIABILITY—READ

Prior to preparing the Journal, it is helpful to analyze the effect of transactions that involve products. The following illustrates the types of accounts and calculations used in the Journal for an invoice entered for the sale of a Rock Fountain. If you access the Products/Services List, you will see that a Rock Fountain sells for $275 and that it costs Craig's Design and Landscaping Services $125.

**Sales**: The amount for which an inventory item is sold is entered into the revenue account. The Rock Fountain was sold for $275 and is recorded as a credit to increase income.

**Inventory Assets**: When a merchandise item is on hand it is an asset. QuickBooks Online uses Inventory Asset as the account. To reduce an asset, you credit the account for the value of the item. QuickBooks Online uses the FIFO method of inventory valuation. As previously illustrated, the cost of the item sold is the cost paid for the oldest (first) item: $125.00.

**Cost of Goods Sold**: Used to calculate the amount the merchandise cost the company. This amount is deducted from sales to determine the amount of gross profit earned when the merchandise is sold. If the Rock Fountain is sold for $275 and the cost to the company $125, the amount of gross profit is $150. (Sales - Cost of Goods Sold = Gross Profit). Since the cost of goods sold will ultimately decrease the revenue, you debit the account.

**Sales Tax**: When sales tax is collected, it is a liability that is owed to the government. To record the liability, you credit the liability account—Sales Tax Payable.

## PREPARE THE JOURNAL—DRILL

The Journal records every transaction entered in Debit/Credit format. It is important to view the Journal to see how the sale of merchandise is recorded.

### *DRILL*

 Continue to use the **Test Drive Company** and prepare the Journal

> With the Inventory Valuation Summary showing on the screen, click **Reports** on the Navigation bar
> You should return to the Manage Products and Inventory screen, click **<All Reports**
> Click the category **Accountant Reports**
> Click **Journal**
> To isolate the transactions you entered, prepare the Journal for the **Current Date**
> - As you examine the transactions, look at Rock Fountain. The Inventory Asset was reduced by crediting the account $125 (the cost of the fountain). The Cost of Goods Sold was increased by debiting the account $125 (the cost of the fountain). Effectively moving the fountain from Inventory Asset into Cost of Goods Sold. Sales of Product Income shows a credit of $275 (the selling price of the fountain).

### Craig's Design and Landscaping Services
#### JOURNAL

| DATE | TRANSACTION TYPE | NUM | NAME | MEMO/DESCRIPTION | ACCOUNT | DEBIT | CREDIT |
|------|------------------|-----|------|-----------------|---------|-------|--------|
| Current Date | Invoice | 1038 | Travis Waldron | | Accounts Receivable (A/R) | $2,038.20 | |
| | | | | Fountain Pump | Inventory Asset | | $10.00 |
| | | | | Fountain Pump | Cost of Goods Sold | $10.00 | |
| | | | | Fountain Pump | Sales of Product Income | | $15.00 |
| | | | | Rock Fountain | Cost of Goods Sold | $125.00 | |
| | | | | Rock Fountain | Inventory Asset | | $125.00 |
| | | | | Rock Fountain | Sales of Product Income | | $275.00 |
| | | | | Garden Rocks | Landscaping Services:Job Materials:Fountains and Garden Lighting | | $1,250.00 |
| | | | | Custom Design | Design income | | $375.00 |
| | | | | | Board of Equalization Payable | | $123.20 |
| | | | | | | $2,173.20 | $2,173.20 |
| Current Date | Invoice | 1039 | Kate Whelan | | Accounts Receivable (A/R) | $225.60 | |
| | | | | Sprinkler Pipes | Inventory Asset | | $12.50 |
| | | | | Sprinkler Pipes | Cost of Goods Sold | $12.50 | |
| | | | | Sprinkler Pipes | Sales of Product Income | | $20.00 |
| | | | | Sprinkler Heads | Sales of Product Income | | $50.00 |
| | | | | Sprinkler Heads | Inventory Asset | | $11.25 |
| | | | | Sprinkler Heads | Cost of Goods Sold | $7.50 | |
| | | | | Sprinkler Heads | Cost of Goods Sold | $11.25 | |
| | | | | Sprinkler Heads | Inventory Asset | | $7.50 |
| | | | | Installation of landscape design | Landscaping Services:Labor:Installation | | $150.00 |
| | | | | | Board of Equalization Payable | | $5.60 |
| | | | | | | $256.85 | $256.85 |
| TOTAL | | | | | | $2,430.05 | $2,430.05 |

> Close the Test Drive Company

## VIEW QUANTITY ON HAND OF PRODUCTS—DO

Prior to recording sales transactions for products/inventory items, it is helpful to know how much quantity is on hand. One way to do this is to prepare an Inventory Valuation Summary report.

### DO

 Open **Your Name's Beach Barkers** and prepare an Inventory Valuation Summary report

Click **Reports** on the Navigation bar
Click the report category for **Manage Products and Inventory**
Click **Inventory Valuation Summary**
Date: **02/01/2016**
- The information shown includes the Quantity, the Asset Value, and the Average Cost.
- Pay special attention to the quantities on hand.

### Your Name's Beach Barkers
### INVENTORY VALUATION SUMMARY
As of February 1, 2016

| | TOTAL | | |
|---|---|---|---|
| | QTY | ASSET VALUE | AVG COST |
| Bones | 350.00 | 700.00 | 2.00 |
| Brushes | 35.00 | 175.00 | 5.00 |
| Collars | 650.00 | 6,500.00 | 10.00 |
| Dog Food-Canned | 485.00 | 1,212.50 | 2.50 |
| Dog Food-Dry | 400.00 | 2,800.00 | 7.00 |
| Leashes | 450.00 | 4,500.00 | 10.00 |
| Sweaters | 325.00 | 4,875.00 | 15.00 |
| Toys & Treats | 3,450.00 | 6,900.00 | 2.00 |
| Vitamins | 450.00 | 1,350.00 | 3.00 |
| TOTAL | | $29,012.50 | |

Close the report without printing. do <u>not</u> close Your Name's Beach Barkers

## EDIT CUSTOMER—DO

Even though customers have accounts with the company, things can change. As you learned previously, customers can be edited and information may be updated, corrected, added, and changed.

In this chapter, debit and credit card transactions will be included as payment methods. You have already included the payment method. When recording a transaction using a debit or credit card remember that the numbers provided in the text are fictitious and may only be used for training purposes. In order to actually process these transactions, a company must set up Online Payments and subscribe to QuickBooks Payments.

---

**MEMO**
**DATE:** February 1, 2016

Edit Customer: Megan Rodriguez. Change her name to Megan Rivera, change the Payment Method to Visa, enter the Visa number: 4929-4327-4096-2308 and Expiration date: 06/2020. Add the name of her dog, Buttercup, into the Note section of her account.

---

<u>*DO*</u>

 Use **Your Name's Beach Barkers** to edit a Customer

Open the **Customers List**, scroll through the list until you see Rodriguez, Megan
Click **Rodriguez, Megan**, click the **Edit** button
Change her Last name to **Rivera**, press **Tab**
Click the drop-down list arrow for **Display name as**
Click **Rivera, Megan**
- Make sure that Print on check as does not have a check mark. If it does, click to deselect.
Click the **Payment and billing** tab
Preferred payment method: click the drop-down list arrow
Click **Visa**
Click the **No credit card information** button
Complete the Credit Card Information screen
- Remember, this is a fictitious credit card number and should only be used for training in the textbook.
Credit card number: **4929-4327-4096-2308**
Expiration date: **06** and **2020**
Name on card: **Megan Rivera**
- Street address and Zip code are correct as shown.
Click **OK**

- Once the credit card has been entered, only the last four digits of the number will be shown.
Review the changes for Megan's account:

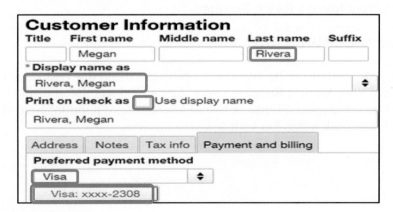

Click the **Notes** tab
Enter: **Dog's Name: Buttercup**

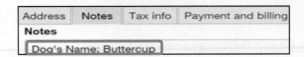

Click **Save** to save the changes for Megan Rivera
- The Note "Dog's Name: Buttercup" is shown just below Megan's address information.

Do <u>not</u> close Your Name's Beach Barkers

## ENTER NOTES IN CUSTOMER ACCOUNTS—DO

Since our customers all have dogs and bring them to us for care, it is a good idea to have the dogs' names listed in each customer's account. This may be done by adding a note to the account.

---

**MEMO**

**DATE:** February 1, 2016

Create Notes to add Dog Names to Customer Accounts for

David De Los Santos: Joe; Sandi Egkan: Daisy; Keith Evans: Boomer; Gloria Gucci: Mishka; Tracy McCarter: Maggie; Carol Russell: Lily; Nick Wagner: Lucky; and Katie Wilson: Suzy.

---

<u>DO</u>

Continue to use **Your Name's Beach Barkers** and add Notes to Customer accounts

Click **David De Los Santos** in the Customers List
Beneath his address click the blue **Add notes**
Enter **Dog's Name: Joe** in the Note text box

Click outside the note text box and the note will be saved
Add the Dog Names for the other customers listed in the Memo
- If you make an error on the Note, simply click it and re-enter it correctly.

Do <u>not</u> close Your Name's Beach Barkers

## ENTER SALES ON ACCOUNT—DO

Now that you have practiced recording invoices for products using the Test Drive Company, you will record transactions in Your Name's Beach Barkers. Since products that are sold incur sales tax, the tax is also included on the invoice. Please note that all credit card information is fictitious and is not to be used except in the work within the textbook.

---

**MEMO**

**DATE:** February 1, 2016

Prepare an Invoice for Megan Rivera for her dog, Buttercup, for 1 Bath, 1 Nails, and 1 Bone $15. Location: Malibu.

Record a sale on account to a new customer: Monroe Miller (Address: 30315 Morning View Drive, Malibu, CA 90265; Email: Monroe@miller.com; Phone: 424-555-5578; Mobile: 424-555-8755; Preferred payment method: MasterCard; 5242-1427-8558-4902; Expiration date: 07/2021; Terms: Net 30; Dog's Name: Max). He purchased 1 Sweater $45, 2 Brushes $25 each, 5 Bones $10 each for his dog, Max. Location: Malibu.

Record the purchase on account from Gloria Gucci, Venice, 5 days of Boarding, 1 Five One-Hour Training Sessions, 1 Bath, 1 Brush $25, 7 Dog Food-Canned $5 each, 1 Vitamins $20.

Record the purchase on account from Tracy McCarter, Malibu, 10 days Boarding, 1 Bath, 1 Nails, 10 Bones $7.50 each, 1 Sweater $75, 3 Toys $10 each.

---

_DO_

Continue to use **Your Name's Beach Barkers** and record Invoices for sales on account

Click the **Plus** icon, click **Invoice** in the Customers column
Select the customer: **Megan Rivera**

- Customers are organized Last name first; however, in transaction information, they will be referred to by first and last name.
- Notice the Online Payment information displayed. "Get set up" means you would need to sign up and pay for QuickBooks Payment Services. When you use this service, you will be charged transaction rates by QuickBooks Online for processing the credit card payments and bank transfers.

Date: **02/01/2016**

- You will be using Locations and Classes when entering invoices. Remember, look at the customer's address and select either Venice or Malibu for the location. Locations will be given if there might be any confusion.

Click the drop-down list arrow for Location, click **Malibu**

- The two classes that were created earlier in the chapter are Dog Care and Boutique. Dog Care is used for all services performed and Boutique is used for all products sold. An easy way to remember this is that the Boutique items are all taxable. Look for the √ in the Tax column.

For Line 1, click the drop-down list arrow for Product/Service, click **Bath**, click in the Class column, click the drop-down list arrow, click **Dog Care**
For Line 2, repeat the steps to select **Nails**, class **Dog Care**
In Line 3 select the Product/Service **Bones**, tab to **Rate**, enter **15**, Class **Boutique**
Once the Product/Service information has been entered, click the drop-down arrow for
   **Select a sales tax rate**
Click **California** to insert a tax rate of 8%

- The sales tax is calculated for the product/inventory item Bones.
- You will see $1.20 as the amount of sales tax. (Do the math: Taxable Subtotal of $15.00 * .08 = $1.20)

Print and or send the invoice as previously instructed
- If you save the invoice, name it **2-Your Name Invoice 1039 Megan Rivera**.

Click **Save and new**

Enter the invoice to the new customer Monroe Miller

Click the drop-down list arrow for Choose a customer

Click **+ Add new**

Enter the name: **Monroe Miller**

Click **+ Details**

Click the drop-down list arrow for Display name as

Click **Miller, Monroe**

Click the checkbox for "Print on check as" to deselect

Enter the Billing address information provided in the Memo

Click **Payment and billing**

Click the drop-down list arrow for Preferred payment method, click **MasterCard**

Click the **Enter credit card details** button, enter the credit card information provided in the Memo
- Make sure Monroe Miller is the Name on card.

Click **OK** on the Credit Card Information screen

Enter the Terms of **Net 30** for Monroe

Click the **Notes** tab

Enter: **Dog's Name: Max**

Click **Save**
- If the blank invoice does not appear on the screen, click the **Plus** icon and click **Invoice**.

Use the information in the Memo and record the purchase on account
- Remember, the location for Monroe is Malibu.

Assign a Class to each line of the transaction
- All of the sales items are marked taxable, so the Class should be Boutique.

Use **California** for the Tax Rate

Print and or send the invoice as previously instructed
- If you save the invoice, name it **3-Your Name Invoice 1040 Monroe Miller**.

Click **Save and new** (Ctrl+Alt+S)

Record the two remaining transactions listed in the Memo
- Do not forget to add Location, Classes, and Sales Tax!

The printed invoices for Gloria Gucci and Tracy McCarter are shown below
- Notice that Location and Class are not shown on the invoices. Those are used for internal purposes. However, the invoice for Gloria Gucci uses Your Name's Beach Barkers Venice address and phone for the invoice and the invoice for Tracy McCarter uses the Malibu address and phone.
- Since sales taxes are calculated for products sold, notice the T next to the Amount for each taxable product and the total amount of Tax (8%).
- Did you select Boutique for the class when the item was marked as taxable and Dog Care for the services provided (no tax)?

Print and or send the invoices as previously instructed
- If you save the invoices, name them: **4-Your Name Invoice 1041 Gloria Gucci** and **5-Your Name Invoice 1042 Tracy McCarter**.

6

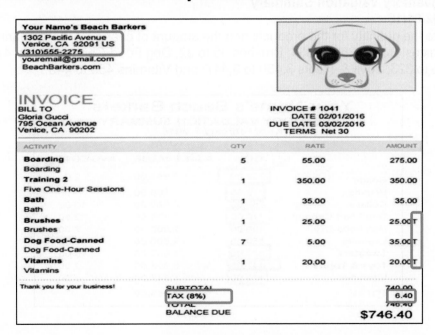

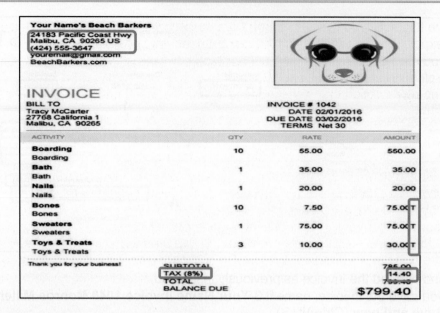

Click **Save and close** (Ctrl+Alt+D)
Do <u>not</u> close Your Name's Beach Barkers

## VIEW INVENTORY VALUATION SUMMARY—DO

To see the effect of the sales of products on the inventory, once again prepare the Inventory Valuation Summary.

### DO

Continue to use **Your Name's Beach Barkers** and prepare an Inventory Valuation Summary report

Go to **Reports**, select **Manage Products and Inventory** for the report category
Click **Inventory Valuation Summary**
Date: **02/01/16**

- Note the quantity for the products and the amount of change since preparing the invoices: Bones 350 to 334; Brushes 35 to 32; Dog Food-Canned 485 to 478; Sweaters 325 to 323; Toys & Treats 3,450 to 3,447; and Vitamins 450 to 449.

### Your Name's Beach Barkers
#### INVENTORY VALUATION SUMMARY
##### As of February 1, 2016

| | QTY | ASSET VALUE | AVG COST |
|---|---|---|---|
| | | TOTAL | |
| Bones | 334.00 | 668.00 | 2.00 |
| Brushes | 32.00 | 160.00 | 5.00 |
| Collars | 650.00 | 6,500.00 | 10.00 |
| Dog Food-Canned | 478.00 | 1,195.00 | 2.50 |
| Dog Food-Dry | 400.00 | 2,800.00 | 7.00 |
| Leashes | 450.00 | 4,500.00 | 10.00 |
| Sweaters | 323.00 | 4,845.00 | 15.00 |
| Toys & Treats | 3,447.00 | 6,894.00 | 2.00 |
| Vitamins | 449.00 | 1,347.00 | 3.00 |
| TOTAL | | $28,909.00 | |

Remove the Date and Time Prepared from the report footer as previously instructed
Print, export, and/or send/submit the report as required by your professor
- If you save the report, name it **6-Your Name Inventory Valuation Summary Ch. 6**.
Do not close Your Name's Beach Barkers
Read the next section then continue to use Your Name's Beach Barkers to prepare the
Journal

## INVENTORY ASSETS, COST OF GOODS SOLD, SALES TAX LIABILITY—READ

Prior to preparing the Journal, it is helpful to analyze the effect of transactions that involve products. The following illustrates the types of accounts and calculations used in the Journal for the purchase of a dog bone by Megan Rivera. In essence, when you record the sale of a dog bone, you are removing the bone from inventory and transferring the cost of the bone into the Cost of Goods Sold account. If you look at the Journal entry for Megan Rivera, you will see that the dog bone cost of $2 was removed from Inventory Asset and entered into Cost of Goods Sold. You will also see that the bone was sold for $15. When it is time to calculate Net Income, the $2 in the Cost of Goods Sold account is subtracted from the $15 in Sales of Product Income to determine Gross Profit of $13 for the sale of the dog bone.

| DATE | TRANSACTION TYPE | NUM | NAME | MEMO/DESCRIPTION | ACCOUNT | DEBIT | CREDIT |
|------|------------------|-----|------|------------------|---------|-------|--------|
| 02/01/2016 | Invoice | 1039 | Rivera, Megan | | Accounts Receivable (A/R) | $71.20 | |
| | | | | Bath | Services:Grooming | | $35.00 |
| | | | | Nails | Services:Grooming | | $20.00 |
| | | | | Bones | Cost of Goods Sold | $2.00 | |
| | | | | Bones | Inventory Asset | | $2.00 |
| | | | | Bones | Sales of Product Income | | $15.00 |
| | | | | | State Board of Equalization Payable | | $1.20 |
| | | | | | | $73.20 | $73.20 |

**Sales of Product Income**: The amount for which an inventory item is sold is entered into the revenue account. The dog bone was sold for $15 and is recorded as a credit to increase income.

**Inventory Assets**: When a merchandise item is on hand it is an asset. QuickBooks Online uses Inventory Asset as the account. To reduce an asset, you credit the account for the value of the item. The Inventory Asset account is reduced by $2. QuickBooks Online uses the FIFO method of inventory valuation, which means that the oldest/first cost paid by the company for the product is used for the value.

**Cost of Goods Sold**: Is used to track the cost of the merchandise sold by the company. Since the cost of goods sold will ultimately decrease the revenue, you debit the account $2. At the end of an accounting period, the amount in the Cost of Goods Sold account is deducted from sales to determine the amount of gross profit earned after the merchandise is sold. For example, the dog bone sold for $15 and cost the company $2 so the amount of gross profit is $13. (Sales - Cost of Goods Sold = Gross Profit).

**Sales Tax**: When sales tax is collected, it is a liability that is owed to the government. To record the liability, you credit the liability account—Sales Tax Payable.

## PREPARE THE JOURNAL—DO

The Journal records every transaction entered in Debit/Credit format. It is important to view the Journal to see how the sale of merchandise is recorded.

<u>DO</u>

Continue to use **Your Name's Beach Barkers** and prepare the Journal

With the Inventory Valuation Summary report still showing on the screen, click **Reports** on the Navigation bar

Click the category **My Custom Reports**

Click **Journal**

- When you customized and saved this report earlier, the Date and Time Prepared were removed from the report footer.

To isolate the transactions you entered, prepare the Journal with Dates From: **02/01/16** and To: **02/01/16**

- Review each of the transactions entered. Pay special attention to the entries for products. The transaction totals are: <u>Megan Rivera</u>, $73.20; <u>Monroe Miller</u>, $191.60; <u>Gloria Gucci</u>, $771.90; and <u>Tracy McCarter</u>, $840.40. The report total is $1,877.10.

Use Landscape orientation to print, export, and/or send/submit the report as required by your professor

- If you save the report, name it **7-Your Name Journal Ch. 6**.

Close Your Name's Beach Barkers

## DELAYED CHARGE—DRILL

QuickBooks Online has a feature that enables you to create a charge for services and/or products that will be converted to an invoice at a later date. This is similar to a Sales Order where a customer calls in an order and the invoice is not prepared until the service is performed or until the product is picked up or delivered. A delayed charge will show up in a customer's register but will not be part of the balance. Once you are ready to convert the delayed charge to an invoice, you may click "Start invoice" in the customer's register or create a new Invoice, enter the customer's name, and click Add for the delayed charge.

> **MEMO**
> **DATE:** February 1, 2016
>
> Use the Current Date to record a Delayed Charge for Geeta Kalapatapu. She wants to have new sprinkler heads installed but isn't quite sure when she can schedule time for the work to be done. In addition to the 15 sprinkler heads, the installation of them will require 1 hour of Maintenance & Repair at $50 per hour.

<u>DRILL</u>

Open the **Test Drive Company** and enter, view, and convert a delayed charge

<u>Enter a Delayed Charge</u>

In the **Test Drive Company**, use the information in the Memo and enter a Delayed Charge

Click the **Plus** icon

Click **Delayed Charge** in the Customers column

Click the drop-down list arrow for "Choose a customer," click **Geeta Kalapatapu**

Enter the **Current Date**

Line 1: Enter the information for 15 sprinkler heads

Line 2: Enter 1 hour of Maintenance & Repair Rate: 50

- Note that the Sprinkler Heads are marked taxable but no tax is included on a delayed charge. Tax is recorded when an invoice is prepared.

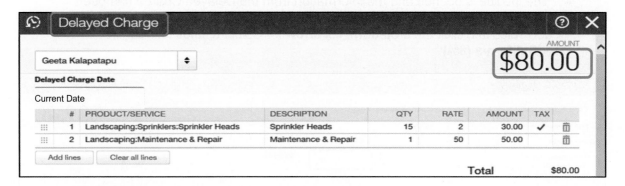

Click **Save and close** (Ctrl+Alt+D)
Do <u>not</u> close the Test Drive Company

## View the Delayed Charge

Once the delayed charge has been entered, it may be viewed in the customer's account register.

 Continue to use the **Test Drive Company** to view the delayed charge in Geeta Kalapatapu's account register

Click **Customers** on the Navigation Bar
Scroll through the list of customers, click **Geeta Kalapatapu** and view her account register
- Her open balance is $629.10, which is the amount owed on Invoice 1033. The Delayed Charge for $80 is shown but not added as an amount due.
- Because of the automatic date changed, the dates shown in the register will be different from your dates.

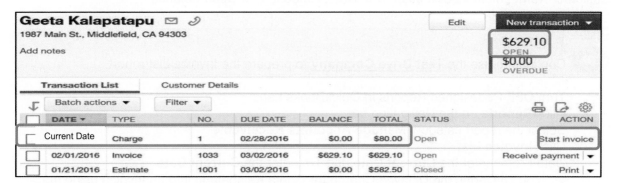

Do <u>not</u> close Geeta Kalapatapu's account register or the Test Drive Company

## Convert Delayed Charge to Invoice

When the work is scheduled to be completed, the Delayed Charge is converted into an Invoice. There are two ways in which to do this: prepare a new invoice and add the delayed charge to it or click Start Invoice in the customer's register.

 Convert the Delayed Charge for Geeta Kalapatapu in the **Test Drive Company**

With Geeta's account register showing on the screen, click **Start invoice** in the ACTION column for the Delayed Charge transaction
- The invoice is opened and the information from the Delayed Charge has been automatically entered using the current date for the Invoice date.

To add sales tax, click the drop-down list arrow for Select a sales tax rate

Click **California (8%)**

Click **Save and close** (Ctrl+Alt+D)
Do not close the Test Drive Company

## INVOICE LIST REPORT

The Invoice List report enables you to see invoices that were prepared for a particular period. Information provided in the report includes the Invoice Date, Transaction Type, Invoice Number, Customer Name, Memo/Description, Due Date, Amount, and Open Balance.

## *DRILL*

Continue to use the **Test Drive Company** to prepare the Invoice List report

Turn **OFF** Redesigned Reports in QuickBooks Labs
Click **Reports** on the Navigation bar
Select the report category **Manage Accounts Receivable**
Click **Invoice List**
Date From: enter the **Current Date** and To: enter the **Current Date**
- You converted the Delayed Charge for Geeta Kalapatapu into an Invoice using the current date.

Click **Run Report**

### Craig's Design and Landscaping Services
#### INVOICE LIST BY DATE
Current Date

| DATE | TRANSACTION TYPE | NUM | NAME | MEMO/DESCRIPTION | DUE DATE | AMOUNT | OPEN BALANCE |
|------|------------------|-----|------|------------------|----------|--------|--------------|
| Current Date | Invoice | 1038 | Geeta Kalapatapu | | 30 Days from Current Date | 82.40 | 82.40 |

Do not close the Test Drive Company

## CREDIT MEMO—DRILL

A credit memo is prepared to show a reduction to a transaction and to notify a customer that a change has been made. If the invoice has already been sent to the customer, it is more appropriate and less confusing to make a change to a transaction by issuing a credit memo rather than voiding an invoice and issuing a new one. When a customer returns an item that is on an unpaid invoice, a Credit Memo is created. QuickBooks Online creates a "Receive Payment" to apply the credit memo to the invoice and to create a link between them.

---

**MEMO**
**DATE:** February 1, 2016

Use the Current Date to record a Credit Memo for Freeman Sporting Goods:0969 Ocean View Road. They returned 3 of the bags of Soil purchased on Invoice 1036 for $10 each.

---

_DRILL_

Continue to use the **Test Drive Company** to prepare a Credit Memo

Click the **Plus** icon, click **Credit Memo** in the Customers column
Customer: **Freeman Sporting Goods:0969 Ocean View Road**
Credit Memo Date: **Current Date**
Enter the information provided in the Memo for the 3 bags of soil
Sales Tax Rate: **California (8%)**

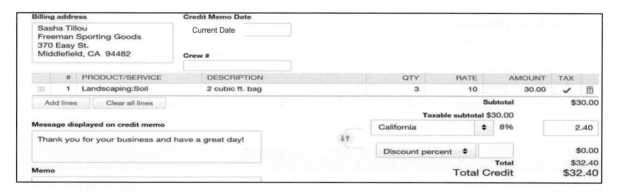

Click **Save and close**
Click **Customers** on the Navigation Bar
Click **Freeman Sporting Goods: 0969 Ocean View Road**
View the Credit Memo in the Customer's account register

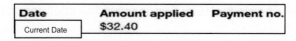

Click the transaction for **Invoice 1036** in the customer's register
At the top of the invoice, click 1 payment made on (Current Date)

| Date | Amount applied | Payment no. |
|---|---|---|
| Current Date | $32.40 | |

- The pop-up shows you the date and amount of the payment, which is the date and amount of the Credit Memo. To see the Credit Memo, click the date.
Close the Test Drive Company

## DELAYED CHARGE—DO

As you just practiced, QuickBooks Online has a delayed charge feature that enables you to create a charge for services and/or products that will be converted to an invoice at a later date. Delayed charges will be prepared for customers in Your Name's Beach Barkers.

---

**MEMO**

**DATE:** February 1, 2016

Record Delayed Charges:

Sandi Egkan: 5 Sweaters $30 each, 5 Leashes $25 each, 5 Collars $25 each, and 5 Brushes $25 each for her dog, Daisy. Location: Malibu. Class: Boutique.

Keith Evans: 1 Brush $20, 1 Leash $50, 1 Collar $75 for his dog, Boomer. Location: Venice. Class: Boutique.

---

_DO_

 Open **Your Name's Beach Barkers** to enter and view a delayed charge

Enter Delayed Charges

 In **Your Name's Beach Barkers**, use the information in the Memo to enter a Delayed Charge

> Click the **Plus** icon
> Click **Delayed Charge** in the Customers column
> Click the drop-down list arrow for "Choose a customer," click **Sandi Egkan**
> Date: **02/01/16**
> Location: **Malibu**
> Enter the information provided in the Memo. The class for each item is Boutique
> • Note that the items are all marked taxable but no tax is included on a delayed charge.

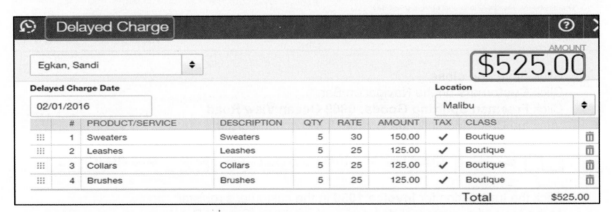

> Click **Save and new** (Ctrl+Alt+S)
> Record the Delayed Charge for Keith Evans using the information provided in the Memo

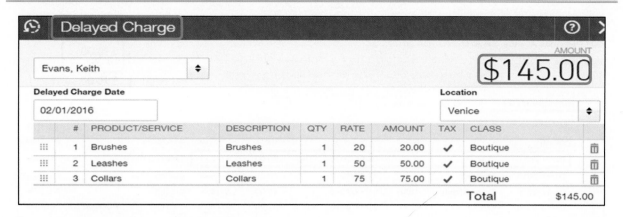

Click **Save and close** (Ctrl+Alt+D)
Do not close Your Name's Beach Barkers

## View Delayed Charges

Once delayed charges have been entered, they may be viewed in each customer's account register.

 Continue to use **Your Name's Beach Barkers** to view the delayed charges for Sandi Egkan and Keith Evans in their account registers

Click **Customers** on the Navigation bar
Scroll through the list of customers, click **Sandi Egkan** and view her account register
- Her open balance is $0.00. The Delayed Charge for $525 is shown but not added as an amount due.

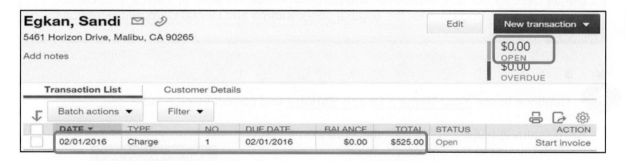

Click **Customers**, click **Keith Evans** and view his account register
- As with the other Delayed Charge transactions, it is shown in his register but not added to his balance.

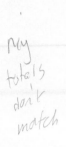

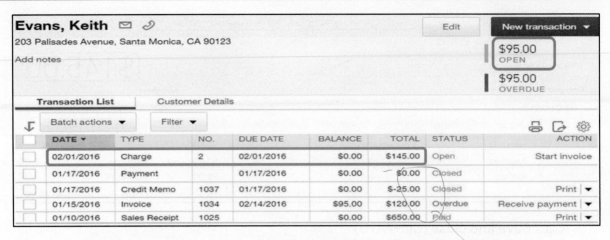

- These two delayed charges will be converted to invoices later in the chapter.
Do <u>not</u> close Your Name's Beach Barkers

## CORRECT INVOICE—DO

As you did when recording sales of services in Chapter 3, invoices for products may be corrected, reprinted, and/or sent.

---

**MEMO**
**DATE:** February 1, 2016

Correct Invoice 1039 to Megan Rivera. In the items shown on the original invoice, only the cost of the Bone needs to be changed. The Bone should have been $12: In addition, she had 1 Dental Care for her dog, Buttercup, and purchased 1 Brush $25, 10 Toys $15 each, and 1 Collar $50. Class: Dog Care for the original service items and Dental Care and Boutique for all others.

---

<u>DO</u>

Continue to use **Your Name's Beach Barkers** and correct Invoice 1039

To return to Invoice 1039, click the **Plus** icon
Click **Invoice** in the Customers column
On the blank invoice, click the **Recent Transactions** icon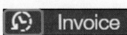
On the list of Recent Invoices, click **No. 1039**
- Invoice 1039 will be opened.
Record the changes to the invoice using the information provided in the Memo

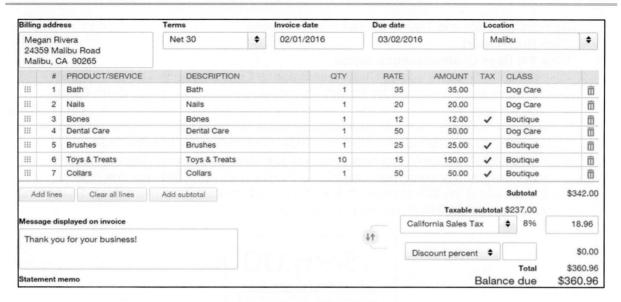

| | # | PRODUCT/SERVICE | DESCRIPTION | QTY | RATE | AMOUNT | TAX | CLASS | |
|---|---|---|---|---|---|---|---|---|---|
| ⠿ | 1 | Bath | Bath | 1 | 35 | 35.00 | | Dog Care | 🗑 |
| ⠿ | 2 | Nails | Nails | 1 | 20 | 20.00 | | Dog Care | 🗑 |
| ⠿ | 3 | Bones | Bones | 1 | 12 | 12.00 | ✓ | Boutique | 🗑 |
| ⠿ | 4 | Dental Care | Dental Care | 1 | 50 | 50.00 | | Dog Care | 🗑 |
| ⠿ | 5 | Brushes | Brushes | 1 | 25 | 25.00 | ✓ | Boutique | 🗑 |
| ⠿ | 6 | Toys & Treats | Toys & Treats | 10 | 15 | 150.00 | ✓ | Boutique | 🗑 |
| ⠿ | 7 | Collars | Collars | 1 | 50 | 50.00 | ✓ | Boutique | 🗑 |

Billing address: Megan Rivera, 24359 Malibu Road, Malibu, CA 90265
Terms: Net 30
Invoice date: 02/01/2016
Due date: 03/02/2016
Location: Malibu

Add lines    Clear all lines    Add subtotal

Subtotal $342.00
Taxable subtotal $237.00

Message displayed on invoice
Thank you for your business!

California Sales Tax   8%   18.96
Discount percent   $0.00
Total $360.96
Balance due $360.96

Statement memo

Print and or send the invoice as previously instructed
If you save the invoice, name it: **8-Your Name Invoice 1039 Megan Rivera Corrected**
Click **Save and close** (Ctrl+Alt+D)
Do <u>not</u> close Your Name's Beach Barkers

## CUSTOMER BALANCE SUMMARY—DO

After a number of sales transactions have been recorded, it is helpful to prepare a Customer Balance Summary report. This report shows the total amount owed by each customer.

_DO_

Continue to use **Your Name's Beach Barkers** to prepare a Customer Balance Summary report

Access the **Manage Accounts Receivable** category in Reports
Click **Customer Balance Summary**
• The report is prepared for **All Dates**.

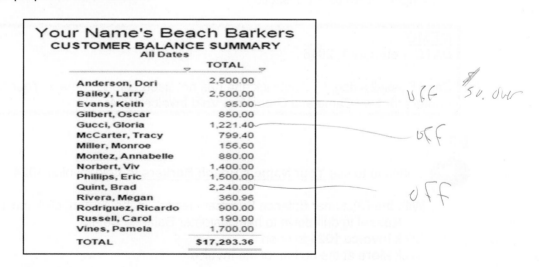

**Your Name's Beach Barkers**
**CUSTOMER BALANCE SUMMARY**
All Dates

| | TOTAL |
|---|---|
| Anderson, Dori | 2,500.00 |
| Bailey, Larry | 2,500.00 |
| Evans, Keith | 95.00 |
| Gilbert, Oscar | 850.00 |
| Gucci, Gloria | 1,221.40 |
| McCarter, Tracy | 799.40 |
| Miller, Monroe | 156.60 |
| Montez, Annabelle | 880.00 |
| Norbert, Viv | 1,400.00 |
| Phillips, Eric | 1,500.00 |
| Quint, Brad | 2,240.00 |
| Rivera, Megan | 360.96 |
| Rodriguez, Ricardo | 900.00 |
| Russell, Carol | 190.00 |
| Vines, Pamela | 1,700.00 |
| **TOTAL** | **$17,293.36** |

Click the **Customize** button

Remove the Date and Time Prepared from the Footer
Click **Run Report**
Click the **Save Customizations** button
Name of custom report: accept **Customer Balance Summary**, click **OK**
To drill-down and view details for an individual customer, click the **95** for **Keith Evans**

- You will see that he has Invoice 1034 for $120 that is due on February 14, 2016. Nothing is shown for the Delayed Charge because it has not been converted into an Invoice.

To drill-down to see the details for Invoice 1034, click the line for **Invoice 1034**

- Invoice 1034 is shown. The total of the Invoice shows that it was prepared for $120 and there is an Amount received amount of $25, which leaves a Balance due of $95.

To find out about the $25 payment that was received, click the blue highlighted **1 payment** made on 01/17/2016 at the top of the Invoice

- You will get a pop-up message showing the Date, Amount applied, and Payment no.

Click the blue highlighted date **01/17/2016**

- The Receive Payment will be shown. Note that the Receive Payment was for $25 that was the result of Credit Memo 1037.

Click the blue highlighted **Credit Memo 1037** to drill-down and open the Credit Memo

- The Credit Memo is marked PAID.

Click the Close button at the top of the Credit Memo

- You are returned to the Customer Balance Detail for Keith Evans.

Click **<Back to Summary Report**
Leave the Customer Balance Summary Report on the screen
Do <u>not</u> close Your Name's Beach Barkers, continue to the next section

## VOID AND DELETE INVOICES—DO

As you learned in previous chapters, business forms may be voided and/or deleted. If you Void a business form, such as an Invoice, it stays in the company's records. If you Delete a business form, it is no longer shown as a transaction.

<u>MEMO</u>
**DATE:** February 1, 2016

Carol Russell's dog, Lily, got sick and has not been able to come to Your Name's Beach Barkers for Day Camp and Grooming. Void Invoice 1024.

<u>DO</u>

Continue to use **Your Name's Beach Barkers** to Void Invoice 1024

With the Customer Balance Summary report on the screen, click the **190** amount for **Carol Russel** to drill-down to her Customer Balance Detail
Click **Invoice 1024** to open it
Click **More** at the bottom of the Invoice

- Note: The procedures to Void or Delete an invoice are the same. The main difference is that a Voided invoice will appear in the company records and a Deleted invoice will not.

Click **Void**, click **Yes** on the "Are you sure you want to void this?" screen

Click **Yes** on the "Closing date" screen

Click **OK** on the "Transaction successfully voided" screen

- If you want to print a voided invoice, you would return to the invoice and print as previously instructed. It is not necessary to print the voided invoice at this time.
- You are returned to the Customer Balance Detail report for Carol Russell, which now shows nothing. This is because the invoice was voided and Carol does not have any other open invoices.

Click **<Back to Summary Report**

- Because she does not have a balance, you will no longer see Carol Russell listed in the report.
- Note: This change to a transaction in a closed period will have an effect on the amount of Net Income recorded as an adjusting entry in Chapter 5. Typically, you would need to correct the adjusting entry you recorded in Chapter 5 for the difference in the net income. However, this will be entered in Chapter 8 when prior to closing the period for February.

Do <u>not</u> close Your Name's Beach Barkers

## CREDIT MEMO—DO

When a customer returns an item that is on an unpaid invoice, a Credit Memo is created and applied to the invoice. Rather than deleting and reprinting invoices when a return is made, preparing Credit Memos enable you to see which customers make returns and to see what is returned. This helps a company to determine if they are buying faulty products or if they have customers who make a lot of returns. QuickBooks Online creates a Receive Payment document to apply the credit memo to the invoice and create a link between them. The Receive Payment form automatically uses the current date.

---

**MEMO**
**DATE:** February 3, 2016

Monroe Miller returned the sweater that he bought for his dog, Max, on Invoice 1040 for $45 because it was too small. Location: Malibu.

---

<u>DO</u>

 Continue to use **Your Name's Beach Barkers** to prepare a Credit Memo

Prepare a Credit Memo as previously instructed
The Credit Memo Date is **02/03/16**
Complete the Credit Memo for Monroe Miller using the information provided in the Memo
Location: **Malibu**, Class: **Boutique**, Sales Tax: **California Sales Tax (8%)**
Click **Save**

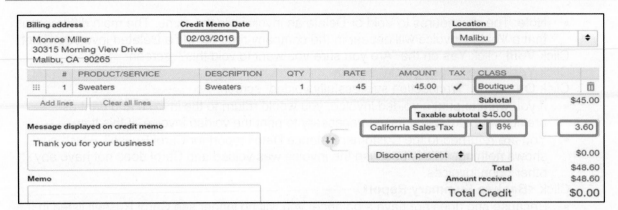

Print and or send the Credit Memo as previously instructed
- If you save a copy of the Credit Memo, name it: **9-Your Name Credit Memo 4013 Monroe Miller**.

Click **Save and close** (Ctrl+Alt+D)
Go to Monroe Miller's account and click the **Payment** for the current date
Change the date to **02/03/16**, which is the same date as the Credit Memo

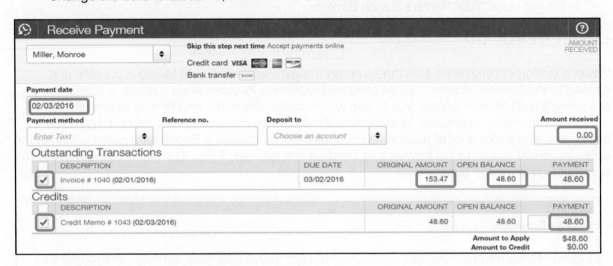

Click **Save and close** (Ctrl+Alt+D)
Do <u>not</u> close Your Name's Beach Barkers

## CONVERT DELAYED CHARGES

A Delayed Charge is converted into an Invoice when the customer is ready to pick up the merchandise. There are two ways in which to do this: prepare a new invoice and add the delayed charge to it or click "Start Invoice" in the customer's register.

---

**MEMO**
**DATE:** February 3, 2016

Convert Delayed Charges for Sandi Egkan and Keith Evans to Invoices.

---

<u>DO</u>

Continue to use **Your Name's Beach Barkers** and convert the Delayed Charges for Sandi Egkan and Keith Evans into Invoices

Click the **Plus** icon, click **Invoice** in the Customers column
Click the drop-down list arrow for "Select a customer," click **Sandi Egkan**
Date: **02/03/16**

- An Add to Invoice pane opens on the right-side of the invoice. Information for Charge #1 is shown.

Click **Add**
- Everything listed on the Delayed Charge was entered into the invoice.

For Select a sales tax rate, click the drop-down list arrow
Click **California (8%)**

| | # | PRODUCT/SERVIC | DESCRIPTION | QTY | RATE | AMOUNT | TAX | CLASS | | |
|---|---|---|---|---|---|---|---|---|---|---|
| | 1 | Sweaters | Sweaters | 5 | 30 | 150.00 | ✓ | Boutique | 🔗 | 🗑 |
| | 2 | Brushes | Brushes | 5 | 25 | 125.00 | ✓ | Boutique | 🔗 | 🗑 |
| | 3 | Collars | Collars | 5 | 25 | 125.00 | ✓ | Boutique | 🔗 | 🗑 |
| | 4 | Leashes | Leashes | 5 | 25 | 125.00 | ✓ | Boutique | 🔗 | 🗑 |

Sandi Egkan
5461 Horizon Drive
Malibu, CA 90265
Net 30 — 02/03/2016 — 03/04/2016 — Malibu

Add lines — Clear all lines — Add subtotal — Subtotal $525.00

Taxable subtotal $525.00

**Message displayed on invoice**
Thank you for your business!

California Sales Tax — 8% — 42.00

Discount percent — $0.00

**Statement memo** — Total $567.00 — Balance due $567.00

Print and or send the Invoice as previously instructed
- If you save the Invoice, name it: **10-Your Name Invoice 1044 Sandi Egkan**.

Click **Save and new**
- The keyboard shortcuts for Save and new—Ctrl+Alt+S—and Save and close—Ctrl+Alt+D—will no longer be shown.

Repeat the steps provided to convert the Delayed Charges for Keith Evans

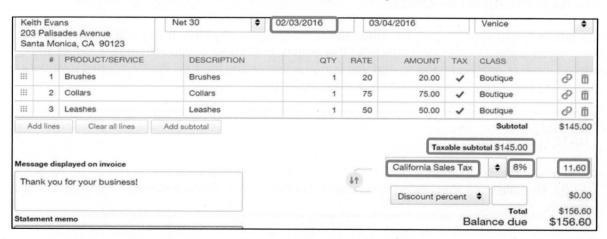

Keith Evans
203 Palisades Avenue
Santa Monica, CA 90123
Net 30 — 02/03/2016 — 03/04/2016 — Venice

| | # | PRODUCT/SERVICE | DESCRIPTION | QTY | RATE | AMOUNT | TAX | CLASS | | |
|---|---|---|---|---|---|---|---|---|---|---|
| | 1 | Brushes | Brushes | 1 | 20 | 20.00 | ✓ | Boutique | 🔗 | 🗑 |
| | 2 | Collars | Collars | 1 | 75 | 75.00 | ✓ | Boutique | 🔗 | 🗑 |
| | 3 | Leashes | Leashes | 1 | 50 | 50.00 | ✓ | Boutique | 🔗 | 🗑 |

Add lines — Clear all lines — Add subtotal — Subtotal $145.00

Taxable subtotal $145.00

**Message displayed on invoice**
Thank you for your business!

California Sales Tax — 8% — 11.60

Discount percent — $0.00

**Statement memo** — Total $156.60 — Balance due $156.60

Print and or send the Invoice as previously instructed
- If you save the Invoice, name it: **11-Your Name Invoice 1045 Keith Evans**.

Click **Save and close**
Do <u>not</u> close Your Name's Beach Barkers

## INVOICE LIST REPORT

The invoices for Sandi Egkan and Keith Evans will show in the Invoice List.

_DO_

Continue to use **Your Name's Beach Barkers** to prepare the Invoice List report

> Open Reports, select **Manage Accounts Receivable** for the report category
> Click **Invoice List**
> Use the Dates From: **020116** and To: **020316** then click **Run Report**
> - All of the invoices prepared in February are shown.
> - Notice that the newly converted invoices are included in the report.

### Your Name's Beach Barkers
#### INVOICE LIST BY DATE
##### February 1-3, 2016

| DATE | TRANSACTION TYPE | NUM | NAME | LOCATION | MEMO/DESCRIPTION | DUE DATE | AMOUNT | OPEN BALANCE |
|---|---|---|---|---|---|---|---|---|
| 02/01/2016 | Invoice | 1039 | Rivera, Megan | Malibu | | 03/02/2016 | 360.96 | 360.96 |
| 02/01/2016 | Invoice | 1040 | Miller, Monroe | Malibu | | 03/02/2016 | 156.60 | 108.00 |
| 02/01/2016 | Invoice | 1041 | Gucci, Gloria | Venice | | 03/02/2016 | 746.40 | 746.40 |
| 02/01/2016 | Invoice | 1042 | McCarter, Tracy | Malibu | | 03/02/2016 | 799.40 | 799.40 |
| 02/03/2016 | Invoice | 1044 | Egkan, Sandi | Malibu | | 03/04/2016 | 567.00 | 567.00 |
| 02/03/2016 | Invoice | 1045 | Evans, Keith | Venice | | 03/04/2016 | 156.60 | 156.60 |

> Change the Dates for the report to From: **010116** and To: **020316**, Run Report
> - You will see all of the invoices prepared in both Chapters 3 and 6.
> Remove the Date and Time Prepared from the Footer
> Use Landscape Orientation to print, export, and/or send/submit the Invoice List as previously instructed
> - If you save the Invoice List report, name it: **12-Your Name Invoice List Ch. 6**.
> Close Your Name's Beach Barkers

## ADD NEW PRODUCTS—DRILL

New products and services may be added to the company at any time. If you add a new product, typically you place an order for it right after it is added. In Chapter 6, you will add a product and enter an initial quantity on hand so that you can practice selling the new item. Ordering inventory items using Purchase Orders will be completed in Chapter 7.

> **MEMO**
> **DATE:** Current Date
>
> Add a new taxable Inventory Item. Name: Garden Lights, Initial Quantity on Hand: 25; As of: 12-31-15; Sales and Purchasing information: Garden Lights; Sales price/rate: 75; Cost: 25. Is taxable: √.

_DRILL_

Open the **Test Drive Company** and add a new Product

> Click the **Gear** icon, click **Products and Services** in the Lists column
> Click the **New** button

Click **Inventory item**
Enter the information for the new item:
- If a field is not listed below, it does not need to be changed or completed.
  Name: **Garden Lights**
  Initial quantity on hand: **25**
  As of date: **12/31/15**
  Sales information: **Garden Lights**
  Sales price/rate: **75**
  Purchasing information: **Garden Lights**
  Cost: **25**
- Make sure "Is taxable" is checked.
Click **Save and close**
- Garden Lights is now shown as an inventory item.

| NAME ▲ | SKU | TYPE | SALES DESCRIPTION | INCOME ACCOUNT | SALES PRICE | COST | TAXABLE | QUANTITY | ACTION |
|--------|-----|------|-------------------|----------------|-------------|------|---------|----------|--------|
| Garden Lights | | Inventory item | Garden Lights | Sales of Product Income | 75 | 25 | ✓ | 25 | Edit ▾ |

Do <u>not</u> close the Test Drive Company, continue to the next section

## RECORD SALES RECEIPTS—DRILL

Not all sales in a business are on account. In many instances, payment is made at the time the merchandise is purchased. This is entered as a cash sale. Payment methods for "cash sales" include cash, debit cards, credit cards, and checks. When entering a cash sale, you prepare a Sales Receipt rather than an Invoice. QuickBooks records the transaction in the Journal and places the amount of payment received in an account called *Undeposited Funds*. The payments received remain in Undeposited Funds until you record a deposit to your bank account. As with sales on account, sales tax is collected for products sold.

<u>MEMO</u>
**DATE:** Current Date

Record a sale to Red Rock Diner for 15 Garden Lights and 3 hours of Landscaping: Installation, paid with Visa number 4532-7253-2209-0557, Expiration date: 07/2021. Sales Tax: California (8%).

<u>*DRILL*</u>

Continue to use the <u>**Test Drive Company**</u> to record Sales Receipts

Click the **Plus** icon, click **Sales Receipt** in the Customers column
Complete the Sales Receipt using the information provided
Customer: **Red Rock Diner**
Sales Receipt date: **Current Date**
Payment method: **Visa**
Click the **Enter credit card details** button
Enter the Credit card number **4532-7253-2209-0557**
Click the drop-down list arrow for Expiration Date Month, click **07**
Click the drop-down list arrow for Year, click **2021**
- Use this credit card in the future for this customer: should be selected.

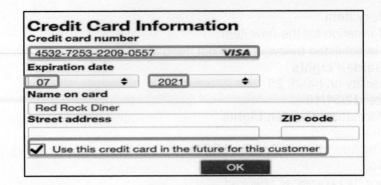

Click **OK**

Complete the Sales Receipt using the information provided in the Memo

- In the customer address, the city of Bayshore is underlined in red. This means that QuickBooks Online thinks that the word is misspelled. If Bayshore is not underlined on your screen, simply read the following steps; then complete the Sales Receipt.

Click in **Bayshore**, right-click **Bayshore** to get the pop up menu

Click **Add to dictionary**

- This will add the word to QuickBooks Online dictionary and it will not be highlighted as misspelled again.

View the completed Sales Receipt

- The Payment method is Visa, below that you see Visa: xxx-0557 for the credit card number. For security reasons, once a credit card number is entered, it is never shown in full again.

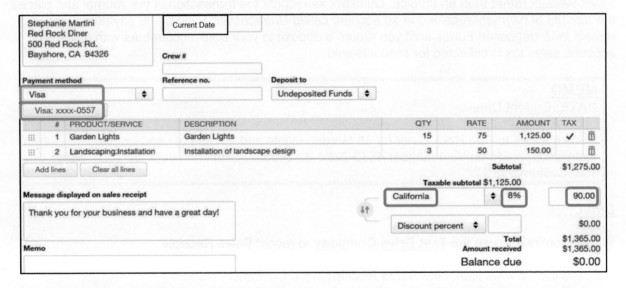

Click **Save and close**

Close the Test Drive Company

## ADD NEW PRODUCTS—DO

New products and services may be added to the company at any time. If you add a new product, typically you place an order for it right after it is added. In Chapter 6, you will add a product and enter an initial quantity on had so that you can sell the new item. In Chapter 7, you will purchase inventory items by preparing Purchase Orders.

If a mistake is made when adding an inventory item, QuickBooks Online allows you to adjust the starting value for it. To make the correction, prepare an Inventory Valuation Detail report, find the line for the item with "Inventory Starting Value" in the Transaction Type column and click it. Make the appropriate changes. An example of when to use this feature would be if you entered an incorrect quantity, as of date, or cost of the inventory item when you first added the inventory item and included a quantity. If you needed to change any of the accounts used or the quantity on hand for anything except the initial starting value, you would edit the item in the Products/Services List. (Both types of corrections will be explored in detail in Chapter 8.)

---

**MEMO**
**DATE:** February 3, 2016

Add two new taxable Inventory Items:

Name: Dog Snacks; Initial Quantity on Hand: 200; As of: 12-31-15; Sales and Purchasing information: Dog Snacks; Sales price/rate: 5; Cost: 1. Is taxable: √.

Name: Dog Bed; Initial Quantity on Hand: 5; As of 12-31-15; Sales and Purchasing information: Dog Bed; Sales price/rate: 65; Cost: 20. Is taxable: √.

---

<u>*DO*</u>

Open **Your Name's Beach Barkers** and add two new inventory items

    Click the **Gear** icon, click **Products and Services** in the Lists column
    Click the **New** button
    Click **Inventory item**
    Enter the information provided in the Memo to enter Dog Snacks
    When finished, click **Save and new**
    If you get a "Closing date" message, click **Yes**
    Use the information in the Memo to add Dog Bed
    Click **Save and close**

| NAME ▲ | | SKU | TYPE | SALES DESCRIPTION | INCOME ACCOUNT | SALES PRICE | COST | TAXABLE | QUANTITY |
|---|---|---|---|---|---|---|---|---|---|
| | **Dog Bed** | | Inventory item | Dog Bed | Sales of Product Income | 65 | 20 | ✓ | 5 |
| | **Dog Snacks** | | Inventory item | Dog Snacks | Sales of Product Income | 5 | 1 | ✓ | 200 |

    Do <u>not</u> close Your Name's Beach Barkers, continue with the next section

## RECORD SALES RECEIPTS—DO

As you just practiced, when merchandise is purchased and paid for at the same time, a sales receipt is prepared to record the transaction as a cash sale. Payment methods have been established for Your Name's Beach Barkers and include cash, debit cards, MasterCard, Visa, and checks. As with sales on account, sales tax is collected for products sold.

---

**MEMO**
**DATE:** February 4, 2016

Record Sales Receipts for the following Cash Sales:

Nick Wagner brought his dog, Lucky, to the Malibu location. He used his MasterCard: 5299-7935-6678-7338, Expiration: 10/2020 to pay for: 10 Day Camp, 1 Ten One-Hour Training Sessions, 1 Leash $25, 1 Collar $25, 14 Dog Food-Canned $5 each, 2 Dog Food-Dry $12.50 each, 1 Vitamins $15; 10 Dog Snacks.

Cash Customer, brought her dog, Coco, to the Venice location. Used Check 1983 to pay for: 1 Day Camp, 1 Bath, 1 Nails, 14 Dog Food-Canned $5, 1 Dog Food-Dry $12.50, 1 Vitamins $15, 10 Dog Snacks.

Katie Wilson brought her dog, Suzy, to the Venice location. She used her Visa: 4175-7880-3245-7211, Expiration: 12/2023 (Address: 4157 Via Marina, # 3; Zip Code: 90202) to pay for: 5 Boarding, 5 Coat Brushing, 1 Bath, 1 Nails, 1 Sweater $30, 2 Toys $10 each.

David De Los Santos brought his dog, Joe, to the Malibu location. He used his Debit Card to purchase 1 Dog Bed, 3 Dog Snacks, 7 Dog Food-Canned $4.50 each, 1 Dog Food-Dry $18, and 1 Vitamins $20.

---

_DO_

Open **Your Name's Beach Barkers** and record Sales Receipts

> Open **Sales Receipts** as previously instructed
> Name: **Nick Wagner**
> Sales Receipt Date: **02/04/16**
> Deposit to account: **Undeposited Funds**
> Location: **Malibu**
> Payment method: **MasterCard**
> Enter Credit Card Details:
> > Credit card number: **5299-7935-6678-7338**
> > Expiration Month: **10** Year: **2020**
> > Name on Card: **Nick Wagner**
> > Address: **23509 Palm Canyon Lane**
> > Zip code: **90265**
> > Use this credit card in the future for this customer: should have a check mark
> Click **OK**

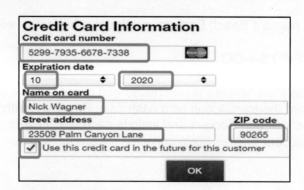

> Complete the Sales Receipt for Nick using the information provided in the Memo
> Deposit to: **Undeposited Funds**
> Location: **Malibu**
> Classes: **Dog Care** or **Boutique**

- Determine which class to use for each item. Remember, if the item has a check in the TAX Column, the Class is Boutique.

Add Sales tax: **California (8%)**

- QuickBooks Online will use the Taxable subtotal in the calculation of the amount of sales tax.

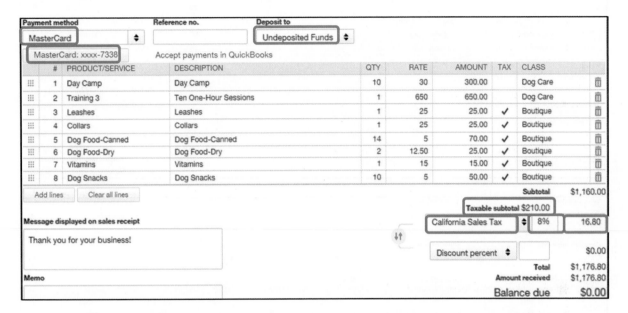

| Payment method | | Reference no. | | Deposit to | | | | |
|---|---|---|---|---|---|---|---|---|
| MasterCard | ⬍ | | | Undeposited Funds ⬍ | | | | |
| MasterCard: xxxx-7338 | | Accept payments in QuickBooks | | | | | | |

| # | PRODUCT/SERVICE | DESCRIPTION | QTY | RATE | AMOUNT | TAX | CLASS | |
|---|---|---|---|---|---|---|---|---|
| 1 | Day Camp | Day Camp | 10 | 30 | 300.00 | | Dog Care | 🗑 |
| 2 | Training 3 | Ten One-Hour Sessions | 1 | 650 | 650.00 | | Dog Care | 🗑 |
| 3 | Leashes | Leashes | 1 | 25 | 25.00 | ✓ | Boutique | 🗑 |
| 4 | Collars | Collars | 1 | 25 | 25.00 | ✓ | Boutique | 🗑 |
| 5 | Dog Food-Canned | Dog Food-Canned | 14 | 5 | 70.00 | ✓ | Boutique | 🗑 |
| 6 | Dog Food-Dry | Dog Food-Dry | 2 | 12.50 | 25.00 | ✓ | Boutique | 🗑 |
| 7 | Vitamins | Vitamins | 1 | 15 | 15.00 | ✓ | Boutique | 🗑 |
| 8 | Dog Snacks | Dog Snacks | 10 | 5 | 50.00 | ✓ | Boutique | 🗑 |

Add lines     Clear all lines

Subtotal $1,160.00

Taxable subtotal $210.00

**Message displayed on sales receipt**

Thank you for your business!

| California Sales Tax ⬍ | 8% | 16.80 |
|---|---|---|

Discount percent ⬍       $0.00

Total $1,176.80

Amount received $1,176.80

**Memo**

Balance due $0.00

Print and/or send the Sales Receipt as previously instructed

- If you save the Sales Receipt, name it: **13-Your Name Sales Receipt 1046 Nick Wagner**.

Click **Save and new**

Enter the three other Sales Receipts using the information provided in the Memo

Sales Receipt Date: **02/04/16**

Deposit to account for all sales receipts: **Undeposited Funds**

Location: Use the one provided in the Memo

- If location is not specified, look at the address to determine which location to select.

Use Classes: Dog Care or Boutique

- Determine which class to use for each item. Remember, if there is a check in the TAX Column, the Class is Boutique. The Class for Service items is Dog Care and no tax is charged.

Add Sales tax: **California (8%)**

- The item Brushing was changed to Coat Brushing in Chapter 3. Did you change the name? If not, change it now.
- Since we are treating Debit Cards the same as checks or cash, we will not be entering the Debit Card number or expiration date.

Print and/or send the Sales Receipts as previously instructed

- If you save the Sales Receipts, name them: **14-Your Name Sales Receipt 1047 Cash Customer**; **15-Your Name Sales Receipt 1048 Katie Wilson**, and **16-Your Name Sales Receipt 1049 David De Los Santos**.

Click **Save and new** to go to the next Sales Receipt

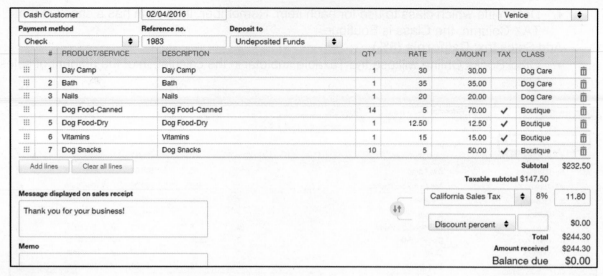

| # | PRODUCT/SERVICE | DESCRIPTION | QTY | RATE | AMOUNT | TAX | CLASS | |
|---|-----------------|-------------|-----|------|--------|-----|-------|---|
| 1 | Day Camp | Day Camp | 1 | 30 | 30.00 | | Dog Care | |
| 2 | Bath | Bath | 1 | 35 | 35.00 | | Dog Care | |
| 3 | Nails | Nails | 1 | 20 | 20.00 | | Dog Care | |
| 4 | Dog Food-Canned | Dog Food-Canned | 14 | 5 | 70.00 | ✓ | Boutique | |
| 5 | Dog Food-Dry | Dog Food-Dry | 1 | 12.50 | 12.50 | ✓ | Boutique | |
| 6 | Vitamins | Vitamins | 1 | 15 | 15.00 | ✓ | Boutique | |
| 7 | Dog Snacks | Dog Snacks | 10 | 5 | 50.00 | ✓ | Boutique | |

Cash Customer   02/04/2016   Venice
Payment method: Check   Reference no.: 1983   Deposit to: Undeposited Funds

Subtotal $232.50
Taxable subtotal $147.50

Message displayed on sales receipt
Thank you for your business!

California Sales Tax 8% 11.80
Discount percent $0.00
Total $244.30
Amount received $244.30
Balance due $0.00

Memo

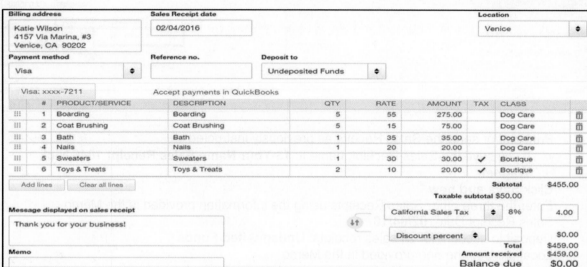

**Billing address**
Katie Wilson
4157 Via Marina, #3
Venice, CA 90202

**Sales Receipt date**
02/04/2016

**Location**
Venice

Payment method: Visa   Reference no.:   Deposit to: Undeposited Funds

Visa: xxxx-7211   Accept payments in QuickBooks

| # | PRODUCT/SERVICE | DESCRIPTION | QTY | RATE | AMOUNT | TAX | CLASS | |
|---|-----------------|-------------|-----|------|--------|-----|-------|---|
| 1 | Boarding | Boarding | 5 | 55 | 275.00 | | Dog Care | |
| 2 | Coat Brushing | Coat Brushing | 5 | 15 | 75.00 | | Dog Care | |
| 3 | Bath | Bath | 1 | 35 | 35.00 | | Dog Care | |
| 4 | Nails | Nails | 1 | 20 | 20.00 | | Dog Care | |
| 5 | Sweaters | Sweaters | 1 | 30 | 30.00 | ✓ | Boutique | |
| 6 | Toys & Treats | Toys & Treats | 2 | 10 | 20.00 | ✓ | Boutique | |

Subtotal $455.00
Taxable subtotal $50.00

Message displayed on sales receipt
Thank you for your business!

California Sales Tax 8% 4.00
Discount percent $0.00
Total $459.00
Amount received $459.00
Balance due $0.00

Memo

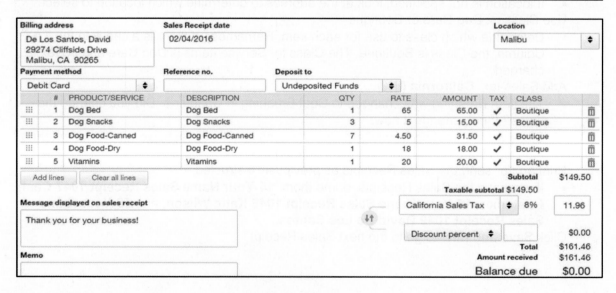

**Billing address**
De Los Santos, David
29274 Cliffside Drive
Malibu, CA 90265

**Sales Receipt date**
02/04/2016

**Location**
Malibu

Payment method: Debit Card   Reference no.:   Deposit to: Undeposited Funds

| # | PRODUCT/SERVICE | DESCRIPTION | QTY | RATE | AMOUNT | TAX | CLASS | |
|---|-----------------|-------------|-----|------|--------|-----|-------|---|
| 1 | Dog Bed | Dog Bed | 1 | 65 | 65.00 | ✓ | Boutique | |
| 2 | Dog Snacks | Dog Snacks | 3 | 5 | 15.00 | ✓ | Boutique | |
| 3 | Dog Food-Canned | Dog Food-Canned | 7 | 4.50 | 31.50 | ✓ | Boutique | |
| 4 | Dog Food-Dry | Dog Food-Dry | 1 | 18 | 18.00 | ✓ | Boutique | |
| 5 | Vitamins | Vitamins | 1 | 20 | 20.00 | ✓ | Boutique | |

Subtotal $149.50
Taxable subtotal $149.50

Message displayed on sales receipt
Thank you for your business!

California Sales Tax 8% 11.96
Discount percent $0.00
Total $161.46
Amount received $161.46
Balance due $0.00

Memo

After the last Sales Receipt, click **Save and close**
Do <u>not</u> close Your Name's Beach Barkers

## RECORD REFUND RECEIPT—DO

Once a customer has paid for an item and it is returned, a Refund Receipt is prepared to record the return and to refund the payment. If the customer used a credit card to pay for the item, the refund is made to the credit card.

> <u>MEMO</u>
>
> **DATE:** February 7, 2016
>
> Sales Receipt 1048 for Katie Wilson included 2 Dog Toys for $10 each. One of the toys was damaged so Katie returned it for a refund. Prepare a Refund Receipt for the <u>1 Dog Toy</u>. Payment Method: Visa, Location: Venice.

<u>DO</u>

Use **Your Name's Beach Barkers** to prepare a refund receipt

Click the **Plus** icon, click **Refund Receipt** in the Customers column
Name: **Katie Wilson**
Refund Receipt Date: **02/07/2016**
Location: **Venice**
Payment method: **Visa**
Refund From: **Undeposited Funds**
- You have not made a bank deposit since receiving the payment from Katie so the account to use is Undeposited Funds. Had the bank deposit been made, the account to use would be Checking.
- The Visa number and other information was recalled automatically by QuickBooks Online.

Enter the information in the Memo for the return of 1 Toy
Sales Tax: **California Sales Tax (8%)**

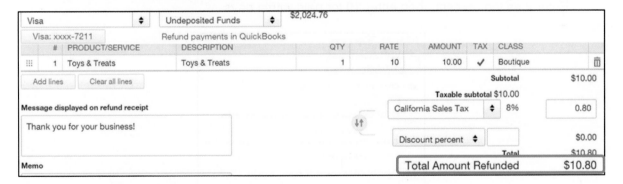

Click **Save and close**
Click **OK** on the "Refund successfully issued" screen
Close Your Name's Beach Barkers

## DISCOUNTS—READ

There are three types of discounts that may be recorded in business transactions: Sales Discount, Merchandise Discount, and Purchase Discount.

**Sales Discount**: Used when you give customers a discount for early payment. Typical terms for early payments are a 1% or 2% discount if paid within 10 days. Sales Discount is categorized as an Income account. Using a sales discount results in a decrease in income because the company will receive less money for a sale. Recording sales discounts is included in this chapter.

**Merchandise Discount**: A discount on inventory sales items purchased for resale. This discount is categorized as a Cost of Goods Sold account because the use of this discount results in a decrease in the amount you pay for the goods (merchandise) you sell. This is used in Chapter 7 for payments for sales items purchased.

**Purchase Discount**: A discount for early payment for purchases made to run the business. Example, a discount on office supplies purchased. A purchase discount is categorized as an Income account because it results in an increase in income since it costs you less to run the business. This is also used in Chapter 7 for payments on purchases made to run the business.

## ADD NEW SALES TERMS—DRILL

When giving a sales discount to a customer, the transaction terms should indicate that a discount is available if paid early. Currently, the Test Drive Company does not have discount terms in the Terms List so the 2% 10 Net 30 Term needs to be added.

*DRILL*

Open the **Test Drive Company** and add discount terms

Click the **Gear** icon, click **All Lists**, click **Terms**
- As you look at the terms list, there are terms for Net 10, 15, 30, 60, and Due on receipt.
Click the **New** button
Enter **2% 10 Net 30** as the name for the New Term
For Due in fixed number of days, enter **30**
Click the check box for **Apply discount if paid early**
Enter **2** as the percent, then enter **10** for paid within days

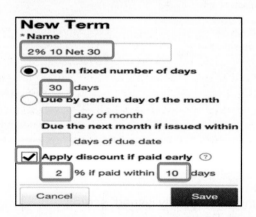

Click **Save**
- If you want 2% 10 Net 30 as the terms for a customer, you would need to go to the customer's account, access the Payment and billing section of the account, and add the Terms. You may also use the 2% 10 Net 30 terms directly on an invoice without adding it to the customer's account.
Open the Customers List, click **Travis Waldron**, click **Edit**
Click the **Payment and billing** tab

Click the drop-down list arrow for Terms, click **2% 10 Net 30**
Click **Save**
Do not close the account register for Travis Waldron
Do <u>not</u> close the Test Drive Company continue to the next section

## RECORD SALES DISCOUNT—DRILL

When recording a sales discount, you return to the customer's invoice and enter the Discount percent at the bottom of the invoice. This is done no matter what Terms you have entered for the invoice. In addition, you will need to select whether or not to apply the discount before or after sales tax is calculated. The appropriate time to record sales discounts is when you receive payment from the customer. If payment is received within ten days after the invoice date and the customer is eligible to receive a discount, you enter the discount percentage on the invoice and then record the payment receipt. It is appropriate to record the discount at the time the payment is received. Therefore, once the discount is recorded, click Save on the invoice, then click Receive payment.

### *DRILL*

 Continue to use the **<u>Test Drive Company</u>** and add a sales discount to an invoice

With the Account Register for Travis Waldron on the screen, click **Invoice 1032**
- Even though you added new terms to his account, the terms used when the invoice was prepared are shown. New invoices will include his new terms of 2% 10 Net 30 but existing invoices will not.

Click the drop-down list arrow for Terms; click **2% 10 Net 30**
For the Discount percent, enter **2**, press **Tab**
- Note that the discount percent is $-7.68 and the Sales tax is $30.72 and the Balance due is $407.04.

Click the light blue circle with the up and down arrows by Sales tax and Discount percent

- The Discount percent text box will appear before California Sales tax. This means that the taxes will be calculated based on the Taxable subtotal <u>after</u> the 2 percent discount is applied. The discount stays at $-7.68; however, the sales tax changes to $30.11 and the Balance due is $406.43.

Click the **Save** button to save the invoice with the 2 percent discount applied before sales taxes are calculated
Do <u>not</u> close the invoice or the Test Drive Company, continue to the next section

## RECEIVE PAYMENTS—DRILL

When you received payments for an invoice, you prepare a Receive Payment form. You may access this form using the Plus icon or from within an invoice. Remember, though, any sales discounts must be entered on the original invoice before recording receive payments.

### *DRILL*

 Continue to use the **<u>Test Drive Company</u>** to record the payment received from Travis Waldron

With Invoice 1032 showing on the screen, click the **Receive payment** button at the top of the invoice

Enter a Payment date that is 10 days after the date of the invoice

- For example, at the time of this writing, the Invoice date was 02/02/16 so the Payment date entered will be 02/12/16.

Click the drop-down list arrow for Payment method, and click **MasterCard**

Click the **Enter credit card details** button

Enter the Cred card number **5152-0967-1708-2500**

Click the drop-down list arrow for Expiration date Month, click **06**

Click the drop-down list arrow for Expiration date Year, click **2019**

- Name on card should show Travis Waldron.

Click **OK**

- Invoice 1032 was marked by QuickBooks Online and the amount of payment is the same that was calculated on the invoice.

Click **Save and close**

Close the Test Drive Company

## ADD NEW SALES TERMS—DO

Currently, Your Name's Beach Barkers has only one Sales Term of Net 30. As you learned in the drill, if the customer qualifies for an early payment discount, the transaction terms should indicate that a discount is available for early payment.

*DO*

Open **Your Name's Beach Barkers** and add discount terms

Click the **Gear** icon, click **All Lists**, click **Terms**

Click the **New** button

Enter **2% 10 Net 30** as the name for the New Term

For Due in fixed number of days, enter **30**

Click the check box for **Apply discount if paid early**

Enter **2** as the percent, then enter **10** for paid within days

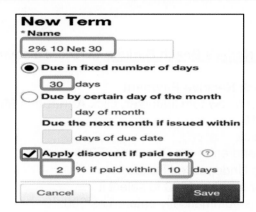

Click **Save**

- If you want 2% 10 Net 30 as the terms for a customer, you would need to go to the customer's account and add it to Terms in the Payment and billing section of the account. You may also use the 2% 10 Net 30 terms directly on an invoice without adding it to the customer's account.

Do <u>not</u> close Your Name's Beach Barkers

## CHANGE CUSTOMER TERMS—DO

To encourage early payment, several of Your Name's Beach Barkers customers should be assigned terms of 2% 10 Net 30 rather than Net 30.

> **MEMO**
> **DATE:** February 7, 2016
>
> Change Terms to 2% 10 Net 30 for the following customers: Keith Evans, Tracy McCarter, and Monroe Miller.

_DO_

Continue to use **Your Name's Beach Barkers** and add discount terms to customer accounts

Open the Customers List, click **Keith Evans**, click **Edit**
Click the **Payment and billing** tab
Click the drop-down list arrow for Terms, click **2% 10 Net 30**
Click **Save**
Repeat the procedure to add Terms of 2% 10 Net 30 to Tracy McCarter and Monroe Miller
Do <u>not</u> close Your Name's Beach Barkers continue to the next section

## RECEIVE PAYMENTS WITHOUT DISCOUNTS—DO

When you receive a payment from a customer who does not qualify for a discount, you may access the invoice and click Receive payment or you may open the Receive payments form.

> **MEMO**
> **DATE:** February 7, 2016
>
> Received Check 7925 from Annabelle Montez in full payment of Invoice 1023.

6

_DO_

 Continue to use **Your Name's Beach Barkers** to record a payment receipt

Click the **Plus** icon, click **Receive Payment**
Click the drop-down list arrow for Customer, click **Annabelle Montez**
Payment date: **02/07/16**
Payment method: **Check**
Tab to Reference no. and enter the Check no. **7925**
- Deposit to remains Undeposited Funds.
Click the check box for **Invoice 1023** to select it
The Amount received is automatically entered as $80.00
- Note that the Original Amount for the invoice was $180.00. In Chapter 3, Annabelle made a partial payment of $100.00. The $80 shown as the Open Balance is the remaining amount due for the invoice.

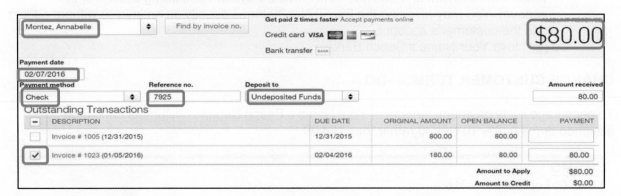

Click **Save and close**
Do _not_ close Your Name's Beach Barkers

## RECORD SALES DISCOUNT AND RECEIVE PAYMENTS—DO

When recording a sales discount, you need to open the customer's invoice and enter the Discount percent at the bottom. This is done no matter what Terms you have entered for the invoice. In addition, you will need to select whether or not to apply the discount before or after sales tax is calculated. If payment is received within the allotted number of days after the invoice date and the customer is eligible to receive a discount, you enter the discount percentage on the invoice and then record the payment receipt. After the discount has been entered, click Save on the invoice. Then, click the Receive payment button at the top of the invoice to record the payment.

---

**MEMO**
**DATE:** February 9, 2016

Received payments from customers qualifying for early payment sales discounts:

Keith Evans paid Invoice 1045 within ten days. Record the discount and the payment he made for $153.47 using his Debit Card.

Tracy McCarter paid Invoice 1042 within ten days. Record the discount and the payment made for $783.41 using her MasterCard No. 5325-4261-2032-5083, Expiration: 02/2018.

Monroe Miller paid Invoice 1040 within ten days. Record the before sales tax discount and the payment made for Invoice 1040 for $104.87 with his MasterCard that is on file.

---

*DO*

> Continue to use **Your Name's Beach Barkers** and add sales discounts to invoices and record payment receipts

Open the Customer Account Register for Keith Evans
Click **Invoice 1045**
- Even though you added new terms to his account, the terms used when the invoice was prepared are shown. New invoices will include his new terms of 2% 10 Net 30 but existing invoices will not.

Click the drop-down list arrow for Terms; click **2% 10 Net 30**
For the Discount percent, enter **2**, press **Tab**
- Note that the discount percent is $-2.90 and the Sales tax is $11.60 and the Balance due is $153.70.

Click the light blue circle with the up and down arrows by Sales tax and Discount percent

- The Discount percent text box will appear before California Sales tax. This means that the taxes will be calculated based on the Taxable subtotal <u>after</u> the 2 percent discount is applied. The discount stays at $-2.90; however, the sales tax changes to $11.37 and the Balance due is $153.47.

Click the **Save** button to save the invoice with the 2 percent discount applied before sales taxes are calculated
- If you get a message that this transaction is linked to others, click **Yes**.

With Invoice 1045 showing on the screen, click the **Receive payment** button at the top of the invoice
Payment date **02/09/16**
Click the drop-down list arrow for Payment method, and click **Debit Card**
- The Debit Card information should appear automatically because it was added to his account.
- Verify that the total amount received is $153.47 and that Invoice 1045 was selected.

Click **Save and close** on Receive Payment and on Invoice 1045
Access **Invoice 1042** for Tracy McCarter
Enter the Terms of **2% 10 Net 30**
Enter **2** for the discount percentage, press **Tab**
Click the icon to make Discount percent before California Sales Tax
Click **Save**
Click **Receive payment**
Payment date: **02/09/16**
Payment method: **MasterCard**
Enter credit card details:
    Credit card number: **5325-4261-2032-5083**
    Expiration: **02/2018**
    Name on card: **Tracy McCarter**
    Street address:**27768 California 1**
    ZIP code: **90265**
    Leave the check mark for Use this credit card in the future for this customer
Click **OK**
- The Amount Received should be $783.41

Click **Save and close** for Receive Payment and for Invoice 1042

Access **Invoice 1040** for Monroe Miller

Change the Terms to **2%10 Net 30**, add the Discount percent **2**, make Discount percent <u>before</u> California Sales Tax

Click **Save**

Click **Yes** on the linked transaction message

- Notice that just below the Receive payment button, there is a message that "1 payment made on 02/03/16. That was for the return of the sweater earlier in the chapter.
- If for some reason you see the current date for the payment, change the date as follows: Click **1 payment**

  Click the current date

  Change the date on the Receive Payment screen to **02/03/16**, press **Tab**

  Click **Save and close** on the Receive Payment screen for the Credit Memo

  Click **Yes** on The transaction you are editing is linked… screen
- You are returned to Invoice 1040 for Monroe Miller.

Click the **Receive payment** button on Invoice 1040

Make sure the Payment date is **02/09/16**

- MasterCard was automatically used for the Payment method. The number on file was inserted, and Invoice 1040 was marked to receive the payment.

Click **Save and close** for Receive Payment and Invoice 1040

Do <u>not</u> close Your Name's Beach Barkers

## RECORD BANK DEPOSIT—DO

Just as you did in Chapter 3, you will record a bank deposit to transfer the payment amounts received from customers out of Undeposited Funds and into Checking.

<u>**DO**</u>

Continue to use **Your Name's Beach Barkers** and record a bank deposit

Click the **Plus** icon

Click **Bank Deposit** in the Other column

- The account should be Checking; if not, select it from the drop-down list.

Enter the Date: **02/09/16**, press **Tab**

- Show payments for this location should be All Locations.

For Select Existing Payments, click the check box next to RECEIVED FROM

- This will insert check marks and select all of the transactions shown.
- The deposit contains all of the payments that were made using cash, checks, debit cards, and Visa and MasterCard credit cards.

Click **Print** at the bottom of the Deposit screen

Click **Print deposit summary only**

- The Deposit Summary may be saved as a pdf file and/or printed. It cannot be exported.
- Note the dates displayed on the preview. On the left side of the report, you will see "Summary of Deposits to Checking on 02/09/2016." On the right side of the report, you will see the current date. This is an instance where QuickBooks Online inserts the current date and you cannot remove it.
- If you save the Deposit Summary, name it **17-Your Name Bank Deposit Ch. 6**.

## Deposit Summary

| | | | | Current Date |
|---|---|---|---|---|

Summary of Deposits to Checking on 02/09/2016

| CHECK NO. | PMT METHOD | RECEIVED FROM | MEMO | AMOUNT |
|---|---|---|---|---|
| | MasterCard | Wagner, Nick | | 1176.80 |
| 1983 | Check | Cash Customer | | 244.30 |
| | Visa | Wilson, Katie | | 459.00 |
| | Debit Card | De Los Santos, David | | 161.46 |
| 1050 | Visa | Wilson, Katie | | -10.80 |
| 7925 | Check | Montez, Annabelle | | 80.00 |
| | Debit Card | Evans, Keith | | 153.47 |
| | MasterCard | McCarter, Tracy | | 783.41 |
| | MasterCard | Miller, Monroe | | 104.87 |
| | | | DEPOSIT SUBTOTAL | 3152.51 |
| | | | LESS CASH BACK | |
| | | | DEPOSIT TOTAL | 3152.51 |

Click **Save and close** on the Deposit screen
Close Your Name's Beach Barkers

## RECORD NSF CHECK—DRILL

A *nonsufficient funds* (*NSF* or *bounced*) check is one that cannot be processed by the bank because there are insufficient funds in the customer's bank account to pay the check. If this occurs, the amount of the check and the associated bank charges need to be subtracted from the account where the check was deposited. Also, the Accounts Receivable account needs to be updated to show the amount the customer owes you for the check that "bounced." In order to track the amount of a bad check and to charge a customer for the bank charges and any penalties you impose, other items may need to be created and an invoice for the amount due for the bank charges must be prepared.

Money received for the bad check charges from the bank and for the Test Drive Company is recorded as income. When the bank account is reconciled, the amount of bank charges will offset the income recorded on the invoice.

Nonsufficient funds, NSF, and bounced check are all used synonymously when referring to a check that does not clear because there was not enough money in the bank account to pay it.

> <u>MEMO</u>
> **DATE:** Current Date
>
> Bill's Windsurf Shop's Check 1053 came back from the bank marked NSF. Record the Bounced Check and the $35 fee that Craig's Design and Landscaping Services charges for an NSF check.

*DRILL*

 Open and use the **Test Drive Company** and record a Nonsufficient Funds (NSF/Bounced) Check and the related charges

<u>Enter New Item for Bounced Check Charges</u>

 Use the **Test Drive Company** and enter new Items that will be used for Bounced Check Charges

Open the Chart of Accounts in the Test Drive Company
Scroll until you get to **Fees Billed**, click the drop-down list arrow for Action, click **Edit**

Change the Category Type to **Other Income**
Change the Detail Type to **Other Miscellaneous Income**
- When you earn income that isn't from normal business operations, such as fees billed for NSF charges, Other Miscellaneous Income should be used to record the income.

Click **Save and Close**
- If you get a warning screen, click **Yes**.

Click the **Gear** icon
Click **Products and Services** in the Lists column
Click the **New** button
- You will be billing Bill's Windsurf Shop for the amount of the bank's NSF service charge plus the $15 you charge for NSF check processing. You will record the total amount as income. When you get your bank statement, you will mark the NSF service charge as Bank Charges, which will offset the amount of income received for Bounced Check Charges.

Click **Service** for the type of item
Enter the information for the new item:
    Name: **Bounced Check Charges**
    Sales information: **Bounced Check Charges**
    Income account: **Fees Billed**
    Click the check box for "Is taxable" to remove the check mark
Click **Save and close**

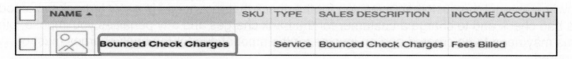

| | NAME ▲ | SKU | TYPE | SALES DESCRIPTION | INCOME ACCOUNT |
|---|---|---|---|---|---|
| | Bounced Check Charges | | Service | Bounced Check Charges | Fees Billed |

Do <u>not</u> close the Test Drive Company, continue with the next step

## Record Journal Entry for Bounced Check

 Use the **Test Drive Company** to record the Journal Entry for a Bounced Check

Click the **Plus** icon, click **Journal Entry** in the Other column
Use the **Current Date**
Line 1: Account: **Accounts Receivable**, Debits: **175**, Description: **Bounced Check**, Name: **Bill's Windsurf Shop**
- This part of the Journal entry puts the $175 from the Bounced Check back into Accounts Receivable. Entering the customer's name, matches the amount of the bounced check with the customer who still owes you $175 because of the NSF check.

Line 2: Account: **Checking**, Credits: **175**, Description: **Bounced Check**
- This part of the transaction removes the $175 that was deposited into the checking account.

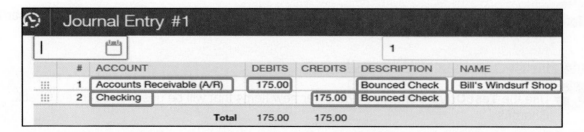

| # | ACCOUNT | DEBITS | CREDITS | DESCRIPTION | NAME |
|---|---|---|---|---|---|
| 1 | Accounts Receivable (A/R) | 175.00 | | Bounced Check | Bill's Windsurf Shop |
| 2 | Checking | | 175.00 | Bounced Check | |
| | Total | 175.00 | 175.00 | | |

Click **Save and close**

If you receive the message regarding "The transaction you are editing is linked to others.",
   click **Yes**
Do not close the Test Drive Company, continue with the next step

## Apply Journal Entry for Bounced Check

 Continue to use the **Test Drive Company** to apply the Journal Entry for a Bounced Check

Access Bill's Windsurf Shop's account register from the Customers List
In the Transaction section, click the **Payment 1053** to open Receive Payment
Click the check box for **Invoice 1002** to remove the check mark
Click the check box for **Journal Entry 1** to enter a check mark
- This removes the $175 payment for Invoice 1002 and applies it to Journal Entry 1.
- Invoice 1002 now shows that it has not been paid.
- Remember that the dates shown in the transaction below will not match the dates you see on your screen.

| Bill's Windsurf Shop ⬍ | | | | | $175.00 |
|---|---|---|---|---|---|
| **Payment date** | | | | | |
| 11/11/2015 | | | | | |
| **Payment method** | | **Reference no.** | **Deposit to** | | **Amount received** |
| Check ⬍ | | 1053 | Checking ⬍ | | 175.00 |

**Outstanding Transactions**

| | DESCRIPTION | DUE DATE | ORIGINAL AMOUNT | OPEN BALANCE | PAYMENT |
|---|---|---|---|---|---|
| ☐ | Invoice # 1002 (10/21/2015) | 11/20/2015 | 175.00 | 175.00 | |
| ☐ | Invoice # 1027 (12/19/2015) | 01/18/2016 | 85.00 | 85.00 | |
| ☑ | Journal Entry # 1 (03/02/2016) | 03/02/2016 | 175.00 | 175.00 | 175.00 |
| ☐ | Invoice # 1039 (03/02/2016) | 03/02/2016 | 35.00 | 35.00 | |
| | | | | Amount to Apply | $175.00 |
| | | | | Amount to Credit | $0.00 |

Click **Save and close**
If you receive the message regarding "The transaction you are editing is linked to others.",
   click **Yes**
Do not close the Test Drive Company, continue with the next step

## Record Invoice for Bounced Check Charges

 Continue to use the **Test Drive Company** to record the Invoice for Bounced Check Charges

Click the **Plus** icon, click **Invoice** in the Customers column
Customer: **Bill's Windsurf Shop**
Terms: **Due on receipt**
Invoice date: **Current date**
Line 1: Product/Service: **Bounced Check Charges**
Description: **Bounced Check Charges**
Qty: **1**
Rate: **35**
- The $35 will cover the bank NSF charge of $20 and will give $15 to Craig's Design and Landscaping Service as income for Fees billed. When the next bank statement arrives, it will show the $20 charge from the bank for the NSF check. This will be put into the Bank Charges expense account. The net result of this will leave $15 as income for Craig's Design and Landscaping Service for processing an NSF check.

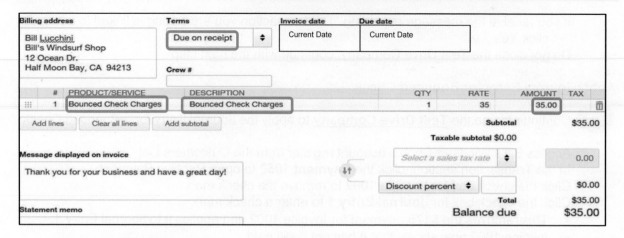

> Click **Save and close**
> Close the Test Drive Company

## RECORD NSF CHECK—DO

As you have just practiced in the drill, recording a *nonsufficient funds* (*NSF* or *bounced*) check requires recording several transactions. First, an income account to use for the fees charged for the NSF check must be selected or added. A Service Item to record Fees Charged for NSF Checks must be created. Then, a Journal Entry must be recorded to add the amount of the bounced check back into Accounts Receivable and remove the amount from Checking. The Journal entry must be selected in Receive Payments for the invoice that was paid with a NSF check. Finally, an invoice must be prepared to charge the customer the fees associated with the bounced check.

> **MEMO**
> **DATE:** February 10, 2016
>
> Check 7925 for $80 from Annabelle Montez was returned as an NSF check. Record the NSF check and the $40 fee that you charge for processing it.

<u>*DO*</u>

 Open and use **Your Name's Beach Barkers** to record a Nonsufficient Funds (NSF/Bounced) Check and the related charges

<u>Enter New Item for NSF Charges</u>

 Use **Your Name's Beach Barkers** and add a new account and a new Service Item that will be used for NSF Charges

> Open the Chart of Accounts
> Scroll through the accounts to see if there is an income account that would be appropriate to
>      use for the fees charged for processing NSF checks
> Since there is not an appropriate account, click **New**
> Add a New Income account:
>      Type: **Other Income**
>      Detail Type: **Other Miscellaneous Income**
>      Name: **Fees Billed**
> Click **Save and Close**

Click the **Gear** icon
Click **Products and Services** in the Lists column
Click the **New** button
- You will be billing Annabelle Montez for the $20 fee the bank charges for an NSF check plus the $20 you charge for NSF check processing. You will record the total amount as Fees Billed in Other Miscellaneous income. When you get your bank statement, you will mark the NSF service charge as Bank Charges, which will offset the amount of income received for Bounced Check Charges.

Click **Service** for the type of item
Enter the information for the new item:
    Name: **NSF Charges**
    Sales information: **NSF Charges**
    Income account: **Fees Billed**
    Click the check box for "Is taxable" to remove the check mark
Click **Save and close**

Do <u>not</u> close Your Name's Beach Barkers, continue with the next step

## Record Journal Entry for NSF Check

 Use **Your Name's Beach Barkers** to record the Journal Entry for an NSF/Bounced Check

Click the **Plus** icon, click **Journal Entry** in the Other column
Date: **02/10/16**
Line 1: Account: **Accounts Receivable**, Debits: **80**, Description: **NSF Check**, Name:
    **Annabelle Montez**
Location: **Venice**
- You do not have a Class for NSF fees so do not include Class in the entry.
- This part of the Journal entry puts the $80 from the Bounced (NSF) Check back into Accounts Receivable. Entering the customer's name, matches the amount of the bounced check with the customer who still owes you $80 because of the NSF check.

Line 2: Account: **Checking**, Credits: **80**, Description: **NSF Check**, Location: **Venice**
- This part of the transaction removes the $80 that was deposited into the checking account.

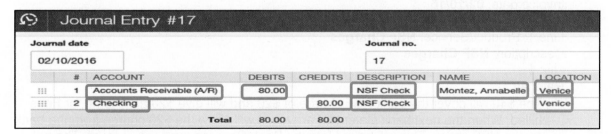

| # | ACCOUNT | DEBITS | CREDITS | DESCRIPTION | NAME | LOCATION |
|---|---|---|---|---|---|---|
| 1 | Accounts Receivable (A/R) | 80.00 | | NSF Check | Montez, Annabelle | Venice |
| 2 | Checking | | 80.00 | NSF Check | | Venice |
| | Total | 80.00 | 80.00 | | | |

Journal Entry #17 — Journal date 02/10/2016 — Journal no. 17

Click **Save and close**
Do <u>not</u> close Your Name's Beach Barkers, continue with the next step

## Apply Journal Entry for NSF Check

 Continue to use **Your Name's Beach Barkers** to apply the Journal Entry for an NSF Check

Access Annabelle Montez's account register from the Customers List
In the Transaction list, click the **Payment 7925** to open Receive Payment
Click the check box for **Invoice 1023** to remove the check mark
Click the check box for **Journal Entry 17** to enter a check mark
- This removes the $80 payment for Invoice 1023 and applies it to Journal Entry 18.
- Invoice 1023 now shows that it has not been paid.

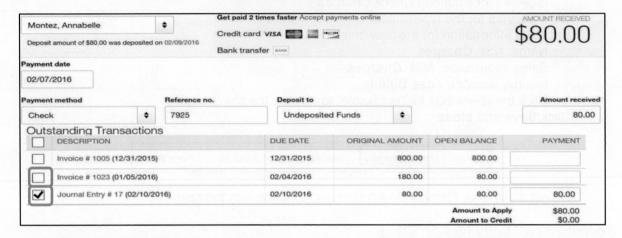

Click **Save and close**
- If you get a message regarding the transaction being linked to others, click **Yes**.
Do <u>not</u> close Your Name's Beach Barkers, continue with the next step

## Record Invoice for Bounced Check Charges

 Continue to use <u>**Your Name's Beach Barkers**</u> to record the Invoice for NSF Charges

Click the **Plus** icon, click **Invoice** in the Customers column
Customer: **Annabelle Montez**
Since you do not have a Due on Receipt Term, click the drop-down list arrow for Terms
Click **+Add new**
   Name: **Due on receipt**
   For due in fixed number of days, click **0**
   Click **Save**
Invoice date: **02/10/16**
Location: **Venice**
Line 1: Product/Service: **NSF Charges**
Description: **NSF Charges**
Qty: **1**
Rate: **40**
- The $40 will cover the bank NSF charge of $20 and will give $20 as income for Fees billed. When the next bank statement arrives, it will show the $20 charge from the bank for the NSF check. This will be put into the Bank Charges expense account. The net result of this will leave $20 as income for Your Name's Beach Barkers for processing an NSF check.

Print and/or send the invoice as previously instructed
- If you save the invoice, name it **18-Your Name Invoice 1051 Annabelle Montez**.
Click **Save and close**
Do <u>not</u> close Your Name's Beach Barkers

## CUSTOMER BALANCE DETAIL

The Customer Balance Detail Report lists unpaid invoices for each customer. The information provided includes the customer name, all invoices with a balance, the invoice date, the invoice number, the amount of each invoice, the open balance (unpaid amount) for each invoice, and the total balance due from each customer.

## <u>DO</u>

Continue to use **Your Name's Beach Barkers** and prepare the Customer Balance Detail report

Access the **Manage Accounts Receivable** category in All Reports
Click **Customer Balance Detail**
Click the **Customize** button and remove the **Date Prepared** and **Time Prepared** from the footer
Click **Run Report**
Since this is a report you prepare frequently, click **Save Customizations**
Name of custom report: **Customer Balance Detail**, click **OK**
Transaction Date: **All Dates**
Review the Unpaid Invoices and the Open Balances
Verify the amounts shown on the following page with the amounts shown in your report
- Is your total for the Amount column $18,679.36? Is the total of your Open Balance column $16,754.36?
Print, export, and/or send/submit the report
- If you save the report, name it **19-Your Name Customer Balance Detail Ch. 6**.

### Your Name's Beach Barkers
#### CUSTOMER BALANCE DETAIL
##### All Dates

| DATE | TRANSACTION TYPE | NUM | LOCATION | DUE DATE | AMOUNT | OPEN BALANCE | BALANCE |
|---|---|---|---|---|---|---|---|
| **Anderson, Dori** | | | | | | | |
| 12/31/2015 | Invoice | 1001 | | 12/31/2015 | 2,500.00 | 2,500.00 | 2,500.00 |
| Total for Anderson, Dori | | | | | $2,500.00 | $2,500.00 | |
| **Bailey, Larry** | | | | | | | |
| 12/31/2015 | Invoice | 1002 | | 12/31/2015 | 2,500.00 | 2,500.00 | 2,500.00 |
| Total for Bailey, Larry | | | | | $2,500.00 | $2,500.00 | |
| **Egkan, Sandi** | | | | | | | |
| 02/03/2016 | Invoice | 1044 | Malibu | 03/04/2016 | 567.00 | 567.00 | 567.00 |
| Total for Egkan, Sandi | | | | | $567.00 | $567.00 | |
| **Evans, Keith** | | | | | | | |
| 01/15/2016 | Invoice | 1034 | | 02/14/2016 | 120.00 | 95.00 | 95.00 |
| Total for Evans, Keith | | | | | $120.00 | $95.00 | |
| **Gilbert, Oscar** | | | | | | | |
| 12/31/2015 | Invoice | 1004 | | 12/31/2015 | 500.00 | 500.00 | 500.00 |
| 01/01/2016 | Invoice | 1022 | | 01/31/2016 | 650.00 | 350.00 | 850.00 |
| Total for Gilbert, Oscar | | | | | $1,150.00 | $850.00 | |
| **Gucci, Gloria** | | | | | | | |
| 01/17/2016 | Invoice | 1036 | | 02/16/2016 | 475.00 | 475.00 | 475.00 |
| 02/01/2016 | Invoice | 1041 | Venice | 03/02/2016 | 746.40 | 746.40 | 1,221.40 |
| Total for Gucci, Gloria | | | | | $1,221.40 | $1,221.40 | |
| **Montez, Annabelle** | | | | | | | |
| 12/31/2015 | Invoice | 1005 | | 12/31/2015 | 800.00 | 800.00 | 800.00 |
| 01/05/2016 | Invoice | 1023 | | 02/04/2016 | 180.00 | 80.00 | 880.00 |
| 02/10/2016 | Invoice | 1051 | Venice | 02/10/2016 | 40.00 | 40.00 | 920.00 |
| Total for Montez, Annabelle | | | | | $1,020.00 | $920.00 | |
| **Norbert, Viv** | | | | | | | |
| 12/31/2015 | Invoice | 1006 | | 12/31/2015 | 2,900.00 | 1,400.00 | 1,400.00 |
| Total for Norbert, Viv | | | | | $2,900.00 | $1,400.00 | |
| **Phillips, Eric** | | | | | | | |
| 12/31/2015 | Invoice | 1007 | | 12/31/2015 | 1,500.00 | 1,500.00 | 1,500.00 |
| Total for Phillips, Eric | | | | | $1,500.00 | $1,500.00 | |
| **Quint, Brad** | | | | | | | |
| 12/31/2015 | Invoice | 1008 | | 12/31/2015 | 1,800.00 | 1,800.00 | 1,800.00 |
| 01/15/2016 | Invoice | 1033 | | 02/14/2016 | 440.00 | 440.00 | 2,240.00 |
| Total for Quint, Brad | | | | | $2,240.00 | $2,240.00 | |
| **Rivera, Megan** | | | | | | | |
| 02/01/2016 | Invoice | 1039 | Malibu | 03/02/2016 | 360.96 | 360.96 | 360.96 |
| Total for Rivera, Megan | | | | | $360.96 | $360.96 | |
| **Rodriguez, Ricardo** | | | | | | | |
| 12/31/2015 | Invoice | 1009 | | 12/31/2015 | 900.00 | 900.00 | 900.00 |
| Total for Rodriguez, Ricardo | | | | | $900.00 | $900.00 | |
| **Vines, Pamela** | | | | | | | |
| 12/31/2015 | Invoice | 1012 | | 12/31/2015 | 750.00 | 750.00 | 750.00 |
| 01/01/2016 | Invoice | 1016 | | 01/31/2016 | 950.00 | 950.00 | 1,700.00 |
| Total for Vines, Pamela | | | | | $1,700.00 | $1,700.00 | |
| **TOTAL** | | | | | **$18,679.36** | **$16,754.36** | |

Do not close Your Name's Beach Barkers

## ADDITIONAL TRANSACTIONS—DO

Record the additional transactions using Your Name's Beach Barkers. All transactions to be recorded were either completed as drills using the Test Drive Company or as transactions for Your Name's Beach Barkers.

### DO

 Continue to use **Your Name's Beach Barkers** and enter the transactions in the Memo box

Specify Location based on the customer's city

Specify Class: Items purchased that are taxed are always Boutique. Everything else is Dog Care until you add a new item for Off-Site. At that point, the Class will be Off-Site for all transportation. Dog care services provided at someone's home will be Off-Site. Boutique items are always classified as Boutique. (Refer to the charts on Page 324.)

Select California Sales Tax as the tax rate for Boutique sales items

Print, save, and submit as you have been requested by your instructor

- Use the same naming structure as previously instructed: Document number, your name, business form and number, customer name. For example, 20-Your Name Invoice 1234 John Doe
- If you correct and print a business document, add Corrected at the end of the document name.

Any cash or checks received should be placed into Undeposited Funds until the bank deposit is made

| |
|---|
| <u>MEMO</u><br>**DATE:** February 12, 2016<br><br>Change the following customer accounts to have terms of 2% 10 Net 30, include payment information as shown, and add the Dog's Name as a note:<br><br>Josh Glass (Debit Card, Dog: Monkey); Anthony Hughes (Check, Dog: Charlie); Colleen Stark (MasterCard: 5444-9255-0737-6193, Expiration 8/18, Dog: Bella), and Taylor Williams (Check, Dog: Riley). |
| Record a Delayed Charge for Taylor Williams, Venice, for 1 Dog Bed for her dog Riley (Class: Boutique). |
| Add a new Class: Off-Site, which will be used when services are performed at someone's home (think dog walking and poop scoop) or when transportation is provided. |
| Record a sale on account for Josh Glass, Malibu, for 5 days of Day Camp (Class: Dog Care), 10 hours Transportation (Class Off-Site) to take his dog, Monkey, to and from Day Care. Josh also purchased 1 Dog Bed (Boutique). |
| Received payment in full from Dori Anderson, Check 7724. |
| Correct Invoice 1044 to Sandi Egkan, add 1 Dog Bed and decrease Quantity of Brushes to 4. |
| Record a cash sale for a new customer: Eugene Fisher (Address: 24755 Vantage Point Terrace, Malibu, CA 90265; Email: Eugene@mbu.com; Phone: 424-555-2751; Mobile: 424-555-1572; Dog's Name: Shadow; Visa: 4175-7880-3245-7211; Expiration date: 12/21; Terms Net 30) 10 Days Boarding, 1 Ten One-Hour Sessions Training, 4 Hours Transportation, 1 Bath, 1 Nails, and 5 Bones for $10 each. Did you include sales tax? Which Location did you use? What Classes did you use—Transportation: Off-Site; Boarding, Bath, Training, and Nails: Dog Care; and Bones: Boutique. |
| Received $14.04 in cash from Cash Customer, Venice, for 1 Dog Snacks $5, and 1 Bone $8.00. |
| Record a sale on account for Colleen Stark, Venice, for 10 days of Day Camp, 20 hours of Transportation to take her dog, Bella, to and from day camp, 2 Bath, 1 Nails, 1 Dental Care, 1 Collar at $45, and 1 Dog Bed. |
| Received Check 2789 from Alice Johnson, Malibu, for the purchase of Dog Food: 30 Cans at $8.95 each and 2 bags of Dry at $50 each. |
| Andrew Nichols, Malibu, is having you come to his house to provide 1 Five One-Hour Sessions of Training, 5 Dog Walking, 5 Poop Scoop. In preparation for Duke's training sessions, he also purchased 1 Collar $35, 1 Leash $30. Used his Debit card for payment. What classes did you use—Training, Dog Walking, and Poop Scoop: Off-Site; Collar and Leash: Boutique. |
| Record Credit Memo to Megan Rivera, Malibu, 2 Toys and Treats $15 each (Class: Boutique). (After recording the Credit Memo, access Megan's Transaction List. Open the Payment for the current date and change the date to 02/12/16. The amount received will show 0.00. This Receive Payment screen is the link between the invoice and the credit memo. Click Save and close.) |

6

Continue recording, saving, and printing transactions.

---

**MEMO**
**DATE:** February 13-15, 2016

Enter the following transactions using the date given in the transaction

February 13: Took Anthony Hughes' dog Charlie to the vet, Malibu. Record a sale on account for 3 hours Transportation (Class: Off-Site). Also include 1 Vitamins for $35 (Class: Boutique).

February 13: Record a Credit Memo to Josh Glass, Malibu, for the return of 1 Dog Bed (Class: Boutique). Go to Receive Payment screen and change the date from the current date to 02/13/16.

February 13: Record refund to Eugene Fisher, Malibu, for 3 Dog Bones for $10 each (Class: Boutique). Account: Undeposited Funds.

February 13: Convert delayed charge from Taylor Williams to an invoice.

February 14: Received payments (Remember, if there is a discount, you must record the discount on the invoice and apply it before sales tax.): Josh Glass (Terms 2% 10 Net 30, Debit Card); Colleen Stark (Terms 2% 10 Net 30, MasterCard), Megan Rivera (Net 30, Visa), Taylor Williams (Net 30, Check 1092). Make sure Receive Payment Date is 02/14/16.

February 14: Bank Deposit. Print the Deposit Summary.

February 15: Check 1092 from Taylor Williams, Venice, was returned marked NSF. Record the NSF check and the $40 fee ($20 that you charge and $20 that the bank charges) for the NSF check with Terms of Due on receipt. No Class is used for NSF check charges.

---

Do *not* close Your Name's Beach Barkers

## PREPARE REPORTS—DO

As with other chapters, reports provide a wealth of information. Some of the reports prepared will give you summary information regarding sales and receivables, while others will provide in-depth information. Since Chapter 6 has been focused on sales and receivables, you will prepare: Customer Balance Summary, shows each customer's total open balance; Sales by Product/Service Summary, shows sales for each item on the Product/Service List; Sales by Class Summary, shows the amount of sales for each Class; Sales by Location Summary, shows the amount of sales for each Location; Journal, shows every transaction entered in debit/credit format; and Trial Balance, proves that Debits equal Credits for February 1-15, 2016.

*DO*

Continue to use **Your Name's Beach Barkers** to prepare the Sales by Product/Service Summary, Sales by Class Summary, Sales by Location Summary, Customer Balance Summary, Journal, and Trial Balance for February 1-15, 2016

### Sales by Product/Service Summary

Prepare the Sales by Product/Service Summary report

Access the **Review Sales** report category and prepare the **Sales by Product/Service Summary**
Remove the Date Prepared, Time Prepared, and Report Basis from the footer
Use the Dates From: **02/01/16** To: **02/15/16**

### Your Name's Beach Barkers
### SALES BY PRODUCT/SERVICE SUMMARY
February 1-15, 2016

| | QTY | AMOUNT | % OF SALES | AVG PRICE |
|---|---|---|---|---|
| | | TOTAL | | |
| Bath | 8.00 | 280.00 | 3.25 % | 35.00 |
| Boarding | 30.00 | 1,650.00 | 19.17 % | 55.00 |
| Bones | 19.00 | 165.00 | 1.92 % | 8.6842105 |
| Brushes | 9.00 | 220.00 | 2.56 % | 24.4444444 |
| Coat Brushing | 5.00 | 75.00 | 0.87 % | 15.00 |
| Collars | 10.00 | 355.00 | 4.12 % | 35.50 |
| Day Camp | 26.00 | 780.00 | 9.06 % | 30.00 |
| Dental Care | 2.00 | 100.00 | 1.16 % | 50.00 |
| Dog Beds | 4.00 | 260.00 | 3.02 % | 65.00 |
| Dog Food-Canned | 72.00 | 475.00 | 5.52 % | 6.5972222 |
| Dog Food-Dry | 6.00 | 155.50 | 1.81 % | 25.9166667 |
| Dog Snacks | 24.00 | 120.00 | 1.39 % | 5.00 |
| Dog Walking | 5.00 | 75.00 | 0.87 % | 15.00 |
| Leashes | 8.00 | 230.00 | 2.67 % | 28.75 |
| Nails | 6.00 | 120.00 | 1.39 % | 20.00 |
| NSF Charges | 2.00 | 80.00 | 0.93 % | 40.00 |
| Poop Scoop | 5.00 | 75.00 | 0.87 % | 15.00 |
| Sweaters | 7.00 | 255.00 | 2.96 % | 36.4285714 |
| Toys & Treats | 12.00 | 160.00 | 1.86 % | 13.3333333 |
| Training 2 | 2.00 | 700.00 | 8.13 % | 350.00 |
| Training 3 | 2.00 | 1,300.00 | 15.10 % | 650.00 |
| Transportation | 37.00 | 925.00 | 10.74 % | 25.00 |
| Vitamins | 5.00 | 105.00 | 1.22 % | 21.00 |
| Not Specified | -2,590.00 | -51.80 | -0.60 % | 0.02 |
| TOTAL | | $8,608.70 | 100.00 % | |

*Add 3*

*#33*

(4) Print, export, and/or send/submit the report as previously instructed
- If you save the report, name it: **33-Your Name Sales by Product-Service Summary Ch. 6**.

## Sales by Class Summary

Prepare the Sales by Class Summary report

Continue to use the **Review Sales** category for reports
Click **Sales by Class Summary**
Remove the Date Prepared, Time Prepared, and Report Basis from the footer
Use the Dates From: **02/01/16** To: **02/15/16**

### Your Name's Beach Barkers
### SALES BY CLASS SUMMARY
February 1-15, 2016

| | TOTAL |
|---|---|
| Boutique | 2,500.50 |
| Dog Care | 4,655.00 |
| Off-Site | 1,425.00 |
| Not Specified | 28.20 |
| TOTAL | $8,608.70 |

- Totals for each Class recorded on sales documents are shown. Not Specified means that a class was not selected for a sales document, which would include the amounts of Sales Discounts and NSF charges.

Print, export, and/or send/submit the report as previously instructed
(5)
- If you save the report, name it: **34-Your Name Sales by Class Summary Ch. 6**.

## Sales by Location Summary

 Prepare the Sales by Location Summary report

Continue to use the **Review Sales** category for reports
Click **Sales by Location Summary**
Remove the Date Prepared, Time Prepared, and Report Basis from the footer
Use the Dates From: **02/01/16** To: **02/15/16**

**Your Name's Beach Barkers**
**SALES BY LOCATION SUMMARY**
February 1-15, 2016

| | TOTAL |
|---|---|
| Malibu | 5,862.10 |
| Venice | 2,746.60 |
| **Total** | **$8,608.70** |

*L 910*

 Print, export, and/or send/submit the report as previously instructed
- If you save the report, name it: **35-Your Name Sales by Location Summary Ch. 6**.

## Customer Balance Summary

 Prepare the Customer Balance Summary report

Access **My Custom Reports** and prepare the customized **Customer Balance Summary** report
Dates: **All Dates**
Compare your totals with the ones shown in the report
- If you need more detailed information about an individual customer, click the total for the customer to drill-down to the individual Customer Balance Detail.

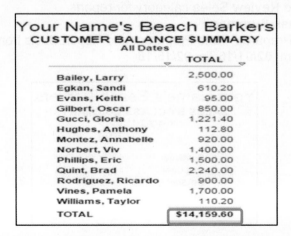

**Your Name's Beach Barkers**
**CUSTOMER BALANCE SUMMARY**
All Dates

| | TOTAL |
|---|---|
| Bailey, Larry | 2,500.00 |
| Egkan, Sandi | 610.20 |
| Evans, Keith | 95.00 |
| Gilbert, Oscar | 850.00 |
| Gucci, Gloria | 1,221.40 |
| Hughes, Anthony | 112.80 |
| Montez, Annabelle | 920.00 |
| Norbert, Viv | 1,400.00 |
| Phillips, Eric | 1,500.00 |
| Quint, Brad | 2,240.00 |
| Rodriguez, Ricardo | 900.00 |
| Vines, Pamela | 1,700.00 |
| Williams, Taylor | 110.20 |
| **TOTAL** | **$14,159.60** |

 Print, export, and/or send/submit the report as previously instructed
- If you save the report, name it: **36-Your Name Customer Balance Summary Ch. 6**.

## Journal

 Prepare the Journal report

Use **My Custom Reports** and prepare your customized **Journal** for February 1-15, 2016
Adjust the column widths:

Point to the sizing handle
Hold down the left (primary) mouse button
Drag to the left to reduce or the right to enlarge the column

| NUM | NAME |
|---|---|

- Are your totals for Debits and Credits $25,555.75?

$25,555.75    $25,555.75

Print in Landscape orientation, export, and/or send/submit the report as previously
instructed
- If you save the report, name it: **37-Your Name Journal Ch. 6**.

## Trial Balance

 Prepare the Trial Balance

Access **My Custom Reports** and prepare your customized **Trial Balance** for
February 1-15, 2016
- Do your Debit and Credit totals match?

### Your Name's Beach Barkers
#### TRIAL BALANCE
As of February 15, 2016

| | DEBIT | CREDIT |
|---|---|---|
| Checking | 71,104.00 | |
| Petty Cash | 107.08 | |
| Accounts Receivable (A/R) | 14,159.60 | |
| Inventory Asset | 28,579.50 | |
| Prepaid Insurance | 1,100.00 | |
| Supplies:Cleaning Supplies | 825.00 | |
| Supplies:Kennel Supplies | 1,950.00 | |
| Supplies:Office Supplies | 628.68 | |
| Supplies:Sales Supplies | 400.00 | |
| Undeposited Funds | 0.00 | |
| Furniture & Fixtures:Depreciation | | 1,625.00 |
| Furniture & Fixtures:Original cost | 15,000.00 | |
| Kennel Equipment:Depreciation | | 2,200.00 |
| Kennel Equipment:Original cost | 21,150.00 | |
| Office Equipment:Depreciation | | 900.00 |
| Office Equipment:Original cost | 11,685.84 | |
| Vehicles:Depreciation | | 3,475.00 |
| Vehicles:Original cost | 32,000.00 | |
| Accounts Payable (A/P) | | 4,214.00 |
| State Board of Equalization Payable | | 199.01 |
| Loans Payable:Equipment Loan | | 1,970.59 |
| Loans Payable:Furniture & Fixtures Loan | | 2,463.24 |
| Opening Balance Equity | | 300.00 |
| Retained Earnings | 1,844.66 | |
| Your Name, Capital | | 119,922.16 |
| Your Name, Capital:Your Name, Drawing | | 0.00 |
| Your Name, Capital:Your Name, Investment | | 53,735.00 |
| Sales of Product Income | | 2,500.50 |
| Services:Boarding | | 2,420.00 |
| Services:Day Camp | | 1,410.00 |
| Services:Grooming | | 1,360.00 |
| Services:House Calls | | 375.00 |
| Services:Sales Discounts | 51.80 | |
| Services:Training | | 5,025.00 |
| Services:Transportation | | 1,225.00 |
| Cost of Goods Sold | 733.00 | |

Continued on the next page

| | | |
|---|---:|---:|
| Advertising | 200.00 | |
| Bank Charges | 16.00 | |
| Equipment Rental | 75.00 | |
| Insurance:Vehicle Insurance | 100.00 | |
| Interest Expense | 18.75 | |
| Laundry | 6.50 | |
| Rent or Lease | 1,500.00 | |
| Repair & Maintenance:Computer Repair | 200.00 | |
| Repair & Maintenance:Vehicle Repair | 212.50 | |
| Supplies Expense:Cleaning Supplies Expense | 100.00 | |
| Supplies Expense:Kennel Supplies Expense | 134.00 | |
| Supplies Expense:Office Supplies Expense | 131.47 | |
| Supplies Expense:Sales Supplies Expense | 100.00 | |
| Telephone Expense | 129.95 | |
| Utilities:Electric | 89.75 | |
| Utilities:Gas-Heating | 189.50 | |
| Utilities:Water | 175.95 | |
| Vehicle Expenses | 109.90 | |
| Fees Billed | | 80.00 |
| Interest Earned | | 78.93 |
| Depreciation Expense | 670.00 | |
| TOTAL | $205,478.43 | $205,478.43 |

Print in Landscape orientation, export, and/or send/submit the report as previously instructed

- If you save the report, name it: **38-Your Name Trial Balance Ch. 6**.

## SUMMARY

In this chapter transactions for sales on account and cash sales of products and services were recorded. A Logo was added to business documents and business forms were customized. Sales Tax was setup and used when invoices and sales receipts were prepared. Terms for 2% 10 Net 30 and Due on Receipt were added and applied to invoices. Sales transactions included information for locations and classes. Delayed charges were created and then converted into invoices. Debit Cards and Credit Cards were added to customer accounts for Payment Methods and used when processing customer payments and cash sales. Customers and accounts were added and edited. New products and service items were added. NSF transactions were recorded. Reports were customized, memorized, and prepared. Preparing reports, such as, the Customer Balance Detail, Customer Balance Summary, Sales by Product/Service Summary, Sales by Classes Summary, Sales by Location Summary, Journal, and Trial Balance provided detailed information regarding sales and receivables.

# END-OF-CHAPTER QUESTIONS

## TRUE/FALSE

ANSWER THE FOLLOWING QUESTIONS IN THE SPACE PROVIDED BEFORE THE QUESTION NUMBER.

_____ 1. If a customer issues a check that is returned marked NSF, you may charge the customer the amount of the bank charges and any penalty charges you impose.

_____ 2. A Logo authorizes you to access custom forms.

_____ 3. Each Location of the business may use a different address and phone number.

_____ 4. Sales discounts are always calculated after sales tax has been entered.

_____ 5. All payments received by QuickBooks Online, including debit cards and credit cards, are placed in Undeposited Funds until the bank deposit is made.

_____ 6. Terms of 2% 10 Net 30 are used for NSF Check penalties.

_____ 7. Sales tax is a fee charged by government agencies on sales of products.

_____ 8. A Delayed Charge is added to the customer's balance.

_____ 9. Locations are allowed to select a descriptive name; such as, Store.

_____ 10. A Customer Note may be added by editing the individual account.

## MULTIPLE CHOICE

WRITE THE LETTER OF THE CORRECT ANSWER IN THE SPACE PROVIDED BEFORE THE QUESTION NUMBER.

_____ 1. Transactions may be categorized based on ___ and ___.
   A. Location and Class
   B. Settings and Class
   C. Locations and Settings
   D. Any of the above

_____ 2. To see the effects of the sales of products on inventory, you prepare a(n) ___ report.
   A. Inventory Asset Account
   B. Sales of Product Income
   C. Inventory Valuation Summary
   D. Cost of Goods Sold Summary

_____ 3. When a customer qualifies for an early payment discount, the discount is recorded ___.
   A. In the Sales Discount register
   B. As a Journal entry
   C. On a new Invoice
   D. On the original Invoice

6

_____ 4. The Sales Tax Center must be set up to include the ___.
    A. Sales Tax Rate
    B. Name of the Sales Tax
    C. Agency collecting the Sales Tax
    D. All of the above

_____ 5. A Sales Discount may be calculated ___ sales tax.
    A. Before
    B. After
    C. Before or After
    D. None of the above

_____ 6. When a customer returns an item from a sale on account, a(n) ___ is completed.
    A. Return Receipt
    B. Credit Memo
    C. Invoice
    D. Sales Receipt

_____ 7. To change the quantity on hand for an inventory item, you ___.
    A. Prepare an Inventory Valuation Detail report
    B. Change the Opening Balance Invoice
    C. Edit the item in the Products/Services List
    D. Edit the Inventory Asset account

_____ 8. To record a sale and the payment at the same time, you prepare a(n) ___ form.
    A. Invoice
    B. Receive Payments
    C. Sales Receipt
    D. Both A and B

_____ 9. The report that lists the unpaid invoices for each customer is the___ report.
    A. Customer Balance Summary
    B. Customer Balance Detail
    C. Collections Report
    D. Open Invoices

_____ 10. Payment Methods are created for ___.
    A. Debit Cards
    B. MasterCard
    C. Visa
    D. All of the above

## FILL-IN

IN THE SPACE PROVIDED, WRITE THE ANSWER THAT MOST APPROPRIATELY COMPLETES THE SENTENCE.

1. The method of inventory valuation in QuickBooks Online is _____.

2. A Delayed Charge is converted into a(n) _____.

3. The three types of discounts available for use in a company
    are _____, _____, and _____.

4. When a product (Dog Bed for example) is sold in Your Name's Beach Barkers, the three accounts used in the Journal are_____, _____, and _____.

5. To record the amount a customer owes for NSF charges, you prepare a(n) _____.

## COMPUTER ASSIGNMENT

REFER TO PRINTOUTS OR USE QUICKBOOKS ONLINE AND YOUR NAME'S BEACH BARKERS TO LOOK UP OR ENTER INFORMATION, AND THEN WRITE THE ANSWERS TO THE FOLLOWING EXERCISES IN THE SPACE PROVIDED

1. What was the amount of sales tax charged on Katie Wilson's Sales Receipt #1048? _____

2. What document did you prepare to record the fees billed for the NSF Check from Taylor Williams? _____

3. What was the Total Credit for Megan Rivera on Credit Memo 1058? _____

4. Prepare an Invoice List by Date report for February 1-15, 2016. What is the amount shown for the Open Balance for Anthony Hughes? (This is the amount that he currently owes.) _____

5. What Location did you use for Sales Receipt 1053 for Eugene Fisher? _____

6. Prepare an Inventory Valuation Summary as of February 15, 2016. What is the total? _____

7. Using the Inventory Valuation Summary as of February 15, 2016, how many Dog Beds are in stock? _____

8. What was the amount of the payment received from Josh Glass on February 14, 2015? _____

9. Refer to Invoice 1055 for Colleen Stark, what is shown for the Balance Due? _____

10. What business form did you prepare to record the payment from Dori Anderson? _____

6

# CHAPTER 6 CHECKLIST

The checklist below shows all of the business forms printed during training. Check each one that you printed, exported, and/or submitted.

| | | | |
|---|---|---|---|
| _____ | 1-Products and Services List Ch. 6 | _____ | 20-Invoice 1052 Josh Glass |
| _____ | 2-Invoice 1039 Megan Rivera | _____ | 21-Invoice 1044 Sandi Egkan Corrected |
| _____ | 3-Invoice 1040 Monroe Miller | _____ | 22-Sales Receipt 1053 Eugene Fisher |
| _____ | 4-Invoice 1041 Gloria Gucci | _____ | 23-Sales Receipt 1054 Cash Customer |
| _____ | 5-Invoice 1042 Tracy McCarter | _____ | 24-Invoice 1055 Colleen Stark |
| _____ | 6-Inventory Valuation Summary Ch. 6 | _____ | 25-Sales Receipt 1056 Alice Johnson |
| _____ | 7-Journal Ch. 6 | _____ | 26-Sales Receipt 1057 Andrew Nichols |
| _____ | 8-Invoice 1039 Megan Rivera Corrected | _____ | 27-Credit Memo 1058 Megan Rivera |
| _____ | 9-Credit Memo 1043 Monroe Miller | _____ | 28-Invoice 1059 Anthony Hughes |
| _____ | 10-Invoice 1044 Sandi Egkan | _____ | 29-Credit Memo 1060 Josh Glass |
| _____ | 11-Invoice 1045 Keith Evans | _____ | 30-Invoice 1062 Taylor Williams |
| _____ | 12-Invoice List Ch. 6 | _____ | 31-Bank Deposit Ch. 6 |
| _____ | 13-Sales Receipt 1046 Nick Wagner | _____ | 32-Invoice 1063 Taylor Williams |
| _____ | 14-Sales Receipt 1047 Cash Customer | _____ | 33-Sales by Product-Service Summary Ch. 6 |
| _____ | 15-Sales Receipt 1048 Katie Wilson | _____ | 34-Sales by Class Summary Ch. 6 |
| _____ | 16-Sales Receipt 1049 David De Los Santos | _____ | 35-Sales by Location Summary Ch. 6 |
| _____ | 17-Bank Deposit Ch. 6 | _____ | 36-Customer Balance Summary Ch. 6 |
| _____ | 18-Invoice 1051 Annabelle Montez | _____ | 37-Journal Ch. 6 |
| _____ | 19-Customer Balance Detail Ch. 6 | _____ | 38-Trial Balance Ch. 6 |

# PAYABLES, PURCHASES, AND INVENTORY

**7**

## LEARNING OBJECTIVES

At the completion of this chapter, you will be able to:

1.  Use Purchase Orders to order inventory items.
2.  Assign discount terms to vendors.
3.  Add new vendors while preparing purchase orders.
4.  Record the receipt of inventory items, close the purchase order, and convert it into a bill.
5.  Add new accounts.
6.  Understand the concepts for computerized accounting for payables and merchandise.
7.  Record partial receipt of Purchase Orders.
8.  Add new inventory items.
9.  Use a company credit card to pay for bills and other purchases.
10. Record purchase discounts and merchandise discounts.
11. Record returns of inventory items and other purchases.
12. Use Petty Cash.
13. Pay Sales Tax Liabilities.
14. Prepare inventory reports such as Inventory Valuation Summary and Purchases by Product/Service Detail.
15. Prepare the Vendor Balance Summary, Unpaid Bills, Check Detail, Bill Payment List, Open Purchase Order List, Journal, Trial Balance reports.

## ACCOUNTING FOR PAYABLES AND PURCHASES AND INVENTORY

When a company sells inventory items, much of the accounting for purchases and payables consists of ordering and paying for the merchandise. In addition, bills for expenses and purchases incurred in the operation of the business must be paid as well. Some of the transactions will be paid for by check, credit card, and petty cash while others will be purchases on account, which will be recorded as a bill. Bills may be paid when they are received or when they are due. If a vendor allows early payment discounts, they may be taken for merchandise (inventory items) and purchases of things used in the operation of the business.

Rather than use journals, QuickBooks Online continues to focus on recording transactions based on the business document; therefore, you use the Enter Bills and Pay Bills features of the program to record the receipt and payment of bills.

When merchandise is ordered, a purchase order is prepared. When the merchandise arrives, a bill is prepared, the items on the purchase order are added to the bill, the purchase order is closed, and the value of the merchandise is added to the Inventory Asset account.

QuickBooks Online uses a Vendor List for all vendors with which the company has an account. QuickBooks Online does not refer to the Vendor List as the Accounts Payable Ledger; yet, that is exactly what it is. The total of the Vendor List/Accounts Payable Ledger will match the total of the Accounts Payable account in the Chart of Accounts/General Ledger.

As in previous chapters, corrections can be made directly on the business form, in the Vendor's Register, or within the account. New accounts, vendors, and inventory items may be added on the fly as transactions are entered. Reports illustrating vendor balances, unpaid bills, inventory valuation, purchases, among others, may be viewed, printed, and exported.

## TRAINING TUTORIAL AND PROCEDURES

Continue to use the Test Drive Company for practice and the fictional company, Your Name's Beach Barkers, to record purchase orders, purchases, and payments. Make payments by writing checks, using the company credit card, and using Petty Cash. In addition to recording transactions, you will also prepare several reports. Use of Your Name's Beach Barkers will continue throughout the text as you explore the different facets and capabilities of QuickBooks Online.

Just as you did in previous chapters, you will enter additional transactions near the end of the chapter. These transactions are similar to the ones you entered in the Test Drive Company and in Your Name's Beach Barkers so no step-by-step instructions will be given. If you need to refer back to the chapter materials to make the entries, you should feel free to do so.

**Pay careful attention to quantities, amounts, and dates as you work through the chapter. A careless error can require a tremendous amount of effort to correct.**

## DATES

Remember that the year used for the screen shots is 2016. Continue to use the same year that you used in Chapters 2-6. In Chapter 7 through the rest of the chapters, the month used will be February. If QuickBooks Online inserts the current date into a transaction, be aware of this and be sure to use the date indicated in the text.

## IMPORTANT NOTE

As has been stated in earlier chapters, QuickBooks Online is constantly evolving and new features, apps, and procedures change frequently. Everything in the text is correct at the time of this writing; however, by the time of publication some changes to the program may occur.

## INVENTORY VALUATION SUMMARY—DRILL

The Inventory Valuation Summary report summarizes key information for each inventory item. The information displayed is quantity on hand, value, and average cost. The report may be customized to remove footer information for Date Prepared and Time Prepared. You may also select whether to include all inventory items, the active inventory items, or the non-zero inventory items.

### *DRILL*

 Open the **Test Drive Company** and prepare the Inventory Valuation Summary report

Once the Test Drive is opened, go to QuickBooks Labs and turn **OFF** Redesigned Reports
Access the Report Category **Manage Products and Inventory**
Click **Inventory Valuation Summary**
- The report is opened and displays the information As of: the current date.
- Because of the automatic date changes in the Test Drive Company, use the current date for this report.

- As you look at this report, you will find several items that do not have much inventory available. Viewing this report will help you determine which inventory items you need to order.

## Craig's Design and Landscaping Services
### INVENTORY VALUATION SUMMARY
Current Date

|  | QTY | TOTAL ASSET VALUE | AVG COST |
|---|---|---|---|
| **Design** | | | |
| **Fountains** | | | |
| Pump | 25.00 | 250.00 | 10.00 |
| Rock Fountain | 2.00 | 250.00 | 125.00 |
| **Total Fountains** | | 500.00 | |
| **Total Design** | | 500.00 | |
| **Landscaping** | | | |
| **Sprinklers** | | | |
| Sprinkler Heads | 25.00 | 18.75 | 0.75 |
| Sprinkler Pipes | 31.00 | 77.50 | 2.50 |
| **Total Sprinklers** | | 96.25 | |
| **Total Landscaping** | | 96.25 | |
| **TOTAL** | | $596.25 | |

Do <u>not</u> close the Test Drive Company

## VERIFY PURCHASE ORDER SETTINGS—DRILL

In order to prepare purchase orders, the Purchase Orders feature must be turned ON in Account & Settings. If it is not ON, the feature may be selected prior to processing your first purchase order.

### *DRILL*

 Continue to use the **Test Drive Company** and verify that Purchase Orders are ON

Click the **Gear** icon, click **Account and Settings** in the Your Company column
Click the **Expenses** tab
- If Purchase orders are Off, click the **Pen** icon, click the **Use purchase orders** check box to select, click **Save**.

| Expenses | | | |
|---|---|---|---|
| | **Purchase orders** | Use purchase orders | On ✎ |

Click **Done** on the Account and Settings screen
Do <u>not</u> close the Test Drive Company

## PURCHASE ORDERS—DRILL

Using the Purchase Order feature helps you track your inventory. When everything on a purchase order is received, it is marked Closed. In essence, a purchase order (PO) is a document you send to a vendor that states your intent to purchase products. The details of the purchase including quantities and prices are included on the purchase order. When the vendor accepts your PO, you have an agreement with them to receive the products ordered. QuickBooks Online Plus is the only version of QuickBooks Online that has the ability to use Purchase Orders and to track inventory.

7

> **MEMO**
> **DATE:** Current Date
>
> After reviewing the Inventory Valuation Summary, you decide to prepare Purchase Orders for 5 Rock Fountains from Tania's Nursery for $125 each.
>
> You are also ordering 100 Sprinkler Heads for 75¢ each and 10 Sprinkler Pipes for $2.50 each from Norton Lumber and Building Materials.

*DRILL*

Continue to use the **Test Drive Company** and prepare Purchase Orders

Click the **Plus** icon, click **Purchase Order** in the Vendors column
Click the drop-down list arrow for Choose a vendor, click **Tania's Nursery**
Because of the automatic date changes in the Test Drive Company, use the **Current Date**
If **Account Details** is expanded, click the title to hide that section on the Purchase Order
If Item Details is not expanded, click the title **Item Details** to expand
- You may see the Item Details information for a previous Purchase Order. If so, delete it. To do this, click the **Trash can** icon at the end of Line 1. Then change the QTY of Rock Fountains to 5.

If you do not see previous items, you will need to complete Line 1 of Item details:
Click in the PRODUCT/SERVICE column for Item details
Click the drop-down list arrow, click **Rock Fountain** in the Item List shown
Tab to QTY and enter **5** for the number of fountains, press **Tab**

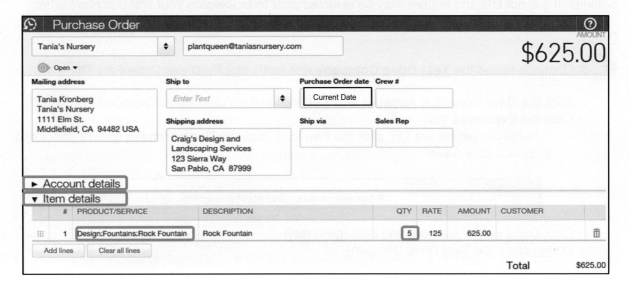

Click **Save and new**
To prepare a second Purchase Order, click the drop-down list arrow for Vendor, click
**Norton Lumber and Building Materials**
Complete the purchase order using the information provided in the Memo
- You may see Item Details information for a previous Purchase Order. If so, delete the 8 Fountain Pumps and the 1 Rock Fountain. Click the **Clear all lines** button beneath the Item Details section.

Complete the Purchase Order

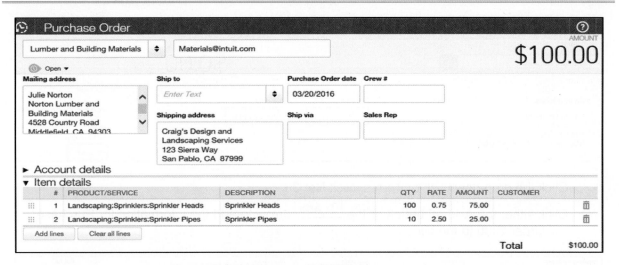

Click **Save and close**
If you get a blank Purchase Order, close it
Do not close the Test Drive Company

## RECEIVE ITEMS ORDERED—DRILL

When you receive the merchandise ordered on the Purchase Order, a bill is prepared and the Purchase Order information is added to it. Doing this closes the purchase order. If you only receive part of the merchandise ordered, a bill is still prepared but the purchase order will not be closed. Because QuickBooks Online does not have a feature in place for receiving partial orders, you will learn a "work around" to create a new purchase order for those items not yet received. Then you will create a bill and close the purchase order for the merchandise that was received.

> **MEMO**
> **DATE:** Current Date
>
> Received the 5 Rock Fountains ordered on Purchase Order 1005 from Tania's Nursery for $125 each.
>
> Received the 100 Sprinkler Heads for 75¢ each from Norton Lumber and Building Materials, Purchase Order 1006. The 10 Sprinkler Pipes for $2.50 each are out of stock and will be delivered at a later date.

*DRILL*

 Continue to use the **Test Drive Company** and record the receipt of inventory items

Click the **Plus** icon, click **Bill** in the Vendors column
Click the drop-down list arrow for Choose a vendor
Click **Tania's Nursery**
- The information for Tania's Nursery is inserted into the bill. Because Terms have not been entered, the current date is inserted for the Bill date and the Due date. An Add to Bill pane appears on the right-side of the bill.

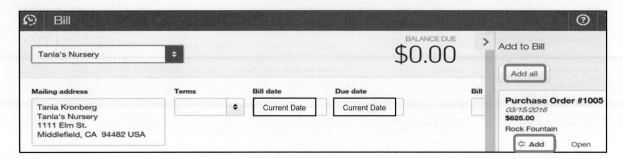

Click the drop-down list for Terms, click **Net 30**

Click either the **Add all** button or the 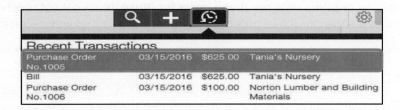 arrow to add the information for Purchase Order 1005 to the bill

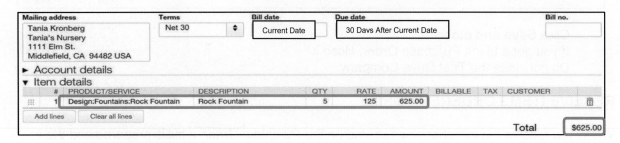

Click **Save and close**
Click the **Recent Transactions** icon next to the Plus icon

Click **Purchase Order No. 1005**
* Notice that the Purchase Order is marked "Closed" and is Linked to a Bill.

Click the Close button for Purchase Order 1005
Click the **Recent Transactions** icon
Click **Purchase Order 1006**
* Part of the order, Sprinkler Heads, was received and the other part, Sprinkler Pipes, was not. To record a bill and close the purchase order for the Sprinkler Heads, a copy of the purchase order must be made and edited.

Click the **More** button at the bottom of Purchase Order 1006
Click **Copy**
* You will see a copy of the purchase order on the screen. With a message that it is a copy.

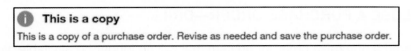

Click the [🗑] icon at the end of Line 1 for the Sprinkler Heads in Item Details
- The Purchase Order now shows just the Sprinkler Pipes that are on backorder (out of stock).

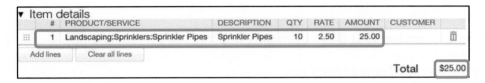

Click **Save and close**
You should be returned to Purchase Order 1006
- If not, click the **Recent Transactions** icon and click Purchase Order 1006.
Click the [🗑] icon at the end of Line 2 in Item Details to remove the Sprinkler Pipes from the Purchase Order
- Purchase Order 1006 now shows just the Sprinkler Heads that were received.
Click **Save and close**
Click the **Plus** icon, click **Bill** in the Vendors column
Click the drop-down list arrow for Choose a vendor, click **Norton Lumber and Building Materials**
Click the drop-down list for Terms, click **Net 30**
- If you have items for Pump and Rock Fountain, click the **Clear all lines** <u>below</u> the Item details section to remove them.
- Notice the Add to Bill pane shows both Purchase Order 1006 for Sprinkler Heads and Purchase Order 1007 for Sprinkler Pipes.
Click the [⇐ Add] button for Purchase Order 1006

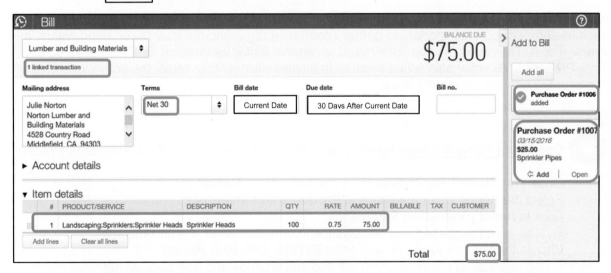

- The information for Purchase Order 1006 was added to the bill. Notice that the bill is linked. Because you added the information from the purchase order, the bill and the purchase order are linked together. Purchase Order 1007 shows that it is still Open.
Click **Save and close**
Do <u>not</u> close the Test Drive Company, continue with the next section.

## MANUALLY CLOSE A PURCHASE ORDER—DRILL

If you have prepared a purchase order for an item that will no longer be available, you manually close the purchase order. It is helpful to retain the purchase order in your records so you know what you ordered and know that it is no longer available from a particular vendor. Because of this, you manually close a purchase order rather than delete it.

*DRILL*

Continue to use the **Test Drive Company** and manually close Purchase Order 1007

> Click the **Recent Transactions** icon
> Click **Purchase Order 1007** for Norton Lumber and Building Materials
> Click the drop-down list arrow for Open
> Click the drop-down list arrow on the Purchase Order status pop up
> Click **Closed**

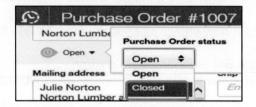

> • The Purchase Order status is now Closed.
> Click **Save and close**
> Close the Test Drive Company

## INVENTORY VALUATION SUMMARY—DO

As you learned in the drill, the Inventory Valuation Summary report summarizes key information for each inventory item. It is important to gather information regarding the quantity on hand, value, and average cost. The report may be customized to remove footer information for Date Prepared and Time Prepared. You may also select whether to include all inventory items, the active inventory items, or the non-zero inventory items.

*DO*

Open **Your Name's Beach Barkers** and prepare the Inventory Valuation Summary report

> Once Your Name's Beach Barkers is opened access **Reports**
> Select the Report Category **Manage Products and Inventory**
> Click **Inventory Valuation Summary**
> • The report is opened and displays the information As of: the current date.
> Click in the text box for As of: and enter **021516**, click **Run Report**
> • As you look at this report, you will find that brushes and dog beds do not have much inventory available. Viewing this report will help you determine which inventory items you need to order.
> • Remember the item name is Dog Bed. When you are ordering or paying for more than one dog bed, it will be referred to as Dog Beds.

### Your Name's Beach Barkers
#### INVENTORY VALUATION SUMMARY
As of February 15, 2016

| | QTY | TOTAL ASSET VALUE | AVG COST |
|---|---|---|---|
| Bones | 331.00 | 662.00 | 2.00 |
| Brushes | 26.00 | 130.00 | 5.00 |
| Collars | 640.00 | 6,400.00 | 10.00 |
| Dog Bed | 1.00 | 20.00 | 20.00 |
| Dog Food-Canned | 413.00 | 1,032.50 | 2.50 |
| Dog Food-Dry | 394.00 | 2,758.00 | 7.00 |
| Dog Snacks | 176.00 | 176.00 | 1.00 |
| Leashes | 442.00 | 4,420.00 | 10.00 |
| Sweaters | 318.00 | 4,770.00 | 15.00 |
| Toys & Treats | 3,438.00 | 6,876.00 | 2.00 |
| Vitamins | 445.00 | 1,335.00 | 3.00 |
| TOTAL | | $28,579.50 | |

Remove the Date Prepared and Time Prepared from the footer then, print, export, and/or send/submit the report as you did in earlier chapters
- If you save the report, name it **1-Your Name Inventory Valuation Summary Ch. 7**.

Do <u>not</u> close Your Name's Beach Barkers

## VERIFY PURCHASE ORDER SETTINGS—DO

Using the Purchase Order feature helps you track your inventory. In order to prepare purchase orders, the feature must be turned ON in Settings when creating a company, or it may be selected prior to processing your first purchase order.

### <u>DO</u>

 Continue to use **Your Name's Beach Barkers** and verify that Purchase Orders are ON

Click the **Gear** icon, click **Company Settings** in the Settings column
Click the **Expenses** tab
- If Purchase orders are Off, click the **Pen** icon, click the **Use purchase orders** check box to select, click **Save**.

| Expenses | | | | |
|---|---|---|---|---|
| | Purchase orders | Use purchase orders | On | ✎ |

Click **Done** on the Settings screen
Do <u>not</u> close Your Name's Beach Barkers

## ADD A NEW VENDOR—DO

As you learned in earlier chapters, it is easy to add a vendor at any time. You may do this by going to the Vendors list or you may add a vendor while preparing purchase orders, bills, and checks.

> **MEMO**
> **DATE:** February 16, 2016
>
> Add a new vendor The Literary Dog, Address: 2975 Main Street, Santa Ana, CA 92701, Email: LiteraryDog@books.com, Phone: 657-555-9723, Web site: www.TheLiteraryDog.com, Terms: 2% 10 Net 30.

*DO*

Continue to use **Your Name's Beach Barkers** and add a new vendor

Click **Vendors** on the Navigation bar
Click the **New Vendor** button
Enter the information in the Memo: in the appropriate fields

## Vendor Information

| Title | First name | Middle name | Last name | Suffix |
|---|---|---|---|---|
| | | | | |

**Company**

The Literary Dog

**Email**

LiteraryDog@books.com

| **Phone** | **Mobile** | **Fax** |
|---|---|---|
| (657) 555-9723 | | |

*** Display name as**

The Literary Dog ⬍

**Other**     **Website**

    www.TheLiteraryDog.com

**Print on check as** ✔ Use display name

The Literary Dog

| **Billing rate (/hr)** | **Terms** |
|---|---|
| | 2% 10 Net 30 ⬍ |

**Address** map

2975 Main Street

| **Opening balance** | **as of** |
|---|---|
| | 📅 |

**Account no.**

*Appears in the memo of all payments*

| Santa Ana | CA |
|---|---|

**Tax ID**

| 92701 | *Country* |
|---|---|

**Notes**

☐ Track payments for 1099

| Cancel | Privacy | Save |
|---|---|---|

When the Vendor Information is complete, click the **Save** button
Do <u>not</u> close Your Name's Beach Barkers, continue to the next section

## ADD A NEW INVENTORY ITEM—DO

In preparation for adding books to our inventory and placing an order with The Literary Dog, a new inventory item for Books must be added. This new item will be used for the purchase order that is created. Since it is a new inventory item, it does not have an opening balance.

> <u>MEMO</u>
> **DATE:** February 16, 2016
>
> Add a new Sales Item named Books. The Cost is $3. There is no opening balance. Use the accounts shown.

*DO*

Continue to use **Your Name's Beach Barkers** and add a new inventory item

Open the Products and Services list, click the **New** button
Click **Inventory item**
Enter the Name: **Books**
There is no Quantity on hand so enter **0.00**
As of date: **123115**
- The 12/31/15 as of date avoids any conflict with dates. If you create a sales item and try to order it on the same date, QuickBooks Online will not let you.

- Be VERY careful to use <u>2015</u> for the year. If you use the current year, you will not be able to order any Books. If you enter the incorrect as of date, delete the product (Open Products and Services list, click the drop-down list arrow next to the product name, click Make Inactive) then re-add the same product as an inventory item.
- If you accidentally enter a quantity of more than 0 and have saved the new item, you must prepare the Inventory Valuation Detail report, select All Dates, Run the Report, click on the product, click the line with Inventory Starting Value in the Transaction Type to open the Inventory Starting Value page, change to 0.00, click Save and Close. You do this in Chapter 8.

Enter the Sales and Purchasing information description: **Books**

- Use the accounts listed: Inventory Asset, Sales of Product Income, and Cost of Goods Sold.
- Is taxable should have a check mark. As you remember, products incur a sales tax when sold.

Enter the Cost: **3**

Click **Save and close**

- If you get a Closing date message, click the appropriate response.

Do <u>not</u> close Your Name's Beach Barkers, continue to the next section

## PURCHASE ORDERS—DO

In essence, a purchase order (PO) is a document you send to a vendor that states your intent to purchase products. The details of the purchase including quantities and prices are included on the purchase order. When the vendor accepts your PO, you have an agreement with the company to receive the products ordered. When everything on a purchase order is received, a bill is prepared and the purchase order is marked Closed. QuickBooks Online Plus is the only version of QuickBooks Online that has the ability to use Purchase Orders and to track inventory.

> <u>MEMO</u>
> **DATE:** February 16, 2016
>
> After creating the new inventory item, Books, you need to order a supply to have on hand for customer purchases. Order 250 books from The Literary Dog at $3 each.

<u>DO</u>

Continue to use **Your Name's Beach Barkers** and create a purchase order for Books

Click the **Plus** icon, click **Purchase Order** in the Vendors column
Click the drop-down list arrow for Choose a vendor, click **The Literary Dog**
Enter the Purchase Order date: **02/16/16**
You will see the text box for Location, leave it blank

- At this time, we are not tracking the location for the inventory purchased. Rather, we will order it from the main office in Venice and stock both locations with the necessary inventory.
- If Account details is expanded, click the ▼ icon to collapse it.
- If Item details is collapsed, click the ▶ to expand it.

In Item details, complete Line 1:
> Click the drop-down list arrow for PRODUCT/SERVICE, click **Books**
> Tab to QTY, enter **250**, press **Tab**

- At this point, we are only interested in tracking Classes for sales so leave the text box for Class blank.

Print and or send the Purchase Order
- If you save the Purchase Order, name it: **2-Your Name PO 1001 The Literary Dog**.
- If you print the Purchase Order, you may or may not notice that the custom formatting you entered for Invoices. If you get the green color on your Purchase Orders, wonderful. If not and your Purchase Order is blue, do not be concerned.

Click **Save and new**

Do <u>not</u> close Your Name's Beach Barkers

## PREPARE ADDITIONAL PURCHASE ORDERS—DO

Additional purchase orders need to be prepared. As you look at the Inventory Valuation Summary, you will see one dog bed 26 brushes in stock. Both of those items need to be replenished.

---

<u>MEMO</u>
**DATE:** February 16, 2016

Prepare a Purchase Order for 25 Dog Beds at $20 each from a new vendor, Pawsitively Elegant (Address: 1520 S. Broadway, Los Angeles, CA 90015, Email: PawsitivelyElegant@dogs.com, Phone: 310-555-2925, Fax: 310-555-5292, Web site: www.PawsitivelyElegant.com, Terms: 2% 10 Net 30.)

You are also ordering 25 Brushes from All About Dogs Supplies.

Bark City Toys has added a new line of toys. Order 50 Toys & Treats for $2 each.

Order 35 Dog Beds at $20 from Canine Supplies.

---

<u>DO</u>

Continue to use **Your Name's Beach Barkers** and prepare Purchase Orders

On the new Purchase Order, click the drop-down list arrow for Choose a vendor, click **+Add new**

Enter the information for the new vendor:

Name: **Pawsitively Elegant**

Click **+ Details**

Remove **Pawsitively** from First name and **Elegant** from the Last name text boxes

Enter the remaining Vendor Information in the Memo to complete the addition of Pawsitively Elegant

- The Opening balance should be left blank.

## Vendor Information

| Title | First name | Middle name | Last name | Suffix | Email |
|---|---|---|---|---|---|
| | | | | | PawsitivelyElegant@dogs.com |

| Company | Phone | Mobile | Fax |
|---|---|---|---|
| | (310) 555-2925 | | (310) 555-5292 |

| * Display name as | Other | Website |
|---|---|---|
| Pawsitively Elegant | | www.PawsitivelyElegant.com |

Print on check as ✓ Use display name | Billing rate (/hr) | Terms
| Pawsitively Elegant | | 2% 10 Net 30 |

| Address map | Opening balance | as of |
|---|---|---|
| 1520 S. Broadway | | |

| | | Account no. |
|---|---|---|
| Los Angeles | CA | *Appears in the memo of all payments* |
| 90015 | *Country* | Tax ID |

Enter the Purchase Order date **021616**
- If Account Details is expanded, click the ▼ icon to collapse it.
- If Item Details is collapsed, click the ▶ to expand it.

Complete Item details Line 1: click in the PRODUCT/SERVICE column

Click the drop-down list arrow, click **Dog Bed** in the Item List

Tab to QTY and enter **25** for the number of dog beds, press **Tab**

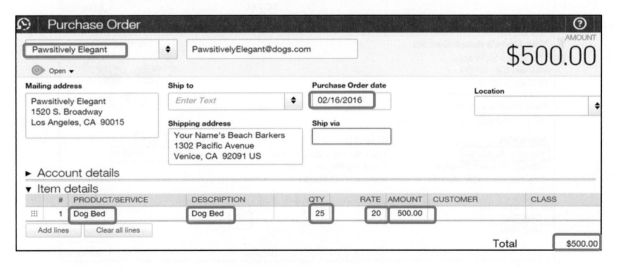

Print and or send the Purchase Order
- If you save the Purchase Order, name it: **3-Your Name PO 1002 Pawsitively Elegant**.

Click **Save and new**

Complete the other Purchase Orders listed in the Memo

Print and or send as previously instructed

Follow the same naming pattern: **4-Your Name PO 1003 All About Dogs Supplies**, **5-Your Name PO 1004 Bark City Toys**, and **6-Your Name PO 1005 Canine Supplies**

- Purchase Orders 1003, 1004, and 1005 are shown in printed format below.

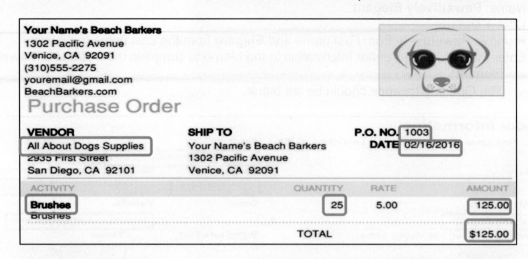

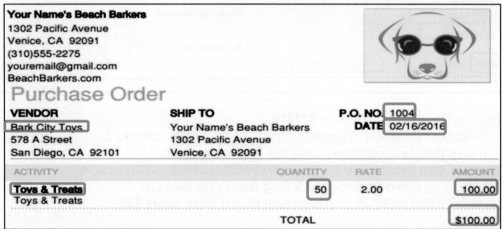

When all purchase orders are complete, click **Save and close**

If you get a blank purchase order on the screen, click the **Close** button

Do <u>not</u> close Your Name's Beach Barkers

## OPEN PURCHASE ORDER LIST BY VENDOR REPORT—DO

When you have prepared several purchase orders, it is important to review the Open Purchase Order List by Vendor report. This report provides information about all purchase orders currently open, the date of the purchase order, the PO number, any memos or descriptions, shipping information, and the amount of the purchase order. If you wish to add additional information, you may customize the report and select from among a variety of columns.

<u>DO</u>

Continue to use **Your Name's Beach Barkers** and prepare the Open Purchase Order List by Vendor report

Click **Reports** on the Navigation bar
Click in the text box for Go to report
Scroll through the list of available reports, click **Open Purchase Order List**
- You could also key in the report name in the text box.
Click the **CUSTOMIZE** button
Click the **Change Columns** button
- Scroll through the list of Available Columns and note the Selected Columns shown.
Click **PO Status** in Available Columns
Click the **Add>** button
- The column will now be shown on the report.
Since we do not have shipping information, click **Ship Via** in Selected Columns
Click the **<Remove** button to remove it from the report
To reorganize the order of the columns shown, click **PO Status** in Selected Columns
Click the down arrow [⌄] to move it down below Num

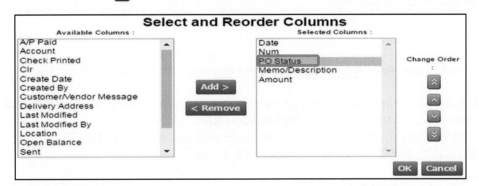

Click **OK**
Click **Header/Footer** on the left side of the Customize screen
Remove the Date Prepared and the Time Prepared, click the **Run Report** button
Click the **Save Customizations** button to save the format changes
Accept the name Open Purchase Order List by Vendor, click **OK**
Review the report

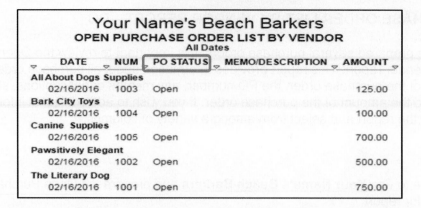

Print, export, and/or send/submit the report as you did in earlier chapters

- If you save the report, name it **7-Your Name Open Purchase Order List Ch. 7**. Note: in order to shorten the file name, by Vendor was not included in the name.

Do <u>not</u> close the report or Your Name Beach Barker's

## EDIT A PURCHASE ORDER—DO

It is possible to drill-down and get information on individual purchase orders by clicking on the PO in the report.

---

**MEMO**

**DATE:** February 17, 2016

You really need to order 35 brushes and cannot remember the quantity you entered for PO 1003 to About All Dogs Supplies.

---

<u>DO</u>

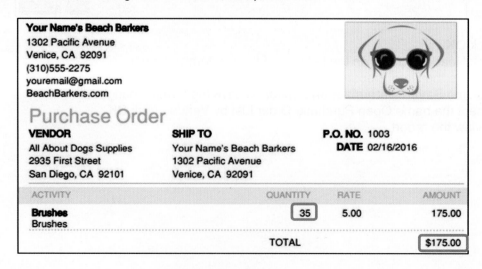

Continue to use **Your Name's Beach Barkers** and edit Purchase Order 1003

With the Open Purchase Order List by Vendor still open, point to the line for **1003** for All About Dogs Supplies, when the line turns **blue**, click it

- The quantity for the Purchase Order is 25 and you want to order 35.

Click in QTY, and change the amount to **35**, press **Tab**

Print and or send the corrected Purchase Order

- If you save the Purchase Order, name it: **8-Your Name PO 1003 All About Dogs Supplies Corrected**.
Click **Save and close**

You are returned to the Open Purchase Order List Report by Vendor
- Notice the amount of PO 1003 changed from $125 to $175.
Do <u>not</u> close the report or Your Name's Beach Barkers

## RECEIVE ITEMS ORDERED—DO

As you practiced in the drill, when the merchandise ordered on the Purchase Order is received, a bill is prepared, and the Purchase Order information is added to it. This closes the purchase order. If you only receive part of the merchandise ordered, a bill is still prepared but the purchase order will not be closed. Because QuickBooks Online does not have a feature in place to receive partial orders, you need to create a new purchase order for the items that were not received. Then you delete the unreceived items from the original PO, create a bill, and close the purchase order for the merchandise that was received.

| MEMO |
| --- |
| **DATE:** February 18, 2016 |
| Received all of the Dog Beds ordered from Pawsitively Elegant. Record the bill. |
| Received all of the Brushes ordered from All About Dogs Supplies. Record the bill. |
| Received 27 of the Dog Beds ordered from Canine Supplies. Record the partial receipt. |

## <u>DO</u>

Continue to use **<u>Your Name's Beach Barkers</u>** and record the receipt of inventory items

Click the **Plus** icon, click **Bill** in the Vendors column
Click the drop-down list arrow for Choose a vendor
Click **Pawsitively Elegant**
- The information for Pawsitively Elegant is inserted into the bill.
An Add to Bill pane appears on the right-side of the bill

Click either the **Add all** button or the ⇐ **Add** arrow to add the information for Purchase Order 1005 to the bill
Enter the Bill date of **02/18/16**, press **Tab**
- The Terms of 2% 10 Net 30 were added to the bill automatically.
- Notice the blue notation "1 linked transaction." This means that the bill and the purchase order are linked together.

7

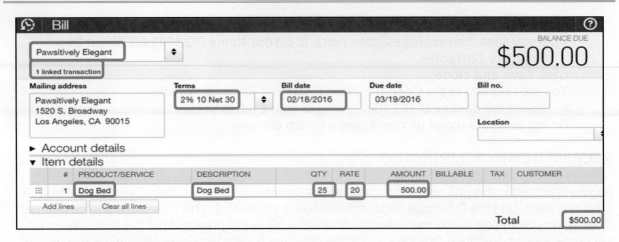

Click **Save and close**

Since you did not close the Open Purchase Order List by Vendor report, it should still be showing on the screen

- Note that PO 1002 for Pawsitively Elegant is no longer shown.

Click the **Recent Transactions** icon next to the Plus icon

Click **Purchase Order No. 1002**

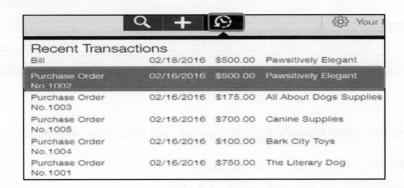

- Notice that the Purchase Order is marked "Closed" and "Linked Bill." This means that all of the merchandise on the purchase order was received and that the purchase order and the bill are linked together.

Click the Close button for Purchase Order 1002

Record the receipt of the bill for PO 1003 All About Dogs Supplies

Enter the information provided in the Memo to record the receipt of all of the brushes ordered

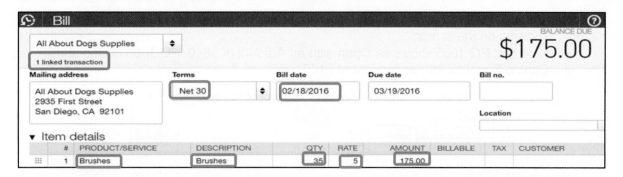

Click **Save and close**
- If the Open Purchase order List by Vendor report is still on the screen, you will no longer see PO 1003 for All About Dogs Supplies.

Click the **Recent Transactions** icon
Click **Purchase Order 1005** for Canine Supplies
- You received 27 of the 35 Dog Beds on order. To record a bill and close the purchase order for the number of dog beds received, a copy of the purchase order must be made and the quantities for both purchase orders need to be edited.

Click the **More** button at the bottom of the Purchase Order
Click **Copy**
- You will see a copy of the purchase order on the screen. With a message that it is a copy.

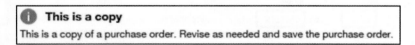

> ℹ **This is a copy**
> This is a copy of a purchase order. Revise as needed and save the purchase order.

Enter the Purchase Order date of **02/18/16**
Change the QTY of dog beds to **8**, press **Tab**
- Do the math: 35 ordered – 27 received = 8 on backorder (the new purchase order).

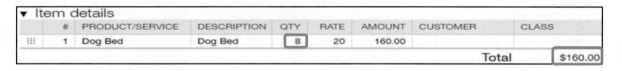

Print and or send the corrected Purchase Order
- If you save the Purchase Order, name it: **9-Your Name PO 1006 Canine Supplies**.

Click **Save and close**
You should be returned to Purchase Order 1005
- If not, click the **Recent Transactions** icon and click Purchase Order 1005.

Change the QTY on the original purchase order to **27**, press **Tab**
- Purchase Order 1005 now shows the dog beds that were received.

Print and or send the corrected Purchase Order
- If you save the Purchase Order, name it: **10-Your Name PO 1005 Canine Supplies Corrected**.

Click **Save and close**

Since you did not close the Open Purchase Order List by Vendor report, it should still be showing on the screen

- Note that PO 1005 shows as Open with an Amount of $540. PO 1006 is also shown for Canine Supplies with an amount of $160.

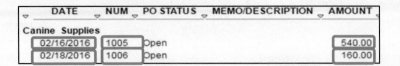

| | DATE | NUM | PO STATUS | MEMO/DESCRIPTION | AMOUNT |
|---|---|---|---|---|---|
| **Canine Supplies** | | | | | |
| | 02/16/2016 | 1005 | Open | | 540.00 |
| | 02/18/2016 | 1006 | Open | | 160.00 |

Click the **Plus** icon, click **Bill** in the Vendors column

Click the drop-down list arrow for Choose a vendor, click **Canine Supplies**

Enter the Bill date of **02/18/16**

- If you have Kennel Supplies shown in Line 1 of Account details, click the **Clear all lines** button below Account details to remove it.
- Notice the Add to Bill pane shows both Purchase Order 1005 for Dog Beds $540 and Purchase Order 1006 for Dog Beds $160.

Since you received 27 Dog Beds, click the [⇦ **Add**] button for Purchase Order 1005

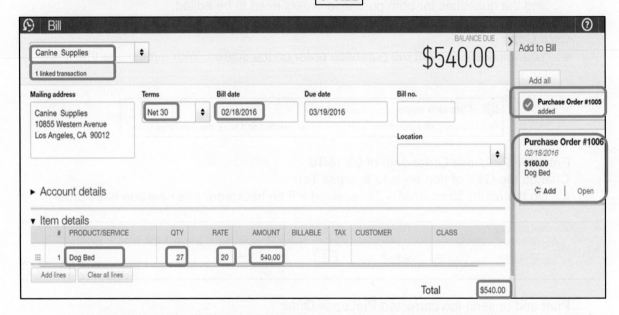

- The information for Purchase Order 1005 was added to the bill. Notice that the bill is linked. Because you added the information from the purchase order, the bill and purchase order are linked together. Purchase Order 1006 shows that it is still Open.
- The description column was intentionally omitted from the screen shot to provide better legibility.

Click **Save and close**

- Notice that the only open invoice for Canine Supplies is 1006.

Do <u>not</u> close Your Name's Beach Barkers

## RECORD A MERCHANDISE RETURN—DO

When dealing with inventory items, there will be times when you order something and it arrives damaged or you may have ordered the wrong item. If this is the case, the vendor issues a credit memo to you and you record a Vendor Credit for the return of merchandise listed on the vendor's credit memo. The amount of the vendor credit is deducted from the amount owed and the merchandise is deducted from the Inventory Asset account.

> **MEMO**
> **DATE:** February 19, 2016
>
> When you were unpacking the Dog Beds you received from Canine Supplies, you notice that two of them had ripped seams. Return the 2 Dog Beds. Received Credit Memo 1596 from Canine Supplies.

*DO*

 Continue to use **Your Name's Beach Barkers** and record the return of the two dog beds

> Click the **Plus** icon, click **Vendor Credit** in the Vendors column
> Click the drop-down list arrow for Choose a vendor
> Click **Canine Supplies**
> Enter the Payment date **02/19/16**
> Enter Canine Supplies Credit Memo number **1596** in Ref no.
> • Purchase Order 1006 is shown in the Add to Vendor Credit pane.
> Since you are not receiving merchandise, click the [ > ] icon to close the pane
> • If Account details is expanded, click the [ ▼ ] icon to collapse it.
> • If Item details is collapsed, click the [ ► ] to expand it.
> Complete Item details Line 1 for the return of 2 Dog Beds

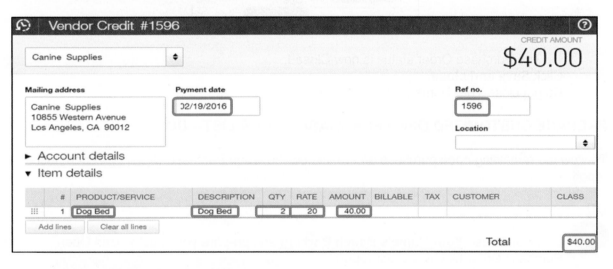

> When finished, click **Save and close**
> Do <u>not</u> close Your Name's Beach Barkers

## CLOSE A PURCHASE ORDER—DO

If you have prepared a purchase order for an item that will no longer be available, you manually close the purchase order. It is helpful to retain the purchase order in your records so you know what you ordered and know that it is no longer available from a particular vendor. Because of this, you manually close a purchase order rather than delete it.

> **MEMO**
> **DATE:** February 19, 2016
>
> Because of a problem with the quality of the dog beds, Canine Supplies discontinued dog beds until they can get a more reliable supplier. Manually close Purchase Order 1006.

<u>**DO**</u>

Continue to use **Your Name's Beach Barkers** and manually close Purchase Order 1006

Click the **Recent Transactions** icon
Click **Purchase Order 1006** for Canine Supplies
Click the drop-down list arrow for Open
Click the drop-down list arrow on the Purchase Order status pop up
Click **Closed**

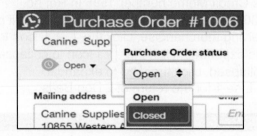

- The Purchase Order status is now Closed.
Click **Save and close**
Do <u>not</u> close Your Name's Beach Barkers

## PREPARE CUSTOMIZED OPEN PURCHASE ORDER LIST—DO

To view the remaining open purchase orders, review the Open Purchase Order by Vendor List report.

<u>**DO**</u>

Continue to use **Your Name's Beach Barkers** and prepare your Customized Open Purchase Order List by Vendor report

If you did not close the report, it will still be showing on your screen
If the report is not showing, do the following:
    Click **Reports** on the Navigation bar
    Click **My Custom Reports** for the report category
    Click **Open Purchase Order List by Vendor**
View the two open purchase orders
- All the purchase orders that were closed by preparing a bill or closing manually will not be shown in the report.

```
┌──────────────────────────────────────────────────────────┐
│              Your Name's Beach Barkers                     │
│          OPEN PURCHASE ORDER LIST BY VENDOR                │
│                      All Dates                             │
│    DATE    ⌄ NUM ⌄ PO STATUS ⌄ MEMO/DESCRIPTION ⌄ AMOUNT ⌄ │
│  Bark City Toys                                            │
│    02/16/2016  1004   Open                        100.00   │
│  The Literary Dog                                          │
│    02/16/2016  1001   Open                        750.00   │
└──────────────────────────────────────────────────────────┘
```

Do not close Your Name's Beach Barkers

## PURCHASES BY PRODUCT/SERVICE DETAIL—DO

There are several reports available that assist you in managing inventory. These include Inventory Valuation Summary and Detail, Product/Service List, Purchases by Product/Service Detail, and Sales by Product/Service Summary and Detail. To group your purchases by inventory item, prepare the Purchases by Product/Service Detail.

## DO

Continue to use **Your Name's Beach Barkers** and prepare the Purchases by Product/Service Detail report

Click **Reports** on the Navigation bar
Click **All Reports**, click **Manage Products and Inventory** to select the report category
Click **Purchases by Product/Service Detail**
Enter the Date From: **020116** and To: **021916**, click **Run Report**
* You will see each merchandise receipt and the accompanying bill or the return and the vendor credit for each item purchased.

```
┌─────────────────────────────────────────────────────────────────────────┐
│                      Your Name's Beach Barkers                            │
│                 PURCHASES BY PRODUCT/SERVICE DETAIL                        │
│                          February 1-19, 2016                              │
│   DATE   ⌄ TRANSACTION TYPE ⌄ NUM ⌄   VENDOR   ⌄ MEMO/DESCRIPTION ⌄ QTY ⌄ RATE ⌄ BALANCE ⌄ │
│  Brushes                                                                  │
│   02/18/2016  Bill              All About Dogs Supplies  Brushes   35.00  5.00   175.00    │
│  Dog Bed                                                                  │
│   02/18/2016  Bill              Canine Supplies      Dog Bed      27.00  20.00   540.00    │
│   02/18/2016  Bill              Pawsitively Elegant  Dog Bed      25.00  20.00  1,040.00   │
│   02/19/2016  Vendor Credit  1596  Canine Supplies   Dog Bed      -2.00  20.00  1,000.00   │
│  TOTAL                                                                    │
└─────────────────────────────────────────────────────────────────────────┘
```
**Partial Report**

Remove the Date Prepared and Time Prepared from the footer and print, export, and/or send/submit the report as you did in earlier chapters
* If Accrual Basis shows in the footer, leave it in the report. At the time of this writing, there was not an option to deselect the report basis from this report.
* If you save the report, name it **11-Your Name Purchases by Product-Service Detail Ch. 7**.
Close Your Name's Beach Barkers

## ADD A COMPANY CREDIT CARD AND VENDOR—DRILL

Some businesses use credit cards as an integral part of their finances. Some companies have a credit card that may be used primarily for gasoline purchases for company vehicles. Other companies use credit cards as a means of paying for expenses, purchasing inventory to sell, and purchasing merchandise or other necessary items for use in the business. In QuickBooks Online, a credit card purchase is recorded as an expense. When you pay the credit card bill, you will need to pay a vendor so the credit card company needs to be added as a vendor.

## DRILL

  Open the **Test Drive Company** and add American Express as a Credit Card account and as a vendor

> Open the Chart of Accounts
> Scroll through the list of accounts to determine if an American Express Credit Card account has been added
> Since there is not an account for American Express, click the **New** button
> Category Type: **Credit Card**
> Detail Type: **Credit Card**
> Name: **American Express**
> Verify the new account details

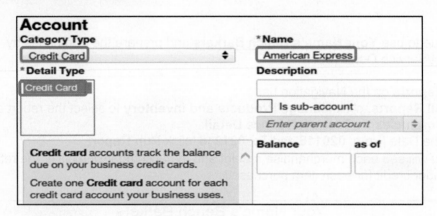

> Click **Save and Close**
> Verify the new American Express Credit Card in the Account List
> Click **Vendors** on the Navigation bar
> Click the **New vendor** button
> Enter the American Express Information:
>> Company: **American Express**
>> Address: **12345 West Avenue**
>> City: **Los Angeles**
>> State: **CA**
>> ZIP: **90012**
>> Phone: **800-555-8155**
> Click **Save**
> Do not close the Test Drive Company

## RECORD CREDIT CARD PURCHASE—DRILL

When a company uses a credit card to make a purchase, the transaction is recorded as an Expense.

> **MEMO**
> **DATE:** Current Date
>
> Record the purchase of $54 of supplies from Computers by Jenni to be used immediately.
> The account is American Express, and the Payment method is American Express.

## DRILL

Continue to use the **Test Drive Company** and record an Expense transaction using a credit card

Click the **Plus** icon, click **Expense** in the Vendors column
Click the drop-down list arrow for Choose a payee
Click **Computers by Jenni**
- A payee is the person or company that will receive the payment.
Click the drop-down list arrow for Checking, click **American Express**
- If Checking is not shown, you may see "Choose an account" or one of the other payment accounts in the text box.
For the Payment date, use the **Current Date**
Click the drop-down list arrow for Payment Method, click **American Express**
- Notice that the Balance is $0.00. This is the first time the credit card is being used.
Complete Line 1 in Account details
- Remember, the Item details section is used only when ordering inventory items for sale.
Click the drop-down list arrow for ACCOUNT
Since the purchase is for supplies to be used immediately, you will select the expense account **Supplies**
Tab to AMOUNT, enter **$54**, press **Tab**

Click **Save and close**
Do <u>not</u> close the Test Drive Company

## RECORD CREDIT CARD CREDIT—DRILL

When something has been purchased and paid for with a credit card, a return is recorded as a Credit Card Credit. This lets you know that your credit card balance and the subsequent bill will be reduced for the amount of the return.

> **MEMO**
> **DATE:** Current Date
>
> Returned $10 of the supplies purchased from Computers by Jenni using an American Express credit card.

*DRILL*

 Continue to use the **Test Drive Company** and record the Credit Card Credit for the return of supplies

> Click the **Plus** icon, click **Credit Card Credit** in the Vendors column
> Click the drop-down list arrow for Choose a payee, click **Computers by Jenni**
> Click the drop-down list arrow for Mastercard, click **American Express**
> * You may see "Choose an account" or Checking rather than Mastercard.
> * The Test Drive Company spells the account as Mastercard rather than MasterCard.
> * Note that the Balance shows $54. That is the amount of the transaction for supplies.
> Leave the Payment date as the Current Date
> * If necessary, expand the Account details area.
> Complete Line 1:
> > Account: **Supplies**
> > Amount: **10**

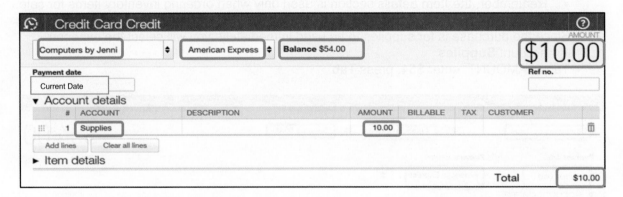

> Click **Save and new**
> * On the blank Expense screen, you will still see American Express for the Account. Notice the Balance of $44.00. This proves that the $10 of the credit was deducted from the amount owed to American Express.
> Do <u>not</u> close the Test Drive Company

## PURCHASE INVENTORY WITH A CREDIT CARD—DRILL

You may purchase inventory and pay for it using a credit card. Using a credit card for inventory can be entered in several ways. If you prepare a PO for the purchase, you record the receipt of the inventory on a bill, as you did earlier in the chapter. Or, you may record the receipt of the inventory on an expense form by adding the PO to the Expense rather than to a Bill. A third way to purchase inventory using a credit card is to record the purchase directly on the expense form without preparing a purchase order.

---

> **MEMO**
> **DATE:** Current Date
>
> Purchased 3 rock fountains from Tania's Nursery for $125 each. Pay with American Express

*DRILL*

 Continue to use the **Test Drive Company** and record the Credit Card purchase of inventory items

With a blank Expense form on the screen, click the drop-down list arrow for Choose a payee
Click **Tania's Nursery**
- If you get a message asking "Do you want to prefill this expense and overwrite your entries using values from this contact's last expense?," click **No**.
- If any previous information has been entered in Account details, click the **Clear all lines** button.

For Checking or Choose an account, select **American Express** if it is not shown
Payment Date: **Current Date**
Payment method: **American Express**
- If necessary, expand Item details.

Click in the PRODUCT/SERVICE text box in Line 1 of Item details
- Remember, Item details is used when you are purchasing inventory items.

Click the drop-down list arrow, click **Rock Fountain**
Change the QTY to **3**, press **Tab**
- The total of $375 is inserted. There is no sales tax on an item you purchase to sell.

Click **Save and close**
To verify that the quantity of Rock Fountains was increased, open the **Products and Services List**
Click the drop-down list arrow for Rock Fountain, click **Run report**
- You will see a Product/Service QuickReport for Rock Fountain.
- Remember, the dates shown in your report will be different from the dates below.

## Craig's Design and Landscaping Services
### PRODUCT/SERVICE QUICKREPORT: DESIGN:FOUNTAINS:ROCK FOUNTAIN
#### Since December 18, 2015

| DATE | TRANSACTION TYPE | NUM | NAME | MEMO/DESCRIPTION | QTY | RATE | AMOUNT | BALANCE |
|------|------------------|-----|------|------------------|-----|------|--------|---------|
| **Inventory Asset** | | | | | | | | |
| 02/20/2016 | Bill | | Norton Lumber and Building Materials | Rock Fountain | 1.00 | 125.00 | 125.00 | 125.00 |
| 02/20/2016 | Invoice | 1037 | Sonnenschein Family Store | Rock Fountain | -1.00 | 125.00 | -125.00 | 0.00 |
| 02/20/2016 | Inventory Qty Adjust | START | | Opening inventory for Rock Fountain | 3.00 | | | 0.00 |
| 02/20/2016 | Invoice | 1035 | Mark Cho | Rock Fountain | -1.00 | 125.00 | -125.00 | -125.00 |
| 02/20/2016 | Inventory Qty Adjust | START | | Opening inventory for Rock Fountain | 3.00 | 125.00 | 375.00 | 250.00 |
| 02/20/2016 | Check | 75 | Hicks Hardware | Rock Fountain | 1.00 | 125.00 | 125.00 | 375.00 |
| 02/20/2016 | Invoice | 1036 | Freeman Sporting Goods:0969 Ocean View Road | Rock Fountain | -1.00 | 125.00 | -125.00 | 250.00 |
| 03/17/2016 | Expense | | Tania's Nursery | Rock Fountain | 3.00 | 125.00 | 375.00 | 625.00 |
| **Total for Inventory Asset** | | | | | | | **$625.00** | |

Close the Test Drive Company

## ADD A COMPANY CREDIT CARD AND VENDOR—DO

As you just practiced, credit cards may be used as a means of paying for expenses, purchasing inventory to sell, or purchasing other necessary items used in the business. In QuickBooks Online, a credit card purchase is recorded as an expense. When you pay the credit card bill, you will need to pay a vendor so the credit card company needs to be added as a vendor.

## <u>DO</u>

Open **Your Name's Beach Barkers** and add a Visa credit card account and vendor

Open the Chart of Accounts
Scroll through the list of accounts to determine if a Visa Credit Card account has been added
Since there is not an account for Visa, click the **New** button
Category Type: **Credit Card**
Detail Type: **Credit Card**
Name: **Visa**
Verify the new account details

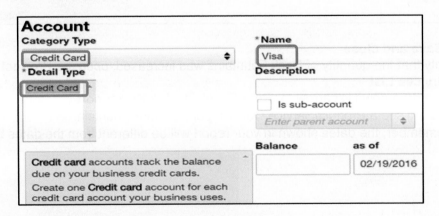

Click **Save and Close**
Verify the new Visa Credit Card in the Account List
- Since the credit card is for something you owe, it is included between Accounts Payable and the Other Current Liabilities.

Click **Vendors** on the Navigation bar
Click the **New vendor** button
Enter the Visa Information:
    Company: **Visa**
    Address: **9501 Los Angeles Avenue**
    City: **Los Angeles**
    State: **CA**
    ZIP: **90012**
    Phone: **800-555-9925**
Click **Save**
Do <u>not</u> close Your Name's Beach Barkers

## RECORD CREDIT CARD PURCHASE—DO

When a company uses a credit card to make a purchase, the transaction is recorded as an Expense.

---

**MEMO**
**DATE:** February 19, 2016

You need to have printer toner cartridges on hand, purchased 5 at $40 each, plus tax for a total of $216.00 from Super Office. Pay for the purchase with the company Visa.

---

<u>DO</u>

Continue to use **Your Name's Beach Barkers** and record an Expense transaction using a credit card

Click the **Plus** icon, click **Expense** in the Vendors column
Click the drop-down list arrow for Choose a payee
Click **Super Office**
- A payee is the person or company that will receive the payment.
- If nothing were shown in the text box next to Payee, you would see Choose an account. Usually, you see one of your acceptable payment methods in this text box. These include: Checking, Petty Cash, and Visa. Simply click the drop-down list arrow and select the payment method of choice.

Click the drop-down list arrow and click **Visa**
For the Payment date, enter **02/19/16**
Click the drop-down list arrow for Payment Method, click **Visa**
- Notice that the Balance is $0.00. This is the first time the credit card is being used.

Complete Line 1 in Account details
- Remember, the Item details section is used only when ordering inventory items for sale.
- If there is any information shown for Account details, click the **trash can** icon at the end of each line of information, or click the **Clear all lines** button below the section.

Click the drop-down list arrow for ACCOUNT
Since the purchase is for supplies to have on hand, you will select the asset account **Office Supplies**
Tab to AMOUNT, enter **216**, press **Tab**
- Do the math: 5 cartridges * 40 each = 200; multiply the cost by the 8% tax: 200 * .08 = $16 tax. Add the cost plus the tax: $200 + 16 = $216 (or 200 * 1.08 = 216 to calculate the cost and include the tax all at the same time).

- When you purchase something and record an expense or a bill, you enter the total amount due. You do not enter separate quantities or tax information.

Tab to or click in Memo, delete any existing Memo and enter: **Printer Cartridges**

- Clicking the Clear all lines button does not have any effect on the Memo.

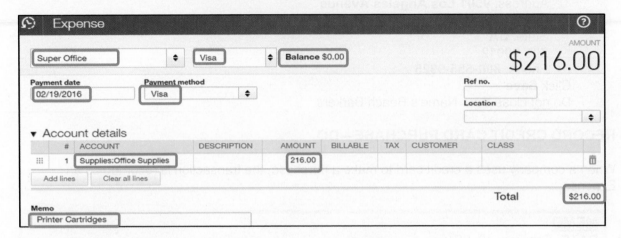

Click **Save and close**
Do <u>not</u> close Your Name's Beach Barkers

## RECORD CREDIT CARD CREDIT—DO

When a credit card purchase, is returned a Credit Card Credit is recorded. This lets you know that your credit card balance and the subsequent bill will be reduced for the amount of the return.

> **MEMO**
> **DATE:** February 19, 2016
>
> Received 1 of the printer cartridges that was the wrong color, $43.20. Record the return for the Visa purchase from Super Office.

<u>DO</u>

Continue to use **Your Name's Beach Barkers** and record the Credit Card Credit for the return of supplies

Click the **Plus** icon, click **Credit Card Credit** in the Vendors column
Click the drop-down list arrow for Choose a payee, click **Super Office**
If Visa is not shown, click the drop-down list arrow for Choose an account, click **Visa**
- Note that the Balance shows $216. That is the amount of the transaction for the printer cartridges.
Payment date: **02/19/16**
- If necessary, expand the Account details area.
Complete Line 1:
    Account: **Office Supplies**
    Amount: **43.20**
    Enter the Memo: **Returned 1 Printer Cartridge**

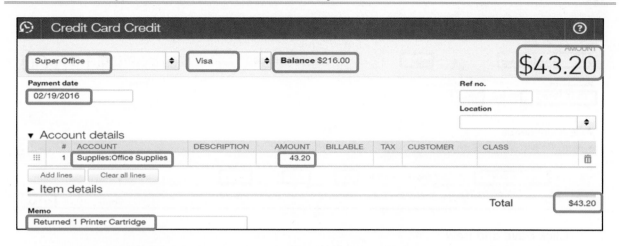

Click **Save and new**
- On the blank Credit Card Credit screen, you will still see Visa for the Account. Notice the Balance of $172.80. This proves that the $43.20 of the credit was deducted from the amount owed to American Express.

Close the blank Credit Card Credit screen

Do not close Your Name's Beach Barkers, continue with the next section

## PURCHASE INVENTORY WITH A CREDIT CARD—DO

As you explored in the drill, you may purchase inventory and pay for it using a credit card. Since you have already created bills from purchase orders, you will complete an Expense form to purchase inventory using a credit card without preparing a purchase order.

---

**MEMO**
**DATE:** February 19, 2016

Use the company Visa to purchase 50 cans of a new line of organic Dog Food-Canned from Pet Supplies Unlimited for 2.50 each.

---

_DO_

Continue to use **Your Name's Beach Barkers** and record the Credit Card purchase of inventory items

Open the **Expense** form, click the drop-down list arrow for Choose a payee
Click **Pet Supplies Unlimited**
- Remember the text box next to Payee is where you select your payment account.
For Choose an account, select **Visa** if it is not shown
Payment Date: **021916**
Payment method: **Visa**
- If necessary, expand the Item details section.
Item details Line 1: click in the PRODUCT/SERVICE text box
- Remember, the section for Item details is used when you are purchasing inventory items.
Click the drop-down list arrow, click **Dog Food-Canned**
Change the QTY to **50**, press **Tab**
- The total of $125 is inserted. There is no sales tax on an item you purchase to sell.

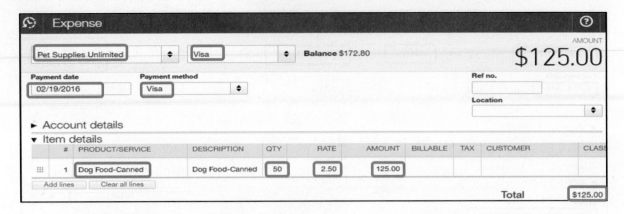

Click **Save and new**

- Is the Balance for your Visa card $297.80?

Click the **Close** button to close Expenses

To verify that the quantity of Canned Dog Food was increased, open the Products and Services List

Click the drop-down list arrow for Dog Food-Canned, click **Run report**

- You will see a Product/Service QuickReport for Dog Food-Canned.

Enter the Date From: **12/31/15** and To: **02/19/16**

### Your Name's Beach Barkers
### PRODUCT/SERVICE QUICKREPORT: DOG FOOD-CANNED
December 31, 2015 - February 19, 2016

| DATE | TRANSACTION TYPE | NUM | NAME | MEMO/DESCRIPTION | CLASS | QTY | RATE | AMOUNT | BALANCE |
|------|-----------------|-----|------|-----------------|-------|-----|------|--------|---------|
| **Inventory Asset** | | | | | | | | | |
| 12/31/2015 | Inventory Starting Value | START | | Opening inventory and value for Dog Food-Canned | | 485.00 | 2.50 | 1,212.50 | 1,212.50 |
| 02/01/2016 | Invoice | 1041 | Gucci, Gloria | Dog Food-Canned | Boutique | -7.00 | 2.50 | -17.50 | 1,195.00 |
| 02/04/2016 | Sales Receipt | 1049 | De Los Santos, David | Dog Food-Canned | Boutique | -7.00 | 2.50 | -17.50 | 1,177.50 |
| 02/04/2016 | Sales Receipt | 1046 | Wagner, Nick | Dog Food-Canned | Boutique | -14.00 | 2.50 | -35.00 | 1,142.50 |
| 02/04/2016 | Sales Receipt | 1047 | Cash Customer | Dog Food-Canned | Boutique | -14.00 | 2.50 | -35.00 | 1,107.50 |
| 02/12/2016 | Sales Receipt | 1056 | Johnson, Alice | Dog Food-Canned | Boutique | -30.00 | 2.50 | -75.00 | 1,032.50 |
| 02/19/2016 | Expense | | Pet Supplies Unlimited | Dog Food-Canned | | 50.00 | 2.50 | 125.00 | 1,157.50 |
| **Total for Inventory Asset** | | | | | | | | | **$1,157.50** |

Close Your Name's Beach Barkers

## ENTER BILLS AND VENDOR CREDITS—DRILL

Whether the bill is to record amounts owed for expenses incurred in the operation of a business, for items purchased for the operation of the business, or for merchandise to sell in the business, QuickBooks Online provides accounts payable tracking for all vendors owed. Entering bills as soon as they are received is an efficient way to record your liabilities.

Frequently, discounts are given from vendors for purchases of merchandise and other expenses in order to inspire early payment. If a Discount Term has not been created, it may be added to the Terms List.

As in previous chapters, there are a few entries that need to be made in order to practice the drill.

---

**MEMO**
**DATE:** Current Date

Add Terms 2% 10 Net 30.

Record a bill for inventory received from purchase order Tim Philip Masonry. Add the Terms of 2% 10 Net 30.

Record a bill from Lee Advertising for an ad campaign, $500. Terms 2% 10 Net 30.

Add discount terms 2% 10 Net 30 to the original bill for $205 from Norton Lumber and Building Supplies.

Record a Vendor Credit for Norton Lumber and Building Supplies for $10 for the return of 1 Pump.

---

*DRILL*

 Open the **Test Drive Company** and add terms, enter bills and vendor credits

Enter Bills

 Record the bills listed in the Memo

>  Click the **Gear** icon, click **All Lists** in the Lists column
> Click **Terms**, click **New**
> Name: **2% 10 Net 30**
> Due in fixed number of days: **30** days
> Click **Apply discount if paid early** to select
> For % enter **2**, press **Tab**, enter **10** for days
> Click **Save**
> Click the **Plus** icon
> Click **Bill** in the Vendors column
> Click the drop-down list arrow to select a vendor, click **Tim Philip Masonry**
> Click the drop-down list arrow for Terms, click **2% 10 Net 30**
> Bill Date: **Current Date**
> Click the **Add All** button on the Add to Bill pane
> • Note: Unused areas on the bill are edited out of the screen shot when possible.

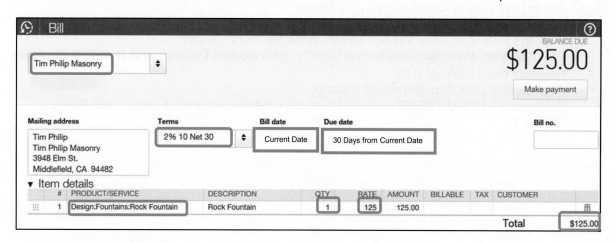

>  Click **Save and new**
> Complete the bill from Lee Advertising using the information in the Memo

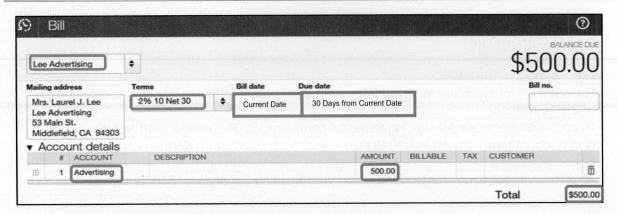

Click **Save and new**
Click the **Recent Transactions** icon at the top-left of the Bill
- Since you are on the form for Bills, this shows you the recent Bill transactions.

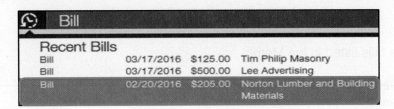

Click the Bill for **Norton Lumber and Building Materials**
Click the drop-down list arrow for Terms, click **2% 10 Net 30**
Click **Save and close**
- If you get a screen about linked transactions, click **Yes**.
- If you get a blank bill, click the **Close** button.

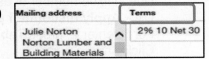

## Enter Vendor Credit

A Vendor Credit is prepared when items or merchandise purchases are returned or when a service is not used and the payment has not been made.

   Record the Vendor Credit listed in the Memo

Click the **Plus** icon, click **Vendor Credit** in the Vendors column
Click the drop-down list arrow for the Vendor, click **Norton Lumber and Building Supplies**
Payment date: **Current date**
If necessary, click **Item details** to expand
Click in the PRODUCT/SERVICE text box, click the drop-down list arrow, click **Pump**
QTY is **1**

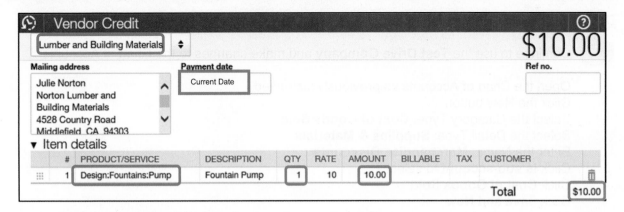

Click **Save and close**
Do <u>not</u> close the Test Drive Company
Read about Discounts then continue with the drill

## DISCOUNTS—READ

In Chapter 6, you allowed customers to take early payment discounts when payment was made within ten days of the purchase date. In Chapter 7, you are the customer purchasing inventory and other items that are used in running a business. The following is a recap of discounts and how they are used in the business. In this chapter you will be using merchandise discounts and purchase discounts.

**Sales Discount** is used when you give customers a discount for early payment. Typical terms for early payments are a 1% or 2% discount if paid within 10 days. Sales Discount is categorized as an Income account. Using a sales discount results in a decrease in income because the company will receive less money for a sale. Recording sales discounts was included in Chapter 6.

**Merchandise Discounts** is used to record discounts for items purchased to resale. This discount is categorized as Cost of Goods Sold because the use of this discount results in a decrease in the amount you pay for the goods (merchandise) you sell. QuickBooks Online has not yet added the same features for merchandise discounts as has been added for invoices. As a result, you do a "work around" and add a Cost of Goods Sold subaccount for Merchandise Discounts. You manually calculate the discount amount. When recording the discount, you use the Merchandise Discounts account and enter the discount amount as a negative number directly on the bill.

**Purchase Discount** is a discount for early payment for expenses or purchases made to run the business. For example, you can have a discount on office supplies purchased. In QuickBooks Online, there isn't a way to automatically record the discount as you do for invoices. Instead, you do a "work around" and create an expense account for Purchase Discounts. You manually calculate the amount of the discount. When recording the discount, you use the Purchase Discounts account, and enter the amount of the discount as a negative number directly on the bill.

## DISCOUNT ACCOUNTS—DRILL

In preparation for taking purchase and merchandise discounts, the Chart of Accounts will need several changes. Since merchandise is purchased to resell, a discount on the merchandise will mean a decrease to the cost of goods sold, which will ultimately increase income. As a result, a Cost of Goods Sold subaccount Merchandise Discounts needs to be added. In addition, a new expense account for Purchase Discounts will also be added. It will be used for discounts on expenses of the business or items purchased for use in the business.

*DRILL*

Continue to use the **Test Drive Company** and make changes to the Chart of Accounts

Open the Chart of Accounts as previously instructed
Click the **New** button
Select the Category Type: **Cost of Goods Sold**
Select the Detail Type: **Supplies & Materials**
Enter the Name: **Merchandise Discounts**
Click **Is sub-account** to select
Click **Cost of Goods Sold**
Click **Save and New**
Since there isn't an appropriate Detail Type in Expenses, select the Category Type: **Other Expense**
Detail Type: **Other Miscellaneous Expense**
Name: **Purchase Discounts**
- If necessary, remove the check mark from Is sub-account.
**Save and Close**
View the two new accounts in the Chart of Accounts

| Cost of Goods Sold | Cost of Goods Sold | Supplies & Materials - COGS |
|---|---|---|
| Merchandise Discounts | Cost of Goods Sold | Supplies & Materials - COGS |
| Purchase Discounts | Other Expense | Other Miscellaneous Expense |

Do **not** close the Test Drive Company, continue to the next section

## PAY BILLS—DRILL

Once bills have been recorded, they should be paid by using Pay Bills from the Vendor column after clicking the Plus icon or by clicking the Make Payment button within a bill. Bills may be paid by using cash, checks, or credit cards. Prior to paying bills, however, the merchandise and/or purchase discounts should be entered as part of the bill.

---

**MEMO**
**DATE:** Current Date

Use a check to pay the bill for inventory received from Tim Philip Masonry. Add the Discount of 2% 10 Net 30 to the bill before paying it.

Use the company Mastercard to pay the bill from Lee Advertising. Include a discount of 2% 10 Net 30 on the bill prior to paying it.

Add the discount of 2% 10 Net 30 to the original bill for $205 from Norton Lumber and Building Supplies. When calculating the amount of the discount, subtract the $10 Vendor Credit prepared for this bill prior to calculating the discount. Pay the bill using the company Mastercard.

---

*DRILL*

Continue to use the **Test Drive Company** and pay the bills you entered earlier

Click the **Recent Transactions** icon, click the bill you prepared earlier for Tim Phillips Masonry for $125
In Account details for Line 1, click in the ACCOUNT text box

Click the drop-down list arrow; click the Cost of Goods Sold subaccount **Merchandise Discounts**

- The bill is for inventory items, so Merchandise Discounts is the discount account to use.
- Calculate the discount: 125 * .02 = 2.50.

Tab to the AMOUNT column for Line 1, enter: **– 2.50**, press **Tab**

- Do not forget to enter the minus – sign in front of the 2.50.
- Notice that the Total changed from $125.00 to $122.50.

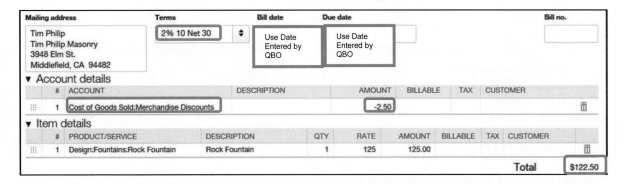

Click **Save and close**

- If you get a message about a linked transaction, click **Yes**.
- If you get a blank bill, click the **Close** button.

Click the **Plus** icon, click **Pay Bills** in the Vendors column
Click the drop-down list arrow for Payment account, click **Checking**
Click in the check box for Tim Philip Masonry to select

- The Payment of $122.50 is automatically inserted.

Click **Save and close**
Click the **Recent Transactions** icon
Click the bill for **Lee Advertising** to open
Repeat the steps to add the 2% discount to the bill from Lee Advertising for $500

- The bill is for advertising so the correct account to use for the discount is the Expense account Purchase Discounts.

Scroll to the bottom of the account list, click **Purchase Discounts**
Calculate and enter the discount

- Do not forget to enter the – .

Click the **Save** button

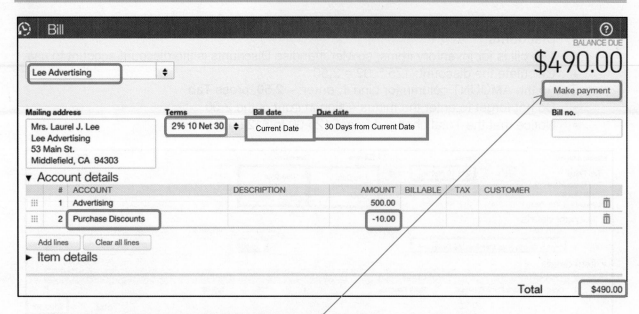

At the top of the Bill, click the **Make payment** button
- You will see a Bill Payment showing the amount paid of $490.00.

Click the drop-down list arrow for Payment account, click **Mastercard**
- Remember, you may see any one of the payment accounts shown. These include Checking, Mastercard, Visa, among others.
- The Test Drive Company spells the account as Mastercard rather than MasterCard.

Payment date: **Current Date**

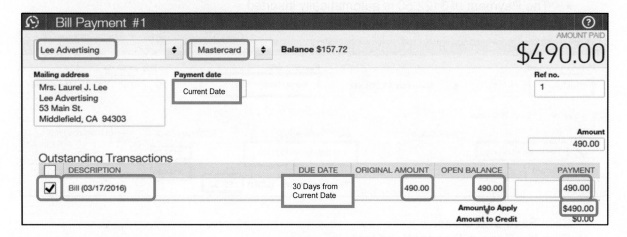

Click **Save and close**
- If you return to the bill, note that the Payment Status is PAID. Click the **Close** button.

Click **Vendors** on the Navigation bar

Open the Register for **Norton Lumber and Building Materials**
- Note the Vendor Credit for the Current Date for $10.00. This was the return of 1 Pump for $10.00 recorded for the Bill for $205.

Open the **Bill** for Norton Lumber and Building Materials for $205

If necessary expand Account details

Line 1: select the Cost of Goods Sold subaccount **Merchandise Discounts**

Calculate and enter the amount of the Merchandise Discounts
- Total $205 – Vendor Credit of $10 = $195. Multiply $195 by .02 to get the discount amount of $3.90.

- Do not forget to enter the − .

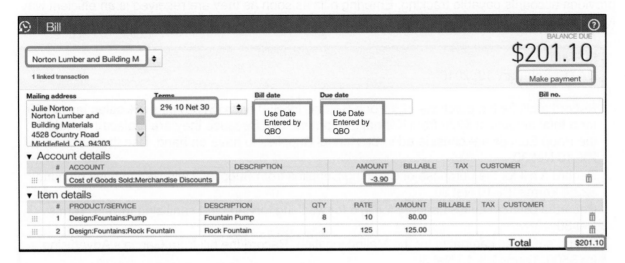

Click the **Save button**
- If you get a transaction linked message, click **Yes**.

Click the **Make payment** button

View the Bill Payment screen

Make sure the Payment Account is **Mastercard**

Payment date: **Current Date**
- This screen shows you the link between the bill and the credit. The bill is shown for the amount due after applying the discount. The Vendor Credit is shown and subtracted from the amount due for the bill. Thus the amount of the payment is $191.10.

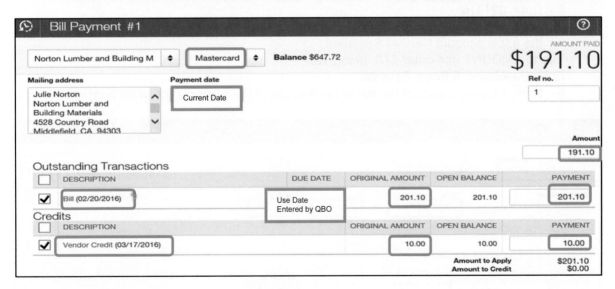

Click **Save and close**
- If you return to the Bill, note that it is marked PAID. Close the bill.

Close the Test Drive Company

## ENTER BILLS—DO

As you practiced in the drills, bills are prepared to record the amounts owed for the costs of expenses incurred in the operation of a business, for the purchase of items used in the operation of the business, and for the purchase of merchandise to sell in the business. QuickBooks Online provides accounts payable tracking. Entering bills as soon as they are received is an efficient way to record your liabilities.

---

**MEMO**
**DATE:** February 19, 2016

Record a bill for the purchase of 5 Poop Scoops for $50 each ($250) plus 8% sales tax of $20 for a total amount of $270 from Kennel Equipment, Inc. Because they are replaced frequently, the Poop Scoops are considered to be Kennel Supplies to have on hand. Use the Terms 2% 10 Net 30.

Record a bill for the purchase of Cleaning Supplies from Supplies Unlimited to have on hand: $225, Terms 2% 10 Net 30.

Record a bill from Lulu's Laundry for $75 for washing, drying, and sanitizing towels. Terms Net 30.

Set up a new ad campaign for the Malibu location. Record the bill from Garcia's Advertising for $500. Terms 2% 10 Net 30.

---

*DO*

Open **Your Name's Beach Barkers** and enter bills

> Click the **Plus** icon
> Click **Bill** in the Vendors column
> Click the drop-down list arrow for Choose a vendor, click **Kennel Equipment, Inc.**
> Terms: **2% 10 Net 30**
> Bill Date: **021916**
> Account details Line 1: Click in the ACCOUNT text box, click the drop-down list arrow; click
>         the asset account **Kennel Supplies**
> Tab to AMOUNT and enter **270**, press **Tab**
> Enter the Memo: **5 Poop Scoops**
> * Note: Unused areas on the bill are edited out of the screen shot when possible.

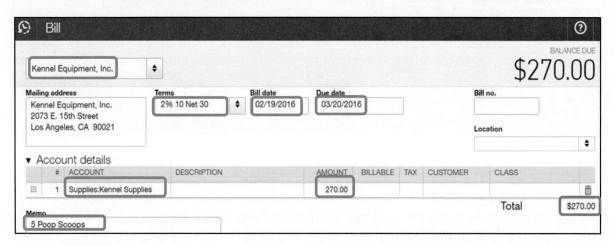

> Click **Save and new**
> Complete the bill from **Supplies Unlimited** using the information in the Memo
> Terms: **2% 10 Net 30**
> Bill date: **021916**

- If Line 1 of Account details already includes information for Cleaning Supplies, simply change the amount.

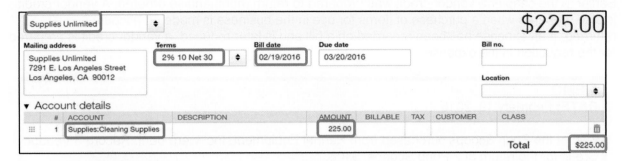

Click **Save and new**
Enter the bill for **Lulu's Laundry** using the information in the Memo
Terms: **Net 30**
Bill date: **021916**

- The next two screen shots do not show the vendor name and balance at the top of the screen. Otherwise, all necessary information is shown.

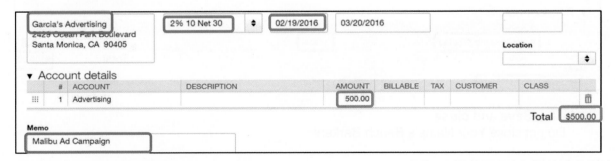

Click **Save and new**
Use the information in the memo and record the bill from **Garcia's Advertising**
Terms: **2% 10 Net 30**
Bill date: **021916**
Enter a Memo: **Malibu Ad Campaign**

- If information is already shown as a Memo, remember to delete it and then enter Malibu Ad Campaign.

Click **Save and close**
- If you see a blank bill, close it.
Do <u>not</u> close Your Name's Beach Barkers

## RECORD VENDOR CREDIT—DO

Earlier in the chapter a vendor credit was prepared to return merchandise ordered. A vendor credit is also prepared when a purchase of items for use in the business is made on account and is returned. If an expense has been recorded on a bill and is later reduced, a vendor credit is prepared for the reduction in the expense.

> ### MEMO
> **DATE:** February 19, 2016
>
> Two of the Poop Scoops purchased from Kennel Equipment, Inc. were bent. Record a Vendor Credit for the return of 2 Poop Scoops, $108.

### DO

Continue to use **Your Name's Beach Barkers** and record a vendor credit

> Click the **Plus** icon, click **Vendor Credit** in the Vendors column
> Vendor: **Kennel Equipment, Inc.**
> Payment date: **02/19/16**
> Account detail Line 1: ACCOUNT: **Kennel Supplies**
> * The asset account is used because these were supplies to have on hand.
> Amount: **108**
> * Do the math: Item cost times quantity: 2 Poop Scoops at $50 each = 100 total cost. Total cost times sales tax rate: 100 * .08 = $8 Sales Tax. Total Cost plus sales tax: $100 + $8 = $108 Amount.
> Memo: **Returned 2 Poop Scoops**

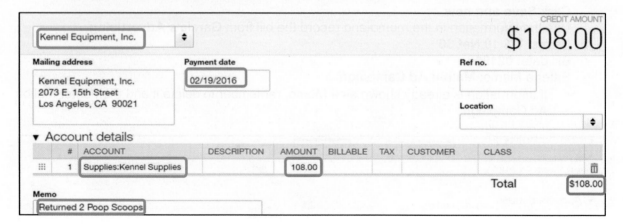

> Click **Save and close**
> Do not close Your Name's Beach Barkers

## DISCOUNT ACCOUNTS—DO

As you practiced in the drill, in order to take purchase and merchandise discounts, the Chart of Accounts will need several changes. Since merchandise is purchased to resell, a discount on the merchandise will mean a decrease to the cost of goods sold, which will ultimately increase income. As a result, the current Cost of Goods Sold subaccount Purchases Discounts account needs to be changed to Merchandise Discounts. Then, a new expense account for Purchase Discounts will be added to be used for discounts on expenses of the business or items purchased for use in the business.

<u>*DO*</u>

Continue to use <u>**Your Name's Beach Barkers**</u> and make changes to the Chart of Accounts

Open the Chart of Accounts as previously instructed
Scroll down to the Cost of Goods Sold subaccount Purchases Discounts
Click the drop-down list arrow for Activities, click **Edit**
Change the Name to **Merchandise Discounts**
Click **Save and Close**
- The account name has been changed.

| Cost of Goods Sold | Cost of Goods Sold | Supplies & Materials - COGS |
|---|---|---|
| Merchandise Discounts | Cost of Goods Sold | Supplies & Materials - COGS |

Scroll back to the top of the Chart of Accounts, click the **New** button
Select the Category Type: **Other Expense**
Detail Type: **Other Miscellaneous Expense**
Name: **Purchase Discounts**
Click **Save and Close**
The new account has been added to the Chart of Accounts

| Purchase Discounts | Other Expense | Other Miscellaneous Expense |
|---|---|---|

Do <u>not</u> close Your Name's Beach Barkers, continue to the next section

## UNPAID BILLS REPORT—DO

It is possible to get information regarding unpaid bills by simply preparing a report. No more digging through tickler files, recorded invoices, ledgers, or journals. QuickBooks Online prepares an Unpaid Bills Report that includes each unpaid bill grouped and subtotaled by vendor. The report includes the Transaction Date, Transaction Type, Number, Due Date, number of days Past Due, Amount of the original bill, and the Open Balance. Evaluating the Unpaid Bills Report enables you to determine which bills should be paid and to know which bills are overdue.

<u>*DO*</u>

Continue to use <u>**Your Name's Beach Barkers**</u> and prepare the Unpaid Bills Report

Access **Reports** as previously instructed, select **All Reports**
- If you see **<All Reports** above a report category, you click it. Otherwise, click **All Reports.**
Click the category **Manage Accounts Payable**
Click **Unpaid Bills**
- You will see the Unpaid Bills for All Dates. You will also see a footer with the Date Prepared and Time Prepared.
- Notice the Past Due column, because we are using specific dates that are not the current date, this column, while valuable in the real world, does not provide relevant information in your training.
Click the **Customize** button

Click the **Change Columns** button

Click **Past Due**, then click **<Remove** to remove the column from the report

Since we are not categorizing bills by location, remove **Location** from the columns

It would be helpful to identify bills that have terms for discounts, in Available Columns click
**Terms** and click **Add>**

- Terms will be positioned just below the column name that is highlighted in Selected Columns.

If necessary, click the Up or Down arrow to position Terms between Num and Due Date

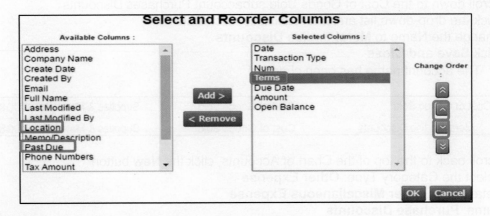

Click **OK**

Click **Header/Footer** on the left of the Customize Unpaid Bills screen

Click **Date Prepared** and **Time Prepared** to remove from the report, unless your instructor
requires this

Click **Run Report**

Click **Save Customizations** to save this customized report

Accept the name Unpaid Bills, click **OK**

## Your Name's Beach Barkers
### UNPAID BILLS
All Dates

| DATE | TRANSACTION TYPE | NUM | TERMS | DUE DATE | AMOUNT | OPEN BALANCE |
|---|---|---|---|---|---|---|
| **All About Dogs Supplies** | | | | | | |
| 310-555-3952 | | | | | | |
| 02/18/2016 | Bill | | Net 30 | 03/19/2016 | 175.00 | 175.00 |
| **Total for All About Dogs Supplies** | | | | | **$175.00** | **$175.00** |
| **Bow-Wow Supplies** | | | | | | |
| 760-555-2951 | | | | | | |
| 12/31/2015 | Bill | | | 12/31/2015 | 2,000.00 | 1,300.00 |
| **Total for Bow-Wow Supplies** | | | | | **$2,000.00** | **$1,300.00** |
| **Canine Supplies** | | | | | | |
| 310-555-6971 | | | | | | |
| 12/31/2015 | Bill | | | 12/31/2015 | 3,000.00 | 2,200.00 |
| 01/24/2016 | Bill | 276 | Net 30 | 02/23/2016 | 189.00 | 189.00 |
| 02/18/2016 | Bill | | Net 30 | 03/19/2016 | 540.00 | 540.00 |
| 02/19/2016 | Vendor Credit | 1596 | Net 30 | | -40.00 | -40.00 |
| **Total for Canine Supplies** | | | | | **$3,689.00** | **$2,889.00** |
| **Computer Town** | | | | | | |
| (310) 555-8816 | | | | | | |
| 01/18/2016 | Bill | 890 | Net 30 | 02/17/2016 | 275.00 | 275.00 |
| **Total for Computer Town** | | | | | **$275.00** | **$275.00** |
| **Garcia's Advertising** | | | | | | |
| 310-555-1879 | | | | | | |
| 01/24/2016 | Bill | 425 | Net 30 | 02/23/2016 | 75.00 | 75.00 |
| 02/19/2016 | Bill | | 2% 10 Net 30 | 03/20/2016 | 500.00 | 500.00 |
| **Total for Garcia's Advertising** | | | | | **$575.00** | **$575.00** |
| **Kennel Equipment, Inc.** | | | | | | |
| 310-555-1156 | | | | | | |
| 02/19/2016 | Bill | | 2% 10 Net 30 | 03/20/2016 | 270.00 | 270.00 |
| 02/19/2016 | Vendor Credit | | Net 30 | | -108.00 | -108.00 |
| **Total for Kennel Equipment, Inc.** | | | | | **$162.00** | **$162.00** |
| **Lulu's Laundry** | | | | | | |
| (310) 555-8789 | | | | | | |
| 02/19/2016 | Bill | | Net 30 | 03/20/2016 | 75.00 | 75.00 |
| **Total for Lulu's Laundry** | | | | | **$75.00** | **$75.00** |
| **Pawsitively Elegant** | | | | | | |
| (310) 555-2925 | | | | | | |
| 02/18/2016 | Bill | | 2% 10 Net 30 | 03/19/2016 | 500.00 | 500.00 |
| **Total for Pawsitively Elegant** | | | | | **$500.00** | **$500.00** |
| **Supplies Unlimited** | | | | | | |
| (310) 555-8529 | | | | | | |
| 01/24/2016 | Bill | 564 | Net 30 | 02/23/2016 | 175.00 | 175.00 |
| 02/19/2016 | Bill | | 2% 10 Net 30 | 03/20/2016 | 225.00 | 225.00 |
| **Total for Supplies Unlimited** | | | | | **$400.00** | **$400.00** |
| **TOTAL** | | | | | **$7,851.00** | **$6,351.00** |

*(handwritten margin note: Total OK)*

Print, export, and/or email or submit the report as required by your professor
- Name the report **12-Your Name Unpaid Bills Ch. 7**.

Do <u>not</u> close Your Name's Beach Barkers

## PAY BILLS—DO

Once bills have been recorded, they should be paid by using Pay Bills. Bills may be paid by using cash, checks, or credit cards. All payments for recorded bills should be made using the Pay Bills feature. However, if a bill has a discount, the merchandise and/or purchase discounts should be entered as part of the original bill. Once the discount is recorded, the bill may be paid by clicking Make Payment within the bill or by going to Pay Bills.

**MEMO**
**DATE:** February 20, 2016

| |
|---|
| Pay the bill for the Dog Beds from Canine Supplies, pay with Check 19. Make sure the vendor credit is used. |
| Use the company Visa to pay the bill from All About Dogs Supplies for the Brushes purchased earlier in the chapter. |
| Add the discount of 2% 10 Net 30 to the original bill for $500 from Pawsitively Elegant. When calculating the amount of the discount, subtract the $10 Vendor Credit prepared for this bill prior to calculating the discount. Pay by check. |
| Pay the bill to Garcia's Advertising for the $500 Malibu Ad Campaign, take the 2% early payment discount and pay with the company's Visa. |
| Use the company Visa to pay for the Poop Scoops purchased from Kennel Equipment, Inc. Be sure to use the credit. Also, subtract the amount of the credit from the bill total and calculate the amount of discount. Record the discount amount. |

*DO*

Continue to use **Your Name's Beach Barkers** and pay the bills in the Memo

Click the **Plus** icon, click **Pay Bills** in the Vendors column
Payment account: **Checking**
Payment date: **022016**
Starting Check: **19**
- If a different check number appears, change it to 19.
Scroll through the list of bills, click the check box for the bill from **Canine Supplies** for $540
- The Credit should have been applied automatically. The payment should be $500.

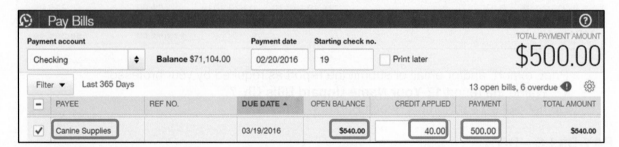

Click **Save and print** (Click the drop-down list arrow next to Save and close to locate)
Click **Print** icon on the Print Checks screen
- The screen should show the Starting check no. 19, the date of 02/20/16, Bill Payment (Check) as the Type, the Payee Canine Supplies, and the Amount $500.
Click **Preview and print**
- If you save the check, name it **13-Your Name Check 19 Canine Supplies**.
Click **Done** on the "Did your checks print OK?" screen
Close Print Checks and return to Pay Bills
Change the Payment account to **Visa**
Payment date: **022016**
Scroll through the list of bills, click the check box for the bill from **All About Dogs Supplies**
- The Payment amount is automatically inserted.

Click **Save and close**
Click the **Plus** icon, click **Bill** in the Vendors column
Click the **Recent Transactions** icon on the Bills screen
Click the $500 bill for **Pawsitively Elegant**

In the Account details for Line 1, click in the ACCOUNT text box
Click the drop-down list arrow; click the Cost of Goods Sold subaccount **Merchandise Discounts**
- The bill is for inventory items, so the Merchandise Discounts is the account to use for the discount.
- Calculate the discount: 500 * .02 = 10.
Tab to the AMOUNT column for Line 1, enter: **– 10,** press **Tab**
- Do <u>not</u> forget to enter the minus – sign in front of the 10.
- Notice that the Total changed from $500 to $490.

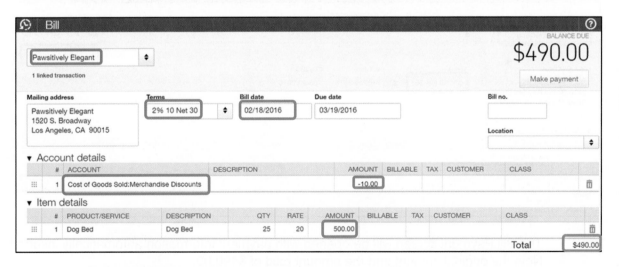

Click **Save and close**
- If you get a message about a linked transaction, click **Yes**.
- If you get a blank bill, click the **Close** button.
Click the **Plus** icon, click **Pay Bills** in the Vendors column
Click the drop-down list arrow for Payment account, click **Checking**
Payment Date: **022016**
Starting check no.: **20**
Click in the check box for the bill for Pawsitively Elegant to select
- The Payment of $490 is automatically inserted.

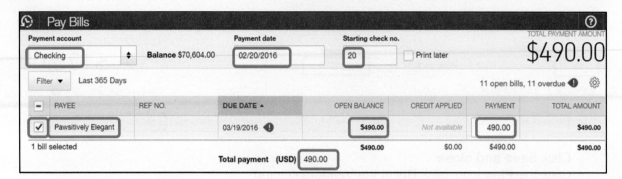

Click **Save and print** (Click the drop-down list arrow next to Save and close to locate)
Click **Print** icon on the Print Checks screen
- The screen should show the Starting check no. 20, the date of 02/20/16, Bill Payment (Check) as the Type, the Payee Pawsitively Elegant, and the Amount $490.

Click **Preview and print**
- If you save the check, name it **14-Your Name Check 20 Pawsitively Elegant**.

Click **Done** on the "Did your checks print OK?" screen
Close Print Checks
Repeat the steps to add the 2% discount to the bill from Garcia's Advertising for $500
- The bill is for advertising so the correct account to use for the discount is the Expense account Purchase Discounts.
- Do <u>not</u> forget to enter the − .

Click the **Save** button
At the top of the Bill, click the **Make payment** button

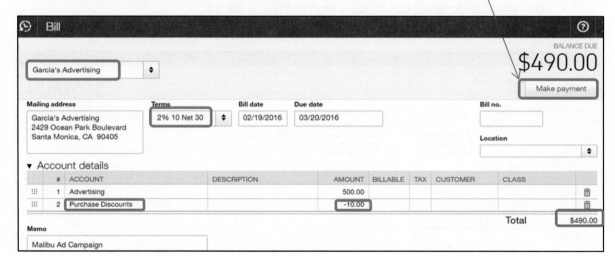

- The Bill Payment screen will be opened with payment information automatically inserted.
- Note the original amount and the amount paid of $490.00.
- If you get an option to add an additional bill, ignore it.
- Because we did not enter a Bill no., the Bill Payment will use 1 for the Ref. no. You may leave this or delete it.

Click the drop-down list arrow for Payment account, click **Visa**
Payment date: **022016**

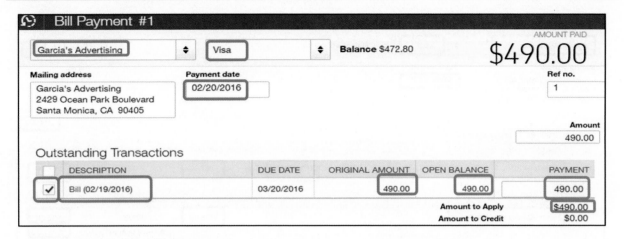

Click **Save and close**
- If the bill for Garcia's Advertising is shown, notice that the Payment Status is PAID.

Close the Bill for Garcia's Advertising

Click **Vendors** on the Navigation bar

Open the Register for **Kennel Equipment, Inc.**
- Note the Vendor Credit for the Current Date for $108.00. This was the return of 2 Poop Scoops for $108.00 recorded for the Bill for $270.

Open the Bill for Kennel Equipment, Inc. for $270

Account details Line 2: select the appropriate Account

Calculate and enter the amount of the Purchase Discounts
- Total $270 – Vendor Credit of $108 = $150. Multiply $150 by .02 to get the discount amount of $3.
- Do <u>not</u> forget to enter the  – .

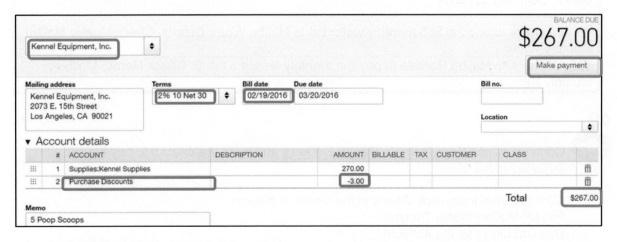

Click **Save**

Click the **Make payment** button

View the Bill Payment screen

Make sure the Payment Account is **Visa**

Payment date: **022016**
- This screen shows you the link between the bill and the credit. The bill is shown for the amount due after applying the discount. The Vendor Credit is shown and subtracted from the amount due for the bill.
- Again, because there was no Bill no., the Ref no. for the Bill Payment is 1. You may leave or delete this number.

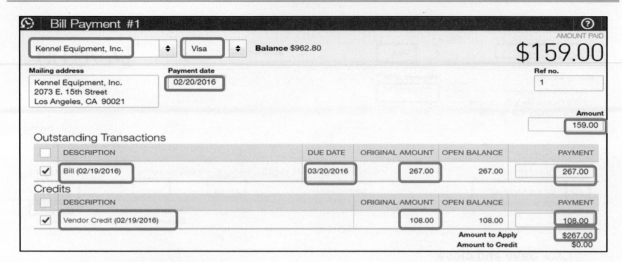

Click **Save and close**

- If you return to the bill for Kennel Equipment, Inc. note that it is marked PAID, then close the Bill.

Do <u>not</u> close Your Name's Beach Barkers

## WRITE CHECKS TO PAY BILLS—DO

Frequently, you will receive a bill and pay it immediately without recording a bill. Typical bill payments that are made in this manner are often rent, utilities, and other regular payments.

---

**<u>MEMO</u>**

**DATE:** February 20, 2016

Write a check to pay the $85 monthly water bill to Malibu Water District. Check Memo: Malibu Monthly Water.

Write a check to Malibu Rentals to pay the monthly rent of $1,400. Check Memo: Malibu Monthly Rent.

---

<u>DO</u>

Continue to use **Your Name's Beach Barkers** and write the checks to pay the bills indicated in the Memo

Click the **Plus** icon, click **Check** in the Vendors column
Payee: **Malibu Water District**
Use **Checking** as the account
Enter the Payment date **02/20/16**
Since the check will be printed as part of a batch (group), make sure Print later has a check
- If it does not, click **Print later** to mark.
In the Account details section, click in the ACCOUNT column for Line 1
Click the drop-down list arrow, scroll through the list of accounts, click the utility expense
    subaccount **Water**
Tab to AMOUNT and enter **85**, press **Tab**
To differentiate the water between Malibu and Venice, enter the Memo: **Malibu Monthly Water**

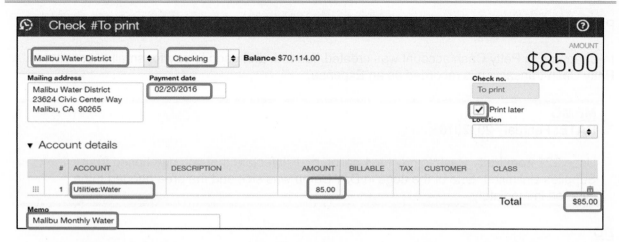

Click **Save and new**

Prepare the check to Malibu Rentals using the information provided in the Memo

- Did you enter a Memo to differentiate the Malibu rent from the Venice rent?

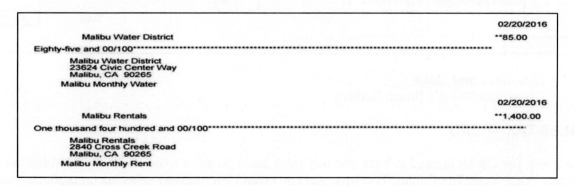

Click **Print Check** at the bottom of the check

Account: **Checking**

Starting check no.: **21**

On first page print: leave at 3 checks

Make sure the check boxes for both checks are marked; if not, click to select

Click the **Preview and print** button

| | 02/20/2016 |
|---|---|
| Malibu Water District | **85.00 |
| Eighty-five and 00/100•••••••••••••••••••••••••••••••••••••••••••• | |
| Malibu Water District | |
| 23624 Civic Center Way | |
| Malibu, CA 90265 | |
| Malibu Monthly Water | |
| | 02/20/2016 |
| Malibu Rentals | **1,400.00 |
| One thousand four hundred and 00/100•••••••••••••••••••••••••••••••••• | |
| Malibu Rentals | |
| 2840 Cross Creek Road | |
| Malibu, CA 90265 | |
| Malibu Monthly Rent | |

- If you save the checks, there will be one document. Name it **15-Your Name Checks 21-22**.

Click **Done** on the "Did your checks print OK?" screen

Close Print Checks; do <u>not</u> close Your Name's Beach Barkers

## PETTY CASH—DO

In Chapter 4, a Petty Cash account was created, funded, and used to pay for small expenditures. A Petty Cash transaction is recorded as an Expense.

---

**MEMO**

**DATE:** February 20, 2016

Used $27 from Petty Cash to pay for 1 gallon of disinfectant that you purchased from Supplies Unlimited. One of the dogs in Day Camp was sick and the area needed to be cleaned immediately.

---

*DO*

Continue to use **Your Name's Beach Barkers** and record the Petty Cash expenditure

Click the **Plus** icon, click **Expense** in the Vendors column
Payee: **Supplies Unlimited**
- If you get a pane to add other transactions, ignore it.
Account: **Petty Cash**
Payment date: **02/20/16**
Click the drop-down list arrow for Payment method, click **Cash**
Account details Line 1: Click in the text box for ACCOUNT, click the Supplies Expense subaccount **Cleaning Supplies Expense**
- Since the disinfectant is for immediate use, it is an expense.
Amount: **27**
Enter the Memo **Disinfectant**

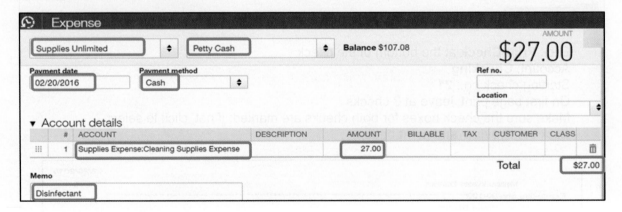

Click **Save and close**
Close Your Name's Beach Barkers

## SALES TAX—READ

The Sales Tax Center is used to track and pay sales tax. You enter sales tax agencies, rates, and settings in the Sales Tax Center. This way, you can collect the required sales tax on products you sell. At the time information was entered for sales tax liability, account(s) were added to the Chart of Accounts for the taxing agencies owed. Periodically, you are required to pay the sales tax you have collected to the appropriate government agencies. This payment is made in the Sales Tax Center.

## SALES TAX LIABILITY REPORT—DRILL

Sales tax reports are available in the Sales Tax Center and include the Sales Tax Liability report. The Sales Tax Liability Report tells you the taxing agency, the taxable amount of sales, and the amount of the tax collected and owed.

### *DRILL*

Open the **Test Drive Company** and prepare the Sales Tax Liability Report

Click **Sales Tax** on the Navigation bar
On the right side of the Sales Tax Center, you will see a blue box with Related Tasks
Click **View sales tax liability report** shown in Related Tasks
- Accept the dates shown in the report.
Tax Agency next to the dates shows All
- Since the Test Drive Company has offices in two states, both of the taxing agencies and tax amounts due are shown.
View the report

### Craig's Design and Landscaping Services
#### SALES TAX LIABILITY REPORT
##### January - March, 2016

|  | TAXABLE AMOUNT | TAX |
|---|---|---|
| **Arizona Dept. of Revenue** | | |
| AZ State tax (7.1%) | 422.00 | 29.96 |
| Tucson City (2%) | 422.00 | 8.44 |
| **Total** | | 38.40 |
| **Board of Equalization** | | |
| California (8%) | 4,711.75 | 376.94 |
| **Total** | | 376.94 |

To see how much tax is owed in California, click the drop-down list arrow for Tax Agency next to the date, click **Board of Equalization**
Click **Run Report**

### Craig's Design and Landscaping Services
#### SALES TAX LIABILITY REPORT
##### January - March, 2016

|  | TAXABLE AMOUNT | TAX |
|---|---|---|
| **Board of Equalization** | | |
| California (8%) | 4,711.75 | 376.94 |
| **Total** | | 376.94 |

To return to the Sales Tax Center, use the keyboard shortcut **Alt + Left Cursor Arrow** two times
Do <u>not</u> close the Test Drive Company, continue with the next section

## PAY SALES TAXES—DRILL

As you record sales transactions involving merchandise, sales tax is added to the invoices and sales receipts that are prepared. As you collect the sales tax from your customers, it is a liability that you owe to a specified government agency. Periodically, you must forward the tax money collected from your customers to pay the liability you have for sales taxes. This is done through the Sales Tax Center.

### DRILL

Continue to use the **Test Drive Company** and record the Sales Tax payment

In the Sales Tax Center, view the information presented
- Notice that the Tax Amount for California is $376.94 and that there has been a payment of $38.50. This leaves a Balance of $338.44. Arizona shows a Tax Amount of $38.40, a Payment of $38.40, and a Balance of 0.00.

Click the **Record Tax Payment** button

View the information presented

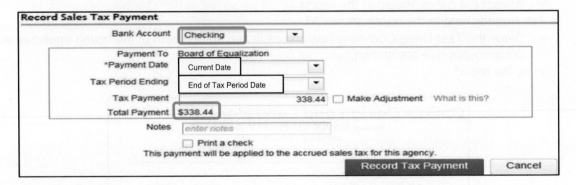

Click the **Record Tax Payment** button
- The tax payment was added to the Recent Sales Tax Payments. Also, in Sales Tax Owed, you will see the Payments made and a Balance of $0.00.

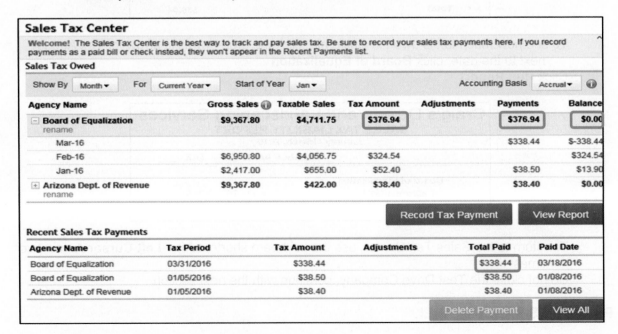

Close the Test Drive Company

## SALES TAX LIABILITY REPORT—DO

As you just practiced, the Sales Tax Liability Report tells you the taxing agency, the taxable amount of sales, and the amount of the tax collected and owed.

_DO_

 Open the **Your Name's Beach Barkers** and prepare the Sales Tax Liability Report

Click **Sales Tax** on the Navigation bar
Click the **View Report** button
Dates From: **010116** To: **033116**
Tax Agency: **State Board of Equalization**
View the report

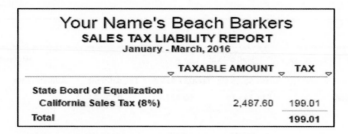

Click the **Customize** button, remove the check marks for Date Prepared, Time Prepared, and Report Basis from the Footer
Click **Run Report**
Print, export, and/or email or submit the report as required by your professor
- Name the report **16-Your Name Sales Tax Liability Ch. 7**.
To return to the Sales Tax Center, use the keyboard shortcut **Alt + Left** two times
- Left means the left cursor key.
Do <u>not</u> close Your Name's Beach Barkers, continue with the next section

## PAY SALES TAXES—DO

As you record sales transactions involving merchandise, sales tax is added to the invoices and sales receipts that are prepared. As you collect the sales tax from your customers, it is a liability that you owe to a specified government agency. Periodically, you must forward the tax money collected from your customers to pay the liability you have for sales taxes. As you have practiced, this is done through the Sales Tax Center.

_DO_

 Continue to use **Your Name's Beach Barkers** and record the Sales Tax payment

In the Sales Tax Center, view the information presented
- Notice that the Tax Amount is $199.01.
Click the **Record Tax Payment** button
View the information presented
Change the Payment Date to **02/20/16**
Click the check box for **Print a check** to select

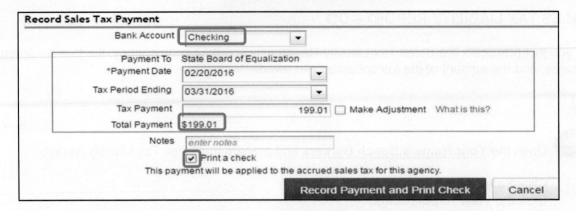

Click the **Record Payment and Print Check** button
- The tax payment was added to the Recent Sales Tax Payments. Also, in Sales Tax Owed, you will see the Payment made of $199.01 and a Balance of $0.00.

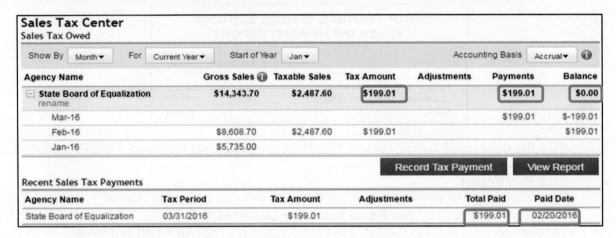

Do <u>not</u> close Your Name's Beach Barkers

## PRINT SALES TAX PAYMENT CHECK—DO

Once the sales tax has been paid and the check written, the check needs to be printed. Do this by using Print Checks.

## *DO*

 Continue to use **Your Name's Beach Barkers** and print the Sales Tax Payment check

    Click the **Plus** icon, click **Print Checks**, in the Vendors column
    Verify the information on the Print Checks screen
    Account: **Checking**
    Starting check no.: **23**
    Sales Tax Payment check is selected
    Click the **Preview and print** button

| | 02/20/2016 |
|---|---|
| State Board of Equalization | **199.01 |
| One hundred ninety-nine and 01/100********************************************************** | |

- If you save the check, name it **17-Your Name Check 23 State Board of Equalization**. Click **Done** on the "Did you checks print OK?" screen
Close Print Checks
Do <u>not</u> close Your Name's Beach Barkers

## ADDITIONAL TRANSACTIONS—DO

As in previous chapters, the following additional transactions will be similar to ones you completed during the chapter. These transactions will be listed in Memos. You will enter them without any specific instructions. If you have questions about how to enter transactions, you may refer back to material presented earlier in the chapter.

## <u>DO</u>

▶ Continue to use **Your Name's Beach Barkers** and enter the following transactions in the Memo boxes

Add Memos to transactions where appropriate
Take discounts when available
Print, save, and submit as you have been requested to do by your instructor
- When using checks, assign the next available check number. The last check written before this section was Check Number 23.
- Use the same naming structure as previously instructed: Document number, your name, business form and number, vendor name. For example, 29-Your Name Check 1234 John Doe.

| MEMO |
|---|
| **DATE:** February 22, 2016 |
| Add an Inventory Item: Name, Sales and Purchasing Descriptions: Dog Dishes and Bowls; Initial quantity on hand: 0; As of date: 12/31/15; Accounts: Inventory Asset, Sales of Product Income, Cost of Goods Sold; Sales price/rate: leave blank; Is taxable: check; Cost: 5. |
| Prepare a Purchase Order for 30 Dog Bowls from a new vendor: Happy Wags (Address: 7925 Broadway, Los Angeles, CA 90011; Email: HappyWags@dogs.com; Phone: 213-555-4897; Fax: 213-555-7984; Website: www.HappyWags.com; Terms: 2% 10 Net 30). |
| Paid <u>cash</u> for windshield wiper blades from Morales Auto Repair, $16.15. (Vehicle Expenses) |
| Prepare a Purchase Order for 40 Dog Cages from Pet Supplies Unlimited for a new inventory item (Name, Sales and Purchasing Descriptions: Dog Cages; Initial quantity on hand: 0; As of date: 12/31/15; Accounts: Inventory Asset, Sales of Product Income, Cost of Goods Sold; Sales price/rate: 125; Is taxable: check; Cost: 25). |
| Use the company's Visa to pay the Bill for Lulu's Laundry. |
| Received all of the Books on Purchase Order 1001 from The Literary Dog. Terms 2% 10 Net 30. |
| Write checks to pay the rent of $1,500 to Venice Rentals, the gas bill of $154 to Southern California Gas Company, the water bill of $125 to Marina Water, and the $75 electric bill to Cal Electric. Print the checks after entering the electric bill. |
| Pay the Bill for 02/19/16 for $225 of Cleaning Supplies to have on hand from Supplies Unlimited with a check. Terms 2% 10 Net 30. (Do not forget to take the discount!) |
| Receive a partial order of 25 toys from Bark City Toys, PO 1004. Print the copy of the purchase order for the backordered items you did not receive. |
| Record a bill from Quality Insurance for $600 (Prepaid Insurance). Terms 2% 10 Net 30. |

Continue recording, saving, and printing transactions

---

**MEMO**
**DATE:** February 23, 2016

Use the company's Visa to purchase $150 of office supplies to have on hand from Super Office. (Did you use the asset account?)

Had paper bags with the logo and company name printed on them. Prepare a bill for the purchase $125 of Sales Supplies to have on hand from Supplies Unlimited. Terms 2% 10 Net 30. (Did you clear any information shown for an earlier bill? Did you use an asset account?)

The toys remaining on the Purchase Order for Bark City Toys were discontinued. Manually Close Purchase Order 1009.

Received all of the Dog Cages on order from Pet Supplies Unlimited.

---

Continue recording, saving, and printing transactions

---

**MEMO**
**DATE:** February 24, 2016

The logos on the paper bags were blurred. Returned all of the bags ($125) on the bill of February 23 from Supplies Unlimited.

Received 25 of the 30 Dog Bowls ordered from Happy Wags on Purchase Order 1007. Terms 2% 10 Net 30. Print the copy of the purchase order.

Use the Visa to pay the Quality Insurance Bill. Terms 2% 10 Net 30.

Returned $30 of office supplies purchased with the company's Visa on February 23 to Super Office.

---

Continue recording, saving, and printing transactions

---

**MEMO**
**DATE:** February 26, 2016

Returned 2 Dog Cages that were the wrong size to Pet Supplies Unlimited.

Pay for the Books received from The Literary Dog. Use Visa and terms of 2% 10 Net 30.

Pay for the 25 Dog Bowls received from Happy Wags use a Check and terms 2% 10 Net 30.

---

Continue to use Your Name's Beach Barkers to complete reports

## INVENTORY VALUATION SUMMARY—DO

After entering several transactions, it is important to prepare the inventory valuation summary. Information is provided for each inventory item including quantity, total asset value, and average cost.

_DO_

Continue to use **Your Name's Beach Barkers** and prepare the Inventory Valuation Summary as of February 26, 2016

Open the **Manage Products and Inventory** category for reports
Click **Inventory Valuation Summary**

Remove the Date and Time Prepared from the footer
Change the As of date to **022616**, click **Run Report**

### Your Name's Beach Barkers
#### INVENTORY VALUATION SUMMARY
##### As of February 26, 2016

| | QTY | TOTAL ASSET VALUE | AVG COST |
|---|---|---|---|
| Bones | 331.00 | 662.00 | 2.00 |
| Books | 250.00 | 750.00 | 3.00 |
| Brushes | 61.00 | 305.00 | 5.00 |
| Collars | 640.00 | 6,400.00 | 10.00 |
| Dog Bed | 51.00 | 1,020.00 | 20.00 |
| Dog Cages | 38.00 | 950.00 | 25.00 |
| Dog Dishes and Bowls | 25.00 | 125.00 | 5.00 |
| Dog Food-Canned | 463.00 | 1,157.50 | 2.50 |
| Dog Food-Dry | 394.00 | 2,758.00 | 7.00 |
| Dog Snacks | 176.00 | 176.00 | 1.00 |
| Leashes | 442.00 | 4,420.00 | 10.00 |
| Sweaters | 318.00 | 4,770.00 | 15.00 |
| Toys & Treats | 3,463.00 | 6,926.00 | 2.00 |
| Vitamins | 445.00 | 1,335.00 | 3.00 |
| TOTAL | | $31,754.50 | |

Print, export, and/or submit as previously instructed

- Name the report **25-Your Name Inventory Valuation Summary Ch. 7**.
Continue to use Your Name's Beach Barkers

## BILL PAYMENT LIST—DO

When a bill is paid, it will be included in the Bill Payment List. The report will show the bill payments made by check and by credit card.

### DO

Continue to use **Your Name's Beach Barkers** and prepare the Bill Payment List for February 1-26, 2016

Access the **Manage Accounts Payable** category in All Reports
Prepare the Bill Payment List
Remove the Date and Time Prepared from the footer
Dates From: **020116** To: **022616**

### Your Name's Beach Barkers
#### BILL PAYMENT LIST
##### February 1-26, 2016

| DATE | NUM | VENDOR | AMOUNT |
|---|---|---|---|
| **Checking** | | | |
| 02/20/2016 | 19 | Canine Supplies | -500.00 |
| 02/20/2016 | 20 | Pawsitively Elegant | -490.00 |
| 02/22/2016 | 28 | Supplies Unlimited | -220.50 |
| 02/26/2016 | 29 | Happy Wags | -122.50 |
| **Total for Checking** | | | $ -1,333.00 |
| **Visa** | | | |
| 02/20/2016 | | All About Dogs Supplies | 175.00 |
| 02/20/2016 | 1 | Garcia's Advertising | 490.00 |
| 02/20/2016 | 1 | Kennel Equipment, Inc. | 159.00 |
| 02/22/2016 | | Lulu's Laundry | 75.00 |
| 02/24/2016 | 1 | Quality Insurance | 588.00 |
| 02/26/2016 | 1 | The Literary Dog | 735.00 |
| **Total for Visa** | | | $2,222.00 |

Print, export, and/or submit as previously instructed

- Name the report **26-Your Name Bill Payment List Ch. 7**.
  Continue to use Your Name's Beach Barkers

## VENDOR BALANCE SUMMARY—DO

In order to see the total amount owed to each vendor, you prepare a Vendor Balance Summary report. For more detailed information that shows all of the bills and credits for each vendor, you prepare the Vendor Balance Detail report. In addition, you could prepare your customized Unpaid Bills report, which would show all of your unpaid bills listed by vendor, the terms, bill amounts, and open balances.

_DO_

Continue to use **Your Name's Beach Barkers** and prepare a Vendor Balance Summary Report

Click **Vendor Balance Summary** in the Manage Accounts Payable Report category
Remove the Date and Time Prepared from the footer

### Your Name's Beach Barkers
#### VENDOR BALANCE SUMMARY
##### All Dates

|                        | TOTAL      |
|------------------------|------------|
| Bark City Toys         | 50.00      |
| Bow-Wow Supplies       | 1,300.00   |
| Canine Supplies        | 2,389.00   |
| Computer Town          | 275.00     |
| Garcia's Advertising   | 75.00      |
| Pet Supplies Unlimited | 950.00     |
| Supplies Unlimited     | 175.00     |
| **TOTAL**              | **$5,214.00** |

Print, export, and/or submit as previously instructed
- Name the report **27-Your Name Vendor Balance Summary Ch. 7**.
  Continue to use Your Name's Beach Barkers

## CHECK DETAIL—DO

Once checks have been printed and petty cash has been used, it is important to prepare the Check Detail Report. In addition to the checks prepared to pay bills, all checks that have been written are included in this report.

_DO_

Continue to use **Your Name's Beach Barkers** and prepare the Check Detail Report

Open the Report category for **Review Expenses and Purchases**, click **Check Detail**
Customize the report to remove the Date and Time Prepared
Enter the report dates From: **02/01/16** To: **02/26/16**
View the Check Detail Report
Does your report show Checks 19-29 and two Petty Cash transactions?
- Note that the checks prepared in Pay Bills have the Transaction Type of Bill Payment (Check) while the checks that you wrote without recording a bill have the Transaction

Type of Check. The check prepared to pay the sales taxes is shown as Sales Tax Payment.

Print, export, and/or submit as previously instructed
- Name the report **28-Your Name Check Detail Ch. 7**.

Continue to use Your Name's Beach Barkers

## JOURNAL—DO

At the end of each chapter, you have prepared the Journal in order to see every entry in debit and credit format. Preparing the Journal report will display this information. In many instances, going through the Journal entries and checking transaction dates, account names, and products/services listed in the Memo column will help you find errors in your transactions. If a transaction does not appear in the Journal, it may be due to using an incorrect date or forgetting to enter it.

In your concepts course, you may have learned that the General Journal was where all entries were recorded in debit/credit format. In QuickBooks Online, you do record some non-recurring debit/credit transactions as a Journal Entry and then display all debit/credit entries no matter where the transactions were recorded in the Journal Report.

### DO

Continue to use **Your Name's Beach Barkers** and prepare a Journal Report

Return to **All Reports**, select **My Custom Reports**, and click **Journal**
Enter the Dates From: **021616** To: **Current Date**
- Scroll through the report and note the transaction dates. The transactions in Chapter 7 began on February 16, 2016 so everything you entered in this chapter should be shown. If you entered transactions for a current date rather than the date provided, those transactions should also be shown. If necessary change any incorrect transaction dates.

Change the report Dates From: **021616** To: **022616**
- Look at the debits and credits carefully, the debit entry is not always shown first. Entries within a transaction may also be shown in a different order.

Verify your Total:

| TOTAL | | |
|---|---|---|
| | $12,958.36 | $12,958.36 |

Use Landscape Orientation to print or export then submit as previously instructed
- Name the report **29-Your Name Journal Ch. 7**.

Continue to use Your Name's Beach Barkers

## TRIAL BALANCE—DO

When all transactions have been entered for the chapter, it is important to prepare the Trial Balance to verify that the total debits equal the total credits.

### DO

Continue to use **Your Name's Beach Barkers** and prepare a Trial Balance

Click **Trial Balance** in My Custom Reports Category
Date: From: **02/16/16** To: **02/26/16**

Do your Debit and Credit balances match the following Trial Balance?

### Your Name's Beach Barkers
**TRIAL BALANCE**
As of February 26, 2016

| | DEBIT | CREDIT |
|---|---|---|
| Checking | 66,232.99 | |
| Petty Cash | 63.93 | |
| Accounts Receivable (A/R) | 14,159.60 | |
| Inventory Asset | 31,754.50 | |
| Prepaid Insurance | 1,700.00 | |
| Supplies:Cleaning Supplies | 1,050.00 | |
| Supplies:Kennel Supplies | 2,112.00 | |
| Supplies:Office Supplies | 921.48 | |
| Supplies:Sales Supplies | 400.00 | |
| Undeposited Funds | 0.00 | |
| Furniture & Fixtures:Depreciation | | 1,625.00 |
| Furniture & Fixtures:Original cost | 15,000.00 | |
| Kennel Equipment:Depreciation | | 2,200.00 |
| Kennel Equipment:Original cost | 21,150.00 | |
| Office Equipment:Depreciation | | 900.00 |
| Office Equipment:Original cost | 11,685.84 | |
| Vehicles:Depreciation | | 3,475.00 |
| Vehicles:Original cost | 32,000.00 | |
| Accounts Payable (A/P) | | 5,214.00 |
| Visa | | 2,639.80 |
| State Board of Equalization Payable | | 0.00 |
| Loans Payable:Equipment Loan | | 1,970.59 |
| Loans Payable:Furniture & Fixtures Loan | | 2,463.24 |
| Opening Balance Equity | | 300.00 |
| Retained Earnings | 1,844.66 | |
| Your Name, Capital | | 119,922.16 |
| Your Name, Capital:Your Name, Drawing | | 0.00 |
| Your Name, Capital:Your Name, Investment | | 53,735.00 |
| Sales of Product Income | | 2,500.50 |
| Services:Boarding | | 2,420.00 |
| Services:Day Camp | | 1,410.00 |
| Services:Grooming | | 1,360.00 |
| Services:House Calls | | 375.00 |
| Services:Sales Discounts | 51.80 | |
| Services:Training | | 5,025.00 |
| Services:Transportation | | 1,225.00 |
| Cost of Goods Sold | 733.00 | |
| Cost of Goods Sold:Merchandise Discounts | | 27.50 |
| Advertising | 700.00 | |
| Bank Charges | 16.00 | |
| Equipment Rental | 75.00 | |
| Insurance:Vehicle Insurance | 100.00 | |
| Interest Expense | 18.75 | |
| Laundry | 81.50 | |
| Rent or Lease | 4,400.00 | |
| Repair & Maintenance:Computer Repair | 200.00 | |
| Repair & Maintenance:Vehicle Repair | 212.50 | |
| Supplies Expense:Cleaning Supplies Expense | 127.00 | |
| Supplies Expense:Kennel Supplies Expense | 134.00 | |
| Supplies Expense:Office Supplies Expense | 131.47 | |
| Supplies Expense:Sales Supplies Expense | 100.00 | |
| Telephone Expense | 129.95 | |
| Utilities:Electric | 164.75 | |
| Utilities:Gas-Heating | 343.50 | |
| Utilities:Water | 385.95 | |
| Vehicle Expenses | 126.05 | |
| Fees Billed | | 80.00 |
| Interest Earned | | 78.93 |
| Depreciation Expense | 670.00 | |
| Purchase Discounts | | 29.50 |
| **TOTAL** | **$208,976.22** | **$208,976.22** |

Print or export then submit as previously instructed

- Name the report **30-Your Name Trial Balance Ch. 7**.

Close Your Name's Beach Barkers

## SUMMARY

In Chapter 7, you learned how to prepare purchase orders to order merchandise and to record a bill to receive the merchandise on purchase order. The company's Visa and checks were used to pay for inventory, bills, and other expenses. The differences between Purchase Discounts and Merchandise Discounts were explored. Payments were made that included discounts for the term of 2% 10 Net 30. Petty cash was used to pay for minor expenses. The Sales Tax Center was explored and the Sales Tax Payment was made. Reports were customized, saved, and used. A variety of reports were prepared throughout the chapter to assess the inventory, liabilities, purchases, and payments made. These include Inventory Valuation Summary, Vendor Balance Summary, Unpaid Bills, Check Detail, Sales Tax Liability, Purchases by Products/Services Detail, Open PO List by Vendor, Bill Payment List, Journal, and Trial Balance.

7

# END-OF-CHAPTER QUESTIONS

## TRUE/FALSE

ANSWER THE FOLLOWING QUESTIONS IN THE SPACE PROVIDED BEFORE THE QUESTION NUMBER.

_____ 1. The total amount of a purchase order shows as an amount due in the vendor's register.

_____ 2. The company credit card may be used to pay bills, pay expenses, or buy merchandise.

_____ 3. Inventory may be purchased and paid for without preparing a purchase order.

_____ 4. To pay sales tax, you click the Plus icon and Checks and then write the check.

_____ 5. The Purchase Discounts account is used for a discount on payments of expenses or bills that are not for merchandise.

_____ 6. To view a list of Open Purchase Orders, you prepare a Vendor List report.

_____ 7. QuickBooks Online automatically calculates and inserts the 2% discount when paying for purchases from vendors.

_____ 8. You can make a bill payment directly from the bill.

_____ 9. A Vendor Credit increases the amount you owe a vendor.

_____ 10. A Purchase Order may never be closed manually.

## MULTIPLE CHOICE

WRITE THE LETTER OF THE CORRECT ANSWER IN THE SPACE PROVIDED BEFORE THE QUESTION NUMBER.

_____ 1. The ___ report tells you the quantity, total asset value, and average cost for inventory items.
   A. Transaction List by Vendor
   B. Inventory Valuation Summary
   C. Inventory Cost Analysis
   D. Unpaid Bills

_____ 2. A(n) ___ is prepared to order merchandise.
   A. Purchase Order
   B. Bill
   C. Inventory List Report
   D. Expense

_____  3. To use a check to pay for a bill that has not been recorded, you access ___ in the Vendors column.
  A.  Pay Bills
  B.  Bills
  C.  Check
  D.  Accounts Payable

_____  4. When you create a new item for a product you sell, it is classified as a(n) ___ item.
  A.  Service
  B.  Non-inventory
  C.  Inventory
  D.  Product

_____  5. Where do you record the 2% discount for early payment of a bill?
  A.  Enter it on the bill
  B.  Prepare a Vendor Credit
  C.  Change the amount of the bill payment check
  D.  Any of the above

_____  6. To pay for small expenses using cash, you use the ___ account.
  A.  Cash
  B.  Transfer
  C.  Petty Cash
  D.  Undeposited Funds

_____  7. If you purchase inventory items and pay for them at the same time, you record the purchase on a(n) ___ form(s).
  A.  Expense
  B.  Purchase Order and Bill
  C.  Bill
  D.  Vendor

_____  8. To take a discount on merchandise ordered, you use the ___ Discount account.
  A.  Sales
  B.  Purchase
  C.  Inventory
  D.  Merchandise

_____  9. Which report shows every transaction recorded in Debit/Credit format?
  A.  Trial Balance
  B.  Journal
  C.  Transaction List by Vendor
  D.  Expenses List

_____  10. With Terms of 2% 10 Net 30 what is the discount amount for a purchase of $500?
  A.  10¢
  B.  $1.00
  C.  $10.00
  D.  $100.00

7

## FILL-IN

IN THE SPACE PROVIDED, WRITE THE ANSWER THAT MOST APPROPRIATELY
COMPLETES THE SENTENCE.

1. If you only receive part of the merchandise ordered you prepare a(n) _____ of the
   original purchase order for the missing amount.

2. A fast way to find your latest purchase orders is to click the _____ in a blank Purchase
   Order.

3. When you return something that was paid for by credit card, you prepare a(n) _____.

4. The names of the three discounts used in the text are _____, _____, and
   _____ Discounts.

5. To view the bills paid by check and credit card you prepare the _____ Report.

## COMPUTER ASSIGNMENT

REFER TO PRINTOUTS OR USE QUICKBOOKS ONLINE AND YOUR NAME'S BEACH
BARKERS TO LOOK UP OR ENTER INFORMATION, AND THEN WRITE THE ANSWERS TO
THE FOLLOWING EXERCISES IN THE SPACE PROVIDED

1. In the Journal refer to the 02/24/16 transaction for Happy Wags. What are
   the three accounts used for the Bill?                                    _____
                                                                            _____
                                                                            _____

2. Prepare your Custom Unpaid Bills report. What are the terms shown for
   Pet Supplies Unlimited?                                                  _____

3. Refer to your Check Detail report to answer which vendor was paid with
   Check 27?                                                                _____

4. Where do you prepare the Sales Tax Liability Report?                     _____

5. What did you use to pay for the windshield wiper blades purchase from
   Morales Auto Repair on February 22, 2016?                               _____

6. What was the discount for the early payment of the bill to The Literary Dog on
   February 26, 2016?                                                      _____

7. Prepare your Custom Open Purchase Order List by Vendor. Which vendor has
   an open purchase order?                                                 _____

8. What account was used for the early payment discount taken for the payment to
   Quality Insurance?                                                      _____

9. Prepare your Custom Profit and Loss report. What was the total amount of rent
   for February?                                                          _____

10. What was the amount of discount taken for the bill payment check to
Happy Wags on February 24, 2016? _____

# CHAPTER 7 CHECKLIST

The checklist below shows all of the business forms printed during training. Check each one that you printed, exported, and/or submitted.

| | |
|---|---|
| _____ 1-Inventory Valuation Summary Ch. 7 | _2_ 16-Sales Tax Liability Report Ch. 7 |
| _____ 2-PO 1001 The Literary Dog | _3_ 17-Check 23 State Board of Equalization |
| _____ 3-PO 1002 Pawsitively Elegant | _____ 18-PO 1007 Happy Wags |
| _____ 4-PO 1003 All About Dogs Supplies | _____ 19-PO 1008 Pet Supplies Unlimited |
| _____ 5-PO 1004 Bark City Toys | _____ 20-Checks 24-27 |
| _____ 6-PO 1005 Canine Supplies | _____ 21-Check 28 Supplies Unlimited |
| _____ 7-Open Purchase Order List Ch. 7 | _____ 22-PO 1009 Bark City Toys |
| _____ 8-PO 1003 All About Dogs Supplies Corrected | _____ 23-PO 1010 Happy Wags |
| _____ 9-PO 1006 Canine Supplies | _____ 24-Check 29 Happy Wags |
| _____ 10-PO 1005 Canine Supplies Corrected | _4_ 25-Inventory Valuation Summary Ch. 7 |
| _____ 11-Purchases by Product/Service Detail Ch. 7 | _5_ 26-Bill Payment List Ch. 7 |
| _____ 12-Unpaid Bills Ch. 7 | _6_ 27-Vendor Balance Summary Ch. 7 |
| _____ 13-Check 19 Canine Supplies | _7_ 28-Check Detail Ch. 7 |
| _____ 14-Check 20 Pawsitively Elegant | _____ 29-Journal Ch. 7 |
| _1_ 15-Checks 21 and 22 | _8_ 30-Trial Balance Ch. 7 |

7

# GENERAL ACCOUNTING, END-OF-PERIOD PROCEDURES, AND BUDGETS

**8**

## LEARNING OBJECTIVES

At the completion of this chapter, you will be able to:

1. Complete the end-of-period procedures.
2. Adjust inventory quantities and starting values.
3. Record Journal Entries for depreciation and the adjusting entries required for accrual-basis accounting.
4. Create budgets using locations.
5. Record owner's equity transactions for a sole proprietor including owner withdrawals and the transfer of net income into the owner's capital account.
6. Reconcile the bank statement; record bank service charges, interest, and automatic payments; and mark cleared transactions.
7. Reconcile Credit Card Statement and pay the balance due.
8. Print reports including Inventory Valuation Detail and Summary, Budget Overview, Budget vs. Actuals, Journal, Trial Balance, Profit & Loss, and Balance Sheet, among others.
9. Close a period.
10. Record a correcting entry after closing a period.

## GENERAL ACCOUNTING, END-OF-PERIOD PROCEDURES, AND BUDGETS

As previously stated, QuickBooks Online operates from the standpoint of a business document rather than an accounting form, journal, or ledger. While QuickBooks Online does incorporate all of these items into the program, in many instances they operate behind the scenes. Most of the end-of-period procedures are the same whether you sell inventory products, services, or both. However, when dealing with inventory, it is important to check your inventory stock on a routine basis to make sure that the number of items you have on hand matches the number of items shown in QuickBooks Online. Sometimes your numbers may not match. This can be due to a variety of reasons: damaged stock that needs to be discarded, miscounting, inaccurate numbers listed on a transaction, and theft, among others. If your numbers do not match, you record inventory adjustments to correct the discrepancies. In addition, if you find an error in a starting value for an inventory item, whether it is the quantity, cost, or date, you may also edit and correct the starting inventory value.

It is important for a business to establish a budget. A budget will help track income and expenses and may be used to make decisions regarding products and services sold and expenses incurred. By having a budget in place, you will be able to see if your projections for profitability are realistic, if you have more expenses than you can sustain, which locations are meeting or exceeding budget expectations, and other relevant data. A budget may be prepared for the company as a whole or it may be broken down by locations, class, or customer.

As you learned earlier in the text, QuickBooks Online does not require special closing procedures at the end of a period. At the end of the fiscal year, QuickBooks Online transfers the Net Income into Retained Earnings and allows you to protect the data for the year by assigning a closing date to the period. Once a period is closed, all of the transaction detail is maintained and viewable, but it will not be changed unless Yes is clicked on a warning screen.

Even though a formal closing does not have to be performed within QuickBooks Online, when you use accrual-basis accounting, several transactions must be recorded to reflect all expenses and income for the period. For example, bank statements must be reconciled and any charges or bank collections need to be recorded. During the business period, the accountant for the company will review things such as adjusting entries, depreciation schedules, owner's equity adjustments, and so on. The changes and adjustments may be entered directly into the company or they may be made by the accountant using QuickBooks Online Accountant. Once necessary adjustments have been made, reports reflecting the end-of-period results of operations should be prepared.

## TRAINING TUTORIAL AND PROCEDURES

Continue to use the Test Drive Company for practice and the fictional company, Your Name's Beach Barkers, to record end-of-period transactions, adjustments, and reconciliations; and to assign a closing date. In certain sections of the chapter, transactions, accounts, and other information will need to be entered into the Test Drive Company before you can complete a drill.

Since you prepared adjusting entries in Chapter 5, the Test Drive practice will be limited. The material entered into Your Name's Beach Barkers will be more complex than the entries for the Test Drive Company. Because you customized the Equity accounts in Chapter 5 and the Test Drive does not include the accounts, it will not be used for practice when entering transactions using Equity accounts. Instructions are given to guide you through the process. In addition to recording transactions, you will also prepare several reports. Use of Your Name's Beach Barkers will continue throughout the text as you explore the different facets and capabilities of QuickBooks Online.

Just as you did in previous chapters, you will enter additional transactions near the end of the chapter. These transactions are similar to the ones you entered in the Test Drive Company and in Your Name's Beach Barkers so no step-by-step instructions will be given. If you need to refer back to the chapter materials to make the entries, you should feel free to do so.

**Pay careful attention to quantities, amounts, and dates as you work through the chapter. A careless error can require a tremendous amount of effort to correct.**

## DATES

Remember that the year used for the screen shots is 2016. Continue to use the same year that you used in Chapters 2-7. In Chapter 8 through the rest of the chapters, the month used will be February. If QuickBooks Online inserts the current date into a transaction, be aware of this and be sure to use the date indicated in the text.

## IMPORTANT NOTE

As has been stated in earlier chapters, QuickBooks Online is constantly evolving and new features, apps, and procedures change frequently. Everything in the text is correct at the time of this writing; however, by the time of publication some changes to the program may occur.

## ADJUSTMENTS FOR ACCRUAL-BASIS ACCOUNTING

As previously stated, the accrual-basis of accounting matches the income and the expenses of a period in order to arrive at an accurate figure for net income or net loss. Thus, the revenue is earned at the time the service is performed or the sale is made no matter when the actual cash is received. Also, an expense is recorded at the time the bill is received or the purchase is made regardless of the actual payment date. Conversely, the cash-basis of accounting records income or revenue at the time cash is received no matter when the sale was made or the service performed.

An expense is not recorded until it is paid. In QuickBooks Online, the Accounting Method selected by default in Settings is Accrual. It may be changed to Cash.

When using accrual-basis accounting, there are several internal transactions that must be recorded. These entries are called adjusting entries. Some items used in a business are purchased and or paid for in advance. When this occurs, they are recorded as an asset and are called prepaid expenses. As these are used, they become expenses of the business. Another example for adjusting entries is in regard to equipment. Since it does wear out and will eventually need to be replaced, an adjusting entry is made to allocate the amount of depreciation of the equipment as an expense for a period.

## ADJUSTING ENTRIES: PREPAID EXPENSES—DRILL

A prepaid expense is an item that is paid for in advance. Examples of prepaid expenses include: Insurance; Office Supplies and Sales Supplies, which are purchased to have on hand and use as needed. (This is different from supplies that are purchased for immediate use.) As noted earlier, a prepaid expense is an asset until it is used. As the insurance or supplies are used, the amount used becomes an expense for the period. In accrual-basis accounting, an adjusting entry is made in the General Journal at the end of the period to allocate the amount of prepaid expenses (assets) used to expenses.

The Test Drive Company does not always have accounts or recorded transactions that are needed to illustrate some of the concepts presented in the text. Prior to recording an adjusting entry for supplies, a purchase of supplies must be entered.

---

**MEMO**
**DATE**: February 28, 2016

Record the purchase on February 5, 2016 of $250 of Supplies to have on hand from Mahoney Mugs. Record an Expense and pay for the purchase with the company Visa.

At the end of the month, there was $200 of Supplies on hand. Record the monthly adjustment for the amount of supplies used.

---

## *DRILL*

 Open the **Test Drive Company** and record the purchase and the adjustment for supplies

Click the **Plus** icon; click **Expense** in the Vendors column
Payee: **Mahoney Mugs**
Account: **Visa**
Payment date: **02/05/16**
Payment method: **Visa**
Account details Line 1: **Prepaid Expenses** (remember this is an Asset account)
- The Test Drive Company does not have separate accounts for prepaid expenses; such as, office supplies, sales supplies, prepaid insurance, etc. Use the Prepaid Expenses account.
Amount: **250**

Click **Save and close**
- Do you remember the keyboard shortcut **Ctrl+Alt+D** to save and close?

Click the **Plus** icon

Click **Journal Entry** in the Other column
- As you remember from Chapter 5 adjusting entries, a Journal Entry requires both a debit and a credit just as you did when you recorded a General Journal Entry in your concepts course.

Enter the date: **02/28/16**, press **Tab**
- The Journal Entry number **1** is shown.

Line 1: Click in the ACCOUNT text box, click the drop-down list arrow, scroll through the accounts, and click the Expense account **Supplies**
- Calculate the amount of the adjusting entry: Supplies Purchased $250 – Supplies On hand $200 = $50 Supplies Used.

Tab to DEBITS, and enter the amount of the adjusting entry **50**

Tab to DESCRIPTION, enter **Adjusting Entry, February**

Line 2: Tab to or click in ACCOUNT, scroll through the accounts, click **Prepaid Expenses**
- The Credit of 50 and the Description are automatically entered by QuickBooks Online. If they do not appear automatically, simply enter them as instructed for the Debit entry.
- This adjusting entry decreases the asset Prepaid Expenses by $50 and increases the expense Supplies.

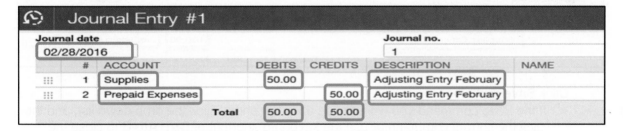

Click **Save and close**

Close the Test Drive Company

## ADJUSTING ENTRIES: PREPAID EXPENSES—DO

As you learned in the drill, a prepaid expense is an item that is paid for in advance. In accrual-basis accounting, a Journal Entry is recorded at the end of the period to allocate the amount of prepaid expenses (assets) used to expenses.

8

<u>MEMO</u>
**DATE:** February 28, 2016

Journal Entry 19: Record the adjusting entry for the use of $100 of Office Supplies.

Journal Entry 20: After taking inventory, you calculate that you have $1,936 of Kennel Supplies on hand. Calculate the amount of supplies used and record the adjusting entry.

<u>DO</u>

 Open <u>**Your Name's Beach Barkers**</u> and record adjusting entries for prepaid expenses

Click the **Plus** icon
Click **Journal Entry** in the Other column
Enter the date: **02/28/16**, press **Tab**
- The Journal Entry number **19** is shown.
Click in the ACCOUNT text box for Line 1
- This adjusting entry is to record the amount of Office Supplies used for the month.
Click the drop-down list arrow, scroll through the accounts, and click the Supplies Expense subaccount: **Office Supplies Expense**
Tab to DEBITS, and enter the amount of the adjusting entry **100**
Tab to DESCRIPTION, enter **Adjusting Entry, February**
Tab to or click in ACCOUNT in Line 2, scroll through the accounts, click the Supplies Asset subaccount: **Office Supplies**
- The Credit of 100 and the Description are automatically entered by QuickBooks Online. If they do not appear automatically, simply enter them as instructed for the Debit entry.
- This adjusting entry decreases the asset Office Supplies by $100 and increases the expense Office Supplies Expense by $100.

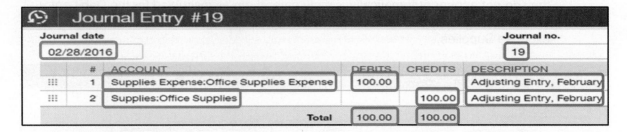

Click **Save and close**
- If the Save command you want to use does not show, click the drop-down list, and then, click the correct command or use the keyboard shortcut of **Ctrl+Alt+D** to close the screen.
Open the Chart of Accounts as previously instructed, and then click **View Register** for the subaccount of Supplies: **Office Supplies**
- The following screen shot shows the register in reverse chronological order. If your register shows in chronological order, click the column heading DATE to reverse the order.

‹ Back to Chart of Accounts          ENDING BALANCE    Reconcile

**Asset Register**    Supplies:Office Supplies  ⬍       **$821.48**

| DATE ▾ | REF NO. | PAYEE | MEMO | CLASS | DECREASE | INCREASE | ✓ | BALANCE |
|--------|---------|-------|------|-------|----------|----------|---|---------|
| | TYPE | ACCOUNT | | LOCATION | | | ⟷ | |
| Add deposit ▾ | | | | | | | | |
| 02/28/2016 | 19 | | Adjusting Entry, February | | $100.00 | | | $821.48 |
| | Journal | -Split- | | | | | | |
| 02/24/2016 | | Super Office | | | $30.00 | | | $921.48 |
| | CC-Credit | Visa | | | | | | |
| 02/23/2016 | | Super Office | | | | $150.00 | | $951.48 |
| | Expense | Visa | | | | | | |
| 02/19/2016 | | Super Office | | | $43.20 | | | $801.48 |
| | CC-Credit | Visa | | | | | | |
| 02/19/2016 | | Super Office | | | | $216.00 | | $844.68 |
| | Expense | Visa | | | | | | |
| 01/31/2016 | 8 | | Adjusting Entry, January | | $125.00 | | | $628.68 |
| | Journal | -Split- | | | | | | |
| 01/20/2016 | 725 | Super Office | | | $21.55 | | | $753.68 |
| | Vendor Credit | Accounts Payable (A/P) | | | | | | |
| 01/18/2016 | 286 | Super Office | | | | $425.23 | | $775.23 |
| | Bill | Accounts Payable (A/P) | | | | | | |
| 12/31/2015 | | | Opening Balance | | | $350.00 | R | $350.00 |
| | Deposit | Opening Balance Equity | | | | | | |

- You will see all of the transactions for Office Supplies from the Opening Balance to Journal Entry 19.
- For the Journal entries, rather than see the Account name, you see -Split-. This means that the transaction was split between two or more accounts. In this case, Office Supplies Expense and Office Supplies were the accounts used.
- While the account register is shown, look at all of the entries that have been recorded for Office Supplies. If your entries do not match, click on the transaction and correct the error. If you are missing an entry, run the report for Office Supplies Expense and see if you recorded the transaction in the wrong account. If so, click on the transaction and change the account name.

Click **<Back to Chart of Accounts** (just above the words Asset Register)

Scroll down to the Office Supplies Expense account, click **Run report**

On the Account QuickReport, enter the date From: **01/01/16** To: **02/28/16**, click **Run Report**

- View the transactions for the account and note the adjusting entry for February. As you did for the asset Office Supplies, check your report to see if your transactions match the ones shown below. If not, correct the transaction.

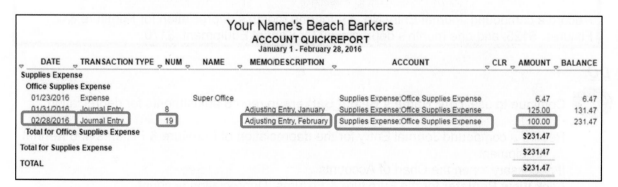

Your Name's Beach Barkers
ACCOUNT QUICKREPORT
January 1 - February 28, 2016

| DATE | TRANSACTION TYPE | NUM | NAME | MEMO/DESCRIPTION | ACCOUNT | CLR | AMOUNT | BALANCE |
|------|------------------|-----|------|-----------------|---------|-----|--------|---------|
| Supplies Expense | | | | | | | | |
| Office Supplies Expense | | | | | | | | |
| 01/23/2016 | Expense | | Super Office | | Supplies Expense:Office Supplies Expense | | 6.47 | 6.47 |
| 01/31/2016 | Journal Entry | 8 | | Adjusting Entry, January | Supplies Expense:Office Supplies Expense | | 125.00 | 131.47 |
| 02/28/2016 | Journal Entry | 19 | | Adjusting Entry, February | Supplies Expense:Office Supplies Expense | | 100.00 | 231.47 |
| Total for Office Supplies Expense | | | | | | | $231.47 | |
| Total for Supplies Expense | | | | | | | $231.47 | |
| TOTAL | | | | | | | $231.47 | |

Reopen the **Chart of Accounts**

Prior to recording the Journal Entry for Kennel Supplies, calculate the amount of the adjusting entry

- The transaction for Office Supplies states that the amount of <u>supplies used</u> is $100. That is the amount of the adjustment to be recorded.

- The transaction for Kennel Supplies states that there is $1,946 of <u>supplies on hand</u>. That is the amount the account balance will be <u>after</u> the adjustment has been recorded.

With the Chart of Accounts open, look at the balance of the asset Kennel Supplies

- The account balance minus the amount of supplies on hand equals the amount of the adjusting entry. ($2,112 - $1,936 = $176)

Record Journal Entry 20 as previously instructed

Date: **02/28/16**

Journal no.: **20**

Line 1: Account: **Kennel Supplies Expense**, Debit: **176**, Description: **Adjusting Entry, February**

Line 2: Account: **Kennel Supplies**, Credit: **176**, Description: **Adjusting Entry, February**

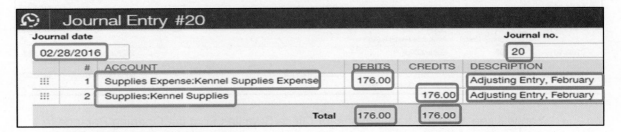

Click **Save and close** (Ctrl+Alt+D)

Do <u>not</u> close Your Name's Beach Barkers, complete the next section

## ADJUSTING ENTRIES—DEPRECIATION—DO

Equipment and other long-term assets lose value over their lifetime. To account for the fact that machines wear out and need to be replaced, an adjustment is made for depreciation. This adjustment correctly matches the expenses of the period against the revenue of the period.

Because you entered the adjustments for depreciation in Chapter 5 and the Test Drive Company requires extra transactions in order to practice, you will not complete a drill in this section.

> **MEMO**
> **DATE:** February 28, 2016
>
> Record a compound Journal Entry No. 21: for one month's depreciation for Furniture & Fixtures, $125; and one month's depreciation for Kennel Equipment, $170.

<u>DO</u>

Continue to use **Your Name's Beach Barkers** to record adjustments for depreciation

Record a compound Journal Entry for the depreciation of Furniture & Fixtures and Kennel Equipment

If necessary, open the Chart of Accounts

Click **View Register** for the Furniture & Fixtures: Depreciation account

- Typically, depreciation would be entered once a year; however, in the text, we are entering it each month.
- Note the amount of the Adjusting Entry for January of $125. You will enter the same amount for February.

Click **<Back to Chart of Accounts**

Click **View Register** for Kennel Equipment: Depreciation account

- Note the amount of the Adjusting Entry for January of $170. You will enter the same amount for February.

Open a **Journal Entry** as previously instructed

- A blank screen for Journal no. 21 should open.

Date: **02/28/16**

Journal Entry: **21**

- It is possible to enter two adjusting entries in the same Journal entry. This is called a compound entry.
- To use the power of the program, the Credit entries to each fixed asset will be entered first. Then, the Debit entry for the total amount of Depreciation Expense will be entered.

Line 1: Account: **Furniture & Fixtures:Depreciation**, Credits: **125**, Description: **Adjusting Entry, February**

Line 2: Account: **Kennel Equipment:Depreciation**

- QuickBooks Online will enter 125 as a Debit. Disregard this.

Click in the **Credits** column, and enter **170**

Description: **Adjusting Entry, February**

- Should be entered automatically.

Line 3: Account: **Depreciation Expense**, Debit: **295**, Description: **Adjusting Entry, February**

- QuickBooks Online should automatically calculate the amount of Depreciation Expense, enter it in the Debits column, and enter the Description.

| | # | ACCOUNT | DEBITS | CREDITS | DESCRIPTION |
|---|---|---|---|---|---|
| ⋮⋮⋮ | 1 | Furniture & Fixtures:Depreciation | | 125.00 | Adjusting Entry, February |
| ⋮⋮⋮ | 2 | Kennel Equipment:Depreciation | | 170.00 | Adjusting Entry, February |
| ⋮⋮⋮ | 3 | Depreciation Expense | 295.00 | | Adjusting Entry, February |
| | | Total | 295.00 | 295.00 | |

Journal Entry #21 — Journal date 02/28/2016 — Journal no. 21

Click **Save and close**

Close Your Name's Beach Barkers

## INVENTORY ADJUSTMENTS—DRILL

QuickBooks Online Plus is the only online version of QuickBooks Online that can track inventory. Beginning inventory quantities were added for each product in Chapter 2. Then in Chapters 6 and 7, you actively started to use inventory tracking. New inventory items and quantities were added. When inventory was purchased, the quantities on hand increased; when merchandise was sold, the quantities on hand decreased.

When adding a new inventory item, it is possible to make an error when entering the starting value of the item. This may be adjusted to change the starting quantity, cost, and/or date if you added the item without preparing a purchase order or a bill. If the new item was added and no value, quantity, or other information was entered until you received the items and recorded the receipt, you may make the change directly on the purchase order, bills, or payment form.

Also, there may be other instances when the quantity of the inventory on hand needs to be adjusted. This might be due to recording an incorrect amount of inventory received or sold, finding that inventory was damaged or misplaced, among other reasons. A Cost of Goods Sold account, Inventory Shrinkage, is added by QuickBooks Online and is used to record the change in quantity.

**MEMO**
**DATE**: February 28, 2016

Add a new Inventory Item: Timers, Initial quantity on hand: 25; As of date: 12/31/15; Sales price: 50; Is taxable, Cost 20. Use the accounts provided by QuickBooks Online.

Change the Inventory Starting Value information for Timers. Quantity: 30, As of date: 01/01/16; Cost: 25.

Discovered two cracked pumps. Adjust the number of Pumps on hand from 25 to 23.

## DRILL

 Open the **Test Drive Company** and record the inventory adjustments

## Add a New Inventory Item

In order to practice inventory starting value adjustments, you need to add a new inventory item.

 Use the **Test Drive Company** and add the new inventory item, Timers

    Open the Products and Services List
    Click the **New** button, click **Inventory Item**
    Enter the information provided in the Memo:
    Name, Sales information, and Purchase information: **Timers**
    Initial quantity on hand: **25**
    As of date: **12/31/15**
    Use the accounts provided by QuickBooks Online: **Inventory Asset**, **Sales of Product**
        **Income**, and **Cost of Goods Sold**
    Sales price: **50**
    Is taxable: should have a check
    Cost: **20**
    Click **Save and close**

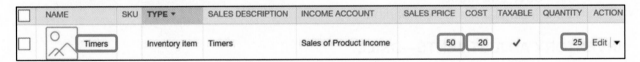

| | NAME | SKU | TYPE ▾ | SALES DESCRIPTION | INCOME ACCOUNT | SALES PRICE | COST | TAXABLE | QUANTITY | ACTION |
|---|---|---|---|---|---|---|---|---|---|---|
| ☐ | Timers | | Inventory item | Timers | Sales of Product Income | 50 | 20 | ✓ | 25 | Edit ▼ |

    Continue to the next section

## Adjust Inventory Starting Value, Quantity, and Date

There are three ways to change the Inventory Starting Value information. In the drill you will do this by preparing the Inventory Valuation Detail Report, and clicking on the "Inventory Starting Value" transaction. You may now change the starting quantity, rate, and date. The other method, which will be used in the DO section, is to open the Product and Services List, click Edit for the item, and click Starting Value. The third way is open the Product and Services List, click the drop-down list arrow in the item's ACTION column, and click Starting Value. This type of adjustment is made only for starting values. If there are changes to quantities due to damage, errors in recording, theft, or other reasons, you adjust the inventory quantity.

 Continue to use the **Test Drive Company** to adjust the starting value, quantity, and date for Timers

Prior to beginning this section, go to QuickBooks Labs and turn **OFF** Redesigned Reports
Click **Reports** on the Navigation bar, select the report category **Manage Products and Inventory**
Click the **Inventory Valuation Detail** report
Date: From: **12/31/15** To: **Current Date**, click **Run Report**
Scroll through the report until you get to **Timers**; click the transaction line for **Inventory Starting Value**

| DATE | TRANSACTION TYPE | NUM | QTY | QUANTITY | AVG COST | RATE | ASSET VALUE |
|---|---|---|---|---|---|---|---|
| **Timers** | | | | | | | |
| 12/31/2015 | Inventory Starting Value | START | 25.00 | 25.00 | 20.00 | 20.00 | 500.00 |

- This will open the Inventory Starting Value #START form.
Change the Inventory Starting Value using the information in the Memo
Change Initial quantity on hand from 25 to **30**
Change As of date from 12/31/15 to **01/01/16**
Change Initial Cost from 20 to **25**
Inventory asset account: **Inventory Asset** (no change)
Inventory adjustment account: **Opening Balance Equity** (no change)
- When inventory is added without preparing a bill and paying for it, a starting inventory value is created. The starting value of an inventory item is always added to the Opening Balance Equity account. Remember, Inventory Asset is increased by the amount of the new inventory item and Opening Balance Equity is also increased by the value of the new item.
- If you add a new inventory item, record a bill, and pay for the item, an inventory starting value transaction is <u>not</u> recorded and the Opening Balance Equity account is not used.

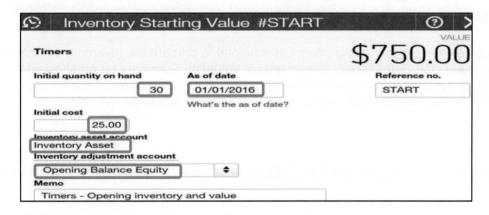

Click **Save and close**
Do <u>not</u> close the Test Drive Company, continue to the next section

## Adjust Inventory Quantities

There are three ways to access the Inventory Quantity Adjustment form to change inventory quantities. One way is to open the Products and Services List, click Edit for the item, and click Quantity. The second way is open the Product and Services List, click the drop-down list arrow in the item's ACTION column, and click Adjust Quantity. The third way is to click the Plus icon and click Inventory Qty Adjustment in the Other column. The drill will access the Inventory Quantity Adjustment form by using the Plus icon.

 Continue to use the **Test Drive Company** to record the quantity adjustment for Pumps

Click the **Plus** icon, click **Inventory Qty Adjustment** in the Other column
Use the **Current Date** for the drill
Use the **Inventory Shrinkage** for the Inventory adjustment account
- Account added by QuickBooks Online.
Line 1: Click in the PRODUCT text box, click the drop-down list arrow, click **Pump**
Tab to or click in NEW QTY, enter **23**, press **Tab**
- Notice that CHANGE IN QTY shows -2.

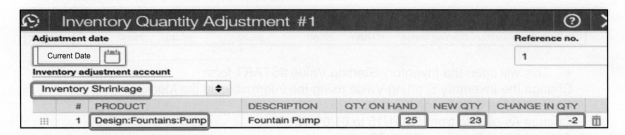

| # | PRODUCT | DESCRIPTION | QTY ON HAND | NEW QTY | CHANGE IN QTY | |
|---|---|---|---|---|---|---|
| 1 | Design:Fountains:Pump | Fountain Pump | 25 | 23 | -2 | 🗑 |

Click **Save and close**
Open the Products and Services List and verify the Quantity

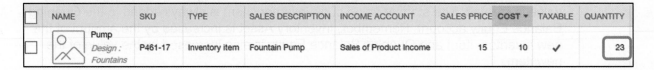

| | NAME | SKU | TYPE | SALES DESCRIPTION | INCOME ACCOUNT | SALES PRICE | COST ▾ | TAXABLE | QUANTITY |
|---|---|---|---|---|---|---|---|---|---|
| | Pump *Design : Fountains* | P461-17 | Inventory item | Fountain Pump | Sales of Product Income | 15 | 10 | ✓ | 23 |

Close the Test Drive Company

## INVENTORY VALUATION SUMMARY—DO

Prior to making changes to inventory items, it is helpful to prepare the Inventory Valuation Summary or Inventory Valuation Detail report. The Inventory Valuation Summary report shows the quantity on hand, value, and average cost for each inventory item. To see the transactions for the individual inventory items, you click the item to drill-down to the item's detailed information.

## DO

Open and use **Your Name's Beach Barkers** and prepare the Inventory Valuation Summary report

Open **Reports**, select **Manage Products and Inventory** for the report category
Click **Inventory Valuation Summary**
Enter the date for As of: **02/28/16**, click **Run Report**
- Notice the quantity and asset value for the item Dog Bed.

## Your Name's Beach Barkers
### INVENTORY VALUATION SUMMARY
As of February 28, 2016

| | QTY | TOTAL ASSET VALUE | AVG COST |
|---|---|---|---|
| Bones | 331.00 | 662.00 | 2.00 |
| Books | 250.00 | 750.00 | 3.00 |
| Brushes | 61.00 | 305.00 | 5.00 |
| Collars | 640.00 | 6,400.00 | 10.00 |
| Dog Beds | 51.00 | 1,020.00 | 20.00 |
| Dog Cages | 38.00 | 950.00 | 25.00 |
| Dog Dishes and Bowls | 25.00 | 125.00 | 5.00 |
| Dog Food-Canned | 463.00 | 1,157.50 | 2.50 |
| Dog Food-Dry | 394.00 | 2,758.00 | 7.00 |
| Dog Snacks | 176.00 | 176.00 | 1.00 |
| Leashes | 442.00 | 4,420.00 | 10.00 |
| Sweaters | 318.00 | 4,770.00 | 15.00 |
| Toys & Treats | 3,463.00 | 6,926.00 | 2.00 |
| Vitamins | 445.00 | 1,335.00 | 3.00 |
| TOTAL | | $31,754.50 | |

Remove the Date and Time Prepared from the footer as previously instructed
Print in Portrait orientation, export, and/or send/submit as previously instructed
- If you save the report, name it: **1-Your Name Inventory Valuation Summary Ch. 8**.
Do not close Your Name's Beach Barkers

## INVENTORY ADJUSTMENTS—DO

As was presented in the drill, QuickBooks Online Plus is the only online version of QuickBooks Online that can track inventory. Beginning inventory quantities and values were added for each product in Chapter 2; then, in Chapters 6 and 7 inventory tracking was used extensively. In those chapters, you added additional inventory items and quantities. When merchandise was sold, the quantities on hand decreased; and, when inventory items were purchased, the quantities on hand increased.

When adding a new inventory item, it is possible to make an error when entering the starting value information for the new item. Adjustments may be made to change the starting quantity, cost, and/or date. Starting values are entered when you add an inventory item and a quantity without entering a bill or a payment for the merchandise. As an example, in Chapter 6, Dog Bed and Dog Snacks were added as new items with quantities on hand. This created a starting value. However, in Chapter 7, you added a new inventory item Books with a quantity of 0. As a result, no starting value was entered.

There may be other instances not associated with the starting values when the quantity of the inventory on hand needs to be adjusted. This might be due to recording an incorrect amount of inventory received or sold, finding that inventory was damaged or misplaced, among other reasons.

**8**

**MEMO**
**DATE**: February 28, 2016

Two dog beds had bleach spilled on them. Reduce the inventory quantity for Dog Bed.

You want to sell towels that have the Beach Barkers Logo on them. Add a new inventory item: Towels; Quantity: 25; As of: 2/20/16; Sales Price 20, Is taxable, Cost 5. Use accounts provided by QBO.

Realized that an error was made when adding the new item Towels. Adjust the Inventory Starting Value to Quantity: 30: As of: 02/28/16; Cost 6.

<u>*DO*</u>

Open <u>**Your Name's Beach Barkers**</u> and record the inventory adjustments

<u>Adjust Inventory Quantities</u>

There are three ways to access the Inventory Quantity Adjustment form to change inventory quantities. The drill used the method of clicking the Plus icon, clicking Inventory Qty Adjustment in the Other column, and making the adjustment. This section will edit the inventory item in the Products and Services List, click Quantity, and enter the adjustment. In the Products and Services List, you may also click the drop-down list arrow for the item's ACTION column, and click Adjust quantity.

Use <u>**Your Name's Beach Barkers**</u> and adjust the quantity of Dog Bed

Open the Products and Services List, click **Edit** for Dog Bed
- If you have Dog Beds as the item name, that is fine.
Click **Quantity** on the Product/Service information screen

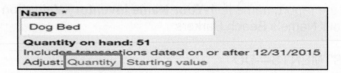

Adjustment date: **02/28/16**
Inventory adjustment account: **Inventory Shrinkage**
- The Inventory Shrinkage account is automatically created by QBO.
Line 1: Click in the PRODUCT text box, click the drop-down list arrow, click **Dog Bed**
Tab to or click in NEW QTY, enter **49**, press **Tab**
- Notice that CHANGE IN QTY shows -2.

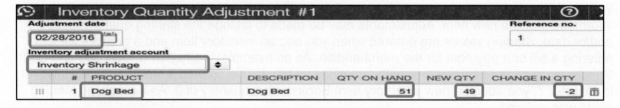

Click **Save and close**
Verify the Quantity in the Products and Services List

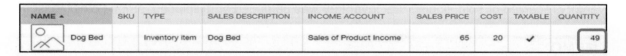

Open the Chart of Accounts, scroll down to **Inventory Shrinkage**, then click **Run Report** to verify the adjustment
Dates From: **020116** To: **022816**

---

**Your Name's Beach Barkers**
**ACCOUNT QUICKREPORT**
**February 1-28, 2016**

| DATE | TRANSACTION TYPE | NUM | NAME | MEMO/DESCRIPTION | ACCOUNT | CLR | AMOUNT | BALANCE |
|------|------------------|-----|------|------------------|---------|-----|--------|---------|
| **Inventory Shrinkage** | | | | | | | | |
| 02/28/2016 | Inventory Qty Adjust | 1 | | | Inventory Shrinkage | | 0.00 | 0.00 |
| 02/28/2016 | Inventory Qty Adjust | 1 | | | Inventory Shrinkage | | 40.00 | 40.00 |
| **Total for Inventory Shrinkage** | | | | | | | $40.00 | |
| **TOTAL** | | | | | | | $40.00 | |

---

- The dog beds cost $20 each. As a result, the cost for the decrease in the quantity was added to the Inventory Shrinkage account.

Do <u>not</u> close Your Name's Beach Barkers

## Add a New Inventory Item

Add a new inventory item to use in adjusting the Inventory Starting Values

Use **Your Name's Beach Barkers** and add the new inventory item, Towels

> Open the Products and Services List
> Click the **New** button, click **Inventory Item**
> Enter the information provided in the Memo:
> Name, Sales information, and Purchase information: **Towels**
> Initial quantity on hand: **25**
> As of date: **02/20/16**
> Use the accounts provided by QuickBooks Online
> Sales price: **20**
> Is taxable: should have a check
> Cost: **5**
> Click **Save and close**

| NAME ▼ | SKU | TYPE | SALES DESCRIPTION | INCOME ACCOUNT | SALES PRICE | COST | TAXABLE | QUANTITY |
|--------|-----|------|-------------------|----------------|-------------|------|---------|----------|
| Towels | | Inventory item | | Sales of Product Income | 20 | 5 | ✓ | 25 |

> Do <u>not</u> close Your Name's Beach Barkers, continue to the next section

## Adjust Inventory Starting Value, Quantity, and Date

As with quantity adjustments, there are three ways to change the Inventory Starting Value. In the drill you prepared the Inventory Valuation Detail Report, clicked on the "Inventory Starting Value" transaction, and changed the starting quantity, rate, and date. In this section, you will use another method. You will access the item in the Product and Services List, click the drop-down list arrow in the item's ACTION column, and click Starting Value. The third way is to open the Product and Services List, click Edit for the item, and click Starting Value. Remember, this type of adjustment is made only for starting values. If there are changes to quantities due to damage, errors in recording, theft, or other reasons, you adjust the inventory quantity.

Use **Your Name's Beach Barkers** and adjust the Starting Value for Towels

> With the Products and Services List showing on the screen, click the drop-down list arrow in the ACTION column for Towels

In the Adjust section, click **Adjust Starting value**

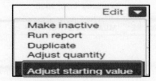

On the "Hold on!" message, click **Got it!**
- This will open the Inventory Starting Value #START form.

Change the Inventory Starting Value using the information in the Memo
Change Initial quantity on hand from 25 to **30**
Change As of date from 02/20/16 to **02/28/16**
Change Initial Cost from 5 to **6**
Inventory asset account: **Inventory Asset** (no change)
Inventory adjustment account: **Opening Balance Equity** (no change)
- When inventory is added without preparing a bill and paying for it, a starting inventory value is created. The starting value of an inventory item is always added to the Opening Balance Equity. Remember, Inventory Asset is increased by the amount of the new inventory item and Opening Balance Equity is also increased by the value of the new item.
- If you add a new inventory item, record a bill, and pay for the item, an inventory starting value transaction is <u>not</u> recorded and the Opening Balance Equity account is not used.

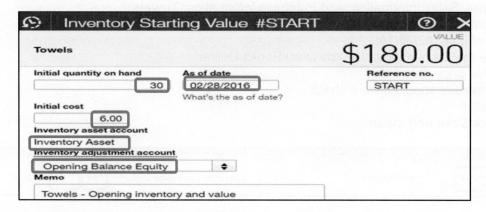

Click **Save and close**
Do <u>not</u> close Your Name's Beach Barkers

## INVENTORY VALUATION DETAIL—DO

Whenever you make changes to inventory quantities, starting values, or other changes, it is important to prepare either an Inventory Valuation Summary or Inventory Valuation Detail report to see the changes made. The Inventory Valuation Detail report lists the transactions for each inventory item within the report dates. The information provided in the report includes the transactions made for adjustments and shows how the transactions affected quantity on hand, value, and cost.

*DO*

Continue to use **Your Name's Beach Barkers** to prepare the Inventory Valuation Detail report

Open **Reports**, select the **Manage Products and Inventory** report category
Click **Inventory Valuation Detail**
Enter the Dates From: **02/01/16** To: **02/28/16**, click **Run Report**
- Scroll through the report and note the adjustment to Dog Bed and the Inventory Starting Value for Towels.
- If you wanted to see the Inventory Starting Value of the original inventory items, you would use 12/31/15 as the From Date.

### Your Name's Beach Barkers
### INVENTORY VALUATION DETAIL
#### February 1-28, 2016

| DATE | TRANSACTION TYPE | NUM | QTY | QUANTITY | AVG COST | RATE | ASSET VALUE |
|---|---|---|---|---|---|---|---|
| **Bones** | | | | | | | |
| Beginning Balance | | | | 350.00 | | | 700.00 |
| 02/01/2016 | Invoice | 1039 | -1.00 | 349.00 | 2.00 | 2.00 | 698.00 |
| 02/01/2016 | Invoice | 1040 | -5.00 | 344.00 | 2.00 | 2.00 | 688.00 |
| 02/01/2016 | Invoice | 1042 | -10.00 | 334.00 | 2.00 | 2.00 | 668.00 |
| 02/12/2016 | Sales Receipt | 1053 | -5.00 | 329.00 | 2.00 | 2.00 | 658.00 |
| 02/12/2016 | Sales Receipt | 1054 | -1.00 | 328.00 | 2.00 | 2.00 | 656.00 |
| 02/13/2016 | Refund | 1061 | 3.00 | 331.00 | 2.00 | 2.00 | 662.00 |
| **Books** | | | | | | | |
| 02/22/2016 | Bill | | 250.00 | 250.00 | 3.00 | 3.00 | 750.00 |
| **Dog Bed** | | | | | | | |
| Beginning Balance | | | | 5.00 | | | 100.00 |
| 02/03/2016 | Invoice | 1044 | -1.00 | 4.00 | 20.00 | 20.00 | 80.00 |
| 02/04/2016 | Sales Receipt | 1049 | -1.00 | 3.00 | 20.00 | 20.00 | 60.00 |
| 02/12/2016 | Invoice | 1055 | -1.00 | 2.00 | 20.00 | 20.00 | 40.00 |
| 02/12/2016 | Invoice | 1052 | -1.00 | 1.00 | 20.00 | 20.00 | 20.00 |
| 02/13/2016 | Invoice | 1062 | -1.00 | 0.00 | 20.00 | 20.00 | 0.00 |
| 02/13/2016 | Credit Memo | 1060 | 1.00 | 1.00 | 20.00 | 20.00 | 20.00 |
| 02/18/2016 | Bill | | 27.00 | 28.00 | 20.00 | 20.00 | 560.00 |
| 02/18/2016 | Bill | | 25.00 | 53.00 | 20.00 | 20.00 | 1,060.00 |
| 02/19/2016 | Vendor Credit | 1596 | -2.00 | 51.00 | 20.00 | 20.00 | 1,020.00 |
| 02/28/2016 | Inventory Qty Adjust | 1 | -2.00 | 49.00 | 20.91 | | 1,020.00 |
| 02/28/2016 | Inventory Qty Adjust | 1 | -2.00 | 47.00 | 20.95 | 20.00 | 980.00 |
| **Towels** | | | | | | | |
| 02/28/2016 | Inventory Starting Value | START | 30.00 | 30.00 | 6.00 | 6.00 | 180.00 |

Partial Report

- At the time of this writing, the ability to change the inventory quantities and values had just been made available. In the Inventory Valuation Detail report, QuickBooks Online shows the Inventory Quantity Adjustment for Dog Bed two times. The first line shows the reduction in Quantity and the second line shows the change in asset value (49 * 20 = 980.00) If the duplicate causes concern, know that when you prepare the Inventory Valuation Summary or look at the item in the Product and Services List, you will see the correct number of dog beds in inventory—49. If you see your adjustment two times, do not be concerned. If you see the information on one line, that is fine, too.
Remove the Date and Time Prepared from the footer
Print in Portrait orientation, export, and/or send/submit as previously instructed
- If you save the report, name it: **2-Your Name Inventory Valuation Detail Ch. 8**.
Do <u>not</u> close Your Name's Beach Barkers

**8**

## TRANSFER OPENING BALANCE EQUITY INTO CAPITAL ACCOUNT—DO

As you may remember from your work in Chapter 5, QuickBooks Online enters all of the values for opening balances into the Opening Balance Equity account. In Chapter 5, you transferred the entire amount of Opening Balance Equity into Your Name, Capital. However, in Chapter 6, you created two new inventory items with quantities—Dog Bed and Dog Snacks— and you just added a new inventory item, Towels, with quantities. Because you added these items without recording a bill or making a payment, the starting values for these items were added to the Inventory Asset and Opening Balance Equity accounts.

It is appropriate to transfer the amount of Opening Balance Equity into Your Name, Capital.

## DO

 Use **Your Name's Beach Barkers** and transfer the Opening Balance Equity into Capital

Open the Chart of Accounts, scroll down until you see the Opening Balance Equity Account
- You should see a balance of $480.
Click **View Register**, for Opening Balance Equity, and scroll through the register
- Note the addition of Towels on 2/28/16 and Dog Bed and Dog Snacks on 12/31/15.
Click **Reports** on the Navigation bar
Prepare your Customized Balance Sheet report for **02/01/16** to **02/28/16**, click **Run Report**
Scroll to the Equity section to view the Opening Balance Equity account balance of $480

| Equity | |
|---|---:|
| Opening Balance Equity | 480.00 |
| Retained Earnings | -1,844.66 |
| Your Name, Capital | 119,922.16 |
| Your Name, Drawing | 0.00 |
| Your Name, Investment | 53,735.00 |
| Total Your Name, Capital | 173,657.16 |
| Net Income | 5,019.21 |
| Total Equity | $177,311.71 |

Click the **Plus** icon, click **Journal Entry** in the Other column
Journal date: **02/28/16**
Journal no.: **22**
Line 1:
    Click in the text box for ACCOUNT, click the drop-down list arrow, and click **Opening Balance Equity**
    Tab to DEBITS, enter **480**
- This is the balance of the account. Remember, Opening Balance Equity has a credit balance. To move the balance to capital, you would debit the account to decrease it.
    Tab to DESCRIPTION, enter **Transfer to Capital**
Line 2: ACCOUNT: **Your Name, Capital**
- The CREDITS should automatically show 480 and the DESCRIPTION should automatically be entered.
- Your Name, Capital is your equity account and the opening balance equity is being transferred into it. Remember, an increase in an equity account is recorded with a credit.

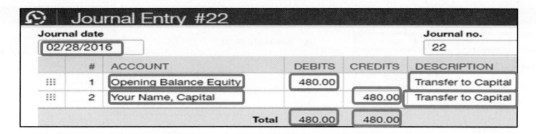

Click **Save and close**
View the change to the Equity section of the Balance Sheet that is still on the screen

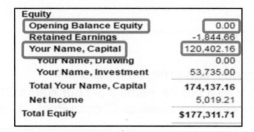

- The Opening Balance Equity shows a balance of 0.00. Your Name, Capital changed from $119,922.16 to $120,402.16, which is an increase of $480.
Do <u>not</u> close Your Name's Beach Barkers

## OWNER WITHDRAWALS—DO

As you practiced and entered in Chapter 5, an owner cannot receive a paycheck because he or she owns the business. In order to provide money to the owner, a withdrawal is made. The withdrawal decreases the amount of cash in the business and the balance of the owner's capital account. Since you already recorded owner withdrawals in Chapter 5, you will not do a drill before recording your semi-monthly withdrawal.

> **MEMO**
> **DATE**: February 27, 2016
>
> You were so busy that you forgot to take your semi-monthly withdrawal in the middle of the month. Record your semi-monthly withdrawal of $500.

<u>DO</u>

Continue to use **Your Name's Beach Barkers** and record an owner withdrawal

Click the **Plus** icon, click **Check** in the Vendors column
Since the owner is not a customer, vendor, or employee, leave the Payee blank
- If you added your name to the Names list, you may use it for the Payee name. If you did not add your name, leave the Payee name blank.
Use **Checking** to pay the check
Payment date: **022716**
Click **Print later** to remove the check mark; if necessary, enter **30** for the Check no.
Prepare Check 30 for the monthly withdrawal as previously instructed
- Remember to use **Your Name, Drawing** as the account.
Add an appropriate note in the Memo

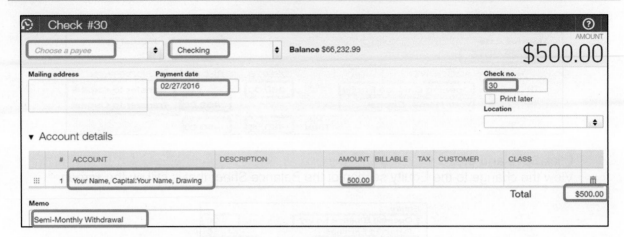

Click **Print check**

Check No. **30**, click **Preview and print**, print the check

- If you save the check as a pdf file, name it **3-Your Name Check 30**.

Click **Close** on Print Preview, click **Done** on Checks Print OK, and click **Cancel** on the print check screen

- You should return to the customized Balance Sheet that you prepared for 020116 to 022816. If not, prepare the report again.

View the Equity section

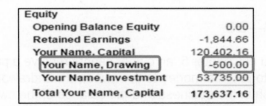

- At the end of January, you transferred the withdrawals for January into Your Name, Capital to practice closing entries. You will do the same at the end of February. For now, the account shows the $500 withdrawal.

Do <u>not</u> close Your Name's Beach Barkers

## NON-CASH INVESTMENT BY OWNER—DO

As you learned in Chapter 5, an owner may make additional investments that are added to the owner's investment account. These investments may be cash or non-cash.

> **MEMO**
> **DATE**: February 28, 2016
>
> You decided to use your new desk, file cabinet, and chair in the office at Your Name's Beach Barkers rather than at home. Record an investment of $2,000 worth of Furniture & Fixtures.

<u>DO</u>

 Continue to use **Your Name's Beach Barkers** and record a non-cash investment

Use the information provided in the Memo to prepare Journal Entry 23
Date: **022816**

Transaction Accounts: **Furniture & Fixtures: Original Cost** and **Your Name, Investment**
Description: **Additional Investment**

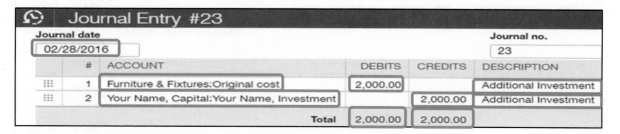

| | # | ACCOUNT | DEBITS | CREDITS | DESCRIPTION |
|---|---|---|---|---|---|
| ⠿ | 1 | Furniture & Fixtures:Original cost | 2,000.00 | | Additional Investment |
| ⠿ | 2 | Your Name, Capital:Your Name, Investment | | 2,000.00 | Additional Investment |
| | | Total | 2,000.00 | 2,000.00 | |

Click **Save and close**
Return to the Balance Sheet and view the Equity section

| Equity | |
|---|---|
| Opening Balance Equity | 0.00 |
| Retained Earnings | -1,844.66 |
| Your Name, Capital | 120,402.16 |
| Your Name, Drawing | -500.00 |
| Your Name, Investment | 55,735.00 |
| Total Your Name, Capital | 175,637.16 |

- Notice that the balance of Your Name, Investment increased by $2,500. Use the amount of investment shown on the previous page to do the math: Your Name Investment balance after additional investment $55,735 – Your Name Investment before additional investment $53,735 = investment amount $2,500.

Do <u>not</u> close Your Name's Beach Barkers

## PREPARE THE JOURNAL—DO

All the transactions recorded for adjusting entries and for Owner's Equity for February, 2016 will show in the Journal.

## <u>DO</u>

Continue to use **Your Name's Beach Barkers** to prepare the Journal report

Go to Reports, use the category **My Custom Reports**, select **Journal**
Enter the Dates From: **02/27/16** To: **02/28/16**, click **Run Report**

8

**Your Name's Beach Barkers**
**JOURNAL**
February 27-28, 2016

| DATE | TRANSACTION TYPE | NUM | NAME | MEMO/DESCRIPTION | ACCOUNT | DEBIT | CREDIT |
|------|------------------|-----|------|------------------|---------|-------|--------|
| 02/27/2016 | Check | 30 | | Semi-Monthly Withdrawal | Checking | | $500.00 |
| | | | | | Your Name, Capital:Your Name, Drawing | $500.00 | |
| | | | | | | $500.00 | $500.00 |
| 02/28/2016 | Journal Entry | 19 | | Adjusting Entry, February | Supplies Expense:Office Supplies Expense | $100.00 | |
| | | | | Adjusting Entry, February | Supplies:Office Supplies | | $100.00 |
| | | | | | | $100.00 | $100.00 |
| 02/28/2016 | Journal Entry | 20 | | Adjusting Entry, February | Supplies Expense:Kennel Supplies Expense | $176.00 | |
| | | | | Adjusting Entry, February | Supplies:Kennel Supplies | | $176.00 |
| | | | | | | $176.00 | $176.00 |
| 02/28/2016 | Journal Entry | 21 | | Adjusting Entry, February | Furniture & Fixtures:Depreciation | | $125.00 |
| | | | | Adjusting Entry, February | Kennel Equipment:Depreciation | | $170.00 |
| | | | | Adjusting Entry, February | Depreciation Expense | $295.00 | |
| | | | | | | $295.00 | $295.00 |
| 02/28/2016 | Inventory Qty Adjust | 1 | | | Cost of Goods Sold:Inventory Shrinkage | $0.00 | |
| | | | | | Inventory Asset | $0.00 | |
| | | | | | Inventory Asset | | $40.00 |
| | | | | | Cost of Goods Sold:Inventory Shrinkage | $40.00 | |
| | | | | | | $40.00 | $40.00 |
| 02/28/2016 | Inventory Starting Value | START | | Towels - Opening inventory and value | Opening Balance Equity | | $180.00 |
| | | | | Towels - Opening inventory and value | Inventory Asset | $180.00 | |
| | | | | | | $180.00 | $180.00 |
| 02/28/2016 | Journal Entry | 22 | | Transfer to Capital | Opening Balance Equity | $480.00 | |
| | | | | Transfer to Capital | Your Name, Capital | | $480.00 |
| | | | | | | $480.00 | $480.00 |
| 02/28/2016 | Journal Entry | 23 | | Additional Investment | Furniture & Fixtures:Original cost | $2,000.00 | |
| | | | | Additional Investment | Your Name, Capital:Your Name, Investment | | $2,000.00 |
| | | | | | | $2,000.00 | $2,000.00 |
| TOTAL | | | | | | $3,771.00 | $3,771.00 |

Close Your Name's Beach Barkers

## BUDGETS—DRILL

QuickBooks Online Plus allows you to create Profit and Loss budgets that track amounts in income and expense accounts. Preparing a budget helps a company plan and view expectations for income and costs for a period of time. It is a useful tool that is used to examine business operations, enable a company to establish operational goals, and take a realistic look at expenditures.

## *DRILL*

 Open the **Test Drive Company** and prepare a budget

Click the **Gear** icon, then click **Budgeting** in the Tools column
The first time you open Budgeting you will complete an interview for Creating a budget
Read the opening screen, then click **Next**

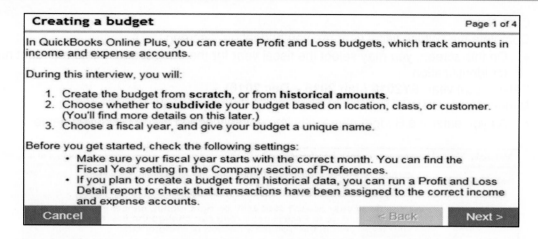

Complete the "Do you want to start with any amounts?" screen

● You have three choices for obtaining and entering your initial budget figures: Actual amounts from This Fiscal Year or Last Fiscal Year; No amounts, which means that you will enter all the amounts for everything you want to budget; or Copy from an existing budget, which may be used if you have already created previous budgets.

Start with: select **Actual amount from**

Click the drop-down list arrow and click **This Fiscal Year**

● If you had a company that had been in business for more than a year, you could select Last Fiscal Year and use your historical data.

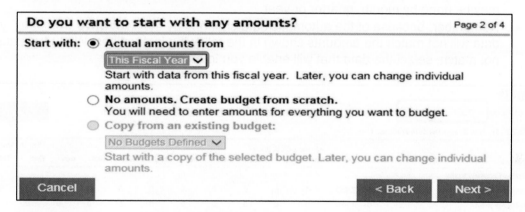

Click **Next**

Complete the "Do you want to subdivide your budget?" screen

● Each budget tracks information by accounts and months. You may and a third component to divide your budget into different areas for tracking. This is used to track by customers, locations, and classes and will be used in the Do section.

Subdivide by: **Don't subdivide**

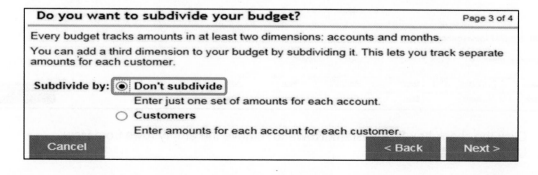

8

Click **Next**

Complete the "Which fiscal year are you budgeting?" screen

- On this screen, you may select the fiscal year for the budget and create a budget name for identification.

Select fiscal year: **FY2016 (Jan 2016 – Dec 2016)**

Budget name: **BUDGET**

- As you enter the Budget name, it is immediately added to the Displayed name.

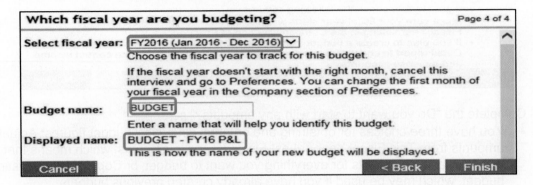

Click **Finish** and the Budgets screen appears

- If your budget does not appear on the screen, click anything on the Navigation bar, then click the Gear icon, and Budgeting. The BUDGET – FY16 P & L should open.
- On this screen, you enter budget amounts for your income and expense accounts. This may be done by month, quarter or year.
- Remember, because of the automatic date changes by the Test Drive Company, your data will not match the amounts shown in the following instructions. When the data does not match, select the data that will enable you to create a budget.

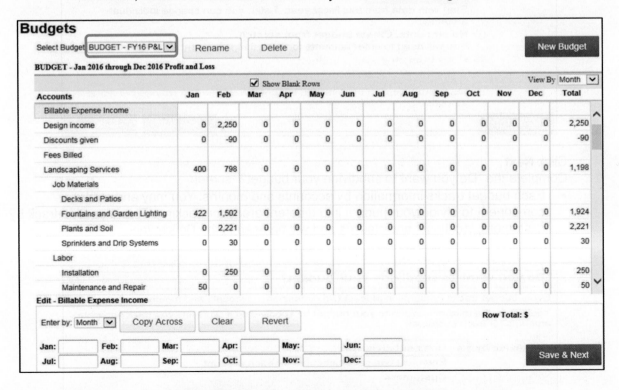

Click the check box **Show Blank Rows** to remove the empty rows from view

Use View By **Month**

To begin entering budget data, click in the month (Feb at the time of this writing) with the highest amount shown for **Design income**
- In the Edit – Design income area at the bottom of the screen, the amounts for Jan: 0 and Feb: 2,250 were entered along with 0 for all other months.

In Edit – Design income section, click in the month with the highest amount (Feb:), click the **Copy Across** button
- The amount for February will be entered for all of the remaining months.

If your Design Income has information for three months, click in the first month with a 0, enter the largest amount shown for the earlier months, click **Copy Across**
- In the following example, Jan was 0, Feb was 1,313, and Mar was 938. You would click on the line for Design Income, then in the Edit – Design Income section click in Apr, enter 1,313 for Apr, then click Copy Across.
- Follow this procedure whenever there are three or more months with amounts.

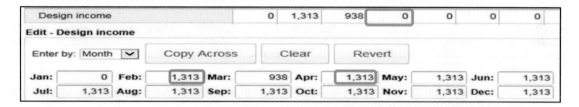

Click **Save & Next**
- Any figures in the next row are automatically entered in the Edit section.

For Edit-Discounts given, click in the month with the highest amount, then click **Copy Across**

Click **Save & Next**

Repeat for all remaining rows

Scroll through the budget and make sure all rows have budgeted amounts, if you missed any rows, enter the budgeted amounts as instructed.

After all rows have budgeted amounts, click **Finished**

Do not close the Test Drive Company, continue with the next section

## BUDGET REPORTS—DRILL

There are two reports available to view budgets in QuickBooks Online. They are Budget Overview, which shows a summary of budgeted amounts for a specific budget, and Budget vs Actuals, which compares your budgeted income and expense account to the actual amounts so you can tell whether you are over or under budget.

## DRILL

 Continue to use the **Test Drive Company** and prepare budget reports

Turn **OFF** Redesigned reports in QuickBooks Labs
Click **Reports** on the Navigation bar
Click the report category **Business Overview** to select

Click **Budget Overview**

- You will see the budgeted amount for each income and expense account for every month of the fiscal year. You will also see totals for each row across and for each column down. This provides you with the total amounts you have budgeted.
- Your figures will not match the example shown. Remember, this is practice.

### Craig's Design and Landscaping Services
**BUDGET OVERVIEW: BUDGET - FY16 P&L**
January - December 2016

| | JAN 2016 | FEB 2016 | MAR 2016 | APR 2016 | MAY 2016 | JUN 2016 | JUL 2016 | AUG 2016 | SEP 2016 | OCT 2016 | NOV 2016 | DEC 2016 | TOTAL |
|---|---|---|---|---|---|---|---|---|---|---|---|---|---|
| **Income** | | | | | | | | | | | | | |
| Design income | 0.00 | 2,250.00 | 2,250.00 | 2,250.00 | 2,250.00 | 2,250.00 | 2,250.00 | 2,250.00 | 2,250.00 | 2,250.00 | 2,250.00 | 2,250.00 | $24,750.00 |
| Discounts given | 0.00 | -90.00 | -90.00 | -90.00 | -90.00 | -90.00 | -90.00 | -90.00 | -90.00 | -90.00 | -90.00 | -90.00 | $ -990.00 |
| Landscaping Services | 400.00 | 798.00 | 798.00 | 798.00 | 798.00 | 798.00 | 798.00 | 798.00 | 798.00 | 798.00 | 798.00 | 798.00 | $9,178.00 |

Return to the report category Business Overview, click **Budget vs. Actuals**

- You will see each month of the fiscal year with columns for Actual, Budget, Over Budget, and % of Budget.

| | JAN 2016 | | | | FEB 2016 | | | |
|---|---|---|---|---|---|---|---|---|
| | ACTUAL | BUDGET | OVER BUDGET | % OF BUDGET | ACTUAL | BUDGET | OVER BUDGET | % OF BUDGET |
| **Income** | | | | | | | | |
| Design income | | 0.00 | 0.00 | | 2,250.00 | 2,250.00 | 0.00 | 100.00 % |
| Discounts given | | 0.00 | 0.00 | | -89.50 | -90.00 | 0.50 | 99.44 % |
| Landscaping Services | 400.00 | 400.00 | 0.00 | 100.00 % | 797.50 | 798.00 | -0.50 | 99.94 % |

- Note the differences between Jan and Feb that are displayed above. Your figures will not match the example shown.

Close the Test Drive Company

## BUDGETS—DO

As you explored in the drill, QuickBooks Online Plus allows you to create Profit and Loss budgets that track amounts in income and expense accounts. For Your Name's Beach Barkers, you will prepare a budget that also shows locations so you can see the profitability of the Venice and Malibu locations. This will help you determine if having two locations is a viable option for Your Name's Beach Barkers.

## DO

 Open **Your Name's Beach Barkers** and prepare a budget

Click the **Gear** icon, then click **Budgeting** in the Tools column
Complete the interview for "Creating a budget"
Read the opening screen, then click **Next**
Complete the "Do you want to start with any amounts?" screen

- You have three choices for obtaining and entering your initial budget figures: Actual amounts from This Fiscal Year or Last Fiscal Year; No amounts, which means you are entering all of the amounts for everything you want to budget; or Copy from an existing budget, which may be used if you have already created previous budgets.

Start with: select **Actual amount from**
Click the drop-down list arrow and click **This Fiscal Year**

- If you had a company that had been in business for more than a year, you could select Last Fiscal Year and use your historical data.

Click **Next**

Complete the "Do you want to subdivide your budget?" screen

- Each budget tracks information by accounts and months. You may add a third component to divide your budget into different areas for tracking. This is used to track by customers, locations, and classes and will be used in the Do section.

Under Subdivide by: click **Locations**

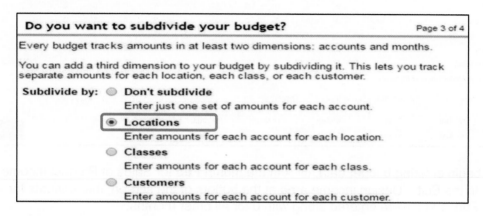

Click **Next**

Complete the "Which fiscal year are you budgeting?" screen

- On this screen, you may select the fiscal year for the budget and create a budget name for identification.

Select fiscal year: **FY2016 (Jan 2016 – Dec 2016)**

Budget name: **BUDGET**

- As you enter the Budget name, it is immediately added to the Displayed name.

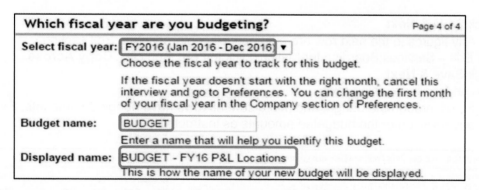

- Notice that Locations was added to the Displayed name.

Click **Finish** and the Budgets screen appears for the location **Malibu**

- If your budget does not appear on the screen, click anything on the Navigation bar, then click the Gear icon, and Budgeting. The BUDGET – FY16 P & L Locations should open.
- On this screen, you enter budget amounts for your income and expense accounts for Malibu. This may be done by month, quarter or year. Once budget information is entered for Malibu, you will need to enter the information for Venice and for Not specified.
- Notice that January has 0 for all income accounts. This is because Locations were not created until February when the Malibu location was opened. Also notice that nothing is shown for expenses. This is because we do not categorize expenses by location.

Click the check box **Show Blank Rows** to remove the empty rows from view

Use View By **Month**

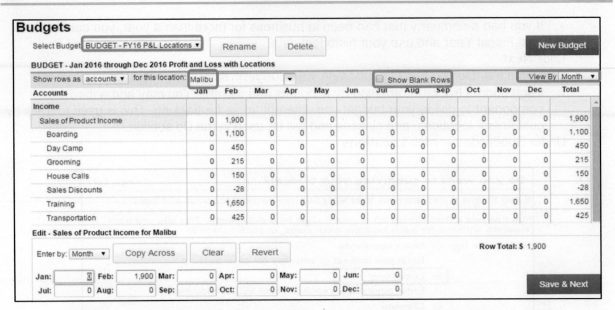

To begin entering budget data, click in the month **Feb** for Sales of Product Income

- In the Edit – Design income area at the bottom of the screen, the amounts for Jan: 0 and Feb: 1,900 were entered along with 0 for all other months.

In Edit – Sales of Product Income, click in **Feb**, click the **Copy Across** button

- The amount for February will be entered for all of the remaining months.

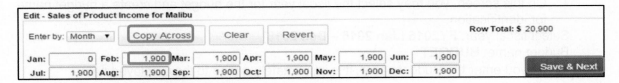

Click **Save & Next**

- Any figures in the next row are automatically entered in the Edit section.

For Edit – Services:Boarding for Malibu, click in **Feb**, then click **Copy Across**

Click **Save & Next**

Repeat for all remaining rows

- Scroll through the budget and make sure all rows have budgeted amounts, if you missed any rows, enter the budgeted amounts as instructed.

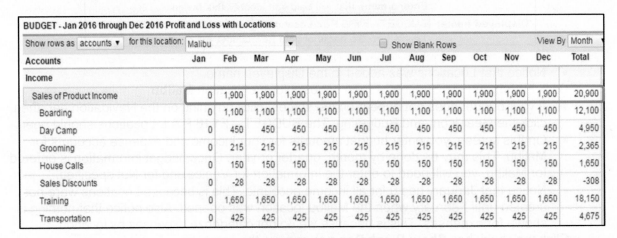

After all rows for Malibu have budgeted amounts, click the drop-down arrow for location, click **Venice**

Repeat the steps as you did for Malibu

- Even though you recorded transactions for Venice during the month of January, they are not shown. This is because you did not establish Locations until February.

| Accounts | Jan | Feb | Mar | Apr | May | Jun | Jul | Aug | Sep | Oct | Nov | Dec | Total |
|---|---|---|---|---|---|---|---|---|---|---|---|---|---|
| **Income** | | | | | | | | | | | | | |
| Sales of Product Income | 0 | 601 | 601 | 601 | 601 | 601 | 601 | 601 | 601 | 601 | 601 | 601 | 6,611 |
| Boarding | 0 | 550 | 550 | 550 | 550 | 550 | 550 | 550 | 550 | 550 | 550 | 550 | 6,050 |
| Day Camp | 0 | 330 | 330 | 330 | 330 | 330 | 330 | 330 | 330 | 330 | 330 | 330 | 3,630 |
| Grooming | 0 | 360 | 360 | 360 | 360 | 360 | 360 | 360 | 360 | 360 | 360 | 360 | 3,960 |
| Sales Discounts | 0 | -24 | -24 | -24 | -24 | -24 | -24 | -24 | -24 | -24 | -24 | -24 | -264 |
| Training | 0 | 350 | 350 | 350 | 350 | 350 | 350 | 350 | 350 | 350 | 350 | 350 | 3,850 |
| Transportation | 0 | 500 | 500 | 500 | 500 | 500 | 500 | 500 | 500 | 500 | 500 | 500 | 5,500 |
| **Cost of Goods Sold** | | | | | | | | | | | | | |
| **Expenses** | | | | | | | | | | | | | |
| **Other Income** | | | | | | | | | | | | | |
| Fees Billed | 0 | 80 | 80 | 80 | 80 | 80 | 80 | 80 | 80 | 80 | 80 | 80 | 880 |
| **Other Expense** | | | | | | | | | | | | | |

*Select Budget: BUDGET - FY16 P&L Locations* — Rename — Delete — New Budget
*BUDGET - Jan 2016 through Dec 2016 Profit and Loss with Locations*
*Show rows as accounts for this location: Venice — Show Blank Rows — View By Month*

Once you complete the budget amounts for Venice, click the drop-down list arrow for location, click **Not Specified**

- Not Specified is used for all transactions that were not entered for specific locations. These include the income accounts for January, and all of the expenses.
- Since income will appear for Venice and Malibu as of February, you will <u>not</u> extend the amount of the income accounts.

Click in the **Feb** column on the line for **Cost of Goods Sold: Merchandise Discounts**

Then, click in the **Feb** (-28) column for Edit – Cost of Goods Sold: Merchandise Discounts for Not Specified, click **Copy Across**, then click **Save and Next**

Click in the **Feb** column on the line for Edit - Inventory Shrinkage for Not Specified

If you have 40 for Inventory Shrinkage in February, copy across as you have been doing

- If your budget does not show 40 for Inventory Shrinkage, click in **Feb** in Edit – Inventory Shrinkage for Not Specified, enter **40** for Feb in the Edit section, click **Copy Across**.

Continue with entering information and always copy across the highest amount

- Not all transactions for February have been entered so you will find instances where January shows a higher amount than February. When this is the case, enter the January amount for March in the Edit section, then Copy Across.

When you get to Cleaning Supplies, the amount for Jan is 100 and Feb is 27, enter the highest amount **100** for **Mar**, then **Copy Across**

8

BUDGET - Jan 2016 through Dec 2016 Profit and Loss with Locations

Show rows as accounts ▼  for this location: Not Specified  ▼        ☐ Show Blank Rows        View By Month

| Accounts | Jan | Feb | Mar | Apr | May | Jun | Jul | Aug | Sep | Oct | Nov | Dec | Total |
|---|---|---|---|---|---|---|---|---|---|---|---|---|---|
| **Cost of Goods Sold** | | | | | | | | | | | | | |
| Merchandise Discounts | 0 | -28 | -28 | -28 | -28 | -28 | -28 | -28 | -28 | -28 | -28 | -28 | -308 |
| Inventory Shrinkage | 0 | 40 | 40 | 40 | 40 | 40 | 40 | 40 | 40 | 40 | 40 | 40 | 440 |
| **Expenses** | | | | | | | | | | | | | |
| Advertising | 200 | 500 | 500 | 500 | 500 | 500 | 500 | 500 | 500 | 500 | 500 | 500 | 5,700 |
| Bank Charges | 16 | 16 | 16 | 16 | 16 | 16 | 16 | 16 | 16 | 16 | 16 | 16 | 192 |
| Equipment Rental | 75 | 75 | 75 | 75 | 75 | 75 | 75 | 75 | 75 | 75 | 75 | 75 | 900 |
| Vehicle Insurance | 100 | 100 | 100 | 100 | 100 | 100 | 100 | 100 | 100 | 100 | 100 | 100 | 1,200 |
| Interest Expense | 19 | 19 | 19 | 19 | 19 | 19 | 19 | 19 | 19 | 19 | 19 | 19 | 228 |
| Laundry | 7 | 75 | 75 | 75 | 75 | 75 | 75 | 75 | 75 | 75 | 75 | 75 | 832 |
| Rent or Lease | 1,500 | 2,900 | 2,900 | 2,900 | 2,900 | 2,900 | 2,900 | 2,900 | 2,900 | 2,900 | 2,900 | 2,900 | 33,400 |

Partial Budget

Click **Finished**
Do <u>not</u> close Your Name's Beach Barkers, continue with the next section

## BUDGET REPORTS—DO

In the drill you practiced preparing the Budget Overview and Budget vs Actuals reports. In this section, you will prepare the reports and customize them in order to get more specific information.

<u>DO</u>

Continue to use **Your Name's Beach Barkers** and prepare budget reports

Click **Reports** on the Navigation bar
Click the report category **Business Overview** to select
Click **Budget Overview**
- You will see the budgeted amount for each income and expense account for every location for the fiscal year. You will also see totals for each row across and for each column down. This provides you with the total amounts you have budgeted.

### Your Name's Beach Barkers
**BUDGET OVERVIEW: BUDGET - FY16 P&L LOCATIONS**
January - December 2016

| | MALIBU | VENICE | NOT SPECIFIED | TOTAL |
|---|---|---|---|---|
| **Income** | | | | |
| Sales of Product Income | 20,900.00 | 6,611.00 | | $27,511.00 |
| Services | | | | $0.00 |
| Boarding | 12,100.00 | 6,050.00 | 770.00 | $18,920.00 |
| Day Camp | 4,950.00 | 3,630.00 | 630.00 | $9,210.00 |
| Grooming | 2,365.00 | 3,960.00 | 785.00 | $7,110.00 |
| House Calls | 1,650.00 | | 225.00 | $1,875.00 |
| Sales Discounts | -308.00 | -264.00 | | $ -572.00 |
| Training | 18,150.00 | 3,850.00 | 3,025.00 | $25,025.00 |
| Transportation | 4,675.00 | 5,500.00 | 300.00 | $10,475.00 |
| **Total Services** | **43,582.00** | **22,726.00** | **5,735.00** | **$72,043.00** |
| **Total Income** | **$64,482.00** | **$29,337.00** | **$5,735.00** | **$99,554.00** |
| **Cost of Goods Sold** | | | | |
| Cost of Goods Sold | | | | $0.00 |
| Merchandise Discounts | | | -308.00 | $ -308.00 |
| **Total Cost of Goods Sold** | **0.00** | **0.00** | **-308.00** | **$ -308.00** |
| Inventory Shrinkage | | | 440.00 | $440.00 |
| **Total Cost of Goods Sold** | **$0.00** | **$0.00** | **$132.00** | **$132.00** |
| **Gross Profit** | **$64,482.00** | **$29,337.00** | **$5,603.00** | **$99,422.00** |

- Since you began recording information for your locations in February, there is no sales information for Venice in January. That information is actually included in Not Specified.
- Prior to February, you did not sell any products only service items. You will note that nothing is shown for Not Specified. The report basically shows you the results of Sales of Product Income for February for both the Malibu and Venice locations.

Click the **Customize** button

Click the drop-down list arrow in Rows/Columns for Show Grid:

| Rows/Columns | |
|---|---|
| Show Grid: | Accounts vs. Locations |
| | Accounts vs. Months |
| Sort By: | Accounts vs. Quarters |
| | Accounts vs. Total |
| | **Accounts vs. Locations** |
| | Locations vs. Months |
| | Locations vs. Quarters |
| Show Rows: | Locations vs. Quarters |

- Notice all of the different options you have for displaying budget information.

Do not make any selections from the list

Scroll down to Header/Footer and remove the Date and Time Prepared, click **Run Report**

- If you still see *Accrual Basis* at the bottom of the report, do not worry about it. Removing the report basis from the report was not an option.

Print in Portrait orientation, export, and/or send/submit as previously instructed

- If you save the report, name it: **4-Your Name Budget Overview Ch. 8**.

Return to the report category Business Overview, click **Budget vs. Actuals**

- You will see columns for Actual, Budget, Over Budget, and % of Budget for each location and for the Total.

| | MALIBU | | | | VENICE | | | |
|---|---|---|---|---|---|---|---|---|
| | ACTUAL | BUDGET | OVER BUDGET | % OF BUDGET | ACTUAL | BUDGET | OVER BUDGET | % OF BUDGET |
| **Income** | | | | | | | | |
| Sales of Product Income | 1,900.00 | 20,900.00 | -19,000.00 | 9.09 % | 600.50 | 6,611.00 | -6,010.50 | 9.08 % |
| **Services** | | | | | | | | |
| Boarding | 1,100.00 | 12,100.00 | -11,000.00 | 9.09 % | 550.00 | 6,050.00 | -5,500.00 | 9.09 % |
| Day Camp | 450.00 | 4,950.00 | -4,500.00 | 9.09 % | 330.00 | 3,630.00 | -3,300.00 | 9.09 % |
| Grooming | 215.00 | 2,365.00 | -2,150.00 | 9.09 % | 360.00 | 3,960.00 | -3,600.00 | 9.09 % |
| House Calls | 150.00 | 1,650.00 | -1,500.00 | 9.09 % | | | | |
| Sales Discounts | -27.90 | -308.00 | 280.10 | 9.06 % | -23.90 | -264.00 | 240.10 | 9.05 % |
| Training | 1,650.00 | 18,150.00 | -16,500.00 | 9.09 % | 350.00 | 3,850.00 | -3,500.00 | 9.09 % |
| Transportation | 425.00 | 4,675.00 | -4,250.00 | 9.09 % | 500.00 | 5,500.00 | -5,000.00 | 9.09 % |
| Total Services | 3,962.10 | 43,582.00 | -39,619.90 | 9.09 % | 2,066.10 | 22,726.00 | -20,659.90 | 9.09 % |
| Total Income | $5,862.10 | $64,482.00 | $ -58,619.90 | 9.09 % | $2,666.60 | $29,337.00 | $ -26,670.40 | 9.09 % |
| **Cost of Goods Sold** | | | | | | | | |
| Cost of Goods Sold | 557.50 | | 557.50 | | 175.50 | | 175.50 | |
| Inventory Shrinkage | | | | | | | | |
| Merchandise Discounts | | | | | | | | |
| Total Cost of Goods Sold | 557.50 | 0.00 | 557.50 | 0.00 | 175.50 | 0.00 | 175.50 | 0.00 |
| Total Cost of Goods Sold | $557.50 | $0.00 | $557.50 | 0.00% | $175.50 | $0.00 | $175.50 | 0.00% |
| Gross Profit | $5,304.60 | $64,482.00 | $ -59,177.40 | 8.23 % | $2,491.10 | $29,337.00 | $ -26,845.90 | 8.49 % |

Partial Report

- Remember, in the column for ACTUAL, you have entered transaction data for January and only part of February. The BUDGET column contains the total budgeted for the entire year.

Click the **Customize** button, click the drop-down list arrow for Show Grid:, click **Locations vs. Quarters**

8

Remove the Date Prepared, Time Prepared, and Report Basis from the footer, click **Run Report**

|  | JAN - MAR, 2016 | | | |
| --- | --- | --- | --- | --- |
|  | ACTUAL | BUDGET | OVER BUDGET | % OF BUDGET |
| Malibu | 5,304.60 | 11,724.00 | -6,419.40 | 45.25 % |
| Venice | 2,571.10 | 5,494.00 | -2,922.90 | 46.80 % |
| Not Specified | -2,856.49 | -9,539.00 | 6,682.51 | 29.95 % |
| Total | $5,019.21 | $7,679.00 | $ -2,659.79 | 65.36 % |

- This report tells you the actual amount and the budgeted amount for each location for the quarter. Remember, the Venice and Malibu locations are budgets for income only. The information shown gives you a more realistic picture of your business results because amounts are shown for a quarter rather than an entire year.

Do not close Your Name's Beach Barkers

## BANK RECONCILIATION—READ

As you remember from Chapter 5, the checking account should be reconciled with the bank statement every month to make sure that the balances agree. The bank statement will rarely have an ending balance that matches the balance of the checking account. This is due to several factors: outstanding checks (written by the business but not yet paid by the bank), deposits in transit (deposits that were made too late to be included on the bank statement), bank service charges, interest earned on checking accounts, collections made by the bank, and errors made in recording checks and/or deposits by the company or by the bank.

Many companies sign up for online banking and use the bank feeds that are matched to recorded transactions. Since Your Name's Beach Barkers is not a real company, we cannot sign up for online banking. As a result, Bank Feeds and Online Banking are not included in this chapter.

In order to have an accurate amount listed as the balance in the checking account, it is important that the differences between the bank statement and the Checking account be reconciled. If something such as a service charge or a collection made by the bank appears on the bank statement, it needs to be recorded in the checking account.

## RECONCILE CHECKING—DO

In Chapter 5, you completed several bank reconciliations. As a result, you will not complete a drill. When you reconcile the Checking account, you are matching the entries in your Checking account with the entries shown on your bank statement. The procedures to Reconcile Checking have been divided into sections marked with green side headings.

> **MEMO:**
> **DATE:** February 28, 2016
>
> Reconciliation the Checking account. The bank statement is dated February 28, 2016.

_DO_

 Use **Your Name's Beach Barkers** to reconcile the Checking account

## Bank Statement Information

Some information appearing on the bank statement is entered into the Begin Reconciliation window. This information includes the statement date, ending balance, bank service charges, and interest earned.

 Use the following bank statement for Your Name's Beach Barkers as you follow the written instructions to reconcile the checking account (Do not try to reconcile the bank statement without following the instructions provided.)

**Beach Bank**
350 Second Street
Venice, CA 90202
310-555-9889

**Your Name's Beach Barkers**
1302 Pacific Avenue
Venice, CA 92091

| Account: 123-321-4566 | | | February 28, 2016 |
|---|---|---|---|
| Beginning Balance, 2/1/2016 | | | $57,940.89 |
| 1/27/2016 Check 14 | | $300.00 | 57,640.89 |
| 1/27/ Check 16 | | 125.00 | 57,515.89 |
| 1/30/2016 Deposit | $3,000.00 | | 60,515.89 |
| 1/30/2016 Deposit | 2,000.00 | | 62,515.89 |
| 1/30/2016 Check 17 | | 500.00 | 62,015.89 |
| 1/31/16 Check 18 | | 600.00 | 61,415.89 |
| 2/09/2016 Deposit | 3,152.51 | | 64,568.40 |
| 2/10/2016 NSF Check | | 80.00 | 64,488.40 |
| 2/14/2016 Deposit | 6,685.80 | | 71,174.20 |
| 2/15/2016 NSF Check | | 70.20 | 71,104.00 |
| 2/15/2016 Equipment Loan Pmt.: Principal $29.53. Interest $8.21: | | 37.74 | 71,066.26 |
| 2/20/16 Check 19 | | 500.00 | 70,566.26 |
| 2/20/16 Check 20 | | 490.00 | 70,076.26 |
| 2/20/2016 Check 21 | | 85.00 | 69,991.26 |
| 2/20/2016 Check 22 | | 1,400.00 | 68,591.26 |
| 2/20/2016 Check 23 | | 199.01 | 68,392.25 |
| 2/22/2016 Check 24 | | 1,500.00 | 66,892.25 |
| 2/22/2016 Check 25 | | 154.00 | 66,738.25 |
| 2/22/2016 Check 28 | | 220.50 | 66,517.75 |
| 2/28/2016 Furniture & Fixtures Loan Pmt: Principal: $36.92, Interest: 10.26 | | 47.18 | 66,470.57 |
| Service Charge | | 56.00 | 66,414.57 |
| Interest | 96.57 | | **66,511.14** |
| Ending Balance | | | **$66,511.14** |

## Begin Reconciliation

As you learned previously, the first part of the reconciliation is to enter the bank statement information.

 Begin the Checking Account Reconciliation for **Your Name's Beach Barkers**

Click the **Gear** icon, click **Reconcile**, in the Tools column

Account: **Checking**

- Notice the two previous checking account reconciliations from Chapter 5.

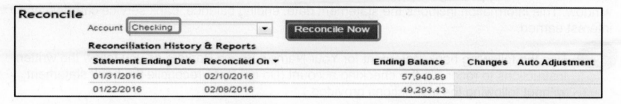

Click the **Reconcile Now** button

Enter the Bank Statement information for the Checking account on the Start Reconciling screen

Statement Ending Date: **02/28/16**

- QuickBooks Online inserts the Beginning Balance of $57,940.89.

Enter the Ending Balance: **66,511.14**

Enter the Service Charge: **56.00**, Tab to Date and enter **02/28/16**, Account: **Bank Charges**

- The normal bank service charge is $16 per month. Each NSF check incurs a $20 bank charge. In February there were two NSF checks for an additional $40 in bank charges.

Enter the Interest Earned: **96.57**, Date: **02/28/16**, Account: **Interest Earned**

- Double-check the dates for Service Charge and Interest Earned to make sure you used 02/28/2016.

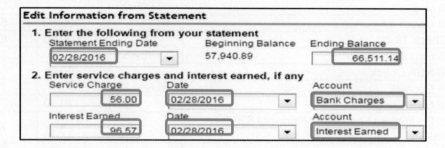

Click **OK**

- You are taken to Reconcile – Checking. Notice that the Service Charge and Interest are shown with a check mark and the statement information entered is shown in the gray summary area.
- As you look at the statement information, you will see a Cleared Balance of 57,981.46 and a Difference of 8,529.68. If you take the Beginning Balance, subtract the service charge and add the interest earned, that becomes the Cleared Balance (57,940.89 - 56.00 + 96.57 = 57,981.46). Subtract the Statement Ending Balance and the Cleared Balance to determine the Difference (66,511.14 – 57,981.46 = 8,529.68). When you complete the Bank Reconciliation, the Difference must be 0.00.

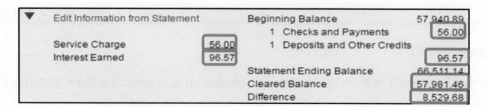

Do **not** close Your Name's Beach Barkers, continue to the next section

- If you do not have time to complete the Bank Reconciliation, click the **Finish Later** button to save your work up to this point. DO NOT click Finish Now!

## Mark Cleared Transactions

Once bank statement information for service charges and interest has been entered, compare the checks and deposits listed on the statement with the transactions for the checking account. Unless all checks and deposits are included on the bank statement, each item should be marked individually by clicking the check box for the deposit or the check.

 Continue with **Your Name's Beach Barkers** Checking Account Reconciliation and mark cleared checks and deposits

Compare the bank statement with the **Reconcile - Checking** window
Click the items that appear on both statements
- The automatic loan payments of $37.74 for the Equipment Loan and $47.18 for the Furniture & Fixtures Loan have not been recorded. So they will appear in the bank statement but not in Reconcile – Checking.
- If you are unable to complete the reconciliation in one session, click the **Finish Later** button to leave the reconciliation and return to it later.
- Under _NO_ circumstances should you click **Finish Now** until the reconciliation is complete and the Difference is 0.00.

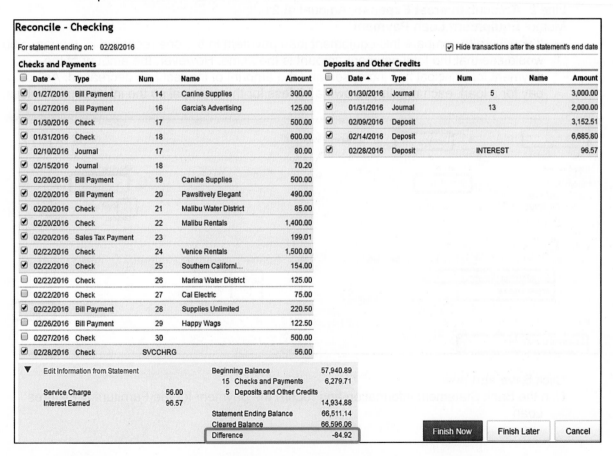

- Notice the Difference of **-84.92**.
Continue to use Your Name Beach Barkers to complete the next section

## Adjusting Entries—Bank Reconciliation

When you have an automatic loan payment setup with the bank, the payment amount will be deducted from your bank account each month. To account for this, you will need to enter the loan payment.

    With **Your Name's Beach Barkers** Reconcile - Checking window still showing, enter the automatic loan payment

Click the **Plus** icon and click **Check** in the Vendors column
Record the check as previously instructed
Payee: **Beach Bank**
Payment Account: **Checking**
Payment date: **02/28/2016**
Click **Print later** to unmark
Check no.: Leave Blank
- You may see information for a previous loan payment. If so, change the accounts and amounts.
Line 1: Account: **Equipment Loan**, Amount: **29.53**
Line 2: Account: **Interest Expense**, Amount: **8.21**
Memo: **Equipment Loan Payment**
- If you were to compare this equipment loan payment to the one recorded in January, you would see that the total payment amount is the same. However, the amount of the payment for principal has increased and the amount of interest has decreased. As you pay for a loan, each month you owe a bit less for the principal so the interest paid is less.

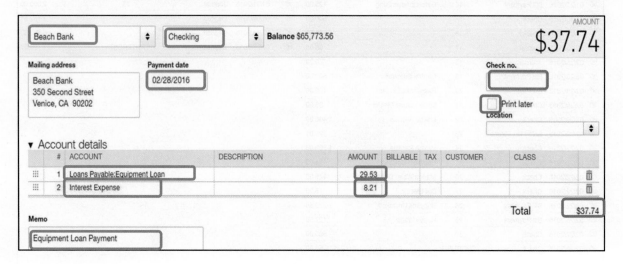

Click **Save and new**
Use the Bank Statement information and record the payment for the Furniture & Fixtures Loan

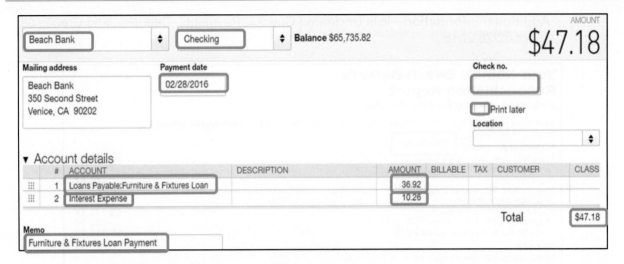

Click **Save and close**; if necessary, close the Check screen
- You should return to the Reconcile – Checking screen. If not, access the Checking Account Register in the Chart of Accounts and click **Reconcile**.

Click the **Checks** you just entered for the automatic loan payments to **Beach Bank**
- The Difference is now 0.00. If your difference is not, find and correct your errors, make sure you marked only those checks and deposits listed in the Bank Statement.

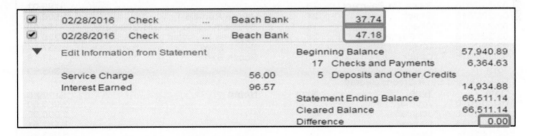

With a Difference of 0.00, click **Finish Now**
After clicking Finish Now, you will return to the original Reconcile screen
You will see the list of all the reconciliation reports you have prepared
Do not close Your Name's Beach Barkers continue with the next section

## Reconciliation Report

 Prepare the Reconciliation Report for **Your Name's Beach Barkers**

In the Reconciliation History & Reports listing, click **02/28/2016**
- For Reconciled On, you will see the current date. Accept the date shown.

| Statement Ending Date | Reconciled On ▼ | Ending Balance | Changes | Auto Adjustment |
|---|---|---|---|---|
| 02/28/2016 | 03/26/2016 | 66,511.14 | | |
| 01/31/2016 | 02/10/2016 | 57,940.89 | | |
| 01/22/2016 | 02/08/2016 | 49,293.43 | | |

The report is divided into three sections:
**Summary**—summarizes Checking account information
**Details**—lists the Checks, Payments, Deposits, and Other Credits cleared

**Additional Information**—lists Uncleared Checks, Payments, Deposits, and Credits as of 02/28/2016

**Your Name's Beach Barkers**
**Reconciliation Report**
**Checking, Period Ending 02/28/2016**

Reconciled on: 03/26/2016 (any changes to transactions after this date aren't reflected on this report)
Reconciled by: ◄—— Your Name

### Summary

| | |
|---|---:|
| Statement Beginning Balance | 57,940.89 |
| Service Charge | -56.00 |
| Interest Earned | +96.57 |
| Checks and Payments cleared | -6,308.63 |
| Deposits and Other Credits cleared | +14,838.31 |
| Statement Ending Balance | 66,511.14 |
| Uncleared transactions as of 02/28/2016 | -822.50 |
| Register Balance as of 02/28/2016 | 65,688.64 |

### Details

Checks and Payments cleared

| Date | Type | Num | Name | Amount |
|------|------|-----|------|-------:|
| 01/27/2016 | Bill Payment | 14 | Canine Supplies | -300.00 |
| 01/27/2016 | Bill Payment | 16 | Garcia's Advertising | -125.00 |
| 01/30/2016 | Check | 17 | | -500.00 |
| 01/31/2016 | Check | 18 | | -600.00 |
| 02/10/2016 | Journal | 17 | | -80.00 |
| 02/15/2016 | Journal | 18 | | -70.20 |
| 02/20/2016 | Bill Payment | 19 | Canine Supplies | -500.00 |
| 02/20/2016 | Bill Payment | 20 | Pawsitively Elegant | -490.00 |
| 02/20/2016 | Check | 21 | Malibu Water District | -85.00 |
| 02/20/2016 | Check | 22 | Malibu Rentals | -1,400.00 |
| 02/20/2016 | Sales Tax Payment | 23 | | -199.01 |
| 02/22/2016 | Check | 24 | Venice Rentals | -1,500.00 |
| 02/22/2016 | Check | 25 | Southern California Gas Company | -154.00 |
| 02/22/2016 | Bill Payment | 28 | Supplies Unlimited | -220.50 |
| 02/28/2016 | Check | | Beach Bank | -37.74 |
| 02/28/2016 | Check | | Beach Bank | -47.18 |
| Total | | | | -6,308.63 |

Deposits and Other Credits cleared

| Date | Type | Num | Name | Amount |
|------|------|-----|------|-------:|
| 01/30/2016 | Journal | 5 | | 3,000.00 |
| 01/31/2016 | Journal | 13 | | 2,000.00 |
| 02/09/2016 | Deposit | | | 3,152.51 |
| 02/14/2016 | Deposit | | | 6,685.80 |
| Total | | | | 14,838.31 |

### Additional Information

Uncleared Checks and Payments as of 02/28/2016

| Date | Type | Num | Name | Amount |
|------|------|-----|------|-------:|
| 02/22/2016 | Check | 26 | Marina Water District | -125.00 |
| 02/22/2016 | Check | 27 | Cal Electric | -75.00 |
| 02/26/2016 | Bill Payment | 29 | Happy Wags | -122.50 |
| 02/27/2016 | Check | 30 | | -500.00 |
| Total | | | | -822.50 |

Print in Portrait as previously instructed
- If you print to a pdf file, save as **5-Your Name Checking Reconciliation Report Ch. 8**.
- You cannot export this report to Excel.

Do not close Your Name's Beach Barkers

## VIEW CHECKING ACCOUNT REGISTER—DO

Once the Checking account and bank statement have been reconciled, it is wise to scroll through the Checking account register to view the effect of the reconciliation on the account. You will notice a column with a check mark. As you scroll through the register, transactions that were reconciled are marked with an R.

 Continue to use **Your Name's Beach Barkers** and view the Checking account register

Open the Chart of Accounts and click **View Register** for Checking
Scroll through the transactions
- Notice that the Service Charge, Interest, Equipment Loan Payment, and Furniture & Fixtures Loan Payment are shown and marked with an R. As you scroll through the register, you will that all of the other transactions selected during the reconciliation are also marked with an R.

Change the column widths to display information in full
Adjust the width of the PAYEE column
Point to the sizing arrow between PAYEE and MEMO and until you get a double arrow
Hold down the primary (left) mouse button, drag to the right to enlarge the column width
- You will see a dark vertical line as you resize.
- Be careful not to click the column heading or you will rearrange the information shown.

Repeat the steps and widen the MEMO column
Make the columns for PAYMENT and DEPOSIT narrower by dragging to the left

| DATE ▾ | REF NO. TYPE | PAYEE ACCOUNT | MEMO | PAYMENT | DEPOSIT | ✓ ⇄ | BALANCE |
|---|---|---|---|---|---|---|---|

Scroll through the register and note that you can see Payees and Memos in full

| DATE | REF NO. / TYPE | PAYEE / ACCOUNT | MEMO | PAYMENT | DEPOSIT | | BALANCE |
|---|---|---|---|---|---|---|---|
| 02/28/2016 | Check | Beach Bank -Split- | Furniture & Fixtures Loan Payment | $47.18 | | R | $65,688.64 |
| 02/28/2016 | Check | Beach Bank -Split- | Equipment Loan Payment | $37.74 | | R | $65,735.82 |
| 02/28/2016 | SVCCHRG Check | Bank Charges | Service Charge | $56.00 | | R | $65,773.56 |
| 02/28/2016 | INTEREST Deposit | Interest Earned | Interest Earned | | $96.57 | R | $65,829.56 |
| 02/27/2016 | 30 Check | Your Name, Capital:Your Name, Drawing | Semi-Monthly Withdrawal | $500.00 | | | $65,732.99 |
| 02/26/2016 | 29 Bill Payment | Happy Wags Accounts Payable (A/P) | | $122.50 | | | $66,232.99 |
| 02/22/2016 | 28 Bill Payment | Supplies Unlimited Accounts Payable (A/P) | | $220.50 | | R | $66,355.49 |

**Partial Register**

Close Your Name's Beach Barkers

## CREDIT CARD RECONCILIATION—DRILL

All asset, liability, and equity accounts may be reconciled. As you did when you reconciled the bank statement and the Checking account, it is especially important to reconcile all charge accounts as well.

You will be reconciling the Visa account for Your Name's Beach Barkers in the Additional Transactions section later in the chapter. In this section, you will complete the reconciliation of the Mastercard for the Test Drive Company. During this reconciliation, you will learn how to make a correction when your entry does not match the statement entry.

**MEMO:**

**DATE:** Current Date

Reconcile the Mastercard account. The credit card statement is dated the Current Date.

*DRILL*

Use the **Test Drive Company** and the following credit card statement to reconcile the Mastercard account

- Since the dates in the Test Drive Company are programmed to change automatically, the credit card statement will not use dates. Instead, the company names and amounts will be shown.

| Fidelity | | | |
|---|---|---|---|
| Mastercard | | | |
| 320 First Street | | | |
| Venice, CA 90202 | | | |
| 310-555-2719 | | | |

**Your Name's Beach Barkers**
1302 Pacific Avenue
Venice, CA 92091

| Account: 123-321-4566 | | | **Current Date** |
|---|---|---|---|
| **Beginning Balance** | | | **$0.00** |
| CC-Credit | 900.00 | | -900.00 |
| Expense: Tania's Nursery | | 158.08 | -741.92 |
| Expense: Chin's Gas and Oil | | 65.00 | -676.92 |
| Expense: Hicks Hardware | | 88.09 | -588.83 |
| Expense: Tania's Nursery | | 54.92 | -533.91 |
| Expense: Tania's Nursery | | 82.45 | -451.46 |
| Bill Payment: Cal Telephone | | 74.36 | -377.10 |
| Expense: Ellis Equipment Rental | | 112.00 | -265.10 |
| Expense: Lee Advertising | | 174.86 | -90.24 |
| Bill Payment: Cal Telephone | | 56.50 | -33.74 |
| Bill Payment: Norton Lumber and Building Materials | | 103.55 | 69.81 |
| Expense: Chin's Gas and Oil | | 52.56 | 122.37 |
| CC Expense: Bob's Burger Joint | | 18.97 | 141.34 |
| CC Expense: Squeaky Kleen Car Wash | | 19.99 | 161.33 |
| CC Expense: Hicks Hardware | | 42.40 | 203.73 |
| CC Expense: Squeaky Kleen Car Wash | | 19.99 | 223.72 |
| CC Expense: | | 34.00 | 257.72 |
| **Ending Balance** | | | **$257.72** |

To access the Reconciliation, click the **Gear** icon, click **Reconcile** in the Tools column
Click the drop-down list arrow for Account, click **Mastercard**, click the **Reconcile Now** button
Enter information for the Mastercard account on the Start Reconciling screen
Statement Ending Date: **Current Date**
- As you have experienced, the Test Drive Company automatically changes transaction dates. As a result, you will need to use the current date for the bank reconciliation.
Enter the Ending Balance: **257.72**

- This is the balance of the credit card statement.

**Start Reconciling**

Account: Mastercard ▼

**Enter the following from your statement**

| Statement Ending Date | Beginning Balance | Ending Balance |
|---|---|---|
| Current Date ▼ | 0.00 | 257.72 |

Click **OK**

Click each item listed on the Reconcile – Mastercard screen **EXCEPT** the expense transaction for **Lee Advertising**

- At this point, the Difference in the gray area is $174.86.
- The amount shown for Lee Advertising in QuickBooks Online is **74.86** and on the credit card statement it is **174.86**.

Point to the transaction for Lee Advertising on the QuickBooks Reconcile – Mastercard screen

When the line turns blue, click the **74.86** transaction (not the check box)

- You are returned to the Expense form where the expense was originally entered.

Click in the AMOUNT text box and change the amount to **174.86**, press **Tab**

Click **Save and close**

- You should return to the Reconcile – Mastercard screen. The amount for Lee Advertising is 174.86.

Click in the check box for Lee Advertising to select it

- The Difference is now 0.00.

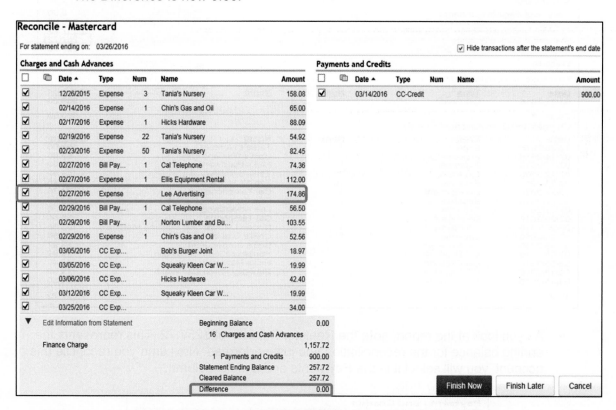

If your reconciliation matches, click **Finish Now**

- If not, find the error and correct it.

- You will get a "Make Payment" screen with three selections: Write a check for the payment now, Enter a bill for payment later, Leave the balance in the reconciled account.

Click **Write a check for the payment now**

Click the drop-down list arrow for Choose a payee, click **Fidelity**

| Fidelity ⬍ | Checking ⬍ | Balance $1,201.00 | $257.72 |
|---|---|---|---|
| **Mailing address** | **Payment date** | | **Check no.** |
| Fidelity | Current Date | | 71 |
| | | | ☐ Print later |

▼ Account details

| # | ACCOUNT | DESCRIPTION | AMOUNT | BILLABLE | TAX | CUSTOMER |
|---|---|---|---|---|---|---|
| 1 | Mastercard | | 257.72 | | | 🗑 |
| | | | **Total** | | | **$257.72** |

Click **Save and close** on the Check

- If you return to the Start Reconciling screen, click the Close button. ⊗

Return to the Reconcile screen, click the drop-down list arrow for Account, click **Mastercard**

Click the Reconciliation History & Report for the current date

**Craig's Design and Landscaping Services**
**Reconciliation Report**

**Mastercard, Period Ending 03/26/2016**

Reconciled on: 03/26/2016 (any changes to transactions after this date aren't reflected on this report)
Reconciled by: Craig Carlson

**Summary**

| | |
|---|---|
| Statement Beginning Balance | 0.00 |
| Payments and Credits cleared | -900.00 |
| Charges and Cash Advances cleared | +1,157.72 |
| Statement Ending Balance | 257.72 |
| Register Balance as of 03/26/2016 | 257.72 |

**Details**

Payments and Credits cleared

| Date | Type | Num | Name | Amount |
|---|---|---|---|---|
| 03/14/2016 | CC-Credit | | | -900.00 |
| Total | | | | -900.00 |

Charges and Cash Advances cleared

| Date | Type | Num | Name | Amount |
|---|---|---|---|---|
| 12/26/2015 | Expense | 3 | Tania's Nursery | 158.08 |
| 02/14/2016 | Expense | 1 | Chin's Gas and Oil | 65.00 |
| 02/17/2016 | Expense | 1 | Hicks Hardware | 88.09 |
| 02/19/2016 | Expense | 22 | Tania's Nursery | 54.92 |
| 02/23/2016 | Expense | 50 | Tania's Nursery | 82.45 |
| 02/27/2016 | Bill Payment | 1 | Cal Telephone | 74.36 |
| 02/27/2016 | Expense | 1 | Ellis Equipment Rental | 112.00 |
| 02/27/2016 | Expense | | Lee Advertising | 174.86 |
| 02/29/2016 | Bill Payment | 1 | Cal Telephone | 56.50 |
| 02/29/2016 | Bill Payment | 1 | Norton Lumber and Building Materials | 103.55 |
| 02/29/2016 | Expense | 1 | Chin's Gas and Oil | 52.56 |
| 03/05/2016 | CC Expense | | Bob's Burger Joint | 18.97 |
| 03/05/2016 | CC Expense | | Squeaky Kleen Car Wash | 19.99 |
| 03/06/2016 | CC Expense | | Hicks Hardware | 42.40 |
| 03/12/2016 | CC Expense | | Squeaky Kleen Car Wash | 19.99 |
| 03/25/2016 | CC Expense | | | 34.00 |
| Total | | | | 1,157.72 |

- As you look at the report, note the Register Balance of $257.72. This represents the ending balance for the reconciliation you just performed. Next time you reconcile this account, you will select it in the Payments and Credits column.

**Payments and Credits**

| ☐ | 🖾 | Date ▲ | Type | Num | Name | Amount |
|---|---|---|---|---|---|---|
| ☐ | | 03/19/2016 | Check | 71 | Fidelity | 257.72 |

Close the Test Drive Company

## CLOSING ENTRIES—READ

In accounting, there are four closing entries made in order to close the books for a period. They include closing all income accounts and expense accounts into Income Summary. Closing the drawing account into Capital The final entry is to close the Income Summary account and transfer the net income or net loss into the owner's capital account.

QuickBooks Online does not close the owner's drawing account so a closing entry is recorded as a Journal Entry. In QuickBooks Online, setting a closing date will replace closing the income and expense accounts. Rather than use an Income Summary account, QuickBooks Online automatically transfers Net Income into Retained Earnings. Retained Earnings contains the amount of all Net Income earned and is separate from Your Name, Capital. According to GAAP, a sole proprietorship should have net income included in the owner's capital account not in retained earnings.

The closing entry for Drawing will be recorded in Your Name's Beach Barkers. All of the other closing entries will be practiced using the Test Drive Company. Reports will be prepared to obtain closing entry information.

## CLOSE DRAWING—DO

The closing entry for Drawing transfers the amount of owner withdrawals into Your Name, Capital. In the Additional Transactions section of the chapter, you will record and close an additional withdrawal.

 Open **Your Name's Beach Barkers** and close Your Name, Drawing

Open the Chart of Accounts and view the balance for Your Name, Drawing

| Your Name, Capital | Equity | Owner's Equity | 175,637.16 |
|---|---|---|---|
| Your Name, Drawing | Equity | Owner's Equity | -500.00 |
| Your Name, Investment | Equity | Owner's Equity | 55,735.00 |

Click the **Plus** icon, click **Journal Entry** in the Other column
Enter the Date: **02/28/16**
Journal no.: **24**
- The Journal number 24 should appear automatically, if not, enter it.
Line 1: Account: **Your Name, Capital**, Debits: **500**, Description: **Close Drawing**
- Remember that a withdrawal reduces owner's equity and that a reduction to owner's equity is recorded as a debit.
Line 2: Account: **Your Name, Drawing**, Credits: **500**, Description: **Close Drawing**

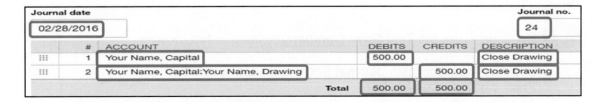

Click **Save and close**
View the account in the Chart of Accounts
- The balance for Your Name, Drawing is 0.00.

| Your Name, Capital | Equity | Owner's Equity | 175,637.16 |
| Your Name, Drawing | Equity | Owner's Equity | 0.00 |
| Your Name, Investment | Equity | Owner's Equity | 55,735.00 |

Close Your Name's Beach Barkers

## BALANCE SHEET—DRILL

As you learned in earlier chapters, the Balance Sheet proves the fundamental accounting equation: Assets = Liabilities + Owner's Equity. Because of the automatic date changes in the Test Drive Company, reports will not match the text unless you use a date range from January 1, 2015 until the current date.

 Open the **Test Drive Company** and prepare the Balance Sheet

Turn **OFF** Redesigned Reports in QuickBooks Labs
Open **Reports**, select **Accountant Reports** as the report category, click **Balance Sheet**
Enter the Dates From: **01/01/15** To: **Current Date**, click **Run Report**
Scroll down to the Equity section of the report
- Because of the changing dates, your amount for Net Income will not be an exact match with the following example. Do not be concerned, simply continue with the closing entries using the amounts shown for Net Income in the Equity section on your report.

| Equity | |
|---|---|
| Opening Balance Equity | -9,337.50 |
| Retained Earnings | 204.17 |
| Net Income | 1,438.29 |
| **Total Equity** | **$ -7,695.04** |

- As you review the Balance Sheet, you will see an amount in Retained Earnings. That amount should be added to the Net Income to determine the amount of the closing entry.
- If Retained Earnings does not have a balance, your closing entry would be for Net Income only.
- Again, if your numbers do not match the ones shown, do not be concerned.
Do <u>not</u> close the Test Drive Company

## TRANSFER NET INCOME—DRILL

At the end of the year, Net Income is transferred into Retained Earnings by QuickBooks Online. Because Craig's Design and Landscape is a sole proprietorship, the amount of Net Income should be included in the Open Balance Equity account not Retained Earnings. A Journal Entry needs to be recorded to transfer Net Income into Opening Balance Equity. If you had Your Name, Capital available for use, this is the account you would use for the transfer of Net Income rather than Opening Balance Equity.

 Continue to use the **Test Drive Company** to transfer Net Income

Click the **Plus** icon, click **Journal Entry** in the Other column
Enter the Date: **Current Date**
Journal no.: **1**
Line 1: Account: **Retained Earnings**, Debits: **1,642.46**, Description: **Transfer Net Income and Retained Earnings**

- At the end of the year, QuickBooks Online automatically transfers Net Income into Retained Earnings. In order to transfer the Net Income into Opening Balance Equity, you will Debit Retained Earnings to transfer both the amount of Net Income and the current amount shown in Retained Earnings. In the future, you would only need to transfer the amount of Net Income.
- The amount of the transaction is calculated by adding the amount shown in Retained Earnings to the amount of Net Income. Again, if your amounts do not match the text, either enter the amounts in your report or just continue by reading the information.

Line 2: Account: **Opening Balance Equity**, Credits: **1,642.46**, Description: **Transfer Net Income and Retained Earnings**

- Opening Balance Equity is used for the account because the Test Drive Company does not save the Owner's Equity capital accounts you created in Chapter 5. When you transfer the Net Income for Your Name's Beach Barkers in the Additional Transactions section of the chapter, Your Name, Capital will be the account used and the closing entry will be for Net Income only.

| ACCOUNT | DEBITS | CREDITS | DESCRIPTION |
|---|---|---|---|
| Retained Earnings | 1,642.46 | | Transfer Net Income and Retained Earnings |
| Opening Balance Equity | | 1,642.46 | Transfer Net Income and Retained Earnings |
| Total | 1,642.46 | 1,642.46 | |

Click **Save and Close**, click the drop down-list arrow if necessary

- You should return to the Balance Sheet. If not, prepare the Balance Sheet again.
- If you get a Message from webpage that the report request could not be completed, click **OK**. Click **Reports** on the Navigation bar, and prepare the Balance Sheet again.

View the Equity section

| Equity | |
|---|---|
| Opening Balance Equity | -7,695.04 |
| Retained Earnings | -1,438.29 |
| Net Income | 1,438.29 |
| **Total Equity** | **$ -7,695.04** |

- Again, your amounts will not match the example above because of the automatic date changes. However, you should still analyze the Equity section in the Balance Sheet.
- Based on the example, the previous amount of Retained Earnings, $204.17, was transferred into Opening Balance Equity. The current amount of Net Income, $1,438.29, shows as a negative in Retained Earnings and as a positive in Net Income.

Change the dates of the Balance Sheet to **01/01/2017** and **Current day and month 2017**

- If the current year happens to be 2017, then use 2018 as the year for this report.

Run the Report

| Equity | |
|---|---|
| Opening Balance Equity | -7,695.04 |
| Retained Earnings | 0.00 |
| Net Income | |
| **Total Equity** | **$ -7,695.04** |

- Amounts for Retained Earnings and Net Income are no longer shown.

Do not close the Test Drive Company

## CLOSE THE BOOKS—DRILL

Rather than record closing entries for income and expense accounts, QuickBooks Online uses a closing date to indicate the end of a period. Once a closing date is assigned, income and expenses are effectively closed. If a transaction involving income or expenses is recorded after the closing date, it is considered part of the new period and will not be used in the calculation of net income (or loss) for the previous period. Conversely, income and expenses for a closed period will not be included in the new period.

If an error is found in a transaction for a closed period, it may be changed but only after acknowledging a warning.

 Continue to use the **Test Drive Company** and close the books for the period

> Click the **Gear** icon
> Click **Account and Settings** in the Your Company column
> - In Your Name's Beach Barkers, you would click **Company Settings**.
> Click the **Advanced** tab
> Click the **Pen** icon for Accounting
> Click the **Close the books** check box to select
> Enter the Closing date **Current date**, press **Tab**
> - Because transaction dates change in the Test Drive Company, you should use the current date.
> Accept the selection of Allow changes after viewing a warning

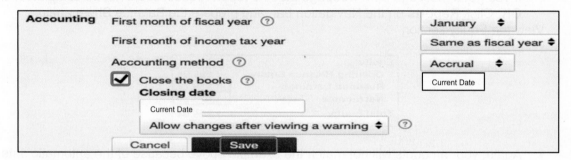

> Click **Save**
> Click the **Done** button in the lower-right side of the Account and Settings screen or click the **Close** button at the top-right of the screen
> Do <u>not</u> close the Test Drive Company

## EDIT CLOSED PERIOD TRANSACTION—DRILL

Even though the month has been closed, transactions still appear in the account registers, the Journal, and so on. If it is determined that an error was made in a previous period, QuickBooks Online allows a correction to be made. In order to save an edited transaction, Yes must be clicked on a warning screen. Changes to transactions involving income or expenses will necessitate changing the amount of net income transferred into the owner's capital account.

---

**MEMO**
**DATE:** Current date

Edit Invoice 1033 to Geeta Kalapatapu. The Quantity for Custom Design should be 5 hours.

Continue to use the **Test Drive Company** to edit an invoice from a closed period and correct the amount of Net Income transferred.

Open **Customers** on the Navigation bar
Scroll through the Customers List and click **Geeta Kalapatapu**
Click **Invoice No. 1033** to Geeta Kalapatapu to open it
For Custom Design change the QTY to **5**, press **Tab**

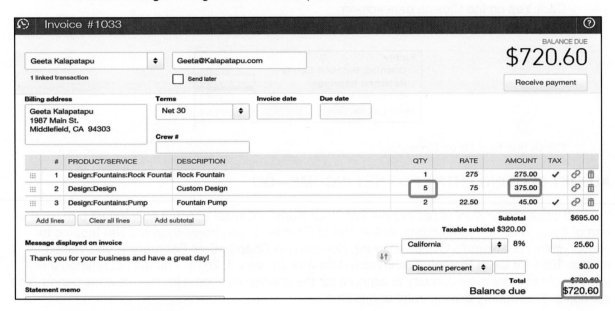

Click **Save and close**
Click **Yes** on the Closing date screen
- If you get a "The transaction is linked to others…" screen, click **Yes**.
- Sometimes the Closing date screen appears before the Transaction linked screen and sometimes it appears after it. Just click Yes whenever it is displayed.

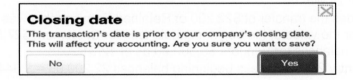

The change in income must be included in the Journal Entry to transfer the Net Income and Retained Earnings into Opening Balance Equity, edit the transaction
Prepare the Balance Sheet report for **01/01/15** to **Current Date**
Look at the amount in Retained Earnings -1,438.29 and the amount in Net Income 1,550.79
- Again, because of the changing dates in the Test Drive Company, your figures will not match. However the amount of change to Net Income, $112.50, should be the same.

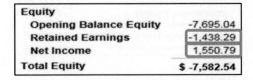

Using the figures shown in the example, calculate the amount for the revised Journal entry:
  Change in income: Net Income 1,550.79 minus Retained Earnings 1,438.29 equals an additional 112.50 in income

The additional income of $112.50 is added to the original transfer amount of $1,642.46 to equal $1,754.96

Click the **Recent Transactions** icon, click **Journal Entry 1**

Correct the adjusting entry

Line 1: Change Debits to **1754.96**

Line 2: Change Credits to **1754.96**

Click **Save and close**

Click **Yes** on the Closing date screen

View the changes to Net Income and Retained Earnings on the Balance Sheet

| Equity | |
|---|---|
| Opening Balance Equity | -7,582.54 |
| Retained Earnings | -1,550.79 |
| Net Income | 1,550.79 |
| Total Equity | $ -7,582.54 |

Close the Test Drive Company

## ADJUST CLOSING ENTRY FOR NET INCOME—DO

You will close the amount of net income into Your Name's Capital account as you just practiced as part of the Additional Transactions. At the end of Chapter 5, you transferred the Net Income for January into Your Name's Capital account. However, in Chapter 6 on February 1, you voided Invoice 1024 for Carol Russell. The invoice date was January 5, 2016. You did not change the transfer of net income for January to account for the change in income for the previous period. You will adjust the January closing entry at this time.

## DO

Open **Your Name's Beach Barkers**, adjust the January transfer of Net Income

Calculate the amount of Net Income for January:

Original Entry: 24,044.66

- This includes the transfer of $22,200 of Retained Earnings that was entered into the account for the value of the beginning balances for Customers $27,500.00 less the beginning balances for Vendors $5,300.00 as of 12/31/2015.
- Original Entry 24,044.66 less beginning balances 22,200.00 = 1,844.66 Net Income for January.

To verify this calculation, you could prepare the Balance Sheet and view the Equity section

- You will see Retained Earnings of **-1,844.66**, which is the amount of Net Income for January. (Remember: Net Income earned for the year will continue to show as a negative amount in Retained Earnings until the next year.)

| Equity | |
|---|---|
| Opening Balance Equity | 0.00 |
| Retained Earnings | -1,844.66 |
| Your Name, Capital | 119,302.16 |
| Your Name, Drawing | 0.00 |
| Your Name, Investment | 56,735.00 |
| Total Your Name, Capital | 176,037.16 |

Reduce the Net Income for January $190.00

- In Chapter 6, you voided Invoice 1024 to Carol Russell (dated January 5, 2016). This decreased the amount of Net Income for January. The voided invoice was for **$190.00**.

Open **Reports** on the Navigation bar, select **Accountant Reports**, prepare the **Journal**

Dates From: **01/31/16** To: **01/31/16**, click **Run Report**
Scroll through the report until you find the Journal Entry to Transfer Net Income and
    Retained Earnings
Click on the transaction
Change the Debit and Credit amounts of the entry to **23,854.66**
- Do the math: $24,044.66 – 190.00 = 23,854.66.
Click **Save and close**, click **Yes** on the Closing date message
Do <u>not</u> close Your Name's Beach Barkers

## ADDITIONAL TRANSACTIONS—DO

Record the additional transactions using Your Name's Beach Barkers. All transactions to be
recorded were either completed as drills using the Test Drive Company or as transactions for Your
Name's Beach Barkers. When you record closing transactions for Drawing, Net Income, and
Retained Earnings, be sure to use Your Name, Capital as the account rather than Opening Balance
Equity.

<u>DO</u>

Continue to use **Your Name's Beach Barkers**, enter the transactions in the Memo boxes,
complete a Credit Card Reconciliation, and record Closing Entries for February 28, 2016

Print as instructed within the Memos
When recording Journal Entries, provide appropriate descriptions

---

**MEMO**
**DATE**: February 28, 2016

Withdrew $600 for the second part of your monthly withdrawal. Print Check 31. (If you save
as a pdf, name it **6-Your Name Check 31**.) (If you added your name to the names list, you
may enter it as the payee name. If not, you may leave the payee name blank.)

Journal Entry 25: Record the monthly adjustment for Prepaid Insurance for your Vehicle
Insurance, $100.

Journal Entry 26: Record the adjusting entry for the amount of Sales Supplies used, $75.

Journal Entry 27: After taking inventory, you calculate that you have $925 of Cleaning
Supplies on hand. Record the adjusting entry.

Journal Entry 28: Use a compound entry to record one month's depreciation for Office
Equipment, $100 and Vehicles, $275.

Found 5 damaged Collars. Record the Inventory Quantity Adjustment. (QuickBooks Online
automatically shows Inventory Shrinkage as the account.)

Journal Entry 29: One of your personal bonds matured. Invest the proceeds in Your Name's
Beach Barkers. Record your additional cash investment of $1,000.

Use the following Credit Card Statement to Reconcile the Visa account. (If the former loan
payment appears when you prepare the check to Beach Bank for the Visa payment, make
sure the Payment date is: 02/28/16; clear the lines; select the Account: Visa; enter the
amount of the payment: $2,639.80; enter the Memo: Visa Payment.) Print the check. If saved,
name it **7-Your Name Check 32 Beach Bank**.

Print the Reconciliation report. If saved, name it **8-Your Name Visa Reconciliation Report
Ch. 8**.

---

This is the Visa credit card statement for February 28, 2016:

**Beach Bank**
**VISA**
**350 Second Street**
**Venice, CA 90202**
**310-555-9889**

**Your Name's Beach Barkers**
**1302 Pacific Avenue**
**Venice, CA 92091**

**Account: 123-321-4566**                                    **February 28, 2016**

| | | | |
|---|---|---|---|
| **Beginning Balance, 2/1/2016** | | | **$0.00** |
| 2/19/2016 Expense Super Office | | 216.00 | 216.00 |
| 2/19/2016 Expense Pet Supplies Unlimited | | 125.00 | 341.00 |
| 2/19/2016 Credit Card Credit Super Office | 43.20 | | 297.80 |
| 2/20/2016 Bill Payment All About Dogs Supplies | | 175.00 | 472.80 |
| 2/20/2016 Bill Payment Garcia's Advertising | | 490.00 | 962.80 |
| 2/20/2016 Bill Payment Kennel Equipment, Inc. | | 159.00 | 1,121.80 |
| 2/22/2016 Bill Payment Lulu's Laundry | | 75.00 | 1,196.80 |
| 2/23/2016 Expense Super Office | | 150.00 | 1,346.80 |
| 2/24/2016 Credit Card Credit Super Office | 30.00 | | 1,316.80 |
| 2/24/2016 Bill Payment Quality Insurance | | 588.00 | 1,904.80 |
| 02/26/2016 Bill Payment The Literary Dog | | 735.00 | 2,639.80 |
| **Ending Balance, 2/28/2016** | | | **$2,639.80** |

When the reconciliation is complete, print and/or save the payment check and the
Reconciliation Report (Refer to the Memo for additional information)
Continue recording, saving, and printing transactions in the following Memos

---

**MEMO**
**DATE:** February 28, 2016

Record Journal Entry 30 for the closing entry for $600 to close the Drawing account. (You
wrote the withdrawal check for the first additional transaction entry.)

Record Journal Entry 31 to Transfer Net Income into Capital (Instructions provided below).

---

Prior to transferring the Net Income into Your Name's, Capital, prepare the Profit and Loss
Report for February, 2016
Verify the Net Income of **$2,661.65**
- This is the amount of the Net Income to be transferred.
Record **Journal Entry 31** as previously instructed to Transfer Net Income into Capital

---

**MEMO**
**DATE:** February 28, 2016

Close the period for February. Use the Closing Date: 02/28/16.

Adjust Invoice #1044 to Sandi Egkan to add 5 days of Day Camp (Dog Care) that had not
been recorded on the invoice. Print the corrected invoice. If saved, name it **9-Your Name
Invoice 1044 Sandi Egkan Corrected**.

Adjust Journal Entry 31 for the Transfer of Net Income into Capital to include the increased
income.

---

Continue to use Your Name's Beach Barkers

2661.65
+  150.00
2676.65

## PROFIT AND LOSS—DO

When the transactions and adjustments for the month are complete, it is helpful to prepare the Profit and Loss report to see your amount of Net Income or Net Loss. Remember Income minus Expenses equal Net Profit or Net Loss.

*DO*

Continue to use **Your Name's Beach Barkers** to prepare the Profit and Loss report for February 1-28, 2016

Access Reports as previously instructed
Click **My Custom Reports** to see all of the reports that have been customized
Click **Profit and Loss** to select the report
Dates are From: **020116** To: **022816**, run the report
- Scroll through the report. Review income and expenses. View the change to Net Income.

| Net Income | $2,811.65 |
|---|---|

*587.40*

*#3*

Print, export, and/or send/submit the report
- If you save the report, name it **10-Your Name Profit and Loss Ch. 8**.
Continue to use Your Name's Beach Barkers

## BALANCE SHEET—DO

After completing all of the adjustments for the month, you need to prepare a Balance Sheet to prove that assets are equal to liabilities and owner's equity. Because this report is for a month, the adjustment for Net Income will appear in both Retained Earnings and Net Income. If, however, this report were prepared for the year, neither account would have balances.

*DO*

Continue to use **Your Name's Beach Barkers** to prepare the Balance Sheet for January 1, 2016 to February 28, 2016 and January 1, 2017 to February 28, 2017

Click **Balance Sheet** in My Custom Reports
Dates From: **010116** To: **022816**, Run Report
- The balances of all accounts for the year are shown. Even if you ran the report for just the month of February, you would still have the same amounts for the account balances shown.
- View and analyze the Equity section after all the adjusting entries have been made:
  After the transfer of Opening Balance Equity for the additional inventory items to Your Name, Capital, the balance of Opening Balance Equity is 0.00.
  The original amount of Retained Earnings, $22,200, was transferred to Your Name, Capital and no longer shows as part of Retained Earnings. The amount of Net Income transferred to Retained Earnings for the year 2016 shows as -4,466.31.
  Your Name, Capital shows $121,923.81, which is the total of the capital without including the Investment.
  Your Name, Drawing was closed into Your Name, Capital so it has a balance of 0.00.
  Your Name, Investment contains the balance of $56,735.00, which shows how much you have invested in Your Name's Beach Barkers.

**8**

Net Income and Retained Earnings were transferred to Your Name, Capital. Since you are still in the same year as the adjusting transaction date, the amount of Net Income shows as 4,466.31 and the amount of Retained Earnings shows as -4,466.31.
The $4,466.31 contains the amount of Net Income for January and for February
- Do the math: Net Income January $1,654.66 plus Net Income February $2,811.65 = $4,466.31.

| Equity | |
|---|---|
| Opening Balance Equity | 0.00 |
| Retained Earnings | -4,466.31 |
| Your Name, Capital | 121,923.81 |
| Your Name, Drawing | 0.00 |
| Your Name, Investment | 56,735.00 |
| **Total Your Name, Capital** | **178,658.81** |
| Net Income | 4,466.31 |
| **Total Equity** | **$178,658.81** |

Print, export, and/or send/submit the report
- If you save the report, name it **11-Your Name Balance Sheet 2016 Ch. 8**.

To see the results of transferring Net Income/Retained Earnings into Capital, change the report dates From: **01/01/17** To: **02/28/17**, Run the Report
- Note that the amount shown for Retained Earnings, Drawing and Opening Balance Equity is 0.00. The amounts shown for Your Name, Capital; Your Name, Investment; and Total Your Name, Capital are all still the same as in the 2016 report.

| Equity | |
|---|---|
| Opening Balance Equity | 0.00 |
| Retained Earnings | 0.00 |
| Your Name, Capital | 121,923.81 |
| Your Name, Drawing | 0.00 |
| Your Name, Investment | 56,735.00 |
| **Total Your Name, Capital** | **178,658.81** |
| Net Income | |
| **Total Equity** | **$178,658.81** |

Print, export, and/or send/submit the report
- If you save the report, name it **12-Your Name Balance Sheet 2017 Ch. 8**.

Continue to use Your Name's Beach Barkers

## BUDGET VS ACTUALS REPORT—DO

The budget was established prior to the end of February. Budget projections were made and recorded for each income and expense account. It is helpful to compare the actual amounts for February with the budgeted amounts. This may be done by customizing the Budget vs Actuals report.

_DO_

Continue to use **Your Name's Beach Barkers** to prepare the Budget vs Actuals report for February 1-28, 2016

Open **Reports**, enter **Budget** in the Search text box for "Go to report"
Click **Budget vs Actuals** on the list that appears
Click the **Customize** button

In the General section of the Customization screen, change the Transaction Date From:
**020116** and To: **022816**
Remove the Date Prepared, Time Prepared, and Report Basis from the footer
Click **Run Report**
- You will see columns for Actual, Budget, Over Budget, and % of Budget for the locations of Malibu, Venice, and Not Specified.

| | MALIBU | | | | VENICE | | | |
|---|---|---|---|---|---|---|---|---|
| | ACTUAL | BUDGET | OVER BUDGET | % OF BUDGET | ACTUAL | BUDGET | OVER BUDGET | % OF BUDGET |
| **Income** | | | | | | | | |
| Sales of Product Income | 1,900.00 | 1,900.00 | 0.00 | 100.00 % | 600.50 | 601.00 | -0.50 | 99.92 % |
| **Services** | | | | | | | | |
| Boarding | 1,100.00 | 1,100.00 | 0.00 | 100.00 % | 550.00 | 550.00 | 0.00 | 100.00 % |
| Day Camp | 600.00 | 450.00 | 150.00 | 133.33 % | 330.00 | 330.00 | 0.00 | 100.00 % |
| Grooming | 215.00 | 215.00 | 0.00 | 100.00 % | 360.00 | 360.00 | 0.00 | 100.00 % |
| House Calls | 150.00 | 150.00 | 0.00 | 100.00 % | | | | |
| Sales Discounts | -27.90 | -28.00 | 0.10 | 99.64 % | -23.90 | -24.00 | 0.10 | 99.58 % |
| Training | 1,650.00 | 1,650.00 | 0.00 | 100.00 % | 350.00 | 350.00 | 0.00 | 100.00 % |
| Transportation | 425.00 | 425.00 | 0.00 | 100.00 % | 500.00 | 500.00 | 0.00 | 100.00 % |
| **Total Services** | **4,112.10** | **3,962.00** | **150.10** | **103.79 %** | **2,066.10** | **2,066.00** | **0.10** | **100.00 %** |
| **Total Income** | **$6,012.10** | **$5,862.00** | **$150.10** | **102.56 %** | **$2,666.60** | **$2,667.00** | **$ -0.40** | **99.99 %** |

Partial Report

Print in Landscape Orientation, export, and/or send/submit the report
- If you save the report, name it **13-Your Name February Budget vs Actuals Ch. 8**.
Continue to use Your Name's Beach Barkers

## JOURNAL—DO

At the end of each chapter, you will always print a Journal so you can view all of the transactions entered during the report dates. As with previous Journals, check each entry carefully, pay close attention to dates, accounts, memos, and amounts. If a transaction does not appear in the Journal, you may have used a current date that is outside the date range of the report.

## DO

Continue to use **Your Name's Beach Barkers** to prepare the Journal for February 1-28, 2016

Click **Journal** in My Custom Reports
Enter the Dates From: **020116** To: **022816**, Run Report
If need be, adjust the width of the Name, Memo/Description, and Account columns so more entries display on one line
- Do your totals for Debits and Credits match the following? If not, double check your entries for correct amounts, dates, accounts, memos.

| TOTAL | | |
|---|---|---|
| | $51,549.05 | $51,549.05 |

Print in Landscape Orientation, export, and/or send/submit the report
- If you save the report, name it **14-Your Name Journal Ch. 8**.
Continue to use Your Name's Beach Barkers

## TRIAL BALANCE—DO

A Trial Balance is printed to prove that debits still equal credits. Post-closing reports are typically prepared as of the last day of the fiscal year after all closing entries for the year have been recorded. Since our closing was simply for a period, this means that income and expenses will be shown in the Trial Balance and in the Profit & Loss reports for February. When you prepare a Trial Balance for the first of the next fiscal year, income and expense accounts will not be shown.

*DO*

Continue to use **Your Name's Beach Barkers** to prepare the Trial Balance for February 1-28, 2016 and February1-28, 2017

Click **Trial Balance** in My Custom Reports
Enter the Dates From: **020116** To: **022816**, Run Report
- You will get the same balances if you run the report for January 1 – February 28, 2016.
- Does your Trial Balance match the following? If not, double check your entries for correct amounts, dates, accounts, memos. Remember, you can click on an account shown in the Trial Balance and access the account register.

### Your Name's Beach Barkers
#### TRIAL BALANCE
##### As of February 28, 2016

| | DEBIT | CREDIT |
|---|---:|---:|
| Checking | 63,448.84 | |
| Petty Cash | 63.93 | |
| Accounts Receivable (A/R) | 14,309.60 | |
| Inventory Asset | 31,844.50 | |
| Prepaid Insurance | 1,600.00 | |
| Supplies:Cleaning Supplies | 925.00 | |
| Supplies:Kennel Supplies | 1,936.00 | |
| Supplies:Office Supplies | 821.48 | |
| Supplies:Sales Supplies | 325.00 | |
| Undeposited Funds | 0.00 | |
| Furniture & Fixtures:Depreciation | | 1,750.00 |
| Furniture & Fixtures:Original cost | 17,000.00 | |
| Kennel Equipment:Depreciation | | 2,370.00 |
| Kennel Equipment:Original cost | 21,150.00 | |
| Office Equipment:Depreciation | | 1,000.00 |
| Office Equipment:Original cost | 11,685.84 | |
| Vehicles:Depreciation | | 3,750.00 |
| Vehicles:Original cost | 32,000.00 | |
| Accounts Payable (A/P) | | 5,214.00 |
| Visa | | 0.00 |
| State Board of Equalization Payable | | 0.00 |
| Loans Payable:Equipment Loan | | 1,941.06 |
| Loans Payable:Furniture & Fixtures Loan | | 2,426.32 |
| Opening Balance Equity | | 0.00 |
| Retained Earnings | 4,466.31 | |
| Your Name, Capital | | 121,923.81 |
| Your Name, Capital:Your Name, Drawing | | 0.00 |
| Your Name, Capital:Your Name, Investment | | 56,735.00 |

| | | |
|---|---:|---:|
| Sales of Product Income | | 2,500.50 |
| Services:Boarding | | 2,420.00 |
| Services:Day Camp | | 1,560.00 |
| Services:Grooming | | 1,360.00 |
| Services:House Calls | | 375.00 |
| Services:Sales Discounts | 51.80 | |
| Services:Training | | 5,025.00 |
| Services:Transportation | | 1,225.00 |
| Cost of Goods Sold | 733.00 | |
| Cost of Goods Sold:Inventory Shrinkage | 90.00 | |
| Cost of Goods Sold:Merchandise Discounts | | 27.50 |
| Advertising | 700.00 | |
| Bank Charges | 72.00 | |
| Equipment Rental | 75.00 | |
| Insurance:Vehicle Insurance | 200.00 | |
| Interest Expense | 37.22 | |
| Laundry | 81.50 | |
| Rent or Lease | 4,400.00 | |
| Repair & Maintenance:Computer Repair | 200.00 | |
| Repair & Maintenance:Vehicle Repair | 212.50 | |
| Supplies Expense:Cleaning Supplies Expense | 252.00 | |
| Supplies Expense:Kennel Supplies Expense | 310.00 | |
| Supplies Expense:Office Supplies Expense | 231.47 | |
| Supplies Expense:Sales Supplies Expense | 175.00 | |
| Telephone Expense | 129.95 | |
| Utilities:Electric | 164.75 | |
| Utilities:Gas-Heating | 343.50 | |
| Utilities:Water | 385.95 | |
| Vehicle Expenses | 126.05 | |
| Fees Billed | | 80.00 |
| Interest Earned | | 175.50 |
| Depreciation Expense | 1,340.00 | |
| Purchase Discounts | | 29.50 |
| **TOTAL** | **$211,888.19** | **$211,888.19** |

Print in Portrait Orientation, export, and/or send/submit the report
- If you save the report, name it **15-Your Name Trial Balance Ch. 8**.

Change the report dates From: **02/01/17** To: **02/28/17**
- You will see the same information and account totals for all of the Asset, Liability, and Equity accounts. Nothing is shown for Income or Expense accounts because the report dates are for the next fiscal year.

This results in a Total of $197,110.19 for both Debit and Credit columns

Do not save or print the report

Close Your Name's Beach Barkers

## SUMMARY

In this chapter the focus was on performing the accounting functions for the end of a period, adjusting inventory, and preparing budgets. Journal Entries were prepared to record the adjusting entries for supplies used, insurance, and depreciation. Adjustments for damaged inventory items were recorded. Adjustments to the starting value of inventory items were recorded. Bank and Checking Account Reconciliations were performed and transactions for automatic payments were recorded during the reconciliation. Credit Card Account Reconciliations were performed and payment checks were issued. The use of Net Income, Retained Earnings, Opening Balance Equity, and Owner's Equity accounts for Capital, Investment, and Drawing was explored, adjusted, transferred, and interpreted for a sole proprietorship. Owner withdrawals and additional investments were recorded. A period was closed and a transaction was changed after the closing. Further adjustments required because of a change after closing were made for Net Income/Retained Earnings. Reports were customized and prepared to provide data for analysis and examination of the results of business operations and end-of-period adjustments.

8

# END-OF-CHAPTER QUESTIONS

## TRUE/FALSE

ANSWER THE FOLLOWING QUESTIONS IN THE SPACE PROVIDED BEFORE THE QUESTION NUMBER.

_____ 1. An adjusting entry for depreciation reduces the value of fixed assets.

_____ 2. In QuickBooks Online Plus you cannot record an adjustment to the quantity of inventory.

_____ 3. If you transfer Net Income into Capital, on the Balance Sheet it will show as a negative in Retained Earnings and a positive in Net Income until the following year.

_____ 4. An owner's withdrawal decreases cash and equity.

_____ 5. You may prepare a budget for locations.

_____ 6. When reconciling an account, if the statement amount is correct and your amount does not match it, you change the amount in your original transaction.

_____ 7. An inventory starting value transaction is recorded when you prepare a purchase order for an inventory item.

_____ 8. After reconciling a credit card account, you may select the option to write a payment check now.

_____ 9. When you have a budget, you cannot purchase office supplies if it is over the budgeted amount.

_____ 10. You can change the amounts shown for account balances on the Balance Sheet by changing the dates to the current month.

## MULTIPLE CHOICE

WRITE THE LETTER OF THE CORRECT ANSWER IN THE SPACE PROVIDED BEFORE THE QUESTION NUMBER.

_____ 1. You may access the Inventory Quantity Adjustment form by ___ and clicking ___.
   A. Clicking the Plus icon, Inventory Qty Adjustment
   B. Opening the item in the Products and Services List, Quantity
   C. Clicking the drop-down list arrow in the item's Action column in the Products and Services List, Adjust Quantity
   D. All of the above

_____ 2. If the adjusting entry to transfer Net Income and Retained Earnings into the owner's capital account is made prior to the end of the year, the Balance Sheet shows ___.
   A. Retained Earnings
   B. Net Income
   C. Both Net Income and Retained Earnings
   D. None of the above because the Net Income and Retained Earnings have been transferred into Capital

_____ 3. The ___ report compares your budgeted income and expenses to the actual amounts.
   A. Budget vs Actuals
   B. Profit and Loss
   C. Budget Overview
   D. Comprehensive Budget

_____ 4. You record adjusting entries for prepaid expenses and depreciation when using ___-basis accounting.
   A. Cash
   B. Accrual
   C. Budget
   D. GAAP Fundamental

_____ 5. To see the Inventory Starting Value transaction, you prepare the ___ report.
   A. Inventory Starting Value
   B. Inventory Valuation Summary
   C. Inventory Valuation Detail
   D. Any of the above

_____ 6. You may ___ to enter your initial budget figures.
   A. Copy a previous budget
   B. Record the amounts individually
   C. Copy amounts from This Fiscal Year or Last Fiscal Year
   D. Any of the above

_____ 7. If inventory was damaged you adjust the ___.
   A. Inventory Starting Value
   B. Item in a Journal Entry
   C. Quantity
   D. Budget

_____ 8. If you create a budget with locations, prior entries are classified as ___.
   A. Prior to Budget
   B. Not Specified
   C. Unknown
   D. Unbudgeted

_____ 9. After editing an invoice in a closed period, you record the change in income by editing the adjusting entry ___.
   A. For the Closing Date
   B. For transferring Net Income and Retained Earnings into the Capital account
   C. Both A and B
   D. You do not edit anything, you record another adjusting entry

_____ 10. Opening Balances for Inventory Items that were added without preparing a purchase order or bill are entered into ___.
   A. Opening Balance Equity
   B. Inventory Assets
   C. Your Name, Investment
   D. Both A and B

8

## FILL-IN

IN THE SPACE PROVIDED, WRITE THE ANSWER THAT MOST APPROPRIATELY COMPLETES THE SENTENCE.

1. In QuickBooks Online Plus you may create a budget that tracks amounts in _____ and _____ accounts.

2. In Your Name's Beach Barkers, the entry to transfer Net Income to Capital is made by debiting _____ and crediting _____.

3. To correct an error in an inventory item's opening balance, you record an adjustment to the _____.

4. You may reconcile all _____, _____, and _____ accounts.

5. The Account Category Type for Inventory Shrinkage is_____.

## COMPUTER ASSIGNMENT

REFER TO PRINTOUTS OR USE QUICKBOOKS ONLINE AND <u>YOUR NAME'S BEACH BARKERS</u> TO LOOK UP OR ENTER INFORMATION, AND THEN WRITE THE ANSWERS TO THE FOLLOWING EXERCISES IN THE SPACE PROVIDED

1. Prepare an Inventory Valuation Summary report to determine the value of Collars after the Quantity Adjustment. What is the quantity on February 28, 2016? _____
   What is the value? _____

2. When you edited Invoice 1044 to Sandi Egkan in the Additional Transactions section, did income increase or decrease? _____

3. What was the amount of the adjusting entry for Cleaning Supplies in February? _____

4. What was the total amount of owner withdrawals for February? _____

5. On what screen do you enter the closing date? _____

6. What is the amount of Total Assets in the Balance Sheet for 2016 prepared after all closing entries and adjustments? (Printed Document 11) _____

7. Refer to your Visa Reconciliation Report ending February 28, 2016. What is the total amount of Charges and Cash Advances Cleared? _____

8. Prepare a Journal report for February 27-28, 2016. What is the total of the Journal? _____

9. What was the amount of Depreciation Expense recorded in the compound adjusting entry for Office Equipment and Vehicles? _____

10. Refer to or prepare the Budget vs Actuals report for the end of the chapter. What was the budgeted amount for Total Net Income for February 2016? _____
    What was the actual amount for Total Net Income for February 2016? _____

# CHAPTER 8 CHECKLIST

The checklist below shows all of the business forms printed during training. Check each one that you printed, exported, and/or submitted.

| | |
|---|---|
| _____ 1-Inventory Valuation Summary Ch. 8 | _____ 9-Invoice 1044 Sandi Egkan Corrected |
| _____ 2-Inventory Valuation Detail Ch. 8 | _____ 10-Profit and Loss Ch. 8 |
| _____ 3-Check 30 | _____ 11-Balance Sheet 2016 Ch. 8 |
| _____ 4-Budget Overview Ch. 8 | _____ 12-Balance Sheet 2017 Ch. 8 |
| _____ 5-Checking Reconciliation | _____ 13-February Budget vs Actuals Ch. 8 |
| _____ 6-Check 31 | _____ 14-Journal Ch. 8 |
| _____ 7-Check 32 Beach Bank | _____ 15-Trial Balance Ch. 8 |
| _____ 8-Visa Reconciliation | |

8

# PAYROLL

## LEARNING OBJECTIVES

At the completion of this chapter, you will be able to:

1. Activate Payroll.
2. Pay employees.
3. Edit paychecks.
4. Add new employees, edit existing employees, and reactivate inactive employees.
5. Delete paychecks.
6. Print Payroll reports including Payroll Summary, Tax Liability, and Employee Details.
7. Pay Taxes and Other Liabilities.
8. Review and edit Payroll Settings for Payroll and Services, Company and Account, and Employees.

## PAYROLL

Payroll is an extremely important part of running a business. Paying your employees is more than simply writing a check. You also take deductions from your employees' pay for state and federal tax withholdings, social security, unemployment, insurance, and various other items that are required to be paid by the employees. As the employer, you are responsible for withholding the correct amounts from your employees and then forwarding the payments to the appropriate agencies and/or companies. In addition, as an employer, there are employer taxes that must be paid and submitted to the appropriate government agencies as well.

Many times, a company begins the process of computerizing its accounting system simply to prepare the payroll using the computer. It is much faster and easier to let QuickBooks Online look at the tax tables and determine how much withholding should be deducted for each employee than to have an individual perform this task. Because tax tables change frequently, QuickBooks Online requires its users to enroll in a QuickBooks Online Payroll plan. Currently, there are two plans available, Enhanced and Full-Service. In order to enroll in a payroll service plan, you must have a company tax identification number. If you do not subscribe to a payroll plan, you must create payroll accounts, calculate and enter the payroll taxes manually, and prepare payroll tax forms and payments by hand. If you choose to enter your payroll manually, there are no payroll reports or tax payment forms available.

Intuit's payroll plans are changed and updated frequently; however, at the time of this writing, details for two payroll plans are:

**QuickBooks Online Payroll Enhanced** is one payroll plan you may use with QuickBooks Online Plus. With this service, you may pay up to 150 employees and prepare 18 different payroll reports. The service includes tax payments and forms for federal and a maximum of one state tax filing. If you need more than one state, there is an additional cost each month. If you bundle QuickBooks Online Plus and Enhanced Payroll, the monthly cost will be $78.95 plus $1.50 per employee per month. Frequently, discounts are available for subscriptions for six months to one year. At the time of this writing, the bundled QuickBooks Online and Enhanced Payroll had a special of 50 percent off.

<u>**QuickBooks Online Full Service Payroll**</u> includes everything in Enhanced Payroll. In addition, your payroll taxes will be completed and filed for you, any previous payroll data will be entered into QuickBooks Online, and there is a guarantee of no tax penalties. If you bundle QuickBooks Online Plus and Full Service Payroll, the monthly cost for both is $138.95 plus $2 per employee per month. Frequently, discounts are available for subscriptions for six months to one year. At the time of this writing, the bundled QuickBooks Online and Full Service Payroll had a special of 50 percent off.

Payroll is an area of accounting that has frequent changes; for example, tax tables are updated, changes in withholding or tax limits are made, etc. As a result, QuickBooks Online is modified via updates to implement changes to payroll. As a word of caution, the materials presented in this chapter are current at the time of this writing. However, it is entirely possible and probable that the amounts in your paychecks, paycheck liabilities, and payroll taxes will <u>not</u> match the figures in the text. While it is possible to enter payroll transactions manually so your figures will match the ones in the text, it is a cumbersome and not very realistic process. As a result, this chapter will focus on how to process payroll using QuickBooks Online and Enhanced Payroll.

## TRAINING TUTORIAL AND PROCEDURES

This chapter will be different from Chapters 2-8 because it will use only the Test Drive Company to explore and enter payroll. Because Your Name's Beach Barkers is a fictitious company, it would not be appropriate to enroll in a payroll program, process payroll, and pay tax liabilities for a company that does not exist.

In previous chapters, all work recorded in the Test Drive Company was for Craig's Design and Landscape Service. In the payroll section of the Test Drive Company, you will be processing the payroll for Collins Paint and Wallpaper Services. As you know, when you close the Test Drive Company, all material entered is erased. Because of this, you will enter a number of transactions in the Test Drive Company and then close the company. When you resume training, you will reopen the company, turn on payroll, and continue with the next material presented. Sometimes, the payroll portion in the Test Drive Company is a bit unstable. If for some reason your computer freezes or you cannot gain access, simply close your Web browser and try again. The data in each section of the chapter is limited so if something happens it will not take a lot of time to re-enter anything that may be lost.

As you did for Chapters 2-8 you will enter additional transactions and print/export documents at the end of the chapter.

**Remember, your totals and dates may not agree with the material in the text. That should not be of concern at this point. The focus of this chapter is for you to learn the procedures for activating payroll, processing payroll, paying payroll liabilities, and preparing payroll reports.**

## DATES

Unlike the other chapters, in Chapter 9, the current date will be used for all transactions. If you see dates in the text that do not match the ones on your screen, use the dates on your screen.

## IMPORTANT NOTE

As has been stated in earlier chapters, QuickBooks Online is constantly evolving and new features, apps, and procedures change frequently. Everything in the text is correct at the time of this writing; however, by the time of publication some changes to the program may occur.

9

## ACTIVATE PAYROLL—DRILL

When working with payroll, you process paychecks, calculate withholdings, and submit payroll tax payments. In QuickBooks Online, when you subscribe to and activate Enhanced or Full Service Payroll, the appropriate liability and expense accounts will be added to the company's Chart of Accounts, Payroll Settings will be created, and payroll reports and tax forms will be made available as well. When using QuickBooks Online Payroll, deductions and taxes are calculated automatically using the latest tax tables.

### DRILL

 Open the **Test Drive Company** and activate Payroll

As usual, prior to beginning work in the Test Drive Company, turn **OFF** Redesigned Reports in QuickBooks Labs
Click **Employees** in the Navigation bar
Click the **Turn on Payroll** button

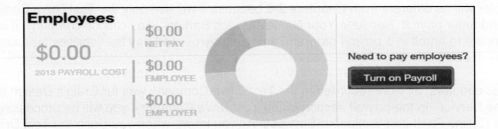

- If you have any difficulties with activating payroll, close your Web browser, reopen it, and then reopen QuickBooks Online.
- Once payroll has been activated you will see a dashboard showing the 2016 Payroll cost to date, the amount of Net Pay, the deductions for the Employees, and the contributions from the Employer. In addition, the three active employees, their pay rates, payment methods, and employment status are listed.

Do <u>not</u> close the Test Drive Company

## PAY EMPLOYEES—DRILL

There are two different methods of compensation, Salary and Hourly. The process for paying an employee whether hourly or salary is very similar and is completed in three steps: Add the employee's hours worked, review the payroll, and submit.

---

**MEMO**
**DATE**: Current Date

Run the payroll for all employees. Use the payroll date provided by QuickBooks Online for the end of the current week. Eloisa Catillo and Bill Lucchini do not have any changes or additions to their payroll information. Kari Steblay worked 40 hours Regular and 5 hours Overtime.

---

### DRILL

 Continue to use the **Test Drive Company** and pay the weekly payroll for all active employees

Now that Payroll has been activated, you will see the three active employees shown on the screen

- Note the information provided for the Active Employees. It includes the employee's name, pay rate, payment method, and status.
- The dates you see on your screen will <u>not</u> match the ones in the textbook. Do not be concerned. Simply use the dates provided by QuickBooks Online.

Click the **Run Payroll** button

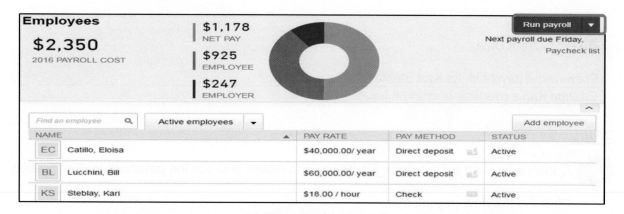

On the Run Payroll: Friday screen, for Kari Steblay enter **40** in REGULAR PAY HRS, press **Tab**, enter **5** in OT HRS, press **Tab**

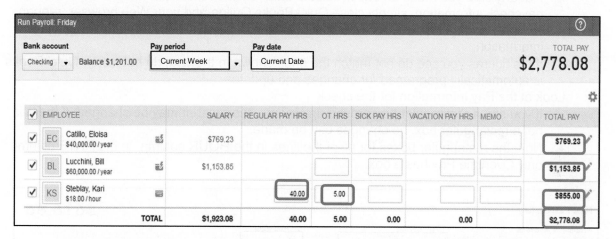

- QuickBooks Online calculated the pay for each employee. While you provided the hours for Kari, you did not need to provide any information for the salaried employees. Unless they are paid for sick and/or vacation time taken, you will not need to enter any hours for them. However, if a salaried employee took one day of vacation, you would record 8 as Vacation Pay Hrs and QuickBooks Online would deduct the amount of vacation hours taken from the vacation hours available. The same process would be used if the employee took off work and was paid Sick Pay.
- You will see the text box for OT HRS for your salaried employees. Salaried employees are not paid for overtime so this will not be used for them.

<u>Immediately</u> continue to the next section without changing or clicking anything, do <u>not</u> close the Test Drive Company

9

## PREVIEW AND EDIT PAYCHECK--DRILL

Immediately after running the payroll, you have the opportunity to preview and edit paychecks. Once a paycheck has been printed, it may not be edited. You may make changes to hours worked, certain types of pay (overtime rates), federal and state withholdings, and voluntary employee deductions. Most taxes and liabilities calculated and entered by QuickBooks Online may not be changed.

> **MEMO**
> **DATE**: Current Date
>
> Preview the paycheck for Kari Steblay.
> Change Kari's overtime hours to 6 hours.

## _DRILL_

 Continue to use the **Test Drive Company** and review and edit the paycheck for Kari Steblay

Click the **Preview payroll** button
Click the **Pen** icon next to the Total Pay for Kari Steblay
You will see the paycheck details for her check

- If at any time you make an uncorrectable error, click on the incorrect screen, or lose your paycheck information, simply close QuickBooks Online and your Web browser, reopen the Web browser and QuickBooks Online, activate payroll, and re-enter the paycheck information.
- If the figures you see do not match the ones shown in the text, do not worry. QuickBooks is automatically programed for changes and updates.

Look at the Pay information for the check

- If you see a rectangular box around an amount, the amount may be changed. If there is not a rectangular box, no changes can be made.
- Note the rectangular boxes for all of the lines in the HOUR column. In the RATE column, only Overtime Pay has a box.

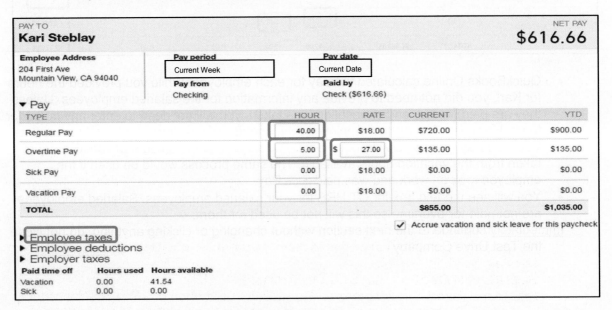

Click **Employee Taxes** to open that section

- Note the rectangular boxes for Federal Income Tax and CA Income Tax. The amount of withholdings may be changed. Do <u>not</u> do this lightly because you will affect the total withholding of income taxes for the year.

| PAY TO | | | NET PAY |
|---|---|---|---|
| **Kari Steblay** | | | **$616.66** |

| **Employee Address** | **Pay period** | **Pay date** | |
|---|---|---|---|
| 204 First Ave | Current Week | Current Date | |
| Mountain View, CA 94040 | **Pay from** | **Paid by** | |
| | Checking | Check ($616.66) | |

▶ Pay

▼ Employee taxes

| TYPE | | CURRENT | YTD |
|---|---|---|---|
| Federal Income Tax | $ | 55.97 | $55.97 |
| Social Security | | $53.01 | $64.17 |
| Medicare | | $12.40 | $15.01 |
| CA Income Tax | $ | 6.51 | $6.51 |
| CA State Disability Ins | | $7.70 | $9.32 |
| TOTAL | | $135.59 | $150.98 |

Click **Employee Deductions** to open that section
- Because these are voluntary deductions, all of the items in the CURRENT column for Employee deductions have rectangular boxes so they all may be changed.

▼ Employee deductions

| TYPE | | CURRENT | YTD |
|---|---|---|---|
| 401K | $ | 42.75 | $51.75 |
| Bright Smile Insurance | $ | 10.00 | $20.00 |
| Good Health Insurance | $ | 50.00 | $100.00 |
| TOTAL | | $102.75 | $171.75 |

Click **Employer Taxes** to open that section
- None of the items in the CURRENT column have rectangular boxes so they may not be changed.

▼ Employer taxes

| TYPE | CURRENT | YTD |
|---|---|---|
| FUTA Employer | $5.13 | $6.21 |
| Social Security Employer | $53.01 | $64.17 |
| Medicare Employer | $12.40 | $15.01 |
| CA ETT | $0.86 | $1.04 |
| CA SUI Employer | $29.07 | $35.19 |
| TOTAL | $100.47 | $121.62 |

Go back to the Pay section and click in the text box for Overtime Hours, change the number of hours to **6**, press **Tab**

Immediately everything for the check was recalculated by QuickBooks

Scroll through and note the following changes:
- Remember: Your figures and amount may not match the following.
  **Net Pay**: $635.59
  **Pay**—Current Overtime Pay: $162.00; Total for Pay: $882.00
  **Employee Taxes**—Federal Income Tax: $59.82; Social Security: $54.68; Medicare: $12.79; CA Income Tax: $7.08; CA State Disability Ins.: $7.94; Total: $142.31

9

Employee Deductions—401K: $44.10; Dental: $10; Medical: $50; Total: $104.10
Employer Taxes—FUTA Employer: $5.29; Social Security Employer: $54.68; Medicare Employer: $12.79; CA ETT: $0.88; CA SUI Employer: $29.99; Total: $103.63
Click the **OK** button for Kari Steblay
<u>Immediately</u> continue to the next section without closing the Test Drive Company

## SUBMIT PAYROLL AND PRINT—DRILL

Once the payroll for the period has been entered and, if necessary, edited, your next step is to submit the payroll.

## *DRILL*

Continue to use the **Test Drive Company** and submit the payroll

Now that the paycheck for Kari Steblay has been previewed and edited, verify the information shown on the Review and Submit screen
- Note that there is one Paper Check (Kari) and two Direct Deposits (Eloise and Bill).
- As you look at the dashboard, you will see the amount of Net Pay for the employees, the amount of Employee Deductions, and the amount of the Employer tax payments.

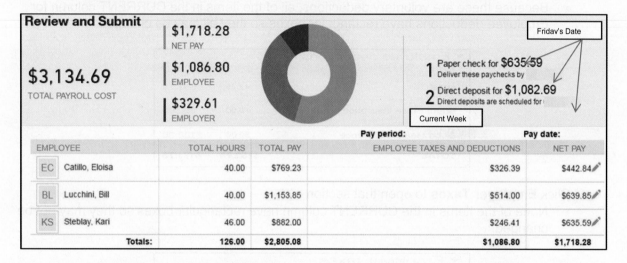

When finished, click the **Submit Payroll** button
- Once the payroll has been submitted, you will see a screen to print paychecks and pay stubs.

Enter **17** for the CHECK NUMBER for Kari Steblay's check
Click the **Print paychecks** button to print the check for Kari Steblay
- Her paycheck and pay stub appears in a new tab in the Web browser.

Friday's Date → **635.59

Kari Steblay

*****Six hundred thirty-five and 59/100

Kari Steblay
204 First Ave
Mountain View CA 94040

| **EMPLOYER** | | | | | **PAY PERIOD** | | |
|---|---|---|---|---|---|---|---|
| Collins Paint and Wallpaper Services | | | | | Period Beginning | | 04/02/2016 |
| 123 Main St. | | | | | Period Ending: | | 04/08/2016 |
| Palo Alto CA 94306 | | | | | Pay Date: | | 04/08/2016 |
| | | | | | Total Hours: | | 46.00 |

**EMPLOYEE**
Kari Steblay
204 First Ave
Mountain View CA 94040

SS#: ...3333

| **BENEFITS** | | **Used** | **Available** | **NET PAY:** | | **$635.59** |
|---|---|---|---|---|---|---|
| Sick | | 0.00 | 0.00 | | | |
| Vacation | | 0.00 | 41.54 | | | |

**MEMO:**

| **PAY** | **Hours** | **Rate** | **Current** | **YTD** | **DEDUCTIONS** | **Current** | **YTD** |
|---|---|---|---|---|---|---|---|
| Regular Pay | 40.00 | 18.00 | 720.00 | 900.00 | 401K | 44.10 | 53.10 |
| Overtime Pay | 6.00 | 27.00 | 162.00 | 162.00 | Bright Smile Insurance | 10.00 | 20.00 |
| | | | | | Good Health Insurance | 50.00 | 100.00 |

| **TAXES** | **Current** | **YTD** |
|---|---|---|
| Federal Income Tax | 59.82 | 59.82 |
| Social Security | 54.68 | 65.84 |
| Medicare | 12.79 | 15.40 |
| CA Income Tax | 7.08 | 7.08 |
| CA State Disability Ins | 7.94 | 9.56 |

| **SUMMARY** | **Current** | **YTD** |
|---|---|---|
| Total Pay | $882.00 | $1,062.00 |
| Taxes | $142.31 | $157.70 |
| Deductions | $104.10 | $173.10 |
| **Net Pay** | **$635.59** | |

Point to the top-right corner of the paycheck, click the **Print** icon 🖨

- If you save the paycheck rather than printing it, name it **1-Your Name Check 17 Kari Steblay**.

Close the browser tab that shows the check

Click the **Print pay stubs** button

- The pay stubs for Eloise Catillo and Bill Lucchini appear in a new tab in the Web browser. (Eloise is shown below.)

Collins Paint and Wallpaper Services
123 Main St.
Palo Alto CA 94306

Pay Stub Detail
PAY DATE:04/08/2016
NET PAY:$442.84

Eloisa Catillo
550 Front Boulevard
Menlo Park CA 94025

| **EMPLOYER** | | | | | **PAY PERIOD** | | |
|---|---|---|---|---|---|---|---|
| Collins Paint and Wallpaper Services | | | | | Period Beginning | | 04/02/2016 |
| 123 Main St. | | | | | Period Ending: | | 04/08/2016 |
| Palo Alto CA 94306 | | | | | Pay Date: | | 04/08/2016 |

**EMPLOYEE**
Eloisa Catillo
550 Front Boulevard
Menlo Park CA 94025

SS#: ...1111

| **BENEFITS** | | **Used** | **Available** | **NET PAY:** | | **$442.84** |
|---|---|---|---|---|---|---|
| Sick | | 0.00 | 0.00 | Acct#....0000: | | $200.00 |
| Vacation | | 0.00 | 41.54 | Acct#....0000: | | $242.84 |

**MEMO:**

| **PAY** | **Hours** | **Rate** | **Current** | **YTD** | **DEDUCTIONS** | **Current** | **YTD** |
|---|---|---|---|---|---|---|---|
| Salary | - | - | 769.23 | 1,538.46 | 401K | 15.38 | 30.76 |
| | | | | | Bright Smile Insurance | 40.00 | 80.00 |
| | | | | | Good Health Insurance | 200.00 | 400.00 |

| **TAXES** | **Current** | **YTD** |
|---|---|---|
| Federal Income Tax | 0.00 | 0.00 |
| Social Security | 47.69 | 95.38 |
| Medicare | 11.16 | 22.31 |
| CA Income Tax | 5.23 | 10.46 |
| CA State Disability Ins | 6.93 | 13.85 |

| **SUMMARY** | **Current** | **YTD** |
|---|---|---|
| Total Pay | $769.23 | $1,538.46 |
| Taxes | $71.01 | $142.00 |
| Deductions | $255.38 | $510.76 |
| **Net Pay** | **$442.84** | |

9

- Disregard the dates shown in the pay stub. Your dates will be for the current week.

Print as instructed for paychecks

- If you save the pay stubs rather than printing them, name the document **2-Your Name Pay Stubs**.

Close the browser tab that shows the pay stubs

Click **Finish payroll** at the bottom of the print checks and pay stubs screen

Depending on the current date, you may get a screen for Tax payments due; if it appears, click the **I'll do it later** button

### Tax payments due
To avoid late fees and penalties, review and pay your taxes on time.

☐ Don't show this reminder again.

[ I'll do it later ]　　　　　[ Review and pay ]

- You are returned to the Employee List.

Immediately continue to the next section without closing the Test Drive Company

## PAYROLL REPORTS

There are 18 different reports available to provide information regarding payroll at the time of this writing. The available reports include Time Activities, Payroll Summary and Detail, Payroll Tax Payments and Liabilities, Employee Details, Payroll Tax and Wage Summary, Payroll Deductions/Contributions, Total Payroll Cost, Paycheck List, among others.

## *DRILL*

Continue to use the **Test Drive Company** and prepare Payroll Summary and Payroll Tax Liability reports

If you did not already turn **OFF** Redesigned Reports in QuickBooks Labs, do so now

Click **Reports** on the Navigation bar, click **Manage Payroll**, click **Payroll Summary**

- The report is shown using Date Range: **Last pay date** and Employee: **Active Employees**.
- The Payroll Summary report shows details for each paycheck you have created and includes information for Net Amount, Total Hours, Taxes Withheld, Deductions, Total Pay, Employer Taxes, Employer Contributions, and Total Cost.

Click the drop-down list arrow next to the button **Share** in the upper-right corner of the report

Click **Printer friendly**

- The report opens in a separate screen.

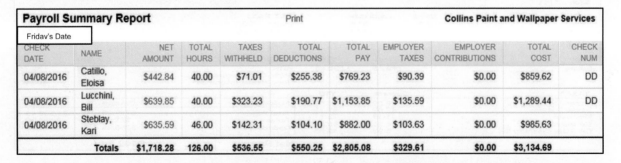

**Payroll Summary Report**　　　　　Print　　　　　**Collins Paint and Wallpaper Services**

Friday's Date

| CHECK DATE | NAME | NET AMOUNT | TOTAL HOURS | TAXES WITHHELD | TOTAL DEDUCTIONS | TOTAL PAY | EMPLOYER TAXES | EMPLOYER CONTRIBUTIONS | TOTAL COST | CHECK NUM |
|---|---|---|---|---|---|---|---|---|---|---|
| 04/08/2016 | Catillo, Eloisa | $442.84 | 40.00 | $71.01 | $255.38 | $769.23 | $90.39 | $0.00 | $859.62 | DD |
| 04/08/2016 | Lucchini, Bill | $639.85 | 40.00 | $323.23 | $190.77 | $1,153.85 | $135.59 | $0.00 | $1,289.44 | DD |
| 04/08/2016 | Steblay, Kari | $635.59 | 46.00 | $142.31 | $104.10 | $882.00 | $103.63 | $0.00 | $985.63 | |
| | **Totals** | **$1,718.28** | **126.00** | **$536.55** | **$550.25** | **$2,805.08** | **$329.61** | **$0.00** | **$3,134.69** | |

If your instructor wants you to print the report, click **Print**, select Landscape orientation and print as previously instructed

If your instructor wants you to export the report to Excel, click the drop-down list arrow for
    the Share button, click **Export to Excel**
Open the report in Excel as usual
If the report opens in Protected View, click **Enable Editing**

> ⓘ **Protected View**   This file originated from an Internet location and might be unsafe. Click for more details.     | Enable Editing |

- If you save the report, name the document **3-Your Name Payroll Summary Ch. 9**.
When finished with the Payroll Summary report, click **Reports** on the Navigation bar
Click **Payroll Tax Liability**
- The report is shown using Date Range: **Last pay date**.
- This report shows you the taxes you need to pay and the ones you've already paid.
- You will see columns for Tax Amount, Tax Paid, and Tax Owed. Notice that Tax Paid
shows 0.00 for everything.

| Tax Liability Report | | Collins Paint and Wallpaper Services | |
| --- | --- | --- | --- |
| | TAX AMOUNT | TAX PAID | TAX OWED |
| **CA PIT / SDI** | **$86.01** | **$0.00** | **$86.01** |
| CA Income Tax | $60.75 | $0.00 | $60.75 |
| CA State Disability Ins | $25.26 | $0.00 | $25.26 |
| **CA SUI / ETT** | **$98.19** | **$0.00** | **$98.19** |
| CA ETT | $2.81 | $0.00 | $2.81 |
| CA SUI Employer | $95.38 | $0.00 | $95.38 |
| **Federal Taxes (941/944)** | **$665.13** | **$0.00** | **$665.13** |
| Federal Income Tax | $235.95 | $0.00 | $235.95 |
| Social Security | $173.91 | $0.00 | $173.91 |
| Social Security Employer | $173.91 | $0.00 | $173.91 |
| Medicare | $40.68 | $0.00 | $40.68 |
| Medicare Employer | $40.68 | $0.00 | $40.68 |
| **Federal Unemployment (940)** | **$16.83** | **$0.00** | **$16.83** |
| FUTA Employer | $16.83 | $0.00 | $16.83 |

Print and/or export to Excel as previously instructed
- If you save the report, name the document **4-Your Name Tax Liability Report Ch. 9**.
After printing or exporting your reports, immediately continue to the next section without
    closing the Test Drive Company

*Do not close*

## PAY TAXES—DRILL

Depending on the number of employees, amount of payroll, and other variables, you will have
specific dates for paying the payroll taxes you deduct from employees and for the taxes you owe as
an employer.

9

## *DRILL*

 Continue to use the **Test Drive Company** and pay Payroll taxes

Click **Taxes** on the Navigation bar, click **Payroll Tax**
- You will open the Payroll Tax Center where you will see the tax type, due date,
e-payment cutoff dates, tax forms, and other activities.

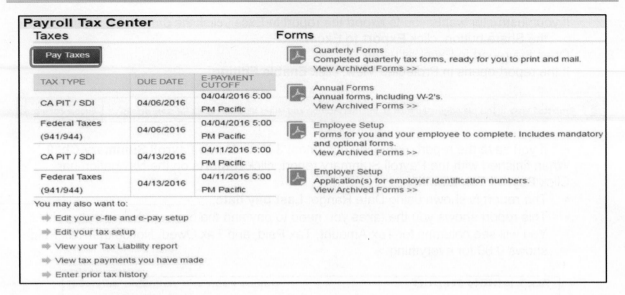

Click the **Pay Taxes** button
- The Pay Taxes screen may show two sections: Tax Payments Due and Upcoming Tax Payments. If you do not see the expanded section, click the ▶ at the end of the heading.
- Your dates will be different from the dates in the text. When dates are different, you may have taxes shown in different categories. If the amounts are different, do not worry QuickBooks Online simply updated tax tables or the dates changed.

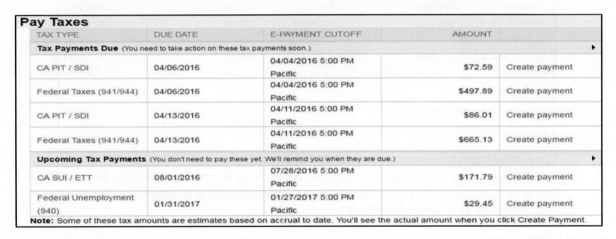

Click CA PIT/SDI to see the details for the tax payment
- You will see that your tax payment will be for CA Income Tax and CA State Disability Insurance with individual amounts for each.

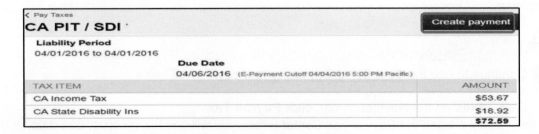

Click the **Create payment** button

- You will see that Pay Electronically is automatically selected.

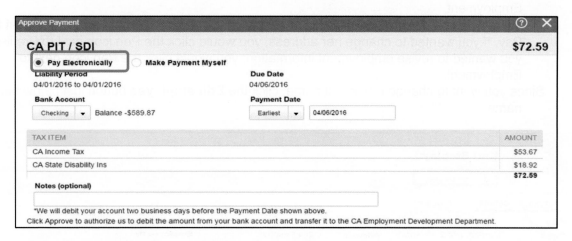

Click the **E-Pay** button at the bottom-right side of the screen
Review the E-Pay screen, click **Done**

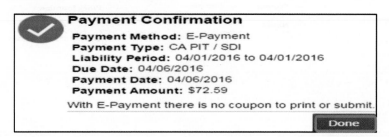

You are returned to the Pay Taxes screen
- Note that the first payment for CA PIT/SDI no longer shows as a Tax Payment Due.
Close the Test Drive Company

## EDIT AN EMPLOYEE—DRILL

Changes can and do occur for employees. As a result, it is possible to edit an employee and change basic payroll information. You may edit the employee to change personal information, pay and withholding information, and employment information.

> **MEMO**
> **DATE**: Current Date
>
> Edit the employee Kari Steblay. Change her last name to Masters, her address to 281 Apricot Lane, add her Mobile phone: 650-555-9238. Change her pay rate to $18.50 per hour.

## _DRILL_

 Open the **Test Drive Company**, activate Payroll, and edit an employee

With the Test Drive Company open, click **Employees** on the Navigation bar, click **Turn On Payroll** to reactivate the feature
- Since you closed the Test Drive Company, all previous payroll information was erased and payroll was deactivated.
Click the employee **Kari Steblay**

9

- Note that you have three distinct areas of information for Kari: Pay, Profile, and Employment.
- If you want to edit information regarding Kari's pay, you would click the Pen icon next to Pay. If you wanted to change her address, you would click the Pen icon next to Profile. If you wanted to revise employment information, you would click the Pen icon next to Employment.

Since you want to change Kari's last name, click the **Edit employee** button just below her name

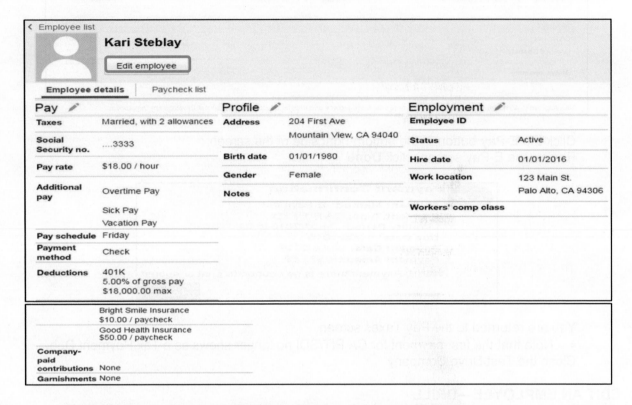

Click in the Last name text box, delete Steblay, then enter **Masters**

- As you look at the items and categories available for Kari in the Pay section, notice the bright yellow circle with an explanation point. This means that information needs to be provided.

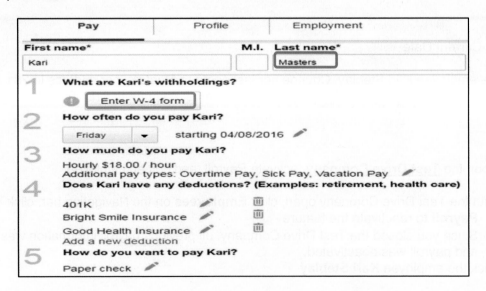

Click the **Enter W-4 form** button

Review the information provided, no changes are needed

- Notice that only the last four digits of Kari's Social Security number are shown. This is done for security reasons.

Click **Done**

- You return back to the Pay section for Kari.

Click the **Pen** icon for Step 3 "How much do you pay Kari?"

Click in the text box that shows 18.00, change the amount to **18.50**

Click **Done**

- You return back to the Pay section for Kari.
- There are no other pay changes required for Kari.

Click **Profile** at the top of screen

Change the Home address to **281 Apricot Lane**

Click in the text box for Mobile, enter **650-555-9238**, press **Tab**

9

| | Pay | Profile | Employment |

**Home address***
281 Apricot Lane

| **City or town*** | **State** | **ZIP code*** |
| Mountain View | CA ▾ | 94040 |

**Email**

> **Want online pay stubs?** ✕
> Give Kari online access to pay stubs!
> Learn about ViewMyPaycheck

**Phone**

| **Home** | | ext. | |
| **Work** | | ext. | |
| **Mobile** | 650-555-9238 | ext. | |

**Gender***      **Birth date**
● Female    01/01/1980
○ Male
**Notes**

Click **Done**
There are no changes required to the Employment section
Click **<Employee list** above Kari Masters' name
- Note the changes for Kari.

| KM | Masters, Kari | $18.50 / hour | Check ▭ | Active |

Do not close the Test Drive Company continue to the next section

## ADD NEW EMPLOYEE—DRILL

Whenever a new employee is hired, the employee is added to the Employees List. Basic payroll information; such as, pay type, voluntary and required deductions and withholdings, sick leave and vacation leave, gender, address, and other information are added for the employee.

> **MEMO**
> **DATE**: Current Date
>
> Add a new part-time employee: Beth Stevens. Pay Section: Item 1: W-4 Info: Social Security number: 100-55-4654; Home address: 244 Carbonera Avenue, Sunnyvale, CA 94086; Single; Allowance: 1. Item 2: How often do you pay Beth: add a new Payroll schedule for Every Other Week; Name the Pay Schedule: Every Other Friday. Item 3: Paid: Hourly @ $15 per hour. Also eligible for Overtime Pay. Profile Section: Mobile Phone: 650-555-7412; Birth date: 03/23/1993. Employment Section: click New Hire Report and Form I-9; Hire date: two weeks before the current date.

## *DRILL*

Continue to use the **Test Drive Company** and add a new employee

Click the **Add employee** button
- You will enter the Pay, Profile, and Employment information for the new employee.
Click in First name, enter **Beth**, press **Tab** two times
In Last name, enter **Stevens**
For Item 1, click the **Enter W-4 form** button
Complete the W-4 form:

Item 1: First name: **Beth**; Last name: **Stevens**; Home address: **244 Carbonera Avenue**; City: **Sunnyvale**; State: **CA**; Zip code: **94086**
Item 2: Social Security number: **100-55-4654**
Item 3: **Single**
Item 4: **1**
Item 5: **0.00**

**What are Beth's withholdings?**
Need blank W-4 forms?

**W-4** Employees Withholding Allowance Certificate **2016**

1. First name* — Beth  M.I.  Last name* — Stevens
2. Social Security number* — 100-55-4654

Home address* — 244 Carbonera Avenue

3. ● Single
   ○ Married
   ○ Married, but withhold at higher Single rate
   ○ Do Not Withhold

City or town* — Sunnyvale  State* — CA  ZIP code* — 94086

4. Total number of allowances you are claiming . . . . . . . . . . . . . . . . . . . . . . . . . . . . . 4. 1

5. 5. $ 0.00
Additional amount, if any, you want withheld from each paycheck . . . . . . . . . . . . . . .

▶ **California state taxes**
We've filled out Beth's state withholding based on the Form W-4 above (They're usually the same).

▶ **Tax exemptions**
These are not common.

Click **Done**
For Item 2, click the drop-down list arrow next to Friday, click **Add new**
- The other employees are paid every Friday. Beth will be placed on the new Pay Schedule of Every Other Week.
Click the drop-down list arrow next to Every Week, click **Every Other Week**
Accept the dates and the pay schedule name shown by QuickBooks Online

**What's Beth's pay schedule?**
How often do you pay Beth?
Every Other Week ▾
When's the next payday?
Friday's Date
When's the last day of work (pay period) for that payday?
Wednesday's Date
What do you want to name this pay schedule?
Every Other Friday
✔ Use this schedule for employees you add after Beth

Click **Done**
For Item 3, enter **15** in the text box for / hour
Click **Add additional pay types**
Click **Overtime Pay**

9

- Since Beth is a part-time employee, she is not eligible for sick or vacation pay.

Click **Done**

For Items 4 and 5, do not make any changes. Click **Done**

Click the **Pen** icon for Profile

Enter Beth's Mobile Phone: **650-555-7412**

For Gender, click **Female**

Click in the text box for Birth date, enter **03/23/1993**. Press **Tab**

- In payroll you must enter the two-digit month, two-digit day, the *I*, and the four-digit year.

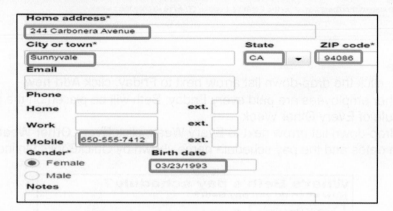

Click **Done**

Click the **Pen** icon for Employment

Click the check box for "Have you filed a new-hire report with the state?" to select

- The new hire report requires the submission of the report to a designated state agency. The information in the report is used to prevent erroneous benefit payments for unemployment, workers' compensation, and public assistance. In addition, the report is used to enforce child support payments.

Click the check box for "Have you stored a completed Form I-9 in your files?" to select

- Form I-9 verifies employment eligibility status.

For Hire date, enter the date for two weeks ago

- The example uses 03/01/2016 and must be entered with the / and the four-digit year.

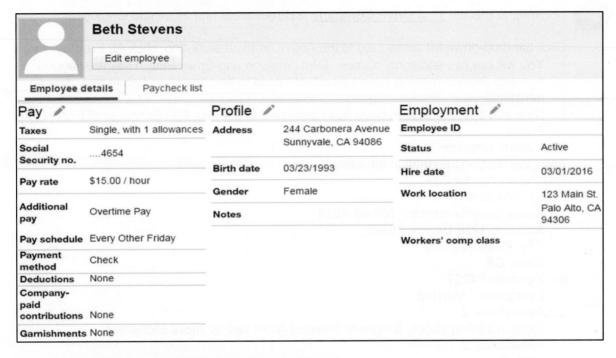

Click **Done**

Review the payroll details for Beth Stevens

Click **<Employee list** just above Beth's name

Do <u>not</u> close the Test Drive Company, continue with the next section

## REINSTATE AND TERMINATE INACTIVE EMPLOYEES—DRILL

If you have employees who have been marked inactive, they may be reinstated. When you reinstate an employee, you must edit the employee and enter any missing details.

9

**MEMO**
**DATE**: Current Date

Activate John Johnson. Pay Section: Item 1: W-4 Form: Social Security number: 100-55-8525; Address: 1270 Dewey Street, Redwood, City, CA 94061; Married, Allowances: 2; CA Filing status: Single or Married (with two or more incomes); Allowances: 2. Item 2: Pay schedule: Every Other Friday. Item 3: Salary: 28,000, Additional Pay Types: Sick Pay: Sick Leave Policy, Balance 40; Vacation Pay: Vacation Policy, Balance 40. Item 4: Dental Insurance: Bright Smile Dental, Monthly 10, Maximum 120; Health Insurance: Good Health Insurance, Monthly 40, Maximum 480. Profile: Mobile number: 650-555-2122; Gender: Male. Employment: Active, New Hire Report and Form I-9.

Mark Emily Platt Terminated. Hire Date 01/02/2016, Termination Date: Current date, Birth Date: 08/03/1995.

## *DRILL*

Continue to use the **Test Drive Company** and reactivate and terminate employees

Click the drop-down list arrow next to the Active employees button, click **All Employees**
- You will see two additional names: John Johnson and Emily Platt. They are flagged because there is missing information that needs to be completed before they may be reinstated.
- Note that both employees have been assigned to the new Pay Schedule of Every Other Friday.

Click **John Johnson**
Enter the missing information for John
Edit the section for Pay
Item 1: W-4 form:
  Social Security number: **100-55-8525**
  Address: **1270 Dewey Street**
  City: **Redwood City**
  State: **CA**
  Zip code: **94061**
  Exemptions: **Married**
  Allowances: **2**
  California Filing status: **Single or Married (with two or more incomes)**
  Allowances: **2**
  Click **Done**
Item 2: should show **Every Other Friday**
Item 3: How much do you pay John?
  Click the drop-down list arrow next to Hourly, click **Salary**
  Enter the salary amount **28,000**
  Click **Add additional pay types**
  Click **Sick Pay** to select, click the drop-down list arrow for No Sick Policy, click **Sick Leave**
  Enter the Current balance: **40**
  Click **Vacation Pay**
  Click the drop-down list arrow for No Vacation Policy, click **Vacation**
  Enter the Current balance: **40**
  Click **Done**
Item 4: Does John have any deductions?, click the **Pen** icon

> Click the drop-down list arrow for Deduction/contribution, click **Bright Smile Insurance – Dental**
> Enter **10** as the Amount per pay period
> Enter the Annual maximum: **120**
> Click **OK**
> Click **Add a new deduction**
> Click the drop-down list arrow for Deduction/contribution, click **Good Health Insurance - Medical**
> Enter **40** as the Amount per pay period
> Enter the Annual maximum: **480**
> Click **OK**
> Item 5: No changes
> Click **Done**
> Click the **Pen** icon for Profile
> Enter his Mobile number: **650-555-2122**, for Gender click **Male**, click **Done**
> Click the **Pen** icon for Employment
>> Click the drop-down list arrow for the Not On Payroll button, click **Active**
>> Click the boxes for New Hire Report and Form I-9 to check
>> Click **Done**
> Click **<Employee list**
> Click the drop-down list arrow for Active employees, click **All employees**
> Click **Emily Platt**
> Click the **Pen** icon for Employment
> Click the drop-down list arrow for the Not On Payroll button, click **Terminated**
> - You will get a marked check box for Show in non-payroll lists.
> Enter the Hire Date of **01/02/2016**
> Tab to Termination date and enter the **Current Date**
> Enter her Birth Date of **08/03/1995**
> Click **Done**
> Click **<Employee list**
> Show **All employees**
> Review your Employee List

| | NAME | PAY RATE | PAY SCHEDULE | PAY METHOD | STATUS |
|---|---|---|---|---|---|
| EC | Catillo, Eloisa | $40,000.00/ year | Friday | Direct deposit | Active |
| JJ | Johnson, John | $28,000.00/ year | Every Other Friday | Check | Active |
| BL | Lucchini, Bill | $60,000.00/ year | Friday | Direct deposit | Active |
| KM | Masters, Kari | $18.50 / hour | Friday | Check | Active |
| EP | Platt, Emily | Missing | Every Other Friday | Check | Terminated |
| BS | Stevens, Beth | $15.00 / hour | Every Other Friday | Check | Active |

> Do not close the Test Drive Company, continue to the next section

## EMPLOYEE DETAILS REPORT—DRILL

Once you have completed the exercises for adding and editing employees, it is important to print the Employee Details report. This report gives you complete information regarding salaries and wages, tax information, deductions, and vacation/sick leave.

9

## DRILL

Continue to use the **Test Drive Company** and prepare the Employee Details report

Be sure to turn **OFF** Redesigned Reports in QuickBooks Labs
Click **Reports** on the Navigation bar, click the category **Manage Payroll**
Click **Employee Details** Report
Review the information shown for each employee

| Employee Details | | Print | | Collins Paint and Wallpaper Services | |
|---|---|---|---|---|---|
| PERSONAL INFO | PAY INFO | | | TAX INFO | |
| | Salary: | $40,000.00/Year | | SSN: | 123-45-1111 |
| | Pay By: | DD, Acct ....0000 | | Fed: | |
| | : | DD2, Acct ....0000 | | CA: | Head of Household/ 2 |
| **Eloisa Catillo** 550 Front Boulevard Menlo Park CA 94025 Hired: 01/01/2016 Born: 01/01/1980 | Deductions: | 401K 2.0% | | | |
| | | Bright Smile Insurance $40.00 | | | |
| | | Good Health Insurance $200.00 | | | |
| | Vac/Sick: | Sick Leave | | | |
| | | Vacation | | | |

**Partial Report**

Click the drop-down list arrow next to the Share button, click either **Printer Friendly** or **Export to Excel** and prepare the report as previously instructed
• If you save the report, name the document **5-Your Name Employee Details Report Ch. 9**.
After printing or exporting your report, <u>immediately</u> continue to the next section without closing the Test Drive Company

## PAY PAYROLL, EDIT, AND DELETE CHECK—DRILL

Now that you have a new payroll schedule in place, you will pay the employees who are on paid on the Every Other Friday schedule. If you make a mistake in processing the payroll, you may delete an individual check if you do so prior to printing the check.

---

**MEMO**
**DATE**: Current Date

Pay the employees on the Every Other Friday schedule—John Johnson and Beth Stevens. Enter 40 hours of regular pay and 2 hours of overtime pay for Beth Stevens.

Edit the paycheck for Beth Stevens. Change her overtime hours to 3.

Realized that you were paying Beth for the incorrect pay period. Delete the paycheck for Beth Stevens.

---

## DRILL

Continue to use the **Test Drive Company** and prepare the Every Other Friday payroll

Click **Employees** on the Navigator bar to return to the Employees List
Click the **Run Payroll** button
Select the **Every Other Friday** schedule if it is not already selected
Click **Continue**
• John Johnson and Beth Stevens will be shown.
Use the dates provided by QuickBooks Online

Enter the hours worked for Beth Stevens: Regular Pay Hrs: **40** OT Hrs: **2**
- Even though Beth is part time and works 20 hours a week. She worked overtime for 2 hours one day to help get a project completed.

Click **Preview payroll**
Click the **Pen** icon for Beth Stevens
Change her overtime hours to **3**
Click **OK**
Click **Submit Payroll**, click **Finish payroll**
- If you get a Tax payments due message, click **I'll do it later**.

Click **Paycheck List** just below the Run payroll button
Click in the check box next to Beth Stevens to select, click **Delete**

Click **Yes** on the message asking "Are you sure you want to delete the selected check?"
- Beth's check is deleted and is no longer shown.

Click the check box for John Johnson to select, click **Print**
- If you save the check, name it **6-Your Name Paycheck John Johnson**.

After printing the paycheck, close the Test Drive Company

*close*

## PAYROLL SETTINGS—DRILL

When you first subscribe to QuickBooks Online Payroll, you go through a series of screens that enable you to make selections regarding pay policies, electronic services, tax setup, deductions, and preferences. These may be edited and changed.

## *DRILL*

 Open the **Test Drive Company** and review and edit Payroll Settings

Click **Employees** on the Navigation bar
Click **Turn on Payroll**
Click the **Gear** icon, click **Payroll Settings** in the column for Your Company
- You will see the Preferences screen for payroll. It is divided into two sections Setup and Setup Overview.

- While both sections allow you to access much of the same information, the Setup Overview provides more details and choices for review and/or change.

<u>Payroll and Services</u>

The selections for Payroll and Services include choices for Payroll, Taxes, and Electronic Services. Review each of the categories within each section and make the changes indicated in the step-by-step directions.

 Use the **Test Drive Company** to review the categories for Payroll and Services and to create a new Pay Schedule

### Payroll

Click **Pay Schedules** in the Payroll and Services list of the Setup Overview section
Click the **Create** button for Pay Schedules to create an Every Other Friday pay schedule
Click the drop-down list arrow for Pay Period, click **Every Other Week**
Click the check box for: Use this schedule as the default for employees I add
- Use the dates inserted by QuickBooks Online. Your dates will not match the ones in the example.

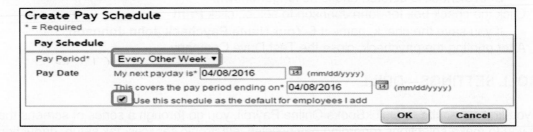

Click **OK**
- You will see a Pay Schedule Confirmation screen showing the Description: **Every Other Friday**, a list of Pay Periods and Pay Dates.

Click **OK**
- Note the addition of the new Pay Schedule.
There are no changes to Vacation and Sick Leave Policies

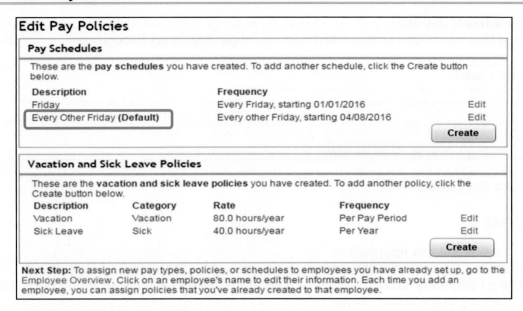

Click the back arrow button by the https URL

Click **Deductions/Contributions**
Review the Deductions/Company Contributions and Employee Garnishments
Click **Edit** next to Good Health Insurance
Delete the word **Good** from the Description

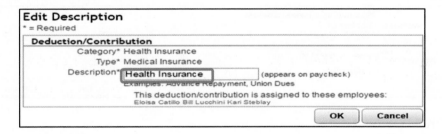

Click **OK**
Review the changes

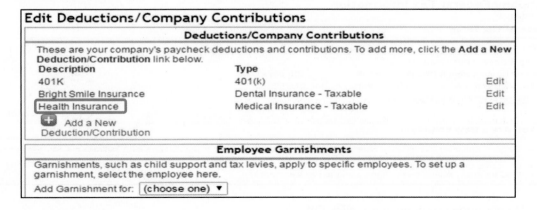

Click the **Back** arrow

Click **Direct Deposit**
Read the information provided on the screen regarding Direct Deposit

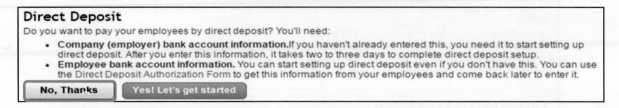

Click **No, Thanks**

**Taxes**

Click **General Tax Information**
For Company type, click the drop-down list arrow for Other, click **Sole Proprietor**
In the Filing Name section, delete the company name and enter **Your Name** (your real
    name) for the Owner Name

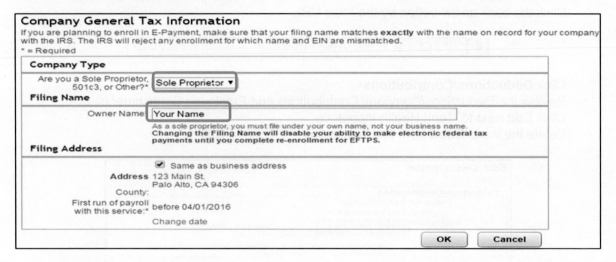

Click **OK**
Click **Federal Taxes**
Review the information presented

No changes are necessary, click **OK**
Click **State Taxes**

Review the information presented

No changes are necessary, click **OK**
Click **Federal Form Preferences**
Review the information presented

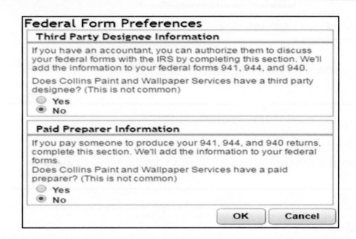

No changes are necessary, click **OK**

## Electronic Services

Click **Update Electronic Services**
Read the information on setting up E-Services

No changes are necessary, click the **Back** arrow

<u>Company and Account</u>

The selections for Company and Account include Business Information and Preferences. Review each of the categories within each section and make the changes indicated in the step-by-step directions.

 Use the **Test Drive Company** to review the categories for Company and Account

### Business Information

Click **Contact Information**
Change the First Name and Last Name to **Your Name** (your real name)
Change and confirm the Email Address: **Your QuickBooks Email** (your actual email)

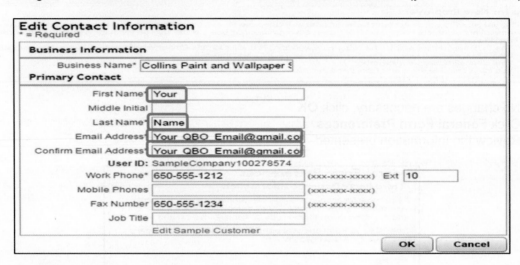

Click **OK**
Click **Work Locations**
Review the material presented, enter **Santa Clara** for the County

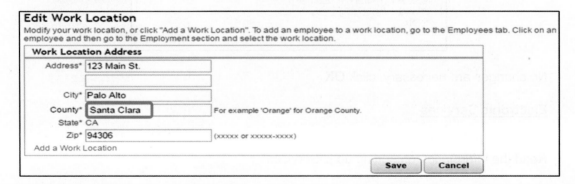

Click **Save**

### Preferences

Click **Accounting**
- The first screen suggests two ways to enter your payroll information: Preferences suggested by QBO or Customize and enter preferences yourself.

Click **Next**

Enter **Checking** as the name for Checking Account
Review the information presented, especially all of the payroll account names

Click **OK** for Accounting Preferences
Click the **Back** arrow after reviewing the Accounting Preferences Summary screen
Click **Paycheck Printing**
Read the information for printing paychecks and pay stubs

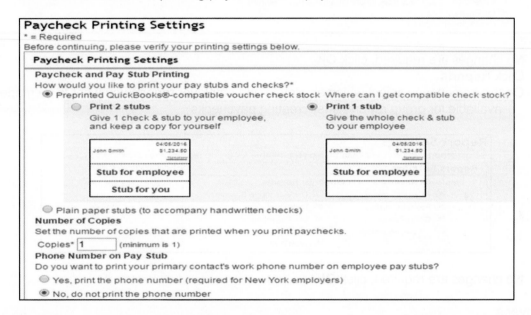

No changes are required, click **OK**
The Printer Setup screen is shown
• This is used to test the Alignment of your Preprinted QuickBooks voucher checks.
You will not test the alignment for paychecks

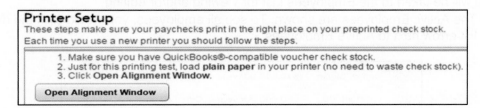

Click **OK**
Click **Form Printing**

This screen is used to select the paper to be used when printing W-2 forms

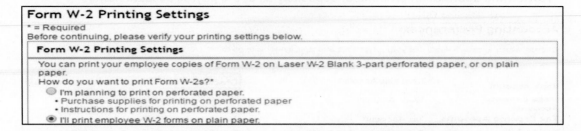

**Form W-2 Printing Settings**

\* = Required
Before continuing, please verify your printing settings below.

**Form W-2 Printing Settings**

You can print your employee copies of Form W-2 on Laser W-2 Blank 3-part perforated paper, or on plain paper.
How do you want to print Form W-2s?\*

  ○ I'm planning to print on perforated paper.
    • Purchase supplies for printing on perforated paper
    • Instructions for printing on perforated paper.
  ◉ I'll print employee W-2 forms on plain paper.

Since you plan on using plain paper, no changes are required, click **OK**

Click **Emails**

On this screen, you select what type of payroll email reminders you want to receive

**Email Preferences**

Issues regarding this payroll account are communicated via email. Reminders are used to help keep you on top of payroll deadlines. Select your preferences for receiving these emails. All fields are optional.

**Email Preferences**

**Reminder Emails**
  ☑ Payday Reminders
  Send the Payday Reminder | the day ▼ | I have to run payroll (For Direct Deposit payrolls, we also send a reminder 2 business days before the payroll has to be run).
  ☑ Tax Payment Reminders
  ☑ Form Filing Reminders

No changes are required, click **OK**

Click **Reports**

On this screen, you select which employee and employer reports you want to be made available for group reports after creating paychecks

**Report Settings**

Select reports you would like to be made available for group reports after creating paychecks.

**Report Settings**

| Employee Reports | Employer Reports |
|---|---|
| ☑ Payroll Summary | ☐ Tax and Wage Summary |
| ☑ Payroll Details | ☑ Total Cost |
| ☑ Deductions | ☑ Tax Payments |
| ☐ Employee Details | ☐ Tax Liability |
| | ☐ Total Pay |

No changes are required, click **OK**

## Employees

### Overview

Click **Employees**

You will be taken to the Employees List for viewing and/or editing

• The Active Employees are shown. To see all employees, you would click the drop-down list arrow next to Active Employees.

| EC | Catillo, Eloisa | $40,000.00/ year | Direct deposit | | Active |
|---|---|---|---|---|---|
| BL | Lucchini, Bill | $60,000.00/ year | Direct deposit | | Active |
| KS | Steblay, Kari | $18.00 / hour | Check | | Active |

No changes need to be made, click the **Back** arrow to return to Payroll Settings
Click **Time Sheets**
You are given the option to enter hours for hourly employees when creating paychecks or
having QBO copy the hours from employee time sheets

| Time Sheets | | |
|---|---|---|
| How do you want to fill in employee hours on paychecks? | | |
| ○ I'll enter hours when I create paychecks | | |
| ● Copy hours from employee time sheets | | |
| **Employee** | **Time Sheets** | **Type of Pay** |
| Kari Steblay | Enabled | Regular Pay |

No changes are required, click **OK**
Close the Test Drive Company

## ADDITIONAL TRANSACTIONS—DRILL

As with the other chapters, you will enter additional transactions now that you have completed the
chapter. In Chapter 9, however, you will continue to use the Test Drive Company to process payroll
and all related reports.

Print and/or Export to Excel as instructed within the Memos and by your professor
- If you save a document, use the same naming structure as previously instructed:
  Document number, your name, business form and number, vendor name. For example,
  29-Your Name Paycheck John Doe.

| MEMO |
|---|
| **DATE**: Current Date |
| Open the Test Drive Company, Turn on Payroll, Turn OFF Redesigned Reports in QuickBooks Labs. |
| Edit Payroll Settings: Create a Pay Schedule for Every Other Week; Use the schedule as the default. General Tax Information: Sole Proprietor; Owner: Your Name. Contact Information: Your Name; Your QBO Email Address. Work Locations: County Santa Clara. Accounting Preferences: Bank account name Checking. |
| Edit the employee: Bill Lucchini. Pay Section: Enter W-4 Form Information: Change allowances to 1. Change Pay Schedule to Every Other Friday. Profile Section: Mobil Phone 650-555-9512; Gender: Male. |
| Add a new employee: Evan Jones. Pay Section: W-4 Information: Social Security number: 100-55-2233; Home Address: 5513 Laura Drive, San Jose, CA 95124; Married, Allowances 2; California State Taxes: Married (with two or more incomes), Allowances 2. Pay: Hourly, $25 per hour; Other Pay Types: Overtime; Sick Pay: Sick Leave, Balance 0.00; Vacation Pay: Vacation, Balance 0.00. Deductions: Dental, $10 per pay period, Maximum $120; Health, $40 per pay period, Maximum $480. Use Paper Check. Profile: Home Phone: 650-555-4789; Gender: Male; Birth date: 02/02/1985. Employment: Check New Hire Report and Form I-9; Hire Date: two weeks before current date. |
| Run Payroll for Every Other Friday employees. Evan Jones worked 80 regular hours and an additional 8 hours in overtime. Bill Lucchini worked his regular amount. |
| Edit the check to Evan Jones. Change his overtime hours to 10. |
| Print Check for Evan Jones (If saved, name it **7-Your Name Paycheck Evan Jones**). Print Pay Stub for Bill Lucchini (If saved, name it **8-Your Name Pay Stub Bill Lucchini**). |

> Pay Payroll Taxes for CA PIT/SDI for the earlier of the two dates shown. (If you see more taxes, do not pay them.) Pay Electronically and use the dates provided by QBO.
>
> Print and/or export Payroll Reports: Payroll Summary for Active Employees (If saved, name it **9-Your Name Payroll Summary Ch. 9**); Employee Details (If saved, name it **10-Your Name Employee Details Ch. 9**).

## SUMMARY

In this chapter a thorough study of processing payroll, paying taxes, and preparing reports was accomplished by using the Test Drive Company. Students practiced paying the payroll, adding new employees, reinstating inactive employees, editing existing employees, deleting employees, editing paychecks, and printing paychecks and pay stubs. In addition, several payroll reports were prepared and include the Payroll Summary, Tax Liability, and Employee Details reports. Payroll settings for Payroll and Services, Company and Accounts, and Employees were reviewed and edited. Finally, additional transactions were recorded for reinforcement.

# END-OF-CHAPTER QUESTIONS

## TRUE/FALSE

ANSWER THE FOLLOWING QUESTIONS IN THE SPACE PROVIDED BEFORE THE QUESTION NUMBER.

_____ 1. You may create Payroll Schedules in Payroll Settings.

_____ 2. A sole proprietor does not use the Company Name as the Tax Filing Name.

_____ 3. A salaried employee is paid overtime.

_____ 4. The payroll plans for QuickBooks Online are updated once a year.

_____ 5. An employee may be added at any time.

_____ 6. A new employee does not have any vacation or sick pay accrued.

_____ 7. For a direct deposit check, you print a copy of the paycheck.

_____ 8. When editing a paycheck, you may change anything shown in a rectangular box.

_____ 9. All payroll reports must be printed before paying payroll taxes.

_____ 10. You activate Payroll by accessing Employees and clicking Turn on Payroll.

## MULTIPLE CHOICE

WRITE THE LETTER OF THE CORRECT ANSWER IN THE SPACE PROVIDED BEFORE THE QUESTION NUMBER.

_____ 1. Information provided for a sole proprietor in the Company General Tax Information preference includes ___.
   A. Company Type
   B. Filing Name
   C. Filing Address
   D. All of the above

_____ 2. In Payroll Settings the Work Location must include the ___ .
   A. Telephone Number
   B. Number of Employees
   C. County
   D. Owner's Home Address

_____ 3. What taxes are paid by both the employee and the employer?
   A. Social Security
   B. Federal Income Tax
   C. State Disability
   D. All of the above

9

_____ 4. The ___ report shows details for each paycheck created and includes total wages, taxes withheld, and deductions.
  A. Tax Liability
  B. Payroll Summary
  C. Employee Details
  D. Payroll Billing Summary

_____ 5. When editing an employee, you enter the phone number in the ___ section.
  A. Employment
  B. Pay
  C. Profile
  D. Personal

_____ 6. An employee's withholding allowances are entered on the ___ form.
  A. W-2
  B. W-4
  C. I-9
  D. ED-44

_____ 7. The ___ report gives you complete information regarding salary and wages, tax information, deductions, and vacation/sick leave for each employee.
  A. Employee Details
  B. Employee Obligations
  C. Paycheck List
  D. Payroll Details

_____ 8. Changes made to an employee's pay rate will be effective ___.
  A. For the Next Pay Period
  B. Immediately
  C. Next Year
  D. Next Quarter

_____ 9. The ___ is used to prevent erroneous benefit payments and to enforce child support payments.
  A. Form I-9
  B. CA PIT/SDI Form
  C. New Hire Report
  D. Employee ID

_____ 10. When you see the Review and Submit screen when processing payroll, you see data for Net Pay, Employee, Employer, and Total Payroll Cost on the ___.
  A. Title bar
  B. Payroll Budget section
  C. Button for Preview
  D. Dashboard

## FILL-IN

IN THE SPACE PROVIDED, WRITE THE ANSWER THAT MOST APPROPRIATELY COMPLETES THE SENTENCE.

1. The two Pay Rate categories used in the chapter are _____ and _____.

2. You pay click the Pay Taxes button in the _____ in order to pay taxes.

3. To verify employment eligibility status, you prepare_____.

4. If you pay CA PIT/SDI taxes _____, you do not have to print or submit a coupon.

5. Payroll Settings have three areas as part of the Setup Overview. They
   are _____, _____, _____.

## COMPUTER ASSIGNMENT

REFER TO PRINTOUTS OR USE QUICKBOOKS ONLINE AND YOUR NAME'S BEACH
BARKERS TO LOOK UP OR ENTER INFORMATION, AND THEN WRITE THE ANSWERS TO
THE FOLLOWING EXERCISES IN THE SPACE PROVIDED

1. Where do you activate payroll?                                        _____

2. Where can you create a new payroll schedule?                          _____
                                                                         _____

3. To print or export a payroll report, you click the drop-down list arrow next to
   the ___ button.                                                       _____

4. What employees appeared in the Payroll Summary report prepared in the
   Additional Transactions?                                             _____
                                                                         _____

5. In which section of the Edit Employee screen do you change an employee's
   status to Terminate?                                                  _____

6. Which report shows you complete information for salaries and wages, tax information,
   deductions, and vacation/sick leave for each employee?               _____

7. What was the Current Total Pay before taxes and deductions for Evan Jones
   after working 10 overtime hours?                                     _____

8. In Payroll Settings, where did you change the Company Type?           _____

9. To get the Net Amount, Total Hours, Taxes Withheld, Total Deductions, Total Pay, Employer
   Taxes and Contributions, and Total Cost, you prepare the ___ report.  _____

10. In the Edit Employee screen you record the employee's social security number
    on the ___ Form in the Pay section.                                 _____

9

# CHAPTER 9 CHECKLIST

The checklist below shows all of the business forms printed during training. Check each one that you printed, exported, and/or submitted.

| | |
|---|---|
| _____ 1-Paycheck Kari Steblay | _____ 6-Paycheck John Johnson |
| _____ 2-Pay Stubs: Elisa Catillo and Bill Lucchini | _____ 7-Paycheck Evan Jones |
| _____ 3-Payroll Summary Report | _____ 8-Pay Stub Bill Lucchini |
| _____ 4-Tax Liability Report | _____ 9-Payroll Summary Report |
| _____ 5-Employee Details Report | _____ 10-Employee Details Report |

# CREATE A COMPANY USING QUICKBOOKS DESKTOP

The QuickBooks Online Program contains many areas that were not explored during the training chapters of the text. The appendices will present information regarding some of these areas. In Chapter 2 a company was created by having QuickBooks Online setup a Chart of Accounts for the company's industry, then data was imported using Excel files.

Another method of company creation is to import your company information directly from QuickBooks Desktop. You may do this within the first 60 days of activating your QuickBooks Online account. In order to perform this import, you <u>must</u> have a copy of QuickBooks Desktop. Both the program and the company file must be up to date. If you do not have QuickBooks Desktop, you may download a 30-day trial version of the program one time.

You must use **Internet Explorer** as your browser in order to Import Desktop Data.

To begin an import of a company file from QuickBooks Desktop, you would use Internet Explorer as your browser and follow all of the steps presented in the first nine pages of Chapter 2 to set up your Intuit ID (email), activate QuickBooks Online, and create Your Name's Beach Barkers. When you get to the section for Purge Company Information, the steps and processes used will be different.

Steps to import your file from QuickBooks Desktop will be shown in the same manner as in the chapters with the exception that the Do button will not be used.

Since the text is written using the company that was created by importing data from Excel spreadsheets in Chapter 2, there will be some differences in the information that you see after a QuickBooks Desktop import. These items will be addressed within this appendix. This will enable you to work in QuickBooks Online using either method of importing data.

## PURGE COMPANY INFORMATION

This is where you will begin working in Appendix A to import your company file from QuickBooks Desktop.

Make sure your QuickBooks Online Plus company, Your Name's Beach Barkers, is open
On the URL of your Internet Explorer, enter **https://qbo.intuit.com/app/purgecompany**
Press **Enter**
- If your number of accounts or the number of days left are different from what is shown below, do not be concerned.

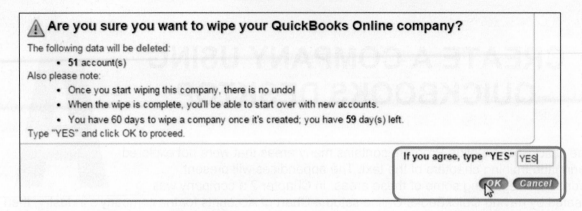

Enter the word **YES**; and then, click **OK**

Scroll through the list of businesses until you get to Miscellaneous Services, click **Pet Care Services**

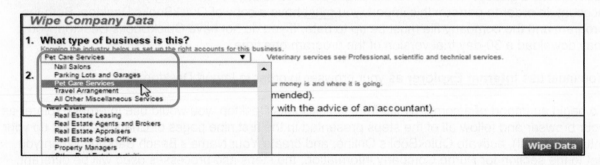

In Step 2, make sure that **Create an empty chart of accounts (select only with the advice of an accountant)** is selected

Click **Wipe Data**

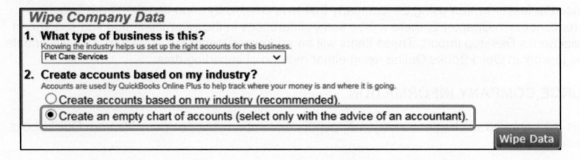

## VIEW CHART OF ACCOUNTS AND PRODUCT SERVICE LIST

Once the purge has been completed, it is important to see which accounts and products and services have been automatically created by QuickBooks Online.

To view the Chart of Accounts and the Products and Services List, click the **Gear** icon
In the column for Settings, click **Chart of Accounts**

- View the two accounts in the Chart of Accounts created by QBO. If you get a third account, Uncategorized Income-1 that is fine.

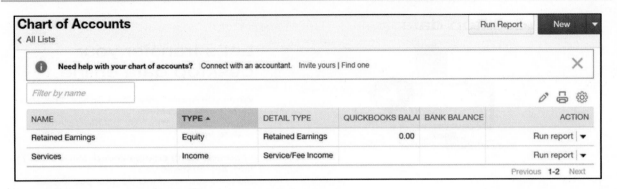

Click the **Gear** icon again
In the column for Lists, click **Products and Services**
View the two items on the list

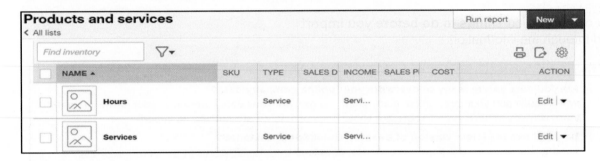

- This proves that the previous data was wiped from the company file.

## IMPORT DATA FROM QUICKBOOKS DESKTOP

Now that the company has been purged, you may import you desktop data. Most of the import process takes place in QuickBooks Desktop; however, QuickBooks Online provides information regarding the import procedures and other pertinent information.

Click the **Gear** icon
Click **Import Desktop Data** on the Tools menu

You will see the Import your desktop data screen
- At the time of this writing, the screens are correct; however, remember that QuickBooks Online is changed and updated frequently. If your screens are not an exact match to the following, do not be concerned. Read the information and perform the steps as they are listed on your screen.

## Import desktop data

# Let's transfer your desktop data online

When you import your QuickBooks data, you can run your business
anywhere, any time. You still have plenty of time to import.

Importing won't change your desktop data. In fact, any changes you
make to your desktop file after you import won't be reflected here.
Now's the time to move online!

▶ Things to do before you import
▶ Step by step instructions
▶ Things you can do after you import

Click on the section **Things to do before you import**
Read through the information

▼ Things to do before you import

- **Are you sure you're ready to overwrite your online company data?**
  When you import your desktop company data, you overwrite any data currently in your online company. If that's why you're here, great! There are some kinds of data we are not able to import.

- **Do you have the latest version of desktop QuickBooks installed?**
  For the best desktop data import experience, download the latest free trial of desktop QuickBooks or update your current desktop QuickBooks version to the latest release. Click **Help > Check for updates.**

  **Note:** We do not currently support importing company data from QuickBooks Enterprise.

- **Do you have payroll due within the next week?**
  We recommend you import after you run payroll from your desktop so you won't feel rushed.

- **Are you currently using desktop QuickBooks in multi-user mode?**
  You'll only be able to import your data if you're running desktop QuickBooks in single-user mode.

- **Is your company file located on your computer's hard drive?**
  To import your data, you'll need a local copy of your company file. If your company file is hosted on a server, make a local copy of the .QBW file and open it from your desktop before you import.

- **Have you already set up direct deposit and e-services for this online company?**
  If you want to bring your desktop company data online, import before you set up these services for your online company. If you have already set these services up and you still want to import desktop data, you'll need to cancel this company and create a new one first.

Click on the sections for **Step by step instructions**
Read the information provided

▼ Step by step instructions

**PC users**
Click **Company > Export company File to QuickBooks Online** and follow the steps on screen.

**Mac users**
Click **File > Export > To QuickBooks Online.**

**NOTE:** If you don't see the option to export your company file, you will need to update your desktop QuickBooks version. See the details under **Things to do before you import.**

We'll send you an email when we've copied and imported your data; then you can sign back in to your online company and check it out.

If you've followed the step-by-step instructions above and your import didn't work, you may be able to find the cause of the problem.

Once you read through the Step by step instructions, click **Things you can do after you import**

---

▼  Things you can do after you import

Feel at home fast, and get the most out of moving online:

- **Have you downloaded the mobile QuickBooks apps yet?**
  Take advantage of the anywhere, anytime benefit of online QuickBooks.
  Check out the Android, Apple, Windows, and Mac apps

- **Are you ready to review your online company settings and preferences?**
  Click the **Gear** icon and select **Company Settings** to get started.

- **Want to give your accountant access to your online company?**
  One of the benefits of moving online is being able to run your business when and how you want.
  Click the **Gear** icon and select **Manage Users** to begin granting others access to your company.

---

- As a note, it is important to know that there is data that does not import automatically. At the time of this writing, this includes: Payroll details, direct deposit, e-filing info; payments account info; customized sales forms and fields; online banking info and connections; memorized reports and reconcile reports; QuickBooks users and permission settings; some inventory data; and detail type for accounts.

If you do not have QuickBooks Desktop, refer to "**Things to do <u>before</u> you import**" regarding download and click "the latest free trial of desktop QuickBooks"

- At the time of this writing, QuickBooks Desktop 2015 was the trial version provided.

Click the link follow the steps shown to download and use the trial version of QuickBooks Desktop

---

# QuickBooks desktop trial links

**IMPORTANT: These links are only trials, so please don't try to register these products because it won't validate and you'll be locked out.**

If you need a QuickBooks Desktop trial to export or import into QuickBooks Online, you can download it here.

## QuickBooks Pro/Premier 2015 - 30 day trial

- **Important**: You can review the system requirements here - System Requirements for QuickBooks 2015.

  - **Note:** It can be installed, but is not supported in Windows 8/8.1 & 10.

- http://dlm2.download.intuit.com/akdlm/SBD/QuickBooks/2015/Latest/QuickBooksPremier2015.exe
- **License number:** 6685-5048-3187-661
- **Product number:** 503-153
- **Trial Validation Code:** 289835

---

Now that you have read the information screens and have QuickBooks Desktop available for use, click **Step by step instructions** again and read the steps:

- Note: The text focuses on PC users.

---

**PC users**
Click **Company > Export company File to QuickBooks Online** and follow the steps on screen.

---

Close QuickBooks Online Plus

## <u>Open and Update QuickBooks Desktop</u>

If QuickBooks is not open, do the following:
Double-click the **QuickBooks Premier** icon on your desk top

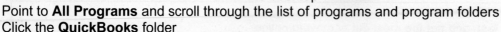

**OR**

Click the **Start** button in the lower-left of the desktop

Point to **All Programs** and scroll through the list of programs and program folders

Click the **QuickBooks** folder

- You may have to scroll down to see all of the folders on your computer.

Click **QuickBooks Premier-Accountant Edition**

When QuickBooks opens, you will get a screen that says Opening QuickBooks

- When opening QuickBooks, you may get a Warning screen showing you how many days you have left to use QuickBooks.

When QuickBooks is open the program name and year will be on the Title bar. For 2015 you see:

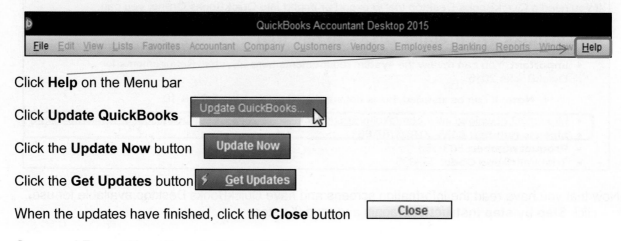

Click **Help** on the Menu bar

Click **Update QuickBooks**

Click the **Update Now** button

Click the **Get Updates** button

When the updates have finished, click the **Close** button

**Open and Export Your Name's Beach Barkers**

Click **File** on the Menu bar
Click **Open or Restore Company…**

Select **Open a company file** and then click **Next**

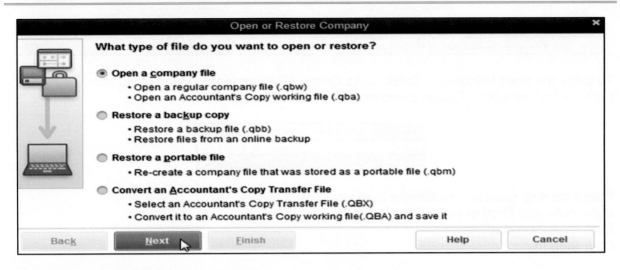

Click the drop-down list arrow for "Look in:"
Click your USB drive
- The text uses (F:)

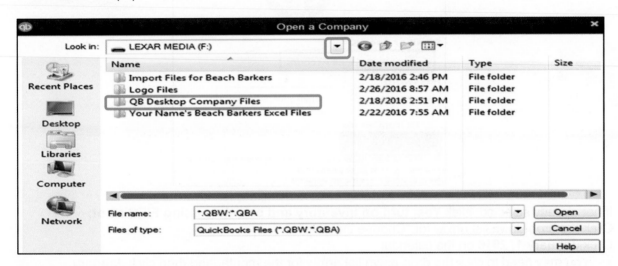

Double-click the folder **QB Desktop Beach Barker Company Files** to open the folder
Click **Your Name's Beach Barkers**, and then click **Open**

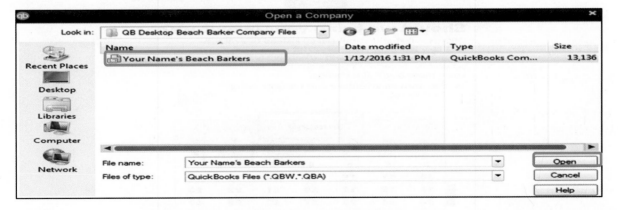

When the company is open, you will see the name on the Title bar next to the program name

To follow the steps indicated by QuickBooks Online, click **Company** on the Menu bar
Click the last menu item **Export company File to QuickBooks Online**

Follow the step given by QuickBooks Desktop
Make sure your Email or Intuit ID is correct
Enter your Password
Click **Sign In**

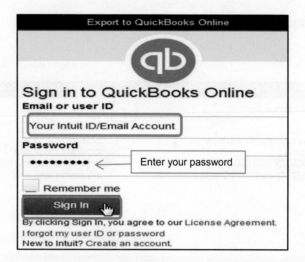

If not already selected, click **Yes, turn on inventory and calculate using FIFO as of:**
Click the drop-down list arrow for "Choose the date"
Click **January 1, 2016** on the calendar
- You may need to click the drop-down list arrow for the month, and then click **January**.

Click the **Continue** button
On the "Let's copy your company file" screen, Replace should be selected
Click the drop-down list arrow and click **Your Name Beach Barkers**
Once you select the company, you should get a "Heads up:" message

> **Heads up:** We'll copy your desktop data over, but you'll need to setup things like direct deposit, e-pay, and e-file again.

Click **Continue**
You will get a message screen telling you "Making a copy of your company file…"

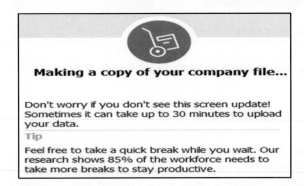

Once the copy of your company file has been created, you will another message "Looks good!"
Click the **OK, got it** button

Click **File** on the Menu bar for QuickBooks Desktop, click **Close Company**
Click the **Close** button **x** in the upper-right corner of the Title bar to close QuickBooks Desktop
After a short time, check your email account for a message from Intuit

| ☐ ☆ ☐ | donotreply | Congratulations! Your data is now available on QuickBooks Online. |

Open the email, read it, then click **Continue to account setup**

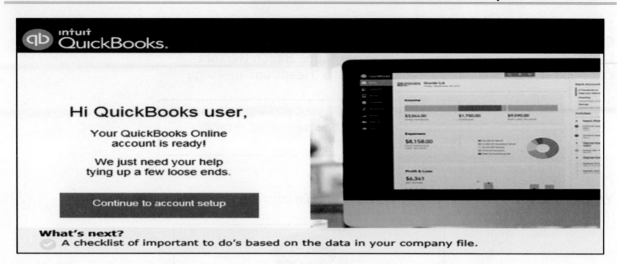

QuickBooks Online will be opened and Your Name's Beach Barkers will show as the company name.

## COMPANY SETTINGS

Once your company file has been imported, there is still work to do. It is important to verify that all of your information came through for the Chart of Accounts, Customers, Vendors, and Products and Services. In addition, Company Settings need to be verified and, if necessary, edited.

Click the **Gear** icon
In the Settings column, click **Company Settings**
- At the time of this writing, the Educational Trial Version of QuickBooks Online shows the column name as Settings; however, the Test Drive Company had been changed to show Account & Settings and included a tab called Billing & Subscription. If Intuit changes the Trial Version to agree with the Test Drive Company, please refer to Chapter 2 to see the different screens.

Click the **Pen** icon for "Company name"
Change the words "Your Name's" to your actual first and last names, repeat for the "Legal name"
- For example, Joe Smith would appear as:

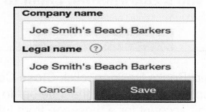

Click the **Save** button
Because we will use this company to perform the work throughout the text, it is important that it matches the company created in Chapter 2 as much as possible
- You may refer to Chapter 2 for more detailed instructions to change settings. Just remember that the changes in Chapter 2 will differ from those required in this appendix.

Additional changes to settings may include:
   **Company**:
      Categories: Track classes change to **Off**—click the **Pen** icon, click the check box for Track classes, click **Save**

**Sales**:

Sales form content: Preferred delivery method **None**, Custom fields **Off**—click the Internal check boxes to remove the checks, Discount **On**, click **Save**

Statements: Show aging table at bottom of statement **Off**, then click the **Save** button

| Customize | Customize the way forms look to your customers | Customize look and feel | |
|---|---|---|---|
| **Sales form content** | Preferred invoice terms | **Net 30** | |
| | Preferred delivery method | None | |
| | Shipping | Off | |
| | Custom fields | Off | |
| | Custom transaction numbers | Off | |
| | Service date | Off | |
| | Discount | On | |
| | Deposit | Off | |
| **Products and services** | Show Product/Service column on sales forms | On | |
| | Track quantity and price/rate | On | |
| | Track quantity on hand | On | |
| **Messages** | Default email message sent with sales forms | | |
| | Default message shown on sales forms | | |
| **Online delivery** | Email options for sales forms | | |
| **Statements** | Show aging table at bottom of statement | Off | |

**Expenses**:

Bills and Expenses: Remove the check from Markup, then click the check box for "Track billable expenses and items as income" to select, then the click **Save** button

| | | |
|---|---|---|
| ✓ Make expenses and items billable ⑦ | | **On** |
| ☐ Markup with a default rate of ____ % ⑦ | | |
| ✓ Track billable expenses and items as income ⑦ | | |

Purchase Orders **Off**, then click the **Save** button

| Bills and expenses | Show Items table on expense and purchase forms | On | |
|---|---|---|---|
| | Track expenses and items by customer | On | |
| | Make expenses and items billable | On | |
| | Default bill payment terms | Net 30 | |
| Purchase orders | Use purchase orders | Off | |

**Advanced**:
 Automation: Pre-fill forms with previously entered content **On**, Automatically apply credits **On**, Copy estimates to invoices **Off**, Automatically apply bill payments **On**, click the **Save** button
 Time Tracking: Add Service field to timesheets **Off**, then click the **Save** button

| Accounting | First month of fiscal year | January | |
|---|---|---|---|
| | First month of income tax year | Same as fiscal year | |
| | Close the books | Off | |
| Chart of accounts | Enable account numbers | Off | |
| | Discount account | Discounts given | |
| | Billable expense income account | Billable Expense Income | |
| Automation | Pre-fill forms with previously entered content | On | |
| | Automatically apply credits | On | |
| | Automatically invoice unbilled activity | Off | |
| | Copy estimates to invoices | Off | |
| | Automatically apply bill payments | On | |
| Time tracking | Add Service field to timesheets | Off | |
| | Add Customer field to timesheets | On | |
| Currency | Multicurrency | Off | |
| Other preferences | Date format | MM/dd/yyyy | |
| | Number format | 123,456.00 | |
| | Warn if duplicate check number is used | On | |
| | Warn if duplicate bill number is used | Off | |
| | Sign me out if inactive for | 1 hour | |

Click the **Done** button at the bottom of the Settings screen

## CUSTOMERS LIST

As you open each customer, you will find that the information for their name and address transferred correctly. It is important to check the Payment and billing information for each customer as well.

Edit Customers List

Click **Customers** on the Navigation Bar (on the left-side of the screen)
Point to **Anderson, Dori**
When you see the name underlined, click the left-mouse button

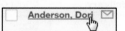

• Dori's account information will be shown.
Click the **Edit** button

Click the **Payment and billing** tab

Click the drop-down list arrow for "Preferred delivery method"
Click **None**

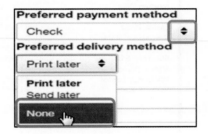

- The Opening balance was entered when you imported the Customers List but will not be shown in Dori's Customer Information screen. The "as of" date will show the current date. Do not change either of these.

View the changes, then click the **Save** button

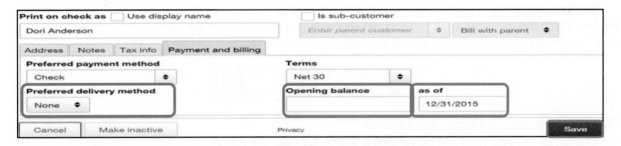

To display the list of Customer names and balances, click the [→☞] next to Dori Anderson
- Notice that the Opening Balance is shown for each customer.

Click **Larry Bailey** and edit his account following the steps shown for Dori Anderson
- Remember, you will see his $2,500 Opening Balance in the list but <u>not</u> in the Payment and Billing information in his Customer Information.

Continue to edit all of the other customers by following the steps shown for Dori Anderson

When finished editing the Customers List, click **Customers** on the Navigation bar, then use the following instructions to print and/or export the Customers List

### Print and/or Export Customers List

Follow the steps listed below to print or export the Customers List
To print a copy of the Customers List, click the **Printer** icon
Make the appropriate selections on the Print menu:

    Destination: should be the printer you will be using
    Pages: All
    Copies: 1
    Layout: Portrait
    Color: Black and white
    Options: Two-sided if available for your printer

| Customer | Phone | Open Balance |
| --- | --- | --- |
| Anderson, Dori | 213-555-7091 | $2,500.00 |
| Bailey, Larry | 818-555-2356 | $2,500.00 |
| Clark, Bunni | 310-555-7961 | $3,500.00 |
| Evans, Keith | 310-555-6314 | $0.00 |
| Gilbert, Oscar | 310-555-8763 | $500.00 |
| Gucci, Gloria | 310-555-9875 | $0.00 |
| Montez, Annabelle | 310-555-8015 | $800.00 |
| Norbert, Viv | 310-555-8651 | $2,900.00 |
| Phillips, Eric | 310-555-1275 | $1,500.00 |
| Quint, Brad | 310-555-9642 | $1,800.00 |
| Rodriquez, Ricardo | 213-555-5421 | $900.00 |
| Stark, Colleen | 310-555-6482 | $3,200.00 |
| Summer, Matthew | 213-555-2594 | $150.00 |
| Vines, Pamela | 310-555-1354 | $750.00 |
| Williams, Taylor | 310-555-8042 | $3,650.00 |
| Wilson, Katie | 213-555-7908 | $2,850.00 |

Click **Print**
- You will see the Customer names, Phone numbers, and Open Balance amounts.
- If the Customer names appear in a new Tab in your browser, close the Tab by clicking the **x** on the Tab.

To export the list to Excel, click the **Export to Excel** icon
Using Google Chrome, you will see at the bottom of your window

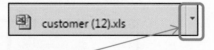

Click the drop-down list arrow for customer
- Customer (12).xls may not be an exact match for your file name.

Click **Open**

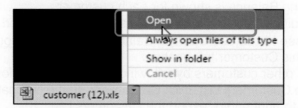

You will see the Customers List in Excel

- The file may open in Protected View. If your file is shown in Protected View, it cannot be saved, click **Enable Editing**.
- In order to see the information in full, you may have to widen the columns in Excel. Do this by pointing between columns until you get ⊞ D ↔ E ⊞ then double-click or drag to the right.

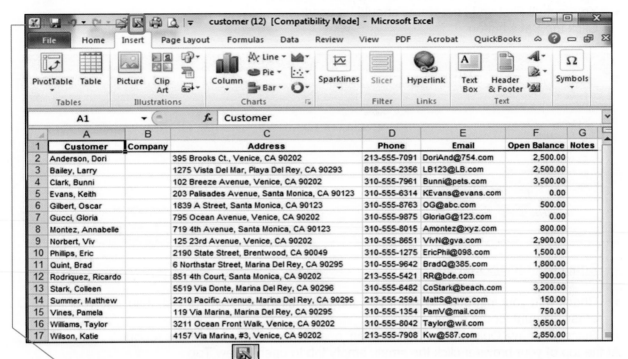

Click the **Save As** button in Excel
Click the location of your USB drive
- F: is the location in this illustration.

Right click in the open pane below QB Desktop Company Files
Point to **New,** then click **Folder**

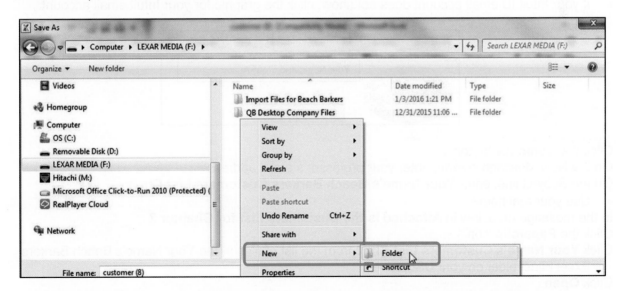

Type **Your Name's Beach Barkers Excel Files** as the name of the folder, press **Enter**
- Your actual First and Last Name should be used rather than "Your Name."

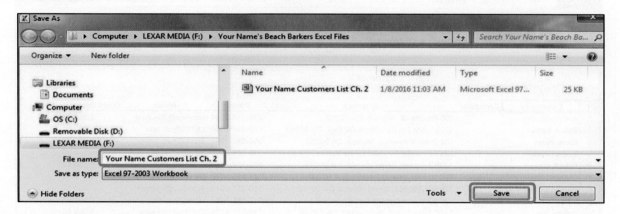

Double-click the folder to open it
Click in the text box for **File name**
Enter **Your Name Customers List Ch. 2** as the file name
- Your actual First and Last Name should be used.

Click the **Save** button

## Email Customers List

- Check with your instructor to see if you should email the Customers List. If so, use your Intuit ID email account for the email.
- Since you have QuickBooks Online open, open a new Tab to email this report.

At the top of your browser click the small, empty tab to open a new Tab

Type **gmail.com** in the URL on the new tab, press **Enter**
- If your Intuit ID email account does not show, click the graphic for your Intuit email account.

Click the **Compose** button
On the New Message screen, enter your professor's email address
On the Subject line, enter **Your Name's Beach Barkers Customers List Ch. 2**
- Use your real name.

In the message area, key in **Attached is the Customers List for Chapter 2**
Click the **Paperclip** icon
Click **Your Name's Customers List Ch. 2** from the list of files in the Your Name's Beach Barkers Excel Files folder on your USB drive
Click **Open**
When the file has been attached, click the **Send** button

- If your instructor wants you to submit your work in batches, add all of the file names in your message. Click the paperclip icon and select each file to be attached. When all the files have been attached, click **Send**.

Close your email account

## VENDORS LIST

Click **Vendors** on the Navigation Bar
Point to **Beach Bank**
When you see the name underlined, click the left-mouse button
- Account information for Beach Bank will be shown.
Click the **Edit** button

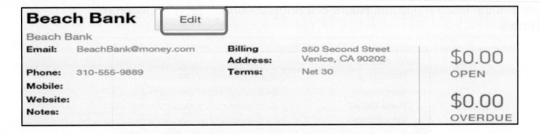

View the Vendor Information for Beach Bank

All of the information imported correctly and completely
Click the **Save** button

Refer to the instructions given for the Customers List to print, and/or export, and submit Your
Name's Beach Barkers Vendors List Ch. 2.

## PRODUCTS AND SERVICES LIST

As with Customers and Vendors, some items in the Products and Services List may need to be
edited, made inactive, or added after the QuickBooks Company File has been imported.

Click the **Gear** icon
Click **Products and Services** in the List Column
Scroll through the list to see all of the products and services you will be selling
- Note: Chapters 3-5 focus on Services and Chapters 6-8 will include both services and inventory
  (products) items.
- As you scroll through the list, you will not see the Service Item "Hours." However, when you try
  to use Hours in a transaction, it shows as part of the Products and Services List; but
  QuickBooks Online will <u>not</u> let you save the business form when you use the item Hours. As a
  result, you will create a new service item Hours-1.
- In the chapters, if you are instructed to use the Service Item "Hours" always use "Hours-1."
Click the **New** button at the top of the Products and Services List
Click **Service** for the type of item
Enter **Hours-1** for the "Name"
Click the drop-down list arrow for "Income account"
- Note that the Income account Hours is a Sub-account of Services Income.
Click **Hours**

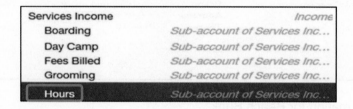

Click **Save and Close**
Scroll through the Products and Services List and note that Hours-1 is now a Service Item
- During the import from QuickBooks Desktop, a Service Item named
  PmntDiscount_Uncategorized Income was added by QuickBooks Online. This item will not be
  used at this time so it needs to be made Inactive.
Click the drop-down list arrow for "PmntDiscount_Uncategorized Income"
Click **Make inactive**

Click **Yes** on the warning screen "Are you sure you want to make PmntDiscount_Uncategorized
Income inactive?"
Print, and/or export, and submit Your Name's Beach Barkers Products and Services List Ch. 2 as
previously instructed
- At the time of this writing, Hours and Hours-1 both show up in the Excel document but not in the
  printed document.

## CHART OF ACCOUNTS

As you scroll through the Chart of Accounts, you will find that a great number of accounts need to be edited. When you import a company from QuickBooks Desktop, the Detail Type is not imported. This necessitates editing the Detail Type for the majority of the accounts.

<u>Add, Rename and Delete Accounts</u>

Click **Transactions** on the Navigation Bar
Click **Chart of Accounts**
Scroll through the Chart of Accounts and look at the accounts that were imported
The account Undeposited Funds needs to be added
Click the **New** button at the top of the Chart of Accounts
Click the drop-down list arrow for "Category Type"
Click **Other Current Assets**
Scroll through "Detail Type"
Click **Undeposited Funds**
The name "Undeposited Funds" is entered by QuickBooks Online
Click **Save and Close**

Verify the new account Undeposited Funds, then continue scrolling through the Chart of Accounts
- You will see several liability accounts added by QuickBooks for Sales Tax Payable and State Board of Equalization Payable. Disregard the accounts at this time. They will be discussed when you set up Sales Taxes in Chapter 6.

Continue to scroll through the accounts until you get to Opening Balance Equity
- When you see Opening Balance Equity, note the 142,362.50 for the QuickBooks balance. As you enter opening balances for the asset and liability accounts, the amounts are also entered into this equity account. Remember, you must have a debit and a credit for each transaction. If you debit the asset for the amount of the opening balance, the Opening Balance Equity account is credited. For a liability, Opening Balance Equity is debited and the liability is credited.
- Remember, Assets = Liabilities + Owner's Equity.

Click **View register** for Opening Balance Equity
Scroll through the register until you see the entry that says "Journal" with the amount of $8,000.00
 Point to **–Split–** on this transaction

- The two accounts used and the amounts are shown. Equipment:Original Cost $8,000.00 and Opening Balance Equity -$8,000.00.

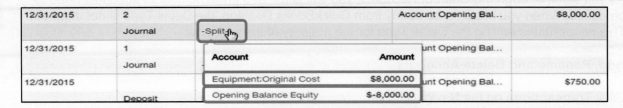

- QuickBooks Online does not show columns for Debits and Credits. Instead, columns are named Increase and Decrease and the transactions are shown based on the entry's effect on the account. In this transaction, the amount of the asset Equipment was increased and the Opening Balance Equity account was also increased. Both accounts are increased because the value of the asset (something you own) increases the value of equity.

Click **Back to Chart of Accounts**

Rename **Opening Balance Equity** to **Your Name, Capital**
Click the drop-down list arrow for Opening Balance Equity, click **Edit**
Delete **Opening Balance Equity** from the Name
Enter **Your Name, Capital**, click **Save and Close**

- Use your actual first and last name.

| Your Name, Capital | Equity | Opening B... | 142,362.50 |
|---|---|---|---|

Rename "Owners Equity" to **Retained Earnings**

- If you get a Please Confirm message: "That name is already being used. Would you like to merge the two?" click **Yes**. The account may not show in the Chart of Accounts, but it is used and shown on the Balance Sheet.
- "Services Income" is named **Services** in Chapter 2. When you try to change the name, QuickBooks Online will not let you. Simply use Services Income rather than Services as you complete the Chapters.

Rename "Discounts given" to **Sales Discounts**, click **Is sub-account** to mark, click **Services Income**

- Note the Detail Type is Discounts/Refunds Given. Do not change this.

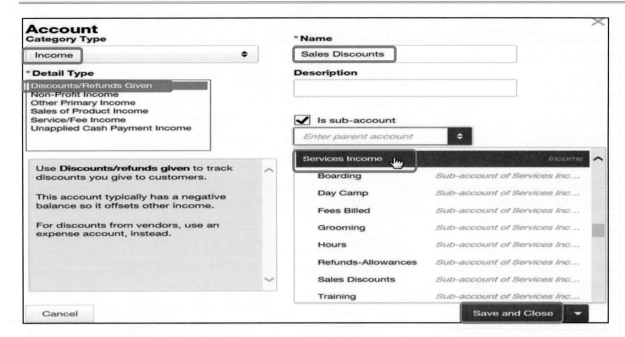

Click **Save & Close**
You do not need both Billable Expense Income and Markup accounts
- QuickBooks Online will not let you delete Markup. To work around this, you will change the name for Markup and then merge the account with Billable Expense Income.

Change the name of "Markup" to **Billable Expense Income** following steps provided above
Click **Save and Close**
You will get a "Please Confirm" message asking "Would you like to merge the two?" click **Yes**

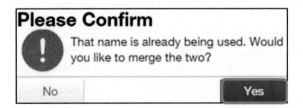

Rename "Insurance Expense" to **Insurance**
Scroll through the accounts until you get to Uncategorized Expense and Uncategorized Expenses
Rename "Uncategorized Expense" to **Uncategorized Expenses**, then Save and Merge the two
    accounts, then edit the merged account name to Uncategorized Expense

## Edit Accounts

Since Detail Type is not part of QuickBooks Desktop, many imported accounts will need to have the correct Detail Type assigned.

Edit and assign Detail Type to the following accounts using the instructions that appear after the chart:
- If you have an account that is not in the chart, it means the account does not need to be edited.

| Account | Type | Detail Type |
|---|---|---|
| Prepaid Insurance | Other Current Assets | Prepaid Expenses |
| Supplies | Other Current Assets | Prepaid Expenses |
| Cleaning Supplies | Other Current Assets | Prepaid Expenses |
| Kennel Supplies | Other Current Assets | Prepaid Expenses |
| Office Supplies | Other Current Assets | Prepaid Expenses |
| Sales Supplies | Other Current Assets | Prepaid Expenses |
| Equipment | Fixed Assets | Machinery & Equipment |
| Equipment:Depreciation | Fixed Assets | Accumulated Depreciation |
| Equipment:Original Cost | Fixed Assets | Machinery & Equipment |
| Furniture & Fixtures | Fixed Assets | Furniture & Fixtures |
| Furniture & Fixtures:Depreciation | Fixed Assets | Accumulated Depreciation |
| Furniture & Fixtures:Original Cost | Fixed Assets | Furniture & Fixtures |
| Kennel Equipment | Fixed Assets | Machinery & Equipment |
| Kennel Equipment:Depreciation | Fixed Assets | Accumulated Depreciation |
| Kennel Equipment:Original Cost | Fixed Assets | Machinery & Equipment |
| Vehicles | Fixed Assets | Vehicles |
| Vehicles:Depreciation | Fixed Assets | Accumulated Depreciation |
| Vehicles:Original Cost | Fixed Assets | Vehicles |
| Loans Payable | Long Term Liabilities | Notes Payable |
| Equipment Loan | Long Term Liabilities | Notes Payable |
| Furniture & Fixtures Loan | Long Term Liabilities | Notes Payable |
| Advertising | Expenses | Advertising/Promotional |
| Automobile Expense | Expenses | Auto |
| Bank Charges | Expenses | Bank Charges |
| Depreciation Expense | Other Expense | Depreciation |
| Dues & Subscriptions | Expenses | Dues & subscriptions |
| Equipment Rental | Expenses | Equipment Rental |
| Freight & Delivery | Expenses | Shipping, Freight & Delivery |
| Insurance | Expenses | Insurance |
| Insurance-Disability | Expenses | Insurance |
| Insurance-Liability | Expenses | Insurance |
| Interest Expense | Expenses | Interest Paid |
| Legal & Professional Fees | Expenses | Legal & Professional Fees |
| License Expense | Expenses | Taxes Paid |
| Office Expenses | Expenses | Office/General Administrative Expenses |
| Other General and Admin Expenses | Expenses | Office/General Administrative Expenses |
| Promotional | Expenses | Advertising/Promotional |
| Rent or Lease | Expenses | Rent or Lease of Buildings |
| Repair & Maintenance | Expenses | Repair & Maintenance |
| Shipping & Delivery | Expenses | Shipping, Freight & Delivery |

| Stationery & Printing | Expenses | Office/General Administrative Expenses |
|---|---|---|
| Supplies Expense | Expenses | Supplies & Materials |
| Cleaning Supplies Expense | Expenses | Supplies & Materials |
| Kennel Supplies Expense | Expenses | Supplies & Materials |
| Office Supplies Expense | Expenses | Supplies & Materials |
| Sales Supplies Expense | Expenses | Supplies & Materials |
| Taxes & Licenses | Expenses | Taxes Paid |
| Telephone Expense | Expenses | Utilities |
| Utilities | Expenses | Utilities |
| Interest Earned | Other Income | Interest Earned |

Click the drop-down list arrow for "Prepaid Insurance"
Click **Edit**

| Prepaid Insurance | Other Current Assets | Other Current Assets | 1,200.00 | | View register ▾ |
|---|---|---|---|---|---|
| | | | | | Edit |

Scroll through the column for "Detail Type"
Click **Prepaid Expenses**, then click **Save & Close**

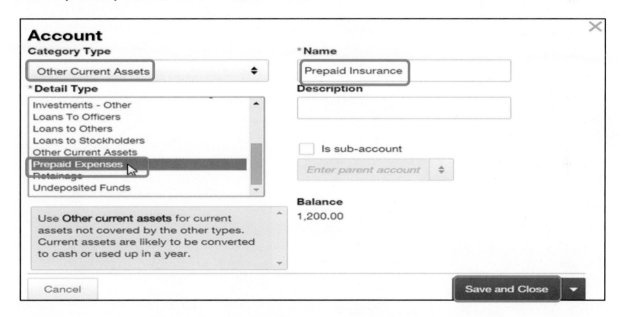

Click **Yes** on the warning screen "Changing the type or detail type…"

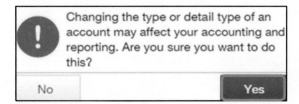

Repeat the steps for all of the accounts listed in the chart
Print, export, and/or submit as previously instructed

Return to Chapter 2 and resume work in the Reports section

- There will be some differences in the reports: (Remember: Report Dates are for **12/31/15**).
- 

**Account Listing**: Appendix A will show the three liability accounts: Sales Tax Payable, State Board of Equalization Payable, and State Board of Equalization Payable:Sales Tax Payable.

**Trial Balance**: Chapter 2 shows Services Credit for $27,500.00 and Appendix A Shows Uncategorized Income Credit for $27,500.00. Chapter 2 shows Miscellaneous Debit for $5,300.00 and Appendix A shows Uncategorized Expense Debit for $5,300.00. In a report for January, both Chapter 2 and Appendix A will not show the above. Instead the total amount of $22,200.00 (27,500.00 – 5,300.00 = 22,200.00) will be shown as a Credit in Retained Earnings.

**Journal**: Entries will be in a different order.

**Profit and Loss**: Chapter 2 shows Services $27,500.00 and Appendix A Shows Uncategorized Income $27,500. Chapter 2 shows Miscellaneous $5,300.00 and Appendix A shows Uncategorized Expense $5,300.00.

**Balance Sheet**: No differences are found.

# GO MOBILE

This appendix will explore the QuickBooks Online Mobile App and is written for you to read. If you wish to follow the steps and examples shown, feel free to do so; however, the appendix is designed as an enhancement rather than actual training. If you actually complete the transactions shown in this appendix for illustration purposes, you will need to remember to delete them at the end of the appendix. If Your Name's Beach Barkers is used for any additional or supplemental assignments, your totals will not match if you keep the transactions as part of Your Name's Beach Barkers.

As part of your QuickBooks Online subscription, you may download the QuickBooks Online Mobile App. It may be used on an iPhone, iPad, Android phone, or Android tablet free of charge. With the App, you may view information, record transactions, receive payments, and prepare Profit & Loss and Balance Sheet reports right on your phone or tablet.

To download the app, you must have an active subscription for QuickBooks Online. Then, depending on your device, you will either download the Free App directly from the Apple Store or from Google Play.

## INSTALL

Open your Web browser and enter **quickbooks.intuit.com/mobile** in the URL, press **Enter**. Scroll through the Web page until you see the area for downloading the App.

Depending on your type of device, tap the icon for either the Apple App Store or the Google Play Store.

<u>Apple Store:</u>

In order to install your Apple device, you must have an ITunes account. If you do not, you must create one before you can download the App.

Tap **View in iTunes**, then tap the **Download Now** button, and complete the installation

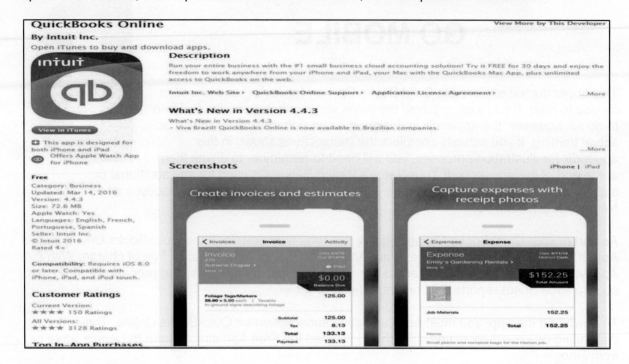

## Google Play

As with Apple, you must have a Google Play account in order to download the App. If you do not, you must create one before you can download the App.

Tap **Install**, and then continue the installation following the prompts provided by Google Play

Once the App is installed, you are ready to use QuickBooks Online Mobile.

## EXPLORE

Please note that the procedures and screens shown are from an Android device. The Apple screens are similar. However, some of the buttons are in different locations and in some instances, you will tap Save rather than Done.

Once the App has been installed, you log in with your QuickBooks Online User Name and Password. When the App is opened, a list of your recent activities will be on the screen. The activities displayed include Invoices, Expenses, Sales Receipts, and Payments. Since you entered transactions for January and February in the chapters, all unpaid invoices will be shown as overdue.

Tap the **Menu** icon ▤ to display the Navigation bar
- The Navigation bar shows you areas that may be accessed. This includes:
  Activities you just viewed.
  Notes and/or photos may be added for customers.
  Products & Services List, Customers List, Vendors List, and Chart of Accounts are available.
    (New items, customers, vendors, and accounts may be added to the lists as well.)
  By tapping Banking, bank and credit card transactions may be imported.
  Expenses, Estimates, Invoices, Sales Receipts, and Payments can be selected to see existing
    transactions and to record new ones.
  Profit & Loss and Balance Sheet reports can be prepared.

Tap **Activity** on the Navigation bar to return to the list of recent activities

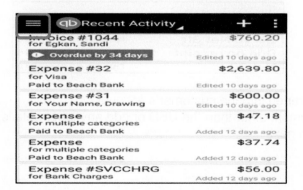

## CUSTOMERS, INVOICES, SALES RECEIPTS, AND PAYMENTS

Using QuickBooks Mobile, you can add and edit customers, prepare invoices and sales receipts, and receive customer payments while using your mobile phone or tablet.

### Add a New Customer

To add a new customer, tap the **Plus** sign at the top of the Recent Activity screen. Tap **Customer** on the Create New screen

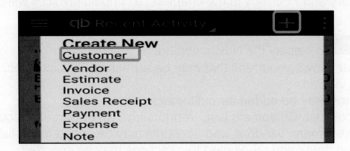

Enter the Customer information for **Donna Nguyen**

When you are ready to add Terms, tap the drop-down list arrow 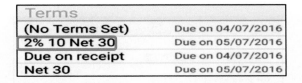 for Terms
Tap the Terms you want to select for the customer
*   Your device will use the current date and will show you the due dates for each of the terms.

| Terms | |
|---|---|
| (No Terms Set) | Due on 04/07/2016 |
| 2% 10 Net 30 | Due on 05/07/2016 |
| Due on receipt | Due on 04/07/2016 |
| Net 30 | Due on 05/07/2016 |

*   The Terms will be inserted into the customer's account.
If you wish to accept payment other than the USD or add any other details, you will select and/or enter that information next

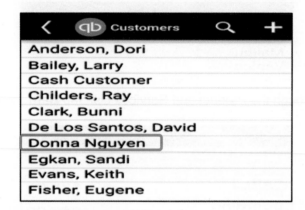

When all information for the new customer has been entered, tap **Done**

## View Customer's Account

Once a customer has been added, you may view the customer's account by tapping the Navigation bar and then tapping **Customers**. Scroll through the Customer's List and view all of the customers used during training. Notice that the new customer, Donna Nguyen, has been added.

Tap **Donna Nguyen** in the Customers List, and tap **Details** to see her account information

## Create an Invoice

At the top of Donna Nguyen's Register, tap the **Plus** icon and then tap **Create Invoice**

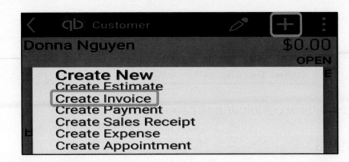

- Her Name and the Terms are entered automatically.

On the Invoice, tap the drop-down list arrow for Location, tap **Malibu**

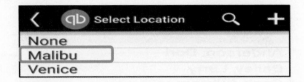

Tap **+ Add Item**, scroll through the Product and Services List, tap **Bath** then tap **Add**

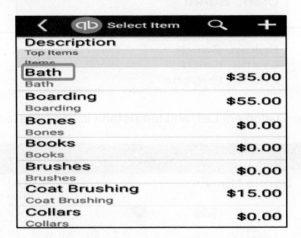

- QuickBooks Online Mobile shows the Quantity of 1 and the price and amount of 35.
- Since Bath is a service item, taxable is not selected.

Click the drop-down list arrow for Class, click **Dog Care**

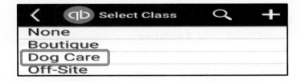

- You will see the completed information for Bath.

To add it to the invoice, tap **Add**

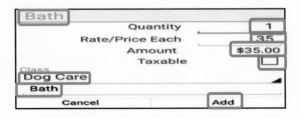

- Bath has been added to the invoice for Donna Nguyen.

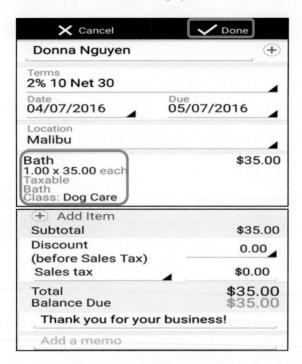

Tap **Done**, when you see the QuickBooks Online Mobile invoice on your screen, tap **More**
- This will display the Invoice number, Terms, and Location.

To preview the printed invoice, tap the ⠿ at the top of the Invoice, tap **Preview**
- Your Preview looks just like the Invoices you prepared in QuickBooks Online.

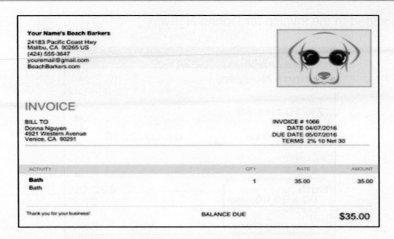

When finished previewing the Invoice, tap the **Back** arrow, tap the **Back** arrow again to exit the
   invoice
Tap the **Menu** icon to return to the Navigation bar

Sales Receipt

As you know from your training in QuickBooks Online, the entries for a Sales Receipt are very
similar to an Invoice.

On the Navigation bar, tap **Sales Receipts**, tap the **Plus** icon, and enter the information for a sales
   receipt
• The invoice was prepared for a service item without sales tax. A product/inventory item is
   charged sales tax.
To sell a product that is taxed, you tap the drop-down list arrow for Sales Tax, and tap **California**

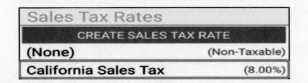

The following screen shot shows you the information for a Sales Receipt to Cash Customer.
**Cash Customer** used **Check 2341** to purchase a **Book** for **$25.99** plus **Tax** and pay for **one** day of
   **Day Camp**
When the Sales Receipt is prepared, the **Location** is selected, the Class of **Boutique** is selected
   for Books and the Class of **Dog Care** is selected for Day Camp.
• View the completed Sales Receipt.

- As in QuickBooks Online, clicking the **Pen** icon allows you to Edit. If you wanted to edit the Sales Receipt, you would click the Pen icon at the top of the receipt and make the changes.

When finished preparing the Sales Receipt, tap the **Back** arrow, tap the **Menu** icon to return to the Navigation bar

## Receive Payments

When you receive a payment without a discount from a customer on account, you select Payments and record the payment receipt in much the same way as QuickBooks Online. When the customer takes a discount on the invoice, the amount of the discount needs to be entered on the invoice prior to payment—just like QuickBooks Online.

To illustrate the discount, tap **Invoices** on the Navigation bar
Tap the invoice being paid
- Donna Nguyen in the example.

Tap the **Pen** icon; tap the drop-down list arrow for **Discount**
Enter the discount percentage **2** for Price; tap the check box for **Is Percentage?** to select, tap **Done**

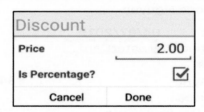

- QuickBooks Online Mobile calculates the amount of the discount and enters it in the Invoice.

Tap **Done** after reviewing the information for the discount
- When you return to the Invoice, notice that the balance is $34.30.

With the invoice showing on the screen, tap ▤ in the title bar for the invoice, then tap **Receive Payment**

The invoice is being paid with a MasterCard, tap the drop-down arrow for Method, and tap **MasterCard**

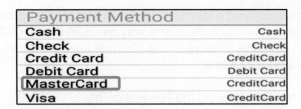

- Once the Method of payment has been selected, review the amount and other information.

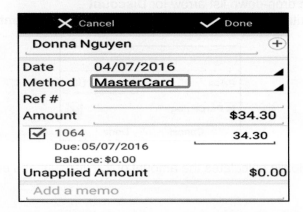

When finished, tap **Done**
Return to the invoice via Donna Nguyen's account in the Customer List
- You will see the Paid Invoice. Notice it is now green rather than blue and is marked PAID.

## EXPENSES

While you cannot record or pay bills in QuickBooks Online Mobile, you may record and pay expenses directly from your phone or tablet.

To illustrate, you went to **Bark City Toys** and purchased some Dog Toys for **$75** specifically for **Ray Childers**. You used the company's **Visa** to pay for the merchandise, the account used is **Cost of Goods Sold**, and the Class is **Boutique**. There is a line for "Anything you need to remember?" which contains the note: **Bought Toys for Customer**.

- Look at the top of the Expense, you will see a Camera icon.
Tap the **Camera** icon, select the **source**, take a **picture** of the receipt, and either tap **Discard** or **Save**

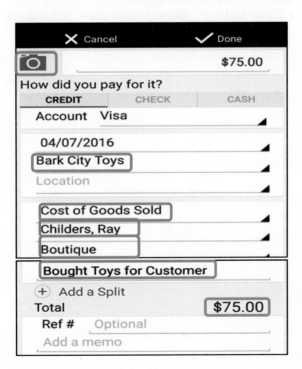

- After tapping **Save**, a picture of the receipt is shown in place of the camera icon.

## REPORTS

When you tap the Navigation bar and scroll through the selections, you will find Profit & Loss and Balance Sheet reports. Tapping on either of these reports will open the report for the current period. You may select a different date range including this Month, Quarter, or Year to Date; Last Month, Quarter, or Year; or Custom where you enter your own date.

<u>Profit & Loss</u>

To prepare the Profit & Loss report, tap **Profit & Loss** on the Navigation bar. The report will be shown using the default setting for This Year to Date. If you wish to change the setting, tap [icon] at the top of the report.

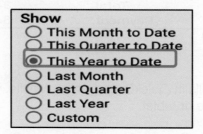

**Tap This Year to Date**

- The report will appear on the screen. As you look at the report, note that the amount of Net Income has changed from the amount you saw in Chapter 8.
- This report includes the amounts for the transactions entered in this appendix.
- As usual, the Profit & Loss report calculates the Net Income:
  Add revenue to determine the Total Income.
  Total Income - Cost of Goods Sold = Gross Profit.
  Gross Profit - Total Expenses = Net Operating Income.
  Net Operating Income + Other Income - Other Expenses = Net Income.

B

### Profit & Loss
### Jan 01, 2016 - Apr 10, 2016

**$14,759.49**
INCOME

Jan 01, 2016 - Apr 10, 2016

**$10,280.89**
EXPENSES

NET INCOME

**$4,478.60**

| INCOME | |
|---|---|
| Sales of Product Inc... | 2,526.49 |
| Services | 0.0 |
| Boarding | 2,420.00 |
| Day Camp | 1,590.00 |
| Grooming | 1,395.00 |
| House Calls | 375.00 |
| Sales Discounts | -52.50 |
| Training | 5,025.00 |
| Transportation | 1,225.00 |
| **Total Services** | **$11,977.50** |
| **Total Income** | **$14,503.99** |

| COST OF GOODS SOLD | |
|---|---|
| Cost of Goods Sold | 811.00 |
| Merchandise Disco... | -27.50 |
| **Total Cost of Goods...** | **$783.50** |
| Inventory Shrinkage | 90.00 |
| **Total Cost of Goods Sold** | **$873.50** |

| GROSS PROFIT | |
|---|---|
| **Gross Profit** | **$13,630.49** |

| EXPENSES | |
|---|---|
| Advertising | 700.00 |
| Bank Charges | 72.00 |
| Equipment Rental | 75.00 |
| Insurance | 0.0 |
| Vehicle Insurance | 200.00 |
| **Total Insurance** | **$200.00** |
| Interest Expense | 37.22 |
| Laundry | 81.50 |
| Rent or Lease | 4,400.00 |
| Repair & Maintenance | 0.0 |
| Computer Repair | 200.00 |
| Vehicle Repair | 212.50 |
| **Total Repair & Maint...** | **$412.50** |
| Supplies Expense | 0.0 |
| Cleaning Supplies E... | 252.00 |
| Kennel Supplies Ex... | 310.00 |
| Office Supplies Exp... | 231.47 |
| Sales Supplies Exp... | 175.00 |
| **Total Supplies Expe...** | **$968.47** |
| Telephone Expense | 129.95 |
| Utilities | 0.0 |
| Electric | 164.75 |
| Gas-Heating | 343.50 |
| Water | 385.95 |
| **Total Utilities** | **$894.20** |
| Vehicle Expenses | 126.05 |
| **Total Expenses** | **$8,096.89** |

| NET OPERATING INCOME | |
|---|---|
| **Net Operating Income** | **$5,533.60** |

| OTHER INCOME | |
|---|---|
| Fees Billed | 80.00 |
| Interest Earned | 175.50 |
| **Total Other Income** | **$255.50** |

| OTHER EXPENSES | |
|---|---|
| Depreciation Expense | 1,340.00 |
| Purchase Discounts | -29.50 |
| **Total Other Expenses** | **$1,310.50** |

| NET OTHER INCOME | |
|---|---|
| Interest Earned | 175.50 |
| **Total Other Income** | **$255.50** |

| OTHER EXPENSES | |
|---|---|
| Depreciation Expense | 1,340.00 |
| Purchase Discounts | -29.50 |
| **Total Other Expenses** | **$1,310.50** |

| NET OTHER INCOME | |
|---|---|
| **Net Other Income** | **-$1,055.00** |

| NET INCOME | |
|---|---|
| **Net Income** | **$4,478.60** |

Accrual basis

## Balance Sheet

The Balance Sheet is just like the ones prepared in QuickBooks Online and proves the fundamental accounting equation: Assets = Liabilities + Owner's Equity. As with the Profit & Loss report, open the Navigation bar, scroll through the selections available until you get to Balance Sheet, and tap **Balance Sheet** and it will appear on the screen.

| ☰  qb  Balance Sheet                ⋮ | |
|---|---|
| As of  Apr 10, 2016 | |
| **TOTAL ASSETS** | **TOTAL LIABILITIES** |
| **$188,329.56** | **$9,658.46** |
| ASSETS | |
| Current Assets | |
| Bank Accounts | |
| Checking | 63,448.84 |
| Petty Cash | 63.93 |
| **Total Bank Accounts** | **$63,512.77** |
| Accounts Receivable | |
| Accounts Receiva... | 14,309.60 |
| **Total Accounts Re...** | **$14,309.60** |
| Other current assets | |
| Inventory Asset | 31,841.50 |
| Prepaid Insurance | 1,600.00 |
| Supplies | 0.0 |
| Cleaning Supplies | 925.00 |
| Kennel Supplies | 1,936.00 |
| Office Supplies | 821.48 |
| Sales Supplies | 325.00 |
| **Total Supplies** | **$4,007.48** |
| Undeposited Funds | 92.37 |
| **Total Other current...** | **$37,541.35** |
| **Total Current Assets** | **$115,363.72** |
| Fixed Assets | |
| Furniture & Fixtures | 0.0 |
| Depreciation | -1,750.00 |
| Original cost | 17,000.00 |
| **Total Furniture & Fi...** | **$15,250.00** |
| Kennel Equipment | 0.0 |
| Depreciation | -2,370.00 |
| Original cost | 21,150.00 |
| **Total Kennel Equip...** | **$18,780.00** |
| Office Equipment | 0.0 |
| Depreciation | -1,000.00 |
| Original cost | 11,685.84 |
| **Total Office Equip...** | **$10,685.84** |
| Vehicles | 0.0 |
| Depreciation | -3,750.00 |
| Original cost | 32,000.00 |
| **Total Vehicles** | **$28,250.00** |
| **Total Fixed Assets** | **$72,965.84** |

| **TOTAL ASSETS** | **$188,329.56** |
|---|---|
| LIABILITIES AND EQUITY | |
| Liabilities | |
| Current Liabilities | |
| Accounts Payable | |
| Accounts Payabl... | 5,214.00 |
| **Total Accounts P...** | **$5,214.00** |
| Credit Cards | |
| Visa | 75.00 |
| **Total Credit Cards** | **$75.00** |
| Other Current Liab... | |
| State Board of E... | 2.08 |
| **Total Other Curre...** | **$2.08** |
| **Total Current Liabil...** | **$5,291.08** |
| Long-Term Liabilities | |
| Loans Payable | 0.0 |
| Equipment Loan | 1,941.06 |
| Furniture & Fixtu... | 2,426.32 |
| **Total Loans Paya...** | **$4,367.38** |
| **Total Long-Term Li...** | **$4,367.38** |
| **Total Liabilities** | **$9,658.46** |
| Equity | |
| Opening Balance E... | 0.0 |
| Retained Earnings | -4,466.31 |
| Your Name, Capital | 121,923.81 |
| Your Name, Drawi... | 0.0 |
| Your Name, Invest... | 56,735.00 |
| **Total Your Name, C...** | **$178,658.81** |
| Net Income | 4,478.60 |
| **Total Equity** | **$178,671.10** |
| **TOTAL LIABILITIES AND EQUITY** | **$188,329.56** |
| Accrual basis | |

# ADDITIONAL FEATURES

This appendix will explore Recurring Transactions, Timesheets, Bad Debts, and Attachments. It is written for you to read. If you wish to follow the steps and examples shown, feel free to do so; however, the appendix is designed as an enhancement rather than actual training. Anything entered into Your Name's Beach Barkers should be deleted after working through Appendix C. If Your Name's Beach Barkers is used for any additional or supplemental assignments, your totals will not match if you keep the transactions as part of Your Name's Beach Barkers.

## RECURRING TRANSACTIONS

For transactions that are recorded each and every month, it is possible to create Recurring Transactions. You may create recurring transactions for a variety of transactions. If you wish to complete the transactions shown as illustrations, it is extremely important that you complete the Create Recurring Transactions section using the current date. Then continue with the Complete Recurring Transactions sections tomorrow.

There are three ways to setup Recurring Transactions: Scheduled, Reminder, and Unscheduled. Scheduled transactions are automatically recorded. Costs such as Rent that recur every month are ideal to set up as a Scheduled recurring transaction. If you schedule a check for the rent, the check is automatically prepared on the date scheduled. Reminder is a good selection if you have transactions with a fixed schedule but different amounts each month, utility bills for example. On the date for the Reminder, you access the Recurring Transactions List, click Reminder, and you will see the transactions with Reminder Templates. Within Reminders, you may complete the recurring transaction. Finally, recurring transactions may be Unscheduled. These transactions are not processed on a particular date; however, the data you choose to save will be available to use as a starting point to finish a transaction.

### Create Recurring Transactions

The examples shown will create a Reminder Bill for the Venice Rent and will create a Scheduled Check for the Malibu Rent.

Open **Your Name's Beach Barkers**
Click the **Gear** icon, click **Recurring Transactions** in the Lists column
Click **New** to set up a recurring transaction for the Venice rent
Click the drop-down list arrow next to Bill, scroll through the list of transactions to see which types can be made recurring
Click **Bill**

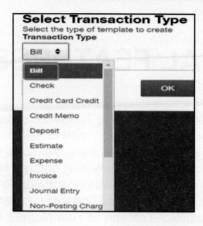

Click **OK**

Create the Recurring Bill template:

Template name: **Venice Rent**

Type: **Reminder**

Remind **0** days before the transaction date

Payee: **Venice Rentals**

Interval: **Monthly** on **day** (tomorrow's date) of every **1** month(s)

- Use the day after the current date. For example, this illustration uses April 8, 2016 as the Start date so the Interval would begin on the 9th day of every 1 month.

Start date: **Current date**

- You cannot select a date earlier than the current date so this example is using April 8, 2016 as the Start date.

End: **None**

Mailing Address: Complete by QuickBooks Online

Terms: **Net 30**

Location: **Venice**

Account: **Rent or Lease**

Amount: **1500**

Memo: **Venice Rent**

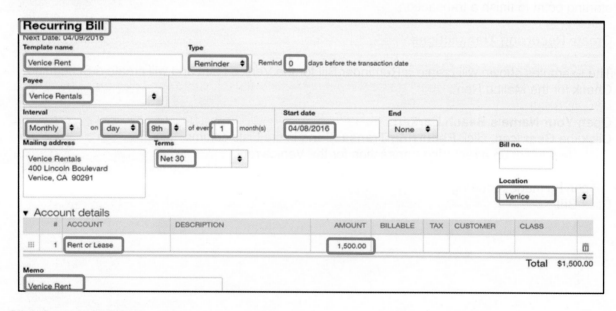

Click **Save template**

Prepare the template for a Recurring Check for Malibu Rent

Template name: **Malibu Rent**

Type: **Scheduled**
Remind **2** days before the transaction date
Payee: **Malibu Rentals**
Account: **Checking**
Interval: **Monthly** on **day** (tomorrow's date) of every **1** month(s)

- Use the day after the current date. For example, this illustration uses April 8, 2016 as the Start date so the Interval would begin on the 9th day of every 1 month.

Start date: **Current date**

- You cannot select a date earlier than the current date so this example is using April 8, 2016 as the Start date.

End: **None**
Mailing Address: Complete by QuickBooks Online
Location: **Malibu**
Account: **Rent or Lease**
Amount: **1400**
Memo: **Malibu Rent**

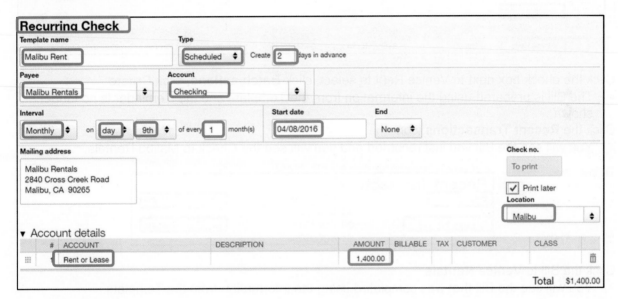

Click **Save template**
On the List for Recurring Transactions, click the drop-down list arrow next to **Reminder List**, click **Run Report**

- You will see the two templates, the next date that the templates should be processed, the name, the accounts used, and the amounts.

### Your Name's Beach Barkers
#### RECURRING TEMPLATE LIST

| TRANSACTION TYPE | TEMPLATE NAME | PREVIOUS DATE | NEXT DATE | NAME | MEMO/DESCRIPTION | ACCOUNT | AMOUNT |
|---|---|---|---|---|---|---|---|
| **Scheduled** | | | | | | | |
| Check | Malibu Rent | | 04/09/2016 | Malibu Rentals | | Checking | -1,400.00 |
| **Total for Scheduled** | | | | | | | $ -1,400.00 |
| **Reminder** | | | | | | | |
| Bill | Venice Rent | | 04/09/2016 | Venice Rentals | Venice Rent | Accounts Payable (A/P) | -1,500.00 |
| **Total for Reminder** | | | | | | | $ -1,500.00 |

- If you are completing this exercise, close Your Name's Beach Barkers and continue with the section for Timesheets. If you are not completing it, continue reading.

## Complete Recurring Transactions

On the scheduled date for the Reminder about the Bill for Venice Rentals, click **Gear**, click **Recurring Transactions** in the Lists column

- If you are doing this exercise, you will complete this on the day after you created the recurring transactions.

Click the **Reminder List** button

- Only the reminder for Venice Rentals is shown.

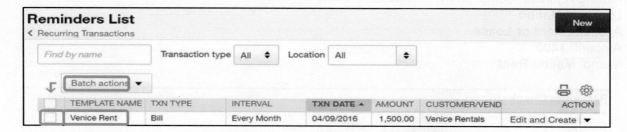

Click the check box next to Venice Rent to select, click **Batch actions**, click **Create**

- The Bill is prepared using the information from the Template and the Reminder is no longer shown.

Click the **Recent Transactions** icon

- You will see the Bill you just recorded and you will see the Check to Malibu Rentals.

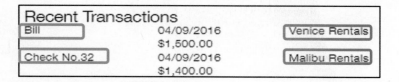

Click the Bill to **Venice Rentals**

- You will see the Bill that was completed using the information from the Template.

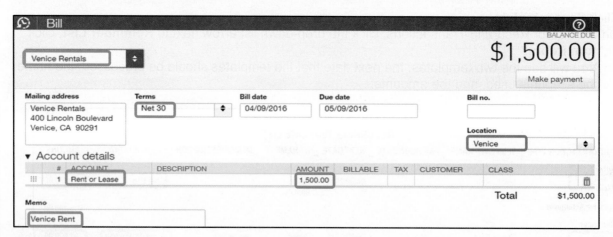

Click **Save and close**

- If you get a message regarding saving changes, click **Yes**.
- If you were to return to the Reminders List, nothing would be shown as a reminder.

Click the **Recent Transactions** icon again, click the check to **Malibu Rentals**

- The check was automatically prepared using the information from the Template.

Click **Save and close**
Close Your Name's Beach Barkers

## TIMESHEETS AND TIME TRACKING

When payroll is active, employees can fill out time sheets to allocate their time among different jobs and/or customers. The timesheets are used to calculate the hours worked and are entered for the payroll hours. In addition, if the hours are billed for a specific customer, they may be added to the customer's invoice.

When you have employees who do specific work for individual customers, you may record the hours worked for each customer on a Timesheet. The Billable hours may then be added to a customer's invoice.

Open the **Test Drive Company** as previously instructed and **Turn on Payroll**
Click the **Plus** icon, click **Weekly Timesheet** in the Employees column
When the timesheet opens, click the drop-down list arrow next to Emily Platt, click **Kari Steblay**
Make sure the dates shown include the current week

- If not, click the drop-down list arrow and select the appropriate dates.

In Line 1, click the drop-down list arrow for **Customer name**, click **Diego Rodriguez**
Click the drop-down list arrow for **Service item**, click **Design**

- Notice the check for Billable, this means that the hours can be billed to the customer at the Rate of $75 per hour. This is not the amount that Kari is paid.

Enter **8** in the text boxes for MON, TUE, and WED
In Line 2, click the drop-down list arrow for **Customer name**, click **Cool Cars**
Select the Service item: **Design**
Enter **10** in the text box for THU and **8** in the text box for FRI

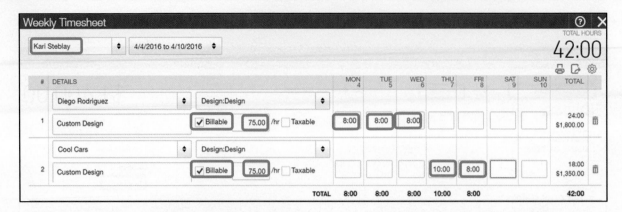

Review the timesheet then click **Save and close**

- You should be returned to the Employees List, if not, access it as previously instructed.

Click **Run Payroll**

Click the check boxes for Eloisa Catillo and Bill Lucchini to remove the check mark

- Notice the hours for Kari: the 42 hours were inserted as regular pay.

Edit the hours for Kari so she has **40** hours for Regular Pay and **2** OT Hrs, press **Tab**

Click **Preview Payroll**

| Review and Submit | | | | | |
|---|---|---|---|---|---|
| **$864.94**<br>TOTAL PAYROLL COST | $559.87<br>NET PAY | | | 1 | Paper check for $559.87<br>Deliver these paychecks by 04/08/2016 |
| | $214.13<br>EMPLOYEE | | | | |
| | $90.94<br>EMPLOYER | | | | |

Pay period: 04/02/2016 to 04/08/2016   Pay date: 04/08/2016

| EMPLOYEE | TOTAL HOURS | TOTAL PAY | EMPLOYEE TAXES AND DEDUCTIONS | NET PAY |
|---|---|---|---|---|
| KS  Steblay, Kari | 42.00 | $774.00 | $214.13 | $559.87 |
| Totals: | 42.00 | $774.00 | $214.13 | $559.87 |

Click **Submit payroll**

- If you get a screen to pay taxes, click **I'll do it later**.

Print the check, then click **Finish payroll**

Click the **Plus** icon, click **Invoice**, and prepare the invoice for **Diego Rodriguez**

- You will see the **Add** pane with three Billable times that may be added to the invoice.

Click **Add all**

- The three days of design were added to the invoice.

Click **Save and close**

You would repeat the steps to add the billable hours to an invoice for Cool Cars

Do not close the Test Drive Company if you are completing the illustrations

## BAD DEBTS

When it becomes clear that you have a customer who is not going to pay the amount owed, you may write off the bad debt. There are two basic ways in which to do this. The first shown is the Direct Method to write off the bad debt. When you use this method, you write off each individual bad debt at the time it occurs. The second and more appropriate method for companies that use accrual-basis accounting is the Allowance for Bad Debts Method.

### Direct Write Off Method for Bad Debts

Before you can write off a bad debt, you need to create an expense account for Bad Debts and add a new non-inventory item named Bad Debt. The account and item will be used when the bad debt is recorded.

Create the Bad Debts account and the Bad Debt non-inventory item:

Continue to use the Test Drive Company
Open the **Chart of Accounts**, click **New**
Category type: **Expenses**
Detail type: **Bad Debts**.
Name: **Bad Debts**

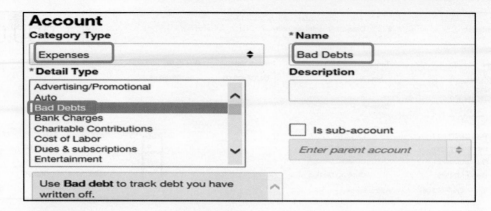

Click **Save and Close**
Create a product/service item called: **Bad Debt**
Open the **Products and Services** List click **New**, select **Non-inventory item**
Name: **Bad Debt**
Income Account: **Bad Debts**
Click to deselect: **Is taxable**

Click **Save**

Bill's Windsurf Shop has not paid Invoice 1027. Since the business was closed and Bill moved out
of state, write off the Invoice by preparing a Credit Memo.

Open a **Credit Memo**
Enter the Customer's information
Click in the text box for PRODUCT/SERVICE, click the drop-down list arrow, and click **Bad Debt**
Tab to AMOUNT and enter **85**, which is the amount of invoice 1027
Memo: **Bad Debt**

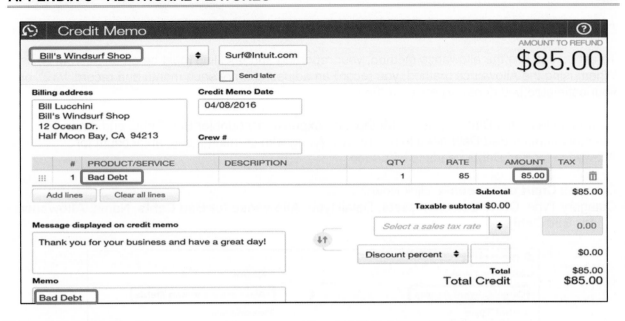

Click **Save and close**

Go to the Account Register for Bill's Windsurf Shop

- You will see Invoice 1027, Credit Memo, and Payment.

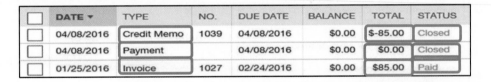

| | DATE ▼ | TYPE | NO. | DUE DATE | BALANCE | TOTAL | STATUS |
|---|---|---|---|---|---|---|---|
| ☐ | 04/08/2016 | Credit Memo | 1039 | 04/08/2016 | $0.00 | $-85.00 | Closed |
| ☐ | 04/08/2016 | Payment | | 04/08/2016 | $0.00 | $0.00 | Closed |
| ☐ | 01/25/2016 | Invoice | 1027 | 02/24/2016 | $0.00 | $85.00 | Paid |

Click the **Payment** to see how the invoice and credit memo are linked together

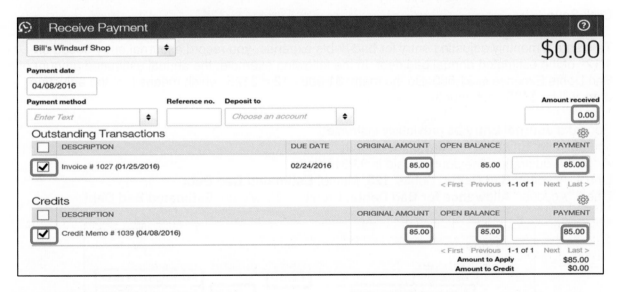

Click **Save and close**

- If you are recording the illustration transactions, you will need to delete the Credit Memo and Receive Payment that you entered in this section before continuing to the next section.

Do <u>not</u> close the Test Drive Company if you are recording the illustration transactions

## Allowance Method for Bad Debts

To set up and use the allowance method, your reporting and tax filing <u>must</u> be on an accrual basis. When using the Allowance method, you record an adjusting entry each month and record 1/12<sup>th</sup> of your estimated bad debts expense for the year.

As was done for the Direct Write Off Method, an expense account for Bad Debts and a non-inventory item for Bad Debt need to be created. Along with creating those, an account for Allowance for Bad Debts needs to be added.

Open the **Chart of Accounts**, click **New**
Category Type: **Other Current Assets**, Detail type: **Allowance for Bad Debts**, Name: **Allowance for Bad Debts**

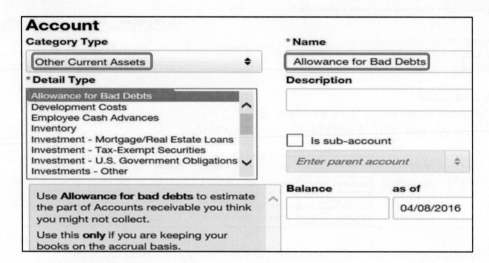

Click **Save**

To create a monthly adjusting entry for bad debts expense, you record a journal entry based on 1/12<sup>th</sup> of the estimated annual bad debt. In the following example, the annual estimated amount of Bad Debts Expense is $1,500. Do the math: $1,500 / 12 = $125, which means that the adjusting entry will be $125 each month.

Record a **Journal Entry** as previously instructed
Journal date: Enter the last day of last month
• In the illustration, the Journal date is 03/31/2016.
Line 1: Account: **Bad Debts**, Debits: **125**, Memo: **Estimated Bad Debt**
Line 2: Account: **Allowance for Bad Debts**, Credits: **125**, Memo: **Estimated Bad Debt**

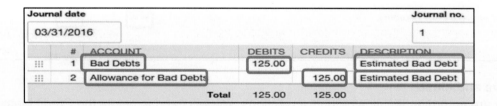

Click **Save and close**

When it is time to write off the bad debt and use part of the Allowance for Bad Debts, a Receive Payments form is completed rather than a Credit Memo.

In the scenario where Bill's Windsurf shop has not paid Invoice 1027 because the business was closed and Bill moved out of state, write off the Invoice by recording Receive Payment.

Open **Receive Payment** as previously instructed
Customer: **Bill's Windsurf Shop**
Payment Method and Reference No. are left blank
Deposit to: **Allowance for Bad Debts**
Amount received: **85**
- Note that Invoice 1027 is shown and selected.
Memo: **Write Off Bad Debt**

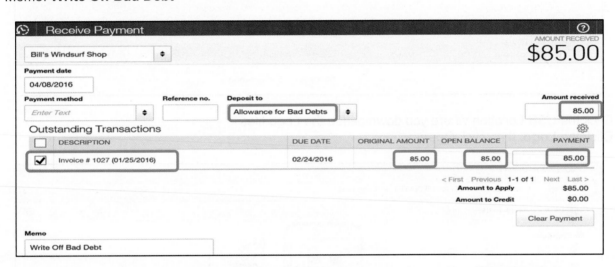

Click **Save and close**
Prepare the Journal as previously instructed to view the transactions for Bad Debts

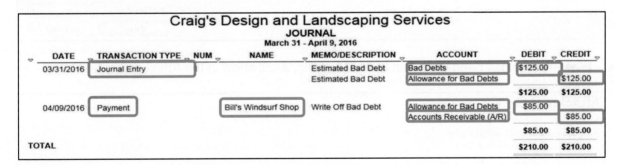

Close the Test Drive Company

## ATTACHMENTS

In QuickBooks Online, you can attachment documents, images, PDFs, and more to transactions. As an example, when working in Appendix B Go Mobile, a picture of a receipt was taken and added directly to the Expense that was being recorded.

Open **Your Name's Beach Barkers** on your computer to Add Attachments
To add a file to the attachment list, click the **Gear** icon, then click **Attachments** in the Lists column
Drag/drop the files from a storage location for your computer or click the **Paperclip** icon and click the **file** in your Documents Library

If you want to use a file from a USB drive, click the **drive**, open any **folders**, and drag the file or click the **file** then click **Open**

For example, the following steps will illustrate Uploading the Beach Barkers Logo as an attachment

With the Attachments List showing, click the **Paperclip**

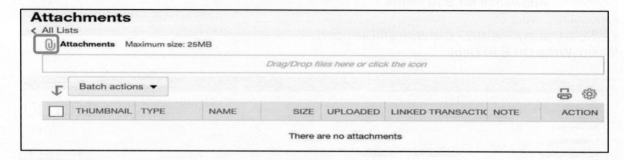

Click the **USB** Location where you downloaded the Logo files
Click the **Logo**, then click **Open**

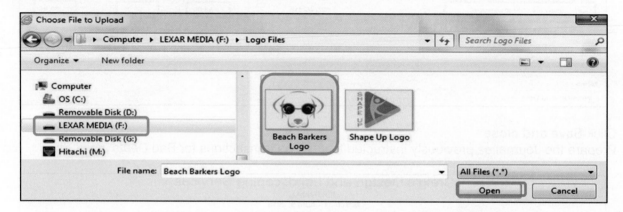

- When the file has been uploaded to Attachments, it will show in the Attachments List.

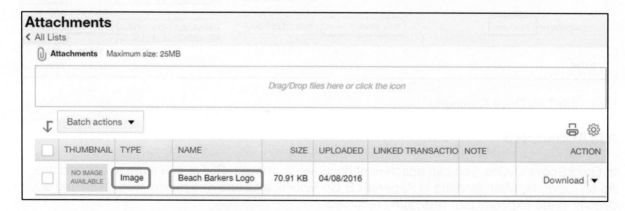

When you want to add an attachment to a business form, an invoice in the example, scroll to the bottom of the form until you find the paperclip
Drag/drop your files from the storage location or click **Show existing** to select a file already inserted into QuickBooks Online
Click the file
The attachment will show in the Add to Invoice pane, click **Add**

- You may need to click the drop-down list arrow for Unlinked, and then click All.

- The attachment has been added to the form.

# Index